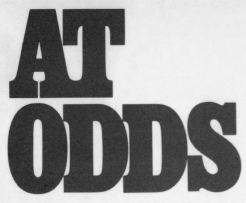

AT ODDS

Women and the Family in America from the Revolution to the Present

CARL N. DEGLER

Pulitzer prize winner Carl Degler has written the first general history of women in America for our generation. "The equality of women and the institution of the family have long been at odds with each other," Degler contends. "Though women and the family have been obviously connected in history as they are in life, in academic studies they have developed almost independently of one another." Linking these subjects for the first time, the book is a brilliant synthesis of what is known today about women and the family. But the book is based not only on recent scholarship; Degler draws on diaries and letters—many of which are excerpted in the book—to give readers an excellent sense of what it was like to be a woman in the last century. In addition, the book brings into historical perspective one climactic question: How is woman's right to equality of opportunity going to be reconciled with the demands of the family which, Degler maintains, still depends on woman's subordinating her

interests to the welfare of her husband?

rn family has been shaped search for greater autonomy mily. *At Odds* shows how that k place, beginning in the late d early nineteenth centuries. n that seminal period, Degler rgence of a new kind of fam- women's roles were primarily to their husbands, moral the family, and nurturers of h children thus occupying a as cherished beings whose nging was a central responsi- nts, it became necessary to umber. Degler explains how decline in fertility took place. zes the character of women's nging patterns of women's e of single women, and the working class, immigrant, ilies, as well as the interrela- women's activities inside the utside, culminating in the age.

is Margaret Byrne Professor History at Stanford Univer- esident of the Organization Historians in 1979-80. He ulitzer Prize in 1972 for his Black nor White; he has also won the Bancroft Prize and was a co-winner of the Beveridge Prize.

ISBN 0-19-502657-8 $25.00

AT ODDS

Women and the Family in America
from the Revolution to the Present

Carl N. Degler

New York   Oxford
OXFORD UNIVERSITY PRESS
1980

Copyright © 1980 by Carl N. Degler

Library of Congress Cataloging in Publication Data

Degler, Carl N
  At odds.
  Includes index.
  1. Women—United States—History.
2. Family—United States—History.
I. Title.
HQ1418.D44   301.41'2'0973   79-17438
ISBN 0-19-502657-8

First printing February 1980

Second printing October 1980

Printed in the United States of America

Preface

This book might be called an exercise in foolhardiness. I say this not only because it seeks to deal in a single volume with two different historical subjects over a long span of time but also because the two subjects are very new. Neither the theory nor the substance of the history of women and the family has been worked out yet. Unlike other historical fields, where the framework of analysis has been well established for many years, in the history of women and the family there is no basic historical text or even an accepted periodization. Peter Laslett of Cambridge University, perhaps the best-known historian of the family, pointed out in 1972 that a comprehensive bibliography on the family listed some 12,000 items published in the 20th century down to 1964. Over half of the titles in the list, Laslett noticed, appeared within the preceding ten years, and 95 per cent of them were published after 1928! And even at that, only 250 titles out of the 12,000 actually dealt with the history of the family. The literature on the history of women goes back somewhat farther than that, but prior to 1965 the production of work in that field had not been much greater than for the history of the family. The most recent bibliography on the history of women in the United States, compiled by Gerda Lerner, runs to almost 80 pages; most of the titles in it were published after 1950.

The novelty of the subject, however, is only one reason for calling this book an exercise in foolhardiness. The strongest reason is that the aim of the book is to integrate these two fields. For the truth of the matter is that, though women and the family have been obviously connected in history as they are in life, in academic studies they have developed almost independently of one another. Historians in one field have generally researched and written their works with only minimal references to the efforts of historians in the other. It is quite common, for example, to read articles and even books on the history of the family without encountering any mention of women and their lives other than the recognition—often indirect at that—that they married men, bore and reared children, and thus were included in every family. Historians of the family, to be sure, calculate and record such things as women's age at first marriage, number of children borne, and age at widowhood; yet they rarely see women as active forces in the development of the family or in its day-to-day activities.

Similarly, historians of women have written whole books on women in the past without more than passing recognition that throughout most of history more women have been involved to a greater extent in the family than in any other institution in Western society except perhaps nunneries, houses of prostitution, and girls' schools. Part of the reason why historians of women have tended to ignore women's role in the family is that women's history until very recently has usually been viewed as just another aspect of traditional history. Thus historians of women have written about those things women have done in the past which were similar to, if not identical with, those things which traditional history has emphasized, such as being active in government, in war, in science, in business, in labor, or in any number of areas outside of the family. After all, until most recently, as Laslett's observation reminds us, the family has not been a concern of historians. Now that it is, the moment has arrived, however foolhardy it might seem, to try to bring together in a single book these two novel fields, the subjects of which are so intertwined.

The purpose of this book, however, extends beyond the goal of bringing together for the first time the history of women and the history of the family in the United States. It seeks to show as well that not only are the two subjects intertwined, but that, in order to understand one, the other must also be understood. In short, the book is designed not only to tell the story of American women and the American family over the last two centuries, but to show as concretely and analytically as possible how the interaction has shaped the family and the life of women down to the present.

As the title suggests, it is at once a primary argument and a basic assumption of the book that the equality of women and the institution of the family have long been at odds with each other. The historic family has depended for its existence and character on women's subordination. Subordination here is intended as neutrally as possible. It means simply that the family's existence assumes that a woman will subordinate her individual interest to those of others—the members of her family. Feminism, or even the less egalitarian term, women's autonomy within the family, calls that assumption into question and, in the case of feminism, seeks its ultimate elimination. Women and the family, in truth, have been in enduring tension for at least two centuries. This book is the story of the evolution of that tension, what it has meant for women and the family in the past, and what it portends for women and the family today and tomorrow.

It is not accidental that the movement for women's emancipation and the emergence of what I call the modern American family occurred at about the same time—namely, at the end of the 18th century and the beginning of the 19th. The interaction of these two developments offers present-day Americans—not only women—an uncertain prospect. The relationship between women and the family is today, I believe, on the verge of potentially fundamental change, but the extent of that change and therefore the future of women's emancipation and the future of the family are quite unclear. It is my belief that to view this enduring tension between women and the family in the long perspective of two centuries may help Americans to make the personal and social decisions the immediate future seems to have in store for us. To understand how one has arrived at the present point not only is a purpose of history but is also a good way to begin to face up to a choice.

As noted already, women's history and the history of the family have not had much to do with one another as disciplines. One sign of that separation has been the different kinds of historical evidence each has relied upon. This is obviously not the place to try to explain why the two fields have moved in different directions, but that they have is germane to at least one thing this book tries to do. By and large, the historians of the family have emphasized the use of statistical evidence, usually data derived from census schedules. Since most historians of the family have come out of disciplines like demography and economics, where statistics are an important part of the tradition of the field, they have naturally emphasized such sources. Very few historians of women, however, make much use of statistical data, for most of them have come out of a tradition of research that has emphasized personal documents like letters, diaries, and literary sources in general. My aim in this book has been to integrate the methods of the two fields as well as the two subjects. Wherever possible I have drawn upon statistical evidence in order to present a broadly based argument; yet I have also tried to flesh out such evidence, especially for the

19th century, with written personal documents, which permit us to learn about feelings, intentions, and reactions of people in the past.

Unfortunately, personal writings for certain kinds of families are much more limited than for others. Few poor, immigrant, or Afro-American families, especially during the 19th century, left letters or other personal sources on which to base a discussion of the internal relationships comparable to that which I have been able to draw on for families of the middle and upper classes. Thus the analysis of these less visible groups in the past will have to rely more heavily upon statistical evidence than I would like.

In that respect, as in so much else in connection with the history of women and the family, this book is only a beginning, not an ending. By trying to construct a synthesis of the history of women and the history of the family, this book, it is hoped, will serve as a stimulus to others to write a more comprehensive and more substantially based synthesis in the future. This effort at combining the two fields will make a contribution to the subject even if it does nothing more than provide scholars with an opportunity to pick holes in it.

Just because this book is a beginning and not a definitive interpretation, throughout it I have tried to make clear to the lay or general reader—for whom the book is really intended—how I have arrived at my conclusions or interpretations. Cognizant of the novelty of the synthesis as well as the recency of the two fields, I have made as clear as I can the logical and evidentiary bases of my analysis. In any case, written history, it seems to me, is most interesting when it is frankly recognized to be a tentative effort to order the myriad facts of the past rather than an immutable narrative that was magically uncovered by some Olympian figure called a historian.

One reason I deplore the lack of personal documents for the writing of the history of working-class, Afro-American, or immigrant families is that only through such evidence can the historian begin to get inside the heads of those who lived in the past and are now dead. One of the central aims of this book is to provide the reader with some sense of what it was like to be a woman in America, particularly in the 19th century, a period now outside the direct experience of the great majority of living persons. As a result, there are chapters on women's activities outside the family as well as inside it, on women's participation in the paid work force, and on efforts of women to control fertility. Several chapters seek to make clear, too, what it meant to be a woman—to bear children, to rear them, to maintain a household, and to minister to a husband. For an important justification of history is that it attempts to give to those who are alive today a sense of what it felt like to live at another time, when different values and personal goals had to wrestle with the same timeless and insistent aspects of human existence—sex, birth, work, and the relations between the sexes—that engage the attention and energies of people today. For that reason I have let Americans of earlier years, particularly 19th-century women, speak in their own words as much as possible.

Having set forth what this book is about, I would now like to say what it does not deal with. For that, too, may help to explain what is to be expected in the pages that follow.

Although the span of the book is some two centuries, no effort has been made to cover all periods equally. In fact, the approach to the subject is essentially topical, as a quick glance at the Contents makes clear. The topics, nevertheless, are ordered chronologically. Moreover, since a large part of the purpose of the book is to explain how and why things changed over these two centuries, chronology is always a part of the story. Yet, inasmuch as changes in an institution like the family are usually quite slow, the 20th-century family is much less fully canvassed in the book than the family of the 19th century. Most readers, after all, know from first-hand experience something of the nature of the 20th-century family. They know nothing directly, however, about 19th-century families or women. Consequently, a good deal of space has been given over to exploring the internal dynamics of families of the 19th century, leaving comparisons with the 20th-century family largely to the reader's own experience. On the other hand, the broad patterns of family behavior in the 1970s are discussed in some detail in the last chapter, where the latest sociological and demographical data are drawn upon, because these are then related to the upsurge in the women's movement in the 1970s.

The character of the so-called sexual revolution since 1960 is not discussed either, for its dimensions and nature have been thrust upon Americans' attention almost to the point of surfeit. But since women's sexuality in the 19th century is much less well known yet deeply important for understanding the development of the family, women's sexuality in that century has a chapter devoted to it. Moreover, the interpretation given there is as central to the book's argument as its contents differ from the conventional view.

Finally, the book raises some theoretical questions about the history of women and the ways in which that history differs from other examinations of human experience. But rather than set forth an abstract, perhaps arid theoretical framework at the outset or even in an appendix, I have elected to discuss such questions at those points in the book where they are pertinent. Thus the question of how women's history must differ from the history of other subordinate groups is discussed in Chapter I, while the relevance of women's sexuality to the explanation of woman's subordination is commented on in Chapter XI. The important but admittedly difficult and speculative question as to why the modern family and women's awakening to self emerged together at the end of the 18th century is tentatively explored in Chapter VIII. Then, in Chapter II my method for studying the internal dynamics of the 19th-century family is critically assessed.

In the end, of course, a book that seeks to pull together the history of women and the family over a span of two centuries must be heavily dependent upon the work of others; a single author cannot gather all the necessary information, much less arrive at the interpretations from his own, unaided efforts. As a result, I have borrowed with both hands from the researches of other scholars. In a number of places in the text I have at least acknowledged my dependence upon them by name, for I think the reader should know of that dependence when it is substantial. At other times I have identified the sources of my information in notes at the back of the book, where they will not distract the general reader who has no interest in sources, but where they can be consulted by a scholar or specialist who may want to verify the basis of my statements in the text. For the convenience of specialists and in order to avoid the necessity of an extensive bibliography, each reference in the notes is given in full the first time it is cited in each chapter. All quotations, moreover, are identified in the backnotes, but otherwise the footnoting is kept to a minimum. Usually items within a given paragraph are grouped together in a single backnote, with the references arranged in order of the appearance of the information in the paragraph. I have not documented all statements in the text, merely those that might not be immediately evident to specialists, either from the mentioning of the author in the text, or from familiarity with the literature of the field.

Stanford, California   C. N. D.
April 1979

Acknowledgments

As I have implied in the introduction, the research for and the writing of this book have depended heavily upon many other people, and institutions. Here it is my pleasure to at last acknowledge what I cannot repay very easily, for without that help this book would not only be different—and worse—but it might not have been completed even now.

First of all, my thanks are owed to those institutions that made it possible for me to live while thinking: The John Simon Guggenheim Foundation for a fellowship in 1972–73, during which I began the research for the book; Stanford University for a sabbatical year (1976–77) that in combination with a generous fellowship from the National Endowment for the Humanities made it possible to complete most of the writing; and the Rockefeller Foundation which provided a wonderful location, generous accommodations, and stimulating companionship for the month of May 1976 at the Villa Serbelloni at Bellagio, Italy, where I began to revise the first draft. Surely, the support of these institutions can be said to constitute the material foundations of the book.

Less material but no less important were those institutions and persons who helped me obtain the intellectual wherewithal from which to construct this book. My gratitude for that help goes to the staff of Stanford University Library, particularly Pat Palmer, and Susan Rosenberg, then assistant curator of the Stanford Archives. My heartfelt thanks also to the staff of the Schlesinger Library at Radcliffe College, where the circumstances of the work and the help from Director Pat King, Curator Eva Mosley, and Bibliographer Barbara Haber made research there a joy. Even

xi

though I was separated from my own family for several weeks while at the Schlesinger, seeking to understand the 19th-century family, that wonderfully hospitable research library was still hard to leave. The Huntington Library, a similar treasure trove of materials, is blessed with even more enticing conditions of work, a fact that was undoubtedly important in bringing me into fruitful association with other scholars in the same field. Between Ray Billington's famous lunches and the choice items that the helpful and accommodating staff brought to my attention, the Huntington Library has earned my thanks many times over. At the Bancroft Library in Berkeley the circumstances of work were truly excellent and I am grateful for the opportunity to draw upon the resources of that major research library. I thank the staff of the Department of Manuscripts and University Archives of the Cornell University Library for their gracious assistance during a brief stay in Ithaca.

I also want to express my gratitude to two women whose relatives play a conspicuous role in this book. I thank Rosamund Gilder for granting me permission to quote from the correspondence between her mother, Helena Gilder, and Mary Hallock Foote; and I thank Molly Schwarz of Golden Eagle, Illinois, for granting permission to quote from the diary of her great grandmother, Mollie Dorsey Sanford.

Several scholars who generously shared with me particular items from their own research I have thanked specifically in the footnotes. Here I want to express my gratitude generally to those scholars without whose work, published and unpublished, a book of this scope could not have been completed in my lifetime.

Once the research and writing had been done, the help of other persons became important, and it is now my pleasure to thank them for that invaluable assistance. Their help took the form of willingness to listen to my ideas and to give me reactions, critical as well as supportive. From these ongoing testings not only did I learn much but the final product gained much. For this help my warm thanks are extended to several groups at Stanford University: the Seminar of the Center for Research on Women, the History Department's Faculty-Graduate Student Seminar, the History Undergraduate Student Association Seminar, and the Stanford Institute in Women's History, at which portions of three chapters of the book were presented as lectures in the summer of 1978. I thank, too, Rice University, and Cornell University for offering me an opportunity to try out portions of the book on formal lecture audiences, the consequence of which was that I received some very helpful feedback on my ideas and some new ideas as well.

One of the often unappreciated perquisites of academia is the willingness of colleagues to appraise critically other scholars' work. I have been especially blessed with an abundance of this "perk." I want here to express my deep thanks to those scholars who took the time and endured the trouble of reading chapters and giving me the benefit of their specialized knowledge and judgment: William O'Neill of Rutgers University, Anne Firor Scott of Duke University, Peter Carroll of Burlingame, California, David C. McClelland and David Miller of Cornell University, and from my own University: Michael Wald, Estelle Freedman, Myra Strober, Carol Jacklin, Robert Sears, and Paul David. Despite the mobilization of all this expertise, errors of fact and mistakes of judgment undoubtedly remain; they are to be charged against me alone, for I have made them all. I was amply warned.

Thanks for another, but no less fundamental kind of support I extend to those several persons who succeeded in putting my various versions and emendations of the manuscript of this book into legible form. Since my prose always seems better when clearly typed and free of interlineations, that source of encouragement should not be minimized. It is therefore my pleasure to thank Emalyn Perkins, who, while bearing the burden of the job, rarely made a mistake; Josephine Garrity, whose speed typing astounded me; and the History Department Trio, Jean Shimaguchi, Loraine Sinclair, and Nancy Ray, whose accuracy as well as speed must have derived from their tolerant familiarity with my idiosyncratic typescript.

Catherine Grady Degler comes in a special place for a variety of reasons. She read virtually the whole large typescript, helping thereby to reshape it into a book a non-historian like herself might find interesting and worthwhile. Her steady encouragement before and after those readings has been only a part of her contribution to this book; after all, we have been debating about women and the family for more than thirty years and we still do not always agree.

Harold Hyman and Leonard Levy have earned my appreciation, not only for having suggested that I write this book but also because their very encouraging reading of the final version came at a time I needed such support. But undoubtedly the great source of encouragement in the final months came from Gerard McCauley and Sheldon Meyer who made it possible for this book to appear under the imprint of the oldest press in the

English-speaking world. For that distinction I am indeed appreciative. To Leona Capeless and Kim Lewis within that distinguished publishing house I want to express my gratitude for their truly creative and thoughtful editing; authors and editors inevitably have an adversarial relationship, so that is no idle compliment.

Finally, I would like to thank the University of North Carolina Press for permission to quote from *The General to His Lady: The Civil War Letters of William Dorsey Pender to Fanny Pender,* edited by William W. Hassler, copyright 1962, 1963, 1964, 1965 by the University of North Carolina Press; and Yale University Press for permission to quote from Robert M. Myers, ed., *Children of Pride: A True Story of Georgia and the Civil War,* © 1972 by Robert Manson Myers.

C. N. D.

Contents

To the memory of Charlotte Perkins Gilman
and to Katharine Stetson Chamberlin,
who were there at the beginning

AT ODDS

I

The Emergence
of the Modern American Family

In every branch of written history, whether that of ancient Egypt, ancient China, medieval Europe, or modern America, the record shows that the family has been the vehicle through which men and women have entered upon life. In the family they have been born, there they have been trained to take a place in society as adults, and from there they go out to begin the cycle all over again with their own children. Even more significant as a measure of the antiquity and fundamental nature of the family is that anthropological studies of cultures far removed in character from so-called civilized societies have turned up virtually none which lacked a family life.

What is meant by a family? It is useful to set forth the essential elements if only because the very omnipresence of the family renders it almost invisible. Because we are truly immersed in the family we rarely have to define it or describe it to one another. For our purposes here the family may be said to consist of five elements. The first is that a family begins with a ritual between a woman and a man, a ceremony that we call marriage, and which implies long duration, if not permanence, for the relationship. The second is that the partners have duties and rights of parenthood that are also socially recognized and defined. For the family has everywhere been the way in which the human being is socialized. There are several other ways to prepare children for adulthood, to be sure, but all of them are very recent in origin (orphanage, kibbutz, commune), and around none of them has a whole society yet been organized. A third element is that husband, wife, and children live in a common place. This aspect, it needs to be said, is the least universal. Anthropologist George P. Murdock in his analysis of

3

the literature on some five hundred different cultures points out that in about one-fourth of them the father lives apart from mother and children at least for a portion of the time. But in the great majority of even those cases the distance between the houses of father and mother is slight. A fourth element in the definition of a family is that there are reciprocal economic obligations between husband and wife—that is, they both work for the family, even though the amount and kind of labor or production may be far from equal. Fifth, the family also serves as a means of sexual satisfaction for the partners, though not necessarily as an exclusive one.

The striking fact is that there are very few societies known to anthropologists in which a family with at least these characteristics does not exist. One of the few exceptions is worth looking at because it is so rare. The Nayars of southern India, in fact, no longer exist as a living culture, so what anthropologists know about them comes from what can be remembered by the people in the area, none of whom live as the Nayars did. Among the Nayars paternity was apparently a one-night thing, offspring being reared by the mother and her female relatives. The actual father of the child was usually not known, since the mother willingly accepted passing visitors as sexual partners. Since the "visiting husbands" came only at night, the relationships hardly involved either a marriage or a common residence. The relationship also lacked any permanence or rights of parentage since all that was expected of the "visiting husband" who acknowledged paternity was that he pay the costs of the midwife! Beyond that there were no reciprocal economic obligations between the parents.[1]

On the face of it, the Nayars had no families, as we have defined them, if what their descendants remembered was in fact the way they behaved. But in the wide spectrum of human cultures the Nayars are such an exception that Murdock, after his survey of the ethnographical literature, still pronounced the family to be universal. And even if one takes the Nayars as an exception, the generalization is changed only to say *almost,* or virtually, universal.

Certainly throughout Western civilization the family has exhibited all of the characteristics set forth in the basic definition. And indeed because these fundamentals are universal, the family has usually been thought of as changeless, as without a history. But when one moves beyond the skeletal definition of the family to examine it in different societies and at different times—even within the Western tradition—it quickly becomes clear that the family has changed over time and therefore, in fact, does have a history. The new field of family history has been interested in discerning both change and continuity in the long history of the family in the West.

One significant consequence of the recent historical interest in the family has been the discovery that the extended family, in which parents and their children live in the same household with their own parents, has not been usual at all. Throughout the national societies of Europe today and as far back as the Middle Ages, at least, the great majority of people has been reared in nuclear families—two parents and their offspring only. Thus a commonplace of sociology of twenty years ago that before industrialization the extended family was the characteristic unit of socialization has been shown to be without basis in fact. No more than one-fifth of all households, so far as present research can tell, has been extended in this sense, and in many societies the proportion has been much less than that. To say this, of course, does not mean that nuclear families have had no contact with grandparents or other kin. In fact, they often had a considerable amount, since kin frequently settled or clustered together. But in the day-to-day life of the family in western Europe and North America since at least the Reformation, the nuclear family has been the primary familial experience of the average person.

If the nuclearity of the family has been unchanged over the last five centuries, other aspects of the family have changed. Prior to the opening of the 19th century the vast majority of people in the world lived on farms or in peasant villages. And for almost all of them the family was a cooperative economic unit, with children and mother working along with husband, even though usually there was a division of labor by gender. This was true whether production was for subsistence or for sale. Even those relatively few families which lived and worked in towns acted as cooperative enterprises in their shops, inns, and other businesses. Home and work were close together, and wife and husband participated in both. Some exceptions existed, to be sure. Here and there, even in medieval times, large enterprises like shipyards, certain kinds of mines, and woolen mills (many hand-powered looms) required male workers to be separated from the family for at least a substantial part of the day or even longer. But the families in which this occurred were a negligible proportion of the population in any society prior to the 18th century. Especially was this true of the English colonies in North America before the Revolution. At that time well over 90 per cent of the people lived outside the few cities, and the number of large-scale enterprises within the cities and towns could be counted on the fingers of two hands. This situation would change dramatically with the spread of the industrial factory system in both Europe and America after the 18th century.

Families in America and western Europe prior to the American Revolu-

tion were thus very much like those anywhere else in the world. Every society on the globe was then pre-industrial or "less developed," to use modern terminology. Yet in two respects families in western Europe differed
from all other families. They differed as to when the families began—that
is, the ages of marriage—and in the proportion of the population which
ever married. The age of marriage in western Europe was substantially
later than in eastern Europe, and the rest of the world. Moreover, the
proportion of women who never married in western Europe was at least
double and not infrequently triple and quadruple that in the societies of
eastern Europe. Let us look at this phenomenon a little more closely.

If a line is drawn across the map of Europe from roughly Trieste on the
Adriatic northward to Leningrad on the Baltic, the countries west of that
line show a significantly higher age at marriage and a lower proportion of
men and women ever married than those countries to the east of the line.
The marriage statistics which John Hajnal, who first discovered this striking difference, has collected are dramatic in their contrast. The pattern is
particularly obvious around 1900, when the registration of vital statistics
achieved some reliability throughout Europe. The contrast is evident in the
following table, which uses Belgium and Sweden as representatives of the
western European pattern, and Bulgaria and Serbia for the eastern European. Notice that 85 per cent of Belgian males were single at age 24, while
only 58 per cent of Bulgarian males were. Similarly, at ages 45–49, some
16 per cent of Belgian males were still unmarried as against 3 per cent of
Bulgarian males. The same differences are apparent in regard to females,
and between Swedes and Serbians.

Per cent single at various ages   1900

Country	Males				Females		
	(20–24)	(25–29)	(45–49)		(20–24)	(25–29)	(45–49)
Belgium	85	50	16		71	41	17
Sweden	92	61	13		80	52	19
Bulgaria	58	23	3		24	3	1
Serbia	50	18	3		16	2	1

Hajnal found that wherever he looked in Europe the differences between
East and West held. Even as late as 1926, despite the modernizing revolution in Russia, the pattern was clear. Only 3 per cent of men and 4 per
cent of women in the U.S.S.R. at that date were still single at ages 45–49

as compared with 11 per cent of men and 12 per cent of women in France in 1900. The pattern of early marriage and a very high proportion of married, Hajnal has shown, also prevailed in Asia and North Africa. As late as 1920, for example, 69 per cent of women in Japan were already married at ages 20–24, while only 2 per cent of them were unmarried at age 45–49. These figures may be compared with the figures from Britain in 1900, when at ages 20–24 only 27 per cent of women were married, and at age 45–49 some 15 per cent remained unmarried.

Apparently, the western European pattern is a modern phenomenon, for the eastern European practice of early marriage and very high proportion of married people was also characteristic of western Europe in the Middle Ages and in antiquity. Why late marriages and relatively low proportions of married people emerged only after the 15th century in western Europe and did not develop elsewhere in the world is not known. But the economic and demographic implications of its development in western Europe are clearly important. Late marriage and a high proportion of people who never married had a direct, downward effect upon the number of children born to a family. And that, in turn, affected the ability of people to save and accumulate wealth for investment and economic growth.[2]

The British colonies in North America in the 17th century constituted a partial, if temporary exception to the pattern in western European societies. In 17th-century America, the age of marriage for women was considerably lower than in contemporary England or on the Continent. In Andover, Massachusetts, for example, the average age of marriage for women married between 1650 and 1675 was 21.3 years, as compared with the mean of 27 years in a contemporary English town. In another New England town, Dedham, the average age of first marriage for women in the late 17th century was 22.5 years. For women born between 1600 and 1700 in Plymouth, Massachusetts, the age of first marriage for females varied between 20.2 and 22.3. Males, on the other hand, seemed to have followed the western European pattern. The mean age of men in Plymouth in the 17th century varied from 27 at the beginning of the century to 24.6 at the end. In Hingham, Massachusetts, the average age of first marriage for men was 27.4 years at the end of the 17th century and 26.4 at the end of the 18th century. Throughout the colonial period the average age of marriage for men in Andover, Massachusetts, was slightly above 26 years. But even for women the average age rose in the course of the 18th century, thus bringing them into line with the pattern in western Europe.

At the time of the American Revolution the average age was 24 for women at Andover and 23.5 at Hingham. A study of some 250 Quaker families at the end of the 18th century showed a high proportion of unmarried persons at age 50, in conformity with the western European practice. Slightly over 12 per cent of the males and almost 16 per cent of the females in these families were unmarried. About 10 per cent of colonial period Andover women never married, a proportion that was somewhat lower than for 19th-century Europe, but considerably higher than any figures for the eastern European countries in 1900.[3] In sum, at the time of the Revolution, according to the somewhat limited, though consistent evidence from several colonial communities, American families exhibited the western European pattern of late marriages, and with around 10 to perhaps 15 per cent of women never marrying at all.

The shift in the age of marriage for women from the 17th to the 18th century was only the beginning of the changes in the American family that are discernible around the time of the Revolution. The family was then on the verge of rather significant alterations, not only in its structure, but in its more important internal dynamics as well.

It is an argument of this book that what today we speak of as the modern American family emerged first in the years between the American Revolution and about 1830. The years are not meant to be taken precisely; they simply suggest the outer limits of the period of transition from the traditional to the modern family in America. And even then the shift is uneven and slow. Yet by the 1830s one can discern quite clearly a form of family that differed in several respects from that which had prevailed prior to the Revolution. This newly emergent family in the 19th century exhibited at least four broad characteristics that had been absent from most families of western European culture in previous centuries. These characteristics will be set forth here only in outline, since it is the job of subsequent chapters to fill out the details and to show more specifically how 19th-century families differed from those of earlier times in America.

One. The marriage which initiated the modern family was based upon affection and mutual respect between the partners, both at the time of family formation and in the course of its life. The woman in the marriage enjoyed an increasing degree of influence or autonomy within the family.

Two. The primary role of the wife was the care of children and the maintenance of the home. Furthermore, the wife, as the mistress of the home, was perceived by society and herself as the moral superior of the husband, though his legal and social inferior. The organizational basis for this relationship was that woman's life was physically spent within the home and with the family, while the man's was largely outside the home, at work. The ideological justification of this division of labor and activity will be referred to as "the doctrine of the two spheres," or "separate spheres."

Three. The attention, energy, and resources of parents in the emerging modern family were increasingly centered upon the rearing of their off-spring. Children were now perceived as being different from adults and deserving not only of material care but of solicitude and love as well. Childhood was deemed a valuable period in the life of every person and to be sharply distinguished in character and purpose from adulthood. Parenthood thus became a major personal responsibility, perhaps even a burden.

Four. The modern family on the average is significantly smaller in size than the family of the 18th and previous centuries, a change that has major consequences for women, as well as for the family.

Because these four elements have continued to be characteristic of the family in the United States in the second half of the 20th century, their presence among a significant proportion of the American population during the opening decades of the 19th century justifies our seeing the emergence of the modern family in those years.

Let us begin to look at the emergence of the modern American family in the order in which the family itself began—with the decision to marry. How was the choice of marital partner made and what was the significance of the basis of the choice? In the half-century after the Revolution the bases of marriage began to change in a decidedly modern direction. Increasingly, free choice by the partners became the basis of family formation. Today it is axiomatic that personal happiness and the affection of the two partners for each other are the only proper foundation for a marriage and the family that follows. Such a conception of marriage has not always been the way in which families were established. Affection was most unlikely to be a basis of marriage if the families of origin of the young people held large amounts of property. For to permit a marriage to take place on the basis of personal or individual preference or whim, rather than by reference to family needs and prospects, threatened a family's holdings and perhaps its long-term future. That was why European crowned heads and noble families insisted that the marriage choices of children be in the hands of parents. Lesser men and women also insisted upon it. In 16th-century Protestant Geneva, for instance, a man could not marry under the age of twenty without his father's consent, or, in case the father was dead, that of his mother or relative. In Catholic France, royal edicts stipulated that parental consent to marry was necessary for a woman until twenty-five and for a man until thirty. As late as 1639 even a son who was over age in France could be disinherited if he married for the first time against his parents' wishes. Historian Lawrence Stone tells of one Michael Wentworth, who, in 1558, stipulated in his will that if any of his daughters did not accept the choice of marital partner named by his executors "but of their own fantastical brain bestow themselves upon a light person" their estate would be reduced from 100 to 66 pounds. Stone called this "powerful posthumous economic blackmail," a practice that American fathers of the 17th century were not hesitant to follow.[4] In Andover, Massachusetts, for instance, fathers who owned land used their control over it to influence, if not to shape, their sons' decisions about marriage. By delaying the turning over of their land to their sons, fathers could determine when and perhaps whom sons would marry.

By the 18th century, however, parental control over the marital choices of their children weakened. Philip Greven, who studied colonial Andover, found that by the mid-18th century fathers were not using their land so frequently to influence their sons' marital decisions. A clearer measure of the decline in parental control over grown children and the corresponding improvement in the children's freedom of choice in marriage is provided by Daniel Scott Smith's study of another colonial town, Hingham, Massachusetts. Smith found that in marriages contracted before 1780 the age of the bridegroom, on the average, was almost two years higher if the father died after age 60 than it was with men whose fathers died before 60. That is, if the father lived beyond the median age of fathers at the marriage of the oldest son (60 years), then the sons' time of marriage was delayed, presumably because the fathers would not let them marry or would not give them the land necessary for the support of a wife and family. In the marriages formed between 1781 and 1840, however, the average difference in the ages of marriage of the two sets of sons was negligible—only three months. This suggests that by the last two decades of the 18th and the opening of the 19th century, a father's influence over a son's choice of decision was much less than it had been before the American Revolution. A study of Concord, Massachusetts, has come up with the same results, though using 1760 as the dividing date. After that date the difference in age of marriage was less than ten months, but before 1760 the difference was 1.5 to 2 years. Moreover, the Concord study found that prior to 1770 the eldest son was twice as likely to succeed to his father's occupation as would be expected by chance. After 1770, the other brothers were more likely to do so than the eldest son, suggesting that the father no longer was able to consider only his own preferences.[5]

In an as yet unpublished investigation of some 100 upper-class families in North Carolina between 1830 and 1860, Jane Turner Censer found that by that period almost no fathers used their power to withhold inheritance from their sons. She reported that even sons who disobeyed their fathers, usually by wasting resources, were not disinherited. Almost half of the fathers actually passed on substantial amounts of property, usually in the form of land, to their sons long before their own deaths, thus facilitating a son's wish to marry without parental influence. Finally, of the 92 wills Censer examined, only two specified a particular occupation that a son ought to follow, but even in these two cases the father added provisions to the will which permitted the son to escape having to follow his father's expectations! In short, even among very wealthy planter families in the South, who certainly had property to conserve, parental power over a son's decisions was not exercised.

Parental control over daughters similarly declined from the 18th to the 19th century. Smith, in his study of Hingham, was able to demonstrate the shift by an examination of the order in which daughters married. He began with the assumption that a father preferred to have his daughters marry in the order of birth; otherwise a prospective suitor might well think something was wrong with an unmarried older daughter. When Smith divided the marriages of daughters according to periods, he discovered that between 1650 and 1750 less than 11 per cent of daughters married out of birth order. But after 1741 over 18 per cent did so, suggesting a substantial increase in the freedom of choice of daughters. Censer in her study of some 100 upper-class families in North Carolina found a similar degree of freedom of choice for daughters. Of 85 women marrying between 1795 and 1865 in 25 families, 30 per cent of them married out of birth order; yet these were families in which the conservation of and control over their substantial wealth certainly gave the father reasons for seeking to control marital choices as well as providing the wherewithal by which to exercise such power.

Finally, Smith advanced a third measure of the shift in parental control from between the 18th to the 19th century. He showed that in Hingham, in the early years of the 19th century, daughters of wealthy parents were actually marrying at a later age than those of poorer parents, though, a hundred years before, the pattern had been just the opposite. Smith's explanation was that in the early colonial period parents with money could marry off their daughters earlier than less wealthy parents simply because the rich had dowries to offer. But by the end of the 18th and opening of the 19th century, young women were making their own decision, and were not permitting their parents to rush them into matrimony any faster than daughters of less well-to-do parents.

By the early years of the 19th century, parental control over the choice of marriage partners of their children was no more than a veto, as it is essentially today in the 20th century. Parents obviously had influence, as in the case of Catharine Beecher, who broke off an engagement with a young man, even though her father, Lyman Beecher, clearly approved of the match. Her father was able to prevail upon her to reopen the relation, and in due course she made a commitment to marry the young man, but the young man's death in an accident intervened. It is nevertheless significant that Catharine never married. Even in the more traditional South, apparently, parental control was weak. Juliet Janin, writing in later life about her own betrothal in 1832 in New Orleans, explained that her suitor, because he was a foreigner, asked her father for her hand before he asked her. "In those days in N.O.," she wrote, "a girl brought up in a measure according to french usages though not coerced was apt to be influenced by . . . the wishes and advice" of her parents or guardian. This, too, was a wealthy family, but clearly considerations of family fortune were not expected to take precedence over the preferences of the young.[6]

If a parent strongly disapproved of his daughter's choice, his principal recourse was either to send her away from home or move the whole family. The second option was apparently being followed by one father in 1857, as recounted by a diarist. The diary-keeper met the daughter on a river boat, where she showed the diarist "the pictures of her lover, from whom she had been ruthlessly torn. Her family actually came West to get her away from him," the diarist wrote indignantly. The limited role of parents and kin in marriage choices is evident, too, in Mary Robart's explanation to cousin Mary Jones of Georgia in 1855, as to why Robart's sister Louisa did not consult the Joneses when she decided to marry a widower with eight children. "Having gained Mother's consent and mine," Robart wrote, Louisa "asked no one else, as she felt she was the best judge of what would promote her own happiness."[7]

Earlier in the century, Elizabeth Southgate, vacationing at a spa far from her parents, met a young man she fell in love with, and though she did not think she could agree to marry him until he had consulted her parents, she knew that her feelings were decisive with her parents. After assuring her mother of her love for the young man, she submitted "herself wholly to the wishes of my Father and you, convinced that my happiness is your warmest wish. . . ." They checked out the young man's reputation and prospects and quickly agreed to the marriage. Even more reflective of the daughter's freedom of choice was the reaction of Mary Peirce's father to the request of Henry Poor for his daughter's hand. Poor had already obtained Mary's consent, he assured the father. Since the Peirces had complete confidence in her judgment, Peirce wrote back, "we submit the subject suggested in your communication entirely to her decision. . . ." [8]

The references to personal happiness in both Mary Robart's and Elizabeth Southgate's letters are significant, for they reveal the goal behind a couple's freedom of choice. Southgate put the matter quite baldly, she thought her suitor "better calculated to promote my happiness than any person I have yet seen." This expression of individualism, as against the collective interest of the family, was made in 1802, and with her parents' tacit acknowledgment of its rightness. The journal of Sarah Ripley of Massachusetts between 1810 and 1812, in which she recorded her movement toward matrimony, also noted that happiness was the expected objective of marriage. Although at one point her meetings with her male friend were less promising than she would have liked, she believed that "hope still soothes my heart and whispers happiness to come." Significant, too, was the fact that throughout the long courtship—five years—her father seemed to play no role at all, except to provide the job that made the marriage possible. Clearly, parents as well as children considered personal, individual happiness the goal of marriage. "There is nothing on this earth that interests me so much as that he may in all respects be worthy of her," wrote a North Carolina planter in 1838 to his son about the suitor of his daughter, "and calculated in mind and morals to make her happy. This is my greatest solicitude." [9]

The role parents played by the latter half of the 19th century was well summed up in a letter in 1871 from Hyland Rice, a young physician, to Robert W. Waterman. In formal, even stilted language, Rice asked Waterman's permission to marry his daughter. "She and I have discovered our mutual affection and have concluded, with the permission of her mother and yourself, to run the two courses of our lives into one." Rice asked permission even though he acknowledged, as he put it in the letter, that Waterman did not think he was "the man suitable above all other men to make her life happier." Nevertheless, Rice promised to do his best to ensure her happiness and to mend his ways in order to achieve that goal.

Once again it is clear that happiness was the purpose of marriage and that mutual affection was its justification. Whatever Waterman's earlier objections to Rice may have been, he did not withold his consent, and apparently Rice had not expected him to once Mary's agreement had been gained. (Something of the weight accorded the personal choice of a son or daughter is measured in the remark of a North Carolina woman on an impending marriage between the daughter of a wealthy planter and a Roman Catholic suitor: "the family (one and all) dislike the match exceedingly," but it went forward nonetheless.[10])

When people in the 19th century spoke of the purposes of marriage, they were most likely to refer to "love" or affection as the basis of the attraction between marital partners and the beginnings of family formation. Love as the basis for marrying was the purest form of individualism; it subordinated all familial, social, or group considerations to personal preference. The idea of love, to be sure, was not new in the 19th century. The Middle Ages had certainly known of it, and the troubadours had sung of courtly love. But significantly enough, not as a basis for marriage. For as Andreas Capellanus, the 12th-century writer, put the matter in his *Art of Courtly Love,* "Everybody knows that love can have no place between husband and wife." Or as he phrased it a little later in the same work: "We declare and hold as firmly established that love cannot exert its powers between two people who are married to each other."[11] In short, love was extra-marital. The idea that love should be the cement of marriages does not figure prominently in Western marriage customs until at least the 17th century. Historian Lawrence Stone tells us that King Charles I and Queen Henrietta Maria were the first English royal couple to be celebrated as a domestic pair rather than as the result of dynastic considerations. Others would follow in subsequent centuries until the high point of royal conjugal love would be reached with Victoria and Albert in the 19th century.

More important as a sign of a new emphasis upon affection within marriage in the 17th century was the stress Puritans placed upon it in their sermons and writings. The Puritan conception was not so much that love ought to be the foundation or origin of marriage as that the couple could expect that time would bring love into their relationship. The Puritan divines asserted the importance of affection, intimacy, and loyalty within marriage, elements that would, of course, become central to the ideal of marriage in America in the 19th century. Margaret Winthrop expressed the idea in quite Puritanical terms when she told her husband, John, the

17th-century governor of the Massachusetts Bay Colony, that the two chief reasons she loved him were "first because thou lovest God; and, secondly, because that thou lovest me. If these two were wanting, all the rest would be eclipsed. But I must leave this discourse," she quickly interjected, "and go about my household affairs. I am a bad housewife to be so long from them; but I must needs borrow a little time to talk with thee, my sweet heart." John's affection for Margaret was no less. In an extant fragment of a letter to her he made clear that she came first in his life. "The largeness and truth of my love to thee makes me always mindful of thy welfare," he began, "and sets me on work to begin to write before I hear from thee. The very thought of thee affords me many a kind refreshment: What will then be the enjoying of thy sweet society, which I prize above all wordly comforts?" The two most popular handbooks on domestic duties in 17th-century England, Lawrence Stone reports, asserted that the purpose of marriage was spiritual intimacy and the avoidance of adultery and fornication outside it. Protestantism, by abandoning the Catholic ideal of celibacy, gave a new emphasis in Christianity to sexual expression, which it then tied to the family.[12]

One consequence of emphasizing affection and loyalty between spouses was an improvement in the position of a woman in marriage. Even in male-dominated Calvinistic Geneva, for example, women were encouraged to sing hymns in church and the old masculine custom of wife-beating was frowned upon. Puritans in Old and New England alike gave recognition to the individual interests of women by making marriage itself a contract, which implied equality. As a contract, rather than a sacrament, marriage could now be dissolved; thus divorce became a matter of public policy, not of religious doctrine. Even so, as John Milton found out, divorce was not easy to obtain, even for a man. But the first step in making marriage responsive to the needs and desires of individuals had been made by Protestantism. Nowhere in the Western world was a divorce easier to obtain than in 17th-century New England.

It is all too easy, of course, to exaggerate the ways in which the Puritans' stress upon personal affection in marriage improved the position of women. To put the proposition into perspective it is only necessary to recollect the explusion of Anne Hutchinson from the Massachusetts Bay Colony in 1638 for presuming to preach. Yet it is worth remembering that it was the Puritans' encouragement of women's participation in church affairs that made it possible for Hutchinson to begin her teaching at all. Protestantism's part in improving the place of women inside and outside the family is best observed in the Quakers, who were, after all, a kind of latter-day Puritans. In them the implications of Puritanism reached their fullest expression. Among the Quakers, women were the religious peers of men. In fact, some of the earliest Quaker missionaries to Puritan Boston were women.

Protestantism's and Puritanism's emphases upon affection in marriage and upon a degree of autonomy for women within the family may have been strong and important, but it would be erroneous to think that the typical American marriage or family even in the 18th century exemplified these ideals. Yet changes were surely in process. In the years after the American Revolution there were more and more signs that affection between spouses and greater freedom for women within marriage were a growing part of family life. Lawrence Stone in his recent history of the family in Britain describes the emergence by the end of the 18th century of what might be called a marriage of companions. And though England is not America, the two countries certainly influenced one another, if only through their common language and common reading. Stone points out that by the end of the 18th century, sons of peers were much less likely to marry wealthy women than in earlier times, a sign of the rise of what he terms "affective individualism." The increase in the expectation of affection in marriage, Stone argues, was also measured in the upsurge in the number of romantic novels published toward the end of the 18th century. Between 1760 and 1779 fewer than twenty such novels were published each year. In the years 1780–89, however, the annual rate was up to almost fifty; by the last decade of the century the figure reached eighty per year. Significantly, many of the novels were written by women—as they would be in the United States in the early 19th century. "Romantic love and the romantic novel grew together after 1780," Stone concluded, "and the problem of cause and effect is one that is impossible to resolve. All that can be said is that for the first time in history, romantic love became a respectable motive for marriage among the propertied classes." [13]

The romantic novel does not become common in America until the 19th century, but in the late 18th century examples of marriages based upon affection and future companionship are not difficult to find. John Dickinson of Pennsylvania wrote his wife of fifteen years in 1784 that she was the "best of women, best of wives, and best of friends." [14] John and Abigail Adams in their correspondence often addressed each other as "friend." The rise in individual affection as a basis for marriage is also measured in a study of some 220 petitions for divorce in 18th-century Massachusetts.

As the century advanced, the study makes clear, the number of petitions increased, even though the law, or the grounds for divorce remained substantially unchanged. More important, the grounds advanced by the petitioners shift as the century moves on. Before 1765 not a single one of the petitioners, male or female, mentioned loss of conjugal affection as a reason for divorce, though they did make other personal accusations, such as that the other party wasted goods or neglected the family. Between 1776 and 1786, however, fully 10 per cent of the 121 suits in that period referred to loss of affection as a justification for divorce. "Ceased to cherish her," said one; another alleged that his wife "almost broke his heart."

Apparently this increased emphasis upon affection in marriage had an effect upon the courts and therefore upon society, much to the benefit of women. Before 1773 not a single petition for divorce by a woman in Massachusetts on the grounds of adultery by a husband was accepted by the courts, though many had been from husbands alleging such behavior on the part of their wives. In 1773, however, two women won full divorces, not merely separations, on the specific ground of adultery by their husbands. Thereafter, other women began to petition, as they had not done before, on the sole ground of adultery, and many now won their cause. In fact, the women's rate of success in divorce petitions in general went from 49 per cent for the years before 1774 to 70 per cent for the years thereafter. During that same period the men's rate of success advanced only from 66 per cent to 73 per cent. In sum, by the end of the 18th century, women's rate of success was almost equal to that of men, pointing to one area in which women's position in marriage, at least in Massachusetts, had come abreast of men's.[15]

Moreover, the increased use by women of the grounds of a husband's adultery clearly reflected a growing emphasis upon personal love and respect as the basis of a marriage. It was putting into practice what the Puritan writers of the 17th century had advocated when they opposed the double standard and defined marriage as a relationship of mutual respect, affection, and companionship. By the last quarter of the 18th century, funeral sermons, too, testified to the ideal of the complementarity of the marital relation and the emotional bonds between marital partners. No longer were women the Eve-temptresses against whom many divines had warned men in earlier times.[16]

Popular writings also reflected this rising emphasis upon love in marriage. A survey of some fifteen magazines published in New England during the last fifty years of the 18th century disclosed that romantic love was widely believed by the writers to be the heart of an ideal marriage. Indeed, the concept was so broadly apparent in the popular literature of the time that it surprised the modern sociologists who were conducting the content analysis of the magazines. They had associated the idea of romantic love with the needs and functioning of an industrial society—that is, a society in which wealth was sufficiently available to permit personal feelings to be the basis of choice of marital partners.[17]

The growing acceptance of affection as the primary ground for family formation was an important stage in the evolution of women's place within the family and in our understanding of how the family has altered over time. It is quite true, as modern observers have pointed out, that most relationships between people involve the exercise of power, and certainly the relationship of marriage is no exception. Yet once affection is a basis of marriage, the marital relation becomes significantly different from other relationships between superiors and inferiors. To begin with, unlike any other subordinate, such as a slave or an employee, a young woman contemplating marriage did have some choice as to who her new master would be. Clearly unsatisfactory possibilities could be ruled out completely, and, from acquaintance at courtship, she had an opportunity to learn who were the undesirable partners. After the marriage, the woman also had an advantage that few slaves or employees enjoyed in dealing with their masters or employers. She was able to appeal to her husband's affection for her, and she, in turn, could use that affection in extracting concessions that a slave or an employee could not. In short, by the very nature of the relation, a woman in the family of affection had more power or influence than any other subordinate one can think of. This is but another way of saying that, simply because women are a sex, the analysis of the history of the family and of women must differ significantly from the ways in which we analyze the behavior of other social groups. Certainly there are valuable analogies to be drawn between the subordination of women and the subordination of other groups, as has often been pointed out. Yet it is essential that the unique elements in the relation between men and women not be forgotten or minimized. By the same token, this caveat should not be read as an invitation to sentimentalize the relations between the sexes; that would only be retrogressive in the study of women or the family.

This modern emphasis upon love in marriage, which by the early 19th century increasingly characterized marriages, was neatly enunciated in 1802 by a young Massachusetts matron of twenty-six when she said that marriage could be a "galling chain. Souls must be kindred to make the bond silken. All others I call unions of *hands, not hearts.* I rejoice," she continued, "that the knot which binds me was not tied with any mercenary feelings, and that my *heart* is under the same subjection as my *hand*." [18]

Marriage for love only was the ideal, and one that many young women tried to put into practice. Mollie Dorsey, in her diary written during the 1850s, epitomized the conflict between love and money as a basis for marriage when the family of origin was not wealthy and, at the same time, the way in which that conflict was probably resolved in most cases. "Aunt Eliza wonders why *I* don't try to captivate Mr. Rucker, as he is rich," Mollie wrote in her journal. Aunt Eliza had admitted that he was not as "nice-looking" as Mollie's lover Byron, "but then, he *owns a farm,* and bless my old darling, he don't own much of anything except those lots and—myself." An indication of how marriages were actually completed comes in her next observation. "My Aunt likes money, but *she* married for love," for her husband had been an impoverished itinerant minister when he asked her to marry him. Aunt Eliza's experience was recapitulated in the marriage of Mollie's sister Dora. Three weeks after Mollie was married, Dora, who was only seventeen, married a man she met for the first time at Mollie's wedding. Her mother was not "reconciled to the suddenness of the affair," Mollie admitted, but her father quietly gathered together a trousseau for Dora, and the wedding went off as and when Dora wished.

Although there is more than a suggestion in Mollie's description that Dora's decision to marry was more emotional than thoughtful, Mollie's own path to matrimony made evident that young women in the middle of the 19th century not only had a choice but also usually exercised it thoughtfully and with realistic expectations. There is no doubt that affection was central to Mollie's decision to marry Byron Sanford. He "loves me tenderly, truly, and . . . I know now that I can place my hand in his and go with him thro life, be path smooth or stormy," she wrote in her diary the night he proposed to her. She fully recognized that their relationship had not been like those depicted in the sentimental novels of the time. "We did not fall madly in love as I had always expected to, but have gradually 'grown into love,' " as the preceding entries in her diary certainly make evident. [19]

Simply because affection was a chief basis for marital choices, courtship in the 19th century was an important stage in family formation. At perhaps no other point in the course of a marriage was a woman's autonomy greater or more individualistically exercised. A brief examination of actual courtships provides some insight into not only how marriages were arranged but what marriage meant for women in the 19th century.

Contrary to what is sometimes thought about the Victorian years, courtship did not have to be formal, excessively restricted, or even chaperoned. Not until late in the 19th century and then only among the urban upper classes was the European practice of chaperoning at all well known. It is true that premarital sexual relations, today so commonplace in America, were rare among all classes of Americans. Even in the 18th century, when premarital pregnancies reached a high not equaled until the late 20th century, no more than 10 per cent of women conceived children that were born less than nine months after the marriage ceremony. And according to the few historical studies on the subject, the proportion of bridal pregnancies in the 19th century was even smaller. Only among black families were premarital pregnancies proportionately high at the end of the 19th century. But even then, the great majority of black couples waited until marriage before conceiving children.[20] Illegitimate births were also low for all groups of society, though of course they occurred.

As we shall see in Chapter IX, means of contraception were rather well known in the 19th century, but they were not sufficiently reliable to protect women from the social stigma which fell like a hammer on those whose sexual relations outside marriage were revealed by illegitimate births. Finally, it should be remembered that premarital sexual relations have not been typical of American courtships for most of the 20th century, either.

If we leave aside premarital sexual experience as a measure of the freedom of courtship, then the Victorian courtship is far from staid. Indeed, as Alexis de Tocqueville and other foreign travelers in America in the 1830s and 1840s pointed out, unmarried women were much freer in public than their married sisters. Middle- and lower-class women moved about not only without chaperones, but also with a certain amount of abandon. Mollie Dorsey, while traveling with her family on a river boat in the late 1850s, reported that she and a newly found female friend "have splendid times—flirt all day." It was not unusual for a young woman to accompany a young man on fishing trips, with no one else along, or to accept invitations for walks together, discussing personal matters. "I am sorry to tell you," one young woman wrote a female friend in 1822, "that I feel remarkably dull this evening having just returned from a long walk of three miles out of town . . . for I was with a gentleman who I am somewhat afraid of, as he is most appallingly sensible and intellectual, and I have been exerting every facility to say something smart." Mollie Dorsey also took a long walk; she stayed out so late with her lover that her father came looking for her. She felt "sheepish to be patrolled home," and her father's reproof "rather spoiled the romance of the thing," she complained. A young man's diary of 1861 similarly revealed young women who were hardly bashful. He told of going to a "Sewing Circle of the North Baptist Church," where he "went over the river with Miss Hutchins. 3 couples of us remained there until 1 ½ in the morning. Came up with Lizzie Green. I don't know how many kisses I had that evening, was almost smothered with sweet things." Two days later he spent an evening with a Miss Albert, who gave "me a sweet kiss before I was aware of the fact; went home with my lady. She too gave me a farewell salute." A dozen years later Anna Haskell in California told in her journal of the several boys who rather regularly came to her room at college at night, even though the practice was quite against the rules. Sometimes Anna would go off alone with one for a walk and talk. Nor was it always necessary for couples to sneak off in order to obtain privacy. When callers came to Mollie Dorsey's house, all her relatives and family quickly left the room so that the couple could be alone.[21]

Late night courting was not limited to the new country or to forward young men. Indeed, as Lester Frank Ward's diary written during the same years in rural eastern Pennsylvania shows, courting in Victorian America could be freer than many have supposed. Again and again Ward reported that he and "his girl," as he referred to the young woman who later became his wife, kissed and caressed each other until the early morning hours. On a Monday night in 1860, when he was nineteen, he left her only "at half past three . . . amid thousands of kisses." Then on the following Wednesday he escorted her home, not leaving again until 3:00 A.M. During that stay, he reported they spent "an hour embracing, caressing, hugging, and kissing. O bliss! O love! O passion, pure, sweet and profound! What more do I want than you?"

Nor was all the initiative his. On a subsequent visit, after an absence of several days, he found her most captivated by him. "She looked at me so gently and spoke so tenderly. 'I love you,' she said, kissing me on the mouth. 'I love this mouth, I love those dear eyes, I love this head,' and a thousand other little caressing pet-names." At around 3:00 A.M., when they became sleepy, they arranged the chairs in such a way that they could lie lengthwise facing each other and he opened his shirt, placing her hand on his bare chest. She said she thought she might be doing something wrong, but, significantly, she did not stop. "As we lay in this position," he noted, "the cocks crowed." Quickly he slipped off to work, where he caught up on his lost sleep. After another equally loving visit, at 4:30 in the morning they heard her father jumping out of bed. Hurriedly they kissed and he ran home.

By early 1861 their physical attraction to one another had become so strong that it began to worry them. "I had a very affectionate time with the girl, kissing her almost all over and loving her very deeply and she *does* me." Two weeks later Ward referred to a "very secret time" with her. "I kissed her on her soft breasts, and took too many liberties with her sweet person, and we are going to stop. It is a very fascinating practice and fills us with very sweet, tender and familiar sentiments, and consequently makes us happy." They talked about their fear that "we might become so addicted in that direction that we might go too deep and possibly confound ourselves by the standards of virtue." Even when he was not with her, he dreamed about her and during the day fantasized about "kissing her sweet breasts and sleeping in her arms." A week later he characteristically, if enigmatically wrote, "I slept in her arms; yes, I lay with her, but did nothing wrong."

Yet, despite the intimacy, the relationship between them was not yet settled, for she was still seeing other young men, a practice that inevitably aroused Ward's jealousy and temporarily reduced her ardor. Gradually, after a long talk, they recognized their mutual attraction and dependence; weeping and kissing, they re-established their old, close relation. Ward was thrown into despair some nights later when he called on her only to find that her brother was home, preventing their usual love-making. Ward managed to get a note to her asking if he could return later. To his delight she wrote back that she wanted to kiss him. When he did return, "closely held in loving arms we lay, embraced, and kissed all night (not going to bed until five in the morning). We have never acted in such a way before. All that we did I shall not tell here, but it was all very sweet and loving and nothing infamous," he assured himself. By the end of that year of rather steady courtship little restraint was left on their emotions. "When I arrived at the house of sweetness, she received me in her loving arms and pressed me to her honey-form, and our lips touched and we entered Paradise together. . . . That evening and night we tasted the joys of love and happiness which only belong to a married life." Early the next year, in 1862, they were married.[22]

Ward's diary is unusually explicit about the physical side of a mid-19th-century courtship; yet even it, by late 20th-century standards, is noticeably circumspect, suggesting the difficulty 19th-century people had in discussing such matters, even privately. It is worth noting, too, that the diary was originally written by Ward in French, a fact that probably accounts for his uncommon explicitness of language. But there is no reason to believe that the behavior he described was rare or exceptional.

The courtship of an older couple, even at the end of the century, could be quite different, though revealing of what marriage meant to certain women. Jerome Hart in 1896 was forty-two years old, but he had never married. Only five years before he had become editor of the *Argonaut,* an important weekly in San Francisco, and a measure of his success as a journalist. In the last month of 1895 he met Ann Clark, a graduate of the University of California Law School and a legal adviser in an insurance and real estate agency in San José, some 45 miles south of San Francisco. Their correspondence over the course of the four years it took them to move from first acquaintance to husband and wife documents the formality that could occur even between lovers, especially when one was a career woman. For the first three months of their correspondence he addressed her only as "my dear Miss Clark." Probably because of her own career, Ann Clark was slow to accept Hart's proposal of marriage. Certainly she gave testimony to the conflict that could arise with the conventional view of marriage when a woman pursued a career. At one point Hart complained that at their last meeting she had seemed cold toward him. She explained herself by writing that "At the last moment how I yearned to say 'Stay' yet you think I do not care for you. You can never realize the terrible temptation I was under to let myself glide into those strong arms of yours and to take all the love and protection you offer me." She then referred to the burdens borne by a single woman in an age when marriage for women was the expected role. "No more would I have to meet perplexities and stumble along in the dark alone."[23]

The courtship of Charlotte Perkins Stetson, the feminist writer, and Houghton Gilman, which took place at about the same time on the opposite side of the continent, was at once different from and similar to that of Hart and Ann Clark. It was different in that in the Stetson-Gilman case the woman was the older of the two by seven years; in 1900, at the time of her second marriage, Charlotte Stetson was forty. It is different, too, in that Stetson was a mother by a previous marriage, and divorced. Like Ann Hart, Charlotte was a career woman who spent much time traveling and lecturing on behalf of women's causes. Houghton was a lawyer and Charlotte's first cousin.

Like Ann Hart, Charlotte Stetson was not prepared to fall in love, though it is also clear that she wanted that love desperately. "O sweet-heart—is it true? Aren't you sorry yet? Surely you could have done better. I ought not to have let you throw yourself away so. You could have had so much happier a life with a *whole* woman who would have been all yours." The last is a reference to her commitment, which Houghton accepted, to her work as feminist and lecturer. But she promised anew that, if she could not be like other wives, "that piece of me from time to time—even most of the time—will make you as happy as all of some one else would. I shall tenderly and remorsefully try to make the piece large and sweet—full of raisins!" At the same time she found it difficult that she was, because of her commitment to Houghton, no longer a complete entity, but now "greatly lacking my other half. It seems vague and funny. I wonder if it will go away. If we have been playing—dreaming—and it will all pass!"

The conflict between the memories of her first marriage, the commitment to her career, and her deep desire to marry Houghton gave a poignancy to this courtship that was probably not usual, but nonetheless illustrative of the ambiguity that many, though certainly not most women of the late 19th century felt about marriage. Charlotte herself had decided that the marriage would not take place for two years, when she had paid off all her accomulated debts. It is also evident that her work came first. "Dear, if I had to choose today between you and my work—two hearts might break, and I might die of the breaking, but I could not choose other than the one way. If I can harmonize love and home with this great calling I shall be happy beyond my wildest hopes." There were also conflicts still in her mind about a wife's proper role, for, as she said in that same letter, she felt "so remorseful and ashamed to think that you, my dear, dear love, are not my first and only. All the piled up ancestral womanheartedness—cries out Treason! I feel I am not truly loving you." In a subsequent letter, when she learned that Houghton's regiment would not be sent to Cuba to fight, she exulted in the sense of security the news brought her. "Guess I'm a woman all right—just like the rest of 'em. 'Tisn't any fun, either," she concluded ruefully. But always there was the commitment to her work, even when it created tension. "If I should lose you, the wound would go deeper than any other of the many I have had. But under and over and around all that poor little woman's heart of mine is this great strong boundless thing that loves and works for all the world. I can't help it—that's me."[24]

Courtship is only one way of gaining an insight into the nature and bases of marriage in 19th-century America. After all, it is only the beginning of a marriage, and, in some ways, the ideal as opposed to the real expression of what marriage meant. A more realistic insight into the nature of marriage during the past century is to see how actual husbands and wives related to one another. That is the subject of the next chapter.

II

Wives and Husbands

One of the hallmarks of the emerging modern family in the early 19th century was the sharply differentiated roles or functions assigned by social custom to wife and husband. Women's activities were increasingly confined to the care of children, the nurturing of husband, and the physical maintenance of the home. Moreover, it was not unusual to refer to women as the "angels of the house," for they were said to be the moral guardians of the family. They were responsible for the ethical and spiritual character as well as the comfort and tranquility of the home. In that role they were acknowledged to be the moral superiors of men. Husbands, on the other hand, the ideology proclaimed, were active outside the home, at their work, in politics, and in the world in general. In fact, it was just this involvement of men in the world that made them in need of women's moral guidance and supervision. Three modern sociologists, after surveying the popular literature published between 1825 and 1850 reported that "all of the discussions advocating power over morality involved the female. . . . The moral superiority of women was a pervasive theme during this period."[1] This sharp division between the roles of husband and wife, which contemporaries called their different spheres, is what is meant by the doctrine of the two spheres, or separate spheres.

Some historians have called the ideology of woman's sphere the "Cult of True Womanhood," a name that reflects their judgment that women's position in the 19th century was not only restricted to the home but that it had declined from earlier times. In the eyes of these historians, the Cult of True Womanhood, by combining piety and domesticity with submissiveness and passivity, controlled women and narrowed their options. And there is no doubt that measured against the opportunities open to women today, the Victorian Cult of True Womanhood did severely circumscribe women's activities. Whether that circumscribing constituted a decline from an earlier position within the family is a more complicated question.

Some contemporaries considered the separation of roles advantageous to women. Tocqueville, for instance, in the 1830s not only documented the existence of the two spheres he also defended it because he thought it reflected mutual respect between husband and wife. Americans, he wrote in *Democracy in America,* did not believe that the two sexes should perform the "same offices, but they show an equal regard for both their respective parts; and though their lot is different, they consider both of them as beings of equal value." As a concrete measure of what he meant, Tocqueville pointed out that in his native France rape was punished only lightly, yet even at that a conviction was difficult to obtain. In the United States, however, he pointedly observed, rape was one of the few capital offenses still remaining. Fredericka Bremer, Swedish feminist and novelist, who visited the United States in the 1840s, also admired the high place accorded women in America. She went on to suggest that one of the sources of this elevation was the important role vouchsafed to women in the family, where they were "the center and lawgiver in the home." And Sarah Josepha Hale, perhaps the leading woman journalist in the nation at the time, proclaimed women to be "God's appointed agent of MORALITY" with a responsibility to use that power within the family to refine man's "human affections and elevate his moral feelings." Catharine Beecher, well-known educator and writer, also believed that women's position in the home was an opportunity and a responsibility to do good.[2]

If only because independent-minded women publicists like Beecher and Hale, not to mention foreign visitors of similar authority, thought highly of woman's sphere, we ought not to conclude too hastily that the separation of the spheres was nothing more than a rationale for the subordination or diminishing of women. In fact, this strict division of influence between the sexes has been interpreted as at least a form of advancement for women. Historian William E. Bridges has pointed out, that Sarah Hale and Catharine Beecher may not have been feminists, but that did not mean their justification of the two spheres was reactionary. On the contrary, Bridges observed, it sprang from "their almost utopian optimism. Far from trying to weaken woman and limit her power," they and other publicists of their persuasion "believed that they were offering the American woman the opportunity to wield incomparable power." There was, to be sure, a discrepancy to be noted in the intentions behind the doctrine as delineated by Bridges or set forth by Catharine Beecher. Yet the fact remains, as Nancy Cott has observed, that within the home women did gain a new recognition and in the process broke the ancient hierarchy that had assigned superiority to men in all spheres of activity.[3] Domesticity, in short, was an alternative to patriarchy, both in intention and in fact. By asserting a companionate role for women, it implicitly denied patriarchy.

Moreover, by confining women's attentions to the home, the doctrine of the two spheres, or domesticity, reflected an improvement in the material situation of women. No longer were women expected to work outside the house, as women did on farms and in less affluent, pre-industrial days. The material improvement was enhanced further by a lightening of women's work within the home. For now commercial manufacturing increasingly produced many of the necessities that had once been women's obligation to make in the home, particularly clothing and foods. As we shall see in later chapters, in the 19th century women began to bear fewer and fewer children, and as early as 1840 the life expectancy of women at birth was higher than men's, something that seems not to have been true in previous centuries. In short, there does seem to have been improvement at least materially in the lot of women accompanying the doctrine of separate spheres. And there was probably some psychological improvement as well.

At the same time, let it be quickly added, insofar as women accepted a separation of roles they denied themselves opportunities for activities outside the home. Inevitably, therefore, a time would arrive when the doctrine of separate spheres would come under attack as repressive and limiting, for in a different time and under different circumstances that is what the doctrine would be. Even before that time arrived, women's special place in the home and the Cult of True Womanhood would be used by some women to justify their working for changes outside the home and within the family. For if the home was to be protected from the world's evil, then it could be argued logically that women had a moral obligation to attack such influences even if that meant acting in the world. Through such logic some women, even in the middle of the 19th century, legitimized their attacks upon social evils like the liquor traffic and prostitution. But that subject is best left to fuller discussion in a later chapter.

The doctrine of the two spheres, like the Cult of True Womanhood, is an ideological construction, not a description of how real people behaved. Its lineaments and content have been derived by historians from what publicists and writers of advice books at the time said the roles of wives and husbands ought to be. The cult, in sum, concerns an image, not necessarily the behavior of people. What we need to know is how the roles of the sexes in the 19th-century family actually functioned. What was the behavioral content, so to speak, of the doctrine of the two spheres? How did real husbands and wives relate to one another?

Marriage has been many things, but at all times it has been a relationship of power, however muted or disguised it may be in any particular case. For in no association between human beings are decisions that affect both arrived at equally. And certainly in the 19th century, when a husband was acknowledged by all to be the head of the family, there can be no doubt that power or the making of decisions was unequally distributed. It was just this aspect of marriage that interested the three recent sociologists, whose work has been cited earlier, in surveying the popular literature of the antebellum years. When they explored the relations between husband and wife as portrayed in popular stories and articles, they found sufficient signs of increasing power for women within the middle-class marriage to conclude "that internal changes concerning the reallocation of power were taking place."[4]

Another way of uncovering the extent of authority, power, or influence of women in the functioning 19th-century household is to examine the correspondence between husbands and wives, and the diaries and journals kept by women. In such sources can be found clues to these elusive yet important relationships that sociologists (and anthropologists) today obtain so much more easily from questionnaires, interviews, and direct observation.

Letters and diaries as sources of information on the internal dynamics of marriages have advantages over other kinds of sources, but they also have serious disadvantages that deserve to be acknowledged. The most obvious advantage is that such documents can reveal people's values, attitudes, and motives as well as their actions. Census or statistical data, which are the kind often used by historians of the family, can tell us what many people did, but they are usually silent on why or how. Statistical information, however, does have one great advantage over written documents: its representativeness can be ascertained or at least its selectivity can be compensated for by a large sample of random cases. Only if one could read hundreds of letters between several hundred couples could literary sources approach the randomness of the census data. And even then that large number of letters—and that large amount of labor—would not allow us to encompass the diversity of the population. For how could we be sure that those who wrote such letters were representative of those whose letters were not saved or did not write letters at all?

But this is making the worst possible case. The fact is that all historical investigation is similarly limited to the evidence that survives, and the fact that even small samples of correspondence corroborate one another suggests that representativeness is not as hard to achieve as it might appear in the abstract. Yet, in the end it has to be conceded that most, if not all, of the couples who wrote to one another or women who kept diaries were probably middle-class people, if only because they wrote at all. Some were actually upper-class persons. The great majority of white Americans it is true, were literate, but most of them probably did not write much. Very few of the extant written sources derive from working-class, black, or immigrant families. Whether such families follow closely or remotely the patterns discerned among middle-class families we cannot tell directly, though there is some reason to believe that middle-class family values and practices penetrated to lower social strata. What is said in this chapter about the relationships between husbands and wives, insofar as it is drawn from written materials, must be presumed to apply mainly to middle-class people, many of whom lived in cities. Since this evidence is particularly rich it seems worthwhile to examine it separately and fully. What connections can be made between this evidence and that available for working-class, black, and immigrant families will be noticed here in passing and more fully in Chapter VI, where the families outside the middle class will be examined in as much detail as the less revealing evidence for those groups permits.

The diaries and letters of the time make it quite clear that husbands accepted the moral superiority of women, which the advice and periodical literature of the early 19th century emphasized. One North Carolina man wrote in the 1820s to a male friend who was contemplating marriage that if he went through with it, he must be "prepared to have his nose occasionally ground . . . and that he must not drink or play cards." The role of women in raising the moral level of men's behavior was also reflected in diaries and letters. Mollie Dorsey, soon after she married Byron Sanford, first heard him swear while traveling by wagon train to their new home in Colorado. Her response was to weep, something she was not prone to do. The effect was as she intended: on a subsequent day, when the oxen were particularly difficult and many of the men let their tongues loose upon them, Byron Sanford did not join in. "My tears had the effect of keeping

By from it, as I've heard no more swearing from him since that day," she observed in her diary. General William Pender proudly wrote his wife during the Civil War that "I have broken myself of using anything like profanity even in telling what someone else might have said, and I very seldom say anything that I would not say in any company." Pender made quite clear that he saw in his young wife—they had been married less than four years—the literal moral arbiter of his life. "Honey," he wrote in the fall of 1862, "whenever I try to reflect upon the future and to resolve to do better, I think of you first and your image rises up . . . so that I have almost come to feel that you are a part of my religion. Whenever I find my mind wandering upon bad and sinful thoughts I try to think of my good and pure wife and they leave me at once. My dear wife you have no idea of the excellent opinion I have of your goodness and sweetness. You are truly my good Angel." [5]

Harriet Beecher Stowe's disciplining of the morals of her husband Calvin was at once more detailed and somewhat less successful, though her moral superiority in his eyes seems not to have been in doubt. Deeply concerned about religion herself, Harriet thought Calvin not sufficiently so, though he was a minister of the gospel. "If you had studied Christ with half the energy that you have studied Luther. If you were as eager for daily intercourse with him as to devour the daily newspapers. If you were drawn towards him and loved him as much as you loved your study and your books then would he be formed in you. . . . But you fancy you have *other* things to do."

Harriet's assertion of her moral superiority included concern about Calvin's sexual urges. At one point she attempted to arouse his guilt in an effort to control his behavior. While on a visit to her brother Henry in the summer of 1844, Henry told her of sexual indiscretions "among high places in the church," she reported to Calvin. Her brother seemed so depressed by the incidents that she began to have "a horrible presentiment. . . . I thought of all my brothers and of you and could it be that the great Enemy has prevailed against any of you." Conceding that she did indeed have a vivid imagination, she began to envision all the despair she would feel if Calvin should "fall." The very thought made her feel "weak and sick. I took a book and lay down on the bed, but it pursued me like a nightmare and something seemed to ask Is your husband any better seeming than so and so?" When she examined herself in the mirror her face appeared "the palest and so haggard that it frightened me. The illusion lasted a whole forenoon and then evaporated like a poisonous mist. . . . I can conceive now of the misery which in one night would change the hair to grey and shrivel the whole frame to premature decrepitude!"

Harriet had no doubt that the danger lay in the difference between men and women, not simply in the power of the devil. "What terrible temptations lie in the way of your sex," she wrote her husband, "till now I never realized it." For, she went on, although before their marriage she had loved him "with an almost *insane* love," she did not then know or feel "the pulsation which showed me that I could be tempted in that way." During their courtship, she continued, "there never was a moment when I felt anything by which you could have drawn me astray" for she then loved him "as I now love God," that is, with the highest of feelings. Indeed, she went on, her own dearth of sexual feelings meant that "I have no jealousy. The most beautiful woman in the world could not make me jealous so long as she only *dazzled* the senses." Even so, she was not going to let Calvin escape the moral responsibilities of his masculine sexuality. He must always recognize its dangers and endeavor to control it. For, "my dear," she continued, "you must not wonder if I want to warn you not to look or *think* too freely on womankind. [He had expressed his interest in pretty women.] If your sex would secure the outworks of thought you would never fall." After all, she concluded, considering the "dizzying" and "astounding . . . advantages which Satan takes, it scarce is implying a doubt to say 'be cautious.' "⁶

Fanny Pender also took her husband to task for letting his sexuality get the better of him. He had told her of gestures of friendship women had made to him at camp and that he had enjoyed flirting with some of the women. Fanny's reaction was one of anger mixed with pain, for she did not understand why he would write to her about his flirting with other women and tell her that women had made overly friendly overtures to him. "My dear, ever dear Husband, do not think this is only a little jealous feeling—I know it will amuse you now, but the time will come when you will remember it." She wondered whether the lady in question would have "made such a remark in my presence? Then it was not proper for you to hear. I never expected to hear you admit that you had been *flirting*. What would you think to hear me use such an expression. And would it be more immoral in me than in you?" Fannie Pender thought that her husband ought to be held to the same moral standard which she observed and that it was her responsibility to call his attention to that standard.⁷

Women may have been the moral governors of their husbands, but that did not mean they were not dependent upon them as well. In the urban family the wife was usually left behind each day when the husband went to work. For some women, the absence of the husband was made considerably lengthier because of his occupation. Wives of seamen, peddlers, and other traveling workers spent much time waiting, worrying, and coping by themselves. And though one might think such isolation would make a woman less dependent on her husband, the record suggests otherwise. The dependence after all was not simply economic or financial, though it was usually that. Principally, it was emotional. Mary Walker, the wife of a missionary living in the Oregon Territory in 1838, feared that her husband, who often left on trips, did not reciprocate her love. "I love my husband so much that almost the only thing that makes me feel unhappy is the fear that he does not love [me] as much. I find it hard to be reconciled to the thought of ever being separated from him," she wrote in her diary.[8]

Seamen's wives expressed their dependence by urging their husbands to come home. Lucy Gray wrote her sea-captain husband in 1823: "Oh Husband I cannot describe to you my feeling the night you left home the house and everything about seem'd melencholly." Although her sister stayed with her, providing some comfort, she could only hope that her chronic ill health and the dangers to which he was exposed would not prevent their seeing one another again. Clearly, her husband did not have the same dependence, for fifteen months later he had not returned, having gone on yet another voyage. Lucy had reconciled herself to his lengthy absence, for it seemed that "as soon as you arrive you will immediately [engage] another voyage but I hope you will not untill I see you; indeed you must not." Now she was willing to consider going with him on his next voyage, something she had apparently refused to do earlier.[9]

As Lucy Gray's description suggested, the night seamen-husbands left on their voyages highlighted most sharply their wives' dependence on them. In 1828 a Salem seaman's wife wrote that "i went down to mothers the night that you went to sea for i could not bear to see the house after It lost its chief attracion." In this particular instance, there was additional concern since she was pregnant with a baby boy, who was born six months later. In informing her husband of his new son, she used the boy as a lure to bring the father home. The child was not "a grate boy but thare is room a nuf to grow. . . . If you ever Live to get home I shall bee happy. But I am afraid that your Boy will say father first."[10]

Lucy Gray was more blunt in urging her husband's return. Taking note of his recent decision to take on a new voyage without coming home, she wondered why that was necessary since he had been doing quite well

financially. "Are you any more contented than you was before you commenced it," she wanted to know. Her own immediate answer was, "It appears you are not." The reason was, she added, that "there is no real satisfaction to be found in the things of this world, for the more we have the
more we shall want." Then she returned to her personal wishes and hopes.
"I think if you knew how much I have undergone this day you would
come home," but if he did not, and she had to continue to "spend my days
alone and in sorrow I hope I shall be reconciled to my lot." Then she
added a mild threat: "But my best advice to you is to come amediately
home and spend 3 or 4 weeks with your family. . . ." Nor was Lucy
Gray's dependence only emotional. At the end of the same letter she
added, "If you go away again dont neglect sending me some money soon
for I have had none to help myself with this winter." [11]

Usually, as the pleas of these women suggest, a large part of the dependence of women on their absent husbands derived from the simple fact
that the women were left with children to care for and sometimes to provide for. Emotional dependence was evident, however, even when children
were not present. When Melville Anderson, a young student of foreign languages, went abroad in 1876 to study, he left behind his wife, Charlena,
who at that time was also a teacher and student. Like the seamen's wives,
Charlena Anderson waited for mail, making trips through the cold to the
post office. "Nothing came this morning. Tonight contrary to . . . my
own judgment I go again. . . . O dear how I miss you sometimes . . . it
is lonesome everywhere without you!" She knew that he would upbraid
her for not being brave and independent as she had promised, but the
loneliness, she wrote, overwhelmed her at times. "I did not know you
were so dear to me. When I think a great deal about you, as I do some
days, I grow so lonesome without you, think I must see you again and talk
with you. How sweet that would be!" [12]

Although it might be thought that the emotional dependence of wives on
their husbands was largely a function of their being left behind at home,
wives who left their husbands behind expressed similar sentiments of dependence. Even though Mary Poor was visiting her parents with her small
children, "Sometimes such a feeling of longing for you, dearest, comes
over me," she wrote her husband in 1846, "that I feel as if I *must* fly to
you." Just like those women whose husbands had left them behind, Mary
Poor found "that the love I feel for you is different from any other love,
that to be with you is my life." At another time she expressed her regret
for his enforced loneliness because she was away, but told him that such

feelings would help him understand hers. "I have been deserted a great deal this Winter," she reminded him. "I grant that I had rather the advantage over you in that the children were left to me, but they are nothing in comparison with you. When you are away I do not enjoy them as I do when you are with me."

These comments were made early in the Poors' marriage and, though Henry and Mary were separated often, principally because of his business, she never became adjusted to it. In 1858, over ten years after their earlier separations, she began a letter to him soon after he had left for Europe: "The longer you are away, the worse I feel about it. It sometimes seems as if I *must* see you. . . . Oh Henry! if I were *half* as sure that I love Jesus as I am that I love you, I should have bright hopes for the eternal world. I can think of nothing to tell you, because when I sit down to write, I have but one thought, and that is, how much I want to see you. That overmasters all others." She knew that she could not possibly hear from him for another two weeks and so she resolved to contain herself, as she had promised. "It is a sin to be wishing these glorious June days away," she confessed, "but it is a sin that I cannot help committing." Then when she did hear from him, she became suddenly aware of how slow and sad the summer was, compared with the last, when he had been able to be with her. "I shall lead a sort of half life till you come back. How could I ever have let you go?" [13]

Their closeness continued and ripened through the 1860s and into the 1870s, though by then their children were grown. In 1863, for example, when he was working in New York City, she admitted the practical necessity of the arrangement only because she knew she was *"infinitely happier to have you away from me while I know that you love me, than I should be with you if ours were such a match as some that I might mention."* Nor had the romance in their marriage dissipated even then. When he returned to New York after an extended visit to their home she wrote that his departure "makes me feel decidedly sentimental and I grieve over your loss like a widowed dove. What a foe to love is business! Do let us retire and live in Andover an Arcadian life, our only business being to make each other happy!" In January 1870 she was still trying to reconcile herself to his absences, promising not "to grieve over your absences again. I ought to be too happy to think that such a being exists, and lives to love me. It is enough for one mortal." [14]

The love and warmth that flowed between Henry and Mary Poor were probably not typical of middle-class marriages of the Victorian era, as

Mary herself at one point suggested. But the affection and emotional dependence were not rare, even among families much less well off, or in which the spouses were less suited to one another. Mary Hallock Foote had a difficult life in the far West, married to a mining engineer who was not always able to support his family, much less provide emotional security. So difficult was his situation—and therefore hers—that he took to drink; Mary Foote was so disgusted that she ran off briefly with her children to Victoria, British Columbia. But that absence brought home to her, as she confessed later, in 1896, to her girlhood chum and confidante, that she could not endure being separated from her husband. "I tried it once in Victoria, as you know, such a little step, but I felt so lost. No," she continued, any long visits away from home "must be both of us or neither." [15]

The emotional dependence of the wife on the husband in the 19th-century family served an important purpose for the husband, just as the ideal of separate spheres prescribed. Her presence provided emotional support, nurturance, and encouragement, if only because he learned thereby of his importance to another human being. The quality and extent of that support or encouragement was most clearly observable when adversity or disappointment struck. Sarah Bell Waller, the wife of a Kentucky lawyer, in 1855 exemplified as well as defined this role. "You seemed so sad and troubled this evening," she wrote soon after he had left home on a business trip. "I longed my dear love to leave all and go with you tonight that I might drive away all your vexations and cares, and cheer you and love you and caress you, till you ceased to feel sad, or troubled." After assuring him that she was the proper one to whom he should bring his troubles, she went on. "T'is to me, you must come for sympathy and consolations, for I am nearest to you and have a right to all these dear confidences. You are my dear sweet husband, whom I love most dearly, and truly, and I cannot be unmoved by what affects you." And when Melville Anderson in 1876 was discouraged about his professional future as he perceived it from his European place of study, he wrote about it to his wife Charlena. Her response was at once supportive and indicative of her emotional need to be with him. "When you come back to America I am going to stay right with you. Don't be discouraged. I am going to follow you to Texas, New Mexico, Alaska or any other place you may be offered a post," she promised. "A year with you would be worth twelve without you," she assured him. [16] The dependence of women had two sides to it: subordination undoubtedly, but also strength and self-reliance. Husbands not only depended on both, but required both.

The dual character of a woman's relationship to her husband was neatly epitomized by an incident in the life of Mollie Dorsey Sanford. When her new husband was ordered to join his company to fight the Indians in New Mexico, she stood beside him "in the midst of those men, only wishing for *one* moment when I could abandon myself to grief," that is, to show her dependence. But before she could find the occasion, the supportive side of her wifely role was called upon. She noticed that her husband's emotions had anticipated hers, for tears were trickling down his cheeks. "Then all the heroic in my woman's nature came [forth] and *I* turned to be the comforter," she proudly recalled.[17]

In the relationship between Mary and Arthur Foote, the strong supportive side of the wife's role was the one more frequently called upon. Because she was a professional writer and artist as well as a mother, Mary Foote was well aware, as she told her confidante Helena Gilder, that she was not a very conventional wife, and so Helena could well "imagine how often I lean very hard upon Arthur's generosity and magnanimity." At the same time, it was Mary who was providing the income for the family when Arthur was unable to. Yet Arthur needed more than income, as she recognized when he reached the depths of his despair and had written to her from the field about his empty future. Filled with remorse for her lack of adequate support, she poured out her feelings to Helena. "My poor old boy is, Heaven knows where—by what lonely water pool in the desert. . . . I fear his own nerve is giving out a little, and small wonder." For if she felt isolated and alone, "what must it have been for him to go back alone, to his dust and wind? . . . I know that for every hard word or sharp word I have ever given him, for every time I have misjudged him I will atone with those tears that we shed in our hearts when it is too late."

In December 1895, her appreciation and support of Arthur reached a high point. "I can say of him," she acknowledged to Helena," as I might of a stranger (for never have I been so critical of anyone as I have been of my husband) that a braver man I have never known; and talking of bitterness—he might be excused for a touch of it, but he grows sweeter and humbler under the hand of discipline." Her hope was that God would reward him for the fight he had made and would continue to make "to the End. He has conquered himself."[18]

In Mary Foote's appreciation of her husband's hard-won strength lay an important measure of the emotional content of the middle-class marriage of the 19th century. Mary and Arthur Foote did not enjoy either the emotional or the financial good fortune of the Poors or even the contentment of the Sanfords or the Andersons, but their shared life together was more than a matter of a convenience or of parallel lives. They supported one another, out of their strengths and despite their individual weaknesses. Mary Foote, who was clearly the stronger and more resilient personality, could yet appreciate the character which adversity ultimately brought out in her weaker and less talented husband. That recognition was not born of subordination, but of intelligence, independence, and strength. Those qualities were as much a part of the character of the Victorian wife as dependence and social subordination.

The supportive qualities and dependence of the 19th-century wife were often matched by similar qualities in her husband. Tocqueville in the 1830s commented on the high degree of companionship he found in the American marriage, noting that mistresses were few in America. During a visit to the United States in 1863, Edward Dicey, the English writer, praised "the great charm which surrounds all family relations in the North. Compared with Europe, domestic scandals are unknown." And at the end of the century, another English traveler remarked that "the average American husband makes a confidante and a companion of his wife." [19] That conclusion was also evident in the letters which husbands wrote to their wives, expressing their dependence on them.

According to Mary Beth Norton's recent study of correspondence between 18th-century husbands and wives that could not have been said about connubial relations in earlier times. Some husbands, Norton observes, actually addressed their wives as "dear child." Others, when separated for a while, wrote not of missing their wives, but of how much they expected the wives missed them! And one husband, in urging his wife to read more, condescendingly reminded her that "my good opinion . . . depends on the *amiable accomplishments* of your *mind.*" Not until the very end of the 18th century, Norton significantly points out, do wives seem to show any resentment of this subordination to their husbands. In the light of these earlier modes of relations between husband and wife, those between spouses in the 19th century seem almost egalitarian as well as companionate. For by then husbands were quite willing to admit dependence upon their wives. [20]

Henry Poor understood why his wife had to absent herself from him while she visited her parents in 1846, but he clearly did not like it. "I have never missed you so much in my life," he wrote at one point. "I do long so much to have you with me." A week later the same sentiment was underscored: "I do *miss* you beyond power of description. By sleeping at home I am continuously reminded of your absence." He compared his impatience for her return to that of "a lover . . . separated . . . from his lady true. The truth is," he told her, echoing the sentiments of the wives who were separated for the first time from their husbands, "I never felt you so completely necessary to my happiness as since you have been absent."

Although Henry Poor was a successful lawyer and businessman, his work neither dominated his life nor overrode his love for his family. "I should be completely miserable did I not know that I *possessed* a *wife* and children, and that they are soon to be united to me." He admitted in one letter that a recent cholera epidemic, which had claimed the lives of the wives of many men he knew, had been on his mind of late. "I wonder at their composure and feel how impossible it would be for me to sustain myself under like circumstances."

Ten years later, in 1858, while in Europe, he sent Mary a stream of letters, in answer to hers. This separation found him closer to her and warmer in his comments than during the first. Now he addressed her as "my dearest *Friend,*" commenting that as he sat down "to commune with my dearest partner friend," he recalled that he had "often, today, written you in thought," and that the feelings aroused then "spring from love and affection," which transcended even the emotions generated by the sunset visible from his window as he wrote.[21]

Henry Waller of Kentucky did not travel to Europe, but he was frequently absent from his wife (Sarah) Bell, upon whom he was emotionally dependent. Her letters, he confessed in 1840, were like meat and drink to him. "And tho' I may be vexed and restive in spirit before, yet when I read those touching evidences of affection, all afterwards is calm, quiet and consoling within." When, at another time that year she threatened not to write because she was not hearing from him as regularly as she thought she ought to, he found it hard to put into words "how depressed I felt." It was not that he disapproved of her remedy, "because it was reasonable and proper; yet the prospect of not hearing from you regularly and at short intervals was very trying to my feelings. I have not been contented since." Thirteen years later their relationship was as close as ever, though the repeated separations were taking their toll. "Oh, how I do long constantly for a love, earnest, ardent, faithful, enduring," he wrote in 1853 from New York City. "How grateful to my tossed and troubled heart are all the evidences you give me of such affection. I am often the prey of great and rapid fluctuations of feelings; more when absent from you than at other times; and I fear it is gaining strength every day. Your constant tenderness can alone save me." At that time Waller was forty-six and married sixteen years.[22]

Melville Anderson, when he was in Europe in 1876, also suffered because he was separated from his wife. He looked to her for emotional support in his worry about his professional future. Although he could not fully express his feelings in a letter—even one to his wife—there is no doubt that she was his confidante. "We cannot trust to a letter," he concluded, "what we might whisper in one another's arms."[23]

The marriage of the Reverend Robert Mallard and Mary Jones Mallard of south Georgia was clearly a more formal relationship than either that of the Poors or the Andersons. Yet Mallard addressed her as "my darling wife" and "my other self." The angushed dependence he felt when Mary was away in 1862 for reasons of health comes through quite clearly in letter after letter. He was, to be sure, always careful to say he did not want to bring her home prematurely and that she should not worry that the household may not have been running properly; his parents were with him while she was away. Still his thoughts about her were so intrusive at times, he confessed, that he could not work upon the composition of his sermons. "I am afraid I sin in allowing your absence such influence," he told her. "I know that my work should be so interesting that time should appear too short for its employments, and yet time moves slowly when you are away." Despite the high cost of postage in the beleaguered Confederacy, he insisted on writing his wife each day, justifying the extravangance on the ground that "writing is the next best thing to seeing you, but a wide interval lies between them. Your absence is an affliction to me, and I long for it to end," he concluded dramatically. Yet he would "not throw a feather in the way of its prolongation" if his wife's medical treatments required more time.[24]

Twenty years later, in the then new family magazine *Good Housekeeping,* the dependence of husbands upon wives was put in general terms by an anonymous male correspondent. "Many a man has hungered for sympathy—the friendship of his wife," the piece began. "Love will not supply its place. It may conceal its absence in the honeymoon, but for the long stretch of every day life it will not suffice. Many a man owes his fortune or his name to the sympathetic assistance of his wife, and many a one has failed because he could not have it."[25]

The dependence of men upon wives and family was not confined to middle- or upper-class people. Andrew Rotter, in a study of diaries of men who made the overland trip to California in 1849, found a "profound psychological dependence upon women and families" among the Forty-Niners; the dependence came out especially when men fell ill. One Overlander, sick with dysentery, wrote that it was "much better if a person is sick to be at home where the wife of his bosom . . . can sympathize with him, and administer to his relief. . . ." Doctors told of ill Forty-Niners breaking out in sobs when they reflected upon their absent wives. Joseph Holt was not a Forty-Niner, but only a simple storekeeper in Indian country in Wisconsin and was neither dying nor even sick when he wrote his teenage daughter that he thought his wife "is quite a woman. Would not exchange her for any ten I know of."[26]

It was not unknown for young husbands to be helpful to as well as appreciative of their wives, as Sam Leland's report to his sister in 1883 showed. The Lelands had just had their first child, whom Addie, the mother, was nursing. Sam took some part in the rearing of the child, apparently, since he could tell his sister the baby's weight and its general progress. "I try to assume charge of affairs when I can," he told his sister, so that Addie might "go out for air and exercise." On an earlier night that week they had had a sitter while they went out for an hour and a half to visit friends. "It seemed to good to be out again," he remarked.

Helping out at home may well have been a regional matter, if the remarks of a southern woman visiting New York can be taken as representative. Juliet Janin chided her husband in 1847 for his lack of domestic interests by observing that she did not think he would ever be "as domestic as some of the husbands at the North are, which means one who aids his wife in housekeeping, in nursing the children and in attending to her in health and in sickness." She was not expecting much in this respect, for she thought "it is carried a little too far here" in New York City. Yet, as a woman she thought it nevertheless "very nice to go half way."[27]

The close affectional ties between husband and wife in the American family of the 19th century mirrored in the foregoing examples did not, of course, preclude disagreements and perhaps profound dissatisfactions in many marriages of the time. Nor should these concrete instances be interpreted as ruling out real meanness or even violence within marriages and families of the 19th century. The kinds of sources relied upon here undoubtedly understate the amount of marital discord or dissatisfaction. Letters and diaries are not the best place to look for such things. A better indication of the degree of dissatisfaction will be encountered in Chapter VII, where the lives of single women—those who rejected marriage and family—and the rise in divorces will be considered. The point here is not to celebrate the Victorian marriage and family, but to show as concretely as possible its affective and companionate aspects, components that need to be appreciated if one is to recognize the reality of women's lives and the bases of their growing autonomy in the family.

That companionship within marriage was important to women comes out in several letters that appeared in the pages of *Good Housekeeping* in 1886. Although the correspondents did not give their names, their tone or their pseudonyms identify them as women. The letters replied to an anonymous letter in an earlier issue, in which a man had emphasized men's dependence upon a wife's sympathy and friendship. The responses noted that if men needed sympathy within marriage so did women. Marriage, they said, was a companionate relationship and not one in which men were to receive all the support. "The first duty of a Man Fit for a Husband," wrote M. H. D., "should be the cultivation of a close companionship with his wife, and the combination with love of that communion of spirit and true sympathy, which is generally considered to be an attribute of friendship." Another correspondent, also anonymous, emphasized the need for equality between the partners and contended that, though it is "traditional that a man wants his wife to be better than he is, the converse should become equally a truism." Marriage, she insisted, should be a relationship "of *mutual* helpfulness." A third writer made the same point in a slightly different and cleverer way. Mothers need to train their sons for marriage as much as their daughters, she argued, for "if women, whose intuitions are admitted to be superior to those of men cannot learn housekeeping by that faculty, how do we expect men to." [28]

Although in the middle-class marriage in 19th-century America there was a mutual dependence on the part of husband and wife, that fact did not preclude differing degrees of autonomy for them. Nor did it necessarily follow that the male member of the marriage would be the dominant or only decision-making member. In the middle 1840s Harriet Beecher Stowe was quite dependent financially upon her husband and burdened by the care of children, who came in rapid succession early in her marriage. Yet she had no trouble in outstripping her husband, Calvin, in the assertion of her own self-confidence and sense of self-reliance. "My love, you do wrong to worry so much about temporal matters," she admonished him in 1844, for it revealed a lack of faith in the Savior. "Every letter of yours contains such unbelieving doubts 'who will take care of us and keep us out of debt?' " Harriet herself harbored no doubts as to who would do it. "My love if you were *dead* this day—and I feeble as I am with five little children I would not doubt nor despond nor expect to starve. . . . Were I a widow standing just as I am I would not have one fear," for she was confident God would take care of them. Then, despite her ostensible reliance upon the deity, she made clear that it was her own will and mind that would take care of them all. "If you will put the affairs all into my hands, let me manage them my own way and give a thought during the winter only to be good and grow in grace, *I'll engage* to bring things out right in the spring," she promised.[29] Although 19th-century society gave all the advantages, all the indicia as well as most of the substance of power to the male, within the family the relationship was, in the end, between two people. Who predominated depended as much on what each was as on the public definition of the institution.

Not all women were as assertive in their marriage as Harriet Stowe. Yet many women made significant decisions about the management of the home. The rearing of children, for example, was almost entirely in the hands of mothers. Wives also participated in deciding where the family would live. Mary Waterman Rice wrote her father in 1876 that she was trying to influence her husband to move from Illinois to California—her old home—rather than to Texas. Hyland Rice's deteriorating health required that he live in a dry climate. But, she went on, the most recent letter from her absent husband indicated that they would be going to Texas. "I am very sorry. I much prefer California," she admitted, while quickly adding that she accepted the biblical rule that a wife should go wherever her husband did. Nevertheless, she did not conceal her hope that they would end up in California. Apparently her reluctance to go to Texas worked its influence; a month later she was packing to go to California to look over possible home sites. As it turned out, her husband's illness postponed that venture, but in 1883 they were in fact living in California, as she had wanted to all along. Where a family lives is one of the crucial decisions a family makes; insofar as women, like Mary Rice, affected that decision they played a decisive role in the family.[30]

Not all women, of course, were as influential as Mary Rice. Some, like Mollie Sanford's sister Dora, had nothing to say about where they lived. One day Dora's husband simply announced that he had a good opportunity for a job in another city and that he and Dora would be leaving immediately. Apparently that was the first that Dora had heard of the possibility. When Byron Sanford, however, was confronted in the fall of 1861 with a chance to become a second lieutenant in a newly formed Colorado regiment mustering for the war, he asked his wife Mollie, "Shall I accept?" Mollie was not ready to offer advice, though she knew that the common gossip was that few men would actually be sent east to fight. "It might be best for By to accept this position," she remarked in her diary, because he had no other job. She believed that her opinion carried weight and, significantly, her husband had asked her for it. As it turned out, Byron Sanford did accept the commission.[31]

Bell Waller of Kentucky also participated in decisions of significance. At one point in 1852, she deliberately raised the question of whether they ought to move from Kentucky, since, as she wrote her husband, the area in which they lived "is visibly declining" and among the inhabitants of the region "there appears to be a settled and growing opinion that the place must go down." Frequently, she wrote, she asked herself whether they were doing justice to their family in staying on in such a place. "To this important question I cannot make a satisfactory answer and I feel that it now requires our serious consideration and direct action." The remainder of her letter is an analysis of what she and her husband wanted out of life and whether their present arrangements will help them achieve them. At the end she asked rhetorically at what other place "could we be happier than we are here" for what she wanted in life—to be able to love him— did not depend on a larger and more varied world. At another time, when Henry Waller was thinking about making a business trip to London, Bell offered her advice, though she promised to abide by his decision. She urged him, nevertheless, to discuss the matter with his father and with a member of the board of directors of his company. And when he raised the question of possibly abandoning the practice of law, she advised against it on the grounds the financial risks were too great. At still another time, Henry noted that "you write to me very solicitously about my finances. I have no desire, dearest, to conceal them from you," but he did not think he ought to burden her with problems additional to her own. "Still," he continued, "there should be no concealment between us; and I think it proper that a wife should have a sufficiently intelligent idea of her husband's condition to enable her to adapt her economical arrangements and expenditures to that condition," he wrote in 1856. He then went on to discuss his financial needs in such a way as to suggest that she was privy to a large part of his business activities. "Your suggestion as to a compromise," he observed at one point, "is a wise one."[32]

Bell and Henry Waller, like the Poors, had an especially close relationship on all levels. Obviously not all Victorian marriages were of that kind. Juliet and Louis Janin's marriage was superficially quite different, yet throughout their correspondence runs an undertone that suggests how a forceful, even assertive wife used the official patriarchalism of the time as a weapon of self-assertion. During the late 1850s and early 1860s Juliet lived abroad, supervising the education of their sons. Although she kept Louis appraised of what was going on, she deliberately played down her own role in making decisions. "I would speak more at large upon this important subject [the boys' plans for schooling] if I thought you had any respect for my judgment upon these subjects. You forget that a mother's love and watchfulness may make her wise." Then she went on to give an accounting of her expenses. "This will show you that I have kept strictly within my allowance," she pointed out.

When war broke out between North and South in 1861, her husband, writing from their home in New Orleans, suggested that she might have to return to the South because of the war. "I have no inclination to return to America in the midst of Civil War," she wrote in May 1861, "and no desire whatsoever to go now to California," a location he was then considering moving to. "I should object very much to leaving here this summer, but shall make up my mind to do so in the Fall . . . if you continue to think it necessary." Then she softened her assertiveness by a bow in the direction of his patriarchal authority. "Of course every other consideration must yield to that." Yet before the letter was finished she was back setting forth conditions. "When *you go to California to* LIVE and are prepared to give me a comfortable home I shall be ready to go there."[33] In July, Louis agreed to her staying in Europe, and two years later she was still there.

In 1863, Louis asked her advice about taking the oath of allegiance to the United States so that he could sell some stock he owned in a California quicksilver mine. Although Juliet eventually gave her advice, she could not refrain from needling him once more about his patriarchalism, an attitude that seems to have been more in her mind than in his behavior, if one can judge from their correspondence. "I have never had any influence over any opinion or action of your life and I could not expect that anything I might say now could change any of your plans, and I refrain from any such useless attempt; but since you have asked me to express myself freely I will do so." She then proceeded to lecture him on his loyalty to the South, where he had prospered. He could sell the stock through an intermediary, after all, she shrewdly advised him, and thus the question of allegiance would not arise. Nor could she let him forget that he came rather late to her. "If before coming to a decision you had asked my opinion (it would seem out' of place to say advice," she slyly added, "and the assumption of a right I never had)," then he might have been able to avoid the dilemma he now found himself in.[34]

Decisions about careers and places of residence came together in a dramatic context in 1849 and after, when many men and families decided to move to California to hunt for gold. Some men went to California without their wives, while others took their families with them. In at least one case, it is clear that the decision for the man to go alone was reversed by the wife. "We were married to live together," she reminded her husband, who had decided to go west without her and the family. She said that she was more than willing to "go with you to any part of *God's Foot Stool*" where he might think he could do best for himself. But, she insisted, he had no right to go where she could not, and, she warned, "if you do, you need never return for I shall look upon you as dead." At that the husband postponed the trip to the gold country until the following year, when she was able to accompany him. Nor was this instance rare, for extant divorce records in California reveal a number of cases of men who obtained divorces from wives in the East who had refused to come west when the husbands decided to seek their fortunes in the gold country.[35]

From the records left by women who did accompany their husbands on the Overland Trail to California, it seems that most of them did not take eagerly to the adventure, whatever their part may have been in the decision to move. It is true that a young woman like Mollie Dorsey, who was still in her teens when her family moved to Nebraska, felt liberated by the new country. She saw it as embodying "a freedom from restraint, and I believe it will be a blessing to we girls." During the first days she took advantage of the new opportunities to explore the woods, catch fish, and help in the garden. She borrowed a riding habit and went riding across the plains, pronouncing it a "delicious sport. I felt like a bird uncaged."

That these were the reactions of a young woman rather than of women in general is made clear by her more sober reactions to the West after her own marriage and the move to Colorado. After telling of an unpleasant encounter on the trail, she wrote, "This is a fair example of the 'novelty' and 'romance' of a trip across the plains that one reads about. Let all try it who are thirsting for the romantic. I just expect to find my head almost white before we get to Denver." Yet at that time she was still a vigorous young woman of twenty-one.[36]

The writings left by women who made the arduous journey overland to California strongly suggest that few of them wanted to make the trip. "What possessed my husband, anyway," wondered one woman, "that he should have thought of bringing [us?] away out through this God forsaken country." Such a woman did not sound as if she had had very much to say about the decision to move west.

Women generally did not see in the West the promise that men did. The adage of the time that the plains were "a heaven for men and dogs but a hell for women and oxen" referred to more than the climate or the monotonous flatness of the land. It referred, also, to the loss of home, of familiar tasks and occupations that made up the world of a married woman. As one woman remarked as she and her family crossed the Continental Divide at South Pass, "Oh, shall we ever live like civilized beings again?" It was not uncommon for women to speak of leaving civilization behind as they entered upon the westward journey. To many women, civilization was more than law, books, or government; it was also pianos, church societies, linens, china, and mirrors; it was home. Not surprisingly, therefore, in the written documents from the overland trek there are many indications that women sought to reproduce their old home-life even when circumstances were hardly conductive. They sought to keep up their knitting or crocheting groups, and other contacts with women. As one woman said when telling of the arrival of an old friend at their camp, "we got out our Daguerreotypes and tried to live over again some of the happy days of 'Auld Lang Syne' " back East. The central place that home held in the minds of women on the trail was captured in the comment of one woman migrant. "Each advanced step of the slow, plodding cattle," she feared, "carried us farther and farther from civilization into a desolate, barbarous country. But our new home lay beyond all this and was a shining beacon that beckoned us on, inspiring our hearts with hope and courage." [37]

At least two conclusions may be drawn from the obvious dissatisfaction displayed by many women who followed the Overland Trail with their husbands, aside from their having little influence over the original decision to migrate. The first is that women seem to have been rather contented with the idea of a sphere of activity separate from men's. For during those weeks and even months of crossing the plains, women had the opportunity to take up many traditional masculine tasks, if only because the exigencies of the trip compelled them to. They labored to push the wagons, gathered fuel, carried water, and managed animals as the need arose. Yet, despite the altered circumstances—that is, the breaking of the crust of custom, so to speak—women did little to seize the opportunity to abandon their traditional role. However willing women may have been to take up those chores usually reserved for men because trail life required it, the great majority of women apparently perceived their assumption of male roles and tasks to be temporary. Neither men nor women, for that matter, considered the overlapping of roles on the trail as either permanent or threatening to the traditional gender division of labor. In fact, as historians Johnny Faragher and Christine Stansell have concluded in their study of women on the Overland Trail, "women fought *against* the forces of necessity to hold together the few fragments of female subculture left to them." [38]

Lillian Schlissel, another student of women in the westward movement, has observed that "the work imposed on women during the six or seven months of travel along the Overland Trail was not merely arduous, but was often felt to be demeaning." Moreover, Schlissel pointed out, women had little to say about where they went, when, or where they stopped for the night, how they set up the camp, or when they resumed in the morning. Such a lack of decision-making by women was in sharp contrast to their freedom to control their daily activities when in their established homes back East. [39]

It might be objected that the period during which women on the trail performed men's tasks was too short to affect women's future activities, that women instinctively, if not consciously, knew that they must take up again the old roles once they reached California. To a certain extent that objection is valid, but not wholly. After all, none of the women knew that the new home would be exactly like the old; it was largely an unsettled region into which they were going. Women might well be able to forge a different and more congenial place for themselves if they were so minded. But in order for that to happen women would have had to be basically unhappy and dissatisfied with their traditional role. Yet if they were so dissatisfied, why did they take up the new "masculine" tasks on the trail with such reluctance, as the documents certainly show they did? Significantly, an unmarried young woman like Mollie Dorsey, as we have seen, immediately took advantage of the liberation that migration to a new country provided her. It would seem, then, that for most married women the domestic role, as the doctrine of the two spheres defined it, may well have offered advantages that they not only recognized but sought to retain. Among other things it provided companionship with other women, a sense of self-worth and personal value, and an independence of men. To have eliminated the segregation by gender between work and home, for example, would have been to weaken that association among women and that sense of identification with other women, which separation of the sexes encouraged.

It is also relevant to notice here that a recent historian of the utopian communities of the early 19th century has concluded that few women wanted to join communities in which segregation by gender was breached. When they did join, it was primarily because their husbands were dissatisfied with the traditional relations between the sexes. Significantly, many of those communities provided for communal household and child care—that is, they would have removed some of the traditional tasks which the doctrine of the two spheres prescribed for married women. Nevertheless, despite the availability of this realistic alternative, few women, apparently, elected to take advantage of the opportunity.[40] (At the same time, it must be remembered that an assertion of domesticity on the part of women, by emphasizing women's gender or their differences from men, weakened their claim to a full range of human experiences. Domesticity, no matter how advantageous it might be for women within the family in the short run, could not lead directly to a feminist or individualistic assertion of women's full humanity. Yet in the short run it could, and probably did improve women's status by increasing their power and enhancing their self-confidence.)

The second point to be made about the women who followed the Overland Trail is that most of them were not upper-class or even middle-class women. Yet they exhibited, as we have seen, the same belief in the proper sphere of women that middle- and upper-class women and the popular literature of the day advanced. Although this point may seem obvious and expected, it is worth making, since it is not always clear that the values and practices of middle-class women have any effect or influence upon the outlook and behavior of working-class people. This "downward" projection of middle-class attitudes and practices, however, should not have been unexpected in a society like that of the United States, where class consciousness was weak, and widespread literacy permitted a large majority of women to inform themselves of the standards of the middle and upper classes.

The as yet unpublished research into California divorce records of the 1870s by Robert Griswold offers additional reason for believing that working-class women accepted the values and emulated the behavior of the middle class. Griswold has shown that two-thirds of the 400 divorce petitions he examined from northern California counties during the 1870s and

1880s were made by working-class men, or by women married to working men, usually farm laborers, artisans, or ordinary farmers. Yet over and over again in their petitions these men and women showed that they believed not only in the separation of the spheres but in the Cult of True Womanhood as well. Both women and men judged women to be "good women" if they performed traditional domestic tasks and eschewed being too forward or self-assertive. Men, on the other hand, were expected to treat women with the deference their moral superiority deserved.[41]

This chapter has argued that though the separation of the spheres was a part of the actual lives of women in the 19th century, the practice ought not to be seen as necessarily either demeaning or unduly subordinating. A truly companionate marriage may not have been yet in being, but the practice was not as far from the ideal as some of the folklore about the 19th-century family would lead us to believe. When a sociologist recently undertook the study of housewives in the 1950s she asked the women she studied to compare their lives with those of their grandmothers in the 19th century. Almost unanimously the women said that they saw a "loss of power by men." The men of three generations earlier, they told her, had been "kings" and "czars" in their families, as they phrased it. The mid-20th-century housewives saw the change as an improvement for women, for in their grandmothers' time, they contended, women had been veritable slaves to men. In fact, so sure were some women that the change was taking place that one even contended that "Men are not men anymore, they are mice."[42] Nor should this myth of the powerful father and subordinate mother in the 19th century be seen as merely private opinion. As one recent sociologist has written, "Freud saw the Victorian father as a stern, forbidding—almost frightening—figure, controlling his wife and children with a firm hand." And apparently the sociologist himself remembered his own family in similar terms. "The writer's family was a Victorian type— all of the money was earned and dispensed by him [the father]," he told his readers. "Children filed their requests with the mother who relayed them to the father. The decision to grant or deny the request would eventually come back via the same route: 'Your father says that he cannot buy you a pair of roller skates this month—but he will try to get them for you next month.' "[43] Such comments remind one of the family depicted in Clarence Day's play *Life with Father*. Perhaps it is time to recognize that Day's Victorian father, like the recent sociologist's and Freud's, was more of a caricature than we have thought.

The relation between husband and wife is certainly a central aspect of marriage, but from the standpoint of women there was more than that to their lives and their place in the 19th-century family. We turn, then, in the next chapter, to look at women's life in the family under the ideal of domesticity, or the two spheres.

III

Wife and Mother

Because the people of 19th-century America often spoke and wrote about mothers and wives in rather extravagant, almost doting, phrases, it is easy to assume that the life of a married woman then was as vacuous as the words with which it was described. The historical truth is quite different. For even when women's activities were confined to the home and children, the responsibilities were still great and the physical burdens heavy. After all, under the doctrine of separate spheres, it was the woman who was charged with maintaining the morality of the home in general and bearing and rearing the children in virtue in particular. On top of those responsibilities there was the onerous and unending task of meeting the physical needs of husband, children, and self.

Given the nature and range of tasks confronting a wife and mother, it is not surprising that many women found the work of the home demanding and not always enjoyable. Although Catharine Beecher was one of the most successful and prominent of the writers of handbooks on domestic life, her sister Harriet Beecher Stowe was not one of the more contented housekeepers. Indeed, it is probably because she was discontented with her lot that we learn so explicitly about the burdensome routine of domestic life. "Since you have gone I have had a great pressure of care upon me," she wrote in 1844 to her husband Calvin. At that time she had five small children. "The arranging of the whole house with reference to the new system, the cleaning, etc. The childrens clothes and the baby have seemed to press on my mind all at once. Sometimes it seems as if anxious thought has become a disease with me from which I could not be free."

At another time she spelled out her morning routine. She rose at 5:30 and ate breakfast at 6:00, since she had a cook as well as another servant. Then at 7:00 she said morning prayers and worked in the garden until 8:00. At that hour she went into the house to check the silverware and table things. At 9:30 she called the children to school, for at that time and in that place schools were not always available and rarely for very young children. The mother was the teacher, and the house the school. At school her children sang "a hymn," and she prayed with them, and gave them "a bible lesson half an hour long." They then spent another half hour on texts for Sunday sermons. She then read with them as a class and spent the remainder of the morning sewing. This was a woman's routine in a house with two servants.[1]

Lest it be thought that Harriet Stowe's schedule was the compulsive activity of the descendant of a New England Puritan, consider an entry from the diary of a South Carolina woman in 1860: "This morning I got up late having been disturbed in the night, hurried down to have something arranged for breakfast. Ham and eggs. . . . Wrote a letter to Charles . . . had prayers, got the boys off to town. Had work cut out, gave orders about dinner, had the horse-feed fixed in hot water, had the box filled with cork; went to see about the carpenters working at the negro houses. . . . These carpenters Mr. Grimball told me he wished me to see about every day, and now I have to cut out the flannel jackets."[2]

Long before Virginia Woolf wrote about a woman's need for a room of one's own, the necessity for it was set forth quite concretely by Harriet Beecher Stowe in a letter to her husband in 1844. On the last day of a long visit with her brother in Indianapolis she reflected on "my state of retirement in this place, in which I have enjoyed what I have long been hoping to enjoy—a season of tranquil vegetation." In the enjoyment of those things which she lacked at home, she remarked, "I have forgotten almost the faces of my children—all the perplexing details of home and almost that I am a married woman." In contrast to the situation at home, at her brother's house she lay down each night "tranquilly, . . . opened my door into the dining room and listened to the ticking of the clock, till I doze, and then slept and slept all night—and then woke next morning without any anxiety or a thought except whether breakfast was ready in the next room. . . . After breakfast, I have read, sewed, talked, and above all *slept* as much as and just when I wished to."[3]

The privacy and rest that Harriet Stowe relished were especially necessary if a woman sought to use her talents, as Stowe did, beyond the rou-

tines of the home, to realize her capabilities in the world. Mary Hallock
Foote, who, like Stowe, was a professional writer, felt the pressures and
demands of the household most keenly when the workers at her husband's
engineering project in Idaho were compelled to stay indoors because of the
weather. Everyone then seemed to be pressing upon her, "and I wished the
house might be cleared of men with all my heart. . . . It will be such a
relief, if that time soon comes, when I can once more 'possess the uses of
my soul.' " For as things were, "I am daily dropped in little pieces and
passed around and devoured and expected to be whole again next day and
all days and I am never *alone* for a single minute!" [4]

The household routine, which the ideal of the two spheres decreed for
the married woman, was unending, even when the household enjoyed the
assistance of servants. When there were no servants, as on the Overland
Trail, women literally had no breaks at all from the circle of labor. For
even when the wagon trains stopped to rest, the work of women continued. "The plain fact of the matter," complained one young woman on
the trail to California, "is *we have no time for sociability*. From the time
we get up in the morning, until we are on the road, it is hurry, scurry to
get breakfast and put away the things that necessarily had to be pulled out
last night." While the train was in motion, no other woman could be in
the wagon, and at noon, when the wagons stopped for meals, the breakfast routine of hurry, scurry was repeated. "At night all the cooking uten-
sils and provisions are to be gotten about the camp fire, and cooking
enough to last until the next night." The men, at this time, sit around the
fire, resting and talking of how far they had come that day.[5] For the ordinary woman at home, there would, of course, be no breaking of camp
each morning, but the routines of daily work would be more elaborate in
caring for children, shopping, preparing meals, cleaning the house, making
and mending clothes. The day would be as long and as full, but the pace
would be slower and somewhat more flexible.

Nor did the demands of the household in the 20th century alter the
character of women's sphere of activities. Margaret Fowler Dunaway was
the wife of a Milwaukee businessman in the late 1920s and had ambitions
to write and read extensively. Yet her complaint to her journal in 1929
would have been familiar to Harriet Beecher Stowe. "I sit down to my
desk in the morning rejoicing that I may write an hour, but the big boy
needs a letter of admonition and encouragement. The little girl needs a
bunny rabbit stitched to take to school . . . and the elder sister must have
a good hot lunch as she eats no breakfast." Dunaway was more easily

reconciled in this instance to the denials of her talents than Mary Foote or Harriet Stowe. Yet she clearly recognized her sacrifice. "I never hear of a successful man, but I think of the great character behind him who had made the necessary sacrifices." In Dunaway's mind the conception of women's role as one of self-sacrifice for the good of the family was as alive and pertinent in the 20th century as it had been in the early 19th. A little later, in 1931, just after the Christmas holiday, she was not quite so contented with her sacrifices. "Cleaning! Baking! Ironing! —When evening arrived I was only a scullery maid, naught left of me, but a deep, intense hunger for something LIVE, something VITAL before the day sinks into oblivion," she complained to her journal. Yet in the next entry one senses her guilt at having not been as compliant as she thought she ought to be. "Against the unspoken wishes of the other four how often have I gone against them to feed this hunger." [6] And so the conflict between self and family, which some women in the 19th century felt and sometimes fought against, still confronted many married women well into the 20th century. In fact it remains today the central, unresolved tension in the life of a woman in the family.

Beneath the ideology and advocacy of the domestic sphere for women in the 19th century there was, of course, one great, fundamental fact that bestowed significance upon all of it. Only women bore children, and only women could properly feed them in the early years of life. No man could perform those tasks, even if he were willing to. Not surprisingly, therefore, the ideology of domesticity stressed that woman's destiny was motherhood. Some medical authorities became almost obsessed with that aspect of a woman's life, saying that the uterus was the central organ of the sex, around which all other facets of a woman's life necessarily revolved. One of the principal objections to contraception by medical and lay persons in the 19th century was that it seemed to call into the question the idea that women were meant to bear children. And in the typical marriage, a birth did occur early on, usually within the first twelve or eighteen months.

Mary Hallock Foote's verbal reaction to the quickening of her first child—what she called "the beginning of life in my little unknown"—captures some of the mystery of pregnancy for a woman. She told her old school friend Helena Gilder in January 1877 of her feelings. She was attending church in San Francisco with some friends when the organ music "made me feel so strangely—Its throbbing seemed to stifle me and for the first time that pulse within me woke and throbbed so strong . . . it took away my breath." She thought she was going to faint, but managed not to.

One of her companions noticed the change in her, but she revealed nothing. "It seems absurd to talk so much about an experience common to every woman," she admitted to Helena, "but I think it one of the *strangest* feelings—that double pulse—that life within a life—I cannot get used to it." [7]

For most of human history, and not only in the West, childbirth has been a peculiarly female experience, not just because women alone bear children but because those present at the birth have almost always been women only. In early modern times, it is true, male physicians were sometimes present at extremely difficult births or because dynastic or other nonmedical reasons imbued the birth with importance. But for most women before the 19th century, childbearing was a female-only experience. Among ordinary women, as among the nobility or royalty, the birth of a child was an occasion in which a number of women would be present, not only as helpers but as visitors and well-wishers. A confinement was an occasion for women to meet, to be convivial as well as supportive. It was, in short, a female ritual and rite, and one which it was not unusual for a woman to return home for if she had moved away when she married. The attending medical figure was also a woman—a midwife, who usually had experience in, and some folk knowledge about, delivering babies. None had any special training, and usually she did no more than cut the umbilical cord, carry away the afterbirth, and, if there was a possibility of a breech delivery, turn the fetus around for a head-first delivery. By and large, childbirth was considered to be a natural, if dangerous and painful, experience. Any woman was deemed capable of assisting at it; during the colonial period in America only New York and Massachusetts had any laws at all regulating midwives, and they were neither significant nor enforced.

Around the time of the Revolution, however, a change in practice and outlook began. As American male doctors learned more in European medical schools and at home about obstetrics, a few of them in cities began to specialize in the field. Dr. William Shippen, Jr., of Philadelphia is usually identified as the first male physician regularly to attend women at childbirth in America. He began his practice in 1763. Some of the male midwives—the word "obstetrician" was later deliberately coined to remove the female connotations of "midwife" from medical attendance at childbirths—openly recommended their own services on the grounds that their knowledge and skills might relieve women of some of the difficulties and pain of parturition. This was particularly relevant when forceps or other instruments were needed. In the process, a subtle change began to come over public attitudes toward childbearing. Whereas before it had been axiomatic, as the Bible said, that women should expect to suffer in childbirth, now ways of avoiding suffering were not only being offered but accepted as well. At one time, wrote one male medical student in 1812, women were "generally looked on by their rugged lords as unworthy of any particular attention," and death itself would not have been seen as "a matter of any importance," but that was no longer true, he concluded. Another male physician simply asked "why should the female alone incur the penalty of God" when some relief through a knowledge of obstetrics was now possible? [8]

As more and more men entered the practice of attending women at births, the number of midwives declined. By 1815 the Philadelphia directory listed 21 women midwives and 23 men as practitioners of midwifery (the term "obstetrics" had not yet been introduced). By 1819 the ratio was down to 13 females to 42 males, while five years later only six females were in the directory. In Boston as early as 1820 midwifery was almost entirely confined to male physicians. These patterns and developments, however, should not be extrapolated to the country at large, for male obstetricians were confined to the large cities. In fact, throughout the 19th century most births were still attended by midwives, not by male doctors. This was so not only because there were not sufficient doctors in the country, but principally because it cost so much to have a doctor present at an event that was at once so common and so "natural." As late as 1910 about half of all births in the United States were still attended by midwives, and in some cities, because of the large numbers of poor immigrant and black women, the proportion may actually have been higher. [9]

Throughout the 19th century, but especially in the opening years of the 20th century, the organized medical profession was concerned about the level of care and cleanliness provided by midwives. Male doctors also worried about the competition midwives brought to their own practices. The general concern reached a crescendo in the first two decades of the 20th century when reliance upon midwives was high because of the large number of immigrant women then entering the country who turned to women of their own ethnic background for assistance during childbirth. Yet many of these midwives, as one investigation at the time reported, were "hopelessly dirty, ignorant, and incompetent." Some public health authorities argued that the proper solution to the lack of cleanliness and knowledge was upgrading of the training of midwives through legal requirements, but the organized body of physicians countered that midwifery did nothing to advance the science of obstetrics. Furthermore, few male physicians relished making permanent the competition to their own practices.

In the end the obstetricians won out, if only because the number of immigrant women declined after 1920. Most middle-class women had long before decided to have regular physicians in attendance, and by the early 20th century a substantial portion of them were going to the hospital to have their babies. On the other hand, there is no evidence that regular doctors in the early 20th century were significantly reducing the infant mortality rate as compared with midwives. And in regard to the number of still births and cases of sepsis, the midwives would seem to have been doing a better job so far as studies at the time showed. The poor continued to depend upon midwives, but in ever decreasing numbers. As late as 1940, a full 48 per cent of all deliveries of non-white women were attended by midwives; at that same date some 60 per cent of all white births were taking place in hospitals. By 1953, however, fewer than one out of five non-white births were carried through by midwives, thus suggesting in another way that the decision to employ a regular physician was largely determined by economic situation.

When male physicians began to enter the delivery room on a regular basis in the early years of the 19th century, the meaning of childbirth inevitably changed for women. It gradually ceased to be a female ritual largely because male doctors brought that to an end. For one thing, they usually reduced the number of women present at the birth, or removed them entirely. For another, male doctors, out of their growing sense of professionalism, did not like the conviviality and conversation that often accompanied labor and birth when women were present. At the same time, the male sex of the physician ensured that the procedure would be formal, cool, and impersonal. No male physician could examine his patient as fully or as freely as a midwife. Proper female delicacy forbade it and most physicians, throughout the 19th century, in order to avoid any charges of impropriety bent over backwards not to appear too familiar. As a result, lights were dim during the examination, and the examination and delivery were by touch only; if instruments were used they had to be manipulated under covers! One male writer even pointed out proudly, in justification of modesty, that one of the greatest male obstetricians had been blind! Thus wherever male physicians entered on the scene, childbirth became a private matter. By the middle years of the 19th century obstetricians were commonly present at births in most middle-class families.

Pregnancy and childbirth were for 19th-century women, as for women in every place and at every time, a profound experience; they separated the sexes more fundamentally than anything else. Unfortunately, the personal meaning of pregnancy in the lives of 19th-century women is not easy to recapture. Few women wrote about their pregnancies, even though middle-class women were incessant correspondents about domestic matters. A modern reader of their most private journals and letters is often brought up short to learn of the birth of a baby, for no previous mention of a pregnancy has been made, though obviously the writer must have known of the impending event for five or six months at the least. Today that kind of modesty appears not only excessive but incredible as well. Yet it is worth recalling that as recently as the 1950s it was not considered polite for obviously pregnant women to appear in public places more than was absolutely necessary. Adrienne Rich in her book on motherhood tells of the cancellation of a poetry reading, for which she was scheduled at a New England boys' preparatory school in 1955, because she was seven months' pregnant. She was told that the boys would not be able to concentrate on her poetry if she appeared in a pregnant state.

When women in the 19th century did refer to their pregnancies, the comments were often tinged with fear, and with a sense of interruption or of the closing of an era in their lives. The sentiment is summed up in the journal entry of Sarah Ripley Stearns in 1813. She was then more than eight months' pregnant with her first child, and had just come back from taking communion with her husband and sister. Anticipating that the event would soon incapacitate her, she noted in her journal that it "will probably be a long time before I have another opportunity of commemorating my Savior's dying love. . . ." But, then, not having faced childbirth before, she recognized that "perhaps this is the last time I shall be permitted to join with my earthly friends." (Nowhere, incidentally, does she link these observations with her pregnancy; their relevance became evident only from an entry three weeks later noting the birth of a daughter!)

Three years later, when Sarah Stearns gave birth to her third child, she was still, perhaps inevitably, conscious of the interruption the birth would bring, noting that "it will most probably be many weeks before I have another opt. to write in this book." But this time there were no references to fears of leaving her earthly friends. And well might she be rather used to the experience of childbirth; in only forty-seven months of married life, she had borne four live children! [10]

Sarah Stearns was one of those women for whom pregnancy was at most an inconvenience, and, at that, only toward the end of the nine months. She even went to church right up until the final weeks. Elizabeth Cabot also seems to have gotten out during the seventh month of her first pregnancy. She wrote her sister in 1858 in regard to a party she expected to attend. "I am allowed a seat where I can creep in and out easily and keep myself out of harm's way. I am not a pretty figure for company," she conceded, "but I hope to manage so as not to be obnoxious." In that Massachusetts community, at least, there was no objection to pregnant women in public. One of the reasons Lizzie Cabot wanted to go to that party was that she found the pregnancy inconvenient. "You don't know how it is to realize," she told her sister, "that from a condition of vigorous health I am suddenly to drop into illness."

This was Lizzie's first pregnancy, too, and, like Sarah Stearns, she worried about her future. "Sometimes I think I must be very frivolous not to keep a steady eye on death and eternity all the time" instead of being so cheerful. But she deliberatley tried not to let the darker side of things dampen her "hope and comfort." Even so, her success was not complete—or else she was just eminently practical. For she told her sister: "I have made my will and divided off all my little things and don't mean to leave undone what I ought to do, if I can help it." [11]

Women, of course, had good reason to be concerned about death from childbirth, for it was always a possibility. And certainly it was a cloud over their lives that shadowed a man's, if it did at all, only through his affection for a woman. Early mortality statistics, limited as they are, offer a measure of what childbearing cost women. The earliest available figures by sex and age are for 1840 and 1850. In those years the death rates for women between the ages of 10 and 35 are greater than those for men, measuring thereby the effects of childbearing on women's chances for life. By the end of the century, however, women at all ages had a lower mortality than men. And even in 1840 and 1850 the life expectancy of a girl at birth was greater than that of a boy, the difference in the 19th century being never more than three years, as compared with more than twice that in the middle of the 20th century. Nevertheless it still suggests that even a century ago women's endurance was greater than men's, just as it is today, despite the greater medical risk in the past. [12]

If pregnancy brought trepidation to many women, to others it brought disappointment and sometimes even stronger negative reactions. For in an age of unreliable contraception and a strong belief in the virtues of child-bearing, family planning was haphazard at best. Elizabeth Cabot told her sister of a common friend, Lizzie, who had "gone the way of all flesh"—her euphemism for pregnancy—and "expects her finale in August and does not like it *at all.* . . . The fact is Lizzie wanted very much to go abroad, and this puts a quietus on all such plans." At no time did unhappy responses to pregnancy burst forth more sharply than when a woman discovered, as Bell Waller did in 1852, that she was not pregnant after all. "I have been sick," she wrote her husband, "for some time—my nervousness was excessive, that alone confirmed me in the belief that I was p——. That thought, amounting to conviction preyed upon me, till the discontentment produced by it became unendurable." At times, she admitted, she felt desperate, particularly because she "felt unable to perform a mother's duty to the children we have and if we had more how could I get through my care. I felt borne down with the thought of the future; it presented only trials and sufferings and worse than all, failures; everything was robed with somber colours, clouds obscured my days, restlessness became a part of me. . . ." And though she was patient, "it was sullen patience, not the gentle endurance of the resigned." Even religion, she confessed was not "able to reconcile me to what I feared was my condition. . . ."[13]

The sure knowledge of a pregnancy evoked similar, if less lengthy expressions of regret. "The knowledge causes no exhilarating feelings," reported a Georgia woman in 1855 when she learned she was definitely pregnant. And the reason was that she knew she would suffer "almost constantly." In the course of the next ten years she had several miscarriages only to find herself in 1865 once again pregnant. "Unfortunately, I have the prospect of adding again to the little members of my household. . . . I am sincerely sorry for it." A North Carolina wife, so fearful of pregnancy that she stayed at the home of relatives for longer and longer periods until her husband ordered her home, referred to pregnancy as "nothing but trouble and sorrow." Another North Carolina woman related her disappointment at finding herself pregnant to the economic burden it would impose. "My heart almost sinks within me at the thought of feeding another child," she wrote her mother in 1845.[14]

These women conceived babies more easily and more often than they wanted. Others found conception more difficult, as the great demand for the services of a well-known gynecologist like Dr. J. Marion Sims make clear. Mary Hallock Foote was a woman who had some difficulty conceiving. Even though she had one child, she was unable to conceive another for years, as she told Helena Gilder, whose pregnancy in 1880 she clearly envied. "I am just as well as possible now and yet I can see no prospect of another child for me. . . . I fancy I am like a fallow field. I rest every day more and more and I never felt better or happier in my life—but I *do* want another baby." Yet for her childbirth was a matter of being "perfectly miserable in body for nine months." [15]

Whatever the prospects of childbirth may have been, the experience was never easy, though not many women actually commented upon it. Not surprisingly, given her own difficulties, Mary Foote called birthing day "Dies Irae." Mary Walker, living in the wilds of Oregon Territory in December 1838, had her first child when her husband was away. Although she knew about when the baby would come, she awoke suddenly at 4:00 A.M. and felt a discharge. "Felt unwilling it should happen in the absence of my husband," she later wrote in her diary. When the pains began, she sent for another missionary's wife, who came with her husband. Between them they made the necessary preparations and left breakfast for her. "I became quite sick enough—began to feel discouraged. Felt as if I almost wished I had never been married. But there was no retreating; meet it I must. About eleven I began to be quite discouraged. I had hoped to be delivered ere then. But just as I supposed the worst was at hand, my ears were saluted with the cry of my child." When her third child was born, in March 1842, she was only somewhat less apprehensive. As before she anticipated the event; she rose at 5:00 A.M. and had an early breakfast and quickly did her housework by nine. "Baked six more loaves of bread. Made a kettle of mush and have a sewet pudding and some beef boiling. . . . May the mercy of the Merciful be with me through the expected scene," she prayed. At nine that evening "was delivered of a son." [16]

Bell Waller was not able to work as well while pregnant, she told her husband in 1844. "I felt great bodily debility last evening; and considerable pain in my back; nature is preparing herself for the crisis. I am feeling daily an increasing lassitude and weakness, it is very gradual. . . . I have nothing of the energy and life which I possessed Christmas week." [17]

After the birth of a child, of course, women often suffered further, though someone like Mary Walker, if only because of her frontier circumstances, seemed to get back to work without more than two or three days' respite. Four weeks after Elizabeth Cabot's first baby was born, she wrote her sister that "I am aware that I have a back and a head, and sometimes for short intervals they each ache, but except these I am as good as new, and more thankful than I can ever tell or think." The baby is "still tormenting me a little each time he nurses," she added, "but less and less and another week will see me through that trouble I think." Moreover, since the medical wisdom of the day called for a protracted convalescence from childbirth, women found themselves incapacitated for another long period *after* the baby was born. Mary Foote admitted after the birth of her first child, when there were some medical complications, that "I could have cried, remembering how gayly" she and her husband had ridden over the hills, and of "the Sundays when I tramped with Arthur, following the steepest trails, without flagging a step. I thought to myself, I can never be a *comrade* any more." And even after the birth in 1886 of her third child, she felt the loss of her "out-door life" which her convalescence required.[18]

Mary Foote's physical incapacity, of course, would not last. But Harriet Beecher Stowe learned from her entry into motherhood that she had entered upon a new and quite different life psychologically than she had known or expected. On the eleventh anniversary of her marriage, in January 1847, she reviewed her feelings in a frank letter to her husband, Calvin. Most of her feelings were regrets. Her first disappointment, she told him, had been his frequent absences from home on behalf of fund-raising for his church. But that disappointment, she went on, was somewhat mitigated by "the hope of being a mother. No creature ever so longed to see the face of a little one or had such a heart full of love to bestow." However, as in the case of her husband, reality did not live up to expectations. "Here came in trail again sickness, pain, perplexity, constant discouragement, wearing, wasting days and nights," not to mention an incompetent and deceitful nurse and an absent husband. "Ah how little comfort had I being a mother—and how has all that I proposed met and crossed and my way ever hedged up!" The lesson she drew from the experience was that God intended "that I should make no family be my chief good and portion, and bitter as the lesson has been I thank Him for it from my very soul." For some women, of course, the consequences of childbirth could be much worse than even Harriet Stowe perceived them. It was surely for Mollie Sanford, who made the following entry in her journal at the birth of her first son: "When I first looked on his little face, he was in his little coffin."[19]

Whether women welcomed their new babies, were surprised by them, or merely regretted them, the household nevertheless inevitably changed with their arrival. "I have little time for writing or serious reflection—with my little family," observed Sarah Stearns in August 1815. In November she wrote that "the care necessarily due to my Infant often detains me at home when I wish to attend the public Ordinances of Religion." And a year and a baby later she complained again about not being able to get to church "but the cares of my babes takes up so large a portion of my time that I have not much time for reading or reflection," even though she had "many things at heart, many devices in my imagination if I could execute any thing." Soon after the birth of her fifth child in 1846, Mary Walker found herself almost overwhelmed by the work it entailed. "The cares of my family so engross my mind," she wrote in her diary, "I have no room to think of anything else. I feel at times scarce courage enough to try to live, because the prospect is of only an increase in care from year to year for years to come." But she was the true wife of a missionary: "Still I trust to find strength equal to my day." Eliza Perkins opened a letter to a female friend with the observation that the friend would understand why she had not written "when you are a wife, and a mother of a crying babe, and feel it necessary to curtail your expenses as it respects help." Simply because her new family had required her to restrict her correspondence "my friends have almost all given me up." And then she went on to delineate one of the consequences of marriage and a family. "It is very painful . . . to be forgotten by friends whom you once knew as your own soul." [20]

Mollie Sanford's lively diary also showed the effects of marriage and motherhood. The death of her first child soon after birth and her second pregnancy seemed to have made her more dependent on her husband than before. While he was away during the Civil War, she boarded with another family. Any delay in his expected return made her restless and anxious. "It is late, and I only write to fill in the time," she confessed in one entry, "for I cannot keep still." And when he did arrive, she reacted exaggeratedly. "And now our life begins again, and if we have but little of this world's goods, I feel rich!!" Another entry made clear that she was almost painfully aware of how her marriage had changed her life. "I spend my time, outside my little housework, rather monotonously. I do not improve much. Where hath my muse departed," she wondered, referring to her earlier habit of writing poems and doggerel in her journal. Although it was only two years since they had come as a newly married couple to Denver, "I feel almost a score of years older." The birth of her second child virtually brought her journal to an end. "I only write now when the mood seizes me," she admitted in April 1863. "I know I am fulfilling the duties of wife and mother." And with the birth of her second living child, the journal does indeed close. "With my two little ones, I will have less time to journalize," she wrote on the last page. "I hope to spend it caring for them in helpless infancy, training their young minds through childhood on up through life." [21]

Charlena Anderson also found the daily round of household chores overwhelming and difficult to organize. She recognized that a mother could not adequately care for the children and maintain a house at the same time. If only she had "relief from the time-consuming details of housekeeping," she wrote her husband in 1887, so that she might spend more time with the children. "Every night when I go to bed my heart sinks at the thought of opportunities lost for drawing out some faculty or doing just a little toward it, for directing them into better habits, or for leaving some pleasant impressions upon minds." Her answer to the problem was that the family should live in a boarding house so that she could "get rid of that 'what shall we eat and drink' and have only the 'wherewithall shall we be clothed' to contend with." Under such circumstances, she told Melville, the problem of properly training her children "would be simple." [22] This prefiguring of what the later feminist Charlotte Gilman would advocate and practice was ahead of the times and probably can be explained by Charlena Anderson's advanced education and experience as a teacher prior to and during the early years of her marriage. But it nevertheless testifies to the way in which a separate and limited sphere of activity filled the life of a woman even though much that was once expected of her was increasingly supplied by others outside the home. For the central task of the married woman in the 19th century, as Charlena Anderson's complaints emphasized, was the rearing of children. That was the job, according to the doctrine of the two spheres, for which women were peculiarly and naturally fitted.

In the next chapter we will therefore look at the role of women in the rearing of children.

IV
Women and Children

Today the United States Census counts any two individuals living under the same roof as a family. Historically, however, the family has usually included children, and that is the way the institution is popularly defined. Despite the centrality of the family in human experience and the obvious social importance of the ways in which children are raised, the history of childrearing is still largely unwritten. From the limited evidence now available, it appears that around the turn from the 18th to the 19th century adults' attitudes toward and practices in regard to children changed dramatically. These were the same years, it will be remembered, in which a comparable change occurred in the character of the family. In fact, the changes in the perception of children constitute another of the reasons for placing the shift to the modern American family at the end of the 18th century.

What were those changes? Perhaps the most notable is that children began to be seen as different from adults; among other things they were considered now more innocent; childhood itself was perceived as it is today, as a period of life not only worth recognizing and cherishing but extending. Moreover, simply because children were being seen for the first time as special, the family's reason for being, its justification as it were, was increasingly related to the proper rearing of children.

This last laid a heavy burden of responsibility upon 19th-century parents. Literary and other manifestations of this novel conception of children and childhood appear around the middle of the 18th century, particularly in the work of Genevan *philosophe* Jean Jacques Rousseau, especially in his book *Émile* (1762). In that book, for example, Rousseau stressed the necessity of fitting education to the special nature of the child, rather than assuming that children were just little adults. Nature, he insisted, "wants children to be children before they are men."[1] Childhood was of value because it was invested with the virtue of being natural. Nature, as the Romantics who followed him would emphasize even more, was good, not evil; children as natural beings were not the depraved incipient adults of Calvinism or Christianity in general. They were beings in their own right. The writings and teachings of the Swiss educator Johann Pestalozzi similarly emphasized the naturalness and individuality of children. Though both Rousseau and Pestalozzi were Europeans, their ideas and writings were well known in the United States. As two recent historians of early 19th-century schooling in Massachusetts have written, "The waning of the harsh Calvinist view of infants, along with the dissemination of Lockean and Pestalozzian notions of the unique emotional, physical, and intellectual needs of pliant but frail young children, fostered the delineation of a distinctive stage of childhood—the preschooler."

Philosophers and educators were not the only harbingers of a new and more favorable conception of children. Present-day literary critics have also discerned in poetry a novel emphasis upon the special virtue of children and childhood. "Until the last decades of the eighteenth century," literary critic Peter Coveney has written, "the child did not exist as an important and continuous theme in English literature. Childhood as a major theme came with the generation of Blake and Wordsworth." William Blake's *Songs of Innocence* (1789) depicted children as lacking the innate wickedness that theology had long insisted upon. With Wordsworth and particularly with his "Ode: Intimations of Immortality" (1807) the transition from the old to the new conception of children was completed. The poem not only denied the innate depravity of children but asserted their essential innocence. In fact, the poem portrayed children as recently arrived from Heaven and thus closest to God and virtue. In Wordsworth's view, as in Rousseau's, growing up was really the corruption of innocence. No longer could the ending of childhood be seen as a good thing. On the contrary, if it could be extended, so much the better. As critic Coveney pointed out, Wordsworth's "Intimations of Immortality" became "one of the central references for the whole nineteenth century in its attitudes to the child."[2]

Literary historian Barbara Garlitz has shown that Wordsworth's ideas—sometimes his precise words—in regard to children's innocence actually turned up in the writing of Americans. James Russell Lowell, for example, wrote of his dead child that "the light of heaven she came from still lingered and gleamed in her hair." Theologians, too, picked up Wordsworth's romantic conception of children as beings recently come from God. A Boston minister lamented in 1855 that the evil influences of the world often lured the young "out of the bright heavenly kingdom which lay around their infancy." And Nathaniel Hawthorne noted in his journal that he had spent many minutes scrutinizing his two-year-old son, wondering if the child had those "recollections of pre-existence" which Wordsworth and the Romantics insisted he had. At least one American publicist in 1841 said that he believed Wordsworth's Ode alone had made parents aware of the value and merit of their children.[3]

Wordsworth's Ode, no more than Pestalozzi's or Rousseau's writings, was not the cause for the new views, but all of them, along with many other Romantic writings, mark the profound shift that had occurred in popular attitudes toward children. A new recognition of the value of children was only one of the elements that comprised Romanticism. Its emphasis upon feeling over reason, the primitive over the sophisticated, the natural over the contrived, and the simple over the complicated made it natural for Romantics to dote upon children and emphasize the need to cherish and love them and rear them with responsibility—even if Rousseau personally failed to practice what he preached.

A more tangible measure of the emergence of a new conception of children at the opening of the 19th century was the publication of books written especially for children and books about their proper rearing. For if children were innocent and natural it followed that parents should learn how to care for them, love them, and instruct them properly. And so in the years after 1820 large numbers of advice books on child-rearing came off the presses in Britain and the United States. And as one authority on the history of child-rearing remarked, parents thought they "were remiss if they did not obtain and study [the] expanding body of literature on child rearing." He quoted one mother early in the 19th century as writing, "There is scarcely any subject concerning which I feel more anxiety than the proper education of my children. It is a difficult and delicate subject, the more I feel how much is to be learnt by myself." Significantly, he concluded, this interest in child-rearing literature "was a new phenomenon" in the 19th century.[4]

Not only was there a new literature on child-rearing, but a new genre of writing designed for children. "No trait in the literary development of the age is more striking," asserted the *Southern Literary Messenger* in 1854, "than the importance which seems suddenly to have attached to what we call juvenile books for children." [5] By the time of the Civil War as many as 300 titles were being published in the United States each year; in England the number of titles issued was at least double that. This outpouring of books and printed materials for children continued through the century, at once reflecting and measuring the continuing interest in children, their education, and their central place in the family.

This cherishing of children as innocent and different from adults, an outlook that certainly seems familiar to us today, was in sharp contrast to the attitudes most parents held in previous centuries. As John Demos pointed out in his study of 17th-century Plymouth, Massachusetts, children then were seen as miniature adults, not special beings whose youth and innocence should be treasured. Children in colonial New England, Edmund Morgan has shown, were quite commonly sent away from home to work in other homes when only ten and eleven years of age. Their parents then took other children into their homes. The origins of this practice, which was widespread in England and went back at least to the 16th century, are obscure. But this willingness, for whatever reason, to let children leave the family so early in life is surely a sign of parents' detachment from their children. This seems to be especially true when it is recognized that by the end of the 18th and beginning of the 19th century children were staying at home much longer. As early as the 1820s, two scholars have recently reported, though from admittedly sketchy evidence, the usual age at which many children left home was fifteen. By the middle of the century, as formal public schooling spread, especially in the North, most children stayed with their parents until well into their teens. Most working girls, for example, continued to live at home even after they went into full-time work between leaving school and marrying. Indeed, if one looks over the history of the ages at which children left home in American middle-class families, the tendency for the age to rise is clear, just what one would expect to happen in a new type of family characterized by the cherishing and even sentimentalizing of children.

Although there are few written historical sources on attitudes of working-class parents toward their children in the 19th century, the limited amount of child labor in the economy does suggest that childhood was seen as a special and different status by working-class parents, too. To say that does not mean that children were not expected to perform chores around the house or farm, for of course they were. A recent study of pre-

At Odds

Civil War Newark, New Jersey, concludes that in one of the most highly industrialized cities in the nation—three quarters of the labor force was engaged in manufacturing—"the best evidence against the widespread use of child labor is that, although many of the craftsmen protested the employment of unskilled teenagers, none complained about competition from child labor." The study goes on to say that working-class families in Newark were as likely to have their sons between the ages of fifteen and twenty living at home as the population in general. In 1850, the proportion staying home in the city at large was 40 per cent; for the working-class families studied, 54 per cent. By 1860 the proportions had risen to 71 per cent and 66 per cent respectively. Recent figures (see table below) on the proportions of children between the ages of 10 and 15 employed throughout the nation similarly suggest that after the Civil War working-class fam-

Children, aged 10 through 15, gainfully employed 1870–1950

	Number (in thousands)			Percentage of children 10 through 15 gainfully employed		
Year	Male	Female	Total	Male	Female	Total
1870	548	191	739	19	7	13
1880	825	293	1,118	24	9	17
1890	700	320	1,020	17	8	12
1900			1,750			18
1910			1,990			18
1920			1,061			8.5
1930			667			5
1940			209			1
1950			701			2

Source: Adapted from David Stern, Sandra Smith, and Fred Doolittle, "How Children Used To Work," *Law and Contemporary Problems* 39 (Summer 1975), 99.

ilies generally kept their children at home at least until the completion of elementary school. Since only those children who actually worked for money are included in the census figures, the great proportion of those reported as working in the following table were probably urban residents. Nonetheless, it is still striking how small was the proportion of children, which included whites, blacks, poor, and rich, who were working for money.

Another study, this time of working-class families only, carried out by the U.S. Bureau of Labor in 1901 showed that even when an investigation was limited to the children of workers the proportion of children in the paid work force was very small. The subjects of the investigation were some 25,000 families in the principal industrial cities in 33 states in which the family head earned no more than $1200 a year. Less than 10 per cent of the children between 10 and 16 years of age were at work.[6]

Other evidence also suggests that by the early years of the 19th century children were seen in a way quite different from that of previous centuries. Increasingly, children were viewed as individuals, as persons in their own right. The new attitude is reflected, for example, in the decline in the practice of naming children after parents. Daniel Scott Smith found that in Hingham, Massachusetts, in the 17th century over 60 per cent of first sons and 70 per cent of first daughters bore the same first name as a parent. By the early 19th century, however, the practice had declined to the extent that by then a different middle name was given the child also; and by the middle of the 19th century only 40 per cent of the sons and 16 per cent of the daughters were still being given the name of a parent. Parents, in short, were seeing their children increasingly as individuals. The same interpretation can be drawn from the abandonment during the early 19th century of naming a living child after a dead one. By the 19th century almost all children, even those who died at birth or in infancy, had their own names, that is, their own individuality. A further sign that children were gaining new recognition as individuals and as special beings was that celebration of birthdays began only in the 19th century. Finally, as one historian of childhood has remarked, prior to the 19th century children were referred to or reported on in letters of adults only in passing or as a formality. "One is struck," this historian concluded, "by how infrequent, brief, casual, and sometimes hard-hearted are the references made to children by eighteenth-century Americans."[7]

A similar casualness about children appears in divorce petitions in the 18th century. In a study of some 220 divorce cases in Massachusetts during the first eighty years of the 18th century, it was found that only a third of the petitions even mentioned children, though probably all of the litigants had children. When offspring were mentioned, it was usually by way of suggesting the previous strength of the marriage, not to arouse concern for the lot of the children. And even when children were mentioned in the petition, the number was rarely given, and the sex of them was never noted. In short, children were used in such cases in the interest of parents and not for themselves.[8]

Another sign of a change in attitudes toward children is that in the transition from the 18th to the 19th century there was a marked decline in recourse to corporal punishment of children. This shift in behavior within the home manifested itself, too, outside the home, notably in the public opposition to corporal punishment in schools. The question aroused a great deal of controversy as early as the 1840s, for by then physical punishment of children was no longer being taken for granted. By then, too, school reformers were making clear their belief in the desirability of prolonging childhood through compulsory school attendance. One of them wrote, for example, that the school was to be an "asylum for the preservation and culture of childhood." Others recommended that the school year be extended to coincide with the years of childhood; failure to attend school was also attacked on the ground that it constituted a deprivation of an important experience of childhood. One historian has explained the well-known unruliness of college students during the early 19th century as a consequence of the permissive discipline of American parents who were thought to be too oriented toward their children and thus acted toward them in a sentimental fashion. Significantly, these parental attitudes and practices were contrasted to the more rigid ones said to have prevailed in preceding centuries.[9] As we shall see in the next chapter, parents in the 19th century, like those in the 20th, still felt it necessary to discipline children, but whippings and other kinds of violence were increasingly frowned upon, not only in the advice literature, but in the practices as well of the middle class.

Although there is little doubt, in contrast with previous centuries, that the 19th was truly "the century of the child," there is much doubt as to why that change to a modern outlook occurred at that particular moment in history. Some historians have related the change to a decline in infant mortality, which was said to have begun in the opening years of the 19th century. Once the likelihood of a particular child's surviving to adulthood had been improved, so the reasoning goes, parents could afford to invest emotion and affection in their children. Hence the change in the conception of children. Appealing as this explanation may be in logic, in fact it falls to the ground simply because there does not seem to have been any decline in infant mortality at any point in the whole century. The few reliable figures available on infant mortality for the middle years of the century in Massachusetts actually show a rise in infant deaths. Furthermore, inasmuch as urbanization spread and fouled the air, contaminated the water supply, concentrated population, and increased the opportunities for the rapid spread of disease, the rise in infant mortality should cease to surprise us. As late as 1900 the rate of infant deaths in Massachusetts was no lower than it had been in 1850. Not until 1920 did it drop significantly at all, when it fell to 79 deaths per thousand births from 141 deaths in 1900. Obviously in such trends there is no support for the argument that by the opening decades of the 19th century parents would have an improved sense of security about the survival of their children. Yet, parents did indeed reduce the number of their children in the course of the 19th century. The reasons for the curtailment are best left for analysis to a later chapter. Suffice to say here that the fall in fertility, like the new attitude toward children, was closely related to other developments in the family, particularly the changing situation of women.

The domestic role of women, which we have been calling the separation of the spheres, went hand in hand with the new conception of children as precious, and different from adults. In ideal and in practice the mother was responsible for carrying out the novel and special view of children. She was not only the bearer but the chief rearer of the children, a task that was increasingly invested with high responsibility and therefore great respect, and even authority. Women, it is true, had always reared children, but in the 19th century it was increasingly recognized as primarily, and, more important, properly woman's task. Students of child-rearing literature in England and America tell us that in the 16th and 17th centuries the father was depicted as the important figure in the rearing of children as well as being the ultimate authority in familial matters. In fact, most of the manuals of those centuries directed their advice to father. By the 18th century, however, the mother was being seen as the primary rearer, though, at that time the recognition, as one systematic study of the literature put it, was made "with some anxiety expressed." Even at that date, no emphasis was placed on an emotional bond between mother and child. (That such emotionality may actually have occurred is shown by the warnings in the literature against excessive emotion or attachment.) By the early 19th century, though, the mother was being frankly identified as "the primary rearer, without anxiety." By then, one study assures us, "almost all of the middle class child-rearing literature spoke only to mothers," referring to the uniqueness of the maternal role and the necessity of it for proper rearing. In the opening years of the 19th century the Protestant clergy also began to refer to the religious influence of mothers without making any references to paternal intervention, though that had been the practice in such literature in earlier centuries.[10]

This increasing and indispensable role for women in the proper rearing of offspring was reinforced by the industrial changes that were removing or simplifying some of women's traditional duties in the home. These changes thus left child care as a growing part of a woman's day and life. And now that children were being perceived as special and precious, society wanted that concentration of attention to continue and grow. For only in that way could the child receive the attentive care the new conception of childhood prescribed. Nor should it be forgotten that it was to women's advantage to encourage this emotional concentration upon children within the family and throughout society, since in that way woman's own role would be enhanced. In effect, the more children were fussed over and cherished the more woman would be honored as the parent most directly and "naturally" concerned with them. It is surely not accidental that the century of the child is also the century of the Cult of True Womanhood. Exalting the child went hand in hand with exalting the domestic role of woman; each reinforced the other while together they raised domesticity within the family to a new and higher level of respectability.

The natural, physical relationships between mother and child ensured that the mother's influence would be primary during the child's early years, that is, down to puberty, at least. Thereafter, especially on the farm, the father's influence expanded, especially with his sons as they sought to find themselves as males and as workers outside the home. Meanwhile daughters continued to look to their mothers for guidance in assuming their gender roles in society. Yet before children of both sexes were eight or nine years of age, the mother was the prime inculcator of values, and perhaps their sole formal educator as well. For "keeping school" appeared in the letters and diaries of women as a common as well as an important responsibility of mothers, and not only those of the urban middle class who might have had servants. In sum, a new emphasis upon children and their proper rearing would be a reason why girls needed to be educated, too: so that they could become adequate teachers of their children. Significantly, as we shall see in Chapter XII, the movement to improve and extend the education of girls also began at the end of the 18th and the beginning of the 19th century.

One measure of the importance of women in the 19th-century middle-class family in general and in child-rearing in particular was the attenuated character of what has often been referred to as the "patriarchal family." The typical husband in the middle-class family was hardly the patriarchal father who gave little recognition to his wife. By definition, the companionate marriage placed limits on the power of the husband.

A similar muting of the meaning and impact of patriarchy is observable when the relationship between father and children is examined. In a well-known passage, Alexis de Tocqueville described how weak patriarchal authority appeared to him when he visited the United States in the 1830s. With the coming of democracy, he contended, "a species of equality prevails around the domestic hearth. . . . I think that in proportion as manners and laws become more democratic, the relation of father and son becomes more intimate and more affectionate; rules and authority are less talked of, confidence and tenderness are often increased. . . ." Tocqueville argued it would be a mistake to imagine that the children's independence of their parents was preceded by any sort of domestic struggle. Instead of that "the father foresees the limits of his authority long before hand, and when the time arrives, he surrenders it without a struggle."[11]

If Tocqueville's conception of "equality around the domestic hearth" is not taken too literally, its truth can be illustrated by the remarks and behavior of people of the time. Mother and father were often seen as equally interested and involved in the upbringing of their children. In 1818, for example, a young North Carolinian wrote to thank his father for letters and gifts received when he was away from home. In the course of his letter he made clear his close relationship to both parents. Ever since his infancy, he wrote, "you and Mama were my best friends and I always try to do my best." When, in 1860, Charles Jones, a Georgia planter and minister wrote his son, then almost thirty years old, to warn him against the evils of drink, he clearly indicated the admonition came also from the mother. "You are our first born, and dear son to your father and mother. You have been in many, many things a great comfort and joy to us. But you know not our solicitude for you that you may escape every danger—the danger of which we have been writing. . . . There are prayers offered for you daily; and often, in the dark and silent hours of midnight . . . your ever anxious and devoted mother is praying for you." Conspicuously absent is any peremptory assertion of patriarchal authority.

The following year, on the occasion of the son's thirtieth birthday, the gentle, even sentimental, character of the father's attitude was again apparent. When he first looked upon his son thirty years before, the father recalled, "I was as conscious of the flowing of a new affection through my soul . . . as I would have been of a warm stream flowing over the most sensitive part of my person." And that feeling, he added, had continued and would continue as long as "my heart continues to beat." Significantly, he concluded as he began, with a plea that his son join the church to which all the other members of the family belonged. It is surely a measure of the limitations on paternal authority that Charles, Jr., never did join the church during his father's lifetime, despite the old gentleman's frequent urgings and personal and professional connection with the church.[12]

An as yet unpublished study by Jane T. Censer of the correspondence of some 100 upper-class families in North Carolina during the antebellum years also documents the reluctance of upper-class fathers to use their substantial financial and psychological power over their children. She suggests that these fathers were caught between their desire to maintain authority within the family and the wish to please their children and thus remain in a friendly relationship with them.

In the family of Joseph and Julia Holt there was no doubt that the mother was the dominant figure. It was the father who provided the psychological support and encouragement to the 19-year-old daughter "Bertie." Julia Holt did the exhorting of the daughter to greater efforts and higher goals. "You can't do everything at once," the mother conceded in a letter in 1873, "but you can make every days work count—and it is your duty to yourself and to us to do it." The parents, she continued, would do their best to support her by their jobs, but it was her responsibility to finish school and "the next 2 or 3 years of your life are to be *specially devoted to it*—everything else, correspondence, reading, company, and everything are subordinate and secondary. . . ." If she would do that, Julia Holt promised, "you would stand a good chance to be a useful, independent and happy woman the rest of your life." But she feared that Bertie was "in great danger of letting just this precious time be frittered away in childish trifling. . . . O dear! I *wish* you could get waked up to appreciate your privileges and improve them." Nor was Julia reluctant to use comparison of Bertie with others as a goad: "If you would work as Nina Gregory does—as conscientiously and self-denyingly you could accomplish as much."

The father, on the other hand, emphasized how much he missed his daughter; he never resorted to the exhortations of his wife. "Be a real good girl," he closed one letter. "We will be together next winter." When her managing of a school election was successful, he wrote exultantly, "I *glory*, of course, in your success at the election. Lots of love and kisses from Father." The character of the relationship among the three can be inferred from the father's telling the daughter of the accommodations she would have when she visited them after school was closed. Her room had "a narrow bedstead in it," he writes. "I'll let you sleep with Mother once a month."[13]

It is true that in one respect Joseph and Julia Holt were hardly a typical couple, since Julia held a job as a teacher; few married white women worked in the 19th century. But Mollie Dorsey's relationship with her father, whose wife did not work at a job, was almost as close or friendly as Bertie's with Joseph Holt. One night, in order to avoid Mollie's being compelled to walk home with an importuning widower, Mollie's father came to pick her up after dinner. As they walked across the prairie, they saw young couples ahead of them, enjoying their walk together, "but none more than I, with my dear Father," Mollie wrote in her journal, "who always enters into my enthusiastic love and admiration of the beautiful in nature." [14]

The relatively democratic role of the father in the 19th-century family was only one of the reasons why mothers occupied a significant place. Another was that husbands were simply not at home as much as mothers, especially in the city home, where the mother's tasks were generally confined to the house. The moral advice and child-rearing books of the 1830s and after backhandedly testified to the small role that fathers actually played in the rearing of children by their deploring of the father's absence at work. The advice literature usually stressed the desirability of the father's active participation in the proper rearing of children, but the point was made in such a way as to make clear that in most middle-class homes the father was indeed absent most of the time. One domestic advice book in 1875, for example, urged fathers to participate in the care of children in order to lighten the burden of work upon mothers. After all, the manual pointed out, fathers love their children and work hard to support them; why should they not also cuddle them on their laps and care for their needs? Most of this advice literature reached urban parents primarily, who made up only a minority of Americans throughout the 19th century. But even among farmers, as Bernard Wishy has observed, fathers were not likely to be around the house enough to take an active part in the rearing of very young children. Thus even on the farm the mother's role in the socialization of the child was predominant.

By and large, men readily recognized the dominant role played by women in the proper rearing of children. In 1845 Horace Bushnell gave a series of sermons in Hartford in which he declared that the careful nurture of children in the home by women was even more important in shaping Christian character than conversion. Henry Waller, after telling in 1856 of some advice he had given to one of their sons, acknowledged to his wife that "I would not have taken such a step without advising with you or notifying you of it. I agree with you perfectly in your views." Two weeks earlier, when he offered a suggestion on child-rearing, he apologized for his interference. "I know, my darling, that if ever mother exerted herself for her children, you certainly do. You must therefore understand that I merely throw out the above suggestions by way of aiding you if I can." The Wallers, incidentally, were not city dwellers; they lived on a farm in Kentucky.[15]

This recognition of the pre-eminence of women in the rearing of children did not mean that mothers sought to exclude the father. In fact, both the advice books and the mothers themselves testified to the wish to include the father as much as possible. The wife of an absent seaman, for example, wrote her husband in 1829 that their newborn son, whom the father had not seen, was "a runing round the room while i am wrighting" and had been told where his "Dear Father" was. A year later she sent to her husband "the Love of your Absent Wife and Son who will bee erly taught to love his absent Father."[16]

One absent father who sought to take a hand in his infant son's upbringing testified at the same time, quite inadvertently, to the primary role of the mother in that upbringing, and in the administering of corporal punishment. William Pender wrote his wife in 1861 that she must not allow his father (the child's grandfather) to spoil their son by protecting him against proper punishment. "He must not interfere when his [the child's] Mama goes to whip him, but think of his youngest son [Pender himself], see what a good boy he is, and think what he might have been if his Mama had not whipped him so much and kept him in such good trim."[17]

As Pender's advice makes clear, fathers sometimes participated in child-rearing, even if, as in this instance, they were physically absent. Their advice generally concerned the health of the children, a matter about which no one in the 19th century was a reliable authority, not even physicians. Henry Waller wrote his wife in Kentucky in 1840 about the illness of their son, the root of which he ascribed to his "eating too much trash." Her remedies for the illness Waller thought inadequate. What the child needed was "a little calomel. Be very careful with his eating—don't let him eat candy and cake and fruit, whilst he is so affected." Pender, too, gave advice on matters of health. He wrote his wife that she was not to bare the infant's feet "according to the most approved style, but put something warm on them." And in 1883 Sam Leland wrote his sister that he, who had once "professed to be so cold on the subject of babies, am a complete convert" now that he had an infant son of his own. In another letter he went on at great length about the child's progress, telling his sister quite knowledgeably of the colic pains his son had suffered early in the morning. "We want him as soon as possible to take only one meal between bedtime and six in the morning," he wrote, expressing a hope that might have been heard in virtually the same words in 1970.[18]

The feeding of infants was almost invariably the responsibility of the mother and not simply because she alone could nurse. For even by the early years of the 19th century "dry-nursing" or, as it was sometimes also called, "raising a baby by hand," was widely, if not commonly practiced. As early as 1820 nursing bottles were cheap and available in most cities and towns. A good baby-food formula was not devised until the second half of the century, and the first rubber nipple was not patented until 1845, but new styles of bottles came on the market fairly regularly, suggesting growing consumer demand. In fact, the vehemence with which an advice book for mothers as early as 1809 inveighed against those "selfish mothers" or "monsters" who did not want to nurse their babies suggests that wet-nursing and dry-nursing were not rare even at that early date. By the 1830s the interest in alternatives to mother's breast-feeding was sufficiently high that most advice books included information on dry-nursing and wet-nursing. Catharine Beecher's widely circulated *Treatise on Domestic Economy,* published in 1841, treated the feeding of a baby "by hand" as almost as likely as by breast. The book included a recipe for making the baby's food out of cow's milk, advising that the milk be taken from a "new-milch cow," mixed with one-third water and sweetened with a little white sugar. The baby, Beecher counseled, was to stay on this formula until the teeth appeared.[19]

Nevertheless, as the attack on mothers who did not nurse their babies suggested, all the advice books as well as individual physicians counseled that women should nurse their infants for their own sakes as well as the children's. And apparently most women agreed. One woman wrote in discreet 19th-century fashion to her mother about an incident she had witnessed. She told of seeing the governor of Georgia at a railroad station holding a crying baby on his knee "trying to shake it into quietude, but failing in his efforts; Mrs. Brown gave it the natural source of comfort." (The statement also suggests that nursing in public was not frowned upon even in the Southern Confederacy.)

The importance attached to breast-feeding by the mother is apparent in the rather painful story of Mary Walker's efforts while serving in the wilds of Oregon in 1838 as a missionary. Her nipples became very sore soon after the birth of the child and then caking occurred within one breast; the pain soon became excruciating. Even though she had to take morphine for the pain, she continued to nurse the child, though at one point her husband had to hold the baby and the breast, so severe was the pain. As she told her parents in a letter, the agony "was so intense that my hands would be clinched and a paroxism produced much like a fit, I think I can with truth say that I never knew what pain was untill then." Finally, she had to give the child over to another woman who was just weaning her own child, but not before she tried unsuccessfully to fashion an artificial nipple from a mare's teat to use with cow's milk. To compound the matter, her failure to be able to nurse her child herself aroused hostility from another missionary's wife on the ground that if her "heart had only been big enough" she could have managed it![20]

The importance attached to breast-feeding comes out, too, in an example from Georgia. Although Ruth Jones was dying of puerperal fever after the birth of her second child, she was aroused several times from her semi-comatose state to nurse the baby. Not until a few days before her death did her physician order the nursing to stop. It is not clear how the infant was fed thereafter, though it is possible, since the family owned a substantial number of slaves, that the infant was given to a slave mother who happened to have milk. On the other hand, there is a suggestion that the child was actually put onto dry-nursing, since only two months later the grandfather reported that the grandmother, with whom the child was living, "put the coconut dipper to her little mouth and she drank heartily like an old person."[21]

The advice books may have thought nursing was desirable, but that did not mean it was always possible. Certainly that was implied in Sam Leland's comment to his sister in 1883 that "fortunately" his wife "seems to have plenty of milk," as if it was not to be taken for granted. He was happy to be able to say, too, that the milk "must be nourishing" since the baby is in excellent health—again a suggestion that some women, at least in the folklore of parents at the time, could not provide sufficient nourishment by nursing alone. William Pender's suggestions to his wife to wean their son early because he thought nursing "might be keeping you down in flesh and strength" implied that some people thought nursing a strain on women. Five months later, when the baby was eleven months old, Pender returned to the subject, saying the boy "is old enough and nursing him will wear you down more than the birth of two." Two days later Fanny Pender did wean the infant because she thought it was taking a toll of her strength. Sam Leland, too, seemed to believe that nursing, for all the emphasis the culture placed upon its value, was debilitating for women. "Isn't it delightful," he wrote to his sister about his wife, "that she is as well as can be, and as fat as a porpoise? It seems quite a marvel that it is so when she is nursing baby."[22]

At the end of the century, advice books were still extolling breast-feeding, but they recommended prompt weaning at ten to twelve months of age, about the same period recommended and practiced at the beginning of the century. By the 1890s, however, bottle-feeding "from the beginning" was recommended as well, suggesting that breast-feeding was less and less successful. Some mothers were apparently interested in early weaning, for one young woman wrote her father in 1876 about the good health of her six-month-old son, though she did "not *now* feed the little one at all." In short, by the opening of the 20th century, breast-feeding was probably considerably less important than it had been.[23]

At the same time, the influence of mothers in child-rearing undoubtedly increased. More and more women by the opening decade of the 20th century were living in urban homes, their husbands out of the house at work. Almost fifty per cent of Americans in 1910 lived in cities, yet no more than 5 per cent of married white women worked outside the home. In social statistics as well as in social ideology the home and the rearing of the children were the domain of women. Before the 19th century the rearing of children and the maintenance of the home had never been a full-time job; there had always been too many other things expected and demanded of the wife and mother. By the opening of the 20th century home and children were the world of most white women and an increasing number of black women as well. It is therefore appropriate to turn now to an examination of the role of women in child-rearing beyond the earliest stages of infant care.

Throughout the 19th century medical knowledge as well as advice books on child-rearing stressed the importance of the mother in the upbringing of children. At the moment of conception, it is true, physicians generally assigned to both parents an equal, if different, influence on the child. But during pregnancy and nursing the mother's attitudes, experiences, and even thoughts were believed to influence and shape the child. It seemed only natural, therefore, that, even after weaning, the mother's role in rearing the child should be dominant. Certainly the child-advice literature left no doubt on this score. "By the mother's forming hand," one manual asserted in 1848, the child "receives its shape to a great extent for all its future existence." A year later, *Mother's Assistant* told its readers that "perhaps there is no proposition that is so hackneyed and at the same time so little understood as that women are the prime cause of all the good and evil in human actions. . . . Yes, mothers, in a certain sense, the destiny of a redeemed world is put into your hands."[24]

Although many of the child-rearing books of the time asserted that the father was clearly the head of the family, they also insisted upon the central role of women in rearing offspring. The apparent contradiction is resolved, as Bernard Wishy has pointed out, by recognizing that "whatever the ultimate or formal supremacy of the father, in most homes during the child's earliest years, the mother was probably far more important than the father as an immediate source of ideals and as a disciplinarian" simply because most fathers were not at home.[25] Indeed, mothers were considered so essential to the moral regimen of the child that many advice books warned mothers against relying upon servants or nurses since they, with their own bad habits, could reduce or eliminate entirely the mother's indispensable control over the child's development. This kind of advice was intended for middle-class women and may actually have been directed against working-class women who were, after all, the servants and nurses.

Perhaps, too, this is the place to raise the question of the extent to which the advice literature and the kinds of sources used here can be related to all social levels. It is quite true that most, if not all, of the advice books were directed at middle-and upper-class families, and certainly most of the correspondence among women and within families has been drawn largely from middle-class people. The fact is that historians know relatively little about the intimate details of working-class family life in these years, principally because the traditional written sources are lacking. Working-class people or immigrants usually did not keep diaries or maintain lengthy correspondence; moreover, even if they did, few were preserved. Yet, as was noted in regard to family correspondence in Chapter II, the middle-class character of most of the evidence does not seriously reduce its usefulness as a reflection of the behavior and attitudes of Americans in general. For one thing, middle-class people were a significant part of the population, probably as much as three-fifths, if commercial farm families are so denominated. For another, the middle class set the cultural tone and level of the society so that it seems reasonable to assume that what middle-class people were doing and thinking about children was influencing people of the working class as well. The great majority of the adult population by the middle of the 19th century was literate. Thus the working class could read the prescriptions and advice of middle-class people as well as observe their behavior. We know, for example, that in the early 20th century working-class and immigrant women read avidly the publications of the Children's Bureau on child-rearing. Their use of this literature comes out in the hundreds of letters from poor women to the Bureau in the years before World War I.[26]

In the 19th century, the letters and diaries of women show that middle-class mothers accepted quite seriously their special role as rearers of children. To a young mother like Sarah R. Stearns there was no question that she was essential to the proper upbringing of her children. In October 1816, as she was reflecting in her journal on how busy she was kept by the need for "constant attention" to the bodily needs of her three children "and the need to cultivate their minds," no mention of the role of her husband in this task was made at all. A month later, when she returned to the subject on the occasion of their fourth anniversary, she coupled her husband's responsibilities with hers, saying God had committed their three children "to our care, to rear, cherish, and prepare for eternity." Earlier she had commented on her daughter's growth "in stature and in knowledge." The child could now understand what was said to her and "already calls for the kind hand of assiduous care, to cultivate her infant reason— may God grant his blessing on her parents' exertions." Here, too, her husband's part was implied, but she seemed principally concerned with her own part in the task. When she commented on what she must do for the child of a distant relative, whom she had recently taken into her home to rear for life, the job was exclusively hers. "I shall study to educate her in the ways of piety, morality, honesty, and sobriety," she vowed.[27]

Sarah Stearns's husband was usually at home, but that did not reduce Sarah's primary responsibility for the moral education of her children. Although Harriet Beecher Stowe's husband was a minister, he was frequently absent. In the mind of Harriet she was the children's moral guardian. She warned Calvin against exaggerating his children's religious nature, reminding him that they are not "a parcel of little saints." In fact, she told her husband, only recently their oldest boy had become so angry with his grandfather for denying him a pleasure he sought "that I had to correct him for it." She conceded, though, that "they do seem at times to be influenced by the religious truths that are constantly and daily inculcated upon them." She left no doubt that it was her instruction, not Calvin's, that was taking hold. She said she trusted that Christ "has accepted the dedication by which . . . I have committed them to him." And given Calvin's absences she was not exaggerating her role.[28]

A more secular way in which mothers sought to inculcate values is revealed in a letter from a mother in Georgia to her son on the eve of the Civil War. Like most slave-holding Southerners, Mary Jones saw no alternative to secession in light of what she believed were the North's attacks upon the South. Consequently, she relieved her sons in January 1861 of a vow she had long before made for them. In Independence Hall in Philadelphia, she wrote, "at the foot of Washington's statue, I pledged you both to support and defend the Union."[29]

Some women were so self-conscious about their responsibilities as mothers that their concern bordered on anxiety. "I lay [awake] all night thinking," Mary Walker wrote in her diary in 1846. "I do not know what course to persue [*sic*] with our children. They need much more care than I can possibly bestow. . . . I hope Providence will dispose of me as is best even if it be to remove me from this place and even to another world." Bell Waller canvassed at length what she saw as her responsibilities as wife and mother when her husband raised the possibility of their leaving Kentucky. After nothing that she was more than willing to "conform to his situation," she went on to say, "my known duty is to the raising and educating my children, this responsibility rests competely with a parent; they are, and must ever be responsible to their God and their children for the principles they instil into those children which God has given them to raise. If I am faithful in the attention I give to my children I have but little time to mingle with the fashionable world," a reference to the possibility of their moving to a large city like Chicago. To properly rear children, she concluded, "is the work of a life."[30]

. The continuity of woman's moral role within the family well into the 20th century is apparent in the journal entries of a middle-class, middle-aged mother in the late 1920s, living first in Milwaukee, Wisconsin, and then in Cambridge, Massachusetts. When her son, a student at the University at Madison, wrote for money she warned him against the "mesmerism of fraternity life." She urged him to read a clipping she enclosed on the life of the new Secretary of the Treasury, Andrew Mellon, who said that his father had been inspired by reading Benjamin Franklin's *Autobiography*. The mother was reading Franklin and urged her son to do likewise. When her daughter "expresses disdain at the sight of a Jewish child across the street" the mother sought to instruct the daughter in the irrelevance of "race difference, superiority, etc." just as Harriet Beecher Stowe might have instructed her child. And much like Sarah Stearns, the 20th-century mother prided herself on the intellectual along with the moral guidance she was providing her children. "I may not be giving my children worldly wealth," she conceded, "but what a heritage is theirs! The best of the world's literature and choicest gems of expressed thought has surrounded them since early years." When a Virginia ham arrived from her traveling-businessman husband, she seized the occasion to sum up the parental division of labor. It has a distinct 19th-century cast to it: "Always a good Provider, plenteous food he has always supplied. The moral sustenance has ever been my chief thought." [31]

The rearing of children required more than simply inculcating proper values or maintaining a good, moral atmosphere in the home. Discipline was also essential, and, though it was never the sole responsibility of the mother, her participation in that aspect of child-rearing in the 19th century was significant, as we shall see in the next chapter.

V

Inducting Children
into the Social Order

A time-honored way of raising children has been to coerce them physically, thereby inculcating not only proper behavior but perhaps proper thoughts as well. And just because the ends were so important, physical disciplining occurred early in the life of the child, not only prior to the 19th century but in the years after 1800 as well. The immediate purpose of this early discipline was to subdue the child's self-assertiveness. Until that was done, it was then believed, little true education or spiritual growth could be expected. Historian Lawrence Stone tells us that in early 17th-century England, schools and parents alike undertook, as contemporaries put it, "to break the child's will." One 17th-century New England minister, for example, ruefully observed that "there is in all children . . . a stubbornness and stoutness of mind, arising from natural pride, which must in the first place be broken and beaten down." He further advised parents that "children should not know, if it could be kept from them, that they have a will of their own." [1]

In 17th-century England whipping was one of the favorite ways of breaking the child's will. The practice was so common that when one theologian sought to be graphic in describing the torments of Hell he said that they were "worse a thousand times than whippings," and that "God's anger is worse than your father's anger." The common use of the whip or cane in disciplining children in the early modern period is suggested by a comment made by King Henry IV of France to the governess of his son, the future King Louis XII. "I have a complaint to make," Henry began, "you do not send word that you have whipped my son. I wish to command you to whip him every time that he is obstinate or mischievous, knowing well for myself that there is nothing in the world which will be better for him than that. I know it from experience, having myself profited, for when I was his age I was often whipped. That is why," the King concluded, "I want you to whip him and to make him understand why." Whipping of children and other dependents persisted well into the 18th century. In the diary of William Byrd children seem to be whipped for little or nothing. And sometimes even more violent methods were used; Byrd claimed to have forced a child to drink "a pint of piss" for wetting the bed.[2]

The idea that it was imperative to "break the will" of the child continued into the 19th century. The new child-rearing literature that began to appear in large quantities in the 1830s and 1840s stressed the need to subdue the child early and at almost any cost. "No child," wrote Theodore Dwight in a book of advice to fathers in 1834, "has ever been known since the earliest period of the world, to be destitute of an evil disposition— however sweet it appears." Dwight's implication, however, that children were innately depraved was not typical of child-rearing thinking at that time. He expressed a line of thought that was by then outmoded. More typical was Lydia Maria Child, writer and abolitionist, who specifically denied any belief in infant depravity, however much she believed in control over the child. It was necessary, she insisted, to provide a good environment if the child's "bad propensities" were to be kept under control until he was able to resist evil on his own. "Evil," she wrote in 1831, "is within and without." By the early 19th century, the breaking of the child's will was as much for the future benefit of the child as for any other consideration. That, too, marked a change from earlier centuries.[3]

The concern expressed in the child-rearing literature for early control over the child appears again and again in the letters of parents as well. In 1860, for example, Mary Mallard described her two-year-old daughter to a close female friend: "She is a child of wonderful life and great activity of mind, so that I have constantly to be on my guard; and she often gets into trouble." She then went on to say it was "no easy matter rightly to control a child," but that she had no doubt that control was essential for proper upbringing. By way of illustration she recounted an incident of a few evenings earlier. After the father had reproved his young daughter for some act of misconduct, the child turned and looked at her father "in the most quizzical way and said; 'Oh, darling, don't talk so; you will scare this child into fits!' " Mary Mallard's pointed conclusion from the incident was that "native depravity shows itself pretty often, but I hope in a few months more she will be quite an obedient little girl."[4] The incident is doubly revealing; it shows not only a clear parental concern for controlling the child, but also a mildness of reaction that is typically 19th-century. No 18th-century parent would have ignored such a challenge. Mary Mallard's mother also testified to a concern about controlling children. In writing to her widower son Charles about his daughter, who was being reared by her, she noted the progress of the two-year-old and concluded with the observation, "I do not think she will ever be a difficult child to govern."[5]

How to "govern" a child was Mary Waterman Rice's concern, too, in 1875 when she wrote to her father about her baby, then only twelve weeks old. After pointing out how attractive he was and how pleased she was to have him, she noted that "the other side of the story is . . . that even at this early age he shows that he possesses a furious temper and a most determined will, and I anticipate trouble in the future, if we [are] not very judicious in his government." The problem of control, of course, could become more serious as the children matured. Thus some mothers, like Juliet Janin, took measures to anticipate problems of discipline and control. When she was in New York in 1847 with her three young sons, she allowed only two of them to take the ferry to Staten Island. "I kept Louis with me because I feared he would be too wild and dispute with his brothers," she wrote her husband. "There is not a milder, better behaved boy than he is when by himself and with those who will give up to him, but with older boys and his brothers who will not, he appears in a different light. He is very self-willed and passionate and unstable to a degree—that is alarming. Those are the worst traits of his character."[6]

Control over her sons was just as important to Charlena Anderson as it was to Juliet Janin, but her confidence was less. In 1881 she wrote her husband that her two sons, neither of whom was yet six years old, were "a great care, the little rascals. Balfour does not mind a whipping in the least," she reported, suggesting that she had tried her hand at that in her husband's absence; "and Playfair is growing bold and it keeps me busy to study out different ways of keeping them in check." Then she offered a succinct statement of her view of the responsibility for discipline and its justification. "I shall be glad when you get with them again to *help* in the responsibility of controlling them, and I know how much their character will depend upon how they are governed."[7]

If concern with subduing the will of the child and "governing" it properly did not alter substantially from the 17th to the 19th century, the way in which that governance was accomplished certainly did. The idea that whipping was good for the child—as Henry IV had said and which many 17th- and 18th-century parents believed—was generally frowned upon by 19th-century middle-class parents and the advice books they read. "Affectionate persuasion addressed to the understanding, the conscience, and the heart," advised Herman Humphrey in *Domestic Education* in 1840, "is the grand instrument to be employed in family government." Whipping, the advice books told them, should be only a last resort. In 1847 Augusta Larned, in her book *Talks with Girls,* put physical punishment at the end of a list of six devices for controlling children. The first, significantly, was "love," the second "reason," and the third "authority." [8] The shift, of course, reflected the new appreciation of children and the sentimentality toward them that had been growing ever since the dawning of Romanticism. Nor was it accidental that the decline of physical punishment coincided with the rise in the importance of women within the family and their increasing concentration upon child-rearing and home. As the gentler sex, traditionally, it was only to be expected that under their aegis a more gentle approach would be taken toward children.

As the listing in *Talks with Girls* makes clear, however, physical punishment was not prohibited even in the late 19th century. Instead there was a shift in priorities rather than an abandonment of physical coercion. In fact, as we saw in the last chapter, as late as the 1860s William Pender was justifying whipping in almost the same terms that Henry IV had used. And one mother in 1834 wrote in *Mother's Magazine* of her efforts to subdue her sixteen-month-old daughter's will, offering us, thereby, a good illustration of how whipping was no longer the first step to control, though it was not dropped entirely. Because the child would not say "dear mama" on her father's orders, the mother banished the child to a room alone. Although she screamed wildly for ten minutes, she still would not comply with the mother's command. It was at that point that the mother spanked the child before putting her back into the room. After four hours of isolation, the child complied with her parent's demand.

A missionary couple, living on the Oregon frontier in the 1840s, also resorted to physical violence to induce proper behavior in their children. When two-year-old Cyrus Walker was told by his father to say please in asking for milk, the child refused, even though denied the milk. "He has gone to sleep with a smile of exultation depicted on his countenance," his mother recorded in her diary. "I hope if he is ever called to suffer at the stake he will be as unrelenting." The parents' reaction to a stubborn child, however, took a different turn with another son in 1846. Again the child was only two years of age; he requested some sugar. The mother told him to say please, but the child would only repeat, "I want some sugar." At that juncture the mother decided "to try the rod which I continued to do with increasing severity till his father came when I delivered him to him, and he followed the same course till noon when the child became so much exhausted that we concluded to let him sleep, but he did not seem to yield at all." After he had awakened, apparently refreshed, they resolved not to give him any food or drink until he said "please." The response was "I don't want to say please." He was then put to bed without food. The next morning he was beaten again until "we feared to longer." No temptations of food or drink moved the child, even though he had been without either for more than twenty-four hours. And apparently he never did yield, though that is not clear since the diary is damaged. But once food and drink had been given him he did say "please" many times. The experience shook the mother's confidence in the use of physical punishment. "I regret the course we pursued," she conceded once he began freely to say "please," even though she did "not perceive that he is much injured by it except for the time but less severity would I think have been just as well." Her reasoning was revealing since it seemed to stem from her equating the child's personality with her own. "I often fear being guilty of the very thing for which I punish my child." [9]

Other more sophisticated 19th-century parents found it necessary to use physical coercion when less violent means failed. But there, too, the use was reluctant. Mary Waterman Rice, who had predicted trouble in governing her newborn child, reported to her father ten years later in 1885 that she had broken his favorite hairbrush while giving her son a spanking. She wrote that since the boy had disobeyed her on two recent occasions, "I saw that a spanking was an immediate and positive necessity, and I do not generally do things by halves, therefore the spanking was a good and complete one, but I did make *halves* out of your brush." [10]

Although physical punishment continued to be used, less violent means were usually relied upon for the control and discipline of children. The internalizing of proper standards of behavior, which John Locke had advocated at the end of the 17th century, had become the practice as well as the ideal by the early 19th century. Rather than continual correction of the child, the Victorian aim was to develop in the child early in its life a proper sense of self that made further correction unnecessary. To achieve this Lockean ideal, 19th-century parents resorted to a variety of devices, not all of them novel, among which physical punishment was the last to be taken up. (Locke himself advised against any physical chastisement.) Much more common were shaming, playing upon the child's guilt, and depriving the child of company, food, or self-respect. Again, the cause for the change probably should be sought in the new prominence of women within the family. It is not surprising that 19th-century women would resort to verbal means of control like shaming, arousing guilt, or denying love.

In Catharine Sedgwick's widely read novel *Home* (1835), the method whereby the rod is spared and the child is saved was graphically depicted. When young Wallace Barclay impetuously threw his sister's kitten into a pot of boiling water because the animal had torn his kite, he was neither whipped nor even deprived of food. Instead he was removed from the company of the family by being sent to his room for all the hours he was not at school. The intention was to cause him to think about the enormity of his deed. After considerably rumination Wallace told his father that he believed he could now resist temptation and control his temper. Twice, he reported to his father, he had been provoked by comrades at school, but in both instances he had successfully resisted. The father gave his blessing to the boy, convinced that the lesson had been well learned.

Real parents used remarkably similar methods to the same end. Harriet Beecher Stowe wrote her husband that one of their daughters, Eliza, had failed to learn her lessons, a deficiency that caused her mother to take away "her dinner privileges and to have only bread and water in her own apartment." Francis Wayland, prominent minister and later president of Brown University, anonymously reported in 1831 on his disciplining of his fifteen-month-old son.[11] Because Wayland was particularly concerned about the growing tendency of fathers to be absent from home and from the upbringing of their own children, Wayland published the incident in a religious journal. The substance of the story, which Wayland told in great detail, concerned the refusal of the child to stop crying when commanded to do so by his father, who was holding him on his lap. To encourage the child to stop crying, Wayland took from him a piece of bread he was holding. At that point the child stopped crying, but when Wayland offered the bread to him, he angrily threw it on the floor. At this show of passion Wayland resolved to "subdue his temper" and so change "his disposition . . . that he would receive the bread *from* me, also be so reconciled to me that he would *voluntarily* come to me." The task he had set himself, Wayland confessed, turned out to be "more difficult than I had expected." In delineating his lesson, Wayland provides us with a concrete example of the intention and method by which a child in the 19th century was made to internalize the standards of his parents.

Although the forms of discipline that Wayland employed were several, at no time did he use physical violence on the child. First he put the fifteen-month-old child in a room by himself and told the remainder of the household that no one was to speak to him or to give him any food or drink. The isolation was begun at eight o'clock in the morning, with Wayland visiting the child once every hour or so, offering the bread and his own open arms. Although Wayland on these occasions spoke to his son "in the kindest tones," the child adamantly refused to do as he was bidden. The increasingly thirsty child would "greedily" drink from a cup held against his mouth, Wayland reported, but he would not touch it. Similarly, he ate crumbs of bread that fell on the floor, but he would not take any food offered by his father. That night he went to bed without having had any food for the preceding twenty-four hours. The next day, by Wayland's own description, the boy was in a pitiable state; hungry, wan, "his breath hot and feverish, and his voice feeble and wailing." Yet he would not accede to his father's importunings. Then at ten o'clock in the morning he finally took a piece of bread, to which his father added a cup of milk.

Wayland, who was apparently in deep anxiety during the ordeal though he says little about his own reactions, "hoped that the labor was at last accomplished." But the job was not yet quite done. The child still refused to come to his father's arms though he took food from him eagerly, even greedily. At this juncture Wayland stopped offering food and put the child back alone in his crib. The hourly visits were resumed until at around one o'clock in the afternoon that same day the child's tone of voice began to change, his crying became less passionate. "You could clearly see in him," Wayland concluded, "the abortive efforts of the will," which it had been Wayland's aim to break. The boy raised his hands, then let them fall; he looked at his father, and then hid his face in the bedclothes, weeping "most sorrowfully" while Wayland addressed him "with invariable kindness." But the child did not respond to these overtures in kind. By now, as Wayland analyzed the sequence of events, the child was beginning to recognize the seriousness of the matter. Consequently, "his distress increased. He would not submit and he found that there was no help without it. It was truly surprising," Wayland confessed, "to behold how much agony so young a being could inflict upon himself."

The child's and Wayland's agony came to an end some two hours later when, after one of his hourly visits, Wayland, as he was about to leave the room, thought he detected a softening in the boy's recalcitrance. Returning, the father put out his hand and asked the child to come to him. "To my joy, and I hope gratitude, he rose up and put forth his hands immediately. The agony was over. He was completely subdued."

Carefully, Wayland spelled out for his readers what the signs and results of submission were. "He repeatedly kissed me, and would do so whenever I commanded." In fact, the child now kissed anyone the father directed him to, "so full of love was he to all the family." The boy's feelings were now so greatly altered, Wayland contended, that the father was preferred to any other person in the family—a situation apparently different from before. Thereafter the child even moaned when his father went away, again a reaction unknown before. Up to the time Wayland wrote about the experience there had been no serious relapses in behavior; the few flare-ups of temper that had occurred had been "easily subdued." The boy was now, contrary to his previous disposition, Wayland reported, "mild and obedient. He is kind and affectionate, and evidently much happier than he was, when he was determined to have his own way."

To put this rather dramatic episode into its proper perspective several comments are in order. First, it would be a mistake to conclude that such protracted disciplining was commonplace. Few parents, as will be shown a little later, could be or were as adamant as Wayland, who admitted that his son was "of unusually unyielding temper." The second is that Wayland fully recognized that the disciplining of the boy was a "trial." His justification, of course, was that the episode was essential to the proper upbringing of a child who could not control himself. "There can be no greater cruelty than to suffer a child to grow up with an unsubdued temper," he informed his readers. The third is that Wayland was relating the incident in a religious periodical in order to demonstrate the joy and value of submission to Christ. It is true that in the metaphor Wayland himself was in the role of Christ, yet as a metaphor of authority even that tendency toward self-righteousness was not without justification. For as Wayland wrote somewhat self-servingly, if the child had been allowed to resist him, as head of the family, "I must have obliged my whole family to have conformed in all their arrangements to his wishes. He must have been made the centre of the whole system. A whole family under the control of a child 15 months old!" This would have been not only unjust to the rest of the family, but it would have also entitled each member to the same authority as the child, thus creating "as many supreme authorities as there were individuals, and contention to the uttermost must have ensued." In Wayland's mind, for all of his excessive logic, more was illustrated by the story than the necessity of maintaining order in the family. Total submission was the only way a sinner could be regenerated, and total submission in the child was the way for him to become a good character. Once that submission took place, Wayland argued, there was "an instantaneous change in his whole character." It was akin to religious conversion, he insisted, for the Christian finds "that happiness can never be obtained by obeying your own will, but that it is obtained only by relinquishing it." And so, by analogy, in Wayland's mind, did the child.

Finally, perhaps the most significant aspect of the episode is the self-consciousness displayed about how one rears a child. Wayland and the editors of the journal thought the episode worth printing because they knew how interested parents were in the matter. And obviously Wayland himself, as his carefully thought-out plan of attack upon his son's intransigence and his later analysis made clear, had been thinking long and hard about the proper way to bring up a child.

Wayland, it is true, was a minister, but men of the cloth were by no means alone in self-consciously thinking about child-rearing in these early decades of the century of the child. Certainly that was true of the Oregon missionaries, the Walkers, who spent so many hours on one lesson. And it is implied in the report of Juliet Janin to her husband about their school-boy son, Edward, in 1844. "He is by no means as passionate as he was and is quiet and gentle in his manners. I fear he has a delicate constitution. He is easily fatigued, complaining of frequent headaches brought on by study—and is actually made sick by noise and disagreeable sights and smells." She then went on to tell of her visit with her three sons to a Chinese junk on exhibition in New York harbor. Two of the boys enjoyed the visit immensely; Edward got a headache. "He is a most interesting child," she continued, "and I regret more than I can express that I can not have him at home with me—his feelings are tender and his tastes refined. He would appreciate and be made happy by a mothers [sic] love and care." [12]

The purpose behind Bronson Alcott's efforts at systematic child-rearing was no more religious than Juliet Janin's, yet Bronson's methods were even more self-conscious than Wayland's. Over a period of five years Alcott kept several journals in which he recorded his experiments in the raising of his own children. Significantly, in some ways Alcott's methods were as cruel—from a 20th-century point of view—as those employed by Wayland. Once, for example, Alcott tried to teach his daughter Anna, then about a year old, the conception of cause and effect. At a time he thought appropriate, he finally allowed her to put her hand into a flame, which for some time had aroused her attention. In his journal Alcott wrote that apparently his daughter felt the pain from the flame, but could not believe it, "for she put her hand again within the blaze in order to satisfy herself, but immediately withdrew it, her eyes suffused with tears and her whole countenance assuming the appearance of chagrin and disappointment." A similar method of instruction was used when she pulled his hair; he retaliated by pulling hers.[13]

The purpose of both Wayland and Alcott was the same: to internalize the standards of behavior. Wayland did it through psychological coercion, as he admitted. Alcott accomplished the same goal by letting his daughter learn that pain would result from certain acts. In neither case was overt whipping or spanking considered necessary or desirable.

Many advice books at the time urged that shame be employed as a way of controlling children and bringing them to what was thought to be the proper level of cultivation. Mary Gardiner Davis, although not a mother herself, often undertook the education of her nieces and nephews, who lived nearby. Quite consciously she recommended the use of shame in handling children. One of the problems she encountered with her nephew Howard was that he often cried when he competed unsuccessfully with others or when he was reprimanded. "He is a regular cry-baby," Davis wrote, "but I have talked so much of the shame of it, that he begins to control himself." The child's mother, though, Davis continued, did "not like to shame him" because she doted upon him as her eldest child and thus excused his crying.[14]

The methods of child-rearing employed by Mary Davis were similar to Wayland's, though hers did not always achieve the same success that Wayland reported, nor were Davis's as rigidly held to as Wayland's. Davis described one incident in such detail that it is worth close examination since it reveals so much about the methods and implications of child-rearing in mid-19th-century America.[15] Moreover, because Mary reported the incident to her mother, the conclusions one can draw from it extend beyond a single episode or example. So far as we can tell her mother approved of her actions, a fact suggesting that the principles and practices followed by Mary Davis were acceptable to, if not commonplace among, middle-class American families and were not simply idiosyncratic actions.

The incident began one morning in 1859 when Sophie, Mary's sister-in-law, sought to leave her son Howard, age eight, with his aunt for the day.

As Sophie prepared to return with the other children to her own house, "Howard screeched and screamed like a mad thing," Mary wrote her mother. But all that the child's mother did to calm him was to inquire of the aunt, in front of Howard, "if I ever saw such an affectionate, passionate nature, and if I thought she ought to go and leave him in this condition or if I thought it would kill him!" Trying to put a good face on what she thought was an error in judgment by Sophie, Mary assured her that Howard was "only a cry-baby" and began to put the other children into their mother's wagon. At this point "Howard really *tore up the earth* in his passion and screamed till I thought he would burst a blood-vessel," all the time struggling in the arms of Mary's husband, William. As soon as the wagon was gone, William hurried the boy upstairs to his room and told him he was to stay there alone until he stopped crying. "You never heard such shrieks in your life as he kept up for nearly ten minutes by the watch," Mary wrote her mother. Gradually he stopped, calling out; "Uncle William, I *feel good;* come and look at me." Mary then went up to him and "soon soothed him down by telling him he acted as if he were mad and I wanted to show him what they did at the Lunatic Asylum for like cases." She ordered him to undress and then "poured two buckets of water over his head." He then washed and dressed himself and she took him into her room to read and talk to him and teach him his Sunday School lesson. After that, she reported, "he was as happy as ever." Later he went down to his uncle, spending the rest of the morning learning about caterpillars. He explained to his uncle what he had learned during his punishment. "I was so excited . . . I did not know what I did," he told his uncle. "I thought when Mother drove off I should *never* see her again, but when you left me alone I remembered I could go tomorrow with Kays [a servant] and the milk [wagon] and see her and come back."

In this episode, although the reformation was quicker and the degree of coercion correspondingly less than in the one recounted by Wayland, the effects upon those meting out the discipline seem to have been more severe. "Such a tragedy," Mary wrote her mother, "upsets me for the day. I had a bad headache, and Howard's eyes were very red and inflamed" even the next morning, and her husband "looked as white as a sheet all the afternoon." The moral she drew was that the child's mother had failed to handle her part of the business properly by not preparing Howard for her departure. Nevertheless there was no doubt in Mary's mind that the remedy she had applied, however great its toll, had been worth it. Howard's temper had been broken, and he emerged from the episode "happy." For even when Sophie did write that it was now all right for Howard to come home, he chose voluntarily to stay at his aunt's in order to play with a neighbor. "I must say I took a great deal of quiet satisfaction in writing Sophie this little fact," Mary commented to her mother.

Mary Davis's moral instruction of her dead brother's children exacted a high toll from her, a measure, no doubt, of the general cost imposed on parents by the 19th-century standards of child care. Child-rearing was a serious business in the life of the family, as the large number of advice books clearly attest, and the close attention to its responsibilities in public print emphasized. It is not unlikely that the price exacted from Mary Davis differed only in degree, not in kind, from that which any parents paid for the new, intense relationship between parents and children. In 1860, for example, after caring for all three of Sophie's children while their mother was away, she confessed that she longed for Sophie's prompt return. "I feel quite exhausted with my school and nursing" (the children had been sick). "The truth is, I feel quite unequal to the reins of government," making that analogy with the general social order that so many rearers of children fell back upon. Apparently, in the minds of parents the very stability and order of the state, as Wayland said quite explicitly, rested upon their proper upbringing of their offspring. The family was but the state writ small. Mary Davis, despite her weariness, confessed that she dared not "let go, lest I should loose [*sic*] my power over them." If she did not keep school for them, she continued, "they get wild as horses," yet no one who has not tried to govern children knows "what tedious work it is. . . . I can't tell you," she told her mother, "how grateful I feel daily that I have no children of my own. It is such endless work, and such close restraint. The same things over and over again. It requires a load of patience and I am principled against showing any impatience to little folks lest it should lessen my influence." [16]

Unlike Wayland, however, Davis had no illusions that a child's adherence to proper behavior and belief could be secured in one mighty effort, however traumatic. Indeed, as she told her mother on this occasion, she fully expected that most of the gains she thought she had achieved in the education of Sophie's children would be lost once they were home again with their permissive mother.

Something of the rationale that lay behind the child-rearing practices in these examples was explicated by Catharine Sedgwick in her novel *Home*, after she had detailed the story of Wallace Barclay's punishment for killing his sister's kitten. When his old aunt suggested, somewhat sentimentally, that perhaps the punishment of isolation was too severe for the infraction, Sedgwick pointed out to the reader that it was not a single act that was being corrected, but a habit, which could be broken only by continuous efforts at control: "Mr. Barclay held whipping, and all such summary modes of punishment, on a par with such nostrums in medicine as peppermint and lavender, which suspend the manifestations of the diseases, without conducing to its cure. He believed the only effectual and lasting government—the only one that touches the springs of action, and in all circumstances controls them, is *self*-government." As the popular theologian Horace Bushnell pointed out at mid-century, the important consideration in child-rearing was to cause the child to want to obey the parents without force of fear. "Let the child be brought to do right because it is right, and not because it is unsafe, or appears badly, to do wrong," he urged.[17] In short, the object of instruction was the internalization of the standard, thus obviating continual correction or punishment. For though internalized standards were not always lived up to, they did help to develop a feeling of guilt if they were not met.

A further remark by Sedgwick offered an explanation for another aspect of American child-rearing in the first half of the 19th century. Again and again foreign visitors who went home to write books about their travels in the United States commented on the undisciplined behavior of American children and the permissiveness of their parents. What Tocqueville praised as independence at an early age, most other European travelers deplored as lack of discipline. A survey of some forty-two foreign travelers' accounts of the United States during the first half of the 19th century concluded that the permissiveness of parents attracted foreigners' attention more than any other aspect of child-rearing practices among Americans. One-fifth of the accounts said right out that children were undisciplined. Catharine Sedgwick explained why foreigners may have arrived at that conclusion. They did not understand what American parents were trying to do. The children under the regime she described in *Home,* Sedgwick pointed out, "might not appear so orderly as they whose parents are like drill sergeants, and who, while their eyes are on the fugelman, appear like little prodigies; but, deprived of external aid or restraint, the self-regulating machine shows its superiority."[18]

Although the behavior of individual parents sometimes fitted the foreigners' observations of permissiveness, the goal of training children in self-control without external constraints was quite consistent with what foreigners called "permissiveness." For it is true that in pursuit of their goals American parents were not rigid in their handling of children. Exceptions to the rules were permitted in the interest of growth in self-control and internalization of values. Harriet Beecher Stowe, for example, in 1844 sent one of her children to bed without her supper, but after dinner she noticed another child "gliding very quietly upstairs with her own saucer full of custard which she had saved up for Eliza." Stowe did not stop her daughter, but commented to her husband, with obvious approval, that "the child is always doing such things." Nor were children indulged only when they broke the rules for someone else. Sometimes even when the adults were put down, the permissiveness still was evident, if the put-down was clever. "Edward came to me the other day and asked me for a lump of sugar, which I refused him," Juliet Janin reported in 1845 to her husband. "Ah mama you promised me some. I promised you some, when pray? Why when I was a baby—so saying he helped himself to the sugar and ate it with great glee." Or take the case of Eva Jones reporting to her mother-in-law on her five-year-old step-daughter's behavior. When the child was blocking the light, Eva told her, "My dear, I *know* your head is empty, but it is not in the least transparent." The child moved slowly away, sat in a rocking chair and then "looking at me quite steadily: 'No, Mama, my head is *not* empty; it is *full* of *sense*—and of all that *poetry* you taught me, *too*!'" By her own admission, Eva was outdone.[19]

An even more striking case of indulgence and its import is evident in Elizabeth Dwight's relationship with her very young nephew. Despite her many tasks each morning, she wrote her sister, her nephew badgered her with: "Aunt Lizzie, I want a stick, Aunt Lizzie, who's that note for? Aunt Lizzie what is Express?" Yet throughout it all, her responses were as calm as she could manage. "I say, 'Don't tease darling, let alone, Wait! Be Quiet!' in a tone of suppressed rage and feel by eleven o'clock as if it would be quite a pleasure for me to wring his neck for him."[20] Throughout, as Mary Davis reported as well, she was displaying the self-control that parents tried to instill in the young in every way possible, including, in this case, by example. In the process, however, she exhibited an indulgence of an importuning child that would have appeared to a foreign visitor as an example of that permissiveness they found so reprehensible yet so common among American parents.

That the attitudes and practices of the early decades of the 19th century persisted into the 20th is suggested by an article by "An American Mother" in the *Ladies' Home Journal* for March 1900 entitled "The Modern Son and Daughter." The burden of the piece raised the same complaint about the permissiveness of American parents that foreigners had made fifty or sixty years before. Nowhere else, the anonymous writer contended, are children so indulged. In the exaggerated tones of the outraged critic, she described the American boy as knowing from his cradle "his importance. There is no rawhide for him, no side-table, no snubbing, no discipline, not even a hint that he has sins, nor any effort made to convert him." Given the looseness of their rearing, she asked, "is it their fault that they are vain, aggressive, and ill-mannered?"[21]

Permissive as American parents may have appeared to the eyes of observers, local or foreign, there was no doubt that they were most eager to start their children's education—moral and secular—early, and to obtain results quickly. One sign that this was a goal—and therefore a problem—was that the advice books in the first half of the century again and again warned parents against pushing their children, physically or mentally. Another sign was that individual parents frequently displayed this tendency. Mary Gardner Davis, for example, was particularly pleased with the determination of her six-year-old niece Eugenie to learn, and to teach her brother and sister as well. To encourage rapid learning Davis established prizes "for *attention* and *well-learned* lessons," and for sewing by the girls. She was distressed, she wrote her mother, that Howard was not making as much progress in school because insufficient demands were being made upon him. "He has never been taught to study," she complained to the child's grandfather, "and it is full time that he was." She therefore undertook to teach him to learn his lessons by himself until he knew all the words without spelling them, a practice, she proudly pointed out, that let him "learn everything of the lessons that nincomdoodle of a school marm teaches him, in . . . less than five minutes." At the beginning, she added, he had taken an hour to learn a lesson.[22]

Howard was eight years old, so that pushing him to learn to study, even if it did result in daily crying, as Davis conceded, was not imposing excessively heavy demands upon him. But Robert Mallard's efforts to impart to his two-year-old son the precepts of Christianity does seem to be starting rather early. As they walked about the grounds of their Georgia plantation, the father asked the child "who made and who died for him, which he answered. . . ." Then, after looking at the steel buckles on his shoes, the boy added, "Papa, God made steel buckles. God made star and sun and moon."[23]

Children were pressed in diverse ways. Grandfather Charles Jones wrote, for example, that a morning ritual was for the grandmother to put granddaughter Ruthie's hands together while she repeated an infant's prayer. "This morning," the child's father was told, "while your mother was repeating it, she held her hands together and looked seriously into her face." By the time the little girl was two years old the grandmother was writing that she "would like a primer or spelling book with pictures for her, as she seems to prefer them to the common picture books." In short, grandmother was ready to teach the child to read. Ruthie's new stepmother, Eva Jones, similarly strove for precocity in the child. Three years later, in 1865, when Ruthie was still only five, Eva was complaining that the little girl was not doing too well with spelling. "I teach her only orally, but she can count to fifty in French and to one hundred in English," Eva told her mother-in-law. "I intend to teach her some French verse soon, so as to accustom her to the pronunciation and accent." She also taught her historical and fictional stories to memorize and recite. "I want to make learning a pleasure and a pastime to Ruthie," she went on. "I never will allow her to repeat her verses if she shows the least want of interest in them."[24]

The elements of child-rearing that have been delineated in this chapter—the permissiveness, the absence or infrequency of physical coercion, the goal of internalization of rules, and the high level of parental affection for children—are quite familiar to Americans today. That familiarity, of course, is but another way of recognizing that the beginnings of the modern American family, at least among middle-class people, are to be found in the early decades of the 19th century. Indeed, recent students of the American family like Philip Greven and Robert Wells have emphasized the similarity in parental attitudes toward children in the 19th and 20th centuries. "The child-rearing literature of the early twentieth century," Wells has written, "was much like that found a hundred years before, with one exception. In addition to being taught that they could influence a child's success, parents were told they could shape his health as well, whereas in the nineteenth century there was little expectation that one could control disease," Wells contends. Actually, even the single exception that Wells mentions turns out not to be one. As early as 1859 Elizabeth Blackwell, contrary to Wells's argument, was urging parents, and mothers in particular, to concern themselves with their children's health simply because there was something they could do about it. After noting the increase in the diseases of women, and the rise in the rate of insanity and of degenerative diseases among women and their offspring, she stressed that these conditions did not have to be endured. "I assert emphatically, that the diseases of women, which have so rapidly increased and are still increasing, with such deplorable results, are directly within our own power radically to cure; for a very large majority of these cases are produced either by an irrational education, which sets at defiance all the natural laws of our being" or by acts of imprudence that could have been avoided if people had been properly informed about their bodies. She was quite specific in the book in recommending better food, proper sleeping rooms, regulated hours, and proper dress as ways parents could use to improve the health of their children.[25]

Blackwell was among those many advisers who thought American parents were pushing their children too hard and fast, calling it "the fatal error of our age—forcing the intellect, and neglecting the development of the body." Children in America, she insisted, were being pushed too fast into adulthood. "The child commences study too soon, and the youth leaves it off too soon; and the young lady enters society at too early an age, marries prematurely, and becomes a mother when she should be preparing for the duties of wedded life." [26]

The modernity of the 19th century's approach to children extended beyond an interest in health. Some of the writers on children, even then, evidenced a more than casual interest in what is often thought of as a solely 20th-century concern: the sexual education of the young. The 19th century, to be sure, was considerably less free in such discussions than the 20th. As we have seen already, sexuality was such a tabooed subject that even pregnancy rarely appeared in private letters or diaries, much less in books and magazines intended for the lay public. And certainly in the years before Sigmund Freud wrote about infantile sexuality it was not to be expected that sexual feelings could receive much attention in books on child-rearing. Yet, in the light of these general presumptions, it is striking to find pointed and even rather well-informed references to the sexuality of children.

The remarks appear in books early and late in the century. "There is not a mother or a nurse who must not have observed the virile member of male infants in the cot or cradle, capable of erection, from the presence of urine in the bladder, or by the slightest physical irritation of that organ," wrote the author of *Philosophy of Marriage* in 1839. At puberty, the book went on, there are some children who "instinctively manipulate certain organs, and some who even make attempts at sexual approach." The remedy, the author calmly suggested, was not to permit children to sleep together. John Kellogg's *Plain Facts for Old and Young* (1881) was certainly not permissive on the subject of sexuality. Yet he recognized the early onset of sexual feelings in children. He warned his readers not to let children of different sexes sleep in the same bed, though he cited cases of that happening in the best-regulated households, even after the children had reached puberty. He recommended that boy and girl children not sleep in the same beds after eight or ten years of age. He spelled out his fears specifically, as when he told of a boy of eight occupying the same bed with three older girls, the eldest of whom used the boy, Kellogg said, to instruct the others in the mechanics of reproduction. Simply because children did such things, Kellogg urged parents to provide some instruction for them on sexual matters. Knowledge in this area, he insisted, was better than ignorance. After all, he wrote, the sexual organs are as natural "as the lungs or the stomach."[27]

Kellogg confronted head-on the common argument that children should be kept in ignorance of such matters as long as possible. "It is doubtless true," he conceded, "that children reared in a perfectly natural way would have no sexual thoughts until puberty at least," revealing in the process his pre-Freudian assumptions. "And it would be better if it might be so, but . . . it is certain that at the present time children nearly always do have some vague ideas of sexual relations long before puberty, and often at a very early age." If sexuality were discussed with them, he concluded, they would obtain proper ideas on the subject, rather than learn about it from "evil sources." At another place he said again that prior to puberty the naturally raised child would "have no sexual notion or feelings," but that was not the way children were in fact raised. In the American homes of the time, he repeated, signs of "sexual passion are manifested before the child has hardly learned to walk."[28]

Elizabeth Blackwell, at once a more careful scientist and more respected adviser of parents than Kellogg, also alerted parents to the presence of sexual feelings in young children. Although she attributed the evidence of sexual feelings in children below the age of 12 to bad example, she clearly recognized it. Masturbation, she warned, occurred before puberty, even among children in well-brought-up, middle-class families. "The very frequent practice of self-abuse occurring in little children from the age of two years old," she warned, "clearly illustrates the fallacy of endeavoring to separate mind and body in educational arrangements."[29]

The ways in which children were raised constituted yet another sign that the beginnings of the modern 20th-century American family are to be found in the 19th century. The emphasis upon children suggests an aspect of the present-day family that has its roots in that century. It is the closeness of the nuclear family, the deep involvement of mother, father, and children with one another, reflecting a closeness that is measured further by the increasing isolation of the nuclear family from the larger society and from kin. Certainly there is nothing more typical of 20th-century American family life than the emphasis upon privatism and separation from society. And in today's highly mobile America kinship ties are even more tenuous.

The true beginnings of the isolation of the nuclear family antedate the 19th century. Historians of the English family, for example, can chart the beginning of the decline in the importance of kinship ties from the 16th century. By the 17th and 18th centuries cousins were no longer of any serious significance for families. Even among the great noble families individual crimes did not taint the family. Henry VIII was the last English king to punish a whole family for the treason of one member. In France such tainting of an extended family because of the acts of individual members survived into the 17th century, though not much beyond that. Alan Macfarlane, in his study of the family life of Ralph Josselin, a 17th-century English clergyman, concluded that, though "there were frequent visits and occasional small loans between kin, economic and ritual activities were not carried by them. When help was needed either in sickness, in economic undertakings, or in the celebration of birth, marriage and death, relatives were only infrequently called upon." Friends and neighbors were the people depended upon.[30]

The weakening of kin connections in England in the course of the 17th century meant that even in the colonial period in America such ties outside the nuclear family were not very strong. John Demos, in his study of Plymouth colony in the early 17th century, reported that the closest ties were with the immediate family and grandparents. "First cousins may have been recognized as such," he concluded, "but the fact implied no special feelings or responsibilities." Sons tended to settle close to fathers in 17th-century Andover, too, another student of early New England communities has shown. But even so, the ties of kinship were not reaching beyond the immediate family. Moreover, since these findings of densely settled kinfolk are based upon records of location, rather than upon personal accounts, it is difficult to know what the actual affective relationship was between kinfolk located fairly close together. An analysis of 770 witnesses in divorce cases in 18th-century Massachusetts does provide some measure and it suggests that the significance was not great. At least half of the identifiable witnesses in the proceedings were neighbors or friends, not kin. Only 11 per cent of the witnesses were related to the principals, suggesting that even in such a time of personal trouble kin were relied upon much less than friends or neighbors.[31] (Since the suits were for divorce, immediate family members were not likely to be called upon.)

It is probable, though the evidence is skimpy, that in the southern English colonies and Southern states, kinship ties beyond the immediate family were more important than in the northern areas. Certainly that has been the traditional view, and Southern novels have frequently described and stressed the importance of kinship among Southern families. An example of it appears in the Charles Jones correspondence. "Do give much love to Aunt Susan, and Cousin Laura; also to Aunt Julia's family," wrote Mary Jones Mallard to her mother in Georgia in 1863. "Aunt Eliza and Aunt Lou send much love to you. Kiss dear little Sister for me, ["Sister" was actually her niece]."[32] And to this day Southerners acknowledge a much more far-flung and more active kin network beyond the family of origin than people in other regions of the United States. Southern blacks, too, even under slavery, exhibited a similar breadth of kinship. Unfortunately, though, the origins and development of this well-recognized propensity in the South for kin connections has been neither systematically delineated nor adequately explained.

The most obvious and important support supplied by kin beyond the immediate family among Americans in general in the 19th century was in the course of the westward movement. When Mollie Dorsey's family decided to leave Indiana for Nebraska, one of the reasons they went, she noted, was that "our two uncles . . . have urged us to come."[33] This practice of following brothers or cousins was especially evident among immigrants from Europe and Asia. Not only did those in America often supply the funds for the movement, but their location in the United States was usually the place of first settlement in the New World. In the immigrant districts and ghettoes of the great cities of 19th- and 20th-century America and in the rural settlements of Italians in California, Swedes and Norwegians in Minnesota, and Germans and Scandinavians in Wisconsin, the strength and significance of kinship ties are measured. Many of the boarders that American families took in during these same years often were relatives getting a start in a new country or a new city. Historian Tamara Hareven has shown in her study of Manchester, New Hampshire, textile mills in the early 20th century that French-Canadian families there often obtained jobs for kin who needed work. It was not unusual for kinfolk to work near one another in the same mill.[34]

In the end, though, perhaps the most significant point to make about kinship ties in the 19th century is that they were weak relative to the intensity of feeling and cohesion within the family of origin. Closeness of the nuclear family was particularly apparent in the strain produced when marriage broke a woman's connection with her family of origin. Some women found the shift hard to accept. Lydia Maria Child never had any children of her own, but in 1863 she gave voice to the difficulties she might have felt if she had a daughter who was about to marry. "My sympathetic thoughts have been with you," she wrote a friend whose daughter was marrying. "I know people are accustomed to congratulate mothers when their daughters are married, but to me it has always seemed the severest trial that a woman can meet, except the death of her loved ones." Certainly everyone expects a daughter to marry, she conceded, "but I can hardly imagine a human heart so unselfish, as not to have some deep pangs mingled with its sympathy for a daughter's bridal happiness." Rebecca Root Buell wrote a friend in 1822 that there was no doubt that she was most happy in her new marriage, but at the same time she testified to the closeness of her family of origin. "I cannot bear to live far from Sister," she confessed, "and by pleading [with husband?] have succeeded in getting Sister Ann with me and this adds very much to my happiness." Mary Mallard, after she had been married for years and had borne two children, still admitted to her mother that the distance between them was something "I do not like to think of. . . ." When Mollie Sanford and her husband first moved to Denver they discovered that Mollie's recently married sister was there, too. When Mollie's husband went away to find work Mollie took comfort from the fact that "I can be with my sweet sister." Moreover, she added, "we *need* each other, too." The sister did not remain long in Denver, however, and when she had gone, Mollie wrote in her journal that she became so homesick for her family that she was ashamed of herself. When she was with her husband she tried to be cheerful in order to spare his feelings, but "he hasn't the family ties that I have and cannot understand. He has no own brothers or sisters living, and that makes a difference," she pointed out.[35]

When Mary Waterman Rice was visiting her husband's relatives in the East in 1875 she became homesick for her family of origin, rather than for her husband. She told her father, in California, "I have cried myself sick, from home sickness again and again; just one week with my own dear Papa and Mama would be such a happiness to me." Although her husband in Illinois wrote her every day or two, she acknowledged that her parents' house was still "home." "I do not know why I should speak of California as 'home' but of course it is because *you* are there, all my dear, *dear* home friends." She closed her letter with a plea that they write her. "Oh, I do not believe my own darling Father and Mother my dear dear sisters and brothers you imagine how deep deep my love for you all is." Nor should it be supposed that the intensity of her feeling was simply a result of being at that time among relative strangers. Almost a year later, when she was once again home with her husband, she wrote her father that she had been reading some of his old letters "and they were such nice loving letters, so much more loving than those you write me now. Do you love me less now than you did then? O I hope not—for it seems to me that I love you all more and more." [36]

Mary Gardiner Davis of Massachusetts was also married, though without any children, yet it is clear from her correspondence with her parents that her relationship with them was still closer and more intimate than that with her husband. Her correspondence with her mother and father while they were traveling in Europe was almost incessant. She left no doubt that she was deeply dependent upon their letters, calling them once in 1859 "meat and drink to me." Frequently she gave no indication to which parent her letter was addressed, because, as she said, "I don't know exactly to whom I am writing—I thought first father because I owe him a letter but then I think the conversation flavors so much of *female* talk that I guess it is to you, I am writing mother. . . ." The inference, of course, is that her relationship with both parents had been so close and undifferentiated that she doubted that "it makes much difference which it is for, as the contents must necessarily be about the same." At another time she addressed them as "My dear People." The correspondence between Mary and her parents implied a common parental relationship to children that is certainly the opposite of patriarchal. A similar conclusion can be drawn from a letter of Charles Jones in 1855 to his son, who had taken his first job at 24 years of age. "We hope that you will ever consider us your best friends, and as such freely and fully communicate with us at all times and on all subjects as you may desire." [37]

The closeness among the members of the 19th-century family, even in the face of marriage outside it, showed itself in the relations between brothers and sisters. If it was only implied in Mary Waterman Rice's letter to her father and family, it came out clearly in the correspondence of Mary Gardiner Davis. When her brother died, she wrote to her father: "No one knows better than you the closeness of the connection between us two children. I never had for any human being anything *like* the tenderness I had for him. I am quite sure if I ever had a child of my own, I can never feel that feeling more strongly developed." A similarly intense relationship between siblings of opposite sexes prevailed between Sam and Minerva Leland, even after Sam was married and a father. Many warm letters passed between them in 1883–84, as he was setting up housekeeping with his new bride in Chicago. He addressed his sister as "My darling Sister Minnie" and often closed with "lovingly" and "immer dein." He kept her informed of new developments in his career and encouraged her in her own intellectual growth and exploration. When the baby arrived he wrote at length of its increase in weight, state of health, and general character.[38]

Traditionally, the network of kin served as psychological or financial support in times of crisis or need. The various members of the nuclear family did support and succor each other. When a mother died it was expected that any children would be reared by other members of the family of origin, even grandparents. Charles and Mary Jones of Georgia immediately took their son's infant daughter into their home upon the death of their daughter-in-law. They reared the child for years until the son married again. When a relative of Sarah Stearns died in 1813, leaving a motherless child, the father's sister took in the little girl. Fathers, apparently, were not expected to rear a small child if a woman could be found to do it. Even unmarried women would take on the nursing of ill relatives, as Mollie Dorsey did when a cousin fell fatally ill. She stayed with her until death came, though the dying woman's stepmother did not approve. Apparently, a sense of kin obligation overrode such objections. The dying girl's mother had been a sister of Mollie's mother.[39]

After Mollie married, her assistance to members of her family of origin, that is, the family into which she was born, continued. When her brother needed a job in the town in which she and her husband lived, her husband was expected to help him find one. Her husband owed a similar obligation to members of his family of origin. When his sister, who had been living with her parents until they died, needed a place to live, she came to By and Mollie's house, for—as Mollie wrote—"she had no home but with strangers." Three months later Mollie's brother came to live with them along with her husband's brother George. As Mollie rightly said, "We are quite a large family," but not out of any sense of being imposed upon.

That was the way one behaved toward members of one's family of origin, when, as she said, "times are hard. . . ." Sometimes this sense of supportiveness was made quite explicit, as when Mary Waterman Rice's father lost an important lawsuit in 1886. His daughter consoled him with the observation that "large and loving families can be a great help to each other in bearing trouble." She urged both of her parents to recognize "that your children all have their arms about you in loving comfort and help in bearing your burdens of all kinds." At that time Mary was herself a widow and thirty-six years of age.[40]

It is, of course, possible to exaggerate the cohesiveness of the 19th-century nuclear family when the documentation consists of letters among family members. Few expressions of lack of close family ties are likely to appear in such sources, since those family members who did not feel a sense of closeness probably did not write at all. Or if they did, they were not likely to give expression to the weakness of their sense of attachment. Fortunately, however, as we have seen, expressions of the closeness of the family of origin also appear in diaries, a source that does not suffer from the one-sidedness of correspondence. In fact, diaries or journals are precisely where one might expect to find expressions of alienation or separation from family. Moreover, beyond personal documents, patterns of migration also attest to the closeness of family ties. The great value of letters and diaries, of course, is that unlike more broadly based sources, such as census statistics, they provide us with concrete, affective expressions of familial attachment.

The internal cohesion of the family of origin, especially when that cohesion is tested against the counter pull of the family of marriage, as has been done here, presents a paradox. Since all families of origin began as families of marriage, how and when did a young woman (or man) make the transition from attachment to her family of origin to an attachment to the family of marriage in which she would become the centerpiece of a new family of origin? Did the transition take place after children were born to her? Apparently not in all cases, at least. For in several of the examples discussed here, the new family of marriage contained babies, yet the mother's ties to the family of origin remained strong and seemingly intact for some years thereafter. Most likely the transition occurred in the course of child-rearing, that is to say, over a period of a decade or more. For as we have seen, child-rearing was the central task of women and the family in both ideology and practice during the 19th century. If that was the period when the transition was accomplished, then the resulting strong internal ties of the new family of origin ought to be seen as a measure of the success as well as the intensity with which the task of child-rearing was carried out. That the process may well have taken some years was a further measure of the closeness of the family of origin as it developed during the 19th century.

Up until now virtually all of the families considered have been composed of native, white people, usually of the middle class. It is therefore time to look at those families in the American population which were less protected from adversity. In families under severe stress we learn not only of the resiliency of the family in 19th-century America but of its diversity as well. It is to families under stress that the next chapter is devoted.

VI

Under Stress:
Families of Afro-Americans
and Immigrants

In discussing families today, it is common for distinctions of class to be drawn. We speak of middle-class, upper-class, and working-class families almost as a matter of course. We refer, also, to differences among ethnic and racial families, talking about Jewish, Italian, and black families. We recognize, in short, that different economic, ethnic, and racial backgrounds foster different life styles and values. In looking at women and the family in the past, it is necessary to recognize such differences as well, insofar as the evidence permits. To treat the middle-class family as *the* American family may well distort the social reality of the past. Middle-class women and families, to be sure, were important numerically as well as socially in the 19th century, but a significant proportion of them in the United States just did not fall into that category. Unfortunately, however, the materials from which to write the history of Afro-American and immigrant women and families are considerably less plentiful than those available for the white, middle and upper classes. It is not yet clear from present research to what extent, if at all, the customs and values of middle-class women and families differed from those of black and immigrant families.

On the basis of what is known now, there certainly were differences between the families of different classes and races. Yet on balance the differences appear to have been less striking or obvious than the similarities. Or, put another way, those aspects of family character that have been studied, such as role of father, or family structure, reveal fewer differences than similarities. But it is conceivable that when more subtle—and perhaps more important aspects—of family life are studied more carefully and fully, the conclusion may be reversed or severely modified. For a variety of social and political reasons, more is known today about the 19th-century black family than the immigrant family, so our examination of families outside the middle class will begin there.

During the first two-thirds of the 19th century the great majority of black women and their families were not legally free. In 1860 almost four million black people were slaves in the fifteen southern states. The remaining half a million Afro-Americans in the United States were free Negroes, as they were then called, divided about equally in their places of residence between North and South. Let us look first at slave families.

Although one might think that enslavement would preclude our having much information about the Afro-American family before emancipation, the truth is that, because of the high scholarly interest in the obsolete institution of bondage, historians today know more about the slave family than they do about the free Negro family of the 19th century. A principal explanation for this is that ever since the days of the abolitionists one of the standard indictments of slavery has been that it disrupted when it did not prevent the coming into existence of families among slaves. Since slaves were legally chattels, subject to unrestricted sale by their owners, disruption of families was built into the institution. To people of the 19th century, who cherished the family as a permanent union and viewed with horror sexual relations outside of marriage, slavery seemed a quintessential enemy of marriage and the family among blacks. (Some white wives of southern slave-masters also recognized the threat that the subordination of black women under slavery posed to the chastity of their own marriage beds, as the divorce records in some southern states make evident.) Moreover, until very recently the standard explanation for the relatively high proportion of female-headed families among blacks in the middle of the 20th century was that slavery had weakened or inhibited the development of a complete family among blacks. In the last ten years, however, historians have begun to revise dramatically our conception of the slave family. The general thrust of that revision has been to affirm an unsuspected completeness and endurance of families among slaves.

Documents by slaves are rare, but, as we shall see a little later, some documentary evidence has survided. Most of our knowledge of slavery in general and of the slave family in particular comes from whites, notably slave-owners. Under the lash of abolitionist criticism, slave-masters often insisted that they were promoting families among slaves rather than destroying them, as the abolitionists charged. And it is true that some masters made it their business to oversee the moral lives of slaves, to supervise marriage arrangements, to prohibit divorces without good reason, and to try to encourage a stable—and, one should add, docile—slave family. A Louisiana slave-owner prohibited remarriage among his slaves unless the divorced person agreed to receive twenty-five lashes. And James A. Hammond of South Carolina in 1840 noted in his diary that on a certain day he had "a trial of Divorce and Adultery cases. Flogged Joe Goddwyn and ordered him to go back to his wife. Dito [*sic*] Gabriel and Molly and ordered them to come together again. Separated Moses and Anny finally." Certainly masters had a strong interest in the development of family among their slaves. It was a convenient way to increase an owner's assets, as the high birth rate among slaves must have reminded them. By giving plots of land, allotting time for the cleaning of family cabins, and by dealing with the slaves in family units, masters gave encouragement to the existence of families.[1] Such encouragement not only returned more slave babies, but most likely also reduced slave dissatisfaction, thereby cutting the likelihood of runaways and the consequent disruption of work schedules. Recent studies show, for instance, that among runaways unmarried males tended to predominate and that many fugitive slaves gave as the reason for their running away the disruption of their family by sale. Certainly not all masters cared about the marital or familial relations of their slaves any more than employers of free Irish workers worried about their workers' family lives. But because of the physical closeness and intimate association of slaves and masters on the plantation or farm a good number of masters and mistresses became heavily involved in the lives of their slaves. Wives of plantation owners often acted as nurses for slaves, many of the slaves were the personal servants of the masters, and the children of free whites and slave blacks literally grew up together on the plantations.

One sign of that involvement appears in the diary of a Mississippi planter, in which he described "for future use," as he put it, the ceremony employed for the marriage of seven slave couples. In the ceremony he asked each person the equivalent of: "Do you agree, before me and these witnesses to take [the woman's and man's name] and to solemnly pledge yourself to discharge toward her the duties of an affectionate husband?" After presenting this vow to each person he then announced that "we have now gone through with every form necessary to authorize me to pronounce each of these several couples as man and wife," which he then proceeded to do. "And in conclusion," he told them, "I enjoin, according to the good old custom of our fathers and mothers, that each bridegroom now salute the bride."[2]

Although the ceremony was obviously modeled on the standard Christian ceremony of whites, it pointedly lacked any promise on the part of the couples to remain faithful forever; nor did the planter call upon God to bless the union. A more cynical, but more honest slave preacher implied the reason for the omission when he pronounced a slave couple married "until death or *distance* do you part." Even more direct was the conclusion pronounced by a black preacher: "Till death or buckra [master] part you."[3]

Sometimes, if the master took an interest in the wedding, the ceremony was part of a larger celebration, as in the case of Tempie Herndon, a black woman who much later recalled her wedding while a slave. "We was married on de front porch of de Big House. Marse George killed a shoat and Mis' Betsy had Georgianna de cook, to bake a big wedding cake all iced up white as snow. . . . De table was set out in de yard under de trees, and you ain't never seed de like of eats." She was dressed in white, including white gloves and veil. She and her betrothed knelt on a white pillow before the altar on the porch. The ceremony itself was performed by the plantation's black preacher. The bride's ring was fashioned by her husband from a red button. "He done cut it so round and polished it so smooth," she recalled, "dat it looked like red satin ribbon tied round my finger." After having worn the ring for about fifty years, she admitted, "I lost it one day in de wash tub when I was washin' clothes."[4]

Most slaves, however, probably did not have either a large celebration or even a religious ceremony at their marriages. The commonest ceremony was "jumping over the broom," a custom that appears in all parts of the South but which has no convincing explanation as to its origins. Nonetheless this simple ritual clearly carried meaning for the slaves; it was their pledge to and the legitimization of the family.

Although whites often participated in or insisted upon marriage between slaves, that is not the same as saying slave marriage and therefore the slave family were merely the result of white influence or example. Some historians agree with John Blassingame that "many slaves adopted white mores regarding courtship, marriage, and weddings."[5] Others, however, are not so sure. The leading authority on the slave family, Herbert Gutman, denied that whites had any influence at all on the slaves in regard to marriage or family practices. This conclusion, however, seems unnecessarily absolute. Masters certainly influenced slaves' weddings, as the examples already quoted show, or as can be seen in this additional instance reported by a white mistress in regard to the forthcoming marriage of her slave. "I have been busy getting her dress ready," she wrote to her mother. "Her heart was set upon a swiss muslin, so I have given her one. She has been a good, faithful servant to me and always a kind nurse to my children, so I felt she was entitled to a nice dress."[6]

The most convincing evidence that masters were not the sole or most significant influence shaping the slaves' conception of marriage is the endurance of slave marriages. No matter how kind or paternalistic a master or mistress may have been, he or she could not promise a slave that the marriage would not be disrupted by sale. Yet most slaves seem to have considered marriage a relationship for a lifetime. Herbert Gutman, for example, found that, on a plantation in South Carolina where the master never sold any of his slaves, marriages of twenty years were not unusual and two lasted thirty-four years. A broader sample is provided by the registration of marriages among slaves undertaken by clergymen who accompanied the Union army into Mississippi and Louisiana during the last years of the Civil War. Over 4600 marriage ceremonies were conducted by these clergymen among the slaves who desired to solemnize their unions. Some 42 per cent of the registrants said that they had been married between five and fourteen years.[7]

Even more striking as evidence of the commitment of slaves to the conception of marriage as enduring was that immediately after emancipation large numbers legitimatized their marriages, even when that act cost them money. In an effort to ascertain just how common among the former slaves was this concern for legitimizing marriage, Gutman compared the number of registrations of marriages in Virginia in 1866 with the total number of possible marriages between black men and women. He did this by pairing off all adult blacks and then asking what proportion the number of registrations for marriage was of this larger figure. In one county the registration equaled only 30 per cent of possible pairings, but in another it was nearly half and in two others as high as 60 and 65 per cent. In seven North Carolina counties Gutman was able to carry out the comparison for a long span of time, from 1867 to 1890. During that period marriages between Negroes constituted 61.3 per cent of the marriages, precisely the percentage of blacks in the population of the seven counties. A marriage license cost one dollar, a not insignificant sum in those days for poor people. Yet apparently former slaves and their children thought enough of marriage to be willing to pay for its official recognition. In thirty-one counties in Mississippi in 1870 a larger proportion of blacks purchased marriage licenses than whites. In Hinds County, Mississippi, fifteen years after emancipation, blacks bought three-quarters of the marriage licenses issued, though they constituted less than three-quarters of the population between 15 and 44 years of age. These couples were primarily the children of slaves; yet the lack of legal marriage under slavery seems to have had little or no effect upon their conviction that marriage was a solemn institution, worthy of the cost of a license and the sanction of the state.[8]

The implication to be drawn from such figures, of course, is that, if marriage had not been an important part of the slaves' lives it would be difficult to account for this strong interest in legitimizing marriage immediately after emancipation. It suggests that it was the slaves' own desire, not something merely insisted upon by the master. By the same token, though, it suggests that they had indeed been influenced by the whites among whom they lived under slavery. For in registering their marriages blacks were doing what 19th-century middle-class society insisted upon: obtaining documentary legitimization of sexual relations as the foundation of a life-long relationship for the purpose of begetting and rearing children. In order to show that they thought their unions were valuable Afro-Americans did not need to register their marriages; paying a fee and obtaining an official piece of paper are not the only ways to demonstrate conviction, but that was certainly the way white society did it.

To sympathetic white observers of the time, however, the high registration rates among blacks was noteworthy and a sign that the former slaves were as moral, or more so, than whites. As Albion Tourgée, the North Carolina carpetbagger, wrote in 1890, "let the marriage bond be dissolved throughout the state of New York today and it may be doubted if as large a proportion of her intelligent white citizens would choose again their old partners."[9]

After emancipation, marriage licenses provided documentary evidence of how interested black people were in lasting connubial relationships. But what about under slavery itself? During those years there were no legal marriages for slaves; the only useful documentary evidence on the nature of the slave family is the plantation records of births. Herbert Gutman has located six sets of plantation records extending over a number of years in which the names of father as well as mother of slave children were specified. On the basis of such records Gutman was able to show that many slave women had their first child outside marriage and by a father different from that of the second and subsequent children, but that thereafter the typical union was long-lived and monogamous. On a plantation in Louisiana between 1807 and 1855, each of twenty-three women bore one child or more by a single father, but twenty other women each had a first child by an unnamed father. The subsequent children of these twenty women, however, had the same father. Thus, if these records are representative, many slave women customarily had intercourse with someone other than their later husbands before they "settled in" to a permanent relationship.[10] Contemporaries recognized this pattern, too. "The negroes had their own ideas of morality and they held to them very strictly," observed Frances Butler Leigh, a former slave mistress, shortly after 1865; "they did not consider it wrong for a girl to have a child before she married, but afterwards were extremely severe upon anything like infidelity on her part." The former slave and later South Carolina politician Robert Smalls confirmed the view when he was asked how many black women had intercourse before marriage. "The majority do, but they do not consider this intercourse an evil thing."[11] In this respect, blacks were *not* following white customs.

Although the great majority of slaves, at least after the marriage of their parents or the birth of the first sibling, lived in two-parent households, not all did. And once again, that deviation from the white ideal was not a serious source of distress for blacks. Thus at the registration of slaves at the end of the war by Union army clergymen, some slave women claimed to be single despite having children. On all of the plantations investigated by Gutman there were some single women who had children by unknown fathers or by different fathers. On one plantation in Louisiana, for example, a quarter of the families were female-headed, a proportion considerably larger than on any of the other plantations whose records Gutman examined, and undoubtedly greater than the proportion among white families of the rural South. A number of male slaves also had more than one wife, a discovery that caused the Union army clergymen to require them to relinquish all but one.[12] In short, not all slaves followed the practices of whites in regard to marriage and the family, but most did, a fact that explains the ease with which blacks after emancipation slipped into the patterns of marriage acceptable to free whites and Negroes alike.

As the attitudes among blacks toward first intercourse suggest, slave women usually had their first child much earlier than free white women, even of the poorer classes. The median age at which black women first gave birth on the plantations studied by Gutman was 18.8 years, which was considerably earlier than that for free white women or European women of pre-industrial times. Seventeenth-century English rural women had a median age of 24 at marriage, and 18th-century French women had a median age of marriage of 26.5; since the great preponderence of first births took place after marriage, the median age for births would be from six months to a year later. Since first menstruation in the 19th century was not until 15 or 16 years of age among white American and European women, it is reasonable to suppose that it was not any lower among slave women, though poor diet could delay the onset. If that assumption is correct, then most slave women were having their first children soon after they became fertile and several years earlier than white women. One contemporary observer opined that slave women became pregnant for the first time three years on the average before white women.[13]

The early pregnancies of slave women are largely explained by the nature of slavery. Slave-masters certainly had an interest in encouraging offspring, an interest that could easily be translated into "the earlier the better." It was well known that masters often rewarded women with a new dress or less work if they were notably fertile. Slave women themselves had an incentive to prove their fertility since it might not only bring rewards, but also would enhance their value and thus reduce the likelihood that they would be sold. Nor were early marriage and motherhood inhibited by any concern about livelihood or economics as they certainly were among free women and men who were personally responsible for the support of offspring. Slave women could count on their children being supported as masters' assets, at least.

Despite the incentives, however, slave families were not as large as might be imagined or expected. On the Stirling plantation in Louisiana, for example, the median number of children per woman between 1807 and 1853 was between four and five. Almost 90 per cent of the children on that plantation grew up in a household with three or more siblings and slightly more than half had six brothers and sisters. On the Good Hope plantation in South Carolina between 1800 and 1849 the numbers were higher, but not extraordinary for 19th-century fertility in general. More than half of the women had eight or more children. One demographer has noted that the ratio of children to women among slaves declined during the 19th century. As he points out, this decline occurred not only in the face of the masters' general interest in more slaves, but also in the face of the rising price of slaves during the 1850s. It suggests, in short, that slave parents were acting with some independence of masters' interest.[14]

Behind the interest of the master in the birth of slave children stood a stark threat to the slave family: the possibility of disruption because of sale. Most masters were reluctant to break up families and especially to separate a mother from a young child. But sometimes masters felt they had little choice because economic reverses made it seem imperative, or because the death of the owner caused the estate to be broken up for distribution among the heirs. Recently some historians have sought to measure quantitatively the extent to which slave families were disrupted by masters. Robert Fogel and Stanley Engerman examined records of slave sales at New Orleans and arrived at a figure of 9 per cent of slave marriages destroyed through sales. This figure, which has been sharply criticized for the methods by which it was arrived at, is probably the lowest any historian has advanced. Yet, even if accepted without murmur, that figure is high when it is recognized as saying that at least one slave marriage in eleven was broken up by sale. That constitutes a risk that could not help affecting the attitudes and the security of the relationships of the other ten. Moreover, it was a threat that no whites or free Negroes had to confront or even consider. Richard Sutch, a critic of the Fogel and Engerman analysis, has put even more pointedly the risk of sale to the slave family. On the average, he writes, a slave would witness in the course of his or her own lifetime the sale of some eleven persons, who were members of the family of origin, or of his or her own family.[15] Another study, based upon the registrations of marriage of some 2880 couples in 1864–65 by the Union army, provides a more specific breakdown of the causes for the disruption of slave marriages. Here the implications are even starker. Only 13.6 per cent of the couples said they had lived together without some sort of disruption. Of the great majority (over 86 per cent) of previous marriages disrupted, almost one-third had been broken by the master, presumably through sale. But the largest number of disruptions by a single cause had come from the death of one of the partners, something which was also true of white families of the time. Slightly over 10 per cent (10.6) of the slave couples said they had disrupted their previous unions by personal choice—that is, what in free society would have been a divorce or desertion.[16] In the middle of the 19th century, divorce among free people was much less common than that proportion suggests. (In 1867, for example, fewer than 10,000 divorces were granted in the whole country. How many deserted, though, is not known.)

A more recent study of some 450 slave marriage registrations in Louisiana reported proportions very similar to those for Mississippi: 35.7 per cent of marriages were broken by master, 51.5 per cent by death of a partner, and 12.8 per cent by choice.[17] Although more separations were caused by death than by the master, the breakup of a marriage by a master had a quite different personal impact than one imposed by death. And in any case, the ever present threat of possible separation was a fact of married life no one but a slave had to live with.

One old black women gave eloquent testimony to what separation had meant to her, though it had taken place more than seventy years earlier. At age 93 Anne Harris told an interviewer that no white person had ever set foot in her house. "Don't 'low it. Dey sole my sister Kate. I saw it wid dese here eyes. Sole her in 1860, and I ain't seed nor hear of her since. Folks say white folks is all right dese days. Maybe dey is, maybe dey isn't. But I can't stand to see 'em. Not on my place." [18]

Anne Harris's enduring animosity toward whites is one measure of the strong attachment that slaves had for kin in spite of the countervailing force exerted by slavery. Occasionally other, contemporary, evidence is also available. One example is a letter from slave Abream Scriven to his wife in 1858. "My dear wife I take the pleasure of writing you . . . with much regret to inform you I am Sold to man by the name of Peterson, a treader and Stays in New Orleans." Although Scriven had not yet been taken to New Orleans, he promised to write her when he arrived there. He wished to send her some things, though he was not sure how he would "get them to you and my children. Give my love to my father and mother and tell them good Bye for me. And if we shall not meet in this world I hope to meet in heaven." Despite the probably truncated ceremony at the time of his marriage, Scriven clearly had his own ideas about the meaning and endurance of marriage and family. "My dear wife for you and my Children my pen cannot Express the griffe I feel to be parted from you all." He closed the letter with words that no master would have been likely to permit in Scriven's marriage vows: "I remain your truly husband until Death." [19]

George Pleasant and his wife were both slaves, he in Tennessee and she in North Carolina; yet their marriage endured. "I hope with gods helpe," Pleasant wrote in 1833, "that I may be abble to rejoys with you on the earth and In heaven lets meet when [God] will[.] I am detemnid to nuver stope praying, not in this earth and I hope to praise god. In glory there weel meet to part no more forever. So my dear wife I hope to meet you In paradase to prase god forever." [20]

Even when one of the partners was free, the marriage was no easier to maintain. Harriet Newby was still a slave after her husband, Dangerfield, had become free. Not unlike other husbands, he did not visit or write her as frequently as she wanted and, like other wives with similar complaints, she urged him to write her. At the same time she expressed her deep affection for him. "I want to see you very much, but am looking forward to the promest time of your coming. Oh, Dear Dangerfield, com this fall without fail monny or no monney. I want to see you so much. . . . Your affectionate wife." Ten days later she repeated her desire to see him: "Com as soon as you can, for nothing would give more pleasure than to see you. It is the grates Comfort I have in thinking of the promist time when you will be here. Oh, that *bless* hour when I shall see you once more." Later that same year, in August, her letters took on a more urgent tone. "I want you to buy me as soon as possible, for if you do not get me somebody else will." Because the other servants were setting her mistress against her, she wrote, and the master was in need of money, she feared she would be sold. "I know not what time he may sell me, and then all my bright hopes of the futer are blasted, for there has ben one bright hope to cheer me in all my troubles, that is to be with you, for if I thought I shoul never see you this earth would have no charms for me." She closed her letter as any mother might write to the absent father of her children. "The children are all well. The baby can not walk yet [at] all. It can step around everything by holding on. It is much like Agnes." We do not know if Dangerfield Newby came to his wife's rescue, for he died helping John Brown at Harper's Ferry in October of that same year.[21]

Sarah Boon, a slave in North Carolina who also was married to a free Negro, found that the arrangement brought strains in their relationship, as it did for the Newbys. Hearing that her husband was sick, Sarah Boon wrote in 1850 that she could get permission from her master to visit him if he needed her. She also felt it necessary to apologize to him for doubting his word in a previous letter. She had been annoyed by his report of a conversation he had with another woman in which he had not defended Sarah to her satisfaction. "My dear Husband, I freely forgive," she wrote confidently. "I have no doubt that you will in the end see that I was rite. I wish it to be banished from our memoreys and it neve to be thought of again and let us take a new start and join on together as we have binn doing for many years." She asked him to "consider my feelings and give me the sentiments of your mind in ancer to this letter." Then she urged him to close his business in Raleigh and move closer to her, for that "would be a great prise to me than all the money you could make." She wanted him to write her when he was coming to visit because she did not think it was "rite" for him to be "sutch a long absence from me if I cant come to join you." After all, as a free Negro he was free to go to her. "I feel very lonesome. be sertin to answer letter as soon as you can get it," she admonished him.[22]

Slave letters and the comments of white masters indicate that the kinship concerns of blacks under slavery extended well beyond spouses and their immediate offspring. Lucy Smith wrote her sister Sarah Boon in 1842 expressing her sadness at the death of their mother, and in the process spelled out the ties they also maintained with other kin. "Your brother sens his love to you. he recieved your letter but has neglected to answer it. his son Garner is married to Jacob Harrises Daughter and has got a son. . . . give our love to Sister, Brother, your Mother's husband and all your family." When Charles Jones's parents' plantation was broken up in November 1865, he told his mother how the former slaves were responding to the change. In the process it is clear that Jones recognized the family ties among the blacks. Little Tom, Jones wrote, "is going with his father to Liberty [another Jones plantation], and his father expects to return to White Oak with Martha, and the rest of the children. William, Kate and family expect to go to Liberty, but not to Montevideo [a third Jones plantation]. . . . Robert and family, Niger and family, Pharaoh and family, and Hannah expect to do the same thing. Maria is going to hunt for Dick. Rose says she is going with Cato. Little Miley goes with her husband, Mary goes with her husband, Elsie and family go to Syphax, [a slave at another plantation]. Hannah goes with Pharaoh."[23]

This recognition by slave-owners of the importance of family and kin to the slaves was also reflected in the advertisements for runaways. One scholar has noted that a third of the almost six hundred advertisements for runaways in 18-century Virginia newspapers which he studied suggested that the runaway might be visiting relatives or family from whom he or she was separated. As already noted, the decision to run away was often precipitated by the selling away of a child or spouse. Although some runaways did try to take spouses with them, few actually did, if only because escape with others was so much more difficult than alone. But when the opportunities for escape improved during the war as the Union armies penetrated the plantation South, slaves came into the military camps mainly in family groups, not as individuals. Over 61 per cent of the first runaways to reach the military camps in northern Virginia in 1862–63 came in family groups. In Louisiana, in January 1863, some 73 per cent of the married males arrived with their wives.[24]

The close concern of slave parents for their children was also evident in the public letters and meetings immediately after emancipation in which parents sought to protect their children against mistreatment or indenture service. And as late as the 1880s, one student of blacks in New Orleans has reported, former slaves were still advertising in newspapers, seeking to locate relatives from whom they had been separated during slavery days or in the course of the war.

Slaves were able not only to maintain their kinship ties in the face of the disruptive forces of slavery, but also to create kinship networks afresh when slavery destroyed them. For in the rapidly expanding and developing cotton economy of the South it was not unusual for plantations to be set up from scratch, the master obtaining his slaves from a variety of sources, a practice that meant most, if not all, of the slaves would be strangers to one another. Herbert Gutman found the records of two plantations, one in Virginia and another in Alabama, in which this was the case. Yet after twenty or thirty years the slaves on these plantations had established the same kind of kinship concerns and patterns that Gutman found on much older plantations. Although the owners of the Virginia plantation, for example, never bought a completed slave family or a young married couple, by the 1850s almost two-thirds of the marriages had lasted at least 13 years; nearly 90 per cent of the children had grown up in two-parent households, and of 52 children born to these slaves nearly two-fifths had names which were the same as blood relatives, a pattern that certainly suggest a continuing sense of kinship.[25]

Perhaps the most imaginative aspect of Gutman's research concerns naming patterns and what they tell us about the internal relationships within the slave family. It was held until very recently that the slave family was virtually dominated by the woman. As Kenneth Stampp in his thorough study of slavery put it, "the typical slave family was matriarchal in form, for the mother's role was far more important than the father's."[26] And there is no question that the mother's relationship to her children was more obvious and significant on a day-to-day basis than that of the father, who, unlike the free white or free Negro father, was not the primary breadwinner. On the contrary, the family's housing, food, and clothing came from the master, not from the father, just as the final authority under which the family lived resided with him. The mother, on the other hand, reared the children, cooked the food, maintained the slave cabin, as well as worked in the fields. On the face of it, the slave father seemed to have no source of authority except perhaps his strength and his gender.

In practice, there may have been more to it than that. Fathers did have hunting or fishing or other skills that they could pass on to their sons and display to their daughters. And if they happened to be artisans, they could supply certain things for the household or earn some cash by selling their work. Even an ordinary field-hand father could raise vegetables on the family plot, hunt, and fish, and thus add something to the food ration supplied by the master. Yet, in the end, the father in the slave family had few of the obvious sources of authority and affection that accrued to the father in a free family where he was the primary breadwinner. Consequently, the mother was probably more important in the slave family than in the free household. But thanks to the research of Herbert Gutman in regard to naming practices, the relationship between mother and father in the slave family does not seem as one-sided as earlier historians had concluded.

Despite the apparent lack of objective bases of authority on the part of the father, on plantation after plantation, Gutman has shown, sons were named after their fathers. On one plantation in North Carolina, for example, almost half of the slave families in which the father had three or more children had a son who bore his father's name. Two-fifths of 103 slave children born between 1803 and 1830 on that plantation had the name of their father or a blood relative. Lest that pattern be seen simply as the result of a lack of originality on the part of those who named the children, it should be said that on that same plantation not a single girl bore the name of her mother, though some had the same name as a grand-mother or a mother's sister. On the Good Hope plantation in South Carolina, out of 29 children, 13 were male; six of the male children had the same names as their fathers. One of these names had been passed down in the family for three generations. Not a single one of the 16 girls was named after her mother, though eight of them were named after the mother's mother. Why this difference in naming traditions between boys and girls developed is not known, but its existence certainly testifies to the slaves' recognition of the father as a significant figure in the family. Apparently the pattern persisted beyond slavery, too, for in the 1880 census Gutman found that in a sample of Southern Afro-American families fewer than 4 per cent of girls carried the names of their mothers, while more than 25 per cent of the sons had the same name as their fathers.

The position of the male in the slave marriage was like that of the whites in other ways as well. It was the male who initiated courtship and pressed the master or mistress for permission to marry. Sometimes the pressure was more than an owner could resist even if he or she wanted to. When Charles Jones's slave Niger indicated his wish to marry a slave on the plantation of Jones's daughter, she complained. "Niger made his appearance this morning with your note," she wrote her mother in 1861. "I was quite suprised to find that matters were to be brought to a focus so soon. I told Niger I did not think the arrangement would suit me at all, for I did not want Tenah to marry. But he seemed to think there could be no valid objections."[27] (And they did marry.) Planters invariably recognized the male as the head of the slave family for the distribution of food and presents as well as for the assignment of work. And after slavery, when contracts for work had to be signed between former owners and former chattels, the signature or the mark of the father was accepted for the whole family. When slave couples lived on separate plantations—a not infrequent burden of slave life—it was the father's plantation that was called the "home house," even though the children were with the mother. Although the phrase "broad wives" was commonly employed to describe wives who lived on another plantation from the husband, a comparable term was never used for husbands, suggesting that only the men went to visit, never the other way around, a pattern that was quite in line with 19th-century white ideas of the proper roles of the sexes. The relation between male and female in the average slave family appears much like that in the free family: the woman was subordinate to the man. Or as Frances Butler Leigh drily commented on the slave family, "the good old law of female submission to the husband's will on all points held good."[28]

Like white folks, too, the slaves were deeply concerned with ties to kin outside the immediate family. Naming patterns reflect this also. About 40 per cent of the 232 children born on the Stirling plantation in Louisiana had the same name as a kinsman or kinswoman. And in the total were included the unnamed fathers whose names may have also been given to their offspring, though we cannot know. Almost all of the names, too, came from blood relations rather than from relatives by marriage. On the Good Hope plantation in South Carolina, where a similar high proportion of names from relatives was carried by children, all of the duplicate names came from blood relatives only.

Perhaps the most striking evidence of the slaves' careful attention to kin is Gutman's failure to find more than a single example of marriage between cousins in the several scores of marriages between slaves he examined. (Other researchers have found a few more, but the general pattern Gutman discerned has not been disputed.) In fact, as Gutman points out, the avoidance of marriage between cousins may have been one of the reasons slaves married off the plantation. This avoidance of marriage to cousins is particularly striking since marrying a cousin was a fairly common practice among upper-class Southerners. It is true that the slaves did not have the incentive of conserving family property holdings through marriage to a cousin, but, given the frequent opportunities for marriage between cousins in the small world of the plantation, the few cases of such marriages strongly suggest that the practice of avoiding marriage to a first cousin was deliberate and therefore reflective of a concern for a particular and significant kinship relationship.

If a good deal of this evidence seems to suggest that masters had little influence on, or were not imitated by the slaves, other evidence suggests a less one-sided conclusion. It has long been recognized that slaves often took their masters' names upon emancipation, if not before. Yet at the same time it has also been known that a large number of slaves did *not* bear the last names of their masters. That failure to accept the master's name has sometimes been explained as a conscious rejection by the slave of his master and may well be part of the reason. But Gutman, having the advantage of records of several generations of slaves, has offered an additional explanation. He contends that slaves with names other than those of their masters at the time of emancipation had actually taken the name of a previous owner, and that the retention of the name of the first master was intended to serve as a basis of identity through life. In that way, Gutman argues, slaves would be able to identify relatives and thus preserve the kin connections they cherished. It is clear, though, that in either case the slaves were taking their masters' names and, to that extent, at least, were adopting white ways. In fact, the adoption of a second name at all was itself a sign of imitation of whites, since surnames were not used in West African societies. The slaves also followed white ways in their choices of first names. Very few African names appear on the lists in the plantation registers unearthed by Gutman. And lists of some 3200 names in the records of the Freedman Bureau for 1866 show almost no African names, though one-quarter consisted of common Christian names like John, George, Elizabeth, Mary, and Sarah. The fifteen most commonly used names were all Anglo-American, suggesting a high degree of acculturation among the slaves.[29] The almost total absence of polygamy among the freed slaves, despite its widespread presence in West Africa, also suggests acceptance of white mores, especially since a few cases among the former slaves show that the practice did cross the Atlantic. And, of course, the overwhelming commitment of the slaves to Christianity further attested to emulation of their masters, though they often reinterpreted Christianity to suit their own needs and purposes.

The recognition of the existence and endurance of the slave family which the new research findings convincingly press upon us, also indicates that in several ways the slaves had some opportunities and ability to shape their own lives, despite the legal power of the master over every aspect of their existence. And the widespread existence of the two-parent houshold among slaves makes it plain that slavery was not the primary cause of the single-parent household among blacks in the 20th century.

From the standpoint of the history of the family in general, perhaps the most striking implication to be drawn from this new evidence is that, even under the extreme duress of slavery, the human urge to create a family endured. Even when families were totally disrupted and new plantations created through purchases of slaves, as we have seen, not only just families but kinship networks as well were constructed afresh. And when it is recognized how precious and important these kinship and family ties were to the slaves another enormity of the institution of slavery is exposed. Throughout the history of opposition to slavery, the threat that bondage inevitably posed to the family has been a frequently raised argument against it. But not even the abolitionists and other opponents of slavery recognized what Gutman's recent research has uncovered. By showing that the kinship ties among slaves spanned generations, Gutman has revealed another measure of deprivation under slavery. Even if a master sold a mother, father, and children together, and thus seemed not to be disrupting a family, painful disruption still occurred in regard to other kin, for those ties, we now have reason to believe, were also highly important in the slaves' lives.

Given the glacial slowness with which fundamental social institutions like the family change, patterns of familial life developed and established during slavery persisted among Afro-Americans after emancipation. Analyses of the censuses of 1880 and 1900 disclose that prenuptial intercourse and bridal pregnancy, and the birth of a child prior to marriage, were as frequent among blacks after slavery as before. Herbert Gutman has shown that in 1900 black women had a considerably higher rate of prenuptial pregnancy (defined as a child born less than eight months after marriage) than native- or foreign-born, urban or rural whites. As we have seen, this had been the pattern under slavery, too. In 1900 in Issaquena County, Mississippi, for example, 17.5 per cent of black mothers age 20–29 had at least one child who was older than the marriage, while only 2.8 per cent of whites in Jones County, Mississippi, did. In Jackson Ward, Richmond, Virginia, 14.5 per cent of black mothers had at least one child conceived before marriage.[30]

Another pattern of family relations which carried over from slavery, but which showed the similarity between black and white families, was the predominance of the two-parent household. Although at one time it had been assumed by sociologists and historians alike that slavery was the source of the female-headed household among blacks after emancipation, that belief has been laid to rest by Gutman's analysis of the plantation registers. The prevalence of the two-parent family among blacks after slavery has been most convincingly established by the work of many scholars, most of whom have based their findings upon the manuscript census records. Although there is a good deal of variation in the proportions of two-parent families among blacks from place to place and time to time, at no place or time before 1950, for which investigations have been made, does the proportion of two-parent households among blacks fall below 65 per cent. In fact, most of the studies show no more than 20–25 per cent of free black households being headed by a single parent. This is generally true whether the place is the rural or urban South or the urban North.

A near exception to this generalization reveals the impact of slavery upon blacks. One scholar examined the character of free black families in seven cities along the Ohio River, both before and after the abolition of slavery in 1865. For the seven cities he found that the average proportion of two-parent households between 1850 and 1880 was 79 per cent. But when he looked into the cities individually he found that in Louisville, Kentucky, the proportion of female-headed households was considerably higher in the two censuses before emancipation than in the two after. In 1870 the proportion was 21 per cent and in 1880 it was 22.9 per cent, but in 1860 it was 32.6 per cent and in 1850 it was 33.8 per cent. The striking difference is explained by the fact that Louisville was in a slave state, while the other Ohio river cities studied were not, and by 1870 and 1880 slavery had been abolished. Apparently under slavery many black women lived alone with their children because the fathers were slaves living on nearby farms or plantations. Once slavery was abolished, those families with absent fathers were reconstituted, as the abrupt rise in two-parent households shows. Significantly, there was no such shift in Cincinnati, for example, which was in a free state.[31]

There is no question that the two-parent household has been characteristic of the free black family, as it was of the slave family and as it still is today. Nonetheless, ever since slavery the proportion of female-headed households among blacks has usually been greater than among other Americans. In 1880, for example, in Atlanta, Georgia, 30 per cent of black families had only one parent present, while for white families the proportion was 21 per cent. (In over 90 per cent of the instances for both races women were at the head of the single-parent household.) In Paterson, New Jersey, in 1880, 6 per cent of native white households and 4 per cent of Irish-American households were headed by a single parent as compared with 9 per cent of black households in Richmond, Virginia, and 13 per cent in Mobile, Alabama. A study of Philadelphia in 1850 and 1880 reported an even more dramatic difference between black families and all other ethnic groups. In 1850, some 22.5 per cent of black households were headed by a woman, as contrasted with 13.4 per cent among Irish, 3.3 per cent among German, and 13.3 per cent among native white Americans. In 1880 the proportions were about the same except that the Germans now counted 8.3 per cent of their households as headed by a female. The difference in this regard between blacks and all other ethnic groups persisted into the 20th century. In 1920, for example, over 26 per cent of black working women in the United States were heads of families as compared with less than 17 per cent of foreign-born whites and 12 per cent of native-born white women with native parents. And almost forty years ago sociologist E. Franklin Frazier wrote, "The 1940 census showed a larger proportion of families with women heads among Negroes than among whites in both rural and urban areas of the South." For the nation as a whole the proportions of female-headed households in 1940 were 7.1 per cent for blacks and 3.0 per cent for whites. Since World War II the difference has widened. The proportion of female-headed households among blacks in 1970 was 20.2 per cent as against 6.2 per cent among whites.[32]

Several explanations of this difference have been advanced. One that cannot be discounted, though it has not been studied carefully or in sufficient detail, is the higher mortality of black males, especially if a comparison between the races is made for all ages. There is no doubt that black males have always died at an earlier age than white males. The study of seven cities along the Ohio River between 1850 and 1880 referred to earlier pointed out that mortality among black males probably accounted for the high proportion of black women over fifty years of age who listed themselves in the census as mothers and heads of households. The proportion was between 27 and 30 per cent of all black women of that age group. The census of 1920 revealed that only 15.4 per cent of white native women were widowed or divorced and 17.4 per cent of foreign-born as against 28.8 per cent of black women.

But, differential mortality among white and black males cannot account entirely for the difference in the proportion of female-headed households among blacks and whites. The basis for such a statement is provided by the comparison made by a group of scholars for Philadelphia in 1880 of ethnic groups for female-headed households but only for ages 30–39, which would thus reduce, if not eliminate, the effects of earlier mortality among black males. The study showed the proportion of households headed by a woman among blacks was still twice what it was for native whites; it was almost twice the proportion among Irish, and over 2.5 times the proportion for German households.

By carrying the analysis one step farther, however, the authors of that study came close to accounting for the difference between the proportions of female-headed households among blacks and other Americans. When they compared black households in which the declared wealth was $1000 or more with households of other Americans with similar amounts of wealth, the differences in proportions of female-headed households narrowed appreciably. For blacks the proportion was 6.3 per cent, which was lower than the 10.1 per cent for native whites. For the Irish the figure at that wealth level was 2.3 per cent and for Germans 3.5 per cent. In short, it would seem that a high proportion of single-parent households was a function of income or wealth, rather than race.[33]

The role of poverty as a primary cause for the disruption of the black family is also strongly suggested in a study of Atlanta households in 1880. There, as in Philadelphia, black families in general reported a much higher proportion of female-headed households than whites. But when the comparison is made between families of similar economic status the difference narrows sharply. When skilled workers' families were compared, the proportion of white households that were headed by a woman was 22.4 per cent as against 24.1 per cent for blacks. Similar results have emerged from a study of Boston families.[34]

All of the historical studies which have suggested that the differences between white and black families in regard to female-headed households were the consequence of income have drawn their data from cities: Philadelphia, Atlanta, and Boston. Yet it would be a mistake to assume that cities have been favorable to blacks. As many recent students of black families have made evident, the opposite is true. It seems that the migration of blacks into the hostile environment of the big city from the rural South has been highly deleterious to Negro family structure. Herbert Gutman studied over 14,000 Southern rural and urban Afro-American households from the census of 1880. He found that 82–85 per cent of the families in rural areas were headed by males, but only 69–74 per cent of those in cities were. It is also the conclusion of the team of students of 19th-century Philadelphia that the urban environment was at the root of the disruption of the relatively large minority of black households after emancipation.

One further consequence of poverty for family structure among blacks is suggested by a study of white and black farm families in Louisa County, Virginia, in 1880. The author of the study noted that the character of the family changed as the family passed through its life cycle. Thus, when white couples first married, 54 per cent of them lived alone, while among blacks only 10 per cent did, presumably because many could not afford to. When children arrived, over two-thirds of the black families lived without any relatives in the household as compared with 59 per cent of the white families. By the time the children were grown and the parents mature, about 65 per cent of the white families were living alone, but only 46 per cent of the black families were, most of them having brought in relatives or boarders. These different changes among black and white families suggest that blacks, because of their poverty, even in rural areas, were more likely to be dependent upon kin than white families. Presumably the kin either provided housing, or functioned as producing rather than consuming members of the black household. Whether this pattern among blacks occurred in other parts of the country is not yet known, but it is consistent with the general poverty of blacks, rural or urban, and therefore probably was a significant pattern among black families.[35]

In the history of the family in America, the black family has undoubtedly experienced greater stress than any other. First slavery and then the burdens of urban life within a climate of racial prejudice pressed hard upon those relations we call the family. Poverty and hostility from whites placed a strain upon many black families that was virtually unknown among the families of the great majority of white, native-born people. Despite these adversities, however, the majority of Afro-American children in the 19th and 20th centuries lived in a nuclear family with both parents present, in which the father was not only the recognized head of the household but the primary breadwinner as well. Many more Negro wives and mothers worked outside the home than white women, but the majority of black mothers did not work outside the home after slavery. In these respects, at least, the statistically average black family resembled the typical middle-class family.

A similar conclusion can be drawn about the families of the immigrant population during the 19th and early 20th centuries. Immigrants never experienced the wrenching effects of slavery, but, like blacks, they felt the stresses of poverty and urban life. Just as it had long been a part of the conventional wisdom among historians that slavery destroyed the black family, so it had long been assumed that the industrial revolution had disrupted the urban working-class family, which in the United States was largely composed of immigrants. Indeed, one of Marx and Engel's most famous indictments of modern capitalism had been that the rise of modern industry virtually destroyed the family among the working class. Recent research has overturned that assumption in regard to both European and American working-class families. Industrial capitalism, like slavery, undoubtedly placed an enormous strain upon the families of farmers and peasants who were compelled to adjust to the new and more rigorous rhythms of the machine, the factory whistle, and the congestion of urban life. But the working-class or immigrant family was able to make the necessary adjustments to survive, just as the Afro-American family endured under the impact of slavery and racial prejudice.

Working-class and immigrant families were not the same, but in this presentation they will be treated as if they were, unless otherwise noted. Sufficient historical research has not been carried out for clear distinctions to be drawn between them. The question of the nature of the family below the middle class is further complicated by the diversity of immigrant families. These distinctions have to be recognized among ethnic groups even if we have been referring, rather cavalierly, to something as general as the Afro-American family. It is a form of historical or sociological license to refer to the black family as if the Afro-American families were all of one kind. But to speak of *the* immigrant family is not only to lose sight of diversity but also to miss the important point that ethnic groups sometimes differed as dramatically in family patterns from one another as they did from families of the native white middle class. Unfortunately, however, no more than three or four, out of the dozen or so, significant immigrant groups can be examined here, for once again the basic historical research has not been done for more than that small number. And even then the information is uneven and limited. With those caveats let us look at the families of immigrants.

Like the Afro-American family, the families of immigrants were at once both similar and dissimilar to families of native white Americans. There were several ways in which the families of all immigrant groups differed from those of native families. For example, natives tended to marry outside their group more than the immigrants. A study of Warren, Rhode Island, for the 1880s found that 86 per cent of Irish men and 85 per cent of French-Canadian men married women of their ethnic group as compared with 79 per cent of native men. Not unexpectedly, English and Scottish men married with other groups even to a greater extent than natives. For them language and religion were not barriers to intermarriage—or, alternatively, bases for ethnic cohesion—as religion was for the Irish and language and religion for the French Canadians. The role of ethnicity was clearer in Cohoes, New York, where in 1880 almost 40 per cent of English-born and native working men married outside their ethnic group, while only 2 per cent of the French Canadians and 7 per cent of the Irish of that same working class did.[36]

Age of marriage varied by ethnic group, but the natives' was generally lower than that of any immigrant group. In part this was a function of class or income. Workers in high-paying jobs tended to marry earlier and to a greater extent than others. In 1860 at the iron works in Troy, New York, 67 per cent of the nailers and spikers, who were among the more highly paid workers, were married as against only 47 per cent of the unskilled laborers. By and large, then as today, wealth or income has generally been an inducement to early marriage, just as poverty has usually been a deterrent. Yet when class was held constant, differences in age of marriage between ethnic groups and natives still showed up, suggesting that cultural traditions were operating. For example, in Troy in 1860, some 51 per cent of American-born unskilled workers were married as against 45 per cent of Irish workers of the same class. Among cotton factory workers in Cohoes, New York, the variation is noticeable among various ethnic groups as well as between natives and immigrants. Only 8 per cent of Irish women between 20 and 29 were married as against 11.5 per cent of French Canadian, 13 per cent of English, and 25 per cent of American-born women. There was a difference by ethnicity in marriage ages among working-class men in Newark, New Jersey as well. In 1860, for example, only 82 per cent of Irish-born craftsmen over 35 were married, while 90 per cent of German workers were. A difference in age of marriage between ethnic groups was evident among Polish and Italian women in Buffalo according to the 1905 state census. At age 30 some 59 per cent of Polish women were still single while only 35 per cent of Italian women were. On the whole, then, immigrant women (and men) tended to marry at a later age than native Americans. Since Americans had always had an earlier age of marriage and a higher proportion of married persons than Europeans, this pattern would seem to be a continuation of practices among groups recently arrived in a new culture.[37]

At the end of the 19th and the beginning of the 20th century, fertility rates also differed between native and immigrant families. The documentation on this is sparse, but it is consistent. An examination of the number of children per 1000 married women in 1880 in two wards of Boston reported that the ratio among native white women was not only lower than among Irish-born women at all age levels but that the drop in the rate occurred at a much younger age among the native women. Native white women between 25 and 29 years of age had 1063 children under five years old per 1000 married women as against 1236 children for Irish women of the same age group. The ratio fell to 627 for the native women at ages 30–34, but actually rose to 1420 for the Irish women of those ages. In Buffalo in 1855 the fertility ratio of Irish women at ages 30–34 was also over twice that of native white women. German women in Buffalo at that time recorded almost as high an overall fertility ratio as the Irish.[38]

Although there were these and probably other differences between the families of native Americans and immigrants, on balance it would seem that, at least in regard to certain gross measures of family life that we can make from this distance in time, immigrant families were more like than unlike native families. The great majority of working-class and immigrant families, for instance, were nuclear in structure—that is, they consisted of two parents and their offspring. Very few of them contained the grandparents or the aunts that the old sociology of the family referred to as the extended family. A near exception seems to have occurred in the early decades of industrialization in Newark, New Jersey, according to the only large study of family structure among the early 19th-century working class. Susan Hirsch, the author of the study, has found that 45 per cent of the families of the craftsmen she studied in Newark in 1850 had people other than husband, wife, and children living in the household. (Most were probably boarders.) Significantly, however, by 1860 slightly over 70 per cent of the working-class families in Newark were nuclear in structure. It is Hirsch's conclusion that the urban working class in antebellum Newark "generally followed the same fashions as other Newarkers. While the Victorian family ideal found its most perfect embodiments in bourgeois homes," she continues, "craftsmen patterned their households on the same lines as their employers." One sign of this, she points out, was that wives stayed at home, for unlike the situation in Britain, the urban household in America may have "lost its centrality in production, but most craftsmen retained the ability to support their families."

A study of working-class families in the cotton textile town of Cohoes, New York, in 1880 reported that extended families comprised no more than 11 per cent of the families among any of the ethnic groups present— that is, native Americans, Irish, French-Canadians, and English. And when nuclear families were counted, immigrant groups showed a higher proportion than native working-class families. Only 60 per cent of the natives lived in such families (26 per cent of them had boarders living with them) as compared with 73 per cent of the Irish, 68 per cent of the French-Canadians, and 78 per cent of the English. An examination of the 1905 census returns on some 2000 Italian families in Buffalo found that 88 per cent were nuclear in structure; the rest included relatives or boarders. A similarly high proportion of nuclear families was reported for Jewish families.[39]

At this point one of the distinctions that needs to be made in discussing immigrant families should be emphasized. Often there was a difference in family patterns between immigrant groups, a fact that suggests that family patterns and structures have to be explained in part, at least, by ethnic traditions. One of these distinctions was that Italian and Jewish families tended to have a higher proportion of families in which both parents were present than black, Irish, or native-born families. And this was true even though the Italian and Jewish heads of household were overwhelmingly unskilled or semi-skilled workers. In short, it was not high economic status that could account for the higher proportion of two-parent households among Italians and Jews. In Troy in 1880, too, Irish iron workers' families showed a lower proportion of two-parent households than English-born or American-born workers, whether they were skilled or unskilled. This tendency of the Irish to have a higher proportion of female-headed households than other ethnic groups has been documented for other cities as well. The reason for the difference is probably that the Irish, as Catholics, could not divorce and remarry. Hence they resorted to desertion to a greater extent than non-Catholics. As we shall see later, cultural values or traditions also differentiated Italian families in other ways from other ethnic groups.

An additional way in which immigrant families in general resembled native families was in the position of the woman. Among the immigrants, as among the black and native families, the wife and mother was the heart of the home; it was she who managed the home and reared the children. Upon her fell the responsibility for seeing that the home was a proper place for the children and an attractive place for the husband. Social worker Margaret Byington in her visits to steel-workers' homes at Homestead in the early 20th century was impressed by the wives' efforts. She noted that even in a five-room house they often kept a "dining room," with the appropriate furniture, though it was rarely used. The kitchen was the center of the home; there the mother was. It usually opened upon a yard or garden so that she could supervise her children's play while she worked. The work, however, was not easy, even though it was almost entirely confined to the house, for most immigrant women by that period were city dwellers, not farm wives. One Pittsburgh woman was quoted as defining a good husband as a man who was careful with his clothes, didn't drink, could read the Bible without spelling out the words, and would "eat a cold dinner on wash day without grumbling." Women's importance in the home was emphasized, too, simply by the absence of the father during a large part of the day. He did not play much of a part in the children's upbringing, and even the management of the family's finances was usually left in the hands of the woman. "His part of the problem is to earn and hers to spend," Byington remarked. When the social worker asked husbands to prepare accounts of their budgets, they usually referred her to their wives. At the time the payments on the house were to be made, it was the wife who "must see that the sum is ready." When Byington compared budgets for good times and bad she found thaat the women managed to cut costs without making comparable cuts in amount of food or nutritional level of meals. Meat and fruit were reduced and replaced by more milk, eggs, and flour.[40]

Jane Addams also reported from her experience with immigrant women at the Hull House settlement in Chicago that "thousands of women . . . make it a standard of domestic virtue that a man must not touch his pay envelope, but bring it home unopened to his wife. High praise is contained in the phrase," she wrote, " 'we have been married twenty years and he never once opened his own envelope' or covert blame in a wife's remark: 'Of course he got into gambling; what can you expect from a man who always opens his own pay?' "[41]

As these remarks suggest, working-class and immigrant women had ways of controlling their men, just as middle-class women did. Thomas and Znaniecki in their monumental study of the Polish peasant in Europe and America conducted just before World War I were not so sure that they liked some of the means Polish women used, but they recognized them, nonetheless. As they wrote, in the traditional family in Poland, a woman had much to say about the management of financial affairs, "almost equal to that of the man, yet in cases of explicit disagreement the man had the formal right of coercing her, whereas she could only work by suggestion and persuasion, or appeal to the large family." But in America a woman gained leverage. Now she could refuse to accept coercion, for neither the man's greater physical strength nor his ability to withhold subsistence could be legally used by him. And an immigrant woman, as Thomas and Znaniecki wrote, "can actually coerce the man into doing what she wants by using any act of violence, drunkenness, or economic negligence of his as a pretext for a warrant. No wonder that she is tempted to use her newly acquired power whenever she quarrels with her husband, and her women friends and acquaintances, moved by sex solidarity, frequently stimulate her to take legal action." And the documentation supplied by the authors of the study from the records of legal aid societies shows that the women did make use of the law in an effort to control husbands' behavior.[42]

Perhaps the most famous example of the way in which immigrant women controlled male behavior is Jane Addams's story of the Devil Baby. Peasant women, she said, would come to Hull House, often with husbands in tow, to see "the Devil Baby," which was supposed to be the monstrous offspring of a man who had announced he was an atheist, or had ripped off a saint's picture from the wall, or had said he would rather have a devil for a child than a seventh daughter. The men had been brought to be shown the results of bad behavior, Addams pointed out; the purpose was quite discernible in the men's relief when told there was no such baby. Sometimes the men came on their own, she continued. "Their talk confirmed my impression that such a story may still act as a restraining influence in the sphere of marital conduct."[43]

Even in the Italian immigrant family, which was known for the dominance of the father, the mother was recognized as the center of the home. As one Italian put it, "if the father should die, the family would suffer; if the mother should die, the family ceases to exist." The close and enduring ties between Italian mothers and their sons, even after the young men married, has been commonly referred to by some observers of the Italian family as "the madonna complex."[44]

Having that important place in the immigrant family exacted a high cost from the mother. Like the middle-class mother, the woman in the immigrant or working class family worked hard and long to make the home attractive to children and husband. Margaret Byington put it concretely in the description of a family she came to know well. "When the men began to come from the mill in the evening, the mother with a fresh apron on and the two children in clean dresses came out on the front porch." The children ran to the father as they recognized him at a distance. After supper the father "smoked contentedly with a child on each knee and talked with his wife of the day's doings. That hour of rest," Byington concluded, "was bought at the price of a busy day for her; she swept off porch and walk, she washed almost daily to keep the dresses clean, she had dinner cooked before he came. A woman must be a good manager and have the courage to appear cheerful when tired, if she is to make the evening at home happy," Byington decided. A further insight into a woman's life in that working-class community was provided by Byington when she noted the women's dependence upon the social insurance lodges, which were "almost their only chance to meet other people and get for a few minutes into a different atmosphere from that of household tasks."[45]

An even greater cost was exacted from the working-class wife when the pay envelopes were thin or did not come in at all. Then she must try to make up the deficiency. Taking in paying boarders was perhaps the quickest and easiest way for a wife to contribute financially to the family. And almost all immigrant nationalities fell back upon it to one degree or another. Polish women, for example, took in boarders to a greater degree than some ethnic groups. But as we will see in the chapter on women's work, all ethnic groups, including the native white families, at one time or another accepted boarders, and not always because of a need for income. Nevertheless, at no time and among no social classes did more than 25 per cent of families actually house boarders.

For some immigrant wives taking in boarders was either not possible or insufficient as a source of income. So they turned to some kind of paid work, either outside the home or done at home. Again the pattern varied by ethnic group, though it should be clear throughout that at no time did a large proportion of immigrant wives of any nationality work outside the home. In Philadelphia in the early 20th century, for example, one investigator has found that among native white women a higher proportion worked than among European immigrant women. In general, Italian and Jewish immigrant wives were less likely to be employed outside the home than Polish or Irish wives. Only about two per cent of Jewish wives in

New York in 1880 took jobs outside the home and by 1905 the proportion was down to one per cent. In 1905 less than six per cent of Italian families in New York reported wives at work. Italian married women would take on work that could be done at home, like sewing, but only rarely would they undertake the domestic work in other people's homes that blacks and Polish women performed. Among Buffalo, New York, Poles at the opening of the 20th century, about two wives worked for every eight men in the community; the comparable rate among Italians was one wife at work for twenty men. Italian women, of all immigrant women, came closest to the European pattern of being isolated in the family and having large numbers of children. One student of immigrant wives in three different cities at the turn of the 20th century found that, even if an Italian woman's husband was unemployed, she usually would not take up outside work as a Negro, Polish, or Irish woman would. A report on immigrant wives in Philadelphia around the time of World War I found that Irish women worked outside the home more frequently than any other nationality—though not more than black women.[46]

Since, in the main, all immigrant families, regardless of ethnicity, were at the bottom of the economic and occupational structure, these variations among ethnic groups in the propensity of wives to work outside the home is largely an ethnic, rather than a class phenomenon. It is undoubtedly related to practices and outlooks learned prior to emigration from the Old World. Irish wives, for instance, had a history of working outside the home in the old country, a tradition that probably influenced their willingness to take on such work in the United States. Moreover, compared with other immigrant groups, the Irish were recognized for their high rate of literacy, and of course, their familiarity with English. Italian wives, on the other hand, came out of a culture in which mothers worked only when they could do so in the company of their children. Agricultural work in Italy had usually been of this kind, with women and children tending vines and picking fruit together. In Buffalo, for instance, Italian wives did work in the canneries in the summer when it was possible for their children to accompany them. But since factory work or domestic service would sever them from their family obligations, few Italian wives took up such work. Italian wives were prevented from working outside the home also because Italian men did not like their wives to work in other men's homes. Put another way, the fact that Italian wives exhibited the lowest proportion of working mothers was probably a measure of the husband's dominance in the Italian-American family.

Despite the diversity in the extent to which immigrant wives worked outside the home, two uniformities are worth noting by way of conclusion. One is that at no time did more than 10 or 15 per cent of wives of any im- migrant nationality work outside the home and usually the proportion was even smaller than that. (Black wives, as we will see in Chapter XV, were always an exception in this respect.) The second conclusion, which spans all ethnic groups, is that, as income rose, the tendency was for even that small proportion of wives who worked to withdraw from the labor force. And in that way, too, immigrant families reflected a pattern that obtained among native families. Even Negro wives, it is worth adding, withdrew from the labor force in the 19th and early 20th centuries when it was financially feasible for them, though at no time to the extent that im- migrant and native married women did.

Finally, immigrant parents tended to relate to their children in some re- spects much as native parents did, or at least as far as we can tell. Unfortu- nately, immigrant children have not been studied as much as children in general have. Consequently, no full or even adequate comparison can yet be made. Nevertheless, the skimpy evidence we do have suggests that treat- ment of and attitudes toward children in immigrant and native families were quite similar. Education, for example, was important to both. Thomas and Znaniecki reported that the Polish families in America ex- pected their children to turn over to the family most of their earnings as at least part payment for the cost of their rearing. But this apparently was not at the expense of the children's education. Byington, for example, was pleased to observe that working-class families in Homestead, which was largely composed of immigrants, did not sacrifice their children's educa- tion to early work. And Michael Katz, writing about mid-19th-century Hamilton, Ontario, noted that the children of immigrants left home at about the same age as native children. But in his study of Newburyport, Massachusetts, Stephan Thernstrom concluded that Irish fathers tended to sacrifice their children's education in favor of accumulating property. And he found that in 1850 perhaps as high as 40 per cent of children of school age of laborers were not in school. More recently, however, in his study of Boston, published in 1973, Thernstrom found that the Irish there were not sacrificing their children's education for property accumulation. In fact in 1900 in Boston, some 80 per cent of immigrants between 10 and 14 were in school. For those of the second generation—that is, children of im- migrants born in the United States—the proportion was 92 per cent, only slightly lower than the 94 per cent recorded for the children of the native born. In New York City the census for 1900 reported that 91 per cent of children aged 6 through 14 whose parents were born abroad were in school. As we saw in Chapter IV, the great majority of children, immigrant and native alike, did not go out to work until primary education was completed.

Of all immigrant groups, the Italians and Irish seem to have been least concerned with education for their children, though this conclusion must be tentative in the face of the thin evidence on the subject. As already noted, in Newburyport, Massachusetts, Thernstrom found Irish children less well schooled than other groups. Elizabeth Pleck found that the proportion of black children at school at the turn of the century in the three different cities she studied was almost double that of Italian children in Chicago in 1900. And when Thernstrom carried his study of ethnicity in Boston into the 20th century he found that the children of Irish and Italians had less education than those of other immigrants and natives. Although part of the discrepancy can be explained by the degree of education of the fathers—that is, fathers with more education tended to have more highly educated children, and many Irish and Italian fathers had little education—that was not the whole story. Even when fathers' educational level was held constant, Swedish and Jewish children had more education than Irish and Italians. The differences Thernstrom attributed to variation in ethnic values. "Jews placed an especially high value on education and careers . . . whereas Catholics [that is, Irish and Italians] were somewhat less dedicated to educational and occupational achievement for their sons than Protestants from the same class and educational background." A recent student of Italian immigrant families has concluded that Italian-Americans, unlike Jewish families, placed higher value upon home ownership than upon the education of their children. In support of her conclusion the author quoted an Italian proverb: "Never make your children better than you are." [47]

That Italians did not view education in the same light as some other immigrant groups is yet another manifestation of the differences in ethnic culture of the immigrants. The cohesiveness of the Italian family was very high; parents often resented efforts to interfere with their control over their children, as certainly the schools threatened to do. In Italy, families were used to working as a unit, and they continued to do so in the new country. Parents were more interested in having their children work with them than in sending them to school. A woman social worker, who was herself of Italian descent, delineated the differences between Italians and natives as well as exposing the Old World roots of the differences. "Although they love their children," she began, "they do not love them in the right way sometimes. They think they must bring in something and that is the Italian idea. They love to have children because they help to lift the burden."[48] And in Italy children were expected to work. Elizabeth Pleck found in her study of immigrants and blacks in three different cities at the opening of the 20th century that Italian families were more likely to send out their children to work than black families were.

The contrast between Italians and others also came through in the way the Italian children worked as compared with children of American-born parents. The American children worked for themselves; when they became tired they quit. Not so the Italian children. They worked because their parents made them, and they could not decide for themselves to quit. Moreover, the money they earned was not for themselves, but went into the family budget. The attitudes of the parents in regard to work, education, and control over their children were neatly epitomized when one Buffalo cannery permitted a school to be set up on its premises. The Italian mothers objected violently because a school meant not only less time for the children to earn money, but compulsory attendance at it was a clear interference with the parents' control over the children.

As the comment by the Italian-born social worker implied, the Italian immigrant family was less democratic than the American family. Yet that contrast, too, pointed up the modernity of the 19th-century family in the United States. The Italian family was simply closer to what the premodern family had been. In time, it, too, would be democratized as the forces of American individualism began to work upon it. A recent study of Italian families documents one aspect of that democratization in the 20th century by noting the rise in the proportion of Italians in school after age 15 in three cities. In 1905, for instance, 25 per cent of Italians aged 15–18 were in school; by 1915 the proportion was up to 32 per cent, and by 1925 it was 51 percent.[49] During the 19th century, as we have seen, the families of other foreign-born nationalities had also displayed differences from those of native Americans. Still, on balance, whatever differences there were seem to have been less significant or obvious than the similarities, even in the years when immigration was still at flood-tide. Or so it appears from the evidence and comparisons currently available to historians.

Although the great majority of immigrants and black women married, as the overwhelming proportion of white native women did, there was still a significant portion of women who never married or, if they did, found marriage unsatisfactory for one reason or another. If we are to understand women's relationship to the family it is necessary to look at those women for whom family did not define their lives. They provide another vantage point from which to assess the relation between women and the family in the 19th century.

VII

Women Challenge the Family

Up to now in examining the nature of the American family as it emerged in the 19th century, the emphasis has been upon the closeness or intensity of the emotional ties between spouses, and between parents and children. Wife and husband were expected to be companions to each other, and loving parents to their children. Women played an increasingly important role as child-rearers as well as moral guides to husband and children, a combination of roles that bestowed on them a certain, if limited degree of authority or autonomy within the family. One argument of this book is that as the 19th century advanced, that area of autonomy within the family expanded for many women. And one reason it did was that some women challenged the family quite directly.

Their challenges took several forms. Some women worked out important relationships with women outside the family. Others spurned marriage and family altogether. And still others abandoned marriage when it did not provide the autonomy or satisfactions they thought necessary. Let us look at these challenges in turn.

If the family was for the great majority of women in the 19th century undeniably important, a significant proportion of them, nevertheless, developed a parallel and in some cases competing relationship with other members of their sex. The lineaments of that alternate relationship, if that is not too strong an adjective, have been imaginatively reconstructed by historian Carroll Smith-Rosenberg from the frequent and often lengthy letters exchanged by 19th-century women. The letters reveal a sense of sisterhood or sorority between the correspondents. The intimate, often highly supportive relationships, revealed in the letters, usually began before the writers married, but not infrequently endured well beyond marriage. Another historian, Nancy Cott, has reported one such relationship that lasted for half a century and for nearly forty years after the marriage of one of the correspondents. Carroll Smith-Rosenberg analyzed the friendship of two women which began when they were girls in their early teens and endured until their old age and throughout the marriages of both. The emotional intensity of the relationship is apparent in the exchanges between Sarah Wister and Jeannie Musgrove. "I can give you no idea how desperately I shall want you" in the coming week, Wister wrote once when she expected to be home alone. At another time, after a visit with Sarah, Jeannie wrote, "Dear darling Sarah! How I love you and how happy I have been! You are the joy of my life . . . I cannot tell you how much happiness you gave me, nor how constantly it is all in my thoughts." Although these last are the words of a single woman writing to a wife, the feelings do not change when Sarah, then a mother, writes in 1870 upon the occasion of Jeannie's marriage at age 37: "Dearest darling—How incessantly have I thought of you these eight days . . . The entire uncertainty, the distance, the long silence [she is writing from London]—are all new features in my separation from you, grievous to be borne . . . Are you married, I wonder? My dearest love to you wherever and *who*ever you are." [1]

Married women could be as erotic in their language as the unmarried. Louise Brackett's letters to Anna E. Dickinson in 1863 are especially noteworthy in this regard. "My own sweet 'Raphael Dickinson'! how much I want to see you: as your letter gave me such exquisite pleasures indeed! I will marry you—run off anywhere with you, for you are such a darling. I can feel your soul—if not your body sweet Anna—do I offend your delicacy?" she finally inquired. Then she closed with, "bye, bye you little soft-cheeked girl—I should love to kiss you, love me and think of me forever." Nine years later Laura C. Bullard, who was also married, told Anna Dickinson that she regretted that Anna had not visited her while Bullard's husband was away, for then "you should have had your place in my bed . . . and I am sorry you didn't . . . Sweet Anna I shall hope to see you soon and kiss your soft, tender lips, either here or at Long Branch." [2]

The references to the physical presence and to actual physical contact make it quite clear that these tender sentiments were more than mere conventionalities of feminine correspondence. Sarah Watson wrote in her diary in 1833 about unexpectedly meeting her old school friend Sarah Bridgman: "took her home with me and *once more* slept with my room mate and friend." The talk that night made the next day a "happy" one, and though Watson was "refreshed," as she recorded, she was "yet not satisfied. How I long this Sunday evening to have her with me now!" Sarah Watson was then only 19. But Sarah Ripley Stearns was 23 and married when her friend Rachel, after whom she would later name her daughter, died. In thinking about her friend Rachel, Sarah did not recall any specific physical relationships, but it is clear their friendship was not being described in sentimental conventionalities. She referred to their friendship as one in which each could "repose their secret thoughts in perfect confidence" in the other. "I have not a friend on earth to who [sic] I could so freely communicate my feelings, at any time" nor did she ever expect to have another such intimate friend. Some years later, in the 1830s, Eliza Schlatter made quite clear her physical longing for Sophie DuPont. "I would turn your *good husband out of bed*—and snuggle into you and we would have a long talk like old times in Pine Street. I want to tell you so many things that are not writable." [3]

When these sororial relationships developed prior to marriage there was always the possibility that marriage would disrupt them. As Bessie Lyman's wedding was approaching in the spring of 1881, her close friend Emily Eliot perceived it as a threat. "Sat with Bessie for an hour in the afternoon," she wrote later in her diary. "She told me 'every passing thought'. . . . What shall I do when she is married?" Three days later they spent more time together. After dinner they "sat on the sofa in the back parlor, her golden head on my shoulder and her hand in mine." That was in early March, three months before the wedding was to take place. After the wedding, as the bridal party drove off, Emily Eliot sadly wrote, "and so I was parted from my dearest friend." [4]

Usually, however, marriage did not disrupt these intense companionships. Even while Elizabeth Dwight Cabot was on her extensive wedding trip in Europe in 1857 she kept up a steady correspondence with her old friend Elizabeth Eliot. She expressed her regret at not having written more and at being separated from her. "The great drawback of travelling is always the necessity of monopolizing the pleasures that would be so much increased by being shared. [A modern reader almost forgets that she is traveling on her honeymoon with her husband.] . . . Darling, do you think every day that in my heart I am *close, close* by your side, though I have wandered so far away . . . that I can be no help to you?" Apparently Elizabeth Eliot responded in kind, because several months later Elizabeth Cabot thanked her for her faithful correspondence. "Beloved darling, don't ever forget how close in my heart I keep you all the time. . . . I certainly live as much with you as if I were with you, but I often think the letters show only my outside doings."[5]

Perhaps the most striking example of the kind of interdependence and love that these relationships could assume even when both people were married to others was the friendship between Mary Hallock Foote and Helena Gilder. They had been schoolgirl chums in the East and continued a remarkable correspondence for some thirty years, during most of which time Mary was in the far West, principally Idaho and California. Historian Carroll Smith-Rosenberg, who has studied the friendship, has no doubt that "Molly and Helena were lovers—emotionally if not physically" prior to their marriages. "I wanted so to put my arms around my girl of all girls in the world," Mary wrote Helena, "and tell her . . . I love her as wives do love their husbands, as *friends* who have taken each other for life." Later, when Helena announced her marriage, Mary confessed, "You know dear Helena, I really was in love with you. It was a passion such as I had never known until I saw you. I don't think it was the noblest way to love you."[6]

Mary's emotional dependence on and corresponding support from Helena suffuse her letters. (Helena's letters are not open to inspection.) At the time of Molly's first pregnancy in 1878 she particularly thanked Helena for her support: "Yours is the warm close clasping woman's hand leading me step by step through the sacred mysteries of wifehood and motherhood. Yes, my darling—even if that last awful mystery must blind my shuddering eyes—I could bear it better because I know that you have borne it and lived and kept your sweet faith whole." The long absences and distances between them, despite their voluminous correspondence, worried Mary, who thought it would be difficult to be with her again, especially since Helena would have new friends and acquaintances. "I always think of you, alone by yourself," Mary wrote in 1887, "as you are in my heart; no one to compare you with or place beside you have I seen or been able to imagine." It troubled her that when they would meet again "there will be always those others." When Mary's husband, at the end of the 1880s, fell into alcoholism and was unable to support the family adequately, the darkest night descended over Mary Foote. Inevitably and naturally, she told all to Helena, seeking emotional support more than counsel, for she was a resourceful woman. Then when the darkness began to lift, she begged to be forgiven for the burden she had imposed. In the process she explained the meaning of their long relationship. "I must not draw too heavily on the bank that holds the savings of years and the riches of friendship," she said; yet she yearned to acknowledge Helena's support all through it. "Now forgive me, and I will hush. I imagine that you kiss me, with a few quiet tears." [7]

There is some evidence that a kind of subculture based upon domesticity and culminating in sorority also developed among women of less education and lower social status than those from whose letters the preceding quotations have been taken. Mollie Dorsey, for example, complained that visitors were few on the plains, and even when a few did come through they were "all men; not one solitary female . . . have we seen . . . but we hear of a family only a mile below, where there is a married lady and single sister. We will hunt them up at once." The emptiness of the prairie caused her at another time to wish that the country would fill up. If only there were "schools or churches, or even some society. We do not see a woman at all. All men, single, or bachelors, and one gets tired of them." The very next day a new family settled nearby, and she and her mother were "delighted to have a family near us, to see a live woman again." [8]

A similar awareness of an underlying attraction among women in the 19th century surfaced during the long ordeal of the Overland Trail to California—and for the same reasons that aroused Mollie Dorsey's yearning for other members of her sex. Suddenly women were confronted by an all male world in which they were neither welcome nor contented. Women traveled in many of the wagon trains that made the journey, but always they were a distinct minority. Their minority position became most obvious, often painfully so, when a wagon would break off from the train for one reason or another. As one woman who left the train with her family wrote, "then I felt that indeed I had left all my friends, save my husband and his brother, to journey over the dreaded Plains, without female acquaintance even for a companion—of course I wept and grieved about it, but to no purpose." Another woman had to leave the train because her husband could not get along with the other families. The day they withdrew from the train, the other women came over to say goodbye to the woman. The effect upon her of leaving was measured in their telling her that "there was no color in my face. I felt there was none," she added. When the last two women of the group "bade me adieu the tears [were] running down their sunburnt cheeks. I felt as though my last friends were leaving me. . . ." [9]

Several things deserve to be said about this sense of sorority or sisterhood among women in the 19th century. The first is that probably not all women continued these relations beyond marriage, if they developed them at all. Certainly those women whose correspondence with their husbands revealed a close and emotional relation, like that between Mary and Henry Poor or between Charlena and Melville Anderson, seem not to have had sororial relationships with other women. Moreover, occasionally, a woman remarked that she preferred the company of her husband to that of other women. Mary Waterman Rice, for example, wrote her father in 1874 that though a little party had been arranged in her honor while her husband was away, "I did not enjoy myself very much. I do not understand how married ladies can enjoy themselves out in society without their husbands. I cannot." [10] Smith-Rosenberg acknowledged that women had important relationships with particular men, like brothers or husbands. Her point is, however, that those relationships "differed in both emotional texture and frequency from those between women." Simply because it is extremely difficult to make comparisons on such a delicate scale, the predominance of sorority must remain open to doubt, though its importance need not. For, as even Mary Rice's unfriendly comment implied, during the 19th century sisterhood was often a significant and integral part of the life of many women, and, as we have seen, not only of upper- or middle-class women.

No thorough study of relationships between women comparable to that which Smith-Rosenberg made for the 19th century has yet been done for either the 18th or 20th century. Nonetheless, the second observation to be made about sorority is that there is some reason to believe that it was peculiar to the 19th century alone. Nancy Cott, for instance, examined some two hundred divorce cases in Massachusetts during the 18th century. Among her findings was that petitions from women for divorce did not call upon women witnesses as frequently as men petitioners did! [11] Yet if there had been a sense of solidarity among women in the 18th century comparable to that which we have noted in the 19th century, just the opposite should have occurred.

Similarly, there is little reason to believe that sisterhood as the 19th century experienced it persisted into the 20th century. In fact, the interest in Smith-Rosenberg's findings today derive largely from the fact that she identified a phenomenon in the 19th century that was largely unknown in the 20th century, at least until the last decade when feminist consciousness has begun to revive the emotion. One early 20th-century feminist, however, described sorority quite well. "There is a kind of Friendship which may exist among women," Dr. Clelia Mosher wrote in her journal in

1919, "where their individual interests are so merged, that each has for the other the same vital interest in the other's success as the mother has in her daughter's affairs; or father in his son's life. It has all the wonderful community interest one finds in ideal marriage and only differs in the absence of the physical relationship. It is emotionally satisfying." But it was her conclusion that is significant for us. "One seldom sees it," she admitted, for it is "only possible to a very high type of woman, spiritually and intellectually." [12]

If sorority is confined to the 19th century—and that is Carroll Smith-Rosenberg's conclusion as well—a question remains. Why did sorority develop first in the 19th century and then virtually disappear in the 20th?

The emergence is easier to account for than the disappearance. The origin seems to be the peculiarly 19th-century idea of domesticity—that is, the confinement of women, by both ideology and practice, to the home and its moral governance. This was an effective force whether one emphasizes the narrowing, oppressive side of domesticity, as Smith-Rosenberg does, or whether one acknowledges the more positive effects of domesticity, as Nancy Cott does. In the former instance, oppression bred its own sense of community and intimacy among women. In the latter explanation, the moral superiority of women, which domesticity decreed, at once segregated them from men while encouraging them to seek intimacy and identification among themselves as the moral center of the home.

If the growth of sorority is thus related to the rise and flowering of the idea of domesticity, the question still remains why it declined after the 19th century. The explanation probably lies in the decline of domesticity itself. As the 19th century came to a close, the place of women in American life was undergoing changes that had been in progress for some time and were accelerated in the opening decades of the 20th century. Long before the 19th century closed, increasing numbers of women worked before marriage. Holding a job tended to weaken if not to sever those exclusive ties between girls that were the origin of sorority in the first half of the 19th century. In fact, by the early years of the next century most young women probably worked for several years before marriage. Thus they did not have a chance to develop relationships which were strong or intense enough to survive disruption by marriage.

Moreover, by the early 20th century the idea of domesticity was much more broadly defined than it had been earlier. A strengthening suffrage movement was under way in many states and, more important, various women's organizations were growing in both number and size. At the end of the 19th century, for instance, the Women's Christian Temperance Union counted 150,000 members, and by 1914, the General Federation of Women's Clubs had a million members. These and other organizations took the place of the older, more intimate but still rather confined relations between individual women, which we have been calling sorority. Something of the spirit engendered by the new organizations comes through in a remark by a member of the Association of Collegiate Alumnae, after graduation from college. "I feel as if I had been flung out into space, and the notices of those meetings were the only threads that connected me with the things I had known." Even more pertinent was the report from a women's club in Arkansas at the end of the 1890s. Though the author got the gender wrong in her description, she knew the feeling of sorority. "All ages, young and old and middle-aged are gathered in the membership and there is a delightful fraternity of spirit among them. The old bring their ripe experiences, the young their youth and eager enthusiasm for knowledge. The result is a blending of social and intellectual life as nearly ideal as can be found in this mortal world." [13]

The 20th-century organizations, to be sure, depended for their existence, just as the sororial relationships had, upon the segregated social position and assumed moral superiority of women. Yet it was precisely this identity of social situation and moral assumptions that drained away from women the need for sororial relationships between individuals. Many of the same satisfactions—and the moral support—could now be obtained by joining women's organizations, rather than through relationships with individual women.

Increasingly, however, in the course of the 19th century, there was a group of women who often did not find their satisfactions in either organizations or the family. They were women who never married at all. By the turn into the 20th century single women were clearly more than the peripheral or ignored persons they had been earlier in American history.

The single woman, the woman who did not help to found a family, and, in a sense, lived outside the family, existed, of course, long before the 19th century. The number of single women in the colonial period, however, was usually severely limited if only because of the paucity of economic opportunities for a woman in an overwhelmingly agricultural society. When a woman failed to marry, she either had to remain with her family of origin, as most of them apparently did, or had to make a living on her own. Unfortunately, the quantitative evidence on the number of unmarried women in the colonial years is thin. But what is available suggests that spinsters were much less numerous then than in the early 19th century. Daniel Scott Smith, for example, located only three out of 89 daughters in 17th-century Hingham, Massachusetts, who failed to marry. In the 18th century the proportion was about twice that, but it still stood at less than 8 per cent. What this suggests is that as the society became more complex the opportunities for unmarried women to find a place in it improved. This supposition is borne out by the more broadly based statistics for the 19th century. A study of marriages in Massachusetts reported that the proportion of women in that state in 1830 who failed to marry before reaching age 50 was less than 13 per cent; by 1870 the proportion was up to almost 18 per cent. A similar increase in the proportion of single women as the 19th century advanced was shown for the country at large by the federal census. The highest proportion of women who never married for any period between 1835 and the present were those born between 1860 and 1880. The proportions ranged between 10.0 and 11.1 per cent.[14]

The striking thing is that this fairly steady increase in women who never married over the course of the 19th century was reversed in the early 20th century. In fact, during the present century the proportion has been declining steadily, from 7.7 per cent of those born at the opening of the century to 4.5 per cent for those born in the early twenties. This reversal in trend is a question that we shall have to consider again before this chapter is concluded. Right now, however, let us look more closely at the increase in the proportion of single women during the late 19th century.

The decision to remain single was not an easy one. For, despite the increase in the number of single women in the last decades of the 19th century, being single or an "old maid" was hardly an honorable status. It was only less maligned than at earlier times. The ambivalence toward the unmarried adult woman comes through in the comment of a popular medical writer, Dr. George Napheys. "Common proverbs portray the character of the spinster as peevish, selfish, given to queer fancies, and unpleasant eccentricities," he told his readers. "In many cases, we are glad to say this is untrue." There are many examples of noble and sacrificing single women, Naphey noted. But then he shifted ground and concluded that on the whole the popular attitude was often only too accurate. Deprived of the natural objects of interest, the sentiments of such women, he contended, were "apt to fix themselves on parrots and poodles, or to be confined within the breast and wither for want of nourishment."[15]

Because of the effective force of the cult of domesticity, Naphey's ambivalence was inevitable. For if the ideal woman was a wife and mother, it followed that there was no proper place for the woman who rejected those roles, or, more accurately, perhaps was never given the chance to assume them. The anomalous place of the unmarried woman in an age of domesticity was well summed up by a single woman, from both her own sad standpoint and that of society. At the end of a twenty-year career, Edith Melvin, one of the few single professional women active among the antisuffragists, wrote, "I regret to state, my life has been more that of a man than of a woman."[16]

In view of the burdens that singleness entailed, it is not surprising that early in the life of a young woman, especially as she approached twenty years of age, a fear that she might be left single for life assailed her. When Mollie Dorsey in 1857 thought of a beau with whom she had recently broken, she also thought of what that rejection of a suitor might mean for her. "Wonder if I'll *ever* have another anyway, or will I settle down here and never marry at all?" But if the thought chilled her, she did not admit it to her journal. "I shall not worry, for I suppose I will do just what *fate* has in store for me." On her nineteenth birthday, a few weeks later, the worry nagged her again: "Or won't I marry at all? If I live to be an *old maid*," she consoled herself, "I will be one of the good kind that is a friend to everybody and that everyone loves."[17]

Not all young women could be as self-confident as Mollie, for, without a husband, life for a woman could be difficult as well as lonely. Anne Firor Scott quotes from the diary of a young woman in Natchez, Mississippi, who thought she wanted to die because she had not found a husband. "I know I would make a faithful, obedient wife, loving with all my heart, yielding entire trust in my husband," she wrote sadly as she put in words the ideal that was supposed to win a husband, but in this case, at least, had not. As Mary Waterman Rice pointed out to her father in 1874, so long as women had to wait upon men's overtures or proposals, marriage was never entirely in the hands of women. "I fear Ella [White] is cut out for an old maid," Mary concluded, "and I am very sorry to think so for she would make some young man an excellent good wife. Her manners certainly are not calculated to please young men," yet she was a young woman worthy of wifehood, Mary believed. "There is better material in Ella than appears on the surface; there is considerable surface there too, Papa, for she weighs 145 lb. . . ."[18]

In the life of the young, unmarried woman we catch a glimpse of what the alternatives to marriage were. Relatively few women, even in the second half of the century, were sufficiently educated or capable of teaching in college or of entering upon the few professional careers open to them. And before 1860 there were few or no careers accessible to women except writing or teaching school. Factory work, as the century advanced, was an opportunity of sorts for single women, but it hardly constituted a career or an inducement to remain unmarried. As long as women lived at home with their family of origin they were expected to help with the housework, or, if their father's employment lent itself, to help there, too. Sarah Ripley, for instance, minded her father's store when she was still unmarried at age 23. But such work by a young woman was not routine, as her comment in 1809 makes clear: "My father has now got a young man in the Store, which has released me." Without her work in the store, Sarah's day was monotonous, as she quite frankly waited or, as her journal makes plain, worked at getting married. "My time continues to pass in the same dull rotation," she wrote in her journal in 1809, "my cares and employments return with each revolving day and with but little variety to enliven the scene." [19]

For women of a social class higher than Sarah Ripley's, the routine could be full, but no less monotonous. The diary of Elizabeth Dwight in the early 1850s offers an example of the routine of a young woman who at the age of 23 would be considered on the edge of being an "old maid." She arose rather late in the morning, around 9:30 or 10 o'clock, took French lessons, practiced on her harp, did some visiting, took walks, and wrote letters. Apparently, since her parents had servants, she was expected to do little housework. Here is her entry for February 24, 1853: "Practised. Went to Aunt Elise's. Read Ellen's [her sister] letter. Went for Jane N—— and Mary L—— and went to riding school. Came home, dressed and went to Mr. L. G. Ward's reception, and to see E. R. C. who came from Newport at one o'clock. Came home. Read, rested, dined, wrote French, worked worsted, read La Robe de Voce and went to bed at eleven."

The routine, however, changed dramatically when illness came to the household, as happened the next year. As she explained to her married sister, the care of old relatives who were ill was taxing and constituted a source of embarrassment to the relatives being cared for. For they see "that four days out of six I cannot touch my harp, that my French lessons have been given up, or that I am busy most of the time. . . ." Her aunt cherished a vision for her of a life that was "literary, musical, social, with time to cultivate my own mind, and enjoy other peoples and it is very hard for her to give it up. . . . I *had* a vision once of such a life, too," she added wistfully, "but I have come to the conclusion that it is not meant for me." Once she had thought there would be ample time for study and musical practice after her sister left to be married, "but it is a positive fact that there have not been two months since you went, when from sickness either of body or mind Anna or Mary or Ned, have not needed a degree of time and strength from me, which has left me but the last end of the day and the last end of my strength for myself." She went on to say she did not regret the burden, because she had learned much about herself "which no books could teach . . . but it costs me an occasional groan to look over the vast seas of ignorance which envelop my mind." Thus her response when urged by her sister to learn German: "I felt perfectly sick, to think how far off that wished for haven still seemed." [20]

Elizabeth Dwight ultimately married, a change of status that could only intensify her confinement to the duties of the home. But those single women who never married or had insufficient training to follow a career or profession enjoyed neither the advantages of domesticity nor those of singleness. "We are leading the lives which women have led since Troy fell," wrote such a woman in the South during the Civil War, "wearing away time with memories, regrets and fears; alternating fits of suppression, with flights imaginary, to the red fields . . . while men, more privileged . . . make name and fortune while helping to make a nation. . . . I am like a pent-up volcano. I wish I had a field for my energies." [21]

The lives of women of the middle and upper classes prior to marriage differed from those of the farming and urban working classes principally in that they were helped by servants. The number of servants in relation to families reached a peak around the 1870s, with one servant for each 6.6 white families. [22] These places were filled by immigrant, black, and poor white girls, usually prior to marriage; among all married women, only black women were significantly represented in the paid labor force after marriage. Increasingly, in the course of the 19th century, urban working girls and farm girls who left for the city found jobs in the expanding factories, shops, and offices of an industrializing America. The proportion of white women working for pay outside their own homes rose from less than 5 per cent in 1800 to 10 per cent in 1850. But when it is recognized that few married white women worked, this figure has to be at least doubled to reflect accurately the proportion of young white women who worked before marriage. If, by this estimate, one-fifth of young white women were employed before marriage in 1850, by the end of the century, on the same calculation, the proportion would be close to 50 per cent. Although there are no comparably accurate figures for black women, the proportion of black women who worked before marriage must have been considerably higher, if only because the incomes of their families of origin were generally so much lower than those of white women, or even immigrant women.

During the last half of the 19th century, an increasing number of middle- and upper-class girls found outlets for their talents and time in secondary school and college. Interestingly enough, for as far back in the 19th century as figures exist, more girls than boys graduated from high school. In 1870 about 9000 girls finished secondary school as compared with 7000 boys. By 1900 the figures were up to 57,000 girls and 38,000 boys. Of course, even at that date no more than 7 per cent of all seventeen-year-olds of both sexes graduated from secondary school. Not until the 1920s was graduation from secondary school a mass phenomenon. On the other hand, throughout the 19th century, young men consistently outnumbered young women in graduation from college. But because collegiate education was barely open to women before the middle of the 19th century, the rise in the number of women attending college was much more rapid than for men. In 1900 about 5000 women graduated from college as compared with 22,000 men.

The great majority of women in 19th-century America, including those who went to college, eventually married. Those who did not either found some form of livelihood or lived with relatives as an extra hand, baby-sitter, or dependent. Working-class women who did not marry probably continued to work at the jobs they had filled as girls—that is, as domestic servants, factory workers, or, increasingly in the 20th century as the economy matured, as office workers. Educated and middle-class single women by the last decades of the 19th century had opportunities in the arts, professions like law and medicine as well as in business, government, teaching, and scholarship.

Unfortunately, the emotional dimension of the life of the single woman of the late 19th century has hardly been studied, though most recently some light has begun to be thrown on it. For example, there is now some evidence that many of the married women who continued to have sororial relationships did so with women who never married. And, as we have seen, that relationship could be warm, intense, and satisfying. Similar relationships also obtained between single women. Single women often lived together, experiencing privately, if not publicly, a relationship with another adult that was quite similar to that of marriage between two members of the opposite sex. Mary Grew made that precise comparison

when she responded to a letter of condolence upon the death of her life-
long friend and companion, Margaret Burleigh, in 1892: "Your words
respecting my beloved friend touch me deeply. Evidently . . . you compre-
hend and appreciate as few persons do . . . the nature of the relation
which existed, which exists, between her and myself. . . . To me it seems
to have been a closer union than that of most marriages." [23]

Although some of these relationships were undoubtedly lesbian, this one
apparently was not, for Mary Grew concluded by saying there had been
such close friendships between men as well as between women. "And why
should there not be? Love is spiritual, only passion is sexual." In any case,
in the 19th century, the law paid little attention to homosexual relations
between women. Laws against "sodomy" or homosexuality appeared on
the statute books of all states from the colonial period on, but the intention behind these laws was to control men, not women. Moreover, as Carroll Smith-Rosenberg has suggested, to seek to define these relationships in
terms of physical or orgasmic reactions may cause us to miss some of the
subtlety of relationships available to people then. "Certain cultures and environments permit individuals a great deal of freedom in moving" between
extreme homosexuality and extreme heterosexuality, Smith-Rosenberg
writes. "I would like to suggest that the nineteenth century was such a cultural environment. That is, the supposedly repressive and destructive Victorian sexual ethos may have been more flexible and responsive to the
needs of particular individuals than those of the mid-twentieth century." [24]
To the American Medical Association, by the end of the 19th century, the
close, affectionate relationships among young women were dangerous simply because they were physical. Speaking of young college women, a report
of the Association in 1899 spelled out the possibilities. "The young girls,
thus thrown together manifest an increasing affection by the usual tokens.
They kiss each other fondly on every occasion. They embrace each other
with mutual satisfaction. It is most natural, in the interchange of visits for
them to sleep together. They learn the pleasure of direct contact, and in the
course of their fondling they resort to cunni-linguistic practices . . . after
this the normal sex act fails to satisfy her." [25]

It is not necessary to ascertain the extent of possible physical contact in
order to appreciate the warmth and deeply emotional character of the relations between some single women. The warmth is apparent even in the letters of a dedicated public activist like Susan B. Anthony to Anna E. Dickinson during the 1860s and 1870s. "So Anna as I love you and you love
me—and we both love the right—I ask you to examine the *'inner light,'* "

to see if she could not bring herself to use her oratorical talents in behalf of woman's suffrage. Then, a year later Anthony wrote, "Anna, I cannot bear to go off without another precious look into your face—*nay Soul* . . . Darling, you know all this is the *over anxiety* of my *mother love* for you." (Anthony was twenty-two years older than Dickinson.) Another year later Anthony urged Dickinson to stop off and visit her in New York. "Do let it be soon—I have *plain quarters* . . . double bed—and big enough and good enough to take you *in*. . . . I do so long for the scolding and pinched ears and everything I know awaits me—what worlds of experience since I last snuggled the wee child in my long arms." Although, as Nancy Sahli has commented, the relationship was later broken off because of their disagreement over politics, as late as the 1890s Anthony recalled with considerable emotion their earlier friendship.[26]

Some single women found their emotional outlets in their brothers. Catharine Sedgwick, for instance, was the most successful American writer in the first third of the 19th century. (So famous was she that Chief Justice John Marshall in 1831 wrote his wife with delight that he had met Sedgwick. "I called on her today," he told his wife, "a complement [*sic*] I pay very few ladies, and she thanked me for it."[27] In short, it was not that she had no work or activity to occupy her.) Yet her closeness to her brothers may well have been a large part of why she did not marry. It probably was not the sole reason, for it is hard to see how as a married woman she could have made for herself the career she in fact enjoyed. Some women, of course, did manage, such as Harriet Beecher Stowe. But even as she admitted, or complained, many times, it was not an easy road with children and a home to run.

In any event, Sedgwick freely acknowledged the importance of her brothers in the shaping of her life. "I am satisfied by long and delightful experience," she informed her brother Robert in 1813, "that I can never love anybody better than my Brothers. I have no expectation of ever finding their equal in worth and attraction; . . . do not be alarmed, I am not on the verge of a vow of celibacy, nor have I the slightest intention of adding any rash resolutions to the ghosts of those that have been frightened to death by the terrors of maiden life." Yet, she warned, they ought not expect her to marry until she changed her mind. And though women had a reputation for being fickle, she admitted, her personal expectation was that she would exercise her womanly virtues as a sister, not as a wife. This future seemed more likely every year, she had began to believe, as her value "depreciates . . . in the market of matrimony." Sixteen years later, still unmarried, she wrote her brother Charles that she knew "nothing of love—of memory—of hope—of which you are not an essential part—if ever I attain any adequate conception of the purity and peace and intensity of heavenly affections it is from that I feel for you."

When her brothers married, neither their closeness nor their familiarity with her could be the same. Yet her dependence persisted, as she admitted in 1853 in the course of a letter to Charles's daughter. "A word—a tone of voice from your father often brings tears to my eyes—and certainly I ought not to need such indications from him of all in the world." Yet she still felt alone, as no married person could, she said, especially when she recalled "my early life when the current of love set towards me on every side, when I was loved and cherished far beyond my deserving—was first to many—and now first to none." She had expressed a similar feeling of being outside any family two years before when asked to write her autobiography for the instruction of a niece. "It is strange and melancholy," she began, "when the memory is called on for domestic events," to discover how few there were. "I have 'boarded around' so much—had my home in so many houses and so many hearts. . . . I have been so woven into the fabric of others, that I seem to have had no separate individual existence."

Upon the death of brother Charles, Catharine Sedgwick offered poignant testimony to her long attachment as a single woman to her brothers. She wrote to Charles's daughter soon after the end of the final six months she was ever to spend with him. "It is all done—my work is all done—and with all the sweet and loving and lurid faces around the house is—oh, how vacant—how cold—the love of my life is gone." A week later she tried to encompass the extent of her loss. "I can never speak—I hardly dare think of what this loss is to me—my heart cries out in darkness and in light—by night and by day for my brother—my brother." [28]

Unlike Catharine Sedgwick, Sarah Ripley did not remain single, but she was well into her twenties before she married. Meanwhile her dependence upon her brother was spread upon the pages of her journal. When he returned to college in 1809 she regretted "his absense at this time more than usual, his society has served to enliven many hours, which I of late have passed." At another time she indicated how truly heavy the hours weighed upon her. "My time passes on, in the same dull round of domestic occupations and I seldom go out or see company, consequently the incidents of my life at present [now that her brother had gone] afford but few materials to commit to writing." [29]

Although some women may have felt excluded, or deeply unhappy because they could not marry, for others remaining single was a conscious choice and one that promised a richness of experience that marriage did not. For a woman to have a life of her own outside of marriage could be not only unusual but liberating. Furthermore, the increase in the proportion of women who remained single during the last decades of the 19th century was surely a criticism of the increasing intensity of familial relationships. To some women, perhaps many, that relationship impeded or stifled the realization of their personal potentialities or aspirations. This became increasingly apparent as opportunities for careers and other kinds of independent work for women opened up. For many such women marriage appeared to be a straitjacket, rather than an opportunity or an improvement in life and status as it may well have seemed in earlier and different times.

Nowhere did this conflict between women's aspirations and marriage surface more obviously than among those women who were graduating from the new women's colleges and coeducational universities during the last half of the century. Elizabeth Blackwell confronted it early in the century. In 1887, after she had become a successful physician—the first woman trained in America—she wrote a young relative about her own youth in the 1840s, when she was making the decision to enter upon a career in medicine. After noting that she had "scarcely ever been free from some strong attraction which my sober judgment condemned," which was the 19th century's way of referring to sexual interests, she told of her internal struggle when the possibility of a career as a physician was raised. At that time, she told her niece, she was going through "an unusually strong struggle between attraction toward a highly educated man with whom I had been very intimately thrown, and the distinct perception that his views were too narrow and rigid to allow any close and ennobling companionship." She resolved the conflict by entering upon her remarkably successful career, which she rightly anticipated put "an insuperable barrier between myself and those disturbing influences which I could not wisely yield to, but could not otherwise stifle." For years thereafter, she remembered, she kept a bunch of flowers, which he had given her, in a package, "which I sentimentally and in all sincerity labelled young love's last dream."[30] Blackwell's inability to reconcile a career with the satisfaction of her emotions in marriage was not unique, only its documentation is. Many other women confronted with a similar choice can be found among the literally scores of single women who taught at Vassar, Wellesley, Smith, Bryn Mawr, and the other women's colleges. For these women, who brought scholarly distinction to their institutions, elected to realize their intellectual and career aspirations rather than accept the limitations that a 19th-century marriage demanded.

Other women, less well-educated than Blackwell and college teachers, also voiced their doubts about marriage or the ways in which its demands contradicted their personal ambitions. Sarah Morgan in 1862 wrote in her diary what she would not say in public. "Why have I never yet fallen in love?" she asked. "Simply because I have yet to meet the man I would be willing to acknowledge as my lord and master." [It is difficult to know whether this hackneyed phrase was written with irony or with a straight face for it was often used by women in ambiguous ways.] In any case, the only man Sarah Morgan could accept as her husband, she contended, was one she would "never have to blush for, or be ashamed to acknowledge, the one that after God I shall most venerate and respect."[31]

Sarah Morgan may have found particular men wanting, but some women who remained single found marriage itself dubious. Eliza Chaplin told a woman friend in 1820 that she simply would not marry at all "rather than be subject to the 'eternal strife,' which . . . prevails . . . where minds are 'fettered to different moulds.' " She vowed to remain always in " 'single-blessedness' and deem it felicity thus to live." Ella White, whom Mary Waterman Rice thought was destined to be an "old maid," was "anxious to get a situation in some seminary to give vocal lessons in music," Mary wrote her father. But that aim was primarily a means to an end that marriage might not have been able to accommodate or satisfy. "Her object is to treat herself to a grand piano and a trip to Boston."[32]

Even in the first half of the 19th century, advice books were beginning to rise to the support of young women who did not marry. One such book denounced the traditional aspersions cast upon old maids as "a species of cruelty . . . which . . . merits unqualified censure. Perhaps, ladies, some of these traduced and persecuted beings have been only more delicate in their choice than you have been. . . . It does not invariably happen that persons remain single because they are not worth having, or that others are married because they are." And in 1847 the former head of the Female Guardian Society wrote that of the errors of the times "there are none more pernicious than those which represent love and marriage not only as essential to the happiness of our sex, but in reality the only end and aim of our existence."[33]

Behind the refusal to marry often lay not only a dissatisfaction with the flatness of married life but also the feeling that married women lacked sufficient autonomy. "O, it's not the worst thing in the world . . . to be an 'old maid,' " wrote the *Female Advocate* in 1854. "Not half as bad as to be the disappointed, wretched wife of something that would disgrace a brute." Mary Jones Taylor, a close friend of Mary Mallard, was plainly of that opinion. As early as age 24 she knew she did not want to marry. In the course of congratulating Mary Mallard on her newborn baby in 1858, Mary Taylor referred to herself as an "old maid" who was "more devoted than ever to spinsterhood." Later in that same letter she offered a clue to her reasons for a decision to which she adhered for the rest of her life. In discussing her reading of *Shirley* by Charlotte Brontë, she found fault with the depiction of heroines who displayed their feelings so openly as to constitute "a perfect outrage on female delicacy." She then went on to say that she saw examples of this kind of behavior in day-to-day life as well. "I have been so disgusted by seeing gentlemen met halfway in their addresses I have to condemn everything that tends to encourage it." [34] Women, in short, ought not to have to throw themselves at men in order to be appreciated or accepted.

This was also the message of Dinah M. Mulock's *A Woman's Thoughts About Women*, which Mary Taylor recommended to Mary Mallard. At the time Mulock wrote the book in 1858 she was unmarried. The English novelist made a strong plea for the autonomy of single women. She deplored the prejudice that consigned women to virtual oblivion if they failed to marry. For that obscurity compelled them to devote their energies to what she called "the massacre of old Time." They seek to "prick him to death with crochet and embroidery needles; strum him to death with piano and harp playing—not music; cut him up with morning-visitors, or leave his carcass in ten-minute parcels at every 'friend's' house they can think of. Finally, they dance him defunct at all sort of unnatural hours; and then, rejoicing in the excellent excuse, smother him in sleep for a third of the following day. Thus he dies, a slow, inoffensive, perfectly natural death." [35]

To Mulock, the active woman was the ideal, the woman who was not dependent on men or marriage though she would be happy if both should come to her. For such women, however, "the 'tender passion' is not to them the one grand necessity that it is to aimless lives; they are in no haste to wed . . . and if never married, still the habitual faculty of usefulness gives them that fixed standing in society, which will forever prevent their being drifted away, like most old maids, down the current of the new generation." [36] Mulock was no outspoken feminist, for she made no objection to those who said that the best education for a woman was to teach her how to depend on a man. For such dependence could be undeniably comfortable and perhaps even pleasant. But, as she quite practically pointed out, not all women found men on whom to depend. In that event, she observed, the training was clearly inappropriate and perhaps worse. She found it particularly unfortunate that single women, who are most in need of what she called "self-dependence," to be "the very last in whom it is inculcated or even permitted." [37]

Mulock's advice to single women like herself was without ambiguity. "We *must* help ourselves." Noticing that marriage "is apparently ceasing to become the common lot, and a happy marriage the most uncommon lot of all," she called for the education of young women. This, she contended, would be much more valuable to women than "any blind clamour for ill-defined 'rights.'" Mulock was not alone in her cause, as the movement to open colleges to and for women during the last half of the 19th century made clear.

A recognition that marriage might well hold disadvantages for an "educated, refined and accomplished" woman also appeared in the columns of so pro-family a publication as *Good Housekeeping* in 1885. A writer from Northampton, who signed herself "Priscilla," told her readers that a woman with such traits might "hesitate a little before stepping out of the sphere of usefulness and earnest living that is the natural environment" of such qualities. For, she continued, an "independent, self-respecting woman has no need to marry for a home or a protector as a weaker might do. Marriage to her means exchanging the possibilities of her single life for the life-work and happiness of the man she marries." For once married, such a woman's "best individual effort and achievement is merged in his save in a few exceptional cases where the woman is an absolute genius." "Priscilla" also pointed out that at that time it was quite possible for two independent women to live together quite contentedly, without worrying about "husband-hunting." Like Mulock, "Priscilla" did not advise against marriage; she merely wanted her readers to recognize that it was not the only path for a woman. "Train the girls to be noble wives by all means," she concluded, "but teach them also 'that her hand may be given with dignity she must be able to stand alone.'" [38]

To historian and journalist Ida Tarbell in the early 20th century singleness was still the key to women's independence. "Four hundred years ago a woman sought celibacy as an escape from sin," she wrote in her book *The Business of Being a Woman* (1921). "Today she adopts it to escape inferiority and servitude; superiority and freedom her aim." Later, in her autobiography, Tarbell linked the single state with her life decisions. "I could never marry. It would interfere with my plan; it would fetter my freedom. I didn't quite know what Freedom meant," she confessed, but she clearly perceived marriage as a threat to her goal of personal freedom. "When I was fourteen," she remembered, "I was praying God on my knees to keep me from marriage." [39]

Vida Scudder, prominent Socialist, writer, and highly successful teacher of English at Wellesley College, was less hostile toward and less threatened by marriage than Tarbell. Yet she, too, recognized what many single women of the 19th and early 20th century learned: marriage was not always a gain for a woman, and singleness offered new worlds and suggested new depths. In her frank autobiography, *On Journey,* she told of being in the Alps on vacation with two women friends "of recognized charm and distinction, each of them happy in a large following of disciples and devotees." After they had discussed all the large questions confronting the world, they moved on to their own personal lives. "Soon each was saying she had never had a love affair. I at least was not mortified by the fact," Scudder recalled; "we were all aware that many women with satisfying and fruitful lives are in the same case. I know that something perhaps, humanly speaking, supremely precious has passed me by; but had it come to me," she recognized, "how much it would have excluded!" And that, of course, was the choice that many educated women at the turn of the century had to make. Which would it be—marriage or career, since it was unlikely they could have both? Given the fact that most men of comparable education, as a matter of course, did enjoy both, it is all the more remarkable how little bitterness these women exhibited. Instead, addressing herself to her male readers, Scudder observed quite matter of factly, "a woman's life which sex interests have never visited, is a life neither dull nor empty, nor devoid of romance." [40]

Those were the attitudes of a mature woman, who had experienced much. But she had not always felt that way. As a girl and young woman she had been subjected to all the influences in favor of sexual experience which any young person was. "Until I was thirty, I wanted terribly to fall in love," she remembered. It was not so much that she wanted to be loved as that she was eager for the experience without which, "all literature assured me, life missed its consummation." In time she recognized that her feeling of lack of fulfillment was related to her "respect for authority, not to any personal sense of lack. And I confess that married life looks to me often as I watch it terribly impoverished, for women. Yet I know that it can be glorious not only in spite of its limitations, but through them." Her perception of marriage was distilled into a single sentence which she offered as advice to her students who were about to marry: "If your marriage is like most I know, it will begin as an indulgence but will proceed into a discipline."

No one spelled out more directly and succinctly the disadvantages of marriage for the educated woman than the early 20th-century sociologist Jessie Taft. College-trained women, she wrote in 1916, are less and less willing to "take on the restrictions of matrimony." Part of the reason was that life without marriage or children was becoming more tolerable "by their discovery that home and companionship are still possible for them. Everywhere we find the unmarried woman turning to other women, building up with them a real home, finding in them the sympathy and understanding, the bond of similar standards and values as well as the same aesthetic and intellectual interests, that are often difficult of realization in a husband, especially here in America." Because men were so often immersed in their businesses, she concluded, they could not meet the standard of the educated woman for a satisfactory husband. "One has only to know professional women," she continued, "to realize how common and how satisfactory is this substitute for marriage." Taft was not unmindful of the cost this solution exacted from women, but she recognized, too, that many were prepared to pay it rather than live the narrowed lives marriage held out to them. "They have worked out a partial solution to their problem," she concluded, "in that they have contrived to combine a real home based on love and community of interests with work in the world, but they have solved it at the expense of men and children." [41]

A broader social indication that by the end of the 19th century many women were perceiving marriage as confining or otherwise unsatisfactory was the upsurge in the divorce rate. Though the ratio of divorces to marriages had been rising ever since the 1840s, in comparison with present-day figures, those for the 19th century are miniscule; as late as 1867 the number of divorces granted that year in the whole country was under 10,000. To measure marital discontent by divorce rate, however, is to use the coarsest gauge, especially in a society like that of 18th- and 19th-century America, when a legal divorce was often difficult to obtain. For example, a recent study of marital separations—not divorces—in the last half of the 18th century discovered over 3300 notices of separation from bed and board in the newspapers, but for a period twice as long, Nancy Cott uncovered only 220 divorces in Massachusetts, where divorce was easier to obtain than in any other jurisdiction. When the ratio of notices of separation to population was calculated, the degree of dissatisfaction with marriage in the late 18th century was about the same as that in the 1870s, when measured by divorce rate. The two measures of discontent, to be sure, are not identical. Divorce is a much more definite, not to say irrevocable statement of discontent than an announcement in a newspaper that one's spouse has left bed and board. But the rising rate of separation notices in 18th-century newspapers reminds us that even before divorce was widespread, marital discontent was not only present, as one might expect, but that married people were expressing it, and to a degree not unlike that a century later. Most significant of all, since 95 per cent of the notices studied were placed by husbands, complaining about their wives' departures, the separations constituted a measure of women's refusal to submit to male control within marriage.[42] The women who resisted were, of course, only a tiny minority, but that the proportion of them rose as the century ended fits in with the argument advanced in the first chapter that the new conjugal family, in which women had a central as well as a more autonomous role, had begun to emerge by the end of the 18th century. For when their autonomy was too limited, the women left.

In the 19th century, the continuation and acceleration of this trend is measured by the increase in divorces. Indeed, the increase was sufficiently noticeable by the 1880s to provoke the first serious study of divorce by an agency of the United States government. Carroll Wright's report on divorce, which appeared in 1889, revealed that between 1870 and 1880 the number of divorces had grown one and a half times as fast as the population and that in 1886 the annual number of divorces was over 25,000. A second government report calculated that during the 1890s the number of divorces was climbing at a rate almost three times that of the increase in the population. Not surprisingly, therefore, by the opening of the 20th century the country entered upon a full-scale debate on the meaning of the rising divorce rate.

To contemporaries, one of the central and disturbing facts in that debate was that though many European countries were also reporting increases in divorces, the United States far outdistanced all of them. Only Japan exceeded the United States in the ratio of divorces to marriage. This preeminence of the United States among European countries in rate of divorce, of course, has continued through the 20th century. Yet, at the same time, it is worth noting that the great upsurge in the divorce rate was completed by

1920. In that year there were about eight divorces for every 1000 married couples in the country, as compared with four in 1900—a jump of 100 per cent in just two decades. But as recently as 1960 the figure was only 9.2 per 1000 married couples, or a mere 15 per cent rise since 1920 and for a period twice as long as the previous one, in which a 100 per cent increase had been registered.[43] Even so, the United States today still leads the world in the ratio of divorces to marriages.

It might be thought that the increase in the number of divorces at the end of the 19th and opening of the 20th century was more a function of changes in laws, rather than being a true measure of social responses to marriage. The states varied greatly then, as they do today, in the grounds on which they permitted a final dissolution of marriage. South Carolina throughout the 19th century, for instance, did not permit divorce on any ground; New York permitted it only on the single ground of adultery. On the other hand, some states not only provided several grounds but also often interpreted them in such a way as to make a divorce quite easy to obtain. Despite all these variations, as one authority at the time pointed out, there was little or no correspondence between the number of variety of grounds and the number of divorces. New York, for example, with a single ground, actually awarded 19 per cent *more* divorces in proportion to population than New Jersey, which offered two grounds. And it is also true that some states, at different periods, like Nevada today, offered easier grounds and looser residence requirements than other states, thus attracting migratory petitioners for divorce. Nevertheless, most divorces in the 19th century, like most of them today, were granted to petitioners in their home states.

Perhaps the most conclusive evidence for believing that the rise in divorce was a true measure of marital discontent and not simply a function of changes in laws or judicial interpretations is the stability of the proportion of divorce petitions that have been successful. In 1887 some 70 per cent of all petitions for divorce resulted in final decrees; in 1950 the figure was 71.2 per cent. Yet in the intervening years many changes in divorce laws occurred in the various states. The only occasion in the course of those sixty years in which the proportion went above 80 per cent was during the years of the Great Depression, and then only for 1930–33 and the single year of 1937.[44]

If, then, the figures on an upsurge in divorces represent a social and not a legal phenomenon, what meaning does that upsurge at the end of the 19th and the beginning of the 20th century have for the history of women and the family? William O'Neill, in his study of the divorce controversy at the opening of the 20th century, has related the rise in the divorce rate to the intensifying demands made upon married couples by the 19th-century family. Where there were low expectations in marriage, he argued, as happened prior to the 19th century, there was little need for divorce. People simply accepted whatever relationship could be worked out. "But when the families become the center of social organization," he contended, "their intimacy can become suffocating, their demands unbearable, and their expectations too high to be easily realizable." At that point, he concluded, divorce becomes "the safety-valve that makes the system workable." Those people who could not meet the obligations or endure the oppressions of the new conjugal family could get out and, if they wished, have another chance. Thus, in O'Neill's view, divorce was an integral part of the new, emotionally intense conjugal family that emerged in the 19th century. Divorce was not a flaw in the system of marriage, as many contemporaries feared, but an essential feature of the system. Without it, the new affective family could not work.[45]

O'Neill's analysis requires only some modification. He refers to the upsurge in divorce as a response to the new *family*. Yet, from what we know about divorces in the late 19th century, most of them dissolved marriages, not families. About 60 per cent of all divorces between 1867 and 1906, for example, did not involve children.[46] But even if one speaks of marriages, rather than families, as the relationships that were being disrupted, O'Neill's insight that divorce was necessary to the success of a system of marriage that emphasized affection and companionship between the partners is still valid.

There is also good reason to see the rise in divorce at the end of the 19th century as another sign of women's drive for greater autonomy within marriage and the family. By the century's end divorce was increasingly a woman's remedy. In the late 1860s, for instance, almost two-thirds of all divorces were granted to women. Since then the proportion has been slowly rising. In 1960 it was up to almost three-quarters of the total.

That women's drive for more autonomy within the family lies behind the upsurge in divorce is also supported by an analysis of the grounds for divorce. During the five years 1872–76 some 63 per cent of all divorces granted to women were for grounds that implied inadequate or inappropriate familial behavior by husbands. The general grounds were cruelty, desertion, drunkenness, and neglect to provide. These were grounds that clearly depended for their validity on the special role males were expected to fill in the 19th-century family. Each of these grounds meant that husbands had failed to offer the support or consideration that women had a right to expect in return for fulfilling their own roles as wives and mothers. Significantly, only 14 per cent of the divorces asked for by women claimed adultery on the part of the husband, even though men's claims against women for this cause constituted the second most frequent ground (33.6 per cent of all male divorces granted). Thirty years later—at the opening of the 20th century—only 10 per cent of women's charges against their husbands cited adultery, but those reasons for divorce which related to men's family responsibilities had risen to 73 per cent of the total. Women, in short, were demanding their rights under the doctrine of separate spheres, but apparently they did not perceive their rights as symmetrical with men's. Men's sexual loyalty was much less important to women than responsible family behavior.

Men's accusations against their wives in divorce suits also reflected a growing assertiveness or drive for autonomy on the part of women within marriage and the family. Over 80 per cent of the grounds cited by husbands in the five-year period 1872–76 concerned wives' failure to live up to the ideal of a submissive subordinant. About one-third of the husbands claimed adultery by their wives; 44.8 per cent cited desertion, and 4.7 per cent cruelty. Thirty years later the proportion that named adultery was down to 27 per cent, but the number citing desertion now constituted 49.6 per cent, a slight increase. The striking change was in regard to cruelty, which increased 1,609 per cent in the thirty years! Only 800 husbands had named that charge against their wives in the 1867–71 period, but, in the five years prior to 1906, almost 13,680 petitioned for divorce from their wives on this ground.

What does this new emphasis upon cruelty tell us about the state of marriage at the opening of the 20th century? What had happened in those thirty years? Certainly it could not mean that wives were literally that much more cruel in 1900 than they had been in 1870. The answer, of course, depends upon the meaning of cruelty in a divorce proceeding. It is true that no precise or fully adequate meaning can be ascribed to the term, which was defined and applied concretely in hundreds of cases before dozens of state courts across the country. Yet we do have some indication of the word's meaning during the last years of the 19th century, and there is no reason to believe that the meaning changed substantially in the first years of the 20th century.

In his study of marriage and divorce for the twenty years prior to 1887,

Carroll Wright included summaries of 29 cases of divorce culled from the original court records in which the wife was the defendant on the single ground of "cruelty." In virtually every one of these cases, the nature of the cruelty was that the wife was breaking out of the standard view of the submissive woman.

About one-third of the 29 cases depicted the wife as physically assaulting the husband: "During the last year defendant has struck plaintiff with pokers, flat-irons, and other hard substances." "Defendant is a powerful woman, weighing 190 pounds; she struck plaintiff with a stove-lid and broke one of his ribs; on another occasion she knocked plaintiff down with a chair." "Defendant took all the covering off the bed, leaving plaintiff to shiver until morning. On one occasion she jumped on him with her knees and ran a knitting needle 4 inches in his arm." Four more of the cases involved threats to the husband, such as "plaintiff once at dinner did not eat; whereupon defendant said to him, 'If you don't eat I'll cut your ——— heart out.' "

Fully half of the cases, however, dwelt upon the wife's failure to perform the traditional duties of a wife, especially as the husband defined them. Usually that included refusal to keep his clothes in repair or to cook his meals. When one husband complained that his wife would not get up in the morning to make his breakfast, or even to wake him, and wanted to eat in restaurants, the court granted the divorce with the observation that it was justified because "the wife has acted in an unwife-like manner." Another woman's "cruelty" was adjudged sufficient to justify her husband's divorce because she had "evinced toward plaintiff a hasty temper." Another husband received the divorce he asked for on the ground of cruelty because no children had been born to the marriage.

Wright also summarized 69 cases in which women charged cruelty on the part of their husbands as grounds for divorce. A large number, 58 of the cases, clearly showed women's unwillingness to resign themselves to the husband's inordinate power within the family. In 29 of the 58 cases, the substance of the cruelty was simple physical assault, sometimes of the most brutal kind. In one case the husband had broken his wife's "nose, fingers, two of her ribs, cut her face and lips, chewed and bitten her ears and face, and wounded her generally from head to foot." One husband forced his wife to beg like a dog. Another husband pounded his wife's head against the wall, while still another "forced plaintiff to open her mouth for the purpose of spitting tobacco juice down her mouth." Sometimes the cruelty was less harsh, such as when a husband cut off the water supply in the house, or forced his wife to stay up at night without heat, or smoked when his wife's chronic headaches were known to be aggravated by tobacco smoke.

The next largest number of cases, 26, concerned mental cruelty, which can be defined as uncomplimentary words or threats of physical violence by the husband. One husband kept a razor under his pillow to harass his wife; another brought a woman to live in the same house with his wife; one woman received a divorce because her husband joined the navy, presumably without gaining her agreement. Because a pregnant wife failed to cook her husband's breakfast, he took all the doors of the house off their hinges, rolled up the carpets, and kept the house in that condition for two weeks.

Ten of the cases went beyond merely responding to husband's acts of cruelty, thereby showing even more plainly the respect or autonomy some women—and the courts—thought ought to be accorded wives. In fact, the definition of cruelty that emerges from these specific cases is the embarrassment of wives by their husbands or the husbands' failure to live up to the level of moral behavior their wives thought they had a right to expect. Among such charges were that the husband kept a saloon, accused his wife's sister of stealing, refused to permit the wife to attend church, failed to speak to his wife civilly, and failed to wash himself. In these particular manifestations of "cruelty" the role of the wife as the moral arbiter of the home comes across clearly. Apparently, divorce was the ultimate sanction behind the role. Women not only believed in the role, but some applied the sanction as well.

That the character of divorce at the end of the 19th century reflected women's special moral role has further significance for the history of women and the family. Usually, in discussing the evolution of the conjugal family of the 19th century, historians have assumed that it was largely a middle-class phenomenon. And, as has been said already, the evidence that the working-class family accepted a similar conception of the family is not weighty. Yet an analysis of the social incidence of divorce suggests that whatever one learns about the conception of women's role in the family from an examination of divorce records applies with particular force to social groups *below* the middle class. For those were the groups that obtained most of the divorces.

In 1909 the Bureau of the Census published a table of some 226,000 divorces granted between 1886 and 1906, arranged according to the occupation of the husband. What is striking to anyone who believes that divorce in the late 19th century was primarily a middle-class remedy for a bad marriage is that one-quarter of the divorces were granted to people in personal service: barbers, domestic servants, laborers, watchmen, and policemen. One-fifth of the divorces were awarded to persons in trade, and another 22 per cent to those in manufacturing. By comparison it might be noted that 5.5 per cent of the divorces were made to professionals. That figure was higher than the proportion that group made up in the work force in 1900, but not by much. They constituted 3.9 per cent of the employed population.

Other more limited but more precise pieces of evidence also testify to the high proportion of working-class people among those obtaining divorces in the 19th century. Robert Griswold, in his as yet unpublished study of divorce records in the 1870s in California, has also shown that two-thirds of the petitions for divorce originated with people from the farm-laboring or working classes. In short, insofar as petitions for divorce reveal an acceptance of separate spheres and the special moral role for women, then that view or outlook was already being accepted on social levels below the middle class.

One further explanation for the upsurge in divorces at the end of the 19th century on into the 20th and, in fact, to our own day needs to be mentioned: the widening opportunities for women to earn a livelihood outside the home. It is difficult to believe that the divorce rate could have risen as it did in the United States, or in Europe, for that matter, unless means had become available for former wives to support themselves financially. Many divorced women in the 19th century depended upon friends or family to take them in. Some divorced women, of course, remarried, but most had to find jobs, just as any unmarried young woman or widow had to. To recognize the importance of the expanding economic opportunities of an industrializing and urbanizing society, however, is not the same as saying that those opportunities "caused" the upsurge in the divorce rate. Rather, those opportunities must be viewed as a necessary but not sufficient condition to explain the increase in divorces. The more active force, as already implied, was a new and higher expectation of what marriage could be and ought to be. These loftier expectations were particularly strong in women, for, though the 19th-century conjugal family constituted, on the whole, an improvement in the autonomy of women, it was only an early stage along the way to women's achievement of independence within the family.

Another change in the lives of women also helps to account for the increase in the divorce rate in the 20th century, though probably not in the 19th. That is the improved chances of life among both sexes, but particularly among women. Around the turn of the 20th century there was a striking improvement in the conditions of health and in the treatment and cure of diseases. This advance in medicine continued so that the number of people who lived into their sixties and even seventies increased dramatically. The effect upon the family was that now many women lived long enough to find flaws in their marriages—and so did men—and thus could seek an alternative through divorce. This explanation or condition, however, cannot be a significant part of the cause for the upsurge in divorces in the 19th century simply because the improvements in health conditions and new medical knowledge that did so much to allow more people to achieve old age did not occur until after 1900.

The improvement in health and medical knowledge in the 20th century had a special bearing on the meaning that divorce held for the family. To Americans at the beginning of the century as well as to many today, an increase in the divorce rate has usually been interpreted as a sign of increasing marital instability. And for those who saw the family as essential to the well-being of society that instability could only be deplored. Indeed, the great public debate about the causes of divorce in the first two decades of the 20th century stemmed from just that concern. During that debate, however, one thing was forgotten: in earlier years, when the divorce rate was lower, marriages were being disrupted to a much greater extent by the death of one of the spouses. Thus in 1860 almost thirty out of 1000 existing marriages in the United States were dissolved either by the death of a spouse or by divorce. In 1950, the comparable figure was slightly less—28.1 dissolutions per 1000 marriages. In 1860, however, divorces constituted only 4.1 per cent of the total, while in 1950, divorce accounted for one-third of the dissolutions. In the interim, the improvement in medicine and health had permitted spouses to live longer, thus allowing a longer time for dissatisfactions with a marriage to develop. Between 1850 and 1950 some 27 years were added to the average life expectancy of Americans (from 42 to 69 years). Of those years, seven were added between 1850 and 1900; the remaining twenty were added in the next half-century. As a result, between 1860 and 1910 the number of marriages broken by death of a spouse fell 13.4 per cent, but during a shorter period 1910–50, the fall was more than double—27.4 per cent.[47]

The conclusion that in a statistical sense the stability of marriages in the United States has not been seriously affected by the increase in the divorce rate because today there are fewer disruptions of marriage by death is, of course, only part of the story. It is an institutional, as opposed to a personal or affective, interpretation. Obviously a spouse who has lost a beloved partner through death has a quite different set of feelings at the disruption of his or her marriage from one whose marriage ends because of a common or individual dissatisfaction with the relationship. Despite this difference, to recognize that dissolution of marriage was as common in the middle of the 19th century as in the middle of the 20th throws a good deal of light on our understanding of what marriage meant to people in the 19th century. Even though divorces were considerably fewer then, there was still a burden of loss to be borne by surviving spouses and children. (Peter Uhlenberg has shown that 13 per cent of children born as late as 1870 and who lived until age 15 lost a father by death, and another 8 per cent lost a mother. For children born in 1950 the proportions were 3 and 1 per cent, respectively.) If today, one of the individual and social costs of divorce is that children are denied the presence of both parents, that situation occurred about as frequently in the 19th century because of the death of one parent. The rise in the divorce rate, until very recently, has not increased the total amount of family disruption, as usually supposed.

The upward trend in divorces can be interpreted even more positively, especially where women are concerned. An increase in divorces was a sign of higher expectations for marriage, and, in the light of the fact that most divorce suits were instituted by women, of a higher standard of marriage by women. If one of the central characteristics of a modern society is the independence of the individual, as the students of modernization assure us, then the improvement in the autonomy of women in the family is a part of that process. Certainly the thrust of women's role in the 19th-century conjugal family was to grant to the wife and mother increasing control over the material management and moral character of the home, including not only the children but the father as well. If the ideal family was one in which husband and wife were attached to one another because of love, mutual respect, and consideration, then it followed that when those qualities were no longer present the marriage ought to be dissolved. William O'Neill saw divorce as a necessary escape hatch from the high demands of the 19th-century family; another way of making the same point is to say that divorce allowed an endless pursuit of the perfect marriage by freeing the individual to consider his or her own needs and expectations.

The rise in the divorce rate was thus a part of the increasing individualization of women within the family. Men had always had divorce at their disposal, but in the 19th century it was a remedy increasingly available to women. And, as we have seen in regard to 19th-century divorce cases, men sought the remedy of marital dissolution when they found women being too independent; women petitioned for divorce when they found their desire for autonomy and self-identification within marriage thwarted by men's insistence upon their subordination to the family. In both cases, therefore, the issue was women's autonomy. If one recognizes that the struggle for women's autonomy within the family was really a struggle for power, then the rise in divorces suggests that women were pressing increasingly for a share of power. It was not that women rejected the home, for the vast majority of them certainly did not, not even those who petitioned for divorce. What an increasing proportion of women did insist upon, so the records of divorce tell us, was a recognition of their proper role in the home without undue subordination.

It can come as no surprise then to learn that the leading 19th-century feminists championed divorce. Susan B. Anthony, Elizabeth Cady Stanton, and Amelia Bloomer, to name only three before the Civil War, all spoke out in favor of easier divorce laws as a necessary condition for the improvement in women's position within marriage. In her usual forthright and incisive manner, Stanton acknowledged the centrality of the marriage relationship in feminism. "It is vain to look for the elevation of woman so long as she is degraded in marriage," she wrote Susan B. Anthony in 1853, just as the organized feminist movement was getting under way. "I say it is a sin, an outrage on our liberal feelings, to pretend that anything but deep fervent love and sympathy constitute marriage. The right idea of marriage is at the foundation of all reforms," she asserted. Throughout her long life as a feminist agitator Stanton argued for easier divorce laws in order to hold the institution of marriage to the high standard she believed it deserved. Even the more conservative Lucy Stone, who tended to shy away from controversial issues like marriage and sex because she feared they might distract the movement from its primary goals, wrote Stanton in 1859, "I wish you would call a convention to discuss divorce, marriage, infanticide, and their kindred subjects." [48]

Finally, of course, the rising curve in the divorce rate is yet another indication that by the opening of the 20th century the principal characteristics of the modern American family were already present. For the United States has continued to have the highest ratio of divorces to married couples of any modern nation. Even Japan's rate is now below that of the

United States. Since World War II the American ratio has been double that of Japan, almost four times that of Great Britain or Canada, and more than three times that of France. Only Sweden's rate of 4.9 divorces per 1000 married couples came close to the American figure of 9.2 in 1960.[49]

The continuation of a high divorce rate throughout the 20th century does not appear to be related to a fundamental dissatisfaction with the institution of marriage as such. In fact, marriage has grown in popularity over the years. It is true that at the end of the 19th century, as the divorce rate rose sharply, an increasing proportion of women did not marry. But by the opening of the 20th century the divorce rate continued its rise, while the proportion of women who remained single began to fall. In the 1970s marriage is more popular than it ever has been, if measured by the number of people who do not try it. As we saw earlier, the proportion of people who have reached the age of 50 without marrying at all is now at the lowest point in the history of U.S. marital statistics. Remarriage rates are at their long-term high, also showing that the institution as such is hardly under attack. Instead, Americans have simply set higher (or more fickle) standards for themselves and their mates within marriage. When those standards are not met, they get divorced and try again.

Finally, we might ask, is there any connection between the fall in the proportion of single women and the continued rise in divorce? One plausible speculation is that, once it became clear that there was an escape from marriage in the shape of divorce, many women who may have been predisposed to shun marriage because they perceived it as too restrictive and too permanent may then have begun to find it acceptable. As a result, so the argument would go, the proportion of women who elected to remain single fell. Improved reliability of and knowledge about birth-control techniques by the early years of the 20th century would have had a similar effect. With control over fertility more likely, women in the 20th century would have less reason to avoid marriage than in previous times. Such connections are consistent with the demographic evidence that we have, but that is all one can say about them. In any event, we shall return to the question of the nature of marriage in 20th-century America in Chapter XVIII, where the relationship of women, work, and the future of the family is examined more fully.

Though in the course of the 19th century some women challenged the family by refusing, or at least failing, to start a family at all, and others sought to expand their autonomy by disrupting an unsatisfactory marriage, the great majority of American women stayed within the bounds of family. But that did not mean women were without influence over its nature. Indeed, as the next chapter seeks to show, there is good reason to see women as central to a major alteration in the structure of the American family during the 19th century.

VIII

Women in the Making
of the Demographic Transition

In the first chapter, it was observed that one of the signs of the emergence of the modern family in the early 19th century was a decline in the size of families. This shift from large families to small, which occurs dramatically within the 19th century, demographers call "the demographic transition."

The existence of this drop in the birth rate, of course, is not news. The earliest historians of colonial America and of the family in the United States noted the shift long ago. More recently, however, students of the colonial family have seriously modified the older views, and these modifications are necessary to know if we are to appreciate the nature of the demographic transition in the early 19th century.

The old view argued that families were virtually as large as biology would allow: historians referred to families with fifteen, twenty, and even twenty-five children. Often these high figures were taken to be averages or common family sizes. The recent, more precise studies of colonial towns and communities now make clear that such high numbers of children were quite unusual. In early 17th-century Andover, Massachusetts, for instance, four-fifths of the families had fewer than twelve children; in Bristol, Massachusetts, in 1689 over 80 per cent of the families had fewer than six children. The average number of children per family in Andover in the late 17th century was 8.1.

Demographers, it should be said, make a distinction between average size of families at one point in time and average size of completed families—that is, at the time the mother reaches menopause (age 45) or dies. From the standpoint of women, the second measure—completed family—

is the more significant, since it tells us how many children the average woman would bear in her lifetime. For Andover at the end of the century the average number of children for completed families was 8.7, with 7.2 surviving to age 21. This rather high survival rate was not unusual for 17th-century New England, where conditions of life were much better than in contemporary Europe. A study of families in Plymouth colony in the 17th century reported a similarly high proportion of survivors into adulthood. Another study for the colonial Massachusetts town of Hingham counted 7.8 children per family surviving to adulthood.

Although the average number of children in 17th-century families was lower than either the maximum possible biologically or what tradition has often told us, it, nonetheless, was noticeably higher than in the average contemporary European family. In one village in late 18th-century France, for instance, the average number of children was 5.2 per family, while in another it was as low as 4.0. About five children per family was the average in Bavaria and in England. Even when the average sizes of households, as opposed to family, are compared, the American colonial household was still conspicuously larger than the contemporaneous English or Continental one. Peter Laslett, the prime student of families in pre-industrial England, has shown that on the average an English family in the 17th and 18th centuries consisted of 4.75 persons. The first United States census in 1790 recorded that the average size of household was 5.7 persons, or one person larger than the average English household of the time.[1]

Despite the larger size of the American household, by the second half of the 18th century the number of children in American families had begun to decline. A study of Rhode Island families living in both cities and farming areas showed that decade after decade from the time of the Revolution to the end of the century there was a steady fall in the average size of families. Another exploration of family size in fifteen towns in Massachusetts and Connecticut before and after 1740 showed a marked decline in average number of births per family. In Gloucester, for example, the births fell from 6.73 for women married before 1740 to 4.57 children for those marrying after that date. In Salisbury, Connecticut, the drop was from 7.86 to 5.78 children. Finally, an analysis of some 271 Quaker families in the late 18th century reinforces the impression that the fall in the average size of families first became conspicuous soon after the Revolution. Robert Wells, the author of the study, grouped the families into three periods according to when the wives were born: pre-Revolutionary or by 1730; Revolutionary or between 1731 and 1755; and finally post-Revolutionary or after 1755. As might be anticipated from the figures already cited, there was a noticeable drop in the average number of children per family as the century advanced. The sharper drop, however, occurred with the middle or Revolutionary era group, those women born between 1731 and 1755. The average number of children per family fell from 6.68 for the pre-Revolutionary group to 5.67 for the second, and then down to 5.02 for the third. Since the change from the first to the second group is, on the average, one child, it would seem that by the last quarter of the 18th century these Quaker women were reducing significantly their number of children.[2]

Whether this Quaker study and the other measures of a decline in fertility in the course of the 18th century are representative of the United States as a whole is not yet known for sure. On the other hand, there is little reason to think that these studies are unrepresentative in more than detail. It would seem, in short, that by the end of the 18th century, fertility was already receding from the high levels of the 17th century.

Despite this decine, however, at the opening of the 19th century the birth rate of the United States was still, as two leading demographers have observed, "markedly higher than that ever recorded for any European country." The rate, they added, "is equalled in reliably recorded data only by such unusually fertile populations as the Hutterites and the inhabitants of the Cocos-Keeling Islands." From that relatively high beginning for 19th-century birth rates, the story thereafter was one of uninterrupted and profound decline. The fall began within the first decade of the century; by the 1850s the birth rate of the United States was below that of Hungary; by 1870 it was lower than Austria's; and by 1880 less than Italy's and Spain's. By then the rate in the United States was equal to that of Britain and nearly as low as Sweden's. As early as 1850, the American birth rate differed from that of almost all European countries in that it was falling while most of theirs were stable. Among European countries in the middle of the 19th century, only France resembled the United States in having a steady decline. France's birth rate had been falling, virtually without interruption, since about 1770.[3]

Demographers measure a nation's fertility in several ways. The crudest is the birth rate, which is simply the total number of births divided by the population. Such a gross figure, however, can give us a distorted picture of what is happening to fertility, since the rate is affected by changes in the proportion of women of childbearing ages in the population. If, for example, all old people were killed off by a disease, the next year the birth rate would rise sharply even though women of childbearing age give birth to the same number of children as in the previous year. This is so because the number of people in the total population would have gone down without having any comparable effect upon the number of children born. In a country like the United States, where immigration introduced some age groups more frequently than others, a simple birth rate does not provide an accurate comparison between periods. A better indicator is what demographers call the total fertility rate, which is the average number of children borne by a woman by the time she reaches menopause. The resulting figure would thus be comparable from period to period, since the same base—women between ages 14 and 45—would be used. Therefore fertility would be measured regardless of what changes had taken place in the mix of ages in the total population. When this measure of fertility is used, it becomes evident that the fertility of white women in the United States fell 50 per cent between 1800 and 1900. In specific numbers the rate fell from 7.04 in 1800 to 3.56 in 1900. (All figures, incidentally, on birth and fertility rates are for the white population, since there are no comparably reliable data in the 19th century for blacks.)

This decline in fertility is certainly the single most important fact about women and the family in American history. The decline since the 19th century, such as between 1900 and 1936, was sharper—a fall of 41 per cent in 36 years—but at no time has the fall been as deep as in the 19th century. Since 1940, of course, fertility actually increased, as we know from the baby boom of the 1940s and 1950s. In 1960, for example, the rate was almost as high as it had been at the end of the 19th century. Since 1970, the rate has begun another precipitous fall.

Simply because the decline during the last century was so deep and so steady, explanations have been looked for. Perhaps the one most commonly advanced as well as the most obvious is that the decline resulted from the onset of urbanization and industrialization. And it is true that urban populations generally have a lower birth rate than rural or farm populations. But however valid the differences in the birth rates of urban and rural people may be in general, in this particular case they alone cannot account for the general decline in birth rates, for the fall in fertility precedes any significant urbanization or industrialization in the United States. In 1850 the United States was only entering upon its life as an industrial society; about 80 per cent of the population lived in rural areas. Yet at that date fertility had fallen from 7.04 children per woman of fertile age in 1800 to 5.42, or a drop of 23 per cent.[4] With a drop of such magnitude while the great majority of the population was still living on farms, fertility must have been falling significantly among rural as well as urban people.

In Europe, too, the fall in fertility often antedated the onset of urbanization and industrialization. The French birth rate, as we have seen already, began its fall even before the Revolution of 1789, long before industrialization had begun there. A decline, though one not as precipitous as that in the United States, occurred during the 19th century in Hungary and Spain, though neither of those countries was industrializing or urbanizing at that time. In fact, even in Britain the drop in fertility does not occur until decades after the onset of industrialization and rapid urbanization.

What evidence we have from local areas or regions of the United States also calls into question the argument that urbanization was the principal cause of the decline. A close demographic analysis of families in counties of southern Michigan between 1850 and 1880 revealed that the decline in the size of households in rural areas was actually more precipitous than for urban and small-town families. (The rural households were larger to begin with, to be sure, but that does not weaken the point that a significant decline in fertility took place over the thirty years.) A study of New York state between 1840 and 1875 found rural birth rates falling faster than urban, and other studies of newly settled regions revealed similar declines in fertility, contrary to the urbanization explanation.[5]

If the fall in fertility, especially that before 1860, cannot be accounted for by reference to the well-known influences of urbanization and industrialization, what other explanations are there? Among economic demographers, perhaps the most widely accepted is that advanced by Yasukichi Yasuba, who argued in a book published in 1961 that the cause of the decline was the lack of available arable land. Yasuba showed that the number of persons per 1000 acres of arable land correlated negatively with white birth rates between 1800 and 1860. That is to say, the higher the number of persons per 1000 acres of arable land, the lower the birth rate. The statistical measures were quite high, running from $-.663$ in 1800 to $-.802$ in 1820 and then to $-.675$ in 1840, and to $-.526$ in 1860, on a scale in which 1.00 is perfect correlation. The negative sign means that the relationship is inverse, so that a perfect negative correlation of 1.00 denotes that an *increase* in the concentration of population on the land would be accompanied by an equal *fall* in the birth rate. All of the measures ("coefficients") of negative correlation he found between availability of land and birth rates are considerably stronger (higher) than between urban population and birth rates for the same years.

Yasuba's explanation of the way in which the lack of arable land influenced the birth rate assumed that the principal means used to bring down the birth rate was postponement or rejection of marriage by men. In that way fewer children would be born because a woman's years of childbearing within marriage would be reduced. And, of course, if fewer men married that would have meant fewer women gave birth to children. The reason men were postponing marriage or rejecting it entirely, according to Yasuba's reasoning, was that with the land filling up they had lower expectations of earning sufficient income to support a family.

A more detailed study of the question was completed in 1972 by Colin Forster and G. S. L. Tucker. This time the relationship between arable land and the fall in fertility was examined within counties, rather than states, and some of the counties were in the older portion of the country, where it might be thought urban influences would be stronger than availability of arable land. But, once again, the relationship that Yasuba found turned up in the new study. Not until at least 1860, Yasuba and then Forster and Tucker showed, was there any significant relationship between industrialization or urbanization and the reduction in births. In fact, Forster and Tucker estimated that about 75 per cent of the national fall in fertility between 1810 and 1860 derived from the decline in rural areas alone; only about 13 per cent, they estimated, was accounted for by a fall in urban fertility; the rest resulted from the shift from rural to urban areas.

Both studies, it should be noted, have relied upon aggregative census data gathered by states or counties. As a result they were not able to segregate individual farm families from urban and town families. Preliminary work by Richard Easterlin in 1977 has remedied this deficiency by a detailed examination of some 21,000 rural households, mostly of white persons, drawn from the manuscript census for 1860 for the northern part of the United States.[6] Although Easterlin carefully checked other possible explanations for the fall in rural fertility, none fitted so well as the lack of arable land. In short, in this more detailed study, the explanation for the decline in births on farms seemed to be that farm men were shaping their decisions about marriage and family size around their prospects for getting land.

Like Yasuba, Easterlin concluded that the way family size was reduced was by postponement of marriage and by the reduction in the number of women marrying. But because Easterlin's information was more detailed and specific than that of previous studies, he was able to show that women in the more settled areas not only married later, thus reducing their number of childbearing years, but also stopped having children earlier. He showed this by comparing the median age of wives in their thirties at most recent birth for the area he designated as most fertile (western) with those he designated as least fertile (eastern). The median age of wives in the two areas is the same, but the median age of women at most recent birth differed to the extent of 1.5 years; for women in their forties the difference was 2 years. Thus he concluded that women in the eastern, or least fertile areas, were curtailing births earlier than women in the western regions. Since what he was measuring here was fertility over discrete decades and not the whole of a marriage, a later age of marriage could not account for the difference in fertility. Some form of deliberate birth control must have been used. Although Easterlin certainly recognized the point, he did not explore the birth-control methods that might have been used, and this is not yet the place to do so. But he did suggest two methods which he designated "the most likely candidates": *coitus interruptus* and abortion.

One further observation might be made here about Easterlin's argument. The method by which births are curtailed can reveal which sex was primarily responsible for the reduction. Thus, if a fall in births resulted from a later date of marriages, it would seem that men were principally responsible, for they were usually the persons who initiated marriage. Social customs were such then, as they are today, that a woman had to be asked; ordinarily she did not propose. Only if one supposed, rather unrealistically, that women were refusing early marriage, can women be the primary determiners of family size through the postponement of marriage. Easterlin's argument, of course, assumed that men were determining the matter, for it was their inability to make a good living because of the relative lack of land that caused them to postpone marriage.

On the other hand, if fertility was being limited through some kind of birth control, as Easterlin suggested, then it seemed likely that women might have had very much to say about it. Unfortunately Easterlin was apparently not interested in distinguishing between the roles of the sexes in this regard, for he loosely lumped together as possible methods of birth control one that was clearly a woman's means and one that was clearly a man's. *Coitus interruptus* obviously required the acquiescence, not to say active cooperation, of the male. Abortion, on the other hand, was clearly a woman's means, for it can be employed even against the will of the male. We shall return later to this distinction between women's and men's methods, for it offers a clue as to responsibility for the decline in fertility during the 19th century.

For the moment, however, let us continue to explore possible explanations, as opposed to means, for the decline in births in rural regions prior to 1860. As Easterlin candidly admits, the motivation behind the correlation between lack of availability of arable land and the decline in births is not at all clear. He examined several alternative explanations, such as that children needed to be educated, or that increased numbers of aged people in the household had to be supported, or that child labor opportunities declined in the older regions. But none of these possible explanations worked when tested against the data for the new and the old areas. There simply are no significant differences between the areas. Only the availability of land correlated with high fertility. Yet the question persists: How did the lack of land cause couples to decide to have fewer children? After all, there was plenty of vacant land farther west during these years, as the division of his households into lowest fertility (eastern) and highest fertility (western) reminds us. The answer Easterlin advanced with some reluctance was that parents wanted their children to settle nearby, but they did not want to subdivide their land. Hence if a son wanted to marry he had to buy land near home which was more expensive than land available to him in the West, so he married late or cut back on the number of his children. Easterlin assumed that, if the parents had not been holding the children nearby, the sons would have naturally moved to the cheaper lands in the West or to more recently settled regions.

There is no direct documentary evidence to support this argument, and one has the feeling that it was derived principally from the fact that the decline in births correlates with the decline in the availability of land. Still, Easterlin's explanation has the merit of being consistent with what we have seen about the nature of the 19th-century family on an individual basis. In the chapter on the family it was noted that the close-knit, companionate nuclear family became the norm of American familial life, particularly of the middle class, which would include commercial farmers. From what we know of the internal relationships in the middle-class family of the mid-19th century, parents would indeed have been sorry to see their children move away, just as the children would have been reluctant to move away. If Easterlin's surmise is correct, then by 1860 that closeness within the family was present among farm families of the North as well as among the largely urban middle-class families whose correspondence we analyzed in earlier chapters.

Economic demographers like Easterlin are especially interested to find some material or at least measurable force to account for the decline in birth rates. The relationship between availability of arable land and births can be studied from this point of view because both variables have been counted in the census. Yet even economic demographers recognize that behind every measurable sign of behavior lies an intangible and perhaps unmeasurable human motive or purpose. And it is purposes that move people. By concentrating upon the actual measurable factor, we may overlook the real or at least the motivational force behind the behavior. Unfortunately, motivation is considerably more difficult to ascertain than the measurement of certain types of behavior or kinds of resources.

Some historians explain the changes in family behavior in these years by invoking the conception of modernization. This rather amorphously defined term is more a description of changes than an explanation, for it means that during these years certain behavioral patterns emerged that are characteristic of modern times. But noting such similarities does not explain why the changes came about at the time they did; no motive or causal force behind the changes is identified. Despite this explanatory weakness, modernization as a conception does have the merit of calling our attention to alterations in the values that lie behind the changes in behavior.

Historical demographer Robert V. Wells has suggested that the explanation for the shifts in fertility between the 18th and 19th centuries should be sought in a shift in values rather than in new techniques, or in social and economic developments. In short, he asked, why do people decide to limit the size of their families, regardless of their social and economic conditions? Is it not possible that they may want to achieve something less tangible than an improved standard of living? [7] This approach to the subject is not unlike Easterlin's point that behind the desire to curtail births because of the dearth of arable land was the desire to remain close to parents. Sons had to be willing to have smaller families so that they could afford to stay near their parents. But the causal motivation for the curtailment of children was not the high cost of land but the desire to remain close to parents. Wells's explanation for the reduction in size of family at the opening years of the 19th century is that families began to believe that they could shape their lives and control their future as they could not earlier. One way that men and women expressed this new concern was to seek deliberately to limit the number of their offspring. Other historians have called this kind of decisive and foresighted act a sign of modernization.

But can the desire and attempt to limit offspring be taken as an indication of modernity? When we look at the recent studies of family history in pre-industrial England, for example, it becomes clear that most men and women have sought to control their fertility long before the early 19th century. Indeed, Norman E. Himes, the well-known historian of contraception, along with most modern demographers, has contended that one of the constants of human history is that families have always wanted to limit fertility. No period of Western history has failed to record significant efforts and some success in limiting offspring.

Once that point is accepted, the inquiry can proceed in only one of two directions. One is to recognize that, though people may have always been interested in controlling fertility, they have not always been uniformly, or even especially, successful until very recently. Therefore, an important consideration in asking why families declined in size in the 19th century as compared with the 18th is whether or not the techniques or methods of contraception or birth control improved. As we shall see in the next chapter, the improvements in technique cannot be the primary explanation simply because there were no significant innovations in methods, though there were some improvements and better communication. There was, for instance, no important new contraceptive device in the 19th century that is comparable in ease of use and efficiency to the anovulant pill of our own day. Technique, in short, cannot give us the answer; motivation or purpose remains the key, for that alone can account for why and how couples made so much more effective use of the available techniques than did the people of the 18th century.

The second route to follow, then, is to ask whether there may have been a change or intensification of the reasons for practicing birth control. When the question is posed in that form, the problem, at least in regard to the United States, is more sharply defined. What new motives or purposes might have arisen at the end of the 18th century?

Although it must be conceded at the outset that we know pathetically little about the motives behind the birth-control practices in pre-industrial societies, demographers generally believe that limitation on food supply or subsistence has played a significant part. Certainly infanticide is widely recognized as a response to inadequate food supply. It follows, therefore, that in societies like those of western Europe, where deeply held religious principles precluded infanticide, limitations on births would be sought as a substitute. This supposition is strengthened when it is recognized that throughout the colonial years the birth rate of Americans far exceeded anything known in Europe. Twenty years before the Declaration of Independence Benjamin Franklin wrote a famous essay on population in which he pointed to the extraordinary high population growth rate in the English colonies, an increase he attributed to the higher standard of living or higher level of subsistence for the mass of people in North America. English parson Thomas Malthus built his theory that population tended to press against the means of subsistence from his knowledge of the high birth rates in the English colonies. Again, the rapid population growth, estimated by Malthus to be equal to a doubling of the population every twenty-five years, was attributed to the availability of land resources. Eventually, Malthus predicted, woman's fecundity would catch up with man's ability to produce food. These contemporary recognitions of the high birth rate of colonial Americans have been amply confirmed, as we have seen, by modern demographic studies.

What we now know, too, is that population came under control or was at least significantly limited in its growth long before the sanction of inadequate subsistence, to which Malthus pointed, came into play. If in pre-industrial Europe one of the principal reasons population control was crucial was the limits on the food supply, in America that motive could not have been significant. Thus, limits on subsistence cannot be the reason why Americans began to reduce the size of their families by the opening years of the 19th century.

The reasons why individual families sought to control their fertility in the 19th century are numerous, but, unlike those who undertook comparable efforts in earlier centuries, the reasons do not have to be inferred. People were quite willing and able to commit their purposes to paper. Foremost among the reasons was the simple fact that one particular group of people—a whole sex, in fact—had a special interest in limiting the number of children since they bore the brunt of their birth, nurturance, and rearing. Surely it is no accident that the movement to limit the size of families coincided with the emergence of a new kind of family in which women occupied a special position and in which children were perceived as different from adults and in need of special and loving care. Yet phrasing the matter in such bald and perhaps prosaic terms distorts or obscures the subtleties of historical reality and the dialectical character of the several forces at work.

Perhaps a more precise way of phrasing the point is to say that as women became more conscious of themselves as individuals, they also sought to control their fertility. They may have wanted to do that before, but generally could not, given their social, economic, and political subordination. Philippe Ariès, for example, cites several instances, drawn from the 16th and 17th centuries, wherein women's personal interest in contraception was clearly evident. Their motives, Ariès pointedly observed, were not merely to improve the standard of living of the family but to avoid having too many children—period.[8] In short, women have always had a reason for limiting children that men have not, but that reason could motivate behavior on a large scale only when women became self-conscious about themselves as individuals—that is, when they began to see themselves as beings separate from their husbands and their families. This was the mental attitude that underlay what in earlier chapters we have called the drive for autonomy for women within the family. Daniel Scott Smith has called it domestic feminism. Robert Wells would see it as a manifestation of modernization.

The idea of individualism in the West has a long history, stretching far back before the 17th century and certainly drawing upon the ideology and social changes symbolized by the Renaissance, Reformation, and the expansion of a capitalist economy. John Locke and Adam Smith celebrated the principles of individual rights and actions, but the individuals they had in mind were men. On the whole women were not then thought of as anything other than supportive assistants—necessary to be sure, but not individuals in their own right. The individual as a conception in Western thought has always assumed that behind each man—that is, each individual—was a family. But the members of that family were not individuals, except the man, who was by law and custom its head. Historian Natalie Zemon Davis has observed that some historians like to describe the changes through which Europe passed from the medieval to early modern times as a shift from Tribal Brotherhood to Universal Otherhood. But, she cogently noted, "Tribal Brothers and Universal Others were not isolated individuals, but family units governed by patriarchal fathers."[9]

For reasons that are still quite unclear, toward the end of the 18th century, individualism, consideration of one's own interest, began to be taken up by women. At bottom, it asserted or assumed that women, like men, had interests and lives that were separate and different in purpose from those of other members of a family.

In the beginning, as might be anticipated, the conception of individualism for women was partial and tentative, as a reading of Mary Wollstonecraft's *Vindication of the Rights of Women* (1792) makes plain when its argument is compared with a modern feminist outlook. Similarly, Abigail Adams's famous admonition to her husband John in the early days of the American Revolution to "remember the ladies" when the new government's laws were being written was far from a feminist plea. "Do not put such unlimited power into the hands of the Husbands," she urged. "Remember all Men would be tyrants if they could. . . . Why then, not put it out of the power of the vicious and the lawless to use us with cruelty and indignity with impunity. . . . Regard us then as Beings placed by providence under your protection and, in immitation of the Supreme Being, make use of that power only for our happiness." [10] This is no assertion of women's rights as equal participants in the world, or politics, or the economy. Rather than denying in any way wifehood or motherhood as the primary role of women, Abigail Adams asked merely for an improvement in the traditional relationship with husbands. When, seventy years later, some women carried the implications of individualism for women to their logical conclusions, as in the Seneca Falls Declaration of Rights of Women in 1848, the mass of American women were unwilling to follow that lead. For in that Declaration all the individualistic rights of men were extended to women, including legal, economic, and political equality. Ultimately, of course, these aims would become the goals not only of radical feminists but of most women. In the context of 19th-century society and its level of consciousness, however, those aims of 1848 were premature. Yet that prematurity ought not to hide from us the recognition that women's reach for autonomy within the family in the 19th century was an important milestone on the road to full equality.

Another sign of the movement toward autonomy by women at the end of the 18th century was the willingness of some men to argue for the individuality or equal rights of women, even though, by the nature of things, men were the oppressors. In America, Charles Brockden Brown's *Alcuin* (1798) was a conspicuous example of an incipient feminist ideology, while, in England, William Godwin offered another defense of women's individualism. Even in remote Königsberg, Prussia, the Mayor, Theodore von Hippel, published a defense of women's civil equality in 1794 that was sufficiently widely known to come under attack. By the middle of the 19th century more men had taken up the cause, with John Stuart Mill the acknowledged intellectual leader with his famous tract *The Subjection of Woman* (1869). As Richard Evans has shrewdly noted, Mill's book was not so much a timeless defense of truth as a direct application to women of

Mill's belief in the individual. For if individualism was right for men, as Mill certainly believed, then it of right ought to be applied to women, too.

The intention here is not to summarize the rise of a feminist ideology but to suggest the implications of that rise for the history of the family. For too long the history of the family has been interpreted as a masculine response to changing cultural and economic circumstances. There is, of course, no denying that men's role in shaping and sustaining the family is important, but, at least over the last two centuries, it has most probably been secondary to that of women. One of the arguments of this book is that the history of the family is best understood by recognizing that changes in the role of women—particularly in what has been called the extension of individualism to women—the awakening to self—have been at the root of that history. As women have changed in their relations to men and children, the family has been altered. For in the end that *is* the family: a congeries of relationships among parents and their children. But instead of considering these alterations merely as responses to exogenous or outside forces, they also need to be acknowledged as flowing from changes in women's self-perception.

It is not difficult to document how and why these changes in women's role came about, for women have not been silent about their situation or their wish to change it. The truly difficult task is to explain why women's sense of individualism emerged when it did. After all, women's subordination to the family in general and to men in particular is an ancient story. Given the long history of the growth of individualism in Western thought, why was that conception of human capability and freedom extended to women only toward the end of the 18th century?

As already observed, at this stage in our understanding of the history of women and the family the answer must be not only tentative but largely speculative. The question has only begun to be canvassed. Yet some of the broad forces in operation can be adumbrated. Certainly Protestantism, particularly Calvinism (Puritanism in England and America), was among the crucial social and intellectual forces, for the Puritans emphasized the family and, most important, the woman's right to respect and affection within it. The dissolution of marriage, which Protestantism introduced, for example, was permitted not only to men, but also, at least theoretically, to women because both sexes had been parties to the contract that was the Puritan definition of marriage.

Considerably more influential was the cluster of ideas and practices that we call, for convenience, the 18th-century Enlightenment. During the middle years of the 18th century the ideas of equality and individualism received a wide and attentive hearing, even though, admittedly, women were not immediately or usually included in such concepts by the leading thinkers. For the first time, during those years, the venerable institution of slavery came under direct and continuous attack. Though the institution would last well into the 19th century, the appeal to freedom for a subordinate class on which the attack rested quickly struck a responsive chord in both the Old World and the New. A similarly positive response was evoked by Adam Smith's demonstration that individual self-interest, contrary to what generations of earlier thinkers had insisted, worked to the enrichment and advancement of society. Individualism, in the developing market economy of late 18th-century Europe and America, was no longer to be equated with mere selfishness.

With freedom and individualism in the air, it is not surprising that those concepts were also applied to women or were taken up by them on their own. Surely it is no mere accident that in the French Revolution, that flowering of the Enlightenment, demands for women's rights were heard with a collective power unknown before in Europe. No fewer than thirty-three of the *cahiers* of complaints on the eve of the Revolution in France called for greater educational opportunities for women. At revolutionary meetings in 1789 and after, women demanded expansion of their rights as individuals. Richard Evans has written that during the French Revolution women for the "first time . . . actually tried to band together to fight for their rights." [11] More formal demands for women's rights appeared in print at the end of the 18th century as we have noted already in the writings of Mary Wollstonecraft, Charles Brockden Brown, and others. The American Revolution itself, with its emphasis upon personal or individual rights, most of which derived from the Englightenment's arsenal of ideas, inevitably sparked new thoughts about women's role, as Abigail Adams's letter to her husband showed.

Sometimes the relative scarcity of women in America in the colonial years has been cited as a more specific cause for the advanced position of women in this country. The assumption has been that when women were scarce, as they tended to be in newly settled colonial America, their leverage in dealing with men was thereby enhanced. Armed with that advantage, they could then press more successfully for greater autonomy inside and outside the family. And it is true that both the laws of the English colonies and the many observations of foreign travelers testified that women did indeed enjoy greater freedom and respect in America than in contemporary Europe. A recent comparative study of women in 17th-century America and England, for example, concluded that "throughout her history, American woman has enjoyed a more attractive position in society than her English counterpart of whatever class. Although all the gains of the seventeenth century were not maintained, this superiority, like so many other lasting American characteristics, was founded during the early generations of the New World." [12]

Tempting as the newness or emptiness of the land in America may be as a part of the explanation for the extension of individualism to women, it requires serious qualification. In other areas of the New World, where the land was equally empty and women were even scarcer, there was no comparable extension of individualism to women. In neither the French nor the Iberian colonies in the New World did women's position improve, as it clearly did in the English colonies. Women's situations in the New World colonies of the various European nations were, in several ways, not comparable at all. Englishmen came to America in families, while Spaniards and Portuguese did not, for the most part. Native Indian and slave Negro women were used much more frequently and much earlier as concubines or sexual companions in the Iberian colonies than in the English colonies of North America. But it is precisely these differences in the situations of women in the New World colonies that make it dubious to ascribe to the empty land, which was characteristic of all of them, a major influence on the development of greater individualism for women in the English colonies.

Much more important than the newness of the land was the corpus of ideas about women, family, and marriage—the cultural baggage, so to speak—which the various European peoples brought with them. What the new land did, then, was to provide a fresh slate on which the ideas of the mother culture could be writ out in new ways or with new terms, or perhaps even be developed into an outlook and practice only implicit in the Old World. This seems to have been what happened in the English colonies. We know, for example, that in the early 17th century, when the English colonies in North America were just being settled, women in England were pressing for increased rights and prerogatives in society and in the family. When these women and the men with whom they were contending came to America, the newness of the society and the scarcity of women gave women fresh opportunity and leverage in challenging the traditional conception of their role.

One ought not push the argument too hard, for obviously the change was a slow one, consuming over a century before its outlines became clear. But the contrast between the relatively advanced position of women in the English 18th-century colonies and the restricted, even oppressed position of women in Portuguese and Spanish colonies should cause us to doubt that empty land in itself had much independent social influence anywhere in the New World. It was as a condition, rather than as a cause, that the openness of the New World made its contribution to the advancement of the idea that women, too, merited autonomy or individuality.

Women's achievement of a sense of individualism, in short, was complex in its development. It cannot be attributed merely to economic conditions in the New World nor only to the impact of ideas, though all played their parts. Moreover, the process has to be seen as dialectical, an interacting of forces and interests. It would be incomplete to explain the growth of individualism among women as simply the result of women's assertion of self-interest. The interaction between men and women needs to be recognized as well. It was, after all, in the interests of men to make their wives—the mothers of their children, as well as their helpmates in the family—content or reasonably satisfied, and thus to respond to their interests. At the same time, women found it possible to assert their self-interest in circumstances in America that were more favorable to that assertion than those in Europe.

Few, if any, men or women envisioned at the outset, or even along the way, the full implications of individualism or a consciousness of self for women. The gains were usually small, the implications remote, and the intentions limited. Furthermore, with each advancement of the idea there were those of both sexes who warned that the integrity of the family, or society, or perhaps civilization itself was put at risk by the idea that women were individuals, with interests that might be different from men's or the family's. And although in every case in the past these prophecies of disaster have proved false, neither the prophecies nor the fears that generate them have died out. For the family and woman's relationship to it are still undergoing change. No social changes seem so threatening as those that take place within the family because the family has been for so long the ultimate sanctuary of men and women. We will return to this large and complicated question of the future of the family in historical perspective in the last chapter when we will be in a better position to take it on. Now we return to the question of family limitation, the issue which caused the recognition that women's growing awareness of their self-interest was at the root of the decline in births during the 19th century.

It will be recalled that demographers have been able to demonstrate a high correlation between density of population on arable land and the fall in birth rates. What is the connection, if any, between this finding and the rise in women's self-consciousness as an explanation for the decline in births? On the surface there does not seem to be much of a connection. Yet, if the density of settlement is taken as a surrogate for a concentration of women, and the further assumption is made that the assertion of individuality by women is encouraged by the presence of other women, then the rise in density would be consistent with an increase in women's sense of confidence to assert themselves within the family. Obviously only with some rather broad assumptions can the connection be made at all, but at least the assumptions are consistent with what we know about the way subordinated persons are encouraged to assert themselves. And the argument does suggest that the two explanations, that offered here and that offered by economic demographers, are not totally irrelevant to one another.

There are less tenuous reasons for seeing women as important in bringing about the decline in the birth rate. As mentioned earlier, women certainly have a personal interest in limiting children that men do not: they are not only the bearers but the rearers of children. Thus when there is a reduction in fertility, just as when there is an increase in births as happened in the 1940s and 1950s, it can be assumed that women preferred it that way. This is not to say that men have not also had an interest in controlling fertility. Of course, they have. But their interest is not sex-linked, as women's always has been. As social beings women have all the interest men have, but, in addition, they have their own interest as women; they are the bearers and nurturers of children.

In the 19th century this special interest of women in limiting births was clearly recognized by advocates of birth control. As Dr. George Napheys wrote in his widely circulated advice book for married couples, it was quite possible that some women might have too many children. After all, he pointedly added, even farmers limited the number of calves their cows bear. In 1864, Dr. Edward Bliss Foote concluded in the course of defending birth control that "excessive child-bearing may be truthfully said to be the bane of general society" because it weakens females and produces defective children. "What is the happiness for a female," wrote Dr. J. Soule in 1856 in his *Science of Reproduction and Reproductive Control,* when "she is in fear every moment of her life, of having to undergo the misery and suffering attendant upon giving birth" to children in rapid succession? Another supporter of birth control wrote in 1855 that if women knew childbirth could be controlled "with what pleasure they could yield themselves in the sexual embrace, if they could only feel that they were no longer the mere victims of fatality." Too many wives, he continued extravagantly, "generally regard marriage as a curse to their sex, and feel that their existence is sacrificed to gratify a passion in the other sex; while their only reward is a burden of cares, crushing them down to an early grave!" And Charles Knowlton, one of the earliest writers on contraception, in the 1830s gave as one of the advantages of his method of contraception that "it is in the hands of the female." In short, the fall in the birth rate during the 19th century needs to be viewed as important a measure of women's improving status as the proportion or number of women who worked outside the home.[13]

Limiting the size of the family was not only advantageous to women, it was also probably advantageous to American society at large. We now know that the nuclear family antedated the onset of industrialization, even in England, and thus was not its product. But a close-knit family, held together by ties of affection, is quite advantageous in a complex, mobile, and often personally threatening industrial society. Indeed, there is reason to believe that the refuge of the affective or companionate family may well have made early industrialization endurable for many individuals. In the face of the alienation, impersonality, and atomistic individualism of modern industrial society, the family was indeed a welcome refuge. It is therefore quite plausible that the modern family may have been a prerequisite for the advance of industrialism even as it was further shaped by those economic changes. In that way, the evolution of the modern American family in the course of the first decades of the 19th century had social and economic consequences stretching far beyond the realm of the home. It helped to create the economic and social structure of an industrial America.[14]

The steady decline in fertility through the 19th century certainly would lead one to conclude that some kind of birth control was being exercised, but the public expressions on the subject lead to precisely the opposite conclusion. For throughout the century the idea of interfering in any way with the natural results of sexual intercourse was vehemently and persistently attacked. Medical doctors, for example, blamed all sorts of illnesses on attempts to prevent conception. One physician cited no fewer than 128 cases he had investigated of sterility, disease, and assorted aches and pains in which he found what he called "sexual Frauds" at the bottom. Dr. Augustus Gardner, one of the most respected physicians writing for a popular audience in the 1870s, flatly informed his readers "that all methods employed to prevent pregnancy are physically injurious." When no specific physical disabilities could be attached to the attempts to counter conception, doctors easily slid into quasi-moral reasons, such as Dr. George Beard's warning that "these devices encourage excess in the act; indulgence is more frequent because more safe." [15]

With no reliable medical evidence for believing that mechanical or chemical contraception harmed anyone physically, it is not surprising that the principal objections were moral or ideological. Even when the ostensible objection was ineffectiveness, the moral objection showed through. Thus John Kellogg in 1881 denounced "the thin rubber or goldbeater's skin" as a snare, quoting the old adage that the condom was "a breastplate against pleasure and a cobweb against danger." Then, significantly, he ended by saying that such methods only reminded one of the brothel and licentiousness anyway. Earlier he had frankly called contraception "conjugal onanism." Catharine Beecher, the educator, denounced, among other evils, "the worldliness which tempts men and women to avoid large families often by sinful means. . . ." One doctor denounced men for "calculating" the dollar cost of children, before and after marriage, and criticized wives for calculating "the trouble and pains of gestation and nursing . . . the temporary privation of social and fashionable enjoyment . . ." and, thus, for concluding "children are a nuisance." Such denunciations occurred even more frequently at the end of the century than at the opening. An editorial in the *New York Medical Journal* in 1883 even went so far as to say that the time would come when not only the life of the fetus would be viewed as sacred, but any attempt to prevent the creation of life—that is, contraception—would be treated as a crime. In 1899, Dr. James Foster Scott stigmatized contraception as "a curse to the good health and the morals of both parties." He advised his readers "that there is no harmless way in which to prevent conception." The hostility to birth control is also measured in the fact that in 1876 Dr. Edward Bliss Foote was indicted and convicted for sending birth-control information through the mails, an action that caused the very large fine for the time of $3000 to be levied against him. He also was required to pay additional costs of $5000. And as late as 1916, G. Stanley Hall, the noted psychologist of Clark University, privately turned down the request of the Massachusetts Birth Control League that he allow his name to be associated with its cause. In his letter, Hall gave his reason for the declination: "I have borne my share of *odium sexicum* for almost a generation of men. . . . I have done my bit in this movement and now I am retiring and am going to have a rest from this trouble for the remainder of my life."[16]

Perhaps the most telling example of the hostility toward contraception in 19th-century America was the opposition from the advocates of woman suffrage and from the advocates of free love. Ezra Heywood, the sexual radical, and Tennessee Claflin, the radical feminist and sister of Victoria Woodhull, both excoriated contraception—as well as abortion—as sinful and harmful. Indeed, historian Linda Gordon, in her social history of birth control, frankly admits the need to explain the opposition of women's groups to contraception since fertility control was clearly in women's interest.

Gordon tried her hand at an explanation, but it is not convincing. She argued that, in a day when marriage was the primary basis of women's livelihood, the principal way a woman attracted a man into matrimony was to maintain the connection between sexuality and reproduction, a connection that contraception would sever. If the connection were broken, Gordon argued, men might not marry as frequently and thereby leave many women without a means of support.

The difficulties with the explanation are several. For one thing, there is no direct evidence that any woman actually considered publicly or privately such a reason for opposing birth control. In fact the argument is so demeaning to a woman that none would think of verbalizing it, and so it probably could have worked only on a subconscious level, if it operated at all. Even if feminists were moved by such thoughts of using children as a way of maintaining a dependent relationship between a woman and a man, the advocates of free love certainly would not have accepted it, yet they, too, vehemently opposed contraception. The whole purpose of radical reformers of marriage, after all, was to see that the relationship between a man and a woman be free, not established and then sustained by deliberately maintaining the connection between sexuality and reproduction. For that would indeed have been a coercive relationship. Finally, the weakness of Gordon's case is particularly exposed by the widespread practice of birth control, despite the refusal of feminists or other women in public life to espouse it. Large numbers of ordinary women, in sum, did not see any significant advantage in keeping the connection between reproduction and sexuality, whatever Gordon and other feminists may have thought. Indeed, if any body of historical evidence can call into serious question the often heard argument that people's actions are shaped largely by what they have been told in the press and by popular opinion, the widespread practice of birth control as measured by the steady fall in fertility throughout the 19th century is certainly a prime candidate for the job.

From our vantage point today it would seem that the principal reasons why feminists and free lovers opposed contraception were the same as those that caused most Americans, at least in public, to do so. The reasons were primarily ideological and moral, and they fall into two large categories. One was a fear that if people practiced contraception they might overindulge in sex, a practice that seemed fraught with unknown consequences. The sexual urge might get out of control. Even an advanced feminist like Charlotte Perkins Gilman had doubts about contraception in the 20th century because she thought it would lead to overindulgence. The second category of argument against contraception was that it represented an interference with nature's as well as God's intentions. According to this line of thought, sexuality presumably had been tied to reproduction for a purpose; to sever that connection was to oppose the natural and religious order as people of the 19th century perceived it. One measure of the presence of such fears and anxieties was the passage of a law in 1873 that excluded from the United States mails all information on birth control. The law was the brainchild of Anthony Comstock, who also obtained from a complaisant Congress the personal authority to enforce it. Thereafter information on birth control was legally classified as "obscene."

Hostile as the law and general opinion certainly were toward contraception, there always was, even after the passage of Comstock's law in 1873, a strong and growing body of opinion that publicly supported the idea of limiting family size, not to mention the untold hundreds of thousands who practiced it in private. In the public defenses are to be found some of the reasons why Americans sought to reduce the size of their families during the 19th century. One early writer in 1839, for example, denied that contraception was against the will of God, as opponents frequently contended, for men had been given reason in order to understand nature and to use that knowledge for their own ends. Animals, another writer pointed out, did not have reason, and their sexuality was confined by nature to limited periods. Since women's was not, he logically concluded, God must have intended human beings to make their own choice of when to indulge in intercourse; hence there was nothing wrong in trying to space children. One imaginative writer justified birth control by reference to the French, who everyone in the English-speaking world thought of as especially given to controlling their fertility. The writer pointed out that, if a people as refined as the French resorted to such practices, birth control could hardly be the immoral or coarse procedure that its opponents asserted![17] Even the staid *Nation* magazine in June 1869 praised the French for the small size of their families, assuring its readers that whatever else they may have heard about the French practice of population control, the weakening of the reproductive powers of the French people was not one of them.

More significant than mere counterings of opposition arguments were those defenses of birth control that offered positive reasons why family limitation was important. Prominent among the reasons was the assertion that it would improve the lot of the poor, that it would help them become socially mobile, in effect. "In how many instances does the hard-working father, and more especially the mother, of a poor family, remain slaves throughout their lives, tugging at the oar of incessant labor, toiling to live, and living but to toil, when if their offspring had been limited to two or three only, they might have enjoyed comfort and comparative affluence!" wrote Robert Dale Owen, son of the British industrialist and reformer, as quoted in A. M. Mauriceau's widely circulated *Married Woman's Private Medical Companion* in 1847. Mauriceau quoted at length from Owen's book, giving it much wider exposure than the philosopher's ideas would have gained on their own. Mauriceau himself was the husband of New York's most notorious woman abortionist, and one of the few men to espouse contraception without reservations. By way of Mauriceau's pages Owen also advanced the argument that the use of birth control would encourage young people to marry for love rather than think about material things such as whether the husband could earn enough money to support a steadily growing family. Mauriceau himself pointed out that though it was possible for a young married couple to live together as brother and sister "as the Shakers do . . . this [remedy] . . . would chill and embitter domestic life, even it if were practicable."

Few medical advisers were as forthright in support of birth control as Mauriceau and Owen, but even Dr. Augustus Gardner, who usually scorned birth control, on occasion had to admit that it was essential that physicians provide their patients with information on the subject. In trying to convince his readers that *coitus interruptus* or withdrawal was dangerous, he told of three husbands he had treated for a general debility stemming from their use of this method of birth control. Two of them already had large families, Gardner noted. Under the circumstances Gardner felt that he needed to do more than make his usual recommendation of continence. He told the two husbands about that period in their wives' fertility cycles when women were least likely to conceive and recommended they confine their marital acts to that span of days.[18]

For our purposes a significant argument made in behalf of birth control was that children would benefit from its practice. At a time when children were being valued as never before, this impulse toward family limitation was important as a cause. For as child-rearing became an important task, the number of children would have to be reduced if parents, particularly mothers, were to give the proper attention to each child. As the number of children was reduced, for whatever reason, the standard of care and attention could rise, thus enhancing the idea that children were indeed at the center of the family.

These assumptions underlay the writings of many contemporaries. Dr. George Napheys, one of the most prominent of mid-19th-century popular medical writers, for example, denied the often heard allegation that the desire to limit offspring arose from "an inordinate desire of indulgence." Those who advance such charges, Napheys contended, "do not know the human heart, and . . . they do it discredit. More frequently the wish springs from a love of children. The parents seek to avoid having more than they can properly nourish and educate. They do not wish to leave their sons and daughters in want." In the pages of Mauriceau's marriage guide, Robert Dale Owen insisted that it was "clearly, incontrovertibly *desirable*, that parents should have the *power* to limit their offspring," even if they choose not to exercise it. "Who can lose by their having this power?" he asked, "and how many *may* gain competency for themselves, and the opportunity carefully to educate and provide for their children!"[19]

Elizabeth Cady Stanton made a similar case in a public speech in New York City in 1870, for, though she, like most feminists, opposed contraception, she strongly believed in "voluntary motherhood," a movement we shall look at more closely in a moment. "There is a good deal said, rather deploringly, today, about the small families of Americans," she began. "When people begin to weigh the momentous consequences of bringing badly organized children into the world there will be fewer still." After all, she continued, merely to reproduce is but an animal function, "but when a mother can give the world, one noble, healthy happy man or woman, a perpetual blessing in the church and the state, she will do a better work for humanity than in adding numbers alone, but with little regard for quality."[20]

Not a few writers who defended limiting births also pointed out the benefits that accrued to women. Frederick Hollick, whose *Marriage Guide* published in 1850 was one of several popular medical advice books he wrote, emphasized the value of birth control for women's health. Certainly it was preferable to abortion, he argued, to which many women were driven in their desire to avoid another child. Some women, he wrote, "rather than have more children . . . even said that they would *die* first. In such cases, therefore," he continued, "there is simply a choice between the two practices of abortion and prevention, and I am confident there are thousands who feel in this way." About the same time J. Soule told his readers of *Science of Reproduction and Reproductive Control* that "no woman shall hereafter be compelled to bear children against her wishes. God knows it is *bad enough* for a woman to bear children when she consents to it, without being compelled, time after time, to bear them when she does not want them. . . . Woman is the better portion of the human race," he went on, echoing the moral precepts of separate spheres, "why should we desire to retain her in suffering?" Then he spelled out what birth control meant to woman: it put her "in a freer, a happier, and more independent position." [21]

Dr. George Napheys also recognized that control over fertility was essential for women's independence. Religion might tell woman, he wrote in 1871, that "it is her duty to bear all the children she can." And some peasant women and perhaps even early American women followed this precept, he conceded, but the modern American wife was constituted differently. " 'If a woman has a right to decide on any question,' said a genial physician in the Massachusetts Medical Society a few years since," Napheys recalled, " 'it certainly is as to how many children she shall bear.' " Then he went on to quote the editors of a medical journal who said that " 'Certainly . . . wives have a right to demand of their husbands at least the same consideration which a breeder extends to his stock.' " There can be no doubt, Napheys continued, that for the woman's sake childbearing must be limited. "There is no lack of authorities, medical and non-medical on this point." Few persons deny that there is such "a thing as too large a family, that there does come a time when a mother can rightfully demand rest from her labors in the interest of herself, her children, and society." [22]

An open defense of birth control was only the most direct sign of a widespread interest in limiting family size. Contemporaneous with it was another body of literature that did not quite advocate contraception, yet nonetheless contended forcefully that women had a right to control their own fertility. The method was to appeal to husbands to exercise sexual restraint. Henry Clarke Wright, the abolitionist, was also a leader in what Linda Gordon has aptly called the Voluntary Motherhood movement. In his several books on the subject Wright never advocated contraception, but he always argued for a woman's right to limit her children and to avoid having "unwanted children." At one place in an 1858 book he quoted from a female correspondent who told him of her daughter whose excessive childbearing had made her detest sexual relations. The daughter, she informed Wright, "thinks it a great misfortune that husbands cannot gratify their sensualism without imposing on their wives the necessity of abortion, or of giving birth to children they do not want, and she lives in constant fear of losing the affection of her husband, if she does not quietly yield to his passion." Apparently what this mother and Henry Wright wanted was for husbands to reduce the frequency of intercourse and to regulate their sexual relations according to the so-called safe period of women's ovulation. Actually, long before Wright popularized the issue, Robert Dale Owen had asserted that "no man ought even to desire that a woman become a mother of his children, unless it was her express wish, and unless he knew it to be for her welfare that she should. Her feelings, her interests should be for him in this matter, *an imperative law.*"[23]

Although most feminist leaders and the feminist movement as a whole in the 19th century never supported contraception, many women, some of whom were feminists, did support the idea of limiting family size, as we have seen Elizabeth Cady Stanton did. In this context it is useful to draw the distinction advanced by Linda Gordon between contraception and birth control—a distinction employed in these pages up to now, as well. Contraception means the use of some method to prevent conception that goes beyond abstention from intercourse. Thus withdrawal or *coitus interruptus* and the condom would, under this definition, be forms of contraception, as well as other, more modern methods that do not require any interference in the sexual act. On the other hand, abstention from intercourse for lengthy periods, prolongation of nursing, delayed time of marriage, and the use of the safe period would be methods of birth control that were not means of contraception. Abortion, although certainly a means of controlling births, is, therefore, not a form of contraception.

Socially and perhaps even psychologically speaking, if contraception was to be used, then an argument in favor of birth control was a necessary precondition. That is why arguments in support of voluntary motherhood, even though they failed to specify any means by which births could be limited, fostered the acceptance in time of true contraception. For once women and men were convinced that a smaller number of children was desirable, for whatever reason, then they would be more likely to be receptive to new means of limiting families.

Even before the Civil War the argument that women had an inherent right to control the number of their offspring was being advanced. After 1865 many women took up the argument publicly, though usually without specifying how those limits were to be achieved. Pauline Davis Wright, a feminist leader, in 1871 denounced law and custom for making "obligatory the rendering of marital rights and compulsory maternity." Another feminist, Isabella Hooker, half-sister of Harriet Beecher Stowe, told her daughter at the time of her marriage in 1869 that she ought to avoid pregnancy until "you are prepared in body and soul to receive and cherish the little one." At about the same time, Victoria Woodhull, radical feminist and advocate of free love, was creating a sensation in New York City and around the country lecturing on the subject of a woman's right to determine when she should have a child. Elizabeth Cady Stanton, during her speaking tours in behalf of the suffrage in the Middle West between 1869 and 1873, frequently held meetings at which only women were permitted. At these meetings she spoke about the desirability for women to limit the size of their families. "What radical thought I then and there put into their heads," she wrote privately. And, she exulted, since no men were present, "these thoughts are permanently lodged there!" [24]

No woman in the years after the Civil War was more outspoken on the subject of a woman's right to her own body than Eliza B. Duffey. Her book *The Relation of the Sexes* was first published in 1876 and was still being issued as late as 1889. The central purpose of the book was to convince women that they had no obligation to have children. To those who said childbearing was God's purpose for women, she responded by turning the usual interpretation of women's biology on its head. Since woman, unlike the lower animals, could become pregnant at any time, God must have intended that she should have a choice in the matter. Whether a woman avoided pregnancy for a month, a year, or a lifetime, Duffey concluded, she "is equally free from blame and simply taking advantage of the law which nature and nature's God have enacted in her behalf, with precisely such a contingency in view." Besides, she said, "avoiding motherhood by legitimate means is evidently not a sin, for no punishment goes with it." [25]

Duffey was never clear about how women were to limit their offspring, though she probably intended them to use either the so-called safe period or restraint on the part of husbands. She certainly thought masculine restraint was called for. "God has not put woman so seemingly at the mercy of men in sexual matters," she insisted, "that man may feel himself justified in giving full play to his animal instincts and compelling her to suffer the consequences." At times she was quite bitter against men for their indulgence and their unconcern for the effects of that indulgence on women. "There is not one man in fifty," she fumed, "who thinks, or cares, or who in his own heart pretends to think, or care, about offspring." When men "talk about the end and aim of marriage being the sexual union, we may possibly believe you are speaking the truth, as regards yourselves; but when you talk about its being your duty to procreate children! Why don't you stop playing the hypocrite and say in plain English 'men find the gratification of sexual passion very pleasant.'" Yet, it will be recalled, Duffey was not hostile to sexual expression; in fact she extolled it—in moderation.[26]

Like Henry Wright before her, Duffey stressed the effects upon children as well as upon women of unwanted offspring. "An unwilling motherhood is a terrible, a cruel, and unjust thing," she told her readers. "This enforced motherhood is the cruelest wrong which women sustain at the hands of men. It embitters their lives and turns into a curse that which should have been a blessing." To those who complained that some women did not want children and therefore needed to be encouraged by public opinion to have them, Duffey's scorn was unrelieved. "Then don't let them have any," she snapped. "Their very lack of desire proves their unfitness. Children, in the hands of such mothers, will only go out into the world to swell the sum of human wretchedness." And to those Pollyannas who blithely said that the Lord would provide for those couples who have more children than they can support, she had a direct and brief retort: "That is all cant. We see constantly that the Lord does *not* provide for those children whom the parents have not taken the precaution to look after."[27]

Alice B. Stockham's *Tokology,* which came out in several editions in the 1880s, also assured women of their right to control their fertility. "Fewer and better children are desired by right-minded parents," Stockham told her readers. She condemned roundly what she called "chance parenthood."[28] Stockham did not approve of certain kinds of contraceptive techniques like *coitus interruptus* and the condom. But neither did she leave her readers with a negative conception of sexuality or with no means of birth control except abstinence. She recommended the safe period, and what she called karezza. The last was really *coitus reservatus,* which John

Humphrey Noyes had perfected and instituted at his Oneida Community before the Civil War. The community was still functioning in 1880. Karezza was sexual intercourse without ejaculation by the male. Its demands upon male control were even greater, in short, than *coitus interruptus,* though it was free from the objection of an interrupted climax. On the basis of this evidence there seems little reason to doubt that at least by the middle of the 19th century women's direct interest in limiting the size of their families was recognized by many people of both sexes. Not all of them, to be sure, were in agreement as to how that reduction in family size was to be accomplished.

Those who did not like the idea of smaller families or birth control usually placed the responsibility for such practices upon women. Elizabeth Evans, for example, though she was assuredly a friend of women, nevertheless blamed women for what she called the "encouragement to license, particularly with reference to the conduct of life in love, marriage and parentage." She attributed the trend to the "emancipation of women" over the previous twenty years. "Women who have married unwisely in their early girlhood now seek to throw off the yoke and save a portion of their lives from the wreck of their fancied happiness," she contended. Other women who think of themselves as "companions of their husbands in intellectual pursuits or political cares, marry with a determination to avoid the hindrances of maternity" and still other women "who have already borne children are tired of the grave responsibilities and petty annoyances which these occasion, and are resolved to prevent any further increase of their families." G. Stanley Hall, the noted psychologist, considerably less understanding of women's situation than Elizabeth Evans, nonetheless also blamed the weakness or self-indulgence of women for their wish to curtail their fertility. "Many women are so exhausted before marriage," he wrote in 1904, "that after bearing one or two children they become wrecks, and while there is perhaps a growing dread of parturition or of the bother of children, many of the best women feel that they have not stamina enough and are embarrassed to know what to do with their leisure." As far as Hall was concerned, men did not share this disinclination toward children. "Perhaps there will have to be a 'new rape of the Sabines,' " he suggested only half jokingly, "and if women do not improve, men will have recourse to emigrant wives, or healthy girls with stamina will have an advantage equal to that of pretty girls now." [29]

Women's role in curtailing fertility is indirectly documented in some statistics on education and birth rates. One scholar who studied illiteracy in the 1840s and 1850s found that it was highly correlated with high birth rates; literate women on the average had fewer children than illiterate women. A study of three Massachusetts cities in 1880 reported a similar correlation between literacy and reduction in fertility. The number of children (four years old or younger) per 1000 literate women was 601 as against 938 for illiterate women. When the fertility of foreign-born women alone was studied, literacy still turned out to be significant, even when the women were divided according to the occupation of the husband. Thus literate women married to men in low-level occupations had lower fertility than illiterate women in that class.

Women's part in reducing fertility was demonstrated in more detail in a study of midwestern families in the middle of the 19th century. Not surprisingly, the study showed that as the educational level of the parents rose, fertility fell. What was not so expected, however, was the further finding that increased education for women reduced fertility more than a comparable increase in educational achievement by men did. For example, men who did not go beyond elementary school averaged 5.65 offspring, while women of that level averaged 5.85 offspring. But when the amount of education reached the level of high school, the relative positions of the two sexes in regard to number of children reversed themselves. The average number of children for males with a high school education was 5.02 but was only 4.57 for females of that level of education. Thus it would seem that wives who had attended high school were acting independently of their husbands in pressing for control over fertility. A similar difference between the fertility of the sexes in discernible in another study in which the subjects were the 19th-century parents of students at the University of California.[30]

Occasionally, more specific individual examples of women's direct interest in controlling fertility appear in personal documents. Benedict Arnold's wife, at the end of the 18th century, made quite clear in writing to her married sister that both Shippen women thought of birth control as naturally a woman's interest and responsibility. "It gives me great pleasure to hear of your prudent resolution of not increasing your family," Margaret Shippen Arnold wrote; "as I can never do better than to follow your example, I have determined upon the same plan; and when our Sisters have had five or six, we will likewise recommend it to them." Unfortunately for us, the method in which they seemed to have so much faith was not revealed! Then there is the instance of the Cormany family of Pennsylvania, in which the wife clearly exercised control over her fertility even though her husband wanted a son. They had one daughter, born in 1862, but though Samuel Cormany had been home for several leaves while in the army no other pregnancies had resulted. In 1865, while still in the army, Cormany wrote in his diary that he had received "a very good letter from Pet this A.M. Oh! how happy I am to learn that Darling has so materially changed her mind on that one great subject of having a Boy—some sweet day, not too far away. Thank the Lord. Finished a letter of 12 pages to my darling." And once Cormany returned home the couple did have a second child, but no more thereafter.[31] Apparently in that family the wife determined whether or not the couple would have additional children. And, though the diary does not inform us of the method, they must also have had a very reliable way of controlling fertility.

To recognize the central role of women in bringing about the reduction in fertility does not require that one must also deny any role to men. Husbands often had economic and other reasons for wanting to restrict the size of their families. In fact, that coincidence of interests helps to account for the remarkable success 19th-century families had in cutting down on the number of children. But generally one may assume, and certainly the writings of the time support the view, a woman's interest was greater than a man's simply because fertility was more immediate to her. A wife had all the economic reasons that a husband did, and in addition she bore and raised the children. Moreover, it should not be forgotten that in the rural areas of the United States, where the birth rate was also falling throughout the 19th century, the usual economic reasons men might have had for cutting back on children would not be so strong as they would be in urban areas. Conventionally it has been argued that farmers had a need for children, which urban families did not.

When one recognizes the special interest of women in limiting family size, a further insight into the evolution of the modern family suggests itself. Present-day sociological studies point out that the successful practice of contraception requires a close and communicative relationship between husband and wife. This conclusion emerged from Lee Rainwater's sociological study of contraception and family planning among present-day working-class men and women, *And the Poor Get Children*. He found that efforts at contraception failed most often because husband and wife could not agree upon method, timing, or intention. On the other hand, when a couple's relationship was cooperative and sympathetic, family limitation was achieved even without contraceptives, as among some Roman Catholic families he studied. In short, successful contraceptive practices implied a closeness and mutual influence between husband and wife, especially when they took place in a social atmosphere like that of the 19th century in which birth control was publicly discouraged and even denounced. Therefore, since the fall in fertility during that century was primarily the result of deliberate effort on the part of the couples, that decline becomes a concrete measure of the closeness of intra-familial relations as well as a sign of women's increasing autonomy within the family. For without such cooperation, mutuality, and female assertiveness, the unreliable and imperfect methods of the time could not have brought about the steep drop in fertility. Thus the decline reinforces the view of the 19th-century family which was delineated in chapters I and II on the basis of individual and personal family records.

When we turn from the reasons for fertility control to the means used to achieve it, the conclusion that the decline in births depended upon the closeness of intra-familial relationships becomes even stronger. The ways in which births were limited in the 19th century are the subject of the next two chapters.

IX

Limiting Fertility

Historical demographers are still not in agreement on how 19th-century Americans managed to reduce the size of their families. There is little doubt, however, that throughout human history efforts at limiting fertility have been virtually constant and widespread. Often these efforts may have involved no more than postponing marriage long after the onset of fertility in women. Since most women are fertile no more than thirty years on the average, the later in a woman's life sexual intercourse occurs the fewer opportunities there are for children to result. Thus, according to the definition of birth control set forth in the last chapter, such a delay in marriage would be designated a form of birth control, though not a use of contraception. Contraception is here defined as a deliberate interference with the process of conception.

Just as the efforts at birth control go back a long time in history, so the use of contraceptives can be traced back to antiquity. The Romans, for example, used a number of substances in the vagina during intercourse to impede the uniting of sperm and egg, though at the time, of course, no one knew the function of the occlusive substance. In fact, the actual medical demonstration of the existence of the egg in the human female was not achieved until 1827, though virtually all societies and cultures—no matter how primitive—recognized a connection between the injection of the semen of the male into a woman's vagina and the subsequent birth of a child. Even the modern condom was known in antiquity, expensive though it was, being made out of an animal's bladder—a circumstance that also made it less desirable because it dulled sensation for the male. Presumably, knowledge of contraceptive techniques, which passed principally by word of mouth, was not lost entirely during the Middle Ages. Modern historical demographers, however, have generally concluded that the principal method used in Europe in the 15th and 16th centuries was *coitus interruptus*. One of the most learned of the modern French students of population decline in his country from the 18th to the end of the 19th century has flatly concluded that the method used "is not a difficult question to answer—*coitus interruptus*." And an English historical demographer reinforces this judgment by noting that as late as the early 20th century the great majority of English women still did not use appliances for controlling their fertility. Only 16 per cent of couples who had married before 1910 used diaphragms or condoms, the remainder, presumably, relying upon either *coitus interruptus* or abortion.[1]

American students of the subject have generally echoed this judgment, even though direct, documentary evidence of the practice of withdrawal has been extremely rare. Sarah Pomeroy, in her study of women in antiquity which reports on several methods of contraception known to, or used by the ancients, looked for evidence that *coitus interruptus* was practiced, but found not a single instance. Page Smith has reported only one example, from the judicial records of colonial Massachusetts. The man admitted to practicing the method in such familiar terminology, however, as to suggest the method was well known. In an effort to establish that he was not responsible for fathering an illegitimate child, the paternity of whom he was charged with, the man admitted in court that he had indeed had intercourse with the mother, but that "I minded my pullbacks." A rare 19th-century example has been kindly supplied to me by another historian, Carol Kammen, from the papers of an upstate New York farm couple. Though the language is characteristically reserved, its import is clear. In 1849 Calista Hall wrote to her husband Pliny in a letter, which she asked him to burn, that "The old maid came at the appointed time," a reference to the beginning of her menstrual flow. "I do think you are a very *careful* man," she added, complimenting him for his skill at avoiding a pregnancy once again. "You must take Mr. Stewart out one side and learn him," she suggested, referring to a neighbor whose wife had too many children.[2]

Those modern historians who believe that *coitus interruptus* was commonly practiced in 19th-century America justify their belief from the fact that so many of the marital and medical advice books of the time denounced it. Moreover, many of those who deplored it often testified at the same time to its popularity as a method. "It is now notorious that in a large proportion of the cases of illegitimate intercourse, and, indeed, of conjugal intercourse," wrote Dr. Horatio R. Storer in 1865, "the completion of the act within the body of the woman is purposely withheld." It so happened that Storer generally opposed contraception, but even those who were positive in their attitudes toward contraception also deplored withdrawal. H. Arthur Allbutt, in *The Wife's Handbook* which was published in London in 1886 specifically for wives of workingmen, recommended both the condom and the pessary, but discouraged *coitus interruptus* on the ground that it was harmful to the nervous system of both sexes, a point made by Storer and others as well. Margaret Sanger, the 20th-century birth-control advocate, was especially hostile to withdrawal because of its "evil effect upon the woman's nervous condition." And it should be remembered that Sanger was both an advocate of birth control in general and the pleasures of sexual expression.[3]

As the great majority of advice books in the 19th century made clear, *coitus interruptus* was disadvantageous for both sexes. It surely required a great amount of control by the male and probably resulted in unsatisfactory orgasms for both males and females. Yet there is no question that it was the easiest method for a couple to use simply because it required no special knowledge or equipment. It probably did not even require much instruction, for it was capable of being "discovered" by a couple on their own. One of the few, if not the only manual published in America to recommend withdrawal, gave a brief description of how to minimize the inconvenience involved. The male was to hold a napkin "during the nuptial act," the book advised. "If you do it at the proper moment, no pleasure is lost to either party; and habit will soon make you expert in this respect," the author assured his male readers. "This is the most certain mode of preventing conception that can be adopted," he concluded.[4]

Modern surveys of sexual habits indicate that withdrawal has been used well into the 20th century by large numbers of couples, both in Europe and the United States. The French have long been thought to rely upon the method for their low birth rate. A study of a small farming community in southwestern Tennessee in 1930 found that 87 per cent of the 94 white families there from whom the local doctor could obtain information on birth control used withdrawal. Only 13 per cent used a contraceptive device. (In that particularly isolated community, even at that recent date, barely a majority of the families knew of any way of limiting births, according to the local doctor.) When the Royal Commission on Population in Great Britain in 1949 studied the effectiveness of various family planning methods it reported that *coitus interruptus* was only slightly less effective than the diaphragm. Those couples using diaphragms averaged 2.6 children, while those using withdrawal averaged 2.7.[5]

The method of birth control most widely advocated in the 19th century, even by those who had doubts about contraception in general, was the so-called safe period. This was the period in a woman's ovulant cycle when she was immune to impregnation because the egg had not yet left the ovary and would not be available for fertilization within the two- or three-day life of the sperm once it had been deposited in the woman's body. Though it was known there was a period during which impregnation was highly unlikely, the precise time in the course of the ovulant cycle it occurred and its duration were not known. As a result, most lay and medical writers, regardless of whether they favored contraception or opposed it, could be quite wrong about the precise span of days when impregnation was least likely. Indeed, Dr. Henry Chevasse stigmatized as "absurd" the view that there was such a thing as a safe period. Then he went on to say that the likelihood of impregnation was greatest immediately before and immediately after the menstrual period! By implication, of course, he was telling his interested reader that the "safe period" was roughly the ten days midway between the ending of one period and the onset of the other. As we know today, that is precisely the period when women are most likely to conceive! No wonder he thought the idea of a safe period "absurd."[6]

Even someone as informed on the physiology of women as Dr. J. Marion Sims, perhaps the leading gynecologist in the United States in the 1860s and 1870s, was shaky in his knowledge of the timing of ovulation. He told his fellow doctors that as the result of his work with women who consulted him for infertility, he advised such women to have intercourse on the third, fifth, and seventh days after the menstrual flow had ceased and on the fifth and third days before it was expected to return. In sum, by implication, Sims believed with Chevasse that the safe period was roughly half way between the ending of one menses and the beginning of the next. He concluded, however, by adding what every physician has said since about the reliability of what today is called the "rhythm method": "I have no doubt that conception may take place at any period whatever relative to the return of the menstruation."[7]

A more popular medical adviser, Dr. Augustus Gardner, in 1870 made clear his own misconception of the ovulant cycle, menstruation, and conception, as well as expressing his firm belief in a safe period. He began by revealing his assumption, which was quite erroneous, that the menses were to be equated with estrus in animals. "Menstruation in woman indicates an aptitude for impregnation, and this condition remains for a period of six or eight days after the entire completion of the flow. During this time only," he asserted boldly, but erroneously, "can most women conceive." Gardner disapproved of mechanical or chemical contraceptives, but he had no objection to advising women on how to avoid pregnancy: "Allow twelve days for the onset of the menses to pass by and the probabilities of impregnation are very slight," he assured his readers. "This act of continence is healthy, moral, and irreproachable." Quite self-consciously he extolled the superiority of the safe period over all the other methods. With the safe period "there need be no imperfection in the conjugal act [a defect of withdrawal, of course], no fear, no shame, no disgust, no drawback to the joys which legitimately belong to a true married life." Besides, he concluded moralistically, it will prevent excessive indulgence as well as limiting the number of children.[8]

This misconception of the timing of the safe period persisted in the popular advice literature right down to the end of the century. As late as 1881, in the twenty-eighth edition of his *Sexual Physiology,* R. T. Trall, for example, was still advocating it as the most effective method for limiting families, though how it could be working is hard to understand since he had the timing wrong. "If intercourse is abstained from until ten or twelve days after the cessation of the menstrual flow," he promised, "pregnancy will not occur." He claimed that the method had "served thousands of married persons with very few failures, adding that he had first advocated the method fifteen years before. The few failures he conceded he attributed to diseased organs in women which slowed down the ovulant process. And in 1886 H. Arthur Allbutt advised women to wait eight days after the ending of the menses; if they did, the likelihood of pregnancy was only "about 5 cases in every hundred." As late as 1910 radical birth-control advocates were still describing the safe period as halfway between menstrual periods.[9]

A few medical men did hit upon the right timing. Dr. George Napheys, for example, advised refraining from intercourse from the tenth day after the cessation of the menstruation until five days before it was expected to recommence. One or two other writers on medical matters for the layman, like Frederick Hollick, also specified what today we recognize as the period of natural sterility in women. Given the many other advisers, including most physicians themselves, who misunderstood the character of the menstrual cycle—they generally saw it as comparable to estrus or "heat" in animals—it is not likely that the safe period could have been the principal way in which fertility was reduced. Insofar as it did reduce births it probably did so by reducing the frequency of intercourse, now recognized by demographers as having just that effect. The frequent references to and advocacy of it in the popular and professional medical writings of the late 19th century more than suggest that many couples must have known about and undoubtedly used it. A study of some 2600 upper-class women in 26 cities in the United States in 1940 revealed that even at that date 11 per cent used the safe period as compared with 14 per cent who used the condom for controlling fertility.[10]

Fundamentally, the safe period method is really only a special case of the more general method of reduced frequency or prolonged abstinence. Paul David and Warren Sanderson, two economic demographers, have recently shown, on the basis of some data on coital habits of married couples in the late 19th century, that if frequency of intercourse falls as low as three or four times a month, the effectiveness of the safe period method improves dramatically.[11] And modern data assure us that reduction in frequency alone usually reduces fertility. From what we know of the Voluntary Motherhood and other marital advice literature of the 20th century, lowered frequency of intercourse was widely recommended. A habit of less frequent intercourse within marriage is also consistent with the upsurge in prostitution in the cities, just as it is consistent with what we have been calling the assertion of women's autonomy within the family. Although reduction in frequency of intercourse cannot be considered a form of contraception, it probably was one of the most widely employed means of controlling fertility during the last century.

A true method of contraception that was also widely used in the 19th century was a douche of the vagina immediately after intercourse. A douche, made with one of several recommended chemical solutions was first advocated by Charles Knowlton, a Massachusetts physician, in his *Fruits of Philosophy*, first published in 1832. Knowlton informed his readers about the condom, which subsequent writers also mentioned, but he did not recommend it, presumably because in Knowlton's day vulcanized rubber was not yet known, and other substances were too thick, thereby deadening the man's pleasure. Moreover, as Knowlton pointed out, a syringe and the chemical solution for the douche were cheap, and involved no loss of pleasure other than that the woman had to get out of bed almost immediately after the completion of intercourse in order to administer the douche. An even more important advantage in Knowlton's eyes, and probably the main reason why douching was widely used, was that its application was entirely in the hands of women, as withdrawal and the condom were not. James Ashton in 1865 made this same point, though he preferred, as we have seen, withdrawal. He said that wives might need other means to give them security and so he recommended a syringe with cold water or "white vitriol." Even the safe period offered no protection to a woman whose husband insisted upon ignoring it. Douching was easily accomplished by a woman even when her husband was unwilling to think about such matters himself. (As late as 1955 a survey of several thousand married women in Indianapolis found that one-fifth of those using some contraceptive method were still using the douche. And those who used it faithfully apparently reduced their risk of conception by 80 per cent. Those women who used a douche only for cleanliness soon after intercourse more than doubled the intervals between their pregnancies as compared with women who used no contraception.) [12]

Knowlton's *Fruits of Philosophy* was not the earliest book printed in America to advocate one or more methods of birth control, for it was preceded by two years by Robert Dale Owen's *Moral Physiology,* usually designated as the first. (Some of the publications of Francis Place, the early British birth-control advocate, circulated in the United States even before that.) Owen's preferred method was *coitus interruptus,* even though he was sensitive to women's vulnerability in sexual relations and well recognized that his preferred method left control in the hands of the male. Knowlton's book seems to have been better known than Owen's, though as we have seen, many of Owen's arguments and pieces of advice got wide circulation through their being reprinted at some length in Mauriceau's popular medical handbook.

Before the 1830s were over, at least one other manual detailing methods of birth control appeared in the United States. In 1839, William Greenfield translated from the French and published *Marriage Physiologically Discussed* by Jean Du Bois. This book listed five methods of varying effectiveness, including some bizarre ones such as having intercourse on an inclined plane so as to avoid dislodging the egg from the ovary. This last was a reference to the false belief that the egg left the ovary only at the time of intercourse. Another of his rather strange recommendations was dancing "smartly" immediately after copulation, or riding horseback over a rough road, a method, he added, which will either prevent conception or bring on an abortion! He mentioned withdrawal, but he could not recommend it because, unlike Owen, he did not think it was easy to accomplish. Du Bois called attention to three methods he thought were effective and reliable. The first was douching with a syringe containing a solution of lukewarm water containing a small amount of vitriol. The second method was one rarely noted in American books and pamphlets on the subject though it figured prominently in the early, underground birth-control literature in England: a sponge placed in the vagina prior to intercourse, with a thread attached for its later removal. The sponge was soaked in a chemical and used to swab out the vagina after intercourse, as well as acting as a barrier to the sperm. The third method was the "Kundum," the "speediest and the least troublesome of all," the book advised. Made of fine silk or bladder skin, it was "fastened on the head of the penis during the act of copulation." Although the book said that such devices were obtainable, cheaply, in all cities, the reference was undoubtedly to France.[13] The device described was presumably the precursor of the true, present-day rubber condom, but had the modern name of glans condom because of its covering only the glans penis. By the time of the Civil War, today's condom made from vulcanized rubber was well known, for as Ashton reported in 1865, they "are now made beautifully with a preparation of India rubber." But, he continued, "the enjoyment of the nuptial act is not so complete as a naked Penis affords, hence the covering or sheath, is not very popular." James Reed in his recent thorough history of birth control asserts that the rubber condom was available at low prices during the 1850s.

Couples interested in learning about means whereby they might restrict their offspring had other sources of knowledge in the years before the Civil War. In 1847, A. M. Mauriceau began the publication of his widely known advice book to wives, which has already been mentioned as a book offering various methods for family limitation. In 1850 Frederick Hollick published the first edition of his *Marriage Guide,* in which he not only advocated birth control but also expanded upon the known methods. He mentioned douching with various chemicals, such as alum, sulphate of zinc, chloride of zinc, and sulphate of iron. He cautiously warned that no method was perfect, including the condom, which he found wanting because it reduced feeling for the male and was not always reliable. The method Hollick recommended as the best was the safe period, but he had to admit no method for ascertaining its timing was entirely reliable. Yet, as we have seen, he came closer than most. Rather pessimistically he concluded his advice on the matter with: "prevention of conception . . . is not so easy as some have supposed and it is not altogether harmless either." A pamphlet by an anonymous physician published in 1855 under the title *Reproductive Control* especially recommended a cold water douche, but frowned on withdrawal and the condom. The pamphlet, incidentally, strongly urged control over fertility on the ground that it enhanced the quality of marriage. No woman could be a companion to a man, a relationship which the pamphlet described as the primary purpose of marriage, if she was wasted "by bearing and nursing children, and the domestic drudgery that a large family always causes. . . ."[14]

At least two other books giving details on methods of birth control appeared before 1861. One was Harry Knox Root's *The People's Lighthouse of Medicine*, the fourteenth edition of which appeared in 1856. It recommended the condom and douching. Although the circulation of the book is not known, the numerous editions suggest that it was hardly obscure. In 1859 Dr. M. Sherman Wharton translated from the French, and Bela Marsh of Boston published Eugene Beckland's *The Physiologist, or Sexual Physiology Revealed*. The book discussed all of the methods already mentioned, adding that an "oiled silk covering" of the penis, which could be bought in any Paris toy store, was quite effective!

In summation, before the Civil War all of the methods of birth control that would be known in the first half of the 20th century, with the single exception of the diaphragm, had been discussed, described, and advocated in books and pamphlets intended for lay readers and to which access was relatively easy. Many of the books were obtainable by mail, as advertisements in the back pages made clear, and so were available to those outside the cities. The diaphragm itself was probably invented before the Civil War, too. Dr. Edward B. Foote, in his *Medical Common Sense*, published in 1864 advocated what he called a womb veil, and which historian James Reed believes was "a true vaginal diaphragm." Significantly, Foote recommended it on the ground that "it places conception under the control of the wife, to whom it naturally belongs; for it is for her to say at what time and under what circumstances she will become the mother and the moral, religious and physical instructress of offspring."[15] Thus, Foote linked voluntary motherhood and contraception.

Even if Foote did invent or discuss the diaphragm, it was not widely used before Margaret Sanger gave it publicity in the early years of the 20th century. One reason for thinking it was not widely used is that the name by which it was known—pessary—was almost universally used in the 19th century to describe various medical devices for holding the womb in place, a nomenclature that would not have persisted if the diaphragm had been common. For to have used one word for both items would have been so confusing that a new word would have been invented, as in fact occurred in the 20th century with "diaphragm."

There can be no doubt that methods of contraception were advocated and described in a number of widely disseminated publications by the middle years of the 19th century. What is not so clear is how widespread the actual practice of contraception was. Indeed, what evidence there is on the practice is almost entirely indirect, derived from the broad social interest in family limitation rather than from any direct interview or statistical information, such as would be relied upon today. The very proliferation of popular medical and marital literature beginning in the 1830s and continuing throughout the century reflects a growing interest in family limitation and probably, therefore, a willingness to employ contraception of some kind. The further fact that many medical writers mounted arguments against birth control suggests that the practice was widespread. The frequent advertisements that appeared in large city newspapers from 1820 to at least 1873, when the Comstock law made it illegal to send contraceptive information through the mails, must also be interpreted as a sign, at least indirectly, of the practice of birth control.

Occasionally, an opponent of birth control inadvertently testified to the widespread interest in and practice of it. William Alcott, the well-known lecturer and writer on marriage, wrote in 1866 that a book on birth control, written some twenty-five years before, the author of which he did not name but who was probably Charles Knowlton, "has a wide circulation. I have found it in nearly every part of our widespread country," Alcott admitted. He then said that the book's advice was being employed successfully in one county in New England where people were especially interested in keeping down the number of children because the husbands were often away for long periods.[16]

Scattered evidence also tells us that contraceptives themselves were fairly easy to obtain, even outside the big cities. In the 1847 edition of Mauriceau's book, there was an offer to sell by mail at $5.00 a dozen condoms imported fron France. Mauriceau also offered to sell M. Disomeaux's "Preventive to Conception," which he claimed would neutralize sperm. The concoction may have been a spermicide or an outright fraud, but the advertisement itself certainly suggests that at least some kinds of contraceptives were possible to obtain.

Even if one accepts on the basis of this indirect evidence that the use of contraceptives was fairly widespread, we still would like to know how far down the social scale the knowledge and practice penetrated. Most historical demographers have believed, on the basis of what we know about the spread of contraceptive knowledge today among social classes, that the upper classes first practiced the more sophisticated—and effective—methods, especially those other than withdrawal. Only later did these other methods reach down to the working class or uneducated. One French writer on the subject in 1870 certainly believed this to be true of France. He wrote that the "laboring classes are generally satisfied with" withdrawal and such methods, being ignorant usually of the condom, while "among the wealthy . . . the use of this preventive is generally known." [17] As we have seen, Ashton in 1865 thought that though condoms were "made beautifully" from India rubber in the United States, they were "not very popular" because they reduced men's pleasure. At the same time, his report that the "best article" could be purchased for about $3.00 a dozen—as compared with the $5.00 a dozen for the imported article offered by Mauriceau twenty years before—suggests that the price may have been coming down as the market expanded. If the price cited by Ashton was correct, by 1865 the cost of condoms was hardly prohibitive for most middle-class American families. If the average frequency of intercourse was twice a week or about 100 times a year, and one condom was used each time, then at $3.00 a dozen the cost per family would be less than $25.00 a year. And that would be the maximum cost, since it did not take into consideration washing and reusing condoms. Since an average non-farm worker in 1865, however, earned on the average only about $500 a year, that cost might be too great for a working-class family to accommodate into its budget.

The real issue in all of this, of course, is not whether contraceptives were available but whether people of all classes used them. Use apparently varied by class and nativity. One statistical study of differential fertility between immigrants and natives during the 19th century, for example, supports the accepted view that the native-born practiced birth control to a greater extent than immigrants. The study compares the number of children per 1000 married women in 1880 in two wards of Boston according to age categories and nativity. The native women, as one might anticipate, had a lower rate than the immigrant women. What was not so expected, however, was the fluctuation in the native women's rates for different age categories. For ages 20–24 the native rate was 763 births per 1000 married women, while the immigrant rate was 1043. But for ages 25–29 the native women's rate jumps to 1063 while the immigrant woman's rate moved up only to 1118. Then for the years 30–34 the native women's rate fell abruptly to 627 while the immigrant woman's rates continued to climb. Clearly, the native women were controlling their fertility in a deliberate way that the immigrant women were not.[18]

What limited information we have on family size among different ethnic groups suggests that control over fertility varied also between immigrant nationalities; some groups apparently made greater efforts than others to limit births. One study of Buffalo, New York, families at the end of the 19th century, for instance, reported that the average number of children born to Italian women (who were now past menopause) was 11, while for Polish women the figure was only 7.8.[19]

Class, as well as ethnic background, affected fertility in the 19th-century family. If the population in the two wards of Boston in 1880 referred to earlier is divided according to the occupation of the husbands, striking differences in fertility emerge. Families in which the fathers held a high-paying job limited their families throughout the fertile years much more than middle-level or low-level income families. And this was true for all age groupings. In the following table notice how the number of children rises as the income falls for women in the 30–34 and 35–39 age groups.

Number of children under five years of age per 1000 married women (two wards in Boston, 1880)

Age group	High income	Middle income	Low income
30–34	852	1161	1188
35–39	500	900	949

A study of 19th-century women made by the Bureau of the Census in 1910 showed similarly sharp differences in number of children between occupational groups. For example, businessmen's wives whose fertility ended in 1885 averaged 3.58 children, while wives of skilled workers averaged 3.97, and wives of farm owners bore 4.84 children on the average.[20]

The explanation for differences in fertility between classes or between ethnic women is complex. In part it may have to do with ethnic inheritances or tradition or class concerns about the costs or advantages of having children. But certainly a part of the explanation was simply lack of sufficient information. Oral interviews with working women whose early fertile years were around the turn of this century suggest that few women of that class knew of mechanical methods of birth control like the diaphragm. For family limitation, they remembered, they had relied upon abstinence or abortion. In fact, some of the women interviewed recalled that abortion was much more commonly talked about among them than contraception as means of family limitation. Margaret Sanger's early campaign in behalf of birth control, just before World War I, was prompted, too, according to her recollections, by the lack of knowledge working-class women had about birth-control methods. Sanger, as historian David Kennedy has pointed out, tended to exaggerate the lack of available information on birth control in the United States, but her experience among working-class women bears out the view that the most reliable methods of contraception were known only spottily by working-class women in the late 19th and early 20th century.

On the other hand, all the evidence points to a broad knowledge about and use of contraception among middle- and upper-class women. Nor ought it to be forgotten that in 19th-century America, the middle class reached down far enough into the social pyramid to comprise probably a majority of the population. The one survey of sexual habits that we have for women born in the 19th century, compiled by Dr. Clelia Mosher between 1892 and 1920, reveals that all but four of the 43 women queried admitted to employing some method of birth control. (Two women did not answer the question.) These women were wives of professional men, and virtually all of them had a high-school education or more, indicating that they were at least middle and probably upper middle class in background. Thanks to the statistical analysis of the Mosher Survey done by Paul David and Warren Sanderson of Stanford University, we can now confidently say that this group of 43 women was representative of the wives of professional men throughout the United States. It follows, therefore, that about 90 per cent of the wives of professional men practiced some form of birth control.

In the light of the argument in this book that women were highly influential in the decision to practice birth control, it is worth noting that the most popular method reported by the Mosher women was douching. Twice as many reported douching as withdrawal, which was about equal in popularity with the condom. The second most popular method, though only slightly more so than withdrawal, was the safe period. Twenty-two of the women reported using "female" methods (douche and pessary), while 17 reported using "male" methods (condom and withdrawal). Eleven women used the safe-period, which was probably the method that required the closest cooperation between the spouses since it meant the man would refrain from intercourse at the time that the wife suggested, while she had to be responsible enough to keep a close record of her period for the method to be effective, providing, of course, that the correct period was known![21]

A direct piece of evidence that married couples did regulate their times for sexual intercourse according to the supposed periods of infertility appears in the correspondence of General William Dorsey Pender and his wife during the Civil War. Their several expressions of concern over whether she was pregnant testify to the strong, sometimes desperate interest young married couples had in controlling their fertility. In February of 1862 General Pender expressed the wish that his wife was indeed about to have a miscarriage, as she thought was possible when she last saw him. He said he hoped her surmise was correct, "for we all have enough to contend with in these times even when we are free from continuous nausea and have to look forward to nine months of pain and general ill-feeling." She did have a miscarriage, for which, he wrote, "I must say I am heartily glad." Since she, too, did not want another baby, he advised her that "if you do not want children you will have to remain away from me, and hereafter when you come to me I shall know that you want another baby." Pender, in short, was not prepared to refrain from intercourse so long as his wife was with him. On the other hand, he contended that he was quite satisfied with only two children, and wanted no more. "The ills of this life are too great for anyone to wish to entail it upon many of his own seed. Two are as many as I want," he assured her. The following year, after his wife had written that it seemed now quite certain that she was once again pregnant, he made clear that they had been using the safe period. "I did hope when you left me that you had escaped," he wrote, "but we poor mortals know so little of the future. Surely we never need make any calculations again." He was not confronted with the problem of what other method he would use because, before his second son was born, Pender was dead at Gettysburg.[22]

One of the few other explicit examples of a use of the safe period was provided by Mary Hallock Foote. In December, 1876 she wrote her confidante, Helena Gilder, that she was undoubtedly pregnant, though she had not wanted to have a baby so soon after her wedding. "I was dismayed at first—but it seemed like fate," she wrote. "No precautions were neglected. The Doctor says change of climate alters everything," a reference, presumably, to the fact that her menstrual cycle was no longer predictable as a result of her moving from New York to California. Some-

thing of her sense of desperation at being pregnant against her will came
out in her remarks. "It is awful, but what can we do. There *must* be some
meaning of it—perhaps in the future, the lives of our children will reveal to
us the meaning." Awed as she may have been on one level, Mary Foote
was not willing to leave her future completely at the mercy of chance, or
Fate, as she called it. "It is a delicate thing to speak of in a letter," she continued, "but Mrs. Hague [her sister-in-law] told me a sure way of limiting
one's family—which is no injury to either father or mother." Because Mrs.
Hague's doctor determined that she must not have any more children for a
number of years, he told her of a reliable method whereby she could avoid
becoming pregnant. Almost painfully aware of the delicacy of the subject,
Mary offered to tell Helena of the method if she had not "provided for the
future to your satisfaction . . . [and] have any miserable uncertainty. . . .
It seems to me to involve no possibility of bad consequences."

Apparently, Helena did have some "miserable uncertainty," for Mary,
in her next letter, proceeded to tell her the new method. "Of course, I
know nothing about it practically and it sounds dreadful; but every way is
dreadful except the one which it seems cannot be relied on. Mrs. H. said
Arthur [Mary's husband] must go to a physician and get shields of some
kind. They are to be had also at some druggists. It sounds perfectly revolting, but one must face anything rather than the inevitable result of Nature's methods." She assured Helena that there was nothing injurious
about these devices and that Mrs. Hague's undeniable fastidiousness ensured that she would hardly submit to an undesirable technique. "These
things are called cundums and are made either of rubber or skin. They are
to be had at first-class druggists." [23]

This unusual letter documents not only the failure of the safe period for
one couple, but it also reveals how it was possible to learn about another
means—and from another woman. Mary Foote passed on the information
to yet another woman, which must often have been the story as necessity
or desperation forced women to seek out such information. In this particular case, it was a western woman in the remote hills of California who told
the wife of a sophisticated editor of a prestigious journal in New York
City what she needed to know. The Foote letter also suggests that even
middle-class women like Mary Foote and Helena Gilder did not read
the marriage and medical literature on contraception though they did
know about the safe period method of birth control. Nevertheless, they did
have other sources of information. And, from a subsequent letter of Mary
Foote, apparently the additional information was put to use. "No—little

Arthur will have no successor for some years yet," she wrote Helena later in 1877 or early 1878. "I haven't the strength and my religion does not interfere with the use of such prevention as is in one's power. I can do nothing myself, but so far the 'French shields' have saved me. Doctors say," she assured Helena, "it is the only means not injurious. Everything is dreadful except nature and Nature is like the letter of the law which faileth." [24]

The dubious reliability of the various methods of contraceptions in the 19th century created more than the "miserable uncertainty" to which Mary Foote referred. It threw a dark shadow over every act of intercourse. Something of the threat was revealed in the sense of release that feminist Charlotte Perkins Gilman voiced when she learned that she might not be able to bear any more children, though she had recently remarried and had expressed a wish someday to have her new husband's child. "Happy thought—take no precautions—take no treatment—all runs smoothly and naturally and nothing happens!!!" [25]

Earlier in the century, Bell Waller's sense of relief at finding that she was not pregnant was even more ebulliently expressed. She wrote her husband in July 1855 that she had "glorious news to communicate," asking him if he could guess. It was that she was not pregnant. "I have positive knowledge, actual demonstration of this, *to me,* important fact, rejoice with me darling—claps hands with delight! for I am so glad!" Apparently she had not told him of her worry, but now she revealed the extent of it. Because her "nervousness was excessive" she was confirmed in "the belief that I was P——, that thought amounting to conviction preyed upon me, till the discontentment produced by it became unendurable. I felt at all times desperate! I felt unable to perform a mother's duty to the children we have, and if we had more, how could I get through my care—I felt borne down, with the thought of the future; it presented only trials and sufferings and worse than all, failures; everything was robed with somber colours, clouds obscured my days. . . ." Not even religion was any help, she confessed. Then with the onset of her menstrual period, all came clear and bright again. That she was in fact exhibiting physical signs of her worry was confirmed by Henry Waller's admission that he had indeed noticed "that you were uneasy, restless, nervous, dissatisfied, unstable, and verging toward despair" even before her letter had arrived telling him of her internal turmoil. [26]

The unexpected or unwanted pregnancy always hit the wife the hardest. General Pender sympathized with his wife when he learned her pregnancy was certain, but he also tried to help her accept it by expressing a wish for a girl this time. A week later he told of reading the Bible and learning that children were a sign of God's blessing. "Ought we to complain so at what is evidently His direct will, for did we not try to oppose it? and with what effect?" he asked his wife. "Let us look upon the bright side of it and be cheerful. I do wish you could go through it without being so sick." When Mary Poor found in August 1863 that she might be pregnant, she vowed "to feel resigned to the fate that Providence assigns to me. It may all blow over after all." But three days later she was inquiring of her husband for Dr. Elizabeth Blackwell's address, "for I may write to her, if things go on much longer as they have done. I do not dare to walk or ride," presumably because she feared to bring on a miscarriage.[27]

The desire to limit the number of children in a family also attested to a growing interest in children, just as an interest in birth control naturally flowed from a growing interest in trying to do one's best by one's children. For by limiting offspring, as Bell Waller told her husband in 1855, parents could do more for each one, materially, educationally, and psychologically. An emphasis upon the value of children, as pointed out in Chapter IV, was another indication of the emergence of the modern family in the United States. Put quite matter-of-factly, as the number of children in a family declined, the emotional investment in and the affection for them were encouraged to rise, just as greater concern for children encouraged women, as rearers of children, to have fewer. Affective cooperation between parents in the course of controlling the number of their children, together with the concentration of their attention and resources upon fewer children, helped to create a family that was as closely knit internally by ties of affection as it was increasingly walled off from outsiders.

Not all intra-familial relationships were cooperative, and certainly not all efforts at birth control, even if cooperatively and lovingly pursued, were successful. It is now time to look at the recourse open to those couples who either did not cooperate or just could not find a successful method to limit their families, though the wife was determined to do so. That will be the subject of the next chapter.

X

Abortion: Women's Last Resort

Spouses in the 19th century might be in complete agreement on the desirability of, or even the necessity for, limiting the number of children, yet the methods at their disposal were often inconvenient or unreliable. Certainly that was true in regard to the so-called safe period. Physicians did not understand enough about the ovulation cycle of women to offer accurate information, or, if they did, no one could be sure that the information was in fact accurate. Hence, whether a couple established the correct infertile period or not was a matter of chance, not a matter of having reliable advice available. Similarly, *coitus interruptus* was a tricky method that could easily fail, though the partners might be in complete agreement about its desirability. For even the slightest amount of semen deposited on the outside of the vagina made impregnation quite possible. Vaginal douches worked only when the spermicide was applied immediately after intercourse. A natural delay on the part of the woman, even if only a matter of minutes, might mean application was too late.

If the partners were not in agreement on either the necessity for, or the means of, contraception, then, of course, the likelihood of failure was even higher. This was especially true for those methods that required the cooperation of the husband, such as the use of the condom, withdrawal, and the safe period. Some husbands undoubtedly resisted agreeing to limit their sexual activity to the so-called safe period.

That contraception failed in practice, or was not tried at all, was dramatically measured in the widespread practice of abortion, especially after 1830. If withdrawal is a peculiarly male form of birth control, then abortion must be acknowledged to be peculiarly female. Unlike all the other forms known in the 19th century, except perhaps douching, abortion was entirely in the hands of the woman, dependent upon neither masculine activity nor masculine acquiescence. So true was this that medical opponents of abortion in the 19th century offered as one of their objections to abortion, as one observed, that "wives will even make the hazardous attempt to keep both husband and physician in ignorance of the procured abortion." They were able to do this because an abortion could be disguised as an illness.[1]

The upsurge in the incidence of abortion in the middle years of the 19th century is a sign of the failure of contraceptive techniques and probably the failure of cooperation between spouses. But above all, it is an indisputable measure of the desire of American women to limit family size. For while it is possible for a man to influence a woman to have an abortion, there are strong reasons why a woman would not consent to one against her own wishes. Moreover, before the 1820s apparently few women had resorted to it. Thus the rise in abortion must be taken as women's last desperate effort to limit their families when all other means failed. Once again, the central interest of women in family limitation by the early years of the 19th century is plain. It is, of course, significant that this additional evidence of women's interest in controlling their fertility first occurred in the 1820s and 1830s—just those decades, as we have seen, when the modern child-centered family in which the woman was the moral guide and guardian was establishing itself.

The sudden increase in abortions became noticeable during the late 1830s and early 1840s. Dr. Hugh L. Hodge felt it necessary in 1839 to warn his students at Pennsylvania Medical School that they must expect to encounter an increasing number of cases of abortions in their practices. Madame Restell, a notorious New York abortionist, began her practice in 1838 and announced in an advertisement that year that she had helped "hundreds" of women with her abortion-producing nostrums. One advocate of contraception wrote in 1846 that a way to reduce the alarming increase in abortion was to encourage birth control.[2]

By the early 1850s many physicians were commenting on how common abortions were in their practices. Dr. Horatio Storer, who would become the leading mid-19th-century authority on, and opponent of, abortion, published the first systematic study of the subject in 1857. Two years later he succeeded in convincing the American Medical Association to go on record against the practice. In 1854 an article in the *Boston Medical and Surgical Journal* had reported that, despite the dangers involved, "there seems no diminution of the evil" of abortion. The killing of unborn children, the article continued, must be "fearfully common everywhere, if the great number of half-grown infants found floating in boxes upon the water, dropped in vaults," and so forth are taken as evidence. In every city, the article added, abortionists abound, and many married women with the concurrence of their husbands patronize them. One medical doctor from Troy, New York, wrote Dr. Storer in the late 1860s that abortion "which forty years ago, when I was a young practitioner, was a rare and secret occurrence, has become frequent and bold." Another, writing from New Hampshire, expressed his awareness of the change with wry exaggeration: "Nowadays, if a baby accidentally finds a lodgement in the uterus, it may, perchance, have a knitting needle stuck in its eyes before it has any." Frederick Hollick, the popular writer on medical subjects, had remarked as early as 1850 that "there are few persons except medical men, who have any idea of the extent to which the revolting practice of abortion is now carried." As a medical man, he said he had seen the horrible effects upon women who had induced abortions in themselves. For all his opposition to abortion, Hollick, as we have seen, was no opponent of birth control. Indeed, one of the reasons he advanced in support of some kind of birth control was that it would provide women with an alternative to abortion.[3]

All commentators on the extent of abortion in the 1850s and 1860s testified to the practice in all classes and particularly among married women. Many women, wrote Morse Stewart in the *Detroit Review of Medicine and Pharmacy* in 1867, know how to abort themselves. "Among married persons," he stated, "so extensive has this practice become, that people of high repute not only commit this crime, but do not even shun to speak boastingly among their intimates, of the deed and the means of accomplishing it." His remarks carried more than the weight of a single witness since he was then speaking to other physicians, and he concluded by asking, "Is there a physician present whose experience does not fully confirm the statement?" At one time, Stewart remembered, abortion was largely confined to the results of illicit intercourse. "Now, however, the exceeding prevalence of the evil is found to be among an entirely different class, and the fruit of legitimate wedlock in every grade of society, high and low, but especially the former, is the prey of this destroying Moloch."

Particularly odious in Stewart's eyes was that many men and women entered marriage with the knowledge of how to terminate pregnancies and without any need, therefore, to call upon a physician.[4]

Abortions could indeed be self-induced, but that fact in itself not only made the procedure dangerous, as the physicians pointed out, but might also mean that the result intended did not occur—that is, no abortion ensued. This was particularly true of such popular practices as jumping off chairs, falling from heights, or, as one medical doctor testified, having someone jump on the pregnant woman's belly. Various kinds of drugs were also commonly used, such as ergot of rye and oil of tansy, most of which acted as strong emetics or mild poisons, thought to be capable of inducing an abortion. Today most of these chemicals are not considered very effective abortifacients, though all are undeniably dangerous to the general health of anyone—man or woman—who might consume them. It is likely that many of the so-called abortifacients retained some credibility because the pregnancies for which they were taken were, in fact, false. Pregnancies were thus believed to have been terminated by the drug when actually no measures were necessary. At least one reference book, Wharton and Still's *Medical Jurisprudence,* published in 1884, referred to certain abortifacients as effective, though without also noting the harmful side-effects. Certainly the willingness of women to use these dubious abortifacients attests to their strong, almost desperate, intention to limit their fertility. Physical devices were also used to induce abortion. Knitting needles, if the frequency with which they were mentioned in the denunciations of physicians is to be taken as indicative, were favorite instruments. Abortionists also advertised in the newspapers concoctions which promised to restore the menstrual flow, as the ads often phrased it, but which were really intended to abort a possible pregnancy. The *Milwaukee Sentinel* of February 2, 1857, carried an advertisement that was typical of its kind. It was for "The Great English Remedy, Sir James Clarke's Celebrated Female Pills." They were promised to cure all female diseases and to remove all obstructions, and bring on "the monthly period with regularity. These pills should not be taken by females that are pregnant, during the FIRST THREE MONTHS, as they are sure to bring on MISCARRIAGE, but at every other time and in every case, they are perfectly safe." Sometimes abortifacients were disguised under the code name "Portuguese" pills, it being well known that the phrase referred to abortifacients, while "French letter" or "French remedy" stood for contraceptive devices.

Then, of course, there were professional abortionists, who also advertised their services, though never explicitly, in the newspapers. They hid behind such disguises as physicians of women's diseases, or as experts on "restoring" women's health, by which they meant the return of an interrupted menstrual cycle. And if the denunciations in the medical journals well into the 1880s are to be taken as indicative, many otherwise quite respectable physicians were willing to perform abortions for their regular patients.

From the amount of discussion among physicians and in the newspapers—the *New York Times,* for example, carried a long condemnatory article on the extent and nature of the business in its August 23, 1871, issue—the practice seems to have been widespread. Unfortunately, however, there are no definite statistics on the extent of abortion during the 19th century. In 1889, one doctor was quoted as saying, on the basis of some 25 years' practice, "that more than one-half of the human family dies before it is born, and that probably three-fourths of these premature deaths are the direct or indirect result of abortion by intent." The doctor who quoted that estimate then continued his denunciation of the practice by lamenting that "even among the married, there are few wives who do not know of some means to destroy the foetus before it comes to full term, and who have not in some manner, and at some time, applied one or more of these means in their own cases. The abortionist plies lucratively his or her trade in nearly every town and hamlet," he concluded.[5] We may doubt that this estimate of extent was strictly accurate, but there can be no doubt that many physicians believed, and presumably for good reasons, that abortion was common throughout the United States.

Certainly that had been the burden of the reports from state medical societies compiled by Stanford E. Chaillé and published in the *Transactions* of the American Medical Association in 1879. In state after state it was disclosed that abortions were rising in number. And in 1872 one respected physician, Dr. Ely Van de Warker, asserted that "the luxury of an abortion is now within the reach of the serving girl. An old man in this city [Syracuse?] performs this service for ten dollars, and takes his *pay in instalments.*" A special committee on Criminal Abortion of the Michigan State Board of Health estimated in the 1890s that 34 per cent of all pregnancies ended in miscarriage. James Mohr, in his recent and thorough study of the crusade against abortion in the last half of the 19th century, estimates that in the middle of the century there was about one abortion for every five or six live births. He contrasts this with his further estimate that during the first three decades of the century the ratio was about one abortion to only 25 or 30 live births. Both estimates are put into perspective by a 1921 study which reported that one out of every two pregnancies was aborted, of which 50 per cent were considered to be criminal abortions. Those figures would work out to about 25 per cent of pregnancies being deliberately aborted, or not far from Mohr's estimate of about 20 per cent for the middle years of the 19th century. About 22 per cent of the women surveyed by Kinsey in the 1950s reported having at least one abortion.[6] Finally, although abortions were undoubtedly easier to obtain in the cities, Mohr's work and the anti-abortion literature of the 19th century make plain that abortions were being performed in the countryside and small towns as well.

Although there is little direct evidence from women as to why they resorted to abortions, a reading of the physicians' denunciations of such women quickly reveals that the desire to control the size of family was the major concern. Although one physician in 1878 was almost contemptuous of women who sought an abortion, his listing of the reasons for their actions, as he saw them, was actually a list, with a little adjustment, of why women might well want to resort to abortion. Among the reasons he cited were "aversion to marriage, fear of pain and perils of child-bearing, anti-maternal hatred of offspring, calculation of the cost of rearing children, unmotherly objection to large families, newspapers advertisements, and other emanations of the press, the obscene literature of 'free love,' the delirium of spiritism, and impulse of passion, the concealment of shame." Another physician writing for a medical journal in 1874 remarked that "so intense is the feeling . . . that some women, expecting to become mothers or loathing the pregnant state will tell you that they will do anything in the world—even suffer death—before they will bear another child." In 1854 (in a Boston medical journal) an article expressing opposition to abortion nonetheless admitted that women who have them think "they have children enough already, or their circumstances forbid an increase of family expenses and responsibilities."[7]

The observation of many physicians that married women constituted by far the largest group seeking abortions further testified to the interest in controlling fertility. One physician, for example, divided women seeking abortions into three categories: prostitutes; "young girls who have been seduced under specious promises" and deserted later, and "by all odds the most numerous, . . . married women, who would resort to the inhuman crime of destroying the fruit of their wombs for no better reason than that children are not to them blessings, but nuisances, interfering with their rounds of fashionable dissipation, or taxing the paternal income." At the end of the century, Dr. James Scott wrote that by far more married women than unmarried sought abortions. He asserted that "it is believed by many physicians that fully seventy-five to ninety percent of criminal abortions are committed by married women." In an analysis of 54 documented cases of abortion in medical journals between 1839 and 1880 James Mohr found that approximately two-thirds of the women involved were married, 60 per cent of whom already had at least one child.[8]

The role of married women in taking the initiative in having abortions is not surprising since they were the potential bearers of children. But it is striking in the light of the oft-expressed argument by historians that family limitation was initiated by husbands interested in reducing costs of child-rearing. Certainly the doctors at the time assumed that the initiative came from the women, not from their husbands. This was also true of an article in *Harper's Magazine* in 1869 in which it was said that women pressed for abortions because children limited their lives. Conservative commentators like Roman Catholic critics of abortion assumed women's initiative, too, when they blamed the incipient women's movement for the increase in abortions. And at least one doctor told of receiving a letter from a woman who deliberately sought to abort herself after hearing a minister speak against abortion. She objected to any clergyman's seeking to restrict her liberty.[9]

Such defenses of abortion were extremely rare. One of the few women to write publicly and understandingly about abortion—and she did it anonymously—explained why some married women had to seek abortion. She was answering Dr. Horatio Storer's contention that women could avoid having abortions if they would time their sexual relations to coincide with their infertile periods. That was all right for the good doctor to advise, said the anonymous woman, but some wives did not have such choices. "They are not independent, but subject; and all teaching tends to keep them so. Here is just where the trouble begins." They cannot save themselves from the cause, she pointed out, but they do have some control over the result—namely, the child. Hence they resort to abortion.[10]

Many physicians were genuinely impressed not only by the fact that women's interest in control over their fertility was intense, but that such women could not be easily dismissed as ignorant or immoral. "Many otherwise good and exemplary women, who would rather part with their right hands or let their tongues cleave to the roof of the mouth," one physician wrote in 1896, "than to commit a crime, seem to believe that prior to quickening it is no more harm to cause the evacuation of the contents of their wombs than it is that of their bladders or their bowels." More than twenty years earlier, another physician made much the same comment. "Astonishing as it may seem," he told his fellow physicians, many of those who sought abortion "are otherwise quite intelligent and refined, with a keen sense of their moral and religious obligations to themselves and to others, deem it nothing amiss to destroy the embryo during the first few months of its growth." Elizabeth Evans, who certainly was a friend of women, nevertheless denounced women who had abortions as "secret criminals." She could not conceal her indignation that "almost all" of these women were were "attendants upon Divine Service, and believers, more or less enthusiastic, in the fundamental doctrines of orthodox Christianity. Nay, the case is not utterly unknown," she assured her readers, "of a clergyman's wife yielding to the same sin." [11]

Physician after physician expressed astonishment at the ease or effrontery with which women asked for abortions. "Mine is but the common story of every physician," began one popular medical writer in 1870. An unknown woman walks into his office, asks for the doctor, and then says, " 'I want you to produce an abortion for me,' as coolly [sic] as if ordering a piece of beef for dinner." Dr. Horatio Storer made clear why women could be so composed. Many of them told him that "the contents of the womb, so long as manifesting no perceptible sign of life, were but lifeless and inert matter: in other words, that being, previously to quickening, a mere ovarian excretion, they might be thrown off and expelled from the system as coolly and as guiltlessly as those from the bladder and rectum." [12]

The testimony of other physicians makes it clear that to many women the destruction of the fetus before quickening—that is, before the fourth month or so of gestation—did not involve the destruction of a living being. The proof of that was attested to by the comment in one popular medical advice book that "destroying a child after quickening . . . is a very rare occurrence in New York, whereas abortions (destroying the embryo before quickening) are of daily habit in the families of the best informed and the most religious; among those abounding in wealth, as well as among the poor and needy." In what is undoubtedly an exaggeration, but one that nevertheless testifies to the physicians' conviction that abortion was common, one doctor told of visiting a woman, just before her death from a self-inflicted abortion, who confessed to him that she had had twenty-one previous self-induced abortions! [13]

As James Mohr has pointed out, for many American women in the 19th century, abortion was not a moral question concerning life and death, as it would be in the 20th century. It was more like contraception—an interference with a natural process, but no more closely related than that to murder and manslaughter. In fact, as we shall see later, it was just because women did not see it in terms of murder that doctors undertook to educate them on the matter. Given this attitude or medical understanding on the part of women in the 19th century, it is very likely that abortion was a much more important way of family limitation than it has been at any time in the 20th century until the legalization of abortion in the 1970s.

When physicians, in their professional literature, discussed abortion, they usually described cases in which some instrument or other outside force had been used, for it was the consequent severe illness of and danger to the life of the woman that brought the doctor into the case. Much less common was actual testimony from married couples of their attempts to abort an unwanted pregnancy. Usually these instances involved drugs, rather than instruments. In fact, one physician, who was a part-owner of a drug store in a large city, said that he personally saw the ease with which these drugs were obtained. "The cool effrontery of young girls and women in speaking to strangers, non-professional, upon this most secret function of her sex is astounding." [14]

In March 1864, Lester Frank Ward and his wife succeeded in aborting her pregnancy with drugs, for that month he wrote in his diary that his wife was "very sick" for two days, "but she is quite well now. . . . The truth is that she was going to have a child, but she took an effective remedy which she had secured from Mrs. Gee. It did its work and she is out of danger." But in the fall she was apparently showing signs of pregnancy once again. He complained that the medicine he had gotten on a trip to Washington, D.C., failed entirely. "I went back to get more, but I do not trust it at all." A month later he noted that "the pills of which I made mention were not good, and I have sent to Syracuse for the instrument advertised in the book I received from the firm." Although he had more confidence in the efficacy of the instrument, it did not produce an abortion either. As a result, in December he went to see a local doctor "concerning secret affairs between me and my wife. He gave me much useful instruction which I plan to put into practice." This was probably contraceptive information for the future, rather than anything to do with abortion, for in June a son was born. [15]

When General Pender's wife told him she thought she was pregnant and made clear that she did not want another child at that time, Pender obtained pills from the camp surgeon to send to her. "Indeed, I did sincerely hope that you had escaped this time," he wrote her, but added that, in view of the precautions they had taken, the probable pregnancy had to be put down to the "positive and direct will of God." Apparently the pills were not true abortifacients but some kind of medicine to stimulate the onset of the menses. "If you are not positively certain" that you are pregnant, he advised his wife, "would it not be well to use Dr. Powell's prescription for if you only use three of the pills and take the baths three days, there could be no harm done if you are as you write"—that is, pregnant. In the Penders' case, the reason for objecting to her pregnancy was almost as trivial as some of the hostile physicians claimed. "It comes in a season of the year," Pender wrote his wife, "when you would like to be able to enjoy yourself, and when I hoped that you would be able to go home somewhere, and have a nice time." As things turned out, Fanny Pender was in fact pregnant.[16]

Both the frequent resort to abortion and the method used by at least one couple appear in a California woman's statement in 1875 in the course of a divorce suit. She asserted that on at least four occasions she had aborted herself, with her husband's knowledge by the "injection of pure water" and at a time before "there was any quickening or life in the foetus whatever." (Her statement was made in rebuttal to her husband's contention that he ought to be granted a divorce because she had aborted herself, thereby showing herself, presumably, to be immoral or criminal.) Elizabeth Evans, who vehemently opposed abortions, asserted that objections to too many children were at the root of women's widespread recourse to abortion, many women recollecting from their own rearing in large families the difficulties and inconveniences of many children. She cited a specific case of a woman who aborted herself when she recalled her own childhood in a big family. And when a woman physician in a medical journal denounced the sexual indulgence to which she ascribed the rise in the number of abortions, a male physician corrected her. Dissatisfaction with maternity among married women, he argued, was not confined to the lower classes, as the woman physician implied, but was much more likely to occur in the upper levels of society. And even then, he stressed, it was "dissatisfaction with the *state of pregnancy* and its attendant inconveniences, and enforced *self-denials*" that were objected to by women, not motherhood itself. Too many pregnancies, in sum, was the issue, not pregnancy itself.[17]

One of the striking social responses to the upsurge in abortions in the

1840s, 1850s, and after was a movement to strengthen the laws against abortion. Prior to the enactment of Connecticut's law against abortion in 1821, no state prohibited abortion by statute, though under the common law inherited from England the destruction of a fetus after quickening or of a child after birth was punishable by fine and imprisonment. (There were also statute laws punishing the killing or concealing the birth of an illegitimate child.) Connecticut's law was an adaptation of the English law of 1803, which was the first statute law against abortion enacted in Great Britain. It prohibited the killing of a fetus by poisoning after quickening. But, unlike a subsequent English law, the Connecticut statute in 1821 did not prohibit an abortion through poisoning *before* quickening. This Connecticut law was amended in 1830 to ban other methods besides poisoning to destroy the fetus, but only after quickening; and for those offenses the penalty was reduced from life imprisonment to seven to ten years in prison. Meanwhile, other states had enacted similar laws. Between 1821 and 1841, for example, ten states and one federal territory had put such laws on their statute books. Alabama's law, enacted in 1841, was typical. It forbade any attempts at causing a miscarriage by any means, and failed to mention quickening, but exempted from the ban any abortion that was deemed necessary to save the life of the mother. This last provision was an American innovation in the law of abortion, for English law at no time during the 19th and early 20th century permitted that discretionary action. At the same time, American law has never abandoned that exception to the prohibition of abortion. Every state law has included it. As a result, one modern commentator has been able to write: "No American state has ever prohibited abortion."[18] Alabama's 1841 statute was also significant because it set only a three- to six-month jail sentence for violators.

As James Mohr has pointed out, most states by the early 1860s had enacted some law against abortion. But most of these legal prohibitions had been introduced as a result of routine legal code revision and not because of a strong campaign or popular upswelling to stop abortions. Most of the statutes did not seek to punish the woman, only the abortionist. In 1860, for example, only three of the twenty states which had laws against abortion punished the mother. And in some cases it was clear that the intent of the law was to protect the woman, rather than the fetus. That, in fact, was the construction put upon New Jersey's law by a court in that state in 1858. "The offense of third persons under the statute," read the opinion of the court, "is mainly against her [the mother's] life and health. The statute regards her as the victim of the crime not as the criminal, as the object of protection, rather than of punishment." Even as late as 1880 a North Carolina court specifically declared that "it is not the murder of a living child which constitutes the offense, but the destruction of gestation by wicked means and against nature." Moreover, some of the laws still did not count as an illegal abortion the destruction of the fetus prior to quickening. A final measure of the slowness with which the states reacted to the upsurge of abortions was that on the eve of the Civil War, thirteen out of thirty-three states in the Union had no statutes against abortion at all.[19]

The situation changed sharply after the Civil War, as the publicity about the widespread incidence of abortion also reached a peak. Between 1860 and 1880 anti-abortion laws went upon the statute books in quick succession around the country. At least forty anti-abortion laws were enacted in states and territories; over thirty were enacted between 1866 and 1877 alone. Significantly, almost all of the new statutes accepted the view that an interruption of pregnancy at *any* stage constituted an illegal abortion. According to James Mohr, the law enacted in Connecticut in 1860 was typical of the new outlook. First of all, it was a special act, designed to deal with a special problem, not merely the product of a routine revision or consolidation of the legal code, as had often been the case in the 1830s. Second, the law designated as illegal an abortion induced at any time, not just after quickening. Third, the potential mother was as liable to punishment as the abortionist. And, finally, the advertising of abortifacients was declared illegal.

One of the main reasons for the burst of anti-abortion legislation after 1860 was that the old laws were not being enforced. Dr. Horatio Storer noted in 1868 that between 1849 and 1858 there had been thirty-two trials of alleged abortionists in Massachusetts, but that not a single conviction had been obtained. Even during the 1870s, Anthony Comstock, the principal single figure tracking down and exposing abortionists, complained privately of the dilatoriness or outright dereliction of duty of district attorneys in prosecuting those accused by Comstock of performing abortions. Comstock said in 1874 that he led a raid in Chicago on a group of abortionists, arresting eleven in three days, but the courts did no more than levy fines on them, although he thought the lawbreakers deserved imprisonment. And later students of Comstock's activities confirmed that the proportion of convictions among accusations against abortionists was lower than for any of his other moral campaigns. Moreover, much to Comstock's chagrin, some of those he managed to convict obtained pardons. Even as late as 1889 another opponent of abortion complained that it was a "well-known fact that [abortionists] are rarely indicted and more rarely convicted." [20]

Since not all persons, by any means, were obeying the laws against abortion, the question naturally arises as to what groups or interests were pressing this new stringency in regard to abortion. Many modern writers on the subject have asserted or simply assumed that the strengthening of the laws against abortion resulted from religious or ecclesiastical considerations and pressures. Modern political struggles over the repeal of those 19th-century statutes would seem to support such an interpretation. Religious groups, particularly the Roman Catholic church, have in the 20th century been in the forefront of defending anti-abortion laws. And it is true, of course, that the Roman Catholic church has opposed abortion as a matter of religious doctrine for centuries. The historical inference drawn from that fact, however, is quite wrong.

It is wrong on two counts. At the time these statutes were enacted in the 19th century, Roman Catholics simply did not constitute a political force of sufficient size and weight to influence the legislatures. Catholics were not powerful enough to enact such legislation against the will of Protestants, who not only far outnumbered the Catholics but occupied virtually all the principal offices of the state and federal governments. In short, all of the anti-abortion statutes of the 19th century must be attributed to the Protestants; Roman Catholics, of course, were quite in agreement with them.

Yet it would be a mistake to emphasize the Protestantism of those who put the laws on the books, for that is the second reason it is wrong to see church influence at work here. No churches of any denomination were especially interested in the matter at the time the laws were passed, whatever they may have become later. James Mohr systematically surveyed the religious press during the 1850s and 1860s, when the campaign against abortion began to cause changes in state laws on the subject. Yet he found very little interest in the cause, even among Roman Catholic newspapers and journals. Indeed, not until 1869 did the American Catholic bishops make a general and broad pronoucement on abortion, one that echoed the general principles laid down that same year by Pope Pius IX. Furthermore, Mohr found that as late as 1871 most Protestant denominations had taken no stand on abortion. Only small and uninfluential denominations like the Congregationalists on the state level had done so.

If religious leaders and denominations were not in the forefront of the movement to reduce or eliminate abortions by legal means, who was? The answer seems to be the medical profession. As we have seen, most of the information on the extent and character of, and attitudes toward abortion during the 19th century has been drawn from the voluminous literature and propaganda produced by individual physicians and medical societies in their efforts to educate the public about the medical facts of abortion and to influence legislators to take strong action against the practice. The issue that particularly distressed the medical profession was the distinction that many people, particularly women, made between an abortion before quickening and one after. Few women were prepared to countenance an interruption of pregnancy after quickening, but at the same time they viewed an interruption prior to quickening as without harm or moment. After all, the common law had long considered the death of a child in the womb after quickening as a serious offense, though usually not as serious as the killing of an infant once it had passed outside the womb. Not until the 1840s did that distinction begin to break down.

The ending of the distinction must be attributed to the educational campaign of the doctors, a campaign that apparently received its primary impetus from new medical knowledge. Not until 1827 was the existence of the human egg established as a scientific fact. Before that time, and as far back as the early 17th century, when the Dutch biologist Anton van Leeuwenhoek first saw human sperm under the microscope, it had been believed by most, though not by all, students of the subject, that the sperm contained a miniature person, which grew into a baby within the "nest," so to speak, of the woman's womb. A minority of scientists, who came to be called "ovists," argued, more from analogy than from observed fact, that human beings also developed from eggs, and that the sperm merely activated the egg's development. Thus what is spoken of today as the moment of conception, the time when egg and sperm unite, had no specific meaning or even conceptualization for people at the opening of the 19th century. About all that physicians and lay people alike knew was that at some point after sexual intercourse the male sperm (or egg) began to develop into a recognizably potential human being. For most of the century there was no reliable medical test of pregnancy for the first few months except the cessation of the menses, and that, of course, was not always reliable, either. The most obvious time when fertilization could be most confidently established was the point at which the mother perceived movement within her belly. Hence the belief by many women, even in the middle of the 19th century, that, until quickening, life had not commenced.

With the scientific establishment of the existence of the ovum and the idea of conception as the moment at which sperm united with egg to begin the process of growth that would eventuate in a baby, the whole matter took on a new aspect. Since the process from conception to birth was now viewed as continuous, whatever sanctity had been attached to the life of the fetus *after* quickening now had to be extended to the full life of the fetus before quickening began, that is, from the moment of conception. This reasoning was clearly evident in the arguments of physicians and laymen alike in their attacks upon the common practice of condoning abortion so long as it occurred prior to quickening. In 1872 Dr. Hugh Hodge admitted that the medical profession had shifted its ground when the new knowledge of conception was gained. "If . . . the profession in former times, from the imperfect state of their physiological knowledge, had, in any degree undervalued the importance of foetal life," he asserted, "they have fully redeemed their error and they now call upon the legislatures of the land . . . to stay the progress of this destructive evil of criminal abortion."[21]

One measure of the influence of the new medical understanding of conception on the actions of physicians is that the literature produced by doctors and their organizations against abortion emphasized this reason, virtually ignoring the dangers to women from abortion. Some physicians, to be sure, did tell women that abortion posed a threat to their health and lives, but it was usually in passing and never the main reason why an abortion was denied. Most argued that the death of the fetus was the principal objection. Again and again physicians told of their having to explain to women who asked them for abortions that life began at conception and therefore an abortion was equivalent to murder. In fact, in 1872 in its Report, the Committee on Criminal Abortions of the New York State Medical Society went so far as to say that it would have liked to denominate abortion "murder" and punishable by death. Only the fear that no convictions would result with such a penalty prevented the committee from making the recommendation. Other physicians were not so pragmatic. "The battle will be more than half won" against abortion, wrote one who referred to the crime as "foeticide," when abortion and infanticide were recognized to be the same and therefore deserved the same penalty—namely, death, "if maliciously committed."[22]

The doctors' lack of primary concern for women in opposing abortion also came through in another way. Frequently the medical opponents of abortion resorted to ideological or philosophical rather than medical or scientific reasons for their objections. In such cases it became clear that new scientific knowledge was not the only impetus behind the campaign against abortion. For to those doctors, abortion threatened the traditional role of women in the family. The Report of the American Medical Association's Committee on Criminal Abortion in 1871 denounced abortion because it violated the laws of God and Nature. Quite unscientifically, one would have thought, it quoted the Bible, and St. Paul in particular, on the need of human beings to multiply. Those women who sought abortions, the report declared, violated their role and purpose in life. Such a woman "becomes unmindful of the course marked out for her by Providence . . . overlooks the duties imposed on her by the marriage contract. . . . Such is *not* the intention of the Deity with regard to woman; such is not the character of her high destiny." [23]

When one physician listed four reasons why abortions were rightly considered a crime, the danger to the health of the potential mother was mentioned only as a proper punishment. Abortion was a crime, he wrote, against the state because it reduced the population; against the family; against women—for any woman "systematically producing abortion upon herself will as assuredly suffer, as that natural laws attach penalties to their transgressions." He concluded the list with an equally non-medical objection to abortion by saying it was a crime "against the welfare of the Soul." At the end of the century, one physician who accepted the idea of a therapeutic abortion—a principle enshrined in every state law on the subject— nevertheless asserted that women were designed for childbirth. "Either let them and the men totally abstain from coition or else consent to be mothers and fathers," he declared. Dr. Augustus K. Gardner, a popular writer on medical matters, called a wife who sought an abortion a "married shirk, who disregards her divinely-ordained duty." One physician was so hostile to the possibility that women might abort themselves that he seriously suggested that schools cease to teach physiology to girls so that they could have no thought or understanding of how to abort themselves. [24]

The logic of the medical men, if not their vehemence, in opposing abortion was widely accepted, as the changes in the laws make clear. One layman writing on marriage set forth the priorities clearly in giving his reasons why abortion must not be permitted: "first, to save the life of a human being [the fetus], and second to rescue you [the husband] but above all, your excellent wife, from the commission of the sin of damnation." Even a friend of women like Alice B. Stockham placed more emphasis upon the threat to the fetus than to women. "The woman who produces abortion, or allows it to be produced," she warned her readers, "risks her own health and life in the act, and commits the highest crime in the calendar, for she takes the life of her own child. She defrauds the child of its right to existence." [25]

As these remarks by Stockham make plain, the life-at-stake argument against abortion carried great weight even with those who might be expected to support abortion because of their interest in women's rights. Even Ezra Heywood, who was an outspoken sexual radical during the 1880s, wrote that "this murderous practice is unworthy of Free Lovers; they accept and rear the child, but take care that the next one be born of choice, not by accident." And Dr. Edward Bliss Foote, who was one of the few medical men to advocate and to disseminate information about contraception, never condoned abortion, even though he recognized that it was "now so prevalent among married people." Eliza Duffey, who could almost always be counted on to defend and expand the rights of women within marriage, as we have seen on several occasions, nonetheless stigmatized abortion as "murder." In short, as Linda Gordon concluded in her history of birth control, during the 19th century feminists and free lovers alike condemned abortion because it destroyed a human being. In fact, they pointed to the prevalence of abortion as a strong reason why voluntary motherhood was necessary; it would protect women against the temptation to commit the crime of abortion. [26]

About the only people who publicly supported abortion in the 19th century were the abortionists themselves, and they usually discreetly confined their advocacy to their deliberately ambiguous advertisements. A. M. Mauriceau, who was married to the most notorious abortionist in New York City, came the closest of anyone to recommending abortion outright. In the hands of "a skilled physician" in the early stages of pregnancy, he advised in 1847, abortion "has proved perfectly safe, recovery following in about three days." He further assured his readers that when properly carried out there was little danger. "A skilful and practised obstetrician will impart no pain," he wrote encouragingly. [27]

Mauriceau's rather back-handed defense of abortion may have been quite rare, but the fact remains that ordinary women were having abortions or aborting themselves. And if the crisis mentality displayed in the writings of the medical profession means anything, the number of abortions was surely rising in the middle decades of the 19th century rather than falling. To ordinary women abortions may have been undesirable, perhaps even criminal, but presumably the interruption of pregnancy was a way out of a situation that was even less endurable.

Already in the 1850s, advocates of voluntary motherhood, like Henry C. Wright, were suggesting that the prevalance of abortion had to be understood as a bad alternative to a worse fate. "It is no matter of wonder," Wright contended in 1858, "that abortions are purposely procured; it is to me a matter of wonder that a single child, undesignedly begotten and reluctantly conceived, is ever suffered to mature in the organism of the mother. Her whole nature repels it." He said that many mothers had told him that they would have "gladly strangled their children, born of undesired maternity, at birth, could they do so with safety to themselves." Addressing himself to husbands, Wright gave voice to the feelings that must have been behind the actions of many women who went to an abortionist. When a husband imposes maternity on his wife, Wright asserted, "she does not feel that it is *her* child. She may regard it as *yours,* but cannot acknowledge it as her own." A wife, forced by her husband into maternity, "is not prepared to bear the cross and endure the crucifixion. Instantly, her soul is filled with murderous intent. She resolves to nip and crush the opening bud of life—to procure abortion,—that is, to commit the deed of ante-natal childmurder." [28]

Not all abortions, of course, originated from this kind of reaction on the part of women, but that Wright found examples of it in his interviews suggests that some married women, at least, were not accepting maternity as something to which they had to submit without consulting their own interest and wishes. Wright told of a woman who was driven to several abortions because of the unthinking lust of her husband. After reading Wright's *Marriage and Parentage,* she raised the matter with her husband, who responded with a promise to be more thoughtful of her interests in the future. [29]

Women themselves, as one might expect, also advanced the kind of argument developed by Wright. An anonymous woman wrote in 1866 in response to Horatio Storer's account of the prevalence of abortion that "abortion is fearfully frequent even more so than Dr. Storer has assumed," and was rapidly increasing. "The true and *greatest* cause of abortion," she insisted, "is one hidden from the world, viz.: unhappiness and want of consideration towards wives in the marriage relation, the more refined education of girls, and their subsequent revolting from the degradation of being a mere thing—an appendage." Recognizing that her argument came close to justifying abortion, she denied that such was intended, but, she asked, what alternative do women have "who are victims of selfish and gross husbands, who are allowed no choice of time or convenience, whose hearts ache with disappointment and degradation . . . who go almost into the shadow of death, and yet return to make the pilgrimage again and again . . . ?" As she wrote in another place, women had a powerful reason to limit their fertility: "if the blessed, benevolent suggestion of the general use of chloroform could be adopted, the world would hear less of abortion." Mere appeals to the duty of women will not convince them, she asserted, for the price women must pay for maternity is too high to be met by mere talk or argument.[30]

Alice Stockham, as we have seen, did not condone abortion, but, like the anonymous woman just quoted, she did not absolve men of responsibility in the matter of abortions. "As long as men feel that they have a right to indulgence of the passions under the law, no matter what the circumstances, what the condition of the wife, or the probabilities of maternity, so long will the spirit of rebellion take possession of women and the temptation to enter their souls to relieve themselves of this unsought burden."[31]

It is impossible to know for sure how widespread the kind of reasoning that lay behind the arguments of the proponents of voluntary motherhood were. But the steady decline in the fertility of American women throughout the 19th century suggests it was not small. And the estimates from James Mohr already mentioned suggest it was rather widespread. Nor, given the vagueness of the evidence, can we tell whether the upsurge that became noticeable in the middle years of the 19th century declined by the turn into the 20th century. Certainly the practice of abortion did not end. Mohr, on the basis of his study of the enactment of stricter and more comprehensive anti-abortion statutes during the last three decades of the 19th century, concluded that fewer and fewer married women resorted to abortion. His reasoning is that improved and more socially acceptable contraceptives reduced the need for abortion as a birth control measure. That may well be, but certainly many married women in the 20th century before abortion was legalized in the 1970s resorted to that answer to their unwanted pregnancies. As we have seen already, a study in the 1920s reported that about one out of four pregnancies ended with a criminal abortion—not very much higher than Mohr's estimate for the 19th century.[32]

Few physicians in the late 19th century thought that the number was falling off. A comment of the *New York Medical Journal* in 1883 suggests, too, the significance of women's continued recourse to abortion. After setting forth elaborate arguments against abortion, the *Journal* closed with the admission that "the great majority of persons," even those of high education and moral sensitivity, would not agree with its opposition to abortion. In fact, the *Journal* continued, "we should be surprised . . . to find one woman, unless educated in medicine, agreeing with us, for in this matter the ordinary conscientiousness of the sex is warped and twisted out of its symmetry by selfish considerations, unconsciously no doubt, none the less, certainly."[33] And, of course, that was precisely what the rise in abortions in the 19th century and after has signified. It was yet another instance of women's push for greater autonomy within the family. What the *Journal* called "selfish considerations" we have been referring to as individuality, a sense of self-interest and identity among women—their recognition that they had interests and identities separate from men, children, and the family as a whole.

The upsurge in abortions in the 19th century was an even more striking measure of women's increasing concern with their own individual interests than the spread of contraception was. For, unlike most means of contraception, abortion does not depend upon male agreement or cooperation. Above all, it asserts the complete sovereignty of woman over her body. It is the supreme assertion of individualism, since the claims of the woman are judged to be superior to those of the man, whose contribution to conception, at least, is precisely equal, genetically, to that of the woman. In fact, one might say that simply because abortion was the assertion of women's complete control over her body, at the expense of both child and husband, the 19th century could not condone it. Not even feminist women were yet far enough advanced in their assertion of women's individuality and self-interest to accept abortion—at least not in public. In private many women did assert that autonomy by simply having abortions even when they were illegal. But clearly it was a last resort, not an asserted right. Most women, so far as we can tell from their public remarks and behavior, accepted the anti-abortion laws that were enacted in the last three decades of the 19th century. To that extent they acquiesced in the principle that women's self-interest was not superior to the interest of the family.

Not until well into the 20th century was the consensus on the undesirability, not to say evil, of abortion broken. In 1910 in *Sex in Relation to Society* Havelock Ellis agreed that most anti-abortion laws were reasonable but suggested that there might be reasons for permitting abortions under certain circumstances. An unconventional physician and writer on sexual matters, Dr. William J. Robinson, was probably the first American to suggest that there were reasons in addition to saving the life of the mother for an abortion. He made the tentative argument in 1911, yet as late as 1917 *Birth Control Review* was still stigmatizing abortion as "child murder." And though there was a rise in abortions in the 1920s and 1930s it was not until the depression years that other physicians picked up Robinson's lead. In fact, in 1933 Robinson himself went far beyond his 1911 statement, arguing in a new public statement that all restrictive laws should be repealed and the protection of the fetus abandoned. It was during the 1930s that popular magazines for the first time felt free to discuss the issue though none then advocated the legalization of abortion. Public acceptance of abortion was still more than a generation in the future.[34]

Seen against the broad canvas of humanitarian thought and practice in Western society from the 17th to the 20th century, the expansion of the definition of life to include the whole career of the fetus rather than only the months after quickening is quite consistent. It was in line with a number of movements to reduce cruelty and to expand the concept of the sanctity of life. The reduction, in the course of the 19th century, in the use, or elimination of the death penalty, the peace movement, the abolition of torture and whipping in connection with crimes all represented steps in that centuries-long movement. The prohibiting of abortion was but the most recent effort in that larger concern.

Measured against that development, the legalization of abortion in the last quarter of the 20th century can only appear as a reversal of a hitherto unreversed trend. For the legalization of abortion once again constricted the definition of life to what it was at the opening of the 19th century. The point here is not to offer an argument against the legalization of abortion but to throw into relief the significance of that reversal for the history of women and the family. It suggests how far women have come in defining themselves as individuals within the family. Their bodies, with the new acceptance of abortion, are truly their own, at the disposal of neither their unborn offspring nor of their husbands. It is quite true that many husbands are as happy as their wives to end an unwanted pregnancy. But that is not the heart of the matter. The laws as they now stand, and the values of the society that enacted those laws, allow a woman to have an abortion even if the husband does not agree. In that sense, the woman is truly the

final authority; she is the sovereign of her body. It is, in short, not accidental that the feminist movement of the late 20th century took up the cause
of abortion. For that was the last legal denial of women's individuality.

The legalization of abortion went beyond equality. It gave to women the
power to veto the husband's act and to extinguish the fetus, which was the
product of that act. To that extent the law and society gave women final authority over the size of the family, for no husband can compel a
woman to have an abortion nor legally deny her the right to have one. In
fact, married women today have it fully in their power to determine
whether they will have a family at all.

Control over fertility was only one aspect of marriage in which 19th-
century women exerted their individuality and affected the interpersonal
relationships that constitute the family. Intimately connected with fertility
is sexuality. In the course of the 19th century, women were able to assert
their individuality and self-interest in regard to sexuality, too. It is to the
complicated question of women's sexuality and its relation to marriage
and the family that we turn in the next two chapters.

XI

Women's Sexuality
in 19th-Century America

If there is one fact concerning the 19th century about which everyone feels
confident, it is that sex was then a tabooed subject. And it is quite true that
sexual feelings and the anatomy of the reproductive organs rarely came in
for the kind of free discussion and analysis that people living in the fourth
quarter of the 20th century take for granted. Yet, to those who are more
than thirty years old, the memory of a time when the discussion of sexual
matters in public was quite taboo must be still quite fresh. But it is not the
unwillingness to discuss sexual matters that distinguishes the 19th from
the 20th century in the popular mind. Rather, it is the effort to repress sexual feelings, particularly in women, that most modern people see as the
hallmark of the 19th century. The popular interpretation which sees the
1920s as the first time respectable women were accepted as sexual beings
sums it up neatly.

To illustrate the 19th century's alleged horror of sex, and particularly
women's sexuality, historians have frequently made use of an account by
the English traveler in Jacksonian America, Captain Frederick Marryat.
He wrote that some American women were so refined that they objected to
the use of the word "leg," using instead the term "limb." He further reported that a schoolteacher at one school he had visited, in order to protect the modesty of her charges, actually dressed all four "limbs" of the
piano "in modest little trousers with frills at the bottom of them!" [1]

So far as the record shows, no other traveler in America ever reported
such a display of modesty, either before or after Marryat. Nonetheless, historians have continued to follow Marryat's lead, even if they do not actu-

249

ally quote him. For example, Steven Marcus in his influential study of Victorian attitudes toward sexuality *The Other Victorians* (1966) and Nathan Hale, Jr. in his acclaimed book *Freud and the Americans* (1971) both draw upon the writings of Dr. William Acton to support their view that women's sexuality was either denied or absent in the middle of the 19th century. Acton's *Functions and Disorders of the Reproductive Organs,* which went through several editions in both England and the United States during the middle years of the 19th century, was undoubtedly one of the most widely quoted books on sexual problems and diseases in the English-speaking world. The book summed up medical opinion on women's sexuality in the following striking language: "The majority of women (happily for them) are not very much troubled with sexual feelings of any kind. What men are habitually, women are only exceptionally." [2] Acton's rather self-revealing dictum was quoted approvingly by contemporaries as well as by historians.

Such agreement between contemporaries and later historians on the absence of, or at least dearth of, sexual feelings in 19th-century women is particularly striking because that had not always been either the popular or medical view of women's sexuality. In writing about women's sexuality in pre-industrial Europe, historian Richard Vann notes that "the physiological theories of the Middle Ages, which still prevailed in modified form, held that women were more capable of sexual pleasure than men. Men were advised to exercise precautions lest the libidinous nature of women break forth." Prior to marriage a woman was to remain chaste to control her sexuality. Once she married, Vann continues, "it was considered her husband's responsibility to ensure his wife's faithfulness by seeing that her libidousness urgings were never aroused." As a result, the marriage manuals of 16th- and 17th-century Europe gave advice, Vann notes, "exactly the reverse of which such books counsel today. They admonished the husband not to arouse his wife to any expectation of sexual pleasure." Rabelais in *Gargantua and Pantagruel* has a chapter in which one of the characters declared that "cuckoldry naturally attendeth marriage." And the reason was that a woman's womb, which he termed "an animal," was so demanding. The only way "that the said animal can be satiated—if it be possible that it can be contented or satisfied," he avowed, was "by that aliment which nature hath provided for it out of the epididymeal storehouse of man." English historian Keith Thomas has pointed out that the rise of witchcraft persecution in the 15th and 16th centuries coincided with the general belief that women were sexually more avid than men. He quoted Robert Burton asking in 1621, "of women's unnatural unsatiable lust, what country, what village does not complain?"[3] Two recent students of American marriage manuals point out that during the 17th and 18th centuries much emphasis was placed upon the sexual arousal, pleasure, and satisfaction of women. The clitoris, for example, was spoken of as analogous to the penis, and the reader was advised to use it to encourage "the action excited in coition until the paroxysm alters the sensation," as one manual put it. *Aristotle's Master Piece,* a work of erotica and pseudo-gynecology that circulated widely in the 18th and very early 19th century, similarly assumed the sexual interest of women. One scholar has counted at least one hundred editions of the book prior to 1830; yet he has not found a single word of complaint about the book in any newspaper or periodical.[4]

Cases of adultery in 18th-century America also reveal the acceptance of the idea that women's sexuality could be strong. In one such suit, for example, the man excused his adultery with a married woman by contending that she had told him "She would Never do without a man" and that if he did not sleep with her "She should with Some other Man." He then went on to say that he had to admit that "She was the best for that game that ever he meet with." In another instance, a male lover was heard to ask "while he was upon her . . . if it felt good." After the lover had gone, the woman "said he was a glorious hand." Some men in the 18th century also gave some thought to women's sexual pleasure: in one of the adultery cases, a lover was reported to have said, "I have not made out so well as I intended to for I have fired my charge too soon." The woman involved was quite understanding. "That is no strange thing," she said, "for my Husband has done so often when he had been gone a few Nights."[5]

This frank recognition of women's sexual needs and desires persisted in the marriage manuals in the early 19th century at least down to the middle of the century. Normal sexual relations for a married couple were placed at four to five times a week by these manuals and they recommended that the wife experience an orgasm along with her husband. The old idea that women's sexual desires were insatiable seems to have lingered on, too, though disguised as an admonition to women and a warning to men. "A modest female," wrote one early 19th-century marriage counselor, "will be found always to possess . . . sufficient degree of effeminate decorum not to outstrip her sex, and play the harlot, even though her passions be strong." By the same token, however, the writer continued, "she ought not to be denied what a healthy husband ought to be able to give." The translator of a French work on marriage in 1839 admitted that it was "a very general impression" that women were more lustful than men, but he did not himself think so. Nevertheless, he later went on to tell of a prostitute who married and remained faithful to her husband. The writer thought that behavior exceptional, given his understanding of women's sexuality. "It is an established truth," he asserted, "that females who have given themselves up to profligacy in their youth can rarely afterwards satisfy their venereal desires in the embraces of one man." Charles Knowlton, in his widely circulated tract on birth control which first appeared in 1832, felt called upon to remind "every young married woman . . . that the male system is exhausted in a far greater degree than the female by gratification." And as late as 1847, one advice book warned young couples that men, as compared with women, were more easily exhausted by sexual activity. [6]

The advice books of the early 19th century could also be quite explicit in describing women's sexual anatomy. Knowlton, for example, asserted quite matter of factly that the male's role in reproduction "consists in exciting the orgasm of the female and depositing the semen in the vagina." The clitoris was described by one handbook in 1839 as analogous to the penis, while Frederick Hollick, a popular medical adviser, called it in 1850 "the principal seat of venereal excitement." Nor were these early writers hesitant in describing that venereal excitement. "In both sexes," wrote Hollick, "when union is really desired and no obstacle interferes," sexual intercourse "leads to the highest and most absorbing excitement that animated beings can experience. Both beings are thrown into a species of mental ecstasy and bodily fever, during which all other thoughts and functions are totally suspended, and all the vital forces are concentrated in the Reproductive system." Hollick admitted that in the female the orgasm is not always experienced, but "when it does occur," he continued, "it is exhibited in the same way as in the other sex, though often much more intensely, being accompanied by cries and convulsive motions of the most energetic character." [7]

If some of these writers merely equated male and female sexuality, others stressed women's interest in sexual expression. Thomas Hersey, for example, in his *Midwife's Practical Directory or, Woman's Confidential Friend,* published in 1836, conceded that women's reproductive powers ceased with the ending of the menses, but, he continued, that was not true of their sexual passion, which "often increased beyond that period, and in many, continues in a greater or less degree to an extreme age." Hersey also observed that, though many women think that they can tell whether they have conceived "from peculiar sensations, nervous tumults, sexual emotions, and exquisite local feelings," in fact, conception does not depend upon women's feelings.[8] Nonetheless, the existence, and one might add, persistence of this folk belief were further evidence that, to the popular mind, as well as to the medical mind, the sexual drives of women were a reality. Hollick even advised his readers that intercourse during menstruation was permissible if neither participant objected on grounds of fastidiousness. He personally concluded that the optimum time was that at which women's organs were receptive, a time he thought occurred immediately after the cessation of the menstrual flow. (For most of the 19th century, as we have observed in previous pages, physicians were confused about the meaning of the menses. Virtually all of them thought it was, as Hollick did here, analogous to estrus, or ovulation, in animals.)

This unanimity on the reality of women's sexuality was broken sometime during the 1840s and 1850s. A whole new literature on sexual behavior then came forward, in which women's sexuality was either played down or virtually denied. Acton's book, cited earlier, was one of the most prominent examples of this literature. It was the sudden emergence of this body of writing that gave birth to the idea, widespread in subsequent years, that women's sexuality was denied or suppressed in 19th-century America. Some historians who later read this literature often took these writings to be expressions of the actual practices and common beliefs of the time rather than what they were: a new ideology of sexual behavior, which was being advanced to counter the traditional one, which had recognized and encouraged women's sexuality. Some of the interpretations by modern historians of that new literature were in error.

To be quite fair, it is not surprising that these new writings on women's sexuality were misinterpreted by some historians. For most of this literature, like Acton's book, was couched in language that reads like description. The writers seem to be describing rather than recommending behavior, and that has been the way historians have interpreted them. But when the books are examined more closely, the prescriptive or normative character of these works comes through. A close reading of Acton's *The Functions and Disorders,* for example, reveals in several places his desire to establish a new and presumably a "higher" standard of sexual attitude and behavior. After pointing out that publicists strongly condemned sexual relations outside marriage, he earnestly asked, "But should we stop there? I think not. The audience should be informed that, in the present state of society, the sexual appetites must not be fostered; and experience teaches those who have the largest means of information on the matter, that self-control must be exercised." But so far, he persisted, no one has "dared publicly to advocate . . . this necessary regulation of the sexual feelings or training to continence." Yet that is precisely, of course, what he would like to have happen, and what he was in fact advocating. Or later, when he was discussing women in particular, it became clear that he was arguing for his own idea of proper behavior and not merely describing prevalent practices. "The *best* mothers, wives, and managers of households," he pointedly observed, "know little or nothing of sexual indulgence. Love of home, children, and domestic duties are the only passions that they feel," he told his readers.[9]

A similar mixture of prescription and description can be found in other works of the second half of the 19th century that played down sexuality. One such was Dr. John Kellogg's *Plain Facts for Old and Young*, which was published in 1881 and sold over 300,000 copies by 1910 in some five editions. Like Acton, Kellogg made clear that he thought sex was too dominant in the thoughts of Americans. As we look around us today, he contended, "it would appear that the opportunity for sensual gratification has come to be, in the world at large, the chief attraction between the sexes. If to these observations we add the filthy disclosures constantly made in police court and scandal suits, we have a powerful confirmation of the opinion," he insisted. It was this excess that he was fighting in his book, which was ostensibly a compendium of information on the relations between the sexes, marriage, and health. One way he sought to achieve his end was forcefully to argue against the view that continence in men was deleterious to health. He admitted that the medical profession at the time was not in agreement on the amount of sexual activity permissible in marriage. "A very few hold that the sexual act should never be indulged in except for the purpose of reproduction, and then only at periods when reproduction will be possible. Others, while equally opposed to the excesses . . . limit indulgence to the number of months in the year." Kellogg's own preference was that human beings should take their cue from animals, who have intercourse for procreation only, and then at widely spaced intervals. But instead of heeding this advice, he noted regretfully, "the lengths to which married people carry excesses is perfectly astonishing."

Kellogg was not alone in using the analogy of animal behavior in advocating the new ideology of restraint in sexual behavior. But he went farther than most by making an overt defense of the analogy. In the course of that defense he revealed that he was pushing a new conception of sexuality and not simply describing the attitudes or practices of the 19th century. He told his readers that, in the modern age of biology, analogies with animal behavior were extremely valuable in ascertaining nature's purpose. "It is by this method of investigation that most of the important truths of physiology have been developed; and the plan is universally acknowledged to be a proper and logical one." Then he launched into a denunciation of those men who used their wives as harlots, "having no other end but pleasure." Among animals, he pointedly observed, reproduction was the only end, and intercourse took place only that one or two times a year when reproduction was possible. But by the time Kellogg reached the place in his book at which he defended the analogy with animals he had already revealed that his purpose in invoking the analogy was reformist and normative, not simply scientific and logical.

In the early pages of his book, in making a different normative point—namely, the need to protect children from premature sexual experience—he told of a parent whose adolescent children often played games in the nude. When admonished for permitting this practice, the parent replied that it was only natural. "Perfectly harmless; just like little pigs!" Kellogg quoted the parent as replying. Kellogg's comment this time, however, was quite different from that which he would make later in his book: "as though pigs were models for human beings!"

In the end, Kellogg virtually admitted that his "plain facts" were neither plain nor facts, but prescriptions and hopes. "There will be many," he concluded, "the vast majority, perhaps, who will not bring their minds to accept the truth which nature seems to teach, which would confine sexual acts to reproduction only." And so in view of that recognition he went on to offer his readers a form of birth control![10]

The advice books of the time were not alone in making references to women's alleged lack of sexual interest. Medical writers did, too. Some doctors, in writing for their fellows, noted that many women showed no interest in sexual relations. Interestingly enough, those who did make such reference usually deplored the phenomenon. Dr. Ely Van de Warker, for instance, stressed the naturalness of orgasms in women; yet he was compelled to admit in 1878 that "there is every reason to believe that there exists a large class of women . . . who remain ignorant through life of these sensations." And in 1882 Dr. Charles Taylor also referred to the view that women have "less sexual feeling than men" and that some people even go so far as to claim that "as a rule women have practically nothing of what is understood as sexual passion." As many as three-quarters of married women, he had been told, took no pleasure in the sexual act. "I admit the facts," he conceded, "but deny the conclusion."

The true character of women's sexuality, Taylor asserted, cannot be ascertained from its manifestations in modern society. Modern civilization, he contended, is "hard on women" because it suppresses their sexuality. It is true that girls do not have the early provocation to sexual activity that boys have with their erections and nocturnal emissions in early puberty, he pointed out. And so the two sexes cannot be expected to have the same interest in sexual activity in the early years. But for mature women, he thought the principal reason for the prevalence of the view that women lacked sexual feelings was the "vigorous repression and mental influences" that are exerted by society from the earliest years to keep women ignorant. He stressed that girls masturbated at an early age, and that other signs of women's sexual feelings made quite clear that their sexual drives are "stronger than the average sentiment accredits them with."

"How then," Taylor quite properly asked, "does the belief obtain that the sexual desire is feeble in women? The fact is, that civilized women live in an atmosphere at once false, strained, and unnatural so far as relates to their sexual life." And the root of the matter, he continued, was "the belief of many that erotic sensations in women are immoral, degrading and to be suppressed by all the power of will." Taylor saw this belief as having two consequences. In the majority of cases, "it diminishes the natural sexual sense; in a certain number it practically destroys it." The second consequence is that, for a minority of women, "directing the attention to the subject, stimulates and increases the feeling, sometimes inordinately. The result is that few women are natural in their sexual lives." This repression of women, he concluded, "is the greatest evil of modern society."

William A. Hammond, onetime Surgeon General of the United States Army, was another physician who recognized as a common conception in 1887 that women had "far less intensity of sexual desire than do men." But, like Taylor, Hammond attributed whatever truth there was to the view to the teachings of society rather than to nature. Women were simply not permitted to express their feeling as men were, or sometimes they were married to unthinking or brutal men, Hammond contended. Better treatment would produce a better result, he advised. Although it was Hammond's view that, generally speaking, "women are slower to reach the height of venereal paroxysm than are men," he thought that "probably in a state of nature there is no difference in this respect between men and women, but civilization has imposed restrictions on the development of the sexual appetite in the one sex, while it has set few or no limits to its exercise in the other." [11]

Although the good doctors were undoubtedly right that women in the 19th century had sexual feelings and that they deserved to be expressed, the further conclusion that society (or men) imposed that repression upon women may not be the full or complete story. There is no question, to be sure, that 19th-century social practices and habits, especially in public forms of expression, played down the outward manifestations of women's sexuality. And it is also true that women's sexuality, unlike men's, could be denied or minimized without endangering women's reproductive capacities. By the middle years of the 19th century it had become clear to physicians, contrary to what most of them had thought previously, that conception did not depend upon a woman's emotional involvement in the sexual act. In fact, Dr. J. Marion Sims, one of the leading gynecologists of mid-century America, in one of his medical publications told how he had overcome a woman's inability to have a baby because sexual intercourse was too painful for her. He recommended that her husband have intercourse while his wife was comatose with chloroform. Sims proudly reported that conception was thereby achieved. If women's emotional involvement in conception was not necessary, then to minimize her sexual feelings entailed no social loss or cost. Manipulation or control of men's sexuality was another matter; it was more difficult to deny since without sexual arousal a man could not procreate at all.

Even though it was and is possible to separate woman's sexuality from her reproductive capacity, it does not automatically follow that men had an overriding interest in denying women's sexuality. In fact, just the opposite might obtain. As noticed already, medical doctors in the 19th century pointed out that husbands often deplored their wives' lack of sexual interest. And generally that is what one would expect. The new ideology of sexual control or denial was not something that answered most men's sexual preferences. On the contrary, it usually resulted in limiting sexual satisfaction for men. Men as a gender, in short, had little or no direct interest in asserting or spreading a new ideology of sexual control. Women and individual men with women's interests at heart, on the other hand, might well have.

Once one begins to think that women may have had an interest in autonomy within the family, it becomes evident that women themselves might well want to minimize or even deny their own sexuality. For one thing it would be a way of reducing pregnancies—the sick headache, as some anonymous wit has said, being the oldest form of birth control. The frequent references in medical and popular journals to illnesses and physical debilities of middle-class women may really have been signs of women's efforts to control their husband's sexuality in the interest of lower fertility. Minimizing or denying women's sexuality may also have been a way of achieving autonomy within marriage. As Nancy Cott has recently pointed out, by asserting their own lack of sexual passion, women gained a certain moral superiority over men, who were thereby relegated to the status of lesser beings simply because they required fairly frequent sexual expression. In short, women would be encouraged to accept a belief in their own sexlessness as a way of enhancing their position within the family. Furthermore, as a class, women would have a tendency to move in this direction if only because sexuality was the primary source of women's subordination to men; it was the force that brought men and women together into marriage, the very institution in which the subordination of women to men was most clearly accomplished.

Although one cannot expect to find many women who have left records of their negative attitudes toward sexuality because of their wish to control their fertility, there are some signs that the connection was consciously made. Alice B. Stockham, in her book *Tokology,* for example, referred to the fallacious theory held by some women "that by avoiding the last thrill of passion herself, during coition, she can prevent the ovules being displaced to meet the male germs." [12] Even those women who were not able to admit consciously to themselves that they did not want to have more children may well have subconsciously projected their dislike of constant pregnancies onto sexual intercourse, which, after all, was the source of the excessive birthings. In short, it is not necessary to see a conscious or rational rejection of sexuality by women to connect that denial to a wish to reduce fertility. The point is that statements about women's lack of sexual interest in the 19th century are quite consistent with the argument made in these pages that in those years women were pressing for greater autonomy and self-respect within the family. Women's own denial or minimizing of sexuality may well have been one of the ways in which that was done.

Although we have been referring to the denial of sexuality on the part of women, that verbal formulation of the matter is undoubtedly too strong. For there is sound reason to believe that the issue was not denial but control of sexuality. One important reason for making that qualification is that, despite the assertion by some 19th-century authorities that women were without sexual feelings, the medical and popular literature throughout the century, as well as the testimony of women themselves, continued to assert that women were indeed sexual beings. The point asserted by most of the so-called repressive literature of the time was that the sexuality of women differed from that of men. And the implications of that assertion were that women's sexual character must not be denied in the name of men's. But first let us listen to those 19th-century men and women who continued to assert women's sexuality.

Various popular and medical writers plainly declared that sexual enjoyment was a legitimate part of married life. Dr. Henry Chevasse told the readers of his popular advice book, *Physical Life of Man and Woman,* published in 1871 that intercourse between married people need not be confined to reproduction. "While its first and most important purpose is the procreation of the species, there can be no doubt that man is permitted this gratification as one of the few legitimate pleasures granted him among so many sorrows and cares." Even more positive was Henry Guernsey in *Plain Talks on Avoided Subjects* (1882): "The sexual relationship is among the most important uses of married life; it vivifies the affection for each other, as nothing else in the world can, and is a powerful reminder of their mutual obligation to each other and to the community in which they live." At the end of the century one medical writer referred to sexual feelings as "this novel instinct which impels love between the sexes, love of progeny, love of home, love of purity, and admiration of true manliness and true womanliness." [13]

Some writers were even more pointed in noting the power of women's sexual needs. James Ashton in 1865, in a book on contraception, admitted that some women did not experience orgasm, "though they are often excited and feel a certain degree of pleasure." But when "orgasm . . . does occur in women, it is even more intense than in the other sex, causing convulsive motions and involuntary cries. . . . It sometimes happens," he continued, "that a female of amative desires is never satisfied with one Orgasm, but craves frequent and repeated intercourse, as the indulgence does not exhaust her as it does her partner." Ashton did not even see any reason for moderation in the female sexual experience. "The female Orgasm, not being produced by any secretion, may be enjoyed without particular injury, though it is sometimes apt to affect the nerves." [14] Elizabeth Evans, writing in *Abuse of Maternity* in 1875, recognized that it is often "assumed that passion is much weaker in the female than in the male of the human species," but she thought a realistic appraisal of the facts would "show that the difference is entirely training. Many courtesans follow their infamous trade because they enjoy it, and many girls called 'virtuous' are so not from choice, but because restraining circumstances are too powerful for them to overcome. Many nuns have gone mad or sunk into premature decline on account of the strength of ungratified passion," she concluded. Dr. Edward B. Foote, perhaps the most outspoken advocate of birth control during the 1870s, even to the point of enduring a heavy fine for resisting Anthony Comstock's attacks upon his publications, also stressed the pleasure of sex for women. "In women," he wrote in 1881, "the clitoris and the erectile tissue of the vagina are the parts, which, when acted upon the electricities already referred to, induce sexual excitement." Medical writers, of course, fully recognized the role of the clitoris as the center of women's sexual excitement and satisfaction, one writer calling it "the most sensitive electrical button." Another sought to emphasize its sensitivity by remarking that the clitoris "is furnished with five times as many nerves as the penis." [15]

Still other writers noted that women were less easily exhausted sexually than men. "Perhaps most men learn this lesson soon enough for themselves," wrote an anonymous physician in 1873 in the pamphlet *Satan in Society*, "but a strongly passionate woman may well-nigh ruin a man of feebler sexual organization than her own." Therefore he advised a woman that, whatever her own feelings, she should be sufficiently circumspect and delicate "to await the advances of her companion before she manifests her willingness for his approaches." One of the few marital guides intended for workingmen's families, published in England in 1886, also pointed out that every woman should know that "a man is sooner exhausted by excessive indulgence than a woman. He should, therefore, never be encouraged to have connection unless he desires." Eliza Duffey in 1889 drily drew the conclusion from these sexual differences between the sexes that they "ought to settle the question of polygamy; for, if either sex may take on plurality of partners, it is plainly indicated by the laws of nature that it is the woman rather than the man who may do so." [16]

Lest it be thought that these proponents of women's sexuality were merely partisans of a cause and therefore suspect as to their representativeness, other, disinterested witnesses can be called upon. For the recognition of women's sexual needs and nature comes through in the writings of those who have no ax to grind in this regard. Instead, women's sexuality is something they assumed in the course of writing or commenting upon quite unrelated subjects. In short, they are neither self-serving nor interested witnesses; they are simply ideal historical reporters.

Among such witnesses were the opponents of birth control. Virtually all writers on birth control condemned *coitus interruptus,* but what is significant for us was that among the reasons for condemnation was that it denied sexual satisfaction to women. This method of contraception, wrote Dr. Henry Chevasse, is "attended with disastrous consequences, most particularly to the female, whose nervous system suffers from ungratified excitement." John Harvey Kellogg quoted approvingly the opinion of a French authority, who warned against the effects of *coitus interruptus* upon women. Whenever this method was employed, the authority stated, all of women's genital organs "enter into a state of orgasm, a storm which is not appeased by the natural crisis; a nervous super excitation persists" after the act. The authority then compared the unreleased tension to that evoked in presenting food to a "famished man" and snatching it away. "The sensibilities of the womb and the entire reproductive system are teased to no purpose." [17]

A similar assumption that women had sexual feelings appeared in discussions of the mechanics of conception. When Dr. J. Marion Sims published *Clinical Notes on Uterine Surgery* in 1866, conception was only beginning to be understood. In explaining how it was achieved, Sims revealed in passing that most people took for granted that women experienced strong sexual feelings, including orgasm. "It is the vulgar opinion, and the opinion of many savants," Sims remarked, "that, to ensure conception, sexual intercourse should be performed with a certain degree of completeness, that would give an exhaustive satisfaction to both parties at the same moment." This sounds like the 20th-century view of optimum sexual performance, for Sims then went on to note that husbands and wives strove for such simultaneity and were unhappy when they failed to have simultaneous orgasms, for then they thought no conception could occur.[18] Sims's point was that conception did not depend upon either the sexual arousal or the sexual satisfaction of the woman. Yet it is quite clear that to Sims, his medical readers, and the patients he treated for infertility, the sexuality of women was taken for granted.

Dr. George Napheys in his popular book of advice for women also alluded to the prevalence of the idea that conception and woman's pleasure were connected. He said that many people erroneously believed that conception could be known to have taken place by the "more than ordinary degree of pleasure" on the part of the woman during the sexual act. In fact, so prevalent was the idea that informed writers on contraception again and again took the trouble to deny it, testimony, once more, to the prevalence of the belief that women's sexuality was a reality.[19] As we have seen, Alice Stockham referred to a theory among some women "that by avoiding the last thrill of passion herself, during coition, she can prevent the ovules being displaced to meet the male germs," a view she rightly stigmatized as fallacious. It was their way, however erroneously based as it may have been, of controlling fertility. (It might also explain why some physicians noticed an increased interest among women in sexual expression after menopause.) Finally, the breadth of the recognition, despite the literature that argued to the contrary, that women indeed had sexual feelings and needs was revealed by the responses of women to an unusual, but important survey of sexual habits, made by Dr. Clelia Mosher. The Mosher Survey of married women's sexual attitudes and habits was begun in 1892 and concluded in 1920. The important point about the 45 women who answered the questionnaire is that 70 percent of them were born before 1870. Thus their attitudes can be said to have been shaped and perhaps solidified in the 19th century, even though many of them did not actually answer the questionnaire until the 20th century.[20]

The number of women queried is small, to be sure. But two considerations suggest that the numbers are not as insignificant as might appear at the outset. The first is that, small as the numbers may be absolutely, the Mosher Survey is the only systematic questioning of women on their sexual habits available for the 19th century. Not even the researches of Kinsey reached women born before 1890. Yet over one-third of the women questioned in the Mosher Survey were born before the Civil War. The second point is that subsequent work by two economic demographers at Stanford University has statistically linked the demographic characteristics of these 45 women to a much larger government survey of wives of professional men, so that it is now reasonable to assume that the attitudes on sexual matters revealed in the Mosher Survey are representative of this much larger group of middle-class women at the opening of the 20th century.

What, then, does the Mosher Survey reveal about the sexual attitudes and practices of middle-class American women at the end of the 19th and the beginning of the 20th century? To begin with, 35 of the 45 women testified that they felt desire for sexual intercourse independent of their husbands' interest; 9 others said they never or rarely felt any such desire. What is more striking is the number who testified to having had an orgasm. According to the standard view of 19th-century women's sexuality, women were not expected to know the term, much less experience one. Yet, in constructing the questionnaire in 1892, Clelia Mosher asked not only whether the respondents experienced orgasm during intercourse, but whether "you *always* have a venereal orgasm [my italics]." The form of the question makes clear that Mosher assumed that female orgasms could be expected. Unfortunately, that form of the query also confused the meaning of the responses. (Incidentally, of the 45 respondents only 2 failed to answer this particular question.) What did "no" mean? It could mean "not always" or "never" or anything in between. Five of the women responded "no" without further comment. The ambiguity of the answer is further heightened when we find that in answer to another question, three of the women who said simply "no" in regard to orgasms said that they felt sexual desire, while a fourth said "sometimes but not often" and the fifth said sex was "usually a nuisance." Luckily, however, most of the women who answered the question concerning orgasm responded more precisely: 35 per cent of them answered "always" or "usually"; another 40 per cent said "sometimes," "not always," or "no," but with specific instances. In short, about three-quarters of the women experienced one or more orgasms sometime in the course of their marriages. If the women born before 1875 are taken as a separate group, about 82 per cent experienced at least one orgasm. This figure is about at the level that Kinsey reported in his survey for women born between 1900 and 1920.

More interesting than the bare statistics are the comments that the women made about their sexual experiences. The questionnaire often asked quite detailed questions, so that only a sampling of responses can be given here to suggest that, among these women at least, sexual expression was desired and enjoyed. One question asked what the women thought was the purpose of sexual intercourse, and whether it was necessary to good health. None of the respondents thought sex was necessary for men only, but 13 thought it was necessary for both men and women; 15 of the respondents thought sexual intercourse was not a necessity for either sex, a point with implications that will be discussed a little later in this chapter. Whereas 24 of the women thought that sex was a pleasure for both sexes, only one thought it was exclusively a pleasure for men.

A few of the women clearly did not desire sex as much as their husbands, or as much as the majority of women in the survey. One woman, for example, said she did not experience an orgasm until the fifth or sixth year of her marriage and that even at the time of her filling out the questionnaire—the early 1890s—she did not experience an orgasm half of the time. She conceded that, because of her love for her husband, she "cultivated the passion" because she thought marriage was a compromise. Another woman commented that she thought a man's needs were at least twice those of a woman's, but that, since she was always in good health, and intercourse "did not hurt me, . . . I always meant to be obliging."

But, as the overall responses, already mentioned, make clear, the women who only tolerated intercourse were in a decided minority. Sexual intercourse "makes more normal people," wrote a woman born in 1857. She was not even sure that children were necessary to justify sexual relations within marriage. "Even if there are no children," she remarked, "men love their wives more if they continue this relation, and the highest devotion is based upon it, a beautiful thing, and I am glad nature gave it to us," she concluded. Another woman, born in 1855, said that a good relationship between married people "cannot exist in perfection without sexual intercourse to a moderate degree." The only respondent who was divorced and remarried testified in 1913 that at age 53 "my passionate feeling has declined somewhat and the orgasm does not always occur," but intercourse, she added, was still "agreeable" to her.

Several of the women even went so far as to reject reproduction as sufficient justification for sexual relations. Said one woman, "I consider this appetite as ranking with other natural appetites and like them to be indulged legitimately and temperately; I consider it illegitimate to risk bringing children into the world under any but most favorable circumstances." This woman was born before 1850 and made her comment after she had been married ten years. Another woman, also born before the Civil War, denied that reproduction "alone warrants it at all; I think it is only warranted as an expression of true and passionate love. This is the prime condition for a happy conception, I fancy." A third woman born before 1861 doubted that sex was a necessity in the same sense as food and drink were, but she had no doubt that "the desire of both husband and wife for this expression of their union seems to me the first and highest reason for intercourse. The desire for offspring is a secondary, incidental, although entirely worthy motive, but could never to me make intercourse right unless the mutual desire were also present." She apparently saw a sharp conflict between the pleasure of intercourse and reproduction—of the sort that modern people refer to as the separation of sexuality from reproduction. It was this outlook, of course, that culminated in the ideas of advanced birth-control advocates like Margaret Sanger in the 20th century. "My husband

and I," this woman said in 1893, "believe in intercourse for its own sake—we wish it for ourselves and spiritually miss it, rather than physically, when it does not occur, because it is the highest, most sacred expression of our oneness. On the other hand, even a slight risk of pregnancy, and then we deny ourselves the intercourse, feeling all the time that we are losing that which keeps us closest to each other."

Although the Mosher Survey is unique in being the only systematic survey of women's attitudes on sex during the 19th century, there are other pieces of evidence to show that women themselves were far from convinced that they lacked sexual feelings or that they had no need for, or right to, sexual satisfaction. In a long essay "Marriage" among the papers of the Grimké sisters are some strong opinions on this matter, written sometime after 1855. (It is not clear which of the sisters, Angelina or Sarah, actually wrote the essay. It is in the hand of Angelina, but the ideas seem to be Sarah's.) Although the Grimké sister was a firm believer in women's having the final say about when intercourse should take place and in generally controlling its exercise, she also had no doubt that the function or purpose of sex extended beyond reproduction. For one thing, she categorically rejected the Shaker notion, which she discussed briefly, that sexual intercourse was the source of original sin. Instead, she asserted, the generative organs should be seen as sacred and instanced the "early Hindoos" who looked upon them "as objects of worship." Only modern misuse and profanation of these organs have "degraded them in our eyes," she asserted. The union of husband and wife "in every true marriage," she went on, "finds it most natural, and most sacred and intense outward expression in that mutual personal embrace which in the order of God, constitutes them Creators, exercising divine functions and ushering into being immortal existence."

Lest there be any doubt about whether or not she thought sexual intercourse should be confined to procreation, she added a long paragraph arguing in favor of intercourse even when children were not intended. Some people, she observed, thought that sexual relations within marriage should stop after a woman was no longer capable of having children. She, however, was not of that opinion. "To me that embrace is as spontaneous an expression of love in husband and wife after that period as before it, and as natural and pure as the kisses pressed by the loving child upon its mother's lips." So long as the force behind the act is strong mutual love between the partners, "why repress this mode of manifestation which will never cease to be natural until disease or the infirmities of age have deadened all physical susceptibilities." After all, she went on, married people who cannot have children are not expected to view "physical connection an inappropriate expression of *their* mutual love." The desire for children, she went on, is certainly a "natural incitement to the sexual act, yet that is weak in comparison with that yearning for *mutual absorption into each other*, which alone gives vitality to every true marriage—and the ceasing to have children does not and cannot destroy this deep abiding feeling." [21]

Other feminist women also attested to the enduring strength of the sex urge in women. Isabella Hooker, sister of Harriet Beecher Stowe, complained to her daughter in 1874 that women "who have scarce known what sexual desire is—being wholly absorbed in the passion of maternity—have sacrificed themselves to the beloved husband as unto God—and yet these men, full of their human passion and defending it as righteous and God-sent, lose all confidence in womanhood when a woman here and there betrays her similar nature and gives herself body and soul to the man she adores." Another feminist, Elizabeth Cady Stanton, complained in her diary in 1883 that Walt Whitman, whose poem "There Is a Woman Waiting for Me" she had just been reading, seemed to think that "the female must be forced to the creative act, apparently ignorant of the great natural fact that a healthy woman has as much passion as man, that she needs nothing stronger than the law of attraction to draw her to the male." [22]

Bell Waller of Kentucky was no feminist, but in her letters to her husband she did not conceal her physical love for him. "Hold your ear 'till I whisper I would give the world to sleep with you and have the exquisite pleasure of being folded to your bosom and there repose during the mystic hours of the night. Is my wish reciprocated?" she asked in 1842. "Would you not like to have me with you? Say yes." Thirteen years later, when Henry was away again, her desire was no less. "I must close, and go to bed, oh my darling, what would I not give to sleep in your dear arms tonight." [23]

Charlotte Perkins Gilman was a feminist, but she was also known publicly for her objections to overindulgence in sexual expression. Yet in her private correspondence she not only recognized women's sexuality, but the important place of sexuality in marriage as well. "It is too bad that you are hungry, dear," she wrote Houghton Gilman in 1898 two years before they were married. "I feel it a little, but not much, consciously." Apparently Houghton had apologized in his letter for having physical longings for her, for she chided him. (His letters have not been preserved.) "I rather resent such tender loving memories of me being denounced as 'the animal side of it'! Good gracious man! What did you expect? To love my astral body? Or to pass your days in intellectual pursuits, lit by a mild glow of Platonic affection?" She then went on to tell him of her own physical feelings for him. "I don't think it is 'an animal side of it' when I remember the look in your eyes—the pressure of your loving arms—your beautiful strong body. Dear—it strikes me that you don't know what the animal side of life is! It is to feel that way just *in general*—so that any woman would do. Apparently such is not your state of mind." [24]

Nor were such expressions of women's need for sexual expression confined to private writings. Eliza Duffey contended that some women's sexual feelings were nipped in the bud by husbands' rough or thoughtless approach to sexual intercourse. "The apple of pleasure will turn to ashes in her taste," under such circumstances, wrote Duffey. As a result, over the years, such a woman would become convinced "that she is denied all passional feelings by nature. If she has given the matter serious consideration, she will feel deep regret that she should have lost out of her life something so essential, which of right belonged to her." But, unfortunately, most women who had that experience with their husbands were not thoughtful. Instead, such a woman "will naturally give herself airs of superiority over her more impassioned sisters, on account of her assumed purity of nature, and be inclined to look with contempt upon all women not equally frigid with herself." [25]

Elizabeth Blackwell, the first woman physician trained in the United States, also made clear her view that women's sexual nature had been misread. "The assertion that sexual passion commands more of the vital force of men than of women," she denounced in 1884 as "a false assertion of the facts of human nature." Later she went on to make her point even more precisely. To compare "the physical development of the comparatively small class of refined and guarded women, and the men of worldly experience whom they marry is a false comparison," she pointed out. These women have been taught by their society to regard sexual passion as sinful, so they cannot be taken as representative of women as a sex. "But if the comparison be made between men and women of loose lives—not women who are allowed and encouraged by money to carry on a trade in vice—but men and women of similar and unrestrained and loose life—the unbridled impulse of physical lust is as remarkable in the latter as in the former. The astounding lust and cruelty of women uncontrolled by spiritual principle is a historical fact," she concluded.

Although she did see differences in attitudes between men and women toward sexual intercourse, Blackwell made clear that she thought it "a well-established fact in healthy loving women, uninjured by the too frequent lesions which result from child-birth, increasing physical satisfaction attaches to the ultimate physical expression of love. A repose and general well-being results from this natural occasional intercourse, whilst the total deprivation of it produces irritability." From her own medical practice (Blackwell never married) she had "known this physical loss severely felt for years after the death of a beloved husband." [26] We also know that the power of sex presented problems to Blackwell personally. As she told a niece in 1887, although she was thought to be tough and unwomanly because of her fight to be accepted as a physician, the greatest fight was against her own sexuality. "From the age of seven, when I first fell in love with a golden-haired rosy-cheeked little fellow in my aunt's school, who seemed to me like a little angel," she confessed, "I have always been keenly susceptible to the influence of sex, both in attraction and repulsion." [27]

Even Ida Craddock, a proponent of the Social Purity movement of the late 19th century, which is today often thought of as hostile to sexuality, entertained no doubt that women's sexual feelings need expression and resolution. Contrary to what some people of the day advised, she wrote, "it is natural and right for a woman who is uniting with her husband . . . to execute various movements of her pelvis during the marital embrace." By refusing to move, she continued, many women reduce the joy of their husbands, thus encouraging them to infidelity. "In fact, a woman who is thoroughly in love with her husband, and who united with him at the proper time of the month, can scarcely help moving," she asserted. At another place in her tract, where she advocated nudity on the part of the wife, she went so far as to say that failure to move was to "violate natural law" and caused women to "become abnormal and debased conveniences for their husbands." Like many writers at that time on sexual matters, Craddock thought that a woman "is most affectionate and most passionate" immediately after the cessation of the menstrual flow. Craddock was at once feminist and positive about women's sexual experiences. "Our final ecstasy should be completely under your control," she told her readers. "It should be induced coincidentally with the ecstasy of your husband." But because a woman took longer to reach climax than a man, she warned, the women "should train him to wait for her, if her own natural functions are to be fulfilled healthfully." In pursuit of this goal, she suggested half an hour of foreplay. "The normal, self-controlled use of the love function (when exercised in moderation)," she promised, "never debilitates, never enervates. It freshens both parties, and renews nervous energy for days thereafter."[28]

It is this clear recognition by male medical doctors, writers of advice books, and women themselves that prevents us from accepting the notion that during the 19th century women's sexuality was generally denied or effectively suppressed. Yet a paradox remains. For at the same time there cannot be any doubt that some medical men and the new prescriptive literature, represented by writers like Acton and Kellogg, certainly portrayed women's sexuality as underdeveloped and perhaps even absent. How can the paradox be resolved? A clue is provided by the prescriptive literature itself, a striking aspect of which is that sexual expression ought to be controlled, especially in males. For the other side of the argument that women were without sexual feelings was the contention that males indulged too freely. Over and over again the argument appears, directly and indirectly, that married couples indulged unduly in sexual relations. Certainly this was one of the main assertions in Acton's book published first in 1857. It was also the message which Sylvester Graham, food faddist and self-appointed adviser to young men, advanced in his *Lecture to Young Men* in 1839. In fact, according to another proponent of sexual restraint, William A. Alcott, it was just this advice by Graham that caused him to be ridiculed and caluminated. Alcott himself was one of the most prolific and popular writers on domestic and marital matters in the middle years of the 19th century. Today the Harvard College Library contains some thirty-two titles of his works. His *Physiology of Marriage,* which was first published in 1855, reached 27,000 copies by 1866, and ran to at least seven editions. That was the book in which Alcott referred to Graham's dictum that sexual intercourse once a week was excessive and that, ideally, sexual relations ought to be confined to once a lunar month—that is, in rhythm with the menstrual cycle of women. Alcott contended that "this doctrine . . . so utterly at war with general habits and feelings of mankind, was almost enough, at the time it was announced to provoke the cry of, Crucify him." Graham, it is worth noting, had other ideas equally divergent from majority opinion, such as his opposition to refined flour and to the eating of meat, which Alcott admitted aroused odium against him. But Alcott was convinced it was "his anti-sexual indulgence doctrines . . . which excited the public hatred and rendered his name a by-word and a reproach."[29]

Alcott was in the forefront of the effort in the 1860s to bring about restraint in sexual expression in marriage. He contended that excessive sexuality not only debilitated the parents but also produced weak children. Henry C. Wright also deplored in books and articles in the 1850s and 1860s the fact that many couples indulged in intercourse without any intention of producing children at all. The aim of men like Wright and Alcott was nothing less than the alteration of the character of marriage. Their goal was to make it a less sensual and more affective institution. Alcott clearly revealed the direction he was moving when he asserted "that one of the very *ends* of marriage is gradually to purify us wholly from sensuality, by bringing our bodies under that law of which Paul makes so much in his writings." By which, he apparently meant that eventually sex would not be needed in marriage at all!

Not all those who followed the lead of Alcott and Wright in seeking to reform marriage by desensualizing it were as extreme as Alcott. But all such advocates thought that less indulgence in sexual expression was desirable. Alice B. Stockham in *Tokology* did not commit herself to Henry Wright's principle that intercourse should be confined to procreation only, but she was certainly partial to the idea. After all, as she wrote, there were other, more intellectual purposes to which that energy could be put. John Cowan, whose *Science of a New Life* was a near best-seller in the 1870s, and John Harvey Kellogg's *Plain Facts for Young and Old,* a widely read book of the 1880s, also argued for confining sexual relations as closely as possible to procreation only. Cowan advised, for example, that sexual intercourse for married couples should cease at the first sign of conception and should not resume until the next menses after weaning, a period, by his own count, of from 18 to 21 months. That, he insisted, is "precisely what Nature intended." Yet he would go beyond even that standard, and, in the interest of the mother, forbid sexual intercourse for three full years after conception. A popular adviser on sexual matters like R. T. Trall suggested that once a week was the outside limit, though adding, almost ominously, that "many cannot safely indulge oftener than once a month." [30]

Lest it be thought that these recommendations stemmed from a general hostility toward sexual expression, it should be recognized that most of the counsels in favor of limitation on sexual activity came from persons who simultaneously expressed positive, even celebratory attitudes toward sexuality. Elizabeth Blackwell, as we have seen already, clearly recognized the power and value of sex in the lives of women and men. Yet in that same book, *The Human Element in Sex,* she wrote that "the amount of nervous energy expended by the male in the temporary act of sexual congress is very great, out of all apparent proportion to its physical results [that is, the amount of semen expelled] and is an act not to be too often repeated." Ida Craddock, Eliza Duffey, and Elizabeth Evans, all of whom recognized or extolled the value of sexual expression in women, nonetheless argued for strict limitations on that expression.[31]

The reason behind the limitation on sexual expression is implied by some of these writers, but it was made quite explicit by the Grimké sister who wrote the essay on marriage, quoted from earlier. In that essay, it will be recalled, she made evident her appreciation of sexual expression, but at the same time she also made plain that she thought husbands overindulged, thereby injuring wives and offspring. "How often," she asked, is a woman "compelled by various considerations to yield to the unnatural embraces of her husband, and thus to endanger the very existence of her embryo babe. How often is it sacrificed to the ungoverned passion of its own father and the health of the mother seriously impaired." Limiting male sexual expression would thus protect women. She then went on to mention women who had had numerous miscarriages, which she thought were the result of their husbands' lust. "Do the beasts of the field miscarry?" she wanted to know. "Why not? *They* are governed by instinct. Are the brutes safe during the period of gestation whilst *Woman* is not?" And even when miscarriages did not result, she continued, worse consequences ensued in the form of "sickly constitutions . . . entailed upon multitudes of children." Dio Lewis at the end of the 19th century was an outspoken advocate of sexual limitations, yet he could praise sexual expression in the following way to a young man recently married: "Your enjoyment of the courtship was intense. It grew out of the sexual instinct. And this was not beastly or wrong. Subordinated to mind and soul, this passion is a great source, not only of the sweetest delights of our earthly life, but of the deepest and most enduring love."[32]

No, it was not the rejection of the pleasure of sexual expression or satisfaction that lay at the root of the argument that sexual indulgence in marriage be limited. The underlying aim in the minds of these marriage reformers—male and female—was to improve the position of women within marriage. For in their minds it was clearly the men, not the women, who pressed for excessive sexual indulgence. It was quite consistent with a broader movement, already noticed, in regard to the family: to enhance the autonomy of women, to give them a greater sense of their own self-interest. That is why the literature of sexual repression in these years should not be seen as opposed to the interest of women. In fact, it ought to be recognized as deriving from a concern for women within the marriage relation. Throughout the writings that argued for a reduction in sexual indulgence in marriage a concern for the welfare of women was strongly present.

Women who wrote on the subject made the point explicitly. The Grimké sister-author of "Marriage" forthrightly asserted woman's right "to decide *when* she shall become a mother, how often, and under what circumstances." Feminist Elizabeth Cady Stanton in 1853 bluntly asserted that "the right idea of marriage is at the foundation of all reforms." She' thought "man in his lust has regulated long enough this whole question of sexual intercourse." Dr. Elizabeth Blackwell observed that throughout the animal kingdom the female regulates procreation, and gentleness is characteristic of the male's relation to her. "Human marriage must be regarded as a life companionship, in which the satisfaction of physical desires forms a secondary, not a primary part. The regulation of sexual intercourse in the best interests of womanhood is the hitherto unrecognized truth of Christianity, towards which we are slowly groping." At another place she took pains to point out that some great men like Honoré de Balzac and members of the Catholic priesthood managed to live full and productive lives without sexual outlets; hence ordinary men ought to be able to manage with limited outlets within marriage. Alice Stockham asserted that "one potent cause of morning sickness is the habit of entering upon sexual relation frequently during gestation." Although some men contended that they were justified in seeking sexual satisfaction outside marriage when their wives did not satisfy their needs, Eliza Duffey, like Blackwell, rejected the argument. Instead of perceiving such a man "as an object of sympathy and commiseration, I should feel more inclined to hold him up for mirth," she snapped. "The discipline of sexual abstinence will certainly never kill him, and may, all things considered, be wholesome." All of these women agreed in equating men's sexuality with that of women, and in rejecting the common male view that men's needs were greater.[33]

Nor were women alone in making this argument. Men reformers also counseled against excessive indulgence in sex in marriage and for the same reasons as the women: it was a derogation of women's rights and autonomy. "The pains, the troubles, the heart burnings, the sickness, the danger of premature death, that woman has to experience through man's lust is beyond all comprehension," wrote John Cowan in his highly popular *Science of a New Life* (1874). "If there is one direction more than another in which 'Woman's Rights' should assert itself, it is in this choice of time for sexual congress," he advised.[34] An earlier writer on marriage reform, Henry C. Wright, put the argument in the mouth of a fictional wife who complained that her husband kept her constantly pregnant and therefore subordinate. "I want to be lovely to you," the wife told her husband, "yet, heretofore, the strongest manifestations of love to you have, usually, had little other effect than to arouse your animal nature." The result has been that she had been made "unlovely; for a wife must become unlovely and repulsive to her husband the moment he ceases to reverence her soul and feels that she is to him but the means of mere sensual gratification." Marriage in Wright's mind was a relationship in which the wife had respect and rights as well as affection. As Lewis Perry has recently shown, Wright drew upon rather extensive conversations with married women who came to his many lectures around the country on marriage. Thus his views need to be seen as more than the views of a lone man; they undoubtedly reflected the views of many women as well. John Harvey Kellogg made the same point as Wright even more succinctly and in startlingly modern language: a woman, he asserted, "remains the proprietor of her own body, though married." Dio Lewis, too, one of the early advocates of sexual restraint in marriage, spelled out in biblical terms the case for women's equality in marriage. Because woman was created after man and from his rib, it was sometimes contended that man was therefore justified in keeping woman as a subordinate in the marriage relationship. Not at all, Lewis crisply retorted. After all, birds, beasts, and fishes were created before man, but no one thinks they were intended to be superior to man. "Rather it would seem," Lewis slyly concluded, "that the triumphs of Creative Genius culminated in woman." Whatever one might say about St. Paul's assertion of the need to subordinate women, Lewis concluded, the fact was indisputable that Jesus never advocated female subjection— "an omission which the great Teacher would not have made, surely, had an ordinance on that subject been divinely enacted."[35]

All through this literature of sexual restraint in behalf of women's interests ran the additional refrain that mutuality was at the heart of sexual pleasure and therefore a happy and fulfilling marriage. The medical doctors quoted earlier, who deplored the sexual suppression of women, for example, often blamed the lack of sexual feeling upon husbands' failures to consider their wives' feelings and sexual rhythms. Dr. Ely Van de Warker concluded in his 1878 article on women's "impotency," as he called their lack of interest in sex, that "so far as my own observation extends, the husband is generally at fault. The more common cause is acute sexual irritability on the part of the husband." (Today that would be called premature ejaculation.) And Dr. Hammond pointed out that men would find their wives much more alive sexually if they recognized women's interest in sex and understood women's sexual rhythms. "Destroy the reciprocity of the union," wrote another medical man in 1887, "and marriage is no longer an equal partnership, but a sensual usurpation on the one side and a loathing submission on the others." Or, as still another medical writer put the issue, men must not force themselves upon their wives or "overpersuade, but await the wife's invitation at this time [during ovulation], when her husband is a hero in her eyes." In this way, the husband "would enjoy more and suffer less," the physician predicted.[36]

Carry Nation, the famous crusader against saloons, also believed that men were at fault in this regard. In her autobiography she told of her disappointment with her first husband, whom she married in 1867. "I did not find Dr. Gloyd the lover I expected. He was kind but seemed to want to be away from me; used to sit and read, when I was so hungry for his caresses and love. I have heard," she went on, "that this is the experience of many other young married women." They found that their husbands changed after marriage. "I believe that men have it in their power to keep the love of ninety-nine women out of a hundred. Why do women lose love for their husbands? I find it is most due to indifference on the part of the husband."[37]

Lack of knowledge of physiology, particularly woman's sexuality, was a common explanation by medical people for the view that women experienced little or no sexual feelings. "Ignorance of the distinctive character of human sex—viz., its powerful mental element," wrote Dr. Elizabeth Blackwell in 1887, was at the foundation of the "prevalent fallacy that sexual passion is the almost exclusive attribute of men and attaches exclusively to the act of coition."[38]

Behind the contention that men's lack of concern for the special needs of their wives stood the further assumption that women had suffered most in the marriage relation because they were subordinated. "The sexual act must be performed with satisfaction to both participants in the conjugal embrace," wrote Denslow Lewis in 1900. A woman writer on marriage reform in 1875 deplored the "fact that the majority of married women are slaves to excessive sexual passion in their husbands, and that any attempt on the part of the wife to assert her own rights in this respect is productive of . . . much domestic infelicity," which she simply endures rather "than see anger and sullenness added to selfishness and lust in her husband's character and conduct." In 1858 Henry Wright contended that "the greatest outrage one human being can perpetrate on another" is for a man "without regard to the wishes and conditions of his wife" to impose maternity upon her, "with all its attendant anguish of body and soul." In another place he asserted, as the Grimké sister had, that no proposition was so clear as "that woman alone, has the right to say when, and under what circumstances, she shall assume the office of maternity, or subject herself to the *liability* of becoming a mother." He urged all maidens to ascertain their future husbands' view on this matter before agreeing to marry. Especially be wary, he warned, of the man who refused on false grounds of modesty or delicacy to discuss the question.[39]

Alice B. Stockham also urged women to discuss the matter with their men, telling of one woman whose marriage was endangered by her husband's insistence upon nightly sexual activity. Once the woman broached the subject to him, however, he was willing to make his desires congruent with hers, and the marriage survived. Stockham remarked, not without significance, that the husband enjoyed sex more after it was confined to about once a month, and the wife now found that she was not pregnant as often. The recognition that there was a connection between the reduction in frequency of intercourse and the reduction in childbearing comes through in another remark by Stockham. This concerned a woman who had a seven-month-old child and then found herself pregnant again. "I was abased, humiliated," the woman was quoted as saying. "The sense of degradation that filled my soul, cannot be described." When she complained to her mother, the mother consoled her with the thought that, after all, the two children would be legitimate. To this remark the woman reacted strongly. "Although my husband is the father of my children, they are not legitimate. No man-made laws, nor priestly rites can ever make an act legitimate that deprives innocent children of their right to life and health."

It angered Stockham that girls were taught *"repression"* while boys were taught *"expression"* by "all the traditions, prejudices, and customs of society." Then, later, men were said to require satisfaction for that expression, including prostitution, while if women committed the slightest indiscretion "they have little hope of remission, even from a just and all-loving God;" she complained. Within marriage, as a result of this training, a woman was not "supposed to have needs in this direction. Neither has she learned that her body is her own and her soul is her Maker's." Instead, the woman was expected to give her soul and body to one man and in the process was "not paid half so well" as the prostitute, whom she resembled in this respect. "Is it too strong language to say she is the one *prostitute* taking the place, for the man, of many, and not like her, having choice of time or conditions?"[40]

Stockham's book *Tokology* was widely read during the last years of the 19th century. Several of the women who answered the questionnaire in the Mosher Survey, for example, mentioned it as one of the few books they had read on physiology or sex. The effort to improve the autonomy of women within the marriage relation, particularly in regard to her control over her own body, was also a theme of the notorious Claflin sisters during the 1870s.

Victoria and Tennessee Claflin became well known during the early 1870s because they opened in New York City what was said to be the first brokerage and investment counseling office in America to be run by women. Victoria had married a man named Woodhull in her youth and was ever after known by that name. The two sisters became notorious because, in addition to the cause of suffrage, they campaigned on behalf of marriage reform, particularly the right of women to control their own bodies. "I would rather be the labor slave of a master, with his whip cracking continually about my ears," Victoria Woodhull announced in 1873, "than the forced sexual slave of any man a single hour." She was at that time a radical on the subject. She proudly announced her willingness to practice what she preached—namely, following love wherever it might lead, regardless of legality or custom. She lived openly with a man not her husband. Her great objection to marriage was that women were expected to submit to their husbands without objection or dissent. "They say I have come to break up the family," she remarked once. "I say amen to that with all my heart."[41]

Few women of the time, of course, were prepared to follow such radical doctrine. But it is not without significance that, when she spoke in public, not only were the halls usually filled to overflowing, but women usually made up at least half the audience. In supporting the broad movement for greater autonomy for women within the family, especially on sexual matters, Victoria Woodhull was more of a prophet than her radical ideas on other subjects might lead one to expect. She was particularly outspoken on the necessity that men recognize women's sexual needs and rhythms in marriage.

Ezra Heywood, another sexual radical of the late Victorian era, also opposed, in the name of women's autonomy, excessive sexuality in marriage. Heywood's pamphlet *Cupid's Yokes,* which reached at least 50,000 in 1887, advocated free love, as did Victoria Woodhull, by which was meant a relationship between members of the opposite sex that was without legal or social compulsion. The trouble with traditional marriage in the eyes of free lovers like Heywood was that it permitted men to indulge their passions. Gleefully Heywood told of a clergyman—for Heywood was an atheist as well—who insisted on having intercourse with his wife six to eight times a day.

The irony was that otherwise conservative writers on marriage like Orson Fowler or William Alcott would have been horrified to be thought to be in the same camp as Victoria Woodhull or Ezra Heywood; yet both sets of writers on marriage were making the same point. As Orson Fowler put it, the phrase "control over her own person" meant that the wife must be able to determine when intercourse took place. The man must wait upon the woman, just as male animals have to wait upon the female, Fowler advised. It is true that the female ought not to refrain entirely from intercourse, for the male has some claims upon her for offspring. But she must be able to choose the time; he is "her sexual servant, not her his." Only in the human world, Fowler contended, "does the male ever obtrude himself upon the unwilling female." [42]

Eliza Duffey was no social or even sexual radical, but on the subject of a woman's right to say "No" to her husband, she agreed with Victoria Woodhull. Duffey, in fact, elevated the wife's negative to an "inborn right." Some wives and hubands might find such "a right to self" new doctrine, she admitted, but upon such a right "is based all the happiness that can possibly be found in the marriage state. The wife's body is unqualifiedly her own," Duffey insisted, "except that she may be guilty of no infidelity to her husband." (Here she departed from Victoria Woodhull.) Contrary to what some men believed, Duffey insisted, "a woman is no more bound to yield her body to her husband after the marriage between them than before, until she feels that she can do so with the full tide of willingness and affection." A similar point, even more strongly expressed was made by Social Purist writer Ida Craddock. "Never, never, never allow yourself to yield to your husband's request for union," she advised young brides, "unless you yourself desire it. For a woman to consent when she does not desire union is to consent to unthinkable degradation; and it places her below the harlot." And the time to begin to exercise that control over their husbands' sexuality, she made clear, was on the wedding night.[43]

R. T. Trall, in his widely circulated handbook *Sexual Physiology and Hygiene,* which first appeared in 1866, neatly brought together the elements in the argument: limitations on sexuality actually enhanced sexual enjoyment while at the same time expanding women's autonomy within marriage. Whatever the object of sexual intercourse—procreation or love—he wrote, "it is very clear that it should be as agreeable as possible to both parties. Indeed, when it is otherwise to either party, it is cruelty." The act itself should take place only when there is "mental harmony and congeniality between the parties. Each must be able to respond to the whole nature of the other—bodily, morally, and intellectually, to the extent that there shall be no sense of discord, no feeling of repugnance."[44] This was the marriage of equals, the idea of the companionate marriage applied to the most intimate of its precincts.

Health reformers, as distinct from sexual or marital reformers, also echoed this demand for restraint on sexual expression in the interest of women. As Regina Morantz has observed in her study of the writings of health reformers, these writers "clearly intended sexual restraint to benefit women and urged them to assert their rights in the sexual sphere. . . . Believing that the male's passion for copulation far out-distanced his wife's, thinkers and educators urged men to follow the sexual rhythm of their more delicate spouses."[45]

The efforts of these individuals and publicists to reshape the internal relationships of the family in behalf of women's autonomy were a part of a much broader, organized reform movement in the second half of the 19th century. And since that movement involves not only women's efforts to control male sexuality, but also women's activities in moral reform it deserves a chapter of its own.

XII

Organizing To Control Sexuality

After the Civil War a number of organizations came into being to press for an improved moral standard within and outside the family. Women played an active and significant part in all of them. Among other things, they mounted campaigns against liquor and prostitution, and in favor of raising the age of consent for girls, and generally asserted and sought to establish a single standard of sexual behavior for men and women. The role of women in the temperance and Prohibition movement is too large a subject to be discussed here; it will be treated in the next chapter in connection with other organizational activities of women. Here the central concern is with a smaller, but no less indicative movement among women seeking to influence the morals of home and society. The movement goes under the general heading of Social Purity, which was really a 19th-century euphemism for sexual purity. The purpose was to raise the level of sexual behavior within the American family through public means. Social Purity, in short, is but the public and organizational expression of efforts to control sexuality that we have already looked at in the last chapter, but there the effort was individual and unorganized.

To anyone who reads the books, pamphlets, and speeches produced by the Social Purity movement in the last two decades of the 19th century, that literature must seem not only sexually repressive but anti-sexual as well. The truth is that the literature of the Social Purity people was similar in argument and content to that discussed in the previous chapter on the desirability of controlling sexuality. Indeed, writers such as Alcott, Evans, and Duffey, to name only three, must be included among the Social Purity proponents even though they may not have been members of formal Social Purity organizations like the White Cross.

Before we turn to an examination of the statements and activities of the Social Purity movement, two observations are worth making in order to give shape and meaning to the variety of its literature. The first is that behind the movement lies the assumption that men's sexuality was as manipulatable as women's—that is, it was susceptible to control and regulation. Once this point is admitted, then efforts to deny sexual expression cease to be simply anti-sexual, either in intent or in tone. Instead, they can then be appreciated as part of a larger purpose to assert a single standard of sexual behavior for both sexes.

The second observation stems from the first. The reason the Social Purists insisted upon the cultural rather than the biological basis of men's sexuality was to give married women greater control over the family, by reducing the power of the husband, even in regard to sexual expression. For women this was a double gain. It was significant ideologically because it reduced the husband's prerogatives within the family while at the same time giving the wife greater opportunity to reduce family size and the incidence of the pain and danger of childbirth. Moreover, the standard which Social Purity advocated was a female one. The ideal insisted upon by society for women—that sexual expression was to be confined to marriage—was now to be the standard to which men would be held. Even more important was the corollary that even within marriage the wife was to be the partner who determined how much sexual activity there would be.

Throughout the literature on Social Purity, as well as in the literature of sexual restraint in general, the assumption was that women desired sexual activity less frequently than men. Whether this assumption was grounded in physiological fact or was simply a socially induced difference is not known for certain even today. But the validity of the assumption is not important. In an age of unreliable contraception, women obviously had an interest in reducing frequency of intercourse that men did not —namely, to reduce the likelihood of pregnancy. "If women had their own way in the matter this physical intercourse would take place at comparatively rare intervals, and only under the most favorable circumstances," wrote Elizabeth Evans in 1875. "Such an arrangement would be of infinite benefit to the race: men would preserve their vigor, and women their beauty and spirits, and though fewer children might be born, their quality would be improved." But, she continued, the way things now stand, "the selfishness of men towards women meets with a heavy punishment in the early failure of the health of wives and the physical and mental shortcomings of offspring." Ida Craddock made the connection between number of offspring and women's interest even more explicitly. "To create a few, a very few children who shall be an expression of the noblest thoughts of yourself and your husband and to give those children all possible advantages of education, travel, and society, is not this doing your duty as a wife and mother better than if you create children at haphazard and by wholesale to such an extent that you can scarcely secure for them a decent living," she asked her readers.[1] The literature of Social Purity specified that in any event it was the woman who was to determine the proper time and frequency of intercourse. In that way men were to be held to a female standard even though, as many in the 19th century believed, women's sexual desires were less insistent than men's. No more persuasive measure of Social Purity's fundamental concern for women could be imagined by any man.

It is not surprising, therefore, that women were prominent in the Social Purity movement. And to the extent that the goals of the movement were ultimately imposed on society it could be said that women exerted their influence outside the home as part of their effort to gain greater autonomy within it. The movement, however, in short, was an excellent example of the successful translation into the social and political arena of the doctrine of the different spheres of activity for the sexes. For if the morality of the home was to be protected from outside forces which threatened it, then those who stood for that morality must go outside the home to ensure that their morality prevailed in the world at large. Carry Nation, the flamboyant crusader against saloons, spelled out the rationale in her autobiography. "We hear 'A woman's place is at home.' That is true," she conceded, "but what and where is home. Not the walls of a house. Not furniture, food or clothes. Home is where the heart is, where our loved ones are. If my son is in a drinking place, my place is there. If my daughter, or the daughter of anyone else, my family or any other family is in trouble, my place is there." A woman would be either selfish or cowardly, she warned, if she "would refuse to leave her home to relieve suffering or trouble. Jesus said, 'Go out into the highways and hedges.' He said this to women, as well as men," she emphasized.[2]

Women's activity in behalf of Social Purity was, therefore, quite in conformity with the doctrine of separate spheres, as other causes, like woman suffrage, would never be. For voting was not a part of domestic morality;

that was man's sphere. That is why many women in the 19th century felt quite comfortable being active in the world of Social Purity or temperance, but would not have been caught dead working for suffrage or any other cause that directly challenged the doctrine of separate spheres, though both activities, of course, brought women "out of the home."

This also helps us to understand why the roots of Social Purity extend back to the early years of the 19th century; such activity fitted quite easily into the doctrine of separate spheres. Traditionally, when historians have treated the Social Purity movement they have directed their attention to the last two or three decades of the century, when the term itself was first used. But if one pays attention to the aims and arguments of the movement rather than to the name, it soon becomes clear that, as an outlook or concern on the part of women, the movement goes back at least to the 1830s.

Carroll Smith-Rosenberg has documented the history of one such organization of women that began in 1834. It was called the New York Female Reform Society and continued to be active and to issue a newspaper until well into the 1850s. By that date it had auxiliaries throughout New England as well as New York. At no time, of course, was the organization particularly powerful or more numerous in membership than a major antislavery society. But its open attacks upon prostitution in the cities and towns foreshadowed the causes that the Social Purity movement at the end of the century would make famous. One method used by the Society in the 1830s and 1840s was to station agents outside brothels to take down the names of patrons, hoping thereby to embarrass them and thus destroy the business. It also encouraged the readers of its journal, *The Advocate,* to send in the names of men in their towns seen frequenting brothels. Sometimes women members would insinuate themselves as domestics into brothels, seeking out the runaway girls they felt sure were hidden or held in the house. And for a while the Society sought to maintain a House of Reception in which prostitutes could be rehabilitated. But that venture was soon abandoned when few women could be found to take advantage of the place. Although there was some hostility toward prostitutes on the part of the organization, it is clear that the primary purpose of the Society was to reform the sexual behavior of men. Smith-Rosenberg, in her analysis of the contents of *The Advocate,* found two themes running through its pages. The first was that males were inherently lascivious and were the principal cause for the downfall of women through seduction and prostitution; the second, that women, as mothers in the home, needed to work together to control the male tendency toward lasciviousness. Not all women would want to work with the Society, it was recognized, but every woman who was a mother could educate her sons in the proper ethical and sexual behavior.

Over and over again *The Advocate* urged women to remember their awesome responsibilities as mothers. A child is an "immortal being, destined to live forever!" one editorial read in 1844. "And who is to make it happy or miserable? You—the mother! You gave it birth, the mother of its body . . . its destiny is placed in your hands." [3] At other times, when the absence of the father from the home was noted, the subordinate role of the father was clearly shown. In short, the very rationale of the Society rested on the idea of separate spheres for women and men, with women in charge of the home and the rearing of the children.

It was just this emphasis upon women's role as moral arbiter in the home and as the rearer of children that vouchsafed to women the right— nay, obligation—to regulate men's sexual behavior. As the purer sex, women had a responsibility to protect the morality of the home. Consequently, as *The Advocate* made evident, women needed to call to account those men who exercised inordinate power within the home. "A portion of the inhabitants of this favored land," one editorial in 1838 commented, "are groaning under a despotism which seems to be modeled precisely after that of the Autocrat of Russia. We allude to the tyranny exercised in the HOME department, where lordly man . . . rules his trembling subjects with a rod of iron, conscious of entire impunity and exalting [*sic*] in his fancied superiority." The trouble with such men, the article continued, was that they denied the ideal relationship between man and woman within marriage. "Instead of regarding his wife as a help-mate for him, an equal sharer in his joys and sorrows, he looks upon her as a useful article of furniture, which is valuable only for the benefit derived from it, but which may be thrown aside at pleasure." [4]

The intention that animated *The Advocate* and its readers was put into bold relief when the paper published a forthright, feminist article by the militant feminist and abolitionist Sarah Grimké. Succeeding issues of *The Advocate* were filled with denunciations from readers of Grimké's arguments. Never again did *The Advocate* publish another piece by an overt feminist. In short, the women who read *The Advocate* were not interested in, or moved by, feminist arguments as such, however much interested they certainly were in maintaining their special moral position in the home. They felt quite justified in going outside the home when necessary to maintain that position, but not for causes that threatened to break down the separation of spheres, as Grimké's feminist argument urged. So long as women confined their attentions outside the home to issues and organizations that were related to their special sphere of activity, men raised few objections. Indeed, the relative lack of male hostility toward organizations like the Female Reform Society or the later Women's Christian Temperance Union attested to the fact that men, too, as we saw in examining the family, conceded to women a pre-eminent, if not dominant, role as moral preceptors in the home. Yet once that superior position had been conceded to women, it could not easily be denied or withdrawn, even when women ventured to exercise that position in such a way as to encroach upon the sexual interests or "needs" of men.

The few hundred women who engaged in incipient Social Purity agitation in the antebellum years cannot, by any stretch of the imagination, be considered a host or even a significant movement. But the beginnings of a major movement of women were certainly there. As Smith-Rosenberg has concluded, "the war for purification of sexual mores was far more fundamental in its implications for women's traditional role than the demand for women's education—or even the vote." [5] The autonomy of women depended upon her position within the family and her relations with men—and both, in turn, revolved around sex, the nexus between them within the family.

The Social Purity movement proper, that which became prominent in late 19th-century America and Britain, was also sparked by the rising popular concern about, and awareness of, prostitution. As early as the 1850s, Dr. William Sanger had conducted a detailed study of prostitution in New York City, the report of which remained for over a generation the most thorough examination of the trade. Sanger's report was itself a sign and a measure of the growth of prostitution before 1860. The Civil War provided new opportunities to the trade, as well as increasing public consciousness of its extent. Prostitutes flocked to the large army camps, even on the edge of battlefields, since women were allowed to follow the armies. Army headquarters in cities behind the lines also attracted brothels. From time to time, both the army and the local police made efforts at suppressing the business, but neither worked at it very hard; in any event, no decline was noticeable. Consequently, during the late 1860s and 1870s, medical men as well as urban police began to call for regulation of the business, rather than continue the futile and costly efforts at suppression. Both the prestigious *Nation* magazine and the influential *New York Times* looked favorably upon regulation in 1867. And even the more moralistic *New York Tribune* came to a similar position by 1876. [6]

Regulation meant confinement of prostitutes to certain areas of the city—the famous "red light districts"—and periodic medical inspection of the prostitutes in an effort to eliminate venereal disease. By the 1870s the medical profession, at least, was much more concerned about the dangers of disease than it was about any threat to public morality. Indeed, that had been Dr. William Sanger's conclusion from his study in the late 1850s. The physicians were often joined in support of regulation by the police, who thought suppression both too difficult and futile. They were joined by those who thought that prostitution was a fact of life and thus could not be eliminated at all, however immoral it might be.

Few, if any, of the proponents of regulations wanted to condone or encourage prostitution, but their willingness to regulate rather than continue to suppress it was taken by many as condoning vice. As a result, women's groups and religious organizations, as well as important individuals, mounted a powerful campaign to prevent regulation from coming to the United States. At that time—in the 1870s—every major European country, including England, practiced some form of regulation of prostitution. Yet, the movement against regulation proved to be so strong and successful that only one American city ever tried it. And even then, the St. Louis experiment lasted for only four years. During the 1870s a number of American cities had started to move in the direction taken by St. Louis, but the antiregulators had stopped them in their tracks. The only other country in which regulation was abandoned during the 19th century was Great Britain, where, significantly, the movement against regulation was led by a woman, the redoubtable Josephine Butler.

The principal arguments for the suppression of prostitution, though sometimes couched in language that smacked of simple opposition to sexual enjoyment, sprang from broader concerns. Fundamentally, of course, a prime intention was to defend women—namely, those who were prostitutes. One defense of prostitutes was that poor economic and social conditions had compelled them to enter the trade. This argument was widely advanced, even though William Sanger's study in the 1850s had pointed out that economic conditions were only a part of the explanation as to why women entered prostitution. Sanger found, for instance, that 525 of the women who answered his questionnaire claimed to have become prostitutes because of "destitution," whereas almost as many—513—admitted that they had done so out of "inclination."

The most common line of defense was to emphasize men's responsibility. "We are forced to the conclusion," one male doctor told his male readers, "that the harlot is less guilty than the seducer; and as we study the causes of her downfall let us ever remember to the unutterable shame of our sex, that women's extremity is man's opportunity." Women Social Purists not infrequently showed a similar sympathy for prostitutes. Elizabeth Duffey, for example, cautioned her women readers not to feel superior to prostitutes, but to place the moral blame where it belonged: on the customers. (She also advanced the feminist argument that the way to prevent women from falling into prostitution was to give them more to fill their lives. "To tell them to wash dishes and make beds is not to the purpose at all. Those are physical labors, but the mind is left as unoccupied as ever. An idle woman, who is encouraged to no intellectual activity," Duffey warned, "is liable to develop into a sensualist.") Feminist Caroline H. Dall followed a similar line in the 1860s, defending prostitutes as "reclaimable." She advised her readers to "put yourself in [the prostitute's] place. Such a woman is no monster, only a gentle-hearted creature, unsupported by God's law, unrestrained by self-control. Your scorn, the world's rejection, *may* make her what you think. Meanwhile, are you above temptation?" [7]

Basically, of course, the Social Purists were right. If there were no men interested in sexual relations outside of marriage there would be no prostitutes. And in that sense the fall of every woman could be laid at the door of a man. One male physician said in 1865 that it was quite common for a married man to visit a prostitute occasionally "that he may preserve his wife from the chance of pregnancy." Eliza Duffey gave the Social Purists' answer to that justification for prostitution when she said that if prostitution was the "only alternative, I think women as a class, would prefer the large families." [8] In short, what the Social Purists insisted upon was a single standard of sexual behavior—and the female one at that. Like the Female Reform Society earlier, the Social Purists sought to control men's sexuality in the interest of protecting women, and in the process they were helping to enhance women's autonomy within marriage.

As one might expect, almost from the outset the fledgling feminist movement, led by Susan B. Anthony and Elizabeth Cady Stanton, took a public position against the mere regulation of prostitution and worked to defeat efforts to bring regulation about. But more significant, though no less expected, was the identification in the 1880s of less militant women's organizations with the crusade against not only regulation but against prostitution in general. Frances Willard, who made the Women's Christian Temperance Union the largest women's organization in the nation, was also a leader of the Social Purity movement.

In an address entitled "Social Purity, the Latest and Greatest Crusade," Willard told how she had been enlisted in the cause. It began by her seeing in Paris the closed, black wagons that carried the prostitutes to their weekly medical inspections. For Paris had long regulated brothels. No English-speaking woman, Willard said, would stand for such an enormity and called upon each young woman to use her sexual attraction—in a Victorian version of Lysistrata—to compel her suitors to "choose between tobacco and me" and between strong drink and me. Here, of course, Social Purity extended the behavioral standards of women to men in still other areas than sexuality while retaining the idea that women must control men morally.

Willard also recognized that women's power over men was limited, even within marriage, for their livelihood still came from men. Hence, as she shrewdly pointed out in the same speech, women can exercise this power only by being "able to earn their own living, ready for an independent life."[9] Thus she unwittingly linked the feminist concerns of a later Charlotte Perkins Gilman or those of an earlier Elizabeth Smith to the cause of Social Purity. The implications of Social Purity were thus carried to their logical conclusion, though few women at that time were yet prepared to follow them out.

Undoubtedly the most dramatic sign of success of the Social Purity campaign was that by the middle 1880s virtually no medical societies or organizations any longer supported the cause of regulation of prostitution. By then, too, discussion of sexual matters, despite the Comstock law of 1873, was more open than it had been for two generations. After all, one could not attack the evils of brothels and prostitution and vice in general without mentioning names, institutions, and practices. That was one consequence of the Social Purity movement no one had anticipated and one that some may well have regretted.[10]

Although all Social Purists were united in their belief that sexual expression needed to be limited, beyond that common principle there could be a range of beliefs about sexual matters. Some became highly exercised about nudity, calling for the draping of statues or the covering up of paintings that depicted unclothed figures. Josiah and Deborah Leeds, for example, campaigned vigorously against any display of flesh or form, including in the ballet. And Frances Willard urged the establishment of boards to preview plays to ascertain their adherence to a code of morals. She also invited the Leeds and Anthony Comstock himself to be superintendents of Pure Literature for the Women's Christian Temperance Union. Eliza Duffey advised her women readers not to disrobe in the presence of their husbands and to have separate beds, because "the close bodily contact under a common bed-covering, in the slight protection which night-clothing affords, is a constant provocation of amorous ideas and sensations to the husband, *if not to both*" (italics added). On the other hand, Ida Craddock extolled nudity within marriage, declaring that "There are times when to be nude in another's [a spouse's] sight is to be chaste." The nude body she referred to as "the human form divine." And other Social Purists during the 1890s began to defend nudity in art as serving good, aesthetic purposes. Craddock also recommended to her female readers that they have their hymens cut prior to marriage in order to ease the first sexual encounter. Vaseline was also a good idea for the first night of marriage, she added.[11] In sum, there was nothing inherent in Social Purity that required its supporters to oppose sexual pleasure or activity, though its principles did lend themselves to those who wanted to put them to that use.

The successful crusade against licensed prostitution was not the only victory for the Social Purity movement. During the 1890s the movement also undertook a campaign in favor of raising the age of consent for sexual activity by girls. The intention, of course, was to protect girls, by legal penalties, from the sexual overtures of men. The issue came to the fore after 1885, when William T. Stead in England exposed the widespread practice of buying and selling girls for sexual exploitation. When the issue was first raised many people were shocked at how low the minimum legal age of consent was in the United States. In many states, for example, it was no higher than ten years. Thanks to the agitation of the women and men of the Social Purity organizations, state after state in the 1890s raised the age. In 1895, for example, Connecticut's minimum age went from 14 to 16; Maine's started at 10 in 1887, then went to 13, and finally to 14 in 1889. In 1893 Arkansas raised its from 12 to 16. By 1900 only two states or territories still retained the limit below 14, while twelve jurisdictions had raised it as high as 18.[12] The Purity movement hoped to get the minimum age up to 21, but few states were prepared to go that far, principally because juries would not convict men who had relations with unmarried women of that age and also because prostitutes would be in too good a position to blackmail their customers were the age placed higher than 18. As it was, though, the general upward movement in the minimum age of consent was not only a triumph for the Social Purity movement but also for the idea that it was more important to protect girls from the sexual aggressions of men than to continue to protect men from the few instances of entrapment by prostitutes. Once again women had reached outside the home—in this case through the law—to maintain the moral integrity of the home, as they saw it. In this instance, too, men's sexuality was being controlled on behalf of women, and on behalf of ultimately achieving a single standard of sexual behavior for both sexes, which was the underlying thrust of the Social Purity movement. "As woman becomes free and wise and self-sustaining," predicted Elizabeth Evans, "she will demand the same purity of man that has always been demanded of herself; and if, in her subjection, her influence has been so immense both for evil and for good, how much greater will be her power when she is universally regarded as man's equal." And as feminist Caroline Dall wrote, "I have not two separate moral standards for the sexes."[13]

The interest of Social Purists in the improvement of the position and conception of women extended quite naturally to aspects other than a single sexual standard for women and men. Social Purists, for example, defended women's rights in employment. In a speech in 1890, later published as a pamphlet, Elizabeth Powell Bond, one of the leaders of Social Purity, stressed "the need for work to promote Social Purity." What she meant by work, as she made evident, was wider opportunities for women in education and employment. When that was done, she promised, it would bring "about a new order of things. Educated women are more and more entering upon independent, self-supporting work." Some might object to this, she admitted, but, since God gave women intelligence, she could be expected to exercise it. Even earlier, another Social Purist, Dio Lewis, had emphasized the need for women's employment in order to free women from their dependence on marriage and men. It would help to make marriage a relationship of affection between companions, he thought, and advance the autonomy of women within it. "If women only had occupations in which they could secure independence," Lewis wrote in 1874, "we should observe a great change in their attitude toward men." Gone would be "their 'low necks and short sleeves,' their padded busts, the dress of their hips, the facial makeup and banter," which revealed their primary purpose. Once women could earn their own living, he continued, "so that they can marry for love, and not for clothes and bread, this sickening connivance will pass away, and woman's moral superiority will pronounce itself, to the infinite advantage of all concerned."[14]

Social Purity seems also to have united women in a new sense of sisterhood, for, as Elizabeth Powell Bond said, "women of cultivation and wealth" were beginning to take up the cause of the underpaid woman.

"Out of this genuine cooperation of the richer with the poorer, the stronger with the weaker, along with the vital influence of the White Cross work, will come a type of civilization that the world has not yet known." Bond may have been overoptimistic, as we know from hindsight, but she was quite correct when she went on to predict that Social Purity contained the seeds of more radical alterations in the relations between the sexes. For this new civilization that Bond predicted would display a new androgyny, in which sex roles would be overlapping rather than sharply delineated. It would be a world with "a womanhood strong as it is fair and sweet; a manhood delicate as it is strong and chivalrous." [15]

David Pivar, in his path-breaking study of the Social Purity movement, has rightly emphasized the new ways of thinking and talking about sex and gender that the movement introduced in American social and intellectual life. Sexuality was now open to freer discussion than ever before; a new movement for sex education in public institutions and in print began; the public became more aware of the need to confront sexual issues frankly and directly. And, of course, Social Purity killed off for good any possibility that licensed or regulated prostitution would be permissible in the United States. The reports on the "social evil" that literally flooded from various municipal commissions across the nation in the fifteen years before 1914 owe their existence to the work of the Social Purists. All of these reports agreed that the "red light districts," against which the Social Purists had campaigned for so long, must go. And so they did. The enactment by Congress of the Mann Act in 1910, which prohibited the transportation across state lines of women for immoral purposes, was likewise a monument to the efforts of the Social Purity movement.

To catalogue the achievements or at least the successes of the Social Purity movement is not the same as saying all that it accomplished or stood for was good or even desirable. It is still an open question whether prostitution can be effectively suppressed and therefore whether it ought to be. And by its very character the Social Purity movement always provided a place for the censor and the kill-joy, and an opportunity for those who took delight in repressing others. Among the Social Purists, Anthony Comstock was always a person in good standing.

From the standpoint of women and the family, however, the significance of the Social Purity movement resides principally in the fact that it was a part of a larger movement in behalf of women's freedom and autonomy inside and outside the family. As Linda Gordon has pointed out, it is difficult to distinguish between Social Purity advocates and feminists. It was not unusual for one to slip easily into the other in the course of the same speech or article. Social Purists often found themselves advocating economic independence for women. Similarly, virtually all feminists espoused Social Purity principles either overtly or indirectly, as when Susan B. Anthony and Elizabeth Stanton came out against regulation of prostitution. Moreover, though Social Purity was primarily concerned with controlling the sexuality of men, it also contained the underlying purpose of moving society in the direction of equalizing the relations between men and women. Few feminists, it is true, concerned themselves with limiting male sexuality—indeed, as we shall see in Chapter XV, the question of intrafamily relations was not something most 19th-century feminists and suffragists knew how to confront. But certainly the idea of equality was something with which feminists did identify. The truth of the intimate relationship between feminist principles and the movement to control male sexuality is demonstrated by a little-known but relevant controversy in Denmark during the 1880s. When the well-known literary critic Georg Brandes came out in support of sexual freedom for *both* sexes (he considered himself a friend of women's rights), he was taken to task by the leading Danish feminist, Elisabeth Grundtvig, on the ground that women could not benefit from that kind of equality. Instead, she insisted, men must learn to control their sexuality. She went on to argue that regulated prostitution must be opposed as well, just as the Social Purity advocates in the United States contended.[16] In short, feminism and Social Purity had a number of things in common, though the two movements assigned different priorities to them.

Linda Gordon has also called attention to a fundamental assumption in Social Purity thought that deserves more elaboration. Today we live in a post-Freudian climate of opinion, an intellectual environment in which sexuality is taken as given, as something that requires full expression in both sexes and even deserves cultivation. Freud himself, to be sure, did not advocate indiscriminate sexual expression. On the contrary, he advised control and sublimation, believing the channeled sexual energy to be the primary source of culture and achievement. Even so, Freud considered sexuality as a force essentially independent of individual will and even human culture. The Social Purity advocates, on the other hand, considered sex as culturally determined. They denied that men were imbued with a stronger or more insistent sexual urge than women. The apparent differences between the sexual drives of men and women they attributed to the fact that men had been allowed to exercise their sexual powers unrestrainedly and excessively. "Continence is not a matter of sex," Elizabeth Evans pointed out in 1875, "but of temperament and will and habit"; that women "are chaste in outward conduct is due to the force of public opinion, which does not allow them to be otherwise without condemnation." Men are unchaste, she continued, because no one has called them "to account for their sins against purity." Moreover, just because "men have always been licentious is no proof that they will always be so." What distinguishes men from animals is that they are not moved by instinct. Thus men, too, can learn to control their sexuality just as women have, she concluded.[17] Therefore, in the interests of women, Social Purists worked to create an intellectual and legal climate in society and in the family in which men's control over their sexual drives would be encouraged. Only by inducing men to control their sexuality could women expect to exert control over their fertility and their bodies. Less frequent intercourse would produce fewer children, as some of the Social Purists pointed out.

On the other hand, if ever it could be demonstrated or proved that physically men required sexual expression more frequently or insistently than women, the opportunity or right of a woman to say "no" to her husband would be seriously undermined, if not destroyed. That is why the issuance in 1895 of a "Medical Declaration of Chastity" was so important to the Social Purity advocates. For in that declaration a group of physicians publicly agreed that male continence was in no way detrimental to health. One historian has recently contended that a reason why the "red light district" disappeared so quickly in the early 20th century was that a principal justification was removed by the increasing professional agreement among physicians that continence was not harmful to men.[18]

The meaning of the Social Purity movement in particular and of Victorian ideas on sexuality in general offered here is not the prevailing historical interpretation. Most writers on Victorian sexual attitudes, notably Steven Marcus and Peter Cominus, have explained the so-called repressive or limited approach to sexual expression quite differently.[19] And just because that view has been widely followed by others, it is worth examining briefly in order to make plain why it is not persuasive.

Cominus and Marcus have contended that the movement to limit sexual expenditure was analogous to the frugal and conserving habits of a nascent capitalist economy, the stage of development of England and the United States in the 19th century. People of the middle class, who are expected to husband material resources, would naturally apply that set of priorities or values to their sexual life as well. Hence their concern about undue indulgence, particularly by men, for whom the sexual act did indeed entail a physical loss.

Superficially, the idea has appeal, if only because the involuntary loss of sperm by men was apparently a troublesome and widespread medical problem in the middle years of the 19th century. Male doctors wrote books about it. But upon closer examination, the interpretation does not fit the nature of the 19th-century economy though on closeness of fit rests its validity. As R. S. Neale has cogently pointed out, the industrial economy of the 19th century was not in especial need of capital accumulation, as Cominus and Marcus' explanation demands. The primary concern was consumption—that is, how to sell the goods that the industrial system was producing in large quantities. Throughout the century the central problem was finding markets for goods, not conserving resources. Cominus and others who have advanced this conception of an industrial society have confused it with the beginnings of capitalism, the period when accumulation of capital was indeed an important consideration. But in 19th-century America, especially after 1850, the concern was not how to husband resources but how to find markets for the goods that were pouring from fields and factories. As economist David A. Wells observed in 1877, "the country . . . is suffering today . . . not because we have not, but because we have; not from scarcity, but from abundance."[20]

Thus the concern to save semen, to which Marcus and Cominus refer, could not have derived from analogous concerns about the economy. In any case, as several proponents of restriction on sexual expression made clear, it was not the loss of semen that was worrying them. Dio Lewis in 1874, for example, said, "It is the sexual excitement more than the emission which exhausts." He also discounted spermatorrhea or involuntary loss of semen as a serious problem, despite what many medical men of the time thought. Dr. Elizabeth Blackwell made a similar point when she wrote that "the amount of nervous energy expended by the male in the temporary act of sexual congress is very great, out of all apparent proportion to its physical results"—that is, the loss of semen.[21] In a sense, both Lewis and Blackwell were anticipating Freud's later argument that sublimation was the reason for restricting the expenditure of sexual energy, that out of such repression came art, science, and culture in general.

If one is interested in an economic model to explain the rise of the Social Purity movement and the development of limits on sexual activity in the Victorian era, a more plausible one has been advanced by Randall Collins and Daniel Scott Smith.[22] Collins and Smith regard marriage as an exchange situation, in which men and women seek to gain advantage from what one has to offer the other. Given the nature of the sex roles in the 19th century, the principal asset of women in this exchange was their sex. As Charlotte Perkins Gilman pointed out in *Women and Economics,* (1898), the fundamental reciprocity was women's sexuality and maternity in exchange for men's financial support. (Housekeeping and cooking were incidental in the exchange since they did not depend upon sex. A hired man could have provided those services.) Once the marriage was made, however, a woman's power was considerably reduced since, as Gilman again pointed out, a woman had no way of economically sustaining herself without a husband. Gilman's answer to the problem was a job, but that was, for reasons that will be clearer later in this book, not a feasible answer in the 19th or early 20th century. A more practical and certainly more immediate solution was for a woman to control her own fertility and her husband's sexual access to her. Children and sexual expression were the "goods" she had to offer; if the supply could be reduced, the "price" would rise. That is to say, to translate the argument into power terms, she would have more influence with her husband and thus could enhance her autonomy. The only way that could be achieved would be to control male sexuality. This, in turn, could be accomplished in several ways, two of which we have already looked at in a different context. The easiest to achieve was to argue that women did not experience sexual pleasure, as writers like Dr. Acton suggested. Women could then appeal to their husbands' sense of guilt. Another way to control men's sexuality was to mount a campaign outside the home calling upon husbands, for a variety of reasons, to control their own sexuality. This was, of course, the Social Purity movement. Viewed in this light, the attack on prostitution became another way in which the power of women was enhanced by denying to men any sexual outlet other than their wives. And certainly this interpretation of the objection to licensed prostitution fits in with the strong hostility that many women and "moral" men displayed toward prostitution then and later.

Such a restrictive attitude toward sexuality by women would change when more reliable means of control over fertility became available and when opportunities for economic independence for women improved. In such a changed social and technological context, limiting sexual expression would not be so closely tied to women's interest in controlling fertility. Then it would be possible to argue, as some feminists in the 1970s have, that women should have the same right to express their sexuality outside marriage as men, and that women's sexual needs are neither less insistent nor less worthy of satisfaction than men's. But, until these social changes took place, most married women found control of male sexuality the best way to protect and advance women's individuality or autonomy within the family—that is, to secure women's interests.

The success that some women achieved in applying a female standard of sexuality to men is suggested by what we know—slim as that body of information may be—about the sexual behavior of married couples at the beginning and at the end of the 19th century. In the Mosher Survey of 45 married women, one question asked what the frequency of intercourse was. Of the 45 women 25 said that they had intercourse once a week or less; ten said they had it once or twice a week, and 9 more said they had it more than twice a week. (One did not answer the question.) In themselves these figures do not tell us how the women felt about these frequencies, whether they were too high or too low. But Mosher included another quite relevant question. She asked the women what they would consider the ideal frequency.

To this question eight women did not offer a response, so total respondents numbered 37. Only eight of the women wanted intercourse as much as once a week or more, and nine said when both partners wanted it. Yet, according to the actual frequencies reported in the first question, nineteen women had engaged in intercourse more than once a week. In short, more than half of the women had engaged in intercourse more frequently than they would have liked. In the early 20th century, Dr. Robert L. Dickinson, well-known birth-control advocate and gynecologist, not only attested to the lower frequency of intercourse desired by women than by men, but also recorded the conclusion that women were in fact restricting their husbands' frequency. As he put it, laconically, "average couple has intercourse twice a week or oftener, the emphasis leaning toward three times. . . . The account of the wife is, approximately, that the husband would like coitus three times a week she would be willing once, and they compromise on twice." [23]

It is possible, of course, to interpret these figures and comments not as a sign of women's influence but as the mutual influence of men and women in matters of sexual activity. And, in a sense, that is the meaning of many of the relations between the sexes in marriage. But there is still some further evidence to suggest more directly that women's efforts to control men's sexuality in the course of the 19th century met with some success. Alfred Kinsey in his book on women's sexual habits noted that the median frequencies of coitus in married couples dropped from 3.2 per week for his born before 1900 group of women to 2.6 per week in the group born after 1900. If one assumes, as Dr. Robert Dickinson had, and the Mosher Survey implied, that women desired a lower frequency than men, then these figures suggest that by the early 20th century women's influence over sexual activity was growing. And this was in part Kinsey's own explanation for the drop in frequency. He related it to a growing willingness on the part of husbands "to consider the wife's desire in regard to the frequencies of coitus." [24] Unfortunately, we do not have comparably full information on frequency for the 19th century, so we cannot be sure whether or not the trend Kinsey measured in the early 20th century was the continuation of an earlier trend or just the beginning of a new one. From what we know of the Social Purity movement and the general atmosphere in favor of limitation on sexual activity during the last half of the century it is plausible to conclude that Kinsey was measuring a long-term trend rather than a novel development.

That this may have been so is suggested by two additional arguments. The first comes from a report by two historians of sexual attitudes. They noted that in the marriage manuals published in the first half of the 19th century the average recommended frequency of intercourse was four to five times a week. [25] If that higher figure can be taken as representative of the early part of the century, then women did indeed have a dampening or restraining influence on men's sexual habits in the course of the century. The second reason for believing that the frequency of intercourse among married couples actually declined during the 19th century is what we know happened to the birth rate. It is well known that a decline in frequency of intercourse is highly correlated with a fall in births. And especially was this likely in the 19th century when, as we saw in Chapter IX, the methods of birth control available to couples were not always reliable. A decline in frequency of intercourse, in short, may well have been a significant cause for the fall in the birth rate. In fact, some economic demographers look to a decline in frequency as perhaps the most important single explanation for the 19th-century decline in fertility. If women generally desired less frequent intercourse in marriage, then the fall in the birth rate is an indirect but important measure of women's influence over male sexual expression.

Phrasing the matter in those terms, however, assumes that males were being put upon. Expressed more neutrally, the trend showed an increase in that sense of mutual consideration which was at the heart of the new ideal of marriage between companions that had begun to emerge in the early years of the 19th century. Presumably, too, as the literature on marriage reform and Social Purity promised, a reduction in the frequency of intercourse was accompanied by an improvement in the quality of sexual satisfaction for both man and woman as a result of taking woman's needs and desires into consideration.

The public movement to enhance women's autonomy within the family by controlling sexuality was merely one organizational activity of women. There were a number of others during the 19th century. The expansion and evolution of women's activities outside the home form an important part of the story of women's awakening to self-interest and individuality. Although many of these activities originated in domestic concerns, they often had effects that ramified far beyond their family origins. It is to that story we turn in the next chapter.

XIII

The World Is Only a Large Home

Throughout the 19th century the idea of a separate sphere for women was the ideological framework within which women lived and worked. At the same time, however, as we have noticed in connection with the Social Purity movement, during most of the century women were in fact active in organizations and in behalf of causes outside the home. Ideologically, this new activity was inherent in the conception of separate spheres: if women were to be effective guardians of the home and its morality, then they might well find it necessary to act in the world in order to protect the home and to preserve its morality. The connection in the popular mind between women and morality provided strong justification for women's participation in organizations and activities outside the kitchen or the nursery.

Almost from the beginning of settlement in the English colonies, religion and the churches were a special sphere of activity for women. This did not mean that women were ministers or even officers of the church, for they were not. In 17th-century Massachusetts, Anne Hutchinson was at once notorious and an exception. Few women in the established churches followed her model of teaching religion, though some time later Quaker women did act as missionaries and leaders within their sect. But if most women did not lead in the churches, they were conspicuous from the outset as members. As early as the 1650s, for example, women outnumbered men in the churches of New England. During the Great Awakening of the 1740s Jonathan Edwards was considered to be a preacher of unusual skill because he converted as many men as women, at a time when women still far outnumbered men among church members. The revivals among the

Baptists and other evangelical sects usually won more women converts than men. During the Second Great Awakening at the end of the 18th and opening of the 19th century, in four Connecticut towns almost two-thirds of the converts were women—usually young and unmarried. In the so-called "Burned-Over District" of upstate New York, which gained its name from the frequency of revivals there, and which was the seedbed of many early 19th-century reform groups, women were conspicuous at the meetings. One observer wrote in 1823 that women outnumbered men two to one among the denominations in the district. In the evangelical churches in the southern states at the end of the 18th century, white women outnumbered men almost two to one, even though men actually outnumbered women in the population.

Even after the Second Awakening had run its course, foreign travelers commented on the disproportionate number of women at the camp meetings and revivals in the back country of the 1830s and 1840s. Significantly enough, these comments came from women and men, and from friends as well as enemies of revivalism. This predominance of women among churchgoers persisted throughout the 19th century. As Mary Poor wrote her husband in 1870, "Yesterday we had a Good Friday service—Our Rev. preached one of his best sermons to one man (Mr. Davis) and a pretty good company of females."[1]

Not surprisingly, churchmen liked the interest women showed in religion, and they recognized and praised the affinity. Many believed women had a special gift for religion and morality. "Their sensibility, their vivacity, and sprightly imagination, their sympathy or tenderness toward distress and those in imminent danger of distress," wrote one minister in 1814, "qualify them, with the grace of God added, to make Christians of the first cast. Their affections are ardent and easily moved; and, when made to move in a religious direction, give them great, and sometimes unspeakable happiness."[2] It was more likely that women's nurturing and supportive role in the home, rather than anything intrinsic in their nature, inclined women to the characteristics the writer pointed to, but, whatever the source of the involvement of women in the churches, it was real and pervasive. Donald Mathews in his recent study of southern religion says that "women made southern Evangelicanism possible." That came through in "almost every surviving local church record as well as from the daily journals, personal letters, and sometimes sentimental memoirs of . . . clergymen." Not only were women the majority of church members in the South, Mathews continues, but "they provided indispensable support to the clergy. Almost every Methodist circuit rider and itinerant Baptist missionary who left an account of his work revealed an impressive reliance upon women for moral support as well as for basic physical comfort."

This intense association between women and the churches laid the bases for married women's movement out of the narrow sphere of the home. The operative word here is "married," for the unmarried woman, usually the young woman prior to marriage, also moved out of the urban home into paid employment. That social migration, however, was economic, not religious in motivation, as we shall see in Chapter XV.

Simply because married women were heavily involved in the work of churches, ministers often encouraged them to undertake tasks of benevolence within their towns or cities. As early as 1805, Janet James has written, "every large city and town had societies supplying soup, sewing, and firewood" to the poor, usually under the direction of women from the leading families. Sometimes these women set up schools to teach the poor.[3] The Sunday School movement owes its origins to the interest and energies of such women. As early as 1804 a number of women from various Protestant denominations formed a "Union Society" for the education of poor girls in Philadelphia on Sunday. This all-woman organization was incorporated in 1808 in the names of twenty-eight women. It flourished for years, having as many as 300 students in one of its several schools. In 1812, in New York City, Joanne Bethune took the initiative with a number of other women to organize what became in 1816 the "Female Union Society for the Promotion of Sabbath-Schools." Although its primary function was teaching religion, it expressed an interest in improving teaching methods and opened its doors to educate female adults who could not attend school during the week. Within one year, the Society had established 21 schools with 250 teachers and 3,163 pupils. As Edwin Wilbur Rice, historian and head of the Sunday School movement, wrote in the early 20th century, without women's "cooperation, it is doubtful whether the modern Sunday-School movement would not have proved a conspicuous failure." Three or four out of every five teachers, he wrote, were women. Women were also active in writing the literature taught in the schools, and usually outnumbered and outproduced the male authors of such books. Sarah Stearns, despite her many pregnancies, took a close interest in the benevolent societies of her Massachusetts town. In 1815, for example, she noted in her journal that "a female charitable Society" had just been formed to help "destitute children and furnish them with the means of attending school and public worship." The same year she also wrote that "a little band of youthful females have . . . formed themselves into a society for improvement in piety." In a number of small cities and towns, like Troy, New York, and Salem and Newburyport in Massachusetts, in the first two decades of the 19th century, women organized and managed orphan asylums.[4]

Literally scores of such benevolent, religiously oriented if not simply religious societies were formed across New England in the years before 1820. Other sections were only a little behind in emulating the practice. During the 1830s and after, even small towns like Cazenovia, New York, and Austinburg, Ohio, had "reasoning" societies and literary groups made up mostly of married ladies who met to discuss politics and economic questions along with religious concerns. Donald Mathews points out that in the South, prayer meetings of women often developed into social and benevolent organizations. He sees such meetings as the foundation of women's public life in the South. Largely because all of these groups stayed well within the traditional moral and "female" sphere, few men or women objected to them. In fact, their religious character and tone won the praise and the support of the religious press and establishment.

As reform organizations, these religious groups and societies were usually quite innocuous. But as alternatives to the home for married women, they were seminal. Women gained experience in organizing themselves and carrying out goals set by themselves. As Mathews has put it, from their religious groups and associations, women gained "psychological and social space." A measure of the significance of the gain, he pointed out, is the hostility that some of the evangelical ministers in the South experienced from husbands because of a wife's desire to convert. He cites one case of a husband who had forbidden his wife to be baptized, and, when her conscience compelled her to do so anyway, he shot the preacher.

The benevolent groups also provided outlets for women's talents and interests that the home could not always satisfy. The members of the societies made social contacts with other women and developed peer associations that provided a sense of identity in a world in which a woman's place depended almost entirely upon her connection with a man. As one woman wrote in 1837 to the New York Reform Society, "I rejoice . . . that I am woman; and I never gloried more in my sex than I do now." Fifteen years later, another woman wrote in a similar vein to a female journal. "I certainly never had a low conception of . . . women, but nothing has raised my ideas of her abilities so high as an acquaintance with the workings of the Home for the Friendless."[5] And because these activities fitted in with the popular belief that women were naturally moral and benevolent no one objected to the organizations. It is highly likely that the participation of many married women in these various activities reinforced the doctrine of separate spheres, while, in turn, the idea of the separate spheres legitimized the activities.

By the end of the 18th century and the beginning of the 19th, some Protestant sects, notably Quakers and Baptists, provided some opportunities to women to be leaders and preachers. The Quakers in particular made few role distinctions between the sexes, so it was not accidental that many of the early women antislavery leaders, like Abby Kelley, Lucretia Mott, and Lydia Maria Child, came out of Quaker backgrounds. This was also true of many of the later suffrage leaders. In short, rather than seeing women's religious organizations and immersion in the church in the early 19th century as a sign of women's conservatism born of the masculine-imposed doctrine of separate spheres, it is worth recognizing that for many married women religious activities opened up new horizons without calling into question their domestic duties or outlook. Such activities were admittedly identified as female rather than human, but, as Nancy Cott has reminded us, that very identification gave women a sense of themselves as women, a development that was indispensable if women were to expand their opportunities still further. The sex as a whole thus carved out a domain for itself that extended beyond the home, even while those activities owed their origins and their justification to domestic duties.

The moral character of these early benevolent societies and concerns encouraged women who worked in them to slip over into activities with a stronger aura of social reform about them. Lydia Andrews Finney, the wife of the famous Oberlin evangelist Charles Grandison Finney, filled her letters with her reform activities in behalf of temperance, education, and the antislavery movement. She was no believer in women's rights in general, nor a feminist, but her social interests tended to undercut those who argued that women should stay away from such outside activities. Yet all of her activities were justified by her religious concerns—that is, precisely those qualities that ministers praised women for exhibiting: compassion, tenderness, sympathy, and humanitarianism. As we saw in a previous chapter, religious principles lay at the root of the New York Female Moral Reform Society, which took upon itself in the 1830s to eradicate prostitution and the double sexual standard. The appeal of the Society to women revealed the central role of religion in its reason for being. "It is the imperious duty of ladies everywhere, and of every religious denomination, to cooperate in the great work of moral reform," the Society's journal asserted. It was a religious impulse that caused the Ladies' Home Missionary Society in the 1850s in New York City to found a kind of early settlement house in the notorious Five Points district. "What no legal enactment could accomplish—what no machinery of municipal government could effect," a male attorney wrote enthusiastically, "women have brought about quietly but thoroughly, and triumphantly."[6] And during the Civil War the Sanitary Commission and similar organizations in the southern states drew upon this reservoir of female benevolence in behalf of soldiers and their families on both sides of the battlefield.

In the years before the Civil War, the reform that most conspicuously attracted women, especially married women, and did the most to move them into public activities was the antislavery cause. The plight of black people under slavery was a natural object of benevolence for women who had been taught to be charitable, to believe in education and in the Christian duty of uplifting the poor and unfortunate. If any group of human beings in America qualified for such benevolence, blacks, both slave and free, certainly did. An astute abolitionist agitator like William Lloyd Garrison made the most of women's reputation for religious benevolence. "The destiny of the slaves is in the hands of American women," he wrote early in his career in 1833, "and complete emancipation can never take place without their cooperation." After noting that the women in England had been active in ending slavery in the British Empire, he urged American women to do the same. He concluded by saying that if "I fail to awaken your sympathies, and secure your aid, I may well despair of gaining the hearts and support of men."[7] Here he was playing with a vengeance upon the doctrine of separate spheres. Women abolitionists, too, were quick to point out that women in particular could be expected to sympathize with the slaves since under slavery women and children were especially debased.

Involvement in the antislavery movement did more than draw upon the religious concerns of women; it also set them thinking about their position within the movement, pushing them, here and there, to seek equality with men. As early as 1836, an Ohio abolitionist assured a woman worker in the cause that "in Jesus Christ there is neither male nor female. . . . A mind whether deposited in a male or female body is equally valuable for all moral and intellectual purposes. Indeed there is no station in life but what may be filled as ably and as beneficially by women as by men."[8] Though this was admittedly a radical statement, which only a few male abolitionists could accept, it was a sign of the intellectual forces that antislavery had let loose. Yet it was no more than a sign. As late as 1840, women were denied the right to appear on the floor of a world antislavery convention in London and at other places in the United States. Most male abolitionists feared that the assertion of equality between men and women within the movement would jeopardize the cause of the slave by frightening away potential supporters. To such abolitionists—and they were in the majority—the greater cause was antislavery; woman's emancipation must wait upon the slave's.

This hostility of men to women's full acceptance within the antislavery movement was a source of consciousness-raising for many women abolitionists. Suddenly, as they fought for the freedom of the slave, they found that they had their own gender's cause to fight. Abolitionist women often obtained their first sense of identity as an oppressed group from their work with fellow abolitionists. In 1837 the first Antislavery Convention of American Women, meeting in New York, resolved "that as certain rights and duties are common to all moral beings, the time has come for women to move in that sphere which Providence has assigned her and no longer remain satisfied in their circumscribed limits which corrupt custom and a perverted application of Scripture has encircled her."[9]

Although that meeting was composed entirely of women, the resolution did not pass unanimously. Women abolitionists, in short, found it difficult sometimes to be accepted by other women, as well as by the world at large. In the beginning, churches and meeting houses denied them pulpits, while newspapers and public figures assailed them for behaving in a manner unbecoming to their sex. Before women abolitionists, led by Angelina Grimké, began speaking in public, virtually no respectable woman, except the notorious social radical Fanny Wright, had appeared on a public platform. But long before the antislavery cause was won, abolitionist women had gained acceptance as public speakers. And those women who were not willing to speak in public, were willing to sign petitions opposing slavery; William Lloyd Garrison said that many more women signed such petitions than men. Though even that amount of public activity was novel, if not threatening to many married women, the very act of signing must have marked a significant step in a signer's movement out of the home and into activities not usually associated with the roles of wife and mother.

One source of consciousness-raising close at hand was the male abolitionists. "I think the tom-turkey ought to do the gobbling," wrote Elizur Wright, Jr., in 1838 in regard to women's speaking in public. "I am opposed to hens crowing, and surely, as a rule, to female-preaching." But, he later admitted, he was not about to become the "executioner of the laws of nature." Even Theodore Weld, one of the most radical and egalitarian-minded of the young abolitionists in the 1840s, had to be taken to task by Angelina Grimké for initially failing to accept women's equal role in the antislavery cause. Contrary to what he thought, she informed him in 1837, it was not the Quaker religion that justified her public speaking against slavery, but "Bible ground and *moral right*. What we claim for ourselves, we claim for *every* woman whom God has called and qualified with gifts and graces." When Weld expressed doubt that it was proper to endanger the cause of antislavery with a concomitant advocacy of women's rights, Grimké's response was quick and sharp. "We will settle *this right before* we go one step further. *The time* to assert a right is the *time* when *that* right is denied. *We must establish this right* for if we do not, it will be impossible for *us to go on with the work of emancipation*."[10] So far as Weld was concerned, Grimké must have successfully established the principle, for the next year they were married. But the question of whether women should or should not put their own cause before that of blacks would continue to bedevil women for another quarter of a century, at least. It lay, for instance, at the root of the division in the suffrage organization into two rival groups in 1869, a division that was not healed until 1890.

The participation of women, married and unmarried, in the reform movement that dominated all others during the antebellum decades was seminal in the growth of women's self-consciousness as well as being a prime example of the way religious involvement brought women into reform work. As the minutes of the Philadelphia Female Anti-Slavery Society phrased the point in 1839, "by the concentration of our efforts in this way, we not only advance the cause of the emancipation of the slave, but . . . the fettered mind of woman is fast releasing itself from the thralldom in which long existing custom has it bound." Furthermore, the minutes continued, as a result of using her talents in behalf of the slave, "woman's intelligence as well as moral being is rising into new life."[11]

It was through the cause of antislavery that some women learned how to speak in public and many women became familiar with public participation as a legitimate role for a married woman. Literally hundreds of mothers and wives gained experience in organizing themselves into groups and absorbing hostile reactions from men and women. And a few women pushed the cause of antislavery to the point where it encompassed equality for women in the name of *human* rights. It is because of this latter development that historian Keith Melder quite properly designates women's participation in the antislavery movement as the training ground for the woman's rights movement, which began with the meeting at Seneca Falls, New York, in 1848. It was that meeting which set forth, in a well-known rewriting of the Declaration of Independence of 1776, the essential elements for the equality of women in American society. The women's Declaration put man in place of George III; in place of the thirty-odd grievances against the King the women listed an equal number of accusations of masculine oppression.

Important as the participation of women in the antislavery movement may have been for raising women's consciousness of self, women probably made up no more than 10 or 15 per cent of the workers in the antislavery societies. In fact, the anti-slavery movement as a whole, men included, was never a mass activity. In short, women's participation was that of a fraction within a fraction. Similarly, the woman's movement throughout the 19th century left untouched the great mass of women, married and unmarried. At no time were more than a few thousand women actively involved in the feminist or suffrage causes. The great preponderance of women either had nothing to do with feminism, or actually scorned it as unnecessary and wrong-headed. Why this was so will be a question we shall explore in the next chapter. Meanwhile, let us look at other activities of women that were, like the religious and benevolent work, more attractive to the majority of married women than either feminism or antislavery.

The key to understanding which activities appealed to middle-class married women in the 19th century is the relation between the activity and the separate sphere of women. The closer a female activity was associated with the moral and domestic responsibilities of women as prescribed by the separate spheres, the more likely that activity was to be condoned and fairly readily accepted by other women and society in general. The church-spawned benevolent activities of women aroused few hostile remarks or resistance, while public speaking by women against slavery often brought opprobrium and denials of pulpits and lecterns. Such activities smacked of masculine practices and were certainly unrelated to domestic routines. Yet an aura of religious commitment and Christian benevolence always surrounded the antislavery movement and its supporters. Religion was their justification. This connection with religion lent support to the idea that women's participation in the antislavery cause was not entirely unrelated to their proper role as guardians of morality and dispensers of Christian benevolence.

Women's role in the family was also a prime reason for women's interest in the antislavery movement. It was widely assumed in the North that under slavery the family could not exist among Negroes and that it was common for white masters to compel slave women to have sexual relations with them. Opposition to slavery seemed, therefore, a natural concern of women, an outgrowth not only of their religious humanitarianism but also of their roles as wives and mothers.

But when the logic of the antislavery involvement pushed some women or men to assert the equality of the sexes, a wall of disapproval and even hostility was quickly erected. From that implication the great majority of women drew back. The necessity to legitimize the activities of women by relating them to their domestic roles would continue to determine the acceptability of women's organizations well into the 20th century.

There was another way in which women's activities moved outside the home in the early 19th century without doing immediate violence to the idea of separate spheres, but which carried within it seeds that, when they sprouted, would split the barriers that separated them. This was the idea that, if women were central to the family and intended to be the principal, if not the only child-rearers, then it followed that they needed to be sufficiently educated to assume that high responsibility. As Catharine Beecher wrote in her famous *Treatise on Domestic Economy,* "the proper education of a man decides the welfare of an individual; but educate a woman, and the interests of a whole family are secured." And insofar as the ideal wife and mother was also a companion to her husband, then it also followed that to fulfill that role, too, she must be adequately educated. What "adequately" meant was susceptible to changing definition, as subsequent history would show. But once the idea had been advanced, it could not be ignored or suppressed; it had set changes in motion.

It is not easy in all of this to separate cause from result. Did women win improved chances for education *because* men recognized the advantages of having an educated companion-wife and an educated mother for their children? Or was it the other way round: because women through their own and others' efforts gained an education, it was increasingly possible to leave the education of children in their hands and to expect that a wife would be more than a household drudge and a bearer of children—that she could also be a man's lifetime companion? Most likely it worked both ways, each development affecting the other dialectically.

What we can be sure about is that around the end of the 18th century there was a marked improvement in the education of girls. This was almost precisely the time, as we have seen, when a new conception of children and a new emphasis upon women's separate sphere were becoming apparent. Before the Revolution even the most rudimentary aspects of girls' education had lagged behind boys'. Prior to the 18th century the literacy of adult women was considerably less than that of men. During the first generation in 17th-century New England perhaps half of adult men could sign their names; only about one-third of women could. By 1776 four-fifths of adult men could sign their names, but only 40 to 45 per cent of women were able to. The education of girls, even of this most rudimentary kind, was probably even less advanced in the remaining English colonies. One authority reported that at the end of the 17th century only one out of three women in Virginia could sign their names as compared with three out of five men. The most recent research informs us that a regression in literacy occurred among rural women between 1705 and 1760, but that an upsurge was evident among men to as high as 80 per cent literate. Yet by 1850, when the census first recorded figures on literacy, over 87 per cent of all white women in America over twenty years of age could read and write. A detailed analysis of northern farm families drawn from the 1860 manuscript census discovered that the literacy of white husbands and wives differed only marginally. Some 94 per cent of white husbands were literate as compared with 91 per cent of wives.[12]

The explanation for the striking improvement in women's literacy since the Revolution is that near the end of the 18th century a movement for the education of girls got under way. When books and articles advocated educating girls on a par with boys in the years after the Revolution, few objections were raised. Instead the need for such education was tied to the needs of a new republic: women would make sure that patriot sons were reared properly. Benjamin Rush, the well-known Jeffersonian and physician in Philadelphia, advocated a special and rigorous education for girls. Where schools for boys could not or would not admit girls, seminaries for females were established. One of the best known was headed by Emma Willard, who founded it in 1821, soon after publishing her *Plan for Improving Female Education* in 1819. Willard's aim was to give women a solid education so that they could be well-trained mothers, and, if necessary, self-supporting as teachers. Even better known was the Hartford Female Seminary, founded in 1823, by Catharine Beecher, sister of the author of *Uncle Tom's Cabin*. Nor were such institutions confined to New England or New York. The Huntsville Female Seminary in Alabama, founded in 1831, was one of the most prestigious schools in the country.

But undoubtedly the most significant development of all was that, as publicly supported education expanded in the first decades of the 19th century, girls were almost invariably included along with boys. Even raw, new towns in the frontier West and South insisted on education for children of both sexes. For the history of women and the family in the United States this social decision ranks among the most fateful. By 1860 it was almost as likely for a white girl as a white boy to attend school, even in the farming regions of the country. The study of the manuscript census returns for northern and western farm families referred to earlier, disclosed that 82 per cent of all white females between 10 and 14 were in school in 1860 as compared with 84 per cent of all white males of those ages. Two historians, in examining the school records of Massachusetts in 1860 and 1880, found to their surprise that more girls than boys attended primary school. As the historians noted significantly enough, "school officials rarely distinguished between girls and boys in talking about early education needs and abilities." [13]

The success of the private female academies and seminaries also ensured that when secondary education surged forward after the Civil War it would also be overwhelmingly coeducation. Secondary education for girls went back much earlier, the first public high school for girls being founded in Worcester, Massachusetts, in 1824. But secondary school education for either sex was not widespread until after 1870. In that year there were only 160 high schools in the whole country. Ten years later, however, the figure was almost 800 and by the close of the century the number was over 6000. One survey of city educational systems at the beginnings of the 1890s reported that out of 628 cities only fifteen had separate high schools for boys and girls. From 1870, when the statistics first began to be kept, until the middle of the 20th century, the girls who graduated each year from high school always outnumbered the boys. It is not surprising, therefore, that the Census of 1880 found that the proportion of literacy for young women was actually higher than for young white men.

The movement for the equal education of girls and boys went forward rapidly and successfully—almost without opposition. The idea fitted easily into the social ideology that women were the rearers of children and the moral companions of men within the family. This acceptance of girls' education, however, stopped short at the collegiate or university level. Prior to the 1830s there was no institution of higher education that permitted young women to enter, though colleges for young men went back to the 17th century. Indeed, during the 18th century and the first three decades of the 19th, there was an upsurge in the founding of colleges, including several state universities in the South. But none of these new institutions, much less the earlier ones, admitted young women. Higher education was a part of man's sphere because the purpose of it was to train ministers, professional men, and political leaders. Girls, it was thought, had no more need for a college education than did a boy intending to be a farmer or a businessman. Even Emma Willard, founder of a famous school for girls in Troy, New York, recognized this point when she wrote in 1819 of "the absurdity of sending ladies to colleges" which were simply modeled after those of men. She sought to train young women to be teachers, but she emphasized how different the education she intended to offer was from that given to men in their colleges.

The total exclusion of women from colleges was broken in 1837, when Oberlin College in Ohio permitted women to enroll with men at its opening. That same year the Michigan legislature, when it passed legislation to found a state university, provided that places be set aside for women, though until 1870 none was actually allowed to attend. In 1852 Antioch College opened its doors to both women and men, and by then several state universities, particularly in the West, included women among their students. But even pioneer Oberlin, it was clear, was moved less by egalitarian principles than by a desire to meet the needs of men. As the founders pointed out, the presence of women would give men an alternative to single-sex education, and women would provide a social outlet for the men, thus encouraging male academic concentration. Moreover, it was believed that the presence of women would have a civilizing and humanizing effect on the male students who, as future ministers, would profit from such influences. The founders referred to the women students, significantly enough, as "the female appendage" to the college; nor was it unusual to refer to the male students as "the leading sex." [14] But whatever the justification for the opening of Oberlin to women, the coeducational college became increasingly common just before and immediately after the Civil War. It was surely a measure of women's influence, if only through their fathers or husbands, who had the ballot, that at least in the states outside the South, as public universities were established by legislatures, women, as a matter of course, were included as students.

Given the relatively large number of public, not to mention private higher educational institutions open to women, the establishment during the 1850s and 1860s of women's colleges cannot be seen simply as a way of supplying places for women who could not otherwise obtain a college education. The primary impetus, rather, was the quality or rigor of the education available. Measured against the standards of the established men's colleges like Harvard, Yale, and Princeton, some of the new state universities were not yet adequate. Moreover, even private colleges that were coeducational, like Oberlin or Cornell, did not treat women as full equals. The central issue, however, was whether women could be educated in demanding subjects like Latin and Greek as men were at the eastern colleges. The first women's college that required classical languages and a full four-year course with a degree of rigor approaching that of the best men's colleges was Mary Sharp College, founded in 1851 in Winchester, Tennessee. Since Mary Sharp College did not survive into the 20th century, the first such women's college to survive to the present is usually taken to be Elmira College, founded in upstate New York in 1855.

The opening of Mary Sharp and Elmira colleges was a "first," but the significant breakthrough in higher education for women did not occur until after the Civil War, with the opening of Vassar College in 1865, with a substantial endowment and well-equipped physical plant. It was followed by Wellesley and Smith Colleges in 1875, Bryn Mawr in 1880, Mills College in California in 1885, and Randolph-Macon in Virginia in 1891. Meanwhile, Harvard had established Radcliffe as a coordinate college, and Columbia had opened Barnard. Mount Holyoke had been a seminary since 1837, but achieved collegiate standing also during the 1870s. A little over half a century after the founding of Mary Sharp College, over 125 women's colleges were in being. By 1910 about 15 per cent of the nation's colleges were for women alone, while another 58 per cent were coeducational.

If by the opening of the 20th century it could be said that higher education for women was accepted, that achievement had not, however, been uncontested. As late as 1858 a report of the Board of Regents of the University of Michigan, which had for twenty years accepted on paper the enrollment of women, opposed instituting coeducation on the ground that it was "contrary to nature" and predicted that "young men would lose a proper sense of dignity of their pursuits" while "the delicacy of the female character would be destroyed." [15] It was widely contended that the very emotional and sensitive nature of women, which made them ideal as moral preceptors of the home and rearers of children, by the same token made them unequal to the intellectual strain of learning Greek or mathematics on the college level. In 1873, Dr. Edward H. Clarke of the Harvard Medical School published *Sex in Education*, in which he contended that women possessed the mental ability to do college work but that their feminine physique was harmed severely when they were trained along the same lines as men. He regaled his readers with horrendous cases of brilliant young women who either died or were incapacitated physically as a result of their intellectual successes at college. Although he repeatedly asserted his belief in the high intellectual capacity of girls, nowhere in his little book did he explain how that capacity could be realized without physical harm. Not surprisingly, a number of women and men who believed in women's education came forward to refute Clarke's assertions and evidence, but *Sex in Education,* in the course of its many editions, exerted a strong negative influence upon women. M. Carey Thomas, later the president of Bryn Mawr College, recalled that "we were haunted in those days by the clanging chains of that gloomy little spectre, Dr. Edward H. Clarke's *Sex in Education.*" [16]

Thomas also remembered vividly the effects of those hostile attitudes on herself. "The passionate desire of the women of my generation for higher education," she recalled in 1907, "was accompanied throughout its course by the awful doubt, felt by women themselves as well as by men, as to whether women as a sex were physically and mentally fit for it." She had no doubt that she wanted to go to college, yet "I was always wondering whether it could be really true, as everyone thought, that boys were cleverer than girls. Indeed, I cared so much that I never dared to ask any grown up person the direct question, not even my father or mother, because I feared to hear the reply." She remembered praying about her doubts and "begging God that if it were true that because I was a girl I could not successfully master Greek and go to college and understand things, to kill me at once." When she read the Bible she wept over the curse pronounced upon Eve because she feared it "might imperil girls' going to college; and to this day I can never read many parts of the Pauline epistles without feeling again the sinking of the heart with which I used to hurry over the verses referring to women's keeping si¹ence in the churches and asking their husbands at home." [17]

The doubts about women's education were so widespread and deeply rooted that for years President John Raymond of Vassar College referred to that institution and its goal of training young women as an "experiment." Yet by 1894, one educational authority could announce that "the old and tiresome question" of women's "intellectual ability is closed." And three years later the Commissioner of Education noted that a quarter of a century earlier there had been grave doubts about women's abilities to be educated. "Since that time, where girls and boys have been educated together," he reported, "it has become an historical fact that women have made rapid strides, and captured a greater number of honors in proportion to their numbers than men." Indeed, ten years after the admission of women into the University of Chicago, 56 per cent of the initiates into Phi Beta Kappa were women. Newly opened coeducational universities in the 1890s, like Chicago and Stanford, witnessed a great upsurge in female enrollments. In 1899, some 40 per cent of Stanford students were women, and, between 1893 and 1902, Chicago's proportion jumped from 24 per cent to 52 per cent.[18]

What brought about the change in outlook? Part of it came simply from observation. Women, when given the opportunity, more than proved themselves. Attitudes changed accordingly. But that does not explain why women were given the opportunity to prove themselves in the first place. For an answer to that question we have to look at the character of the developing 19th-century family and the central role increasingly assumed by women.

When Vassar opened, it was clear that many women saw in the new college opportunities for their daughters which had been denied to them. "When I remember my own meager opportunities," wrote a woman in 1862, seeking to have her fourteen-year-old daughter admitted, "I shall rejoice that a better time is coming." Another woman wrote that she had three daughters to educate "and have long looked forward to Vassar and been thankful they would find advantages denied to older women." Mary Jones of Georgia did not refer to college, but she voiced a mother's interest in her daughter's education when she wrote in 1862 about two young women who were engaged in intellectual endeavors even though married. "I do admire to see ladies keep up their literary tastes, although I am myself a striking example of the opposite practice," she wrote her daughter, "and feel to my shame and sorrow the rust and ruin which have accumulated upon a neglected mind. All that I can now do is to warn my daughters and grand-daughters, that they may not become as I am. For years and years I had intellectual cravings that made me almost miserable; but starvation has quenched the pangs of hunger, and I am now content with the Book of Books and daily striving to fulfill the ordinary duties of life. I hope none of you will ever pattern after such an example." [19]

Mothers were not the only persons interested in educating young women. As the *New York Tribune* observed at the time of the founding of Vassar College, "no man but would prefer that his mother or his wife should be an educated woman; none that does not rejoice in giving the highest advantage to his daughters." President John Raymond of Vassar pointed out the advantages more directly when he wrote that "the larger the stock of knowledge and more thorough the mental discipline a woman actually attains, other things being equal, the better she is fitted to fill every womanly duty, at home and in society." Or as Charles McIver, a North Carolina educator, chose to phrase the same idea at the end of the century: "Educate a man and you have educated one person; educate a mother and you have educated the whole family." [20]

The close relationship between the higher education of women and their important place in the family is shown, too, by the outcry against the education of women when that education seemed to be interfering with the traditional role of women in the family. The occasion was the discovery toward the end of the 19th century that college-educated women did not marry to the same extent as other women. No matter who collected the statistics, the figures always showed that at least a fourth of women who graduated from college never married, a proportion that was more than double that for non-college women. And because many college women, if they married at all, did so at a later age than other women, the charge continued, they produced fewer children. (That both things were also true of college-educated men was rarely mentioned because men's primary role was not fatherhood.) Furthermore, it was married college women who knew most about and practiced contraception and other means of family limitation, so that even when they did marry at a young age they bore fewer babies. Also, since immigrant and lower-class women usually had more children, higher education for women came under attack for class as well as family reasons.

Because college education seemed to prevent women from marrying or having as many children as non-college women, women's education was criticized for having a subversive influence upon the traditional conception of women and the family. By arousing women's sense of self and identity, higher education seemed to be undermining one of the chief reasons for opening colleges to women—that is, to make them into better wives and mothers. And certainly by the opening years of the 20th century and for decades thereafter the colleges themselves had proclaimed their primary mission to be just that. After all, the great majority of college women did marry and become mothers. As Charles Richmond said at his inauguration as president of Skidmore College in 1925, "One of the chief ends of college for women is to fit them to become the makers of homes; whatever else a woman may be, the highest purpose of her life always has been . . . to strengthen and beatify and sanctify the home." And that was in the middle of the "roaring twenties." [21]

Yet, like the benevolent activities of religious societies, a college education was susceptible to many uses; once certain doors had been opened, low expectations raised, and new skills taught, how women used their education or what conclusions they drew from it were not always what their teachers or the founders of the colleges had intended. As historian Keith Melder well phrased it, "not every educated woman was a rebel, but nearly every rebel had been educated." [22]

The spread of women's education was only one of the ways in which the idea of separate spheres and the institution of the closely knit, companionate family encouraged women, ironical and unintended as they may have been, to expand their activities beyond the home. Indeed, by the last decades of the 19th century, thanks to the spread of education, the expanding religious activities of women, the growth of cities and the expansion of urban life, more and more married women found the time, the energy, and the inclination to form or join a whole range of organizations that sought to reshape, if not actively reform, American society. In Chapter IX we saw one example of this in the Social Purity movement. Now it is time to look at some of the other organizations that depended upon the new extrafamilial concerns of wives and mothers. None of the causes served by these organizations was more important nor more reflective of the close relationship in women's activities between home and the world than the war against drink.

Temperance had a long history in 19th-century America. Concern over drinking had become sufficiently widespread before the Civil War, that several states enacted laws against the sale of alcoholic beverages, beginning with Maine in 1851. In some of the temperance organizations, women had been active during the 1840s, particularly in the so-called Martha Washington societies. But the antislavery movement and then the Civil War distracted public attention away from the issue.

The post-Civil War movement to ban the consumption of alcohol began in 1873 in the little town of Hillsboro, in southern Ohio, when a group of one hundred middle- and upper-class married women appeared before the saloons of the town, praying and urging the owners to close their doors for good. The women's visits, begun just before Christmas, were interrupted for the holiday and then resumed immediately thereafter, continuing for many weeks. Spontaneously, a similar vigil took place before saloons in

Washington Courthouse, Ohio, and in Fredonia, New York. In the beginning there were no organizations and no leaders. The women in each town simply decided among themselves to take action. Very soon thereafter, however, the idea caught on and spread to other towns in Ohio, New York, Massachusetts, Pennsylvania, Illinois, and elsewhere. By March of 1874 the eastern metropolitan newspapers were reporting fully on the vigils; what had once been treated as a joke now began to be perceived as a groundswell of sentiment that in some places was even affecting the outcome of local elections.

The Woman's Uprising, as one historian called these vigils involving hundreds of women, lasted about six months before it died away. In the course of it, perhaps as many as 3000 saloons were closed—at least temporarily. One national magazine reported that in Ohio and Indiana the federal revenue from excise duties fell off by $350,000 for January and February in 1874. Temperance bills now gained consideration in Congress. Perhaps the most enduring consequence of the "Uprising" was the formation of the Women's Christian Temperance Union, soon to become the largest women's organization in 19th-century America.

At the time it was widely recognized, as it has been since, that the impetus behind women's opposition to drink was concern for the moral wellbeing of the home. Not only was the saloon the place in which husbands spent their wages on liquor, but it was also the recognized site of gambling and prostitution. The saloon was a man's world, one in direct competition with the home, the proper sanctuary of the family—that is, all the family; not only mother and children but the father as well. The goal of destroying the saloon, which increasing numbers of married women rallied behind, was as much a part of the attempt to control the behavior of men as the contemporary Social Purity movement. Both sought to realize a new ideal for the family, one in which the women may have been the moral preceptors, but the men were expected to be responsible and contributing family partners as well. Thus even those women whose husbands may have been as temperate or teetotaling as themselves saw in the movement against liquor a way of spreading proper ideas about family life and responsibility to others less fortunate. Certainly one of the aims of the temperance people was to have working-class and immigrant families follow their example. It is true that the WCTU was primarily a middle-class organization, but a study of some of its local leaders in 1885 revealed that the husbands of almost 30 per cent of them were skilled and unskilled workers.[23] This suggests some success in reaching women of different classes.

Simply because of the doctrine of the two spheres, in the name of which the women undertook the temperance crusade, it was difficult, if not impossible, to object to women's increasing participation in the war on liquor. For this was one of those activities that women needed to attack even if it meant they formed organizations outside the home; it was clearly a legitimate extension of their moral guardianship. Even when women obviously broke the law in pursuit of their temperance goals, few men were prepared to denounce them. During the Uprising of '74, for example, many women had trespassed on private property as they sought to close down saloons, but very few were arrested. Although one reason they were not was that many of the offending women were married to socially or politically prominent husbands, in many towns the male leaders of opinion and government favored the women because they were perceived as carrying out a religious duty. The mayor of Cincinnati, for example, said as much when he directed that the women should be protected in the public square of the city during their protests. The liberal *Nation* was less favorably disposed toward women, but no more willing to interfere. "The women have triumphed over the law," the magazine pointed out. It was significant, too, that in justifying the violation of law by the temperance women, the press often excused the infractions by noting that these women were not agitating for the suffrage.[24] Presumably, if they had been, support would not have been forthcoming.

The substantial and rapid growth of the Women's Christian Temperance Union soon after its founding in 1874 was a concrete and telling measure of women's interest in the cause of temperance. It far outdistanced women's organizations in behalf of woman suffrage. By the 1890s there were ten times as many women in the New York WCTU groups as in suffrage organizations. In 1911, the WCTU counted 245,000 members; it was then the largest women's organization in the United States. It tapped not only women's involvement with the home but also their religious concerns. Churches supported the organization as they would not support the suffrage cause; moreover, many prominent church women were also active in the WCTU, thus lending an additional aura of respectability. And many men found the cause not only a respectable one but one that was quite consistent with what they considered the proper domestic concerns of their wives, mothers, and sisters.

The women's temperance crusade, however, like education and church work, could not be held strictly to its original intention. The women who became involved in it saw things and learned things that moved them in new, often quite unexpected and even unsettling directions. One southern temperance leader called the WCTU "the golden key that unlocked the prison doors of pentup possibilities . . . the discoverer, the developer of southern women." Mary Livermore, president of the Massachusetts WCTU, looking back in 1883 on the "Uprising of '74," contended that through it women were "floated . . . to a higher level of womanhood. It lifted them out of a subject condition where they had suffered immitigatible woe . . . to a plateau where they saw that endurance had ceased to be a virtue!" One may doubt that the situation of women before 1874 was quite as bad as Mary Livermore remembered, but there can be little doubt that the WCTU raised the consciousness of many women as to their capabilities and potentialities for effecting changes. Moreover, the WCTU was strictly a women's organization, giving women broader chances for leadership, and experience in working with other women, uninhibited by the presence of men. As Frances Willard, its most famous leader, was fond of saying, the WCTU was "of the women, by the women, but for humanity." [25]

The most dramatic sign that the cause of temperance moved many women in new directions is Frances Willard's success in inducing the WCTU to support a truly feminist cause like woman suffrage. At the founding, the leaders of the WCTU wanted to have nothing to do with the "extreme" cause of votes for women; but, from the beginning, Frances Willard worked from within the organization to change this outlook. As she tirelessly pointed out to the members, if women were to be effective in behalf of temperance they must be able to exert their influence where it counted—namely, in the voting booth. To do this they required the suffrage. After five years of agitation within the WCTU, Willard in 1879 was elected national president, an office she was to hold for eighteen years. As one of the truly outstanding organizational leaders of the 19th century, Willard also worked to weld the loosely structured WCTU into a dues-paying, tightly organized, smoothly articulated society, a goal she achieved in 1881 when a new constitution was adopted. Although passionately interested in achieving a temperate America, she envisioned the WCTU as extending beyond temperance, of being an organization for all women. In 1880 she frankly invited women to join the organization even if they had little interest in temperance! She inaugurated what she called the "Do-Everything Policy" in which she provided causes other than temperance for members to work for. By 1889 she had 39 departments in the WCTU, organized under headings like labor, women, health, social purity, peace and arbitration, as well as temperance.

Willard's aim of having the WCTU stand for woman suffrage, however, was not achieved easily. When she made her first plea for the suffrage, her words were met with silence, as if she had announced a catastrophe. When she had finished, the presiding officer hastened to announce that Willard spoke only for herself. Later the president told Willard, "You might have been a leader, but now you'll only be a scout." And in 1881, when Willard managed to have feminist Susan B. Anthony invited to speak before the WCTU, many conservative members left the organization. But by 1885 the Union's journal, *Union Signal,* was saying that when prohibition had been achieved women's public work would still not be accomplished until the ballot had also been given to women.[26]

The WCTU never did become the major force behind the drive for the suffrage, but it was an excellent example, nonetheless, of how women's involvement in a cause close to the home and to the traditional sphere of women could lead women to support causes that were neither traditional nor home-related. The process could be observed in the lives of many individual women. Julia Tutwiler of Alabama and Rebecca Fenton of Georgia began their public lives in the WCTU, but in the 1880s they also became interested in ending the convict lease system in southern prisons as a result of what they had learned about the practice during their fight against alcohol. Carrie Chapman Catt and Anna Shaw, both leaders in the last stages of the fight for woman suffrage, began their public work in the temperance cause.

Because so many women were associated with temperance, those men who supported prohibition were spurred to support woman suffrage. The assumption was that if women gained the ballot they would vote for prohibition. Thus as early as 1872 the Prohibition party came out for woman suffrage, the first political party to do so. In return, the WCTU endorsed the Prohibition party. Soon after the Anti-Saloon League was founded in 1896, it announced its support of woman suffrage, principally on the ground that women could be counted on to vote against the liquor interests. And there is some evidence that many did when they got the chance. Of the fourteen states that adopted Prohibition before the passage of the Eighteenth Amendment, in ten of them women already had the vote. As Alice Stone Blackwell, feminist Lucy Stone's daughter, wrote, "in the main, suffrage and prohibition have the same friends and the same enemies."[27]

Although one of the principal drives behind the extension of higher education to women was the desire to improve the quality of wives and mothers, education acted in as unpredictable ways on women as temperance and religious societies. The ramifications that stretched out from education, however, were more numerous and extensive. The very fact that literally thousands of women in the course of the 1870s and 1880s were brought together in colleges and universities laid the ground for a fresh outlook among women. For one thing, the college experience set them apart from other women of their age and from their mothers and previous generations of women. Many of them wanted to continue this new relationship somehow, and also to put to social and individual use their newly acquired skills and awareness.

One immediate consequence was the formation of organizations of college women. The Association of Collegiate Alumnae was founded in 1882, for example, to perpetuate in some fashion that special association young women had discovered in college. Its founding purpose was to maintain high standards for women's education, but its practical purpose was to give several thousand young women who had graduated from college a sense of community and identity as women. In 1903 the Southern Association of College Women was formed to do for educated women of the South what the ACA had been doing for northern college women.

The most obvious and important connection between the new educational opportunities for women and organizations of women was the settlement movement. The earliest settlement house was founded in the United States in 1889, derived from the prototype erected in a London slum. The idea was to have young, socially conscious middle-class men and women live in the poor, working-class, and immigrant districts of the great cities in order to bring understanding, practical help, entertainment, and some intellectual experience to the inhabitants. The settlement houses offered instruction in baby care, sewing, and nutrition, as well as providing recreational facilities and cultural activities for the neighborhood. Although many men went into settlement work, the striking thing about the most famous settlements of the late 19th century—Hull-House in Chicago and the Henry Street Settlement in New York—was that they were run and staffed mainly by women. Usually they were college-trained women who wanted to put their education to use and, above all, wanted to expand their talents and find an identitiy beyond the immediate family. Certainly the most famous—and most successful—of the settlement workers was Jane Addams. In her life she exemplified to an almost exaggerated degree the impact of higher education upon young women. Her aimless search, while plagued by what today would be recognized as various psychosomatic illnesses, for something to do after graduation from Rockford

College, is sufficiently familiar that it does not need to be retold here. Once she and her classmate Ellen Starr hit upon the idea of establishing Hull-House among the immigrant tenements of Chicago, her life took on a meaning and acquired a drive that made her one of the leading reformers of the Progressive era, not only in the United States but in Europe as well.

Jane Addams's life, like her success, was not representative of the woman social worker. Addams never married and spent almost all of her active life at Hull-House. Yet, as Allen Davis's study of the lives of some 300 social workers has shown, about half of women social workers married, and most of them spent less than five years in a settlement house. And even if they did not marry, they stayed, on the average, only about ten years; no more than 22 persons out of the 300 in Davis's sample followed Jane Addams in making a lifetime career out of settlement work. Interestingly enough, though, sixteen of those twenty-two were women, and fourteen of the sixteen never married. Ten years earlier those fourteen women would not have had that alternative to marriage and family.

For our purposes here, the important point about the new profession of social work was not only that it appealed to women but also that it was quickly accepted as a proper occupation for women. As the work and writings of Jane Addams and Lillian Wald and those of other well-known settlement-house women testified, the primary concerns of these women were the situations and lives of poor women and children. They welcomed the opportunity to exercise their humanitarian, nurturing, and compassionate qualities, thereby offering to slum dwellers those qualities women generally were expected to provide for their families. The settlement house, in short, was the extension of women's traditional role into the tenement and the slum. It enlisted all the sympathy, understanding, warmth, and emotion which were ascribed to women by the principle of separate spheres. Although settlement-house work was literally outside the home, and a profession that not infrequently deflected women from marriage and motherhood, it nevertheless was easily accommodated to the idea of separate spheres. It did not contradict the popular view that women and men were different and properly engaged in different spheres of work. At the same time, however, settlement work clearly offered a career and useful service to the educated woman.

The origin and expansion of settlement work at the end of the 19th century was only in part a response to the increasing number of women being graduated from colleges and universities. Its primary roots were embedded in the city and the factory, those visible signs of industrialization. Other women's organizations were equally direct responses to the radical social transformation engendered by industrial expansion. In 1866 the Young Women's Christian Association was formed in Boston to help young women who came to the city to find work; by the mid-1870s over 35 cities reported such associations. During the 1880s some philanthropic women sponsored the organizing of Working Girl Clubs to provide medical care, libraries, classes in dress-making, and stenography for young women seeking work in the cities. Before the decade was out, Philadelphia, Chicago, St. Louis, and several cities in New England counted such clubs in their midst.

The most important women's organizations that clearly were responses of women to the stresses of industrialization were the National Consumers' League and the Women's Trade Union League. Both of them consisted of middle- and upper-class women, usually college-educated, and usually married, who wanted to work with, and assist working women. The Consumers' League was founded by Josephine Shaw Lowell, an energetic, socially motivated widow, member of a prominent Massachusetts family. The original purpose of the Consumers' League was to raise the level of wages and improve the conditions of work for young women in department stores. The scope of its work expanded greatly in short order to include a wide variety of women's occupations and working conditions. It was highly effective in achieving many of its goals and in bringing altruistic, educated women into fruitful cooperation with working women. In 1899 Florence Kelley, one of the great figures in the women's movement during the first twenty-five years of the 20th century, became the general secretary of the National Consumers' League. She raised the organization to the level of a public power in economic and political affairs. Well-known women friends of labor like Pauline and Josephine Goldmark and Frances Perkins, later the first woman Cabinet officer (in Franklin Roosevelt's four administrations), began their careers with the League.

Even more closely allied with working women was the Women's Trade Union League, founded in New York in 1903. The broad question of women in trade unions will be discussed in Chapter XVI as a part of women's employment outside the home, but the WTUL was not a trade union and so it is appropriately discussed here. It was, much like the Consumers' League, an organization of middle- and upper-class married women who were interested in using their talents in behalf of their sisters who worked for wages. The purpose of the WTUL was to help in the organizing of women workers on the assumption that it would improve their status and conditions of work. The League was closely affiliated with the labor movement and at no time did the League seek to organize women outside the established unions. It organized no unions of its own, even though at times it was not able to accept all the policies of the conservative American Federation of Labor. The League, for example, refused to endorse the exclusion of Asian immigrants, though the A.F. of L. did.

The League's most notable work was during the great organizing drives among working women in the garment industry in New York City in 1909–10. Its members walked in the picket lines, represented the workers in court, sent out publicity, raised funds, and acted as organizer for the striking workers. After the strikes were won the International Ladies' Garment Workers' Union presented the League with a silver cup in recognition of its substantial aid.

Eventually, working-class women like Rose Schneiderman and Leonora O'Reilly took over the leadership of the League from the middle-class matrons who had founded it and had run it for years. In that sense, the National Women's Trade Union League was one of the few women's organizations of the early 20th century that actually could point to working women among its leadership. The League was unusual, if not unique, too, in that it managed to bridge the gulf of class that generally divided women. Virtually all of the women's organizations in the 19th century, as in the 20th, whether for feminist or other causes, have been composed of middle-class women. Indeed, the feminist movement throughout American history has been overwhelmingly middle class and white. The very uniqueness of the WTUL in breaching the class barrier testifies to the difficulties inherent in any broad conception of sisterhood among women transcending class lines. For, like men, but unlike blacks and other minorities, women are distributed throughout the social and class structure. Class thus acts as a divisive force for them as it has not for blacks nor for immigrant groups. Historically, blacks and immigrants have been disproportionately concentrated in the lower economic levels of society, and though they may not have been united by class, at least they have not been seriously divided by it. The history of women's organization in the early 20th century, as well as the history of more recent women's groups, suggest that the ideal of a bond of sisterhood that transcends the divisions between working-class and middle-class women is a utopian conception, however appealing and even essential the idea may appear to many women.

Women's organizations at the close of the 19th and the opening of the 20th century were not restricted to those that grew up out of a reaction to urbanization or industrialization. Women also formed social organizations because they had been excluded from or ignored by men's groups. In 1876, for example, the Ancient Order of the Eastern Star was established by the wives of the all-male Masonic Order. In 1883, the Women Relief Corps was organized by the wives of members of the Civil War veterans' Grand Army of the Republic. The founding of the secret women's organization P.E.O. at Iowa Wesleyan College in 1869 was clearly an effort to bring to young women the kind of "mystery" organization that many men reveled in but from which women were excluded. The Daughters of the American Revolution was established in 1890 because the Sons of the American Revolution would not admit women. The Junior League, made up of urban debutantes interested in civic improvement or philanthropic endeavors, was founded in New York City in 1901; soon other cities created their own Junior Leagues.

The decade of the nineties was a period of organization-founding of all kinds, and women avidly participated in the activity. During that decade were founded the Colonial Dames, the United Daughters of the Confederacy, and the National Congress of Mothers, which later metamorphosed into the Parent-Teacher Association. Black women, too, formed organizations, usually because they were excluded from the organizations of their white sisters. The National Association of Colored Women was founded for that reason in 1896. By the opening of the 20th century, William O'Neill has observed, "half of the important American women's organizations had been established, most of them in the 1890s."[28]

During the first twenty years of the new century many professional women's organizations came into being, too, in response to the growing number of women in various kinds of employment. Among such organizations were the National Organization of Public Health Nurses (1912), the International Association of Policewomen (1915), the Medical Women's National Association (1915), the Federation of Teachers (1916), the National Association of Deans of Women (1916), and the National Federation of Business and Professional Women's Clubs (1919).

If access to higher education and the impact of urbanization and industrialization made possible or encouraged myriad women's organizations, the most pervasive and important single force or circumstance behind the formation of women's groups was the increased leisure of the middle-class wife and mother. That leisure, of course, was a function of the urbanization of society and the consequent reduction in the household chores of women. Not the least of the reductions was the steady and significant drop throughout the 19th century in the number of children in the white family. Alongside this general development must be placed the long history of assigning women to a special moral role in the family. It was this role that married middle-class women—with their increased leisure—sought to fill in society through what has been called the women's club movement.

Women's clubs began inconspicuously enough in the 1860s, and without any long-range purpose behind them. But by the 1890s they had become a force of significance in many communities, where the club women became active in all kinds of civic improvement and municipal reforms. Some women's clubs, to be sure, never rose above the level of a garden group or a loosely defined and loosely run book-reviewing meeting of middle-class women who had more time than serious thought at their disposal. Other clubs were simply educational meetings for the members, introducing them to subjects usually believed to be beyond the province and competence of women, such as international relations, economics, or municipal corruption. Many, however, were literally forces for change, sometimes single-handedly bringing kindergartens, playgrounds, public laundries, public baths, parks, and libraries to their communities. In a big city like New York the Women's Municipal League undertook in 1906 to investigate the immigration process in an effort to protect new arrivals from harassment and fraud. Women's clubs were also instrumental in getting the streets cleaned and in improving the quality of milk. As Mary Beard pointed out in 1915, middle- and upper-class married women had more leisure for observation and investigation of such matters as well as more opportunities for the "cultivation of social sympathies" than the men of the same classes.[29] Often it was the women's clubs which not only brought civic needs or problems to the attention of the municipal authorities but saw to it that the remedies were rigorously applied as well.

The rapid growth in the membership of the women's clubs offered striking testimony to the changes within the middle-class home by the turn of the century. By 1896, some 100,000 women were affiliated with clubs; by 1898 the 800 delegates to the National Convention of the clubs were said to represent 160,000 members. That year the national organization sent its first petition to Congress—a socially innocuous one in behalf of protecting wild birds. More significantly, that same year Jane Addams and Beatrice Webb, the British Fabian Socialist, addressed the biennial meeting on "The Industrial Problem as It Affects Women and Children." The meeting then adopted standards for women and children working in industry, and each affiliated club undertook to set up committees to check on local compliance with these standards. Thereafter the national organization of women's clubs became increasingly immersed in social and economic reform, particularly in regard to women and children. By 1910 the national membership reached 800,000, and Congress had awarded a national charter to the General Federation of Women's Clubs. When the war broke out in Europe, the Federation counted over a million members.

Yet it was not until 1914—very late in the game, so to speak—that the General Federation endorsed woman suffrage. Although by then women's clubs had become active in virtually all kinds of social and economic reforms, the suffrage was still seen as outside the proper role for women. When the clubs finally endorsed the suffrage the goal had almost been achieved. Not much courage was required for a women's group to come out for the suffrage in 1914.

The broad spectrum of activities in which the women's clubs engaged constituted a rough measure of where middle-class women stood just before the suffrage was won. On the one hand, the wide range of activities available to married, middle-class women offered a mode of expression for many and diverse talents. Yet, on the other hand, despite the undeniable breadth of the opportunities, virtually all of them fell within the traditional pattern of women's activities. The club women were primarily involved with issues concerning the welfare of children, education, diet, purity of foods, housing, and sanitation. These causes, like the family and the home, depended upon women's allegedly nurturant, compassionate, enduring, and supportive qualities. They still reflected the separate spheres.

William O'Neill, in his book *Everyone Was Brave: The Decline and Fall of Feminism in America,* has given the name "social feminist" to those women whose primary concern was service to others and to society, as contrasted with the feminists whose primary object was the achievement of individual opportunities for women, regardless of the end to which the opportunities might be put. Feminists, he wrote, rejected "the social feminist compromise that enlarged women's sphere of action while channelling their energies" in socially acceptable directions. He defined the dichotomy neatly: "Social feminists wanted the vote on the perfectly reasonable ground that it would advance their reforms. Ardent suffragists wanted it for its own sake." [30]

In social feminism and its growth, O'Neill has located the primary reason for the failure of the women's movement in the United States. "The chief feature of social feminism was that it created roles for women that militated against their full emancipation," he writes. "Their benevolent enterprises met women's desire for useful and satisfying work without touching the sources of their inequality."[31] Since, in O'Neill's view only a thoroughgoing social change could bring about the full emancipation of women, he faults the early 20th-century feminists for failing to recognize what was required if they were to achieve their goals. That is why, he argued in his book, the Socialist party, just because it did support fundamental change, was a more likely political home for the feminists than the traditional parties. To this question of how, if at all, full equality for women can be achieved, we shall return in the last chapter. Suffice to say here that O'Neill is quite right when he concluded that, despite the broad range of activities open to women by the first two decades of this century, true equality of opportunity was neither achieved by them then nor since.

The simple fact is that, though the Social Purity advocates, the social feminists, and the suffragists at one time or another all recognized, however dimly, that the family was a central problem in the advancement of women's equality, none was able to confront that fact directly. It was simply too radical. Instead, organized women hitched the cause of emancipation to a remedy that was certainly necessary for women, but which was quite incapable of dealing with the heart of the problem, that is, women's subordination in the family. Thus to answer the question of why "feminism failed," or more accurately, why a new feminist movement was necessary in the 1970s, we must now look at the reform which consumed most of the energy and time, and drew so heavily upon the skills of organized women during the first twenty years of this century—the struggle for the vote.

XIV

The Suffrage Fight:
The Last Step
Was Really the First

The story of the achievement of woman suffrage is shot through with paradoxes. Not the least of those paradoxes is that, though the suffrage cause in the 19th century became increasingly central to the feminist cause, suffrage, once achieved, had almost no observable effect upon the position of women. To listen to the advocates of woman suffrage in the decade or so before the ratification of the Nineteenth Amendment in 1920, one would have thought that the millennium would result once women were permitted to vote. All sorts of reforms and social improvements were to be instituted, and all kinds of evils such as war, imperialism, crime, and vice were to be reduced or eliminated. Of course, none of these things happened. In fact, as we shall see in more detail later, women did not even make as much use of the ballot as expected, much less bring about any significant social or economic changes. As political historians have pointed out more than once, women armed with the vote divided in their political preferences about as their husbands or fathers did. As the anti-suffragists had predicted, women with the vote doubled the electorate without altering its results. Why?

William O'Neill, in *Everyone Was Brave* (1969), sought to provide an answer to the question of why feminism's promise was not realized, or at least not as predicted. His answer was that the 19th-century feminists had concentrated upon suffrage as the means of achieving women's equality with men, but that the vote alone was inadequate to the job that had to be done. To O'Neill, the equality of women was ultimately dependent upon the place women occupied in the family, upon the nature of the relation they had with their husbands. The right to vote simply did not—and could not—affect women's role within the family, one way or the other. O'Neill contended that the family was the arena in which the battle had to be fought and won. At one time in the 19th century some women leaders like Elizabeth Cady Stanton, Victoria Woodhull, and her sister Tennessee Claflin had identified the family as the central issue in the achievement of women's emancipation. Only when women were equal within the family could they expect to be equal outside. This approach to the question of equality was too strong for most feminists, according to O'Neill, especially after Victoria Woodhull in 1872 exposed Henry Ward Beecher's affair with a woman parishioner, who was also the wife of a close friend. In exposing Beecher, Woodhull made clear that she approved of such behavior so long as the two people concerned loved one another; marriage, she insisted, ought not to be binding without love. A marriage based merely upon legal ties was no marriage at all, she asserted. This was carrying marriage reform to lengths too extreme for the great majority of women and for most feminists as well. A few staunch allies, like Elizabeth Cady Stanton, to be sure, stood by Woodhull's right to her opinion, but most of the leading feminists repudiated her. The lesson they learned from the incident, O'Neill says, was that tampering with the traditional family was too risky; it was safer, even if less central, to concentrate upon suffrage as the means for achieving women's equality. O'Neill therefore castigates the late-19th-century feminists for having abandoned the one avenue to success open to the achievement of the feminist goal of equality. The result may have been the achievement of the franchise, but at the same time that success decreed the failure of feminism. That is why, O'Neill insists, a revival of feminism in the 1960s was inevitable; the winning of woman suffrage fifty years before had simply not accomplished the emancipation of women.

With O'Neill's conclusion there is no reason to quarrel. It is quite true that the full achievement of equality for women depended then and still does today upon the transformation of woman's place within the family. What is at issue, though, is whether the feminists of the 19th century really had any choice about the road they followed. To be sure, they need not have put all their eggs in the basket of suffrage, asserting as many did that once women had the vote all sorts of magical things would occur to equalize the opportunities of the sexes. They could have been more circumspect and realistic both in their language and their claims, but inflated rhetoric is only a venial, not a mortal, sin. Given the difficulty and the length of the struggle to win the vote, it is understandable why women made the extravagant claims for the ballot they did.

And one can even understand in historical context the racist and class-conscious arguments that were trotted out on behalf of the suffrage from time to time. As early as 1868, Elizabeth Cady Stanton wrote in the suffragist magazine *The Revolution:* "Think of Patrick and Sambo and Hans and Ung Tung who do not know the difference between a Monarchy and a Republic, who never read the Declaration of Independence or Webster's spelling book, making laws for Lydia Maria Child, Lucretia Mott or Fanny Kemble." The argument was advanced even more pointedly by Olympia Brown at the suffrage convention of 1889. "The last census shows, I think, that there are in the United States three times as many American-born women as the whole foreign population, men and women together, so that the votes of women will eventually be the only means of overcoming this foreign influence and maintaining our free institutions. There is no possible safety for our free schools, our free churches, or our republican government, unless women are given the suffrage and that right speedily." And in 1893 the reunited woman suffrage organization pointed out in a resolution that "in every state there were . . . more white women who can read and write than all negro voters; more American women who can read and write than all foreign voters; so that the enfranchisement of such women would settle the vexed question of rule by illiteracy, whether of home-grown or foreign-born production." [1]

O'Neill is right to find the suffragists morally and politically wanting in resorting to such arguments in the name of their own enfranchisement. But his further contention that they ought to have stuck with the reform of marriage and family is difficult to accept as a historically valid criticism of 19th-century feminists. Given the obstacles to the acceptance of woman suffrage even *without* directly attacking the contemporary family, it is hard to see how the suffragists would ever have gained the vote if they had insisted upon carrying the additional burden of open hostility to the traditional family. The historical fact seems to be that feminists of the 19th century had no real alternative; they had to achieve the suffrage before they could hope to renovate intra-familial relations in the direction of equality between husband and wife. They may have been mistaken to have ignored or to have played down the centrality of the family to the achievement of feminist goals, but that was a practical necessity given the general and strong hostility to woman suffrage. (It is true, as O'Neill implies, that many feminists did not even recognize the connection between the family and their achievement of emancipation. But there is also some reason to believe, as we shall see a little later, that even someone like Elizabeth Cady Stanton, who did demand reform of the family, did not appreciate how difficult it would be to put such reform into practice.)

This brings us to the heart of the matter about the suffrage. Why did it take so long for women to win the franchise? The fight extended over seventy years, from 1848 when woman suffrage was first called for by an organized body of women and men at Seneca Falls down to 1920 when it was agreed to for the nation by constitutional amendment. Such a long struggle is without analogue in the entire history of suffrage in the United States, which on the whole was extended to group after group without much dissent and with hardly a hitch in the steady expansion of the size of the electorate. Not until the late 1890s was that remarkable expansion interrupted by the disfranchisement conventions of the southern states, which sought to remove blacks and some poor whites from the electorate. Prior to that decade the number of voters had been steadily expanding, first by the removal of property and other qualifications and then by the extension of the suffrage to former male slaves in the South and free male blacks throughout the country. This second expansion was accomplished even though the blacks were socially segregated and discriminated against in both parts of the country. Almost a dozen states extended the suffrage to aliens during the 19th century; yet not a single state granted it to women until the 1890s. During the 19th century the United States led the world in pushing for universal *manhood* suffrage, regardless of race, nativity, property, or even citizenship in some states. The resistance to granting woman suffrage is even more striking, as historian Eleanor Flexner has pointed out, when contrasted with the opposition to women's opportunities in other respects. "By comparison, opposition to women in education or professional work was guerilla-like in nature," Flexner observes in her history of women's rights, "sporadic, largely concealed, and evinced in obstacles and restrictions which toughminded women would overcome" The opposition to woman suffrage, on the other hand, Flexner continues, "instead of weakening . . . actually stiffened, becoming more active and more articulate." [2] Why, then, the refusal for so long and so adamantly to extend the vote to women? In the territories of Wyoming and Utah, and in some countries, in fact, the vote came to women with little or no agitation at all. New Zealand, New South Wales in Australia, and Finland, for example, extended the vote to women even before they asked for it. So the reluctance to do so in the United States was not simply a matter of male opposition on grounds of gender alone.

And even in the United States, the improvement in the position of women over the course of the 19th century suggested that there ought not to have been any serious objection from men to woman suffrage. Throughout much of the 19th century, beginning in the 1840s, there was a steady improvement in the legal status of women. The first state to give married women control over their own property, contrary to the common law inherited from England, was Mississippi in 1839. Soon many other states followed. Between 1869 and 1887 some thirty-three states and the District of Columbia granted married women control over their own wages and earnings, while thirty of the states specifically provided for a separate estate for women. During those same years Louisiana, Texas, New Mexico, Arizona, and California adopted the law of community property, wherein the property of a family was deemed to be held in equal shares by husband and wife. Later, community property was adopted in Washington and Idaho as well. A married woman's property law was not adopted in England until 1882, long after most states in the United States had done so. Furthermore, in some states, like New York in 1860, women were declared to be the joint guardians with the father of their children, with equal rights and duties. Susan B. Anthony and Ida H. Harper in their *History of Woman Suffrage* summed up what they called the "decided progress" in married women's legal rights by 1900 as follows: "the wife now may own and control her separate property in three-fourths of the states, and in the other fourth only one Northern State is included. In every State a married woman may make a will, but can dispose only of her separate property. In about two-thirds of the states she possesses her earnings. In the great majority she may make contracts and bring suit. The property rights of unmarried women always have been nearly the same as those of unmarried men." The husband's right to life-use of his wife's real estate (curtesy), the report continued, "has now been abolished in over one-half of the States . . . and the wife's separate estate has been made so liberal that in comparatively few States is she left in the helpless condition of olden times." As a result, they concluded, the many changes in the state laws regarding married women "represented a complete legal revolution during the past half century."[3]

In sum, by 1900, when the suffrage was still far in the future and accepted by only four states, married women's rights were greatly improving in almost every state. Surely one of the reasons the property rights of married women received these legal protections is that male legislators were responding to the interests they had as fathers and brothers in the property of their female relatives. For, unlike any other disadvantaged group in society, women have always enjoyed the support and protection of their "oppressors," simply because those "oppressors" have an emotional and sometimes an economic interest in protecting them. The money or property that married women possessed at the time of marriage or during a marriage may well have come from a male relative, or would come from them at some time in the future. "The ease with which such legislation went through," according to historian David Morgan, "was eloquent testimony of the male support it recruited. This is not to say that it was a very clear and simple case of male self-interest, but rather that there existed a co-incidence of interest" of women and men.[4]

It is true, too, that the improvement in the legal status of married women during the 19th century fell far short of equality, however remarkable the improvement may have been. As late as 1930, for example, women still did not enjoy equality of rights in regard to sale of real estate in seventeen states, and, even in the community property states, a husband legally managed the joint property and legally determined the place of residence of the couple. In 1940 a quarter of the states did not permit a wife to make a contract and almost half of them exempted women from jury duty. The Women's party during the 1930s compiled a list of over 1000 state laws that discriminated against women. The point here, however, is not that married women's rights at the opening of the 20th century were everywhere and in all respects on a par with married men's. Of course they were not. Rather, the point is that throughout the 19th century there had been a steady and, as even feminists at the time attested, striking improvements in the legal status of married women. Yet the very same legislators—all male—who enacted these improvements refused to accord the vote to women.

A similar paradox appears when one reflects on the long and expanding history of women's organizations, which have been examined in the preceding chapter. By the opening of the 20th century, women had been admitted to all levels of education, undergraduate and graduate, professional and technical, and they were organizing themselves into all kinds of groups and participating in a wide variety of activities. There still were some occupations closed to women, and hostility to their employment in certain jobs continued, but the picture differed markedly from that of the suffrage fight. The suffrage drive had almost no trophies to display, while social feminism's efforts in bringing women's influence to bear upon the world of the city, government, labor, and social betterment had many. Why this disparity of achievement? Part of it, of course, stems from the interest that men, who permitted or encouraged these changes to take place, often had in protecting and advancing the opportunities open to their daughters or sisters. More important still, however, all of these changes, from the opening of educational opportunities to the acceptance of women in social work were quite in accord with the traditional role of women in organized groups. They were activities fully consonant with woman's role in the family as mother; nothing that the social feminists advocated or did seriously threatened the traditional division between the activities of men and women. As William O'Neill has put it, the social feminists, for all their activities outside the home, actually undermined the drive for true equality for women by fulfilling roles that were largely extensions of women's activities within the home. "Their benevolent enterprise," he charged, "met women's desires for useful and satisfying work without touching the sources of their inequality."[5]

Today, when historians and others look back upon the rhetoric of the suffrage movement they are struck by the contrast between the high expectations for the improvement in women's state that the vote was said to promise and the little that changed once the Nineteenth Amendment went into effect. "The addition of women to the electorate," historian Aileen Kraditor has drily remarked, "has not significantly altered American patterns as the suffragists predicted it would."[6] Clearly, woman suffrage did not liberate women. And because so little changed after 1920, historians have tended to deride the suffrage as not a radical measure at all. The opposition to woman suffrage, so the argument goes, was as grossly misplaced as was the expectation of substantial change. Political scientist Alan Grimes, in fact, published a book in 1967 in which he argued that the vote was gained for socially conservative reasons by conservative middle-class women and men. He contended that woman suffrage came in Wyoming Territory in 1869 and then in Utah Territory in 1870 largely to preserve the status quo, not to advance a liberal reform. In both places, he argued, men used woman suffrage as a way of keeping the social or political situation stable and favorable. This was especially true, he continued, in Utah, where Mormon men wanted to be sure to have the votes necessary to overwhelm potential Gentile opposition. Similarly, he said, many advocates of woman suffrage in the early 20th century pushed for the vote for women in order to counterbalance the influence of male immigrants, who were the mainstay of urban political machines, and of male blacks in the South. Woman suffrage, in short, was advocated by women and accepted by men as a conservative device for preserving the white, Protestant, Anglo-Saxon politics of the early 20th century.

Such admittedly conservative arguments may help to explain why support for woman suffrage was stronger in the 20th century, as immigration shot up and southern states moved to disfranchise blacks, but it is difficult to believe that it was adopted *because* it was socially conservative. For, if that had been the case, then why was it delayed for so long? It is the delay that requires explanation, not the final acceptance. For certainly those who benefited from the status quo were the ones who were in a position to grant the suffrage, but did not. That supporters of woman suffrage expressed socially conservative and even racist arguments is admittedly a measure of the depth of their frustration and desperation, but such arguments do little to account for the long delay. In fact, as we shall see later, they are more helpful in accounting for the final acceptance of votes for women.

That such arguments were advanced does call attention to the truth that from the outset and down to the present the women's movement as a whole and the suffrage cause in particular have been white middle-class affairs. One suffragist who worked closely and sympathetically with working-class and immigrant women once called attention to what must have been obvious to many women outside the middle class. "I have rarely heard a ringing suffrage speech," Florence Kelley told a suffrage convention in 1906, "which did not refer to the 'ignorant and degraded' men, or the 'ignorant immigrants' as our masters. This is habitually spoken with more or less bitterness," she went on. "But this is what the workingmen are used to hearing applied to themselves by their enemies in times of strike." [7] Not surprisingly, there were few working-class women and even fewer blacks or immigrants interested in woman suffrage or other feminist issues, just as today there are few black or working-class women pressing for the ratification of the Equal Rights Amendment. It is not so much that the middle-class character of the proponents offends or repels them as that the causes supported by feminists do not seem immediately germane to the everyday lives of working-class women. Yet other reforms advocated by middle-class men and women were achieved without the support of immigrants and the working class; why not woman suffrage?

Certainly the delay in the acceptance of the suffrage is striking. As late as 1910 only four states granted full suffrage to women, and all of them were small and western: Wyoming, Utah, Idaho, and Colorado. Yet woman suffrage leaders had been crisscrossing the country in almost endless speaking tours for over a generation. Seventeen states, it is true, granted suffrage to women in the election of school boards, while four states extended the vote to women when a special financial measure, like a bond issue, was to be voted upon by taxpayers. But these achievements were hardly signs of success. At the same time, the delay in the achievement of the full suffrage for women concealed another paradox. For though women generally could not vote, they nevertheless had long exercised substantial and growing influence in politics.

In a sense, as Linda Kerber has suggested, the founding of the United States by a Revolution and as a free Republic propelled women into politics, but from inside the family only. For the Revolution did not bring women publicly into political affairs. In permitting women taxpayers to vote under its first constitution until 1807, when the right was withdrawn, New Jersey was an anomaly. No other state followed its example. But increasingly during the early Republic, mothers were exhorted to take up the responsibility of rearing sons to be patriots and daughters to marry good Republican citizens. One commencement speaker told the young women in his audience in 1795, "while you thus keep our country virtuous, you maintain its independence." The aim of integrating domesticity and politics, Kerber tells us, was something new in the world of European culture. Theretofore ordinary women had not been seen as having any political function even within the family. In the United States the wife and mother was now to become a political being as part of her familial obligations. She was shaping those who would participate, even if she herself did not participate.[8]

That opening wedge into politics was only the beginning. For as early as the 1830s young working women at the Lowell mills were actually participating in politics by attending rallies, discussing issues and candidates, and displaying in their dress the symbols of the campaigners. Candidates, in turn, did not ignore women, even though at that time no woman could vote. As the *National Anti-Slavery Standard* summed up one campaign in 1841, the election had worked a revolution "in behalf of women. We have seen her invited to take a part in the getting up of political machinery, to influence elections. We have listened to her eulogies and poems in behalf of the people's candidates." A recent historian of the Dorr War in Rhode Island in 1842 also documented the activity of women in that cause.

"Women staged political rallies, organized clambakes, drafted petitions and otherwise publicized the Dorrite cause," he tells us. "They did this in defiance of martial law," apparently on the assumption that the Draconian laws against any kind of agitation would not be applied to them as severely as to men.[9]

During the agitation for the ten-hour day in New England in the mid-1840s women were publicly active. Their principal organization, the Female Labor Reform Association, sent representatives to appear before legislative committees, cooperated with male organizations, and mounted petition campaigns. On one petition almost 90 per cent of the signatures were of women, though none of them was a voter. At a meeting in Manchester, New Hampshire, in 1845, two-thirds of the more than a thousand workers present were women.

Individual women, too, often became heavily involved in politics, despite their lack of the vote. Bell Waller of Kentucky was apparently such a woman, for her husband, Henry, sometimes filled his letters with political news and election results. "I know you are so good a Whig," he wrote in August 1840, "that the following election news will be very gratifying."[10] Wives of political figures, of course, were also often interested in and influential with their husbands in regard to politics.

At no time during the 19th century was women's weight in public political activity more noticeable than during the upheaval among southern and western farmers in the 1880s and 1890s. Even in the 1870s the National Grange, another farmer's organization, had permitted women to work within the organization along with men, though it put restrictions on the offices and jobs open to women in the organization. The Farmers' Alliance provided more opportunities for women to work beside men than any contemporary organization. The WCTU and the women's clubs were limited to women, and, though that kind of experience was valuable, it was less realistic socially than the bi-gender experience to be gained in Alliance work.

The participation of women in the Alliance was extensive. At first some women had difficulty in working with men in political activities, as the self-conscious, overly diffident comments from some of them show. "I am but a female," one woman apologetically began a letter to an Alliance newspaper in the 1880s. "Being a farmer's wife," wrote another, "I am not in the habit of writing for the public prints." Still a third thought that "your many subscribers will not expect much from a female correspondent." But these women did write and they did participate. By the

1890s the women correspondents were usually omitting the apologetic openings. "We can work just as well as the brethren," one woman wrote proudly to the newspaper. In some local groups in the North Carolina Alliance, women made up one-third to one-half of the total membership. A recent historian of the Southern Alliance has estimated that as many as a quarter of the regional members were women. Few women, however, held offices in the Alliance. Texas was the only southern state in which women held state office; there two women were state officials. The only woman to hold office on the national level of the Alliance was Mrs. R. A. Southworth of Colorado, but that was not until 1894, when the order was no longer significant. No woman headed any of the local Alliance groups in North Carolina, but women did hold lesser offices as well as acting as lecturers, discussion leaders, or keynote speakers. They also worked within the Alliance in behalf of expanding the kinds of education available to women. They advocated training in typing, bookkeeping, telegraphy, and shorthand, generally scorning what they thought of as "finishing school" subjects. They sought, in sum, to make farm women more self-sufficient through the acquisition of skills other than those associated with housework; but the women were not expected to leave the home.[11] The Alliance men did not want their women to be other than farm wives or farm managers, just as they themselves did not want to leave farming. After all, to help the family farm survive was the primary purpose of the Farmers' Alliance.

On the national scene, when the Alliance became the Populist party in 1890, women were again prominent, especially as public speakers. Mary Elizabeth Lease, who has passed into history as the Populist orator who told farmers "to raise less corn and more hell," was only one of scores of women who toured the hustings and the crossroads of the West and the South spreading the Populist gospel. Among them were Annie L. Diggs of Kansas, Eva McDonald of Minnesota, Marion Todd of Chicago, and Sarah Emery of Michigan. Virtually all of these women were accomplished writers and sometimes trained professionals as well. Annie L. Diggs was a major political leader in the Kansas People's party. Even for the ordinary farm woman, as the experience of the Alliance showed, the Populist movement was a catalyst to political activity by women. "No other movement in history—not even the antislavery cause," wrote the novelist Hamlin Garland about the Populist party, "appealed to the women like this movement here in Kansas."[12]

Close behind the farmers' movement as a stimulant to, or occasion for, women's political activity was the temperance cause. Even during the 1870s and 1880s, when women did not enjoy the ballot in a single state (Utah and Wyoming were then territories), they were nonetheless recognized as effective in pressing men to vote for temperance or Prohibition. In Iowa, in 1882, for example, every county contained an organized group of women to get men to vote against liquor. Herbert Hoover in his memoirs recalls being brought to the polls in Iowa by his Quaker mother to "make the men vote themselves dry." And during the last days before Prohibition was added to the Constitution, a New York newspaper provided a graphic example of how women worked their influence at the polls even without the vote. The occasion was an election in North Carolina on Prohibition. Hundreds of women and children stationed themselves outside the polls, along with some male ministers. "When a voter came within range he was immediately surrounded by ministers and the women and children," the reporter noted. "The clergymen employed words of advice and confined their activities to the proprieties. But the women and children were less tactful. The clutched at the coats of the voter. They importuned him to vote the dry ticket. A phrase constantly employed was: 'Mister, for God's sake don't vote for whiskey,' " the reporter wrote. "A few of the wets ran the gauntlet of the women and children to whom they were personally known, but the greater majority of the voters viewed the conflict from afar and returned to their offices and homes. The drys won the day."[13]

When one has canvassed the participation of women in politics of the 19th century, not to mention their wide-ranging activities in reform work, the long delay in the acceptance of a woman suffrage in the United States is more difficult than ever to understand or explain. The traditional explanations have something to add, but they are ultimately not persuasive. The suffrage leaders were fond of pointing to the liquor interests as their pre-eminent opponents. As Carrie Catt wrote, as early as 1881 the brewers had decided that Prohibition was "far less dangerous . . . than woman suffrage because prohibition could be repealed at any time but woman suffrage would insure the permanency of Prohibition." And it is true that those who opposed Prohibition thought that granting the vote to women would surely bring Prohibition in its wake. The prominence of women's groups like the WCTU and the early endorsement of women's suffrage by the Prohibition party all gave credence to their fears. And so, as one leader of the liquor and brewing industry from South Dakota succinctly put it, "we have defeated county option by the vote of the people, at three different times. We have defeated woman suffrage at three different times."[14]

The brewers and distilleries undoubtedly supplied funds for the anti-suffragists but they were simply not sufficiently wealthy or influential to be a major obstacle to the achievement of woman suffrage, especially since the liquor interests were spending most of their energy and money trying to stop Prohibition. More potent as opponents of woman suffrage were broader social groups, which also feared that a vote for women would indeed bring restrictions upon the consumption of alcohol. German immigrant groups were particularly opposed for that reason. In Kansas even German liberals denounced the ballot for women because they thought it would strengthen "the fanatical regime of preachers and priests," as one newspaper wrote. The president of the Michigan German-American Alliance put it more sharply at the time of a referendum on woman suffrage. "If the suffrage would be laid into the hands of the native-born American women . . . the results which surely will follow can easily be predicted," he warned. "Narrowmindedness will triumph everywhere, fanaticism will flourish, prohibitionists easily set for dictators in the State." But, again, the Germans, or even immigrants in general, were not sufficiently numerous or influential politically to make up more than a fraction of the opposition.[15]

The fact of the matter is that the most powerful and concentrated opposition came from those who *favored* Prohibition, the Southern states. Ironically enough, the states which were most interested in denying themselves access to liquor were also the states most immovable on the subject of the vote for women. In the end only ten states refused to ratify the Nineteenth Amendment: nine of them were in the South and the tenth was Delaware, which was almost southern. Yet everyone of these states ratified the Eighteenth Amendment, which brought Prohibition. This anomaly has been explained in David Morgan's recent book on the Democratic party and woman suffrage. For, as late as 1916, the Democratic party, which was dominated by the South, refused to endorse woman suffrage by constitutional amendment, though by then both the Republican party and the Progressive party had done so. Even the head of the party and incumbent President, Woodrow Wilson, himself southern-born, had endorsed woman suffrage by 1916. The source of the South's adamantine resistance, Morgan showed, was the fear that woman suffrage would reopen the race question in the South. By doubling the black vote many white Southern leaders apparently thought that the disfranchisement of blacks, which had only recently been accomplished, would be called into question. Many feared that the kind of coercion and violence that had been routinely used against black males who tried to vote or otherwise upset the political status quo would not be as easily or as effectively invoked against black women. Further than that, southern politicians from textile-producing states feared that if women received the vote white middle-class women might seek to reduce or eliminate the child labor that many southern textile and other industrial enterprises depended upon.

The problem that Morgan addresses—namely, why the South resisted to the very end—is quite satisfactorily answered by his analysis. But that particular issue does not really speak to the larger social question of causation that we have been pursuing here: Why was woman suffrage not achieved in any more than four states prior to 1910? The fight for the constitutional amendment was a dramatic struggle, simply because the South, which dominated the Democratic party, refused to recognize the handwriting on the political wall. For by 1915 the long struggle was essentially over; it was only a matter of time before the day would be won. Morgan's close examination of southern attitudes after 1910, however careful and thorough it admittedly is, does not help us to understand why the vote for women was so much longer delayed than the vote for propertyless men or for black men.

The answer has to be sought in what most historians have been rather reluctant to concede. Suffrage for women was more radical than is generally supposed. As noted already, the radical character of woman suffrage is difficult to recognize simply because nothing much changed socially or politically as a result of women's winning the franchise, whatever the suffragists may have predicted. But to many people at the time, opponents as well as supporters, significant changes were anticipated if women gained the vote. It is true that radicals like Mother Jones and Charlotte Perkins Gilman recognized that putting the ballot into the hands of women would not do more than give middle-class women a chance to influence social and economic policies concerning women and that it would do little or nothing to help working-class or poor women. And in that sense woman suffrage was clearly not a radical measure that would change society or the economic order in any significant way. And those doubters of the radical character of the ballot were right. Votes for women could not and did not change the social structure. Yet, that gauge is not the only meaning of "radical" insofar as resistance to the suffrage is concerned. To many men and women the suffrage *appeared* radical because, unlike all other activities in which women engaged outside the home, as Ellen Du Bois has pointed out, it could not be accommodated to the idea of the separate spheres. In fact, the aim of woman suffrage, it might be said, was to break down the barriers or separation between the two spheres. That is why even an advanced social thinker on the question of women like Frances Willard, at least in the beginning of her work with the WCTU, was careful to stay away from outspoken suffragists like Susan B. Anthony and Elizabeth Cady Stanton. In 1874, although Willard actually favored woman suffrage, she joined with other prominent public women to form the Association for the Advancement of Women, which pointedly ignored the suffrage and equally pointedly excluded from membership Stanton and Anthony and other outspoken suffragists of the time.

Men certainly did not want to see the idea of separate spheres abandoned, but it was women's fears of what the franchise might lead to that needs to be recognized as the real measure of the radical character of woman suffrage. A dramatic sign that women feared the implications of the vote is that even those women who might have been expected to push for the suffrage did not. Thus the many women who were active in the Dorr War agitation in Rhode Island, even though that struggle was directly occupied with the expansion of male suffrage, never asked for suffrage for themselves. They were eager to fight in the cause, but apparently they did not see suffrage as pertinent to them. The same point can be made about the women in the Farmers' Alliance and the Populist party, which were contemporaneous with the national woman suffrage movement. One historian of women's activities in the movement has commented that, despite all kinds of activities engaged in by women in the other two groups, no movement for suffrage for women emerged from their involvement. And, despite the efforts of Frances Willard, the Populist party failed to endorse woman suffrage in 1892. In short, even politically active women frequently did not see the vote as acceptable to them. Why not?

There seem to be two interrelated reasons. One was that married women accepted as adequate for their current purposes the doctrine of the separate spheres. It gave them a degree of autonomy at home, a substantial influence with their husbands, and sufficient role flexibility to permit them to engage in many different kinds of activities outside the home, including working with political parties and in social causes. In fact, as one male leader of the Southern Alliance made plain, under the concept of the separate spheres women were actually indispensable to any successful reform effort. "If our organization means anything," he wrote in 1888, "it means a moral reformation. . . . The ladies are and always have been the great moral element in society; therefore *it is impossible to succeed without calling to our aid the greatest moral element in the country.*"[16] No conservative advocate of the nature of the separate spheres would have defined the doctrine any differently.

The second, and more important, reason why most women did not support woman suffrage was that it threatened the family as people of the 19th century understood that institution. The suffrage was the essence of feminism in that it asserted the individuality of women and assumed and asserted a woman's self-interest. Throughout the 19th century feminists recognized that at the heart of women's rights lay the recognition of her selfhood, her existence as a separate person, different from that of a man and different from that of other women. One of the earliest feminist writers put it clearly. "Would that women would learn to recognize their own individuality—their singleness of thought," Elizabeth Oakes Smith wrote in *Woman and Her Needs* in 1851. "Our right to individuality is what I would most assert. Men seem resolved to have but one in our sex," she complained, when in fact, women vary as much as men. When women acknowledged themselves as individuals, she continued, then they would not be dependent upon marriage or their relation to men, then a woman "should be truly, nobly woman. . . . Whether we wear this or that costume, or go to the polls or stay away, seems of less importance than a radical understanding of our true selves."

Another early feminist writer, Caroline Dall, advanced a similar argument in 1867. "We have not laid a secure foundation for any statement on this subject unless we have made it clear that 'woman's rights' are identical with 'human rights'; that no father, brother, or husband can have all the privileges ordained for him of God, till mother and sister and wife are set free to secure them according to instinctive individual bias." [17] That is, until women were acknowledged, and acknowledged themselves to be individuals.

Elizabeth Cady Stanton pressed the same point. In 1892 she told her audience that the principal argument she wished to make concerned "the individuality of each human soul." In discussing the rights of women she continued, there were four things to be considered. The first is "what belongs to her as an individual, in a world of her own, the arbiter of her own destiny. . . . Her rights under such circumstances are to use all her faculties for her own safety and happiness." The second was that she must have the same rights as all other citizens, and the third was that as a woman she was an "equal factor in civilization," and her rights and duties were the same as those of anyone else—that is, to achieve "individual happiness and development." The fourth "is only the incidental relations of life, such as mother, wife, sister, daughter"—that is, those that pertained to the family. As Stanton well recognized, what she placed as last and "incidental," society put first: women's obligations as family members. This conflict between the individual woman and the family, Dr. Mary Putnam Jacobi, a well-known physician, confronted directly and clearly. Contrary to what opponents of the suffrage asserted, she wrote in 1894, the American state was based on "individual cells," not households. "Confessedly, in embracing in this conception women, we do introduce a change which, though in itself purely ideal, underlies all the practical issues now in this dispute," she admitted. "In this essentially modern conception, women also are brought into direct relations with the State, independent of their 'mate' or 'brood'."[18]

What Jacobi was saying had been put quite directly by Caroline Dall in 1867 in *The College, the Market, and the Court*. "Our reform is unlike all others; for it must begin in the family, at the very heart of the society." For after all, she continued, it was the relationship between men and women that was at the heart of feminist aspirations for equality. Elizabeth Cady Stanton, too, made no attempt to conceal the conflict between feminism and the traditional family. John Stuart Mill, she told an audience in New York City in 1870, contended that most males cannot "tolerate the idea of living with an *equal* at the fireside, and here is the secret of the opposition to women's equality in the state and the Church; men are not ready to recognize it in the home. . . . Conservatism cries out we are going to destroy the family. Timid reformers answer that political equality will not change it. They are both wrong. It will entirely revolutionize it. . . . When woman is man's equal," Stanton accurately concluded, "the marriage relation cannot stand on the basis it is on today. . . . Let us remember that womanhood is the great fact, wifehood and motherhood its incidents."[19]

Stanton charged men with being unable to countenance the effects which the equality of women would have on the family. But there were not many women who were prepared to disrupt or seriously alter the traditional family and woman's role in it. Even someone as radical in her feminism as Caroline Dall could not abandon completely women's traditional role; she simply wanted women to take on men's opportunities *in addition* to women's obligations. "There is no excuse for neglecting any home duty for the most desirable foreign pursuit," she counseled her women readers. "Let button and shirt-bosoms have their day, the lexicon or grammar its own also. Let the dinner-table be carefully spread; the food, not only well cooked, but gracefully laid—before we seek the more precious nutriment of culture; and this, not so much because anyone has a right to say it *shall* be so, as out of our own tender regard to the needs of others, and a desire, though every possible self-sacrifice, to make the common road easier, and turn recreant public opinion to its proper vent." [20]

Nor was Elizabeth Cady Stanton, for all her brave words about making womanhood the center of woman's life and wifehood and motherhood merely incidents, very clear about how that division of labor was to be worked out. She personally managed to be an active worker in the world while bearing and rearing seven children, but she was much more than an average woman in energy, intelligence, and commitment. Even an advanced feminist couple like Angelina Grimké and Theodore Weld fell into the old domestic patterns. "We keep no help and are therefore filling up 'the appropriate Sphere of woman' to admiration," Angelina wrote with some irony to a female friend in 1838, "in the kitchen with baking pans and pots and steamers, etc., and in the parlor and chamber with the broom and duster. Indeed, I think our enemies would rejoice could they look in on us day to day, and see us in our domestic life, instead of lecturing to promiscuous audiences." (The "we" referred to herself and her sister Sarah, not to Theodore.) And some outspoken feminists, even in the 20th century made clear that family came before career. Florence Kelley, her biographer Josephine Goldmark tells us, never put her feminism ahead of her concern for the family. "She was, in the intensity of that belief," Goldmark concedes, "what might today be called old-fashioned. She was against wage earning for mothers of young children." [21]

The fact is that none of the 19th-century feminists ever argued that women should cease to be the primary rearers, as well as the bearers of children. Yet if women continued to fill that role, they shut themselves out of all sorts of professions and occupations, not to mention careers. It was not until Charlotte Perkins Gilman raised the issue directly with her book *Women and Economics* in 1898 that the practical problems got any attention at all. Gilman was one of the few prominent feminists, even in the early 20th century, who insisted upon writing and lecturing about cooperative kitchens, professional house maintenance, and professional baby care as ways of permitting women to have careers equivalent to men's without giving up the joys and satisfactions of marriage and family. Most feminists simply failed to confront the elementary fact that their arguments assumed that women would take on two jobs in life, instead of the single one men filled. What most women did who wanted careers or lifetime occupations was either not marry at all or else begin a career only after their family responsibilities were largely over. In neither case, however, were such women enjoying opportunities equal to those open to men.

Although few feminists or suffragists recognized the practical difficulties confronting the great majority of women seeking to combine family and career, many of them did recognize that the suffrage cause aroused anxiety and fear among women for the future of the traditional family. Elizabeth Cady Stanton and Mary Putnam Jacobi could boldly grasp the nettle of family disruption without flinching, but most feminists, as historian Ellen DuBois has pointed out, "regularly denied the anti-suffragists' charge that woman suffrage meant a revolution in the family." Yet even those who denied the conflict had to recognize that most women were at best apathetic, and at worst, hostile to the suffrage. "O, how much I do wish we could rally the women to the necessity of doing something for their own case," wrote one suffragist privately to another in the 1890s. " 'The women don't want the vote' is the 'stunner' that we friends of the cause have to meet at every hand," she admitted. And all through the polemical literature in support of woman suffrage runs the refrain that the vote is a matter of justice and not to be decided by merely counting the heads of women who favor it. Right down until the very end of the long struggle, suffragists were at pains to show that thousands of women signed petitions in support of the suffrage in an effort to counter the frequently heard claim that most women did not want the vote. As late as 1902, Susan B. Anthony and Ida H. Harper wrote in their history of woman suffrage that "in the indifference, the inertia, the apathy of women lies the greatest obstacle to their enfranchisement." Both feminists admitted that, in the end, it was women, not men, who slowed down the acceptance, even though men technically had the final word, since only their votes could bring it about. "The average man would not vote against granting women the suffrage if all those of this own family and the circle of his intimate frineds brought a strong pressure to bear upon him in its favor," they observed.[22]

The same point was made from a slightly different angle in 1915 by another feminist. "In none of the four suffrage states first enfranchised in this country, Wyoming, Utah, Idaho, and Colorado, in Australia or in New Zealand," observed labor writer Alice Henry, "did any large proportion of women ask for or desire their political freedom."[23] In short, even on the eve of the acceptance of the suffrage, it was hard to make a case for a compelling interest among women in achieving the vote. One modern commentator has pointed out that even in 1915 the number of women who were members of the Women's Christian Temperance Union was more than double the number who were members of the National American Woman Suffrage Association, the principal suffrage group in the country. Anti-suffragists delighted to point out that even in states in which women did have the vote they usually did not exercise it. In Massachusetts, for example, after forty years of school suffrage for women, only 5 per cent of eligible women cast ballots. Yet in one year, in which a religious issue was prominent, women came out in great numbers, suggesting that in the other years they simply had no interest in participating in elections. The most devastating piece of evidence from the anti-suffragists' point of view was the special referendum in Massachusetts in 1895. In order to settle the question of women's wish for the suffrage, the legislature permitted women to vote for or against the suffrage, along with men. And the results were to be tabulated by sex. The "no" vote overwhelmed the "yes" vote, as one might have expected—187,000 to 110,000—but the embarrassing aspect was that 87,000 males voted *for* the suffrage as compared with only 23,000 females! The suffragists explained away the embarrassment by saying they had urged their supporters to boycott the election, a piece of advice that some probably followed. But the advice and results showed that the suffragists had little faith that most women would support their cause.[24]

The greater number of women in the WCTU as compred with those in the suffrage organization offers a means of finding out why women had so little interest in the suffrage. Some years ago Janet Zollinger Giele wrote an imaginative doctoral dissertation comparing the leadership and the publications of the WCTU and those of the NAWSA. In many ways, Giele found, the women leaders and the literature turned out by their respective organizations were remarkably alike. In both sets of leaders, for example, were to be found a high proportion of highly educated women, many of whom were teachers and lecturers. Both groups also agreed that women had roles to play in society which men either could not or would not assume. And the two organizations usually stood together on improving the position of women in the home. Both wished to give women proper recognition for what they did in the home and both sought ways to protect women from men who would exploit their dependence or their affections. Both of them generally saw women as morally superior to, and as socially more vulnerable than, men. The two movements also shared a number of leaders. Frances Willard was the best known, but others included Mary Livermore of Massachusetts, J. Ellen Foster of Iowa, Caroline Merrick of Louisiana, and Zerelad Wallace of Indiana. Some of the most prominent woman suffrage leaders actually had begun their public careers in the temperance movement, women like Carrie Chapman Catt, Anna Howard Shaw, Catharine Waugh McCullock, and Susan B. Anthony herself.

When Giele probed more deeply into the activities of the leaders and into the contents of their respective journals, however, differences appeared which provide clues as to why temperance was a more popular woman's cause than suffrage. When she asked what other causes the leaders of the two primary groups were engaged in, the temperance women turned out to be most active in causes dealing with personal issues, such as charity, cruelty to animals and children, or Social Purity, while the suffragist leaders were active in what Giele called structural reforms, like labor-union organization, education, and municipal government. Giele's comparative analysis of the content of the suffragists' *Woman's Journal* and the WCTU's *Union Signal* revealed a similar division of interest. For example, 31 per cent of the articles in the *Woman's Journal* between 1885 and 1915 dealt with the intellectual and civic equality of women; only 3 per cent of the pieces in the *Union Signal* did. Giele concluded that the women in the two groups differed significantly in outlook. "The temperance women," she wrote, "were oriented primarily to the warm affectional world in which they stood. In humanitarian endeavor, they turned to helping the weak rather than to interceding with the powerful. They were happy with the image of the traditional woman and rather than change her, they wanted only to pull up imperfect man to her level. And finally, their explicit reform objective was much more strongly directed at consolidating woman's status within the home, rather than trying to find a place for her outside of it." [25]

Simply because the activities and interests of the temperance women fitted so snugly the traditional role of women they were rarely denounced for alleged masculinity, despite their active participation in the world outside the home. The suffragist women, however, frequently had such charges hurled at them. "The womanliness of temperance women," Giele commented, "was seldom if ever questioned." Temperance, as a women's movement, always seemed "other-serving," while suffrage seemed "self-serving," as it was intended to be. It rested, after all, on the assumption that a woman could not be represented by anyone but herself. Alice Henry phrased the point well; the suffrage was necessary "because men, even good men, cannot be trusted to take care of women's interests." [26]

It was this individualistic or admittedly "self-serving" aspect of the suffrage that aroused much of the hostility to votes for women. It was the one demand of the women's movement of the 19th century that could not be subsumed under the heading of woman's traditional role as mother, wife, and sustainer of the family. In fact and by implication the suffrage promised to open to women a role so traditionally male and so straight-forwardly individualistic that it was totally unacceptable to most Americans. As Mary Putnam Jacobi recognized, it "introduced a change" in the role of woman in society.

This is but another way of saying that men could not accept the suffrage, for they could not help recognizing that it might alter sharply their place in politics and, more threatening still, in the family. The suffrage was a direct attack upon the doctrine of the separate spheres. As such it could be expected to be resisted by men. Most suffragists and virtually all historians of the suffrage struggle have blamed men for the primary resistance to the vote. And, in a formal sense, that is where the blame must lie; men had the votes necessary to sanction it. Yet, at the same time, that explanation cannot be the full one. As Susan Anthony and Ida Harper pointed out in 1902, if women as a sex really wanted the suffrage, their influence upon men within the family was such that they could have brought it about much sooner. Moreover, making men wholly or mainly responsible, incorrectly reduces or minimizes women's role in the making of history. For an emphasis upon men's opposition ignores that there was not only a great "silent majority" of women who had little or no interest in the suffrage, but a sizable minority of women who were far from silent in their opposition.

Although the active opposition of thousands of women was one of the most striking aspects of the struggle for the vote, comparatively little historical attention has been paid to it. Jane Jerome Camhi's recent doctoral dissertation "Women Against Women" is the only substantial and careful study that has been written on the subject, and it has yet to be published. Historians who favor woman suffrage have either ignored the anti-suffragists or dismissed them as women who were merely expressing the opposition of their husbands. But the size, persistence, and activities, not to mention the character of the leadership of the anti-suffrage groups, beginning in the 1890s, belie the argument that the opposition was male-directed. Men were in the movement, to be sure, but, as Camhi informed us, "the anti-suffrage movement was organized, staffed, and run primarily by women." And though the size of the membership of all the anti-suffrage organizations is not known, some of the state organizations reported large numbers. The New York State group, for example, was said to have

20,000 members in the 1890s, and in 1907 the Massachusetts organization reported 12,500 members. Since, at bottom, the anti-suffrage women were defending the status quo, their organizations went out of existence when there was no threat to traditional practices. Unlike the suffrage women, who were pressing for change, the "Antis," as they were often called, came into being only when the "Suffs" were pushing a particular bill or convention. Nonetheless, the influence of the Antis was inadvertently suggested by Carrie Chapman Catt's observation that the strongest suffrage organizations were in Massachusetts, New York, New Jersey, Pennsylvania, Ohio, Indiana, Illinois, and Iowa, "where the woman suffrage appeal was continual during these forty years," but where "no suffrage referendum was secured." As Jane Camhi pointed out, "it was not just coincidental that these very states witnessed the highest levels of anti-suffrage activity."[27] Among the well-known opponents were some of the prominent public women of the time, like Annie Nathan Meyer, writer and economist; Ida Tarbell, journalist and historian; Minnie Bronson, a special agent of the U.S. Labor Department; Mariana van Rensselaer, writer and art critic; Kate Barnard, prison reformer; Caroline Corbin, writer, and one of the founders of the Association for the Advancement of Women; and Priscilla Leonard, poet and labor-law reformer.

The existence of a strong anti-suffrage movement among women is a unique development among reform groups. English historian and feminist Constance Rover has commented on a similar phenomenon in Great Britain. Although groups of men have been "apathetic concerning the acquisition of voting rights," Rover wrote in *Women's Suffrage and Party Politics in Britain, 1866–1914,* "there was no organization of men opposing their own enfranchisement." And at the time the point was not lost on contemporaries. "It is somewhat remarkable," commented the *Indianapolis Journal* in reviewing Helen Kendrick Johnson's anti-suffrage tract, *Women and the Republic* (1897), "that the most vigorous arraignment of, and attack upon the woman-suffrage movement should come from a woman."[28]

The reason why women, alone of all social groups, organized against their own political emancipation is that many women perceived in the suffrage a threat to the family, a threat so severe that the vote did not seem worth the possible cost. Although the anti-suffrage case comprised almost an infinite number of arguments and justifications—as the pro-suffrage case did, too—behind all the arguments and justifications loomed the fear that bestowing the ballot upon women would force an alteration in the traditional family. The argument runs all through the anti-suffrage literature from the 1880s right down to 1920.

Underlying the anti-suffrage arguments was the fundamental assumption that the natures of women and men were different. As an anti-suffrage document submitted to the Illinois legislature in 1897 phrased it, the pivotal question is that "of sex. We believe that men are ordained to govern in all forceful and material matters, *because they are men,* physically and intellectually strong, virile, aggressive; while women, by the same decree of God and nature, are equally fitted to bear rule in a higher and more spiritual realm, where the strong frame and the weighty brain count for less, but the finer fibre of the woman's body and the spiritual uplift of her affection and her soul are the indications of a power not less than that of a man, and even more necessary to the progress and elevation of the race."[29] This was, of course, a biological justification of the old principle of the separate spheres. And though it denied the identity of the sexes, it asserted their equality, with perhaps a slight edge to women.

Some anti-suffragists were even more precise in equating the intellectual abilities of men and women, while asserting their basic difference in character. "You cannot dodge the fact women have work in the world that men cannot do, and it is equally true that men have work that women cannot do," contended Ann Watkins in 1912. "Neither man nor woman is superior or inferior to the other; the two are just different, positive and negative, two great manifestations of a still greater force."[30]

One reason for insisting on the equality of women with men was to counter the oft-heard suffrage argument that women were morally superior to men. Henry Blackwell, writing in the suffragist *Woman's Journal* in 1895, made the point quite explicitly. "Government need the women. . . . Women differ from men in nature, position, and training. They are superior to men in certain qualities. They are more peaceable, temperate, chaste, economical and law-abiding. These qualities are needed in our legislation." Suffragist leader Anna Howard Shaw's answer to those who feared that fewer women would be active in charitable work if women gained the suffrage was: "Thank God, there will not be so much need of charity and philanthropy" once women can vote. Florence Kelley thought "the enfranchisement of women is indispensable to the solution of the child labor problem." And the Congressional Union asserted in a pamphlet that "a government responsible to all women, as well as all men, will be less likely to go to war, without real necessity." Even as advanced and sophisticated a feminist as Charlotte Perkins Gilman insisted that women needed to be brought into the work of the world, including that of government, because the man-made world of the time lacked the special attributes and character of women. In short, suffragists often made as much of the difference between the sexes as the "Antis."[31]

What differentiated the Antis from the Suffs was not their conceptions of the differences between men and women, but the Antis' denial of *individual* differences in women. The Antis thought and acted much as racists—they assumed that all people in a given biological category—in this case women —were alike and so much so that social policy—the suffrage—should be based on that assumption. "The Anti-Suffragists grant the equality of sexes," wrote a well-known Anti in 1909. "Men are no better than women and science assures us that they are no more intelligent. But the Anti insists that the *difference* between the sexes shall not be ignored." The work of the two sexes, wrote another anti-suffragist, was "not to be measured by the same standard of values." It was their differences that made "any home a symmetrical thing. . . . We do those things for which we are best fitted by physical and mental powers." The response of the Antis to the suffragists' contention that sex had nothing to do with work, she continued, was that "*sex happens to be the pivot upon which the whole question turns.* It has fixed our place in the home and in the world, and no matter how far astray we go mentally from our right appreciation of this truth, sex will inexorably drive us back to wifehood and motherhood until the world ends." It was the feminists' and suffragists' counter-assertion that some women could perform the work of men that fully exposed the quasi-racist, anti-individualist assumptions of the Antis. "That woman could develop better under masculine conditions of life," contended Margaret Robinson in 1916, "is a totally unsupported theory. Woman cannot become man— she can only become a poor imitation. She develops best along the lines of her aptitudes and instincts."[32]

Nothing revealed the anti-individualistic assumptions of the anti-suffragists more than their repeated assertion that "the interests of men and women are identical," as one Anti put it. (Recall suffragist Alice Henry's remark, quoted earlier, that no man, not even a good man, could represent a woman.) The interests were identical in the minds of Antis, because men and women were united in the family. "Today there is not a single interest of woman which is not shared and defended by men," argued Clara T. Leonard before a Massachusetts legislative committee in 1884. Alice George, the leader of Massachusetts Antis, denounced the suffrage in 1915 as wrong because it rested on the assumption that there was "a definite sex division of interests." On the contrary, she continued, "there is no rivalry between men and women; in the economy of life they have different duties, but their interests are the common interests of humanity. Women are not a class, they are a sex whose interests in a well-ordered government are represented, automatically and inevitably, by the men of their social group." A Brooklyn anti-suffrage group made the argument even more explicitly when it asserted that the "household, not the individual is the unit of the State, and the vast majority of women are represented by household suffrage." Lily Foxcroft conceded in 1917 that certain social groups, like the rich and the poor, the native and the foreign-born, the ignorant and the intelligent, might need the ballot to protect their interests, but "the interests of men and women do not clash, and their relations are so close that the men of each class may truly be said to represent the women of that class."[33]

Alice George thought the suffrage must disrupt the family because of its emphasis upon women's individuality. Should the vote be granted, she wrote, "the whole sweep of relations of the sexes must be revised, if the woman's vote is to mean anything more than two people doing what one does now." For if women simply duplicated the votes of men there would be no purpose in giving them the suffrage. Yet if women used the vote as individuals with interests different from those of their husbands, then we "reinforce those who clamor for individual rights" and "strike at the family as the self-governing unit upon which the state is built." In 1903 Frances J. Dyer made a similar point when she said that granting the suffrage to women would "shift the basis of our government from the family as a unit to the individual. So fundamental and important a change as this we believe would prove inimical to the highest interests of the home." To Helen Johnson, the fundamental threat of the suffrage was that it brought "the possibility of civil war . . . to the door of every family."[34]

If the suffragists worried about the lack of interest the mass of women showed in achieving the suffrage, the anti-suffragists made capital out of it. The more perceptive of them recognized the women's apathy or hostility toward the suffrage stemmed from the threat it posed to the family. Caroline Corbin, one of the leading anti-suffragists in Illinois, made the point in the form of a question as early as 1887. If women become politically and economically independent, she inquired, "what then becomes of marriage and the home? Is there any escape from the conviction that the industrial and political independence of women would be the wreck of our present domestic institutions? May it not be possible," she asked, "that an intuitive sense that woman suffrage is incompatible with the present relations of men and women in the home, has something to do with the fact that . . . an overwhelming majority of women do not desire the ballot?"[35] She might have added that the refusal of most suffragists and feminists to acknowledge the conflict between the family and women's emancipation was in itself a sure sign that there was a threat.

Ida Tarbell, historian and journalist, writing in 1909 did more than pose a question; she explained the resistance of the average middle-class married woman on the ground that most women perceived women's rights to be a threat to the family. "It was not bigotry or vanity or a petty notion of their own spheres that kept the majority of the women of the '40s from lending themselves to the Woman's Rights Movement," she began. "It was a fear to destroy a greater thing which they possessed"—namely, their lives as wives and mothers. "It was the woman's life which barred the way most effectually to the growth of the cause of Woman's Rights." What that life entailed, Tarbell insisted, was the "dependence of man and child—the necessity of themselves—to know that upon them depended the health, the character, the happiness, the future of certain human beings, to see themselves laying and preserving the foundations of so imposing a thing as a family. . . . They might not have been able to state it, but all their instincts and experiences convinced them of the supreme and eternal value of their place in the world. They *dared* not tamper with it."[36]

In the end, then, the conflict between the Suffs and the Antis was over whether women ought to be treated as individuals or as subordinates who served the family. Sometimes and anti-suffragists made precisely that point in their objections. Women "do the neglected work, they remember the forgotten duty, they bring light and help to the dark places," wrote Priscilla Leonard. "And all this they do, not for their own sakes or their own glory, but for the common good." The motto of women, she concluded, was, significantly enough, "Not to be ministered unto, but to minister." The Antis attacked Elizabeth Cady Stanton's *Woman's Bible* because it frankly emphasized women's thinking of themselves rather than of others—that is, acting as self-interested individuals. "What sort of a 'next generation' would evolve," asked the *Anti-Suffragist* in 1909, "if all women considered their 'first duty' to be themselves, and overlooked the fact that their strongest power and highest possibility is that of unselfish—and often unnoticed—service." This is also why many anti-suffragist women were among the leaders in the opposition to easier divorce laws, for they saw in divorce not only a sign of family instability but a heightened sense of self among women, which they could only deplore. Helen K. Johnson, the author of a major anti-suffrage book, for example, was also a leader in the opposition to any easing of the divorce laws. The Antis also asserted that divorce was easier in those states where woman suffrage prevailed.[37]

We know today that the fears of the anti-suffragists were unfounded. Granting the franchise to women did not disrupt the family. And the reason it did not is that women did not use it in any way that would alter their place within the family. In fact, it is hard to see how the suffrage alone could have made any serious change in intra-familial relations. It is true that in projecting women into politics the suffrage broke the barrier between the spheres of women and men in a novel way. But as voters, women tended to behave like their husbands or fathers, not as self-interested persons with different interests from their menfolk. It is true that, in insisting upon a separate vote for women, the feminists seemed to threaten to divide the family. Indeed, that had been the great fear of the Antis. In practice, however, the threat was only theoretical or symbolic, not real. So theoretical was it that most suffragists did not recognize it and usually explicitly denied any such intention or implication. The Antis, on the other hand, exaggerated the implications of the suffrage, asserting that the vote was going to set wife against husband because in theory the suffrage recognized women's individuality and self-interest. They naturally interpreted that as disruptive because in the traditional family the woman had indeed subordinated her individuality to her husband's.

If a perceived threat to the family explains why women were reluctant to support the suffrage, we are still left with the question of how it was that the suffrage finally was accepted in 1920. Two kinds of reasons suggest themselves.

First of all, there was the powerful and well-organized campaign mounted by the suffragists, especially after 1910. Just about then a decision was made by the suffrage leadership to abandon the fifty-year-long campaign to win the suffrage state by state and to concentrate upon amending the federal Constitution. After all, as late as 1910 no more than four states, all of them small and western, had enacted full suffrage for women. Once the decision was made to fight for a federal amendment, the suffrage leaders moved to win over Congress and the President, much more concentrated targets than some forty state legislatures. Notable in this regard was the intense and often violent campaign of the radical wing of the suffragists in 1913–14, led by the indefatigable Alice Paul. Emulating the passive-resistance tactics of the contemporary English women's movement, suffragists picketed the White House, chained themselves to fences, and, when taken to jail, went on hunger strikes. There they resisted the brutality of forced feeding and, when freed, went back to jail immediately and eagerly. Meanwhile membership in the more conventional organizations swelled, and the propaganda and political pressure mounted. Although in 1915 referenda on woman suffrage were defeated in four eastern states, the proponents came close to winning. They captured 46 per cent of the total in Pennsylvania, 42 per cent in New York and New Jersey, and 35 per cent in Massachusetts. President Wilson himself supported suffrage when he voted that year in New Jersey. Membership in the National American Woman Suffrage Association reached almost two million members, with a gross income of three-quarters of a million dollars a year. In short, by 1915 the suffrage had been raised to a national political issue, causing the Progressive and Republican parties officially to endorse the suffrage in time for the election of 1916.

The highly organized activities of the suffragists and the disruptive and attention-gaining tactics of the radicals may have made the men willing to concede that further resistance was counterproductive, but there was no evidence that the mass of women were any more interested in the suffrage than ever. Even women who had the vote prior to 1920 did not exercise it as expected. In 1914, in Chicago, for example, only a third of the eligible women bothered to register as against two-thirds of the men. And after suffrage was achieved, women's participation was lower than men's. The proportion of women voters, according to the Gallup poll, did not equal that of men until 1956—36 years after the winning of the suffrage—and at that date women in the population outnumbered men. Thus, proportionately, they were still not voting to the same extent as men. A more striking measure of the lack of interest by women in the suffrage was the small number of women who have been elected to public office since women obtained the vote. Although many women candidates have presented themselves for office, women have not voted for them. Contrary to what the Antis feared, and the Suffs expected, women have not voted as a sex. As a result, the number of women in the House of Representatives has never amounted to more than a handful, and, even in the age of the new feminism in the 1970s, only one woman sits in the United States Senate. In retrospect, in short, the suffrage does not seem to have been an ardently desired goal of most women, not even by 1920.

The second reason why resistance to the suffrage was finally overcome has to do with a decline in the fear that the suffrage threatened the family. During the first decade or so of the 20th century it became increasingly clear that, whatever the suffrage might portend in theory, in fact it was not a threat to the family. By 1910 woman suffrage had been tried in four states for over a decade; yet there nothing much had changed, one way or another. Indeed, the anti-suffragists were fond of taunting the suffragists with the truth that not even the social improvements promised by the social feminist suffragists had taken place. Gambling and prostitution were as safe and as rife in Colorado *with* woman suffrage as they had been *without* it. And as municipal suffrage spread throughout the country, city bosses learned, too, that they had little to fear from women voters and that Prohibition was not an automatic political reflex of women voters. By 1919, a recent historian of the politics of the Progressive era has concluded, "virtually all of the nation's major Democratic urban political machines had come to accept female suffrage, regardless of their earlier views."[38] In sum, woman suffrage was accepted at long last simply because it was no longer perceived as likely to produce the effects upon women's behavior and the relationships within the family that the suffragists had hoped for and the anti-suffragists had feared.

The most important reason of all why many women could forget about their apprehension that the suffrage threatened the family was that the justifications for the suffrage shifted ground in the early 20th century. The original and most common argument on behalf of woman suffrage in the 19th century had been that which has been sketched in previous pages— namely, that votes for women symbolized their individuality, their sense of self-interest, their need to be able to speak politically as individuals. Feminists and suffragists like Elizabeth Cady Stanton pushed that argument hard, contending that no man could speak for a woman, any more than a white person could speak for a black. Suffrage was justified on the grounds that women were individual human beings, who must express their own preferences individually.

By the opening years of the 20th century, however, the original suffragist leaders had passed from the scene, and the old appeal to individual rights as the basis for the suffrage for women was gradually abandoned. The principal reason it was dropped was that it was not working. It was winning neither votes from men nor support from women. At the same time, the advancement of women in education, business, professions, and in a great variety of social and reform organizations by the early 20th century suggested a more practical argument in support of the suffrage. The new justification was that women had a special contribution to make to society, something that men could not provide. This special contribution, so the argument went, came from their character as women—as wives and mothers, as homemakers. Jane Addams, for example, pointed out early in the 20th century that the problems of modern cities were those that women had long been familiar with: child labor, unsanitary housing, adulterated food, and so forth. "May we not say," she asked, "that city housekeeping has failed partly because women, the traditional housekeepers, have not been consulted as to its multiform activities?" And in 1914 Alice Stone Blackwell urged woman suffrage on the ground that it would have a salutary effect on foreign policy because women were different from men. "Let us do our utmost to hasten the day when the wishes of the mothers shall have their due weight in public affairs, knowing that by so doing we hasten the day when wars shall be no more." [39] In short, politics and voting were but an extension of the home, so they needed the special character of women to improve them. Suffrage now became a way of extending women's special sphere to society, rather than being a way of providing political expression for women's self-interest as individuals. Those suffragists who advanced such a defense of the suffrage were, in effect, arguing that women's character as a sex should be represented, but not a woman's interest as an individual. This new justification for the suffrage was thus very close to the Antis' assertion that women as a group were basically different from men. In the process, of course, that assertion played down, if it did not deny outright, a woman's individuality. It fitted in well, however, with the idea that woman's place in the family was as helper and nurturer of others, and thus supported, rather than threatened, the traditional relation between husband and wife in the family.

One of the striking social manifestations of this belief that women were different from men and that their primary function in society as wives and mothers was the enactment of protective labor legislation in behalf of women workers. The best known justification for such laws was made by Louis Brandeis in his famous brief before the Supreme Court in the case of *Muller v. Oregon* in 1908. Brandeis, as attorney for several women's organizations, contended that as potential mothers women needed and deserved special legislation to protect them from jobs or occupational situations that might be injurious to their health. Such legislation was not to apply to men because they were stronger and would never be mothers. One of the new justifications for the ballot for women was that if women were enfranchised they could compel legislators to enact such protective legislation. In short, the suffrage was now being justified on the ground that it protected the family and women's traditional role within it.

Thus by the time the fight for the suffrage reached a climax in 1918, the argument that the vote would enhance each woman's individuality had been replaced by a more traditional one, which frankly drew upon the view that women had a special nature, deriving from their being mothers and wives. Thus neither women nor men need any longer consider the suffrage as a threat to the family. Hence it could be accepted and become a part of the Constitution. Parenthetically, as Richard Evans and others have pointed out, suffrage for women in a number of other countries was enacted for similarly conservative reasons. In Finland and Norway, for instance, woman suffrage came as a means of advancing nationalism in societies then under foreign domination. Similarly in Utah and Wyoming it seems to have been pushed by men because they thought it would encourage the stabilizing influence of women and the home over single men and outsiders. (This is the argument advanced by Alan Grimes referred to earlier.) And the same conservative purpose, deriving from woman's traditional role in the family, seems to be at the root of the rapid acceptance of woman suffrage in Australia at the end of the 19th century.

Finally, the transformation of the suffrage into a conservative cause by obscuring its potentialities as an expression of woman's individuality can be seen in the United States in another way. Within three years after the ratification of the Nineteenth Amendment, Alice Paul, a radical feminist who had been perhaps the most militant of the supporters of the suffrage during the final years of the campaign, proposed a new amendment to the Constitution. She called it the Equal Rights Amendment, for it would forbid any state or the federal government from discriminating in any way between males and females. The amendment would require the law to recognize and to treat women as individuals, not as members of a sex.

To Alice Paul the Equal Rights Amendment was simply a return to the original principle that had been the justification for woman suffrage—that is, of seeing women as individual human beings. But to the great majority of women who had campaigned and had brought about the passage of the Nineteenth Amendment, the Equal Rights Amendment was a betrayal of all they had worked and struggled for. And it was true that, if the Equal Rights Amendment were ratified, it would nullify all the special protective legislation in behalf of women that had been enacted in the preceding twenty years or more. As a result, women leaders of the day like Carrie

Chapman Catt, Florence Kelley, and Jane Addams, all of whom had been in the forefront of the fight for the ballot, rejected the Equal Rights Amendment. To these leaders the important thing was to protect women as women—that is, as a sex, not as individuals. And so for another half-century the Equal Rights Amendment was vehemently opposed by most of the leaders of women's organizations on the ground that it was harmful to women, their essential nature, and their place in society. And it is that long period of opposition to the ERA by suffragists themselves that points up once again how profoundly suffragists had shifted their arguments in support of the suffrage. That opposition offers also a measure of how necessary it was that the individualistic implications of the suffrage be obscured or denied if enfranchisement was to be accepted. For, until that was done, suffrage for women was generally perceived as a threat to the traditional subordinate role of women in the family. The result was that the achievement of suffrage for women took longer than any other effort to expand the electorate in American history.

To explain the achievement of suffrage for women in this way constitutes no minimizing of the monumental effort mounted by the suffragists to put the Nineteenth Amendment into the Constitution. As Carrie Chapman Catt later recalled, "to get that word, male, out of the Constitution, cost the women of the country 52 years of campaigning. During that time they were forced to conduct 56 campaigns of referenda to male voters; 480 campaigns to urge Legislatures to submit suffrage amendments to voters; 47 campaigns to induce State constitutional conventions to write women suffrage into State constitutions; 277 campaigns to persuade State party conventions to include woman suffrage planks; 30 campaigns to urge presidential party conventions to adopt woman suffrage planks in party platforms, and 19 campaigns with 19 successive Congresses to get the federal amendment submitted and ratified.[40] But one important reason the struggle took so long and was so difficult was that most women were either hostile or apathetic. The women opponents were, as the Antis liked to say, 'a silent majority'."

Because the predictions about the suffrage's effects turned out to be wrong, the threat to the family implicit in the suffrage has generally been ignored by historians. As a consequence, the suffrage fight has been treated as a conservative reform, which is certainly the way it was defended in the last stages of the campaign. In fact, though, the suffrage was the political side of a drive for woman's individuality that was reshaping the traditional family. The suffrage may have been only a first step in the achievement of women's equality, rather than the last one that the suffragists contended. Yet it was certainly an integral and necessary part of that long revolution concerning woman's place through which American society is still passing.

Another essential part of that revolution was the movement of women out of the urban home into the paid work force. That, too, like the campaign for the suffrage, was a 19th- and 20th-century phenomenon, but its most profound effects upon women were not felt until the second half of the 20th century. It is that transformation in women's lives to which the next three chapters are devoted.

XV

Women's Work:
The First Transformation

Traditionally, historians and sociologists alike have measured the activity of women in the world outside the home by the number, or proportion, of women working for pay. That particular gauge is misleading in that, as we have seen in earlier chapters, women could be quite active in the world without receiving pay. They formed organizations of their own, fought for political and social reforms, and generally helped in shaping the world. To measure women's work by whether it was paid for or not is misleading in another sense. Even when women did not receive pay, they nonetheless worked hard. The maintenance of the home and the care of children throughout American history for the great majority of women, including middle-class women, can only be described as demanding, arduous, and time-consuming. As has been observed before, the Victorian lady of leisure so beloved by novelists and critics of the age was representative at best of a minuscule proportion of all women.

Nevertheless there is good reason for examining the history of women's participation in the economy since it reveals yet another side of the long evolution of women and the family over the last two centuries. Work for money, as opposed to work for family, generates different attitudes and relationships among family members, and the intra-familial relationships as well as the role of women in the economy are central subjects in this book. In looking at women's work in this chapter the emphasis will be upon the years prior to 1900. Those were the years when women began to follow men out of the home into the industrial and commercial work places. The chapter after that will look at women's relationship to various economic institutions, especially in the first half of the 20th century. Then, Chapter XVII will examine the transformation in women's work since World War II.

Throughout the colonial years, the great majority of women, regardless of age or status, were principally involved in the non-money sector of the economy, that is, they worked at jobs in the home that earned them no money, and the products of which did not enter the market. Neither of those propositions, however, should give the impression that women were not heavily engaged in producing goods and services. Prior to the Revolution and for some decades after, the great majority of American families— probably as high as 90 per cent—lived on farms. With the economy overwhelmingly agricultural, the great preponderance of the labor force was dedicated to raising crops for family consumption and for sale. With the exception of the southern plantation, where, ever since the end of the 17th century, black slaves supplied the bulk of the labor, the farm was typically a family enterprise. Although all members of the family worked at a common activity, that did not mean they interchanged jobs. On the contrary, there was a sharp division of labor between the sexes. Certain tasks were peculiarly women's, while others were men's. This division of labor by gender was as old as human history, extending back even to the hunting societies that antedated the invention of agriculture. All societies known to anthropologists today still manifest this clear division of tasks, as did the rural colonial economy and the rural European economy of the 17th and 18th centuries.

As far as women were concerned, their tasks were not only diverse but almost endless. Over the long term of a lifetime they were probably more arduous and demanding than those performed by men. One traveler in 18th-century Carolina reported that "the ordinary women take care of Cows, Hogs, and other small Cattle, make Butter and Cheese, spin cotton and flax, help to sow and reap corn, wind silk from the worms, gather Fruit, and look after the House."[1] Looking after the house was itself a heavy task, since that included not only cleaning the physical interior but the washing and mending of the family's clothes, preparing meals under the handicaps of an open fireplace and no running water, preserving various kinds of foods, making all the soap, candles, and most of the medicines used by the family, as well as all the clothes for the family. And then, as the quotation suggests, the woman had to be ready at planting or harvest time to help in the fields. On top of all this, of course, was the bearing and rearing of children. During the colonial years, when families of at least six children were common, this task was close to a full job in itself. It was this almost unending congeries of jobs that probably gave birth to the well-known tag line that a woman's work is never done. Unlike the work of the husband-farmer, women's work went on after dark and at an undiminished pace throughout the year.

Given the nature of most women's work in agricultural America, the image of women, especially on the frontier, where most Americans lived in the 18th century, was hardly that of a frail or delicate creature. William Byrd, well-known diarist and planter of tidewater Virginia, wrote in 1710 of being entertained in the back country by a fairly well-to-do woman. "She is a very civil woman and shews nothing of the ruggedness, or Immodesty in her carriage" that he had noticed in other frontier women he had encountered in the course of his surveying trip. "Yett she will carry a gunn in the woods and kill deer, turkeys, etc., shoot down wild cattle, catch and tye hoggs, knock down beeves with an ax and perform the most manful Exercises as well as most men in those parts." [2]

From an economic standpoint, the significance of women's work on the farm was that she was the principal manufacturer. While the husband of the typical married woman busied himself with raising crops for home consumption and for sale, women were weaving cloth from which the underclothes, coats, pants, dresses, tablecloths, blankets, and shawls of the family were fashioned. Few homes were without a spinning wheel for the manufacture of thread, and most also had looms for the weaving of woolen or linen cloth. Some women bartered these products with neighbors or at stores for manufactured goods. A few women in the 18th century did custom work for wealthier women who did not want to make their own homespun or sew their own clothes. Yet throughout the colonial years and well into the 19th century most of the clothes worn by the average American family were made by women at home. Indeed, if one allows for a little exaggeration, the observation of one economic historian is about right: "during the colonial period, agriculture was in the hands of the men, and manufacturing, for the most part, in the hands of women." [3] Actually, some kinds of manufacturing, like shoe-making, iron forging, and leather-working, were almost exclusively male occupations, and some manufactures were always imported from Europe. Yet the role of women was significant in manufacturing simply because the largest volume of such goods during the late 18th century were made in farm homes, where women's role was pre-eminent.

Although during the colonial years, 90 per cent of Americans lived on farms, there was also a small but slowly growing urban population. In a town or city the work of women inevitably contracted, since many of the things that farm or frontier women had to make for themselves could be purchased in shops; the cash incomes of urban people—whatever might be said of their total income—was generally larger than that of rural families. At the same time, though, the city or town offered a range of new occupations open to women. One historian has counted at least 35 women physicians during the colonial years; 17 women physicians appear in the official records of the New England colonies alone. He also found several dozen women who owned printshops in their own right; six of them were the official printers for the colonial governments; sixteen of them published newspapers. An unspecified number of women worked as silversmiths, papermill workers, distillers, woodworkers, leather workers, and barbers. One researcher has located some thirty different crafts that women engaged in for purposes of sale in Philadelphia alone in the years before 1776. Women were especially noticeable as tavern owners and operators. The so-called "she-merchants," as they denominated themselves in colonial New York, actually issued, at one point, public protest against sex discrimination. In Philadelphia in the 1760s as many as 17 per cent of the licenses for taverns went to women, and in the single year of 1717 about a third of all shopkeepers applying for the "freedom" of the city were women.[4] In short, women were economically active in cities as well as on the farm and frontier.

To draw this conclusion, however, is not to say that most city women perceived such activity as normal. In fact, there is reason to believe that most of the women who were "she-merchants," shopkeepers, or craft workers, were widows who were taking over from their dead husbands. It was usually the death of a husband that was crucial in bringing a woman's talents into play. Certainly this was the case for one widow who took over her husband's Long Island whaling business in the 18th century and made it into a success. It was also true of Polly Spratt Provost, who was only twenty-six when her husband died, leaving her with three children. She immediately assumed the running of his importing business, which she continued to operate after she remarried. How she managed the double work load was suggested by her second husband, James Alexander, in a letter he wrote at the time of the birth of their first child. She "does more than can be Expected of any woman," Alexander told her brother in 1721, "for till within a few hours of her being brought to bed she was in her Shop and ever Since [the birth was two days earlier] has given the price of goods to her prentice, who comes to her and asks for it when customers come in. The very next day after she was brought to bed She Sold goods to above thirty pounds value." Alexander admitted that she had carried on the business "without the Least help from me." Ultimately she gave birth to six more of Alexander's children—ten all told from the two marriages.[5]

Inasmuch as most of the women proprietors we know about were widows, it is, at best, misleading to see the work of these women as typical or representative of the occupational roles open to the sex. That widows did take over their husbands' businesses in this manner certainly attests to the acceptance of women in such roles when necessity required it. But then most people recognized that in such small businesses wives were often as much a part of their husbands' enterprises as farm women were of their husbands'. This was especially true of inns, taverns, and shops, where the work of the house and child-rearing was in close proximity to the work of the husband. That widows did take over the businesses of their husbands when they died is silent but effective testimony to their familiarity with their husbands' enterprises.

The extent of that familiarity, however, can easily be exaggerated, as Mary Beth Norton has warned us in her study of some 470 colonial women.[6] The women she studied were Loyalists during the Revolution who made claims for compensation to the British government. All of the claims studied were entered by women in their own behalf, without the intercession of men. Thus the documentary evidence analyzed by Norton was the testimony of women, not men. The first point to notice is that only 9 per cent of the 470 women actually had income of their own, that is, were earning money; and half of that 9 per cent were without either a living or a healthy husband. In other words, half of that small number actually entered business only when their husbands no longer could run the business.

A second and more interesting point is that women, in their petitions, clearly implied their acceptance of the general view that woman's place was in the home, not at the shop counter or work bench. For instance, very few of the women, when questioned by Crown officials, could give details of their husbands' business, such as the value of their homes, lands, or shops. Again and again, Norton found, the women had to refer the inquirers to men for the necessary facts about their husbands' businesses. (By the same token, men without their wives present could not list individual items of furniture, dishes, and so forth—a clear measure of how sharp the separation of spheres was. Women could easily list in detail the items that men lumped under the general heading "furnishings.") Sometimes the women gave direct expression to their self-image as persons peripheral to the world of work and business: one woman described herself as "a poor weak Woman unused to business." Yet, despite that description, that woman later returned to the United States to press her claim on the spot, something that most male Loyalists were fearful of doing! The disparity is in part a reflection of a stereotype, but it may also have been a measure of a woman's preference for the home. Certainly that was the meaning of a remark one woman (not one of the Loyalist women) wrote in her diary in 1809. Although she commonly worked with her husband, she preferred the home. "A Storm is most welcome, for then I can stay at *home,* which has more charms for me than any other place." [7]

If during the colonial years most married women did not cross the line separating men's and women's work, the labor of women was still important to the economy. Even at the end of the 18th century, the primary role of women in the manufacture of cloth was well recognized. "It is computed in a number of districts," Alexander Hamilton noted in his famous Report on Manufactures in 1791, "that two-thirds, three-fourths, and four-fifths of all the clothing of the inhabitants are made by themselves." Albert Gallatin, one of Hamilton's successors in the office of Secretary of the Treasury, testified to the continuing influence of women in this branch of the economy. "It is probable that about two-thirds of the clothing, including hosiery and of the house and table linen worn and used by the inhabitants of the United States, who do not reside in cities," Gallatin wrote in 1810, "is the product of family manufactures." This was about ten times, by value, of what was produced outside the home, Gallatin estimated. [8]

Hamilton's and Gallatin's comments were made in the context of trying to encourage women to leave the home for the factories. In one of his more famous asides, Hamilton concluded that "women and children are rendered more useful by manufacturing establishments than they otherwise would be." And the history of early textile manufacture in the United States testifies that women were indeed useful. By 1816 well over half of the labor force in the cotton mills in the United States was female. Out of the 100,000 workers estimated in 1822 to be employed in the manufacture of cotton cloth in the United States, about 65,000 were women and girls.

Textiles were undoubtedly the most advanced form of manufacturing in the first three decades of the 19th century, but women workers were also important in a variety of other manufacturing enterprises. Among the seventy different businesses in which women were significantly employed before 1830 was the fabricating of furniture, shoes, gunpowder, buttons, gloves, shovels, and tobacco. Not all of these items were manufactured in factories; some could be fashioned at home, thus allowing women to tend their home chores as well. By 1850, women were working in nearly 175 industries, mostly manufactures of one kind or another. Virtually all these women workers were white, for most black women during the first half of the 19th century, it will be remembered, were slaves, who worked as farm laborers.

The labor of women was an impetus to the industrial revolution in America. In any agricultural society in which the productivity of workers is low, manufacturing is difficult to get started because the preponderance of labor is tied up in the production of food and other needed agricultural commodities. This was especially true in a relatively unsettled country like the United States, where the going wage was higher than in England, which, at that time, was the major manufacturing country in the world. It was the recognition of these basic economic facts that caused Hamilton and other early proponents of manufacturing to look to women's labor as a major national resource. And for most of the 19th century, women workers supplied the bulk of the labor force in textiles and a substantial portion in several other industries.

By the early 1830s working women were sufficiently common for one Boston newspaper to complain that "the times are out of joint." Now, the *Boston Courier* asserted, "women are assuming the prerogatives and employments which, from immemorial time, have been considered the attributes and duties of the other sex."[9] Certainly the incentive for women to work in factories was not a desire to replace men or to violate conventional gender roles, yet the textile millowners and the women both gained from the movement of women into the paid labor force. The women obtained better wages than they could command in domestic service or by staying at home, while the millowners cut costs since women worked for considerably lower wages than men. In fact, the lower wages made it possible for the American mills to compete with English textiles. Generally speaking, the lower wages paid to women in the early days of industrialization must be counted as a signal contribution to the beginnings of a modern American economy, whatever else it may say about the inequities of that economy. Since factory wages were generally higher than women's wages in other enterprises, over the long run they tended to raise the wages of women in other segments of the economy as well.

Although factory labor by women began in the northeastern section of the country, particularly New England, by the middle of the 19th century manufacturing had spread even into the South and West. By 1850 over a million workers were employed in manufacturing, of whom women made up a quarter—the highest proportion at any time in the century, and another measure of the importance of women in the early industrialization of the nation. Most of these women workers were in cotton textiles, where women always outnumbered men until the 1880s. In Massachusetts in 1850, for example, some 20,000 women were employed in cotton textiles as against fewer than 10,000 men. Interestingly enough, this same predominance of women prevailed in the southern states, though there the total number of women workers was smaller. In 1850, for example, 1400 women worked in Georgia's textile mills as compared with fewer than 900 males. Throughout the fifteen slaves states in 1850, almost 9000 women were employed in textile manufacturing alone; some 22,000 women were employed in manufacturing of all kinds, constituting a little over 13 per cent of the labor force in southern manufacturing.

By 1860, although more women than ever were employed in manufacturing, they constituted a smaller proportion—about 20 per cent—of the workers in all branches of manufacturing. The proportions varied from section to section, but the figure for the South was not as insignificant as sometimes thought. In New England, to be sure, women constituted about one-third of the workers in manufacturing, while in the South the proportion was only one-third of that. Although the antebellum slave South is generally perceived as a place of white ladies and black slaves, and an economy of plantations and no factories, that image is justified only by comparison with industrializing New England and the Middle Atlantic states. When compared with the agricultural Northwest—what today would be called the Middle West—the proportion of women workers in southern manufacturing is strikingly high. On the verge of the Civil War the slave states counted a larger proportion of women working in manufactures than the agricultural West with which it properly should be compared. According to the Census of 1860, women constituted 10 per cent or more of the work force in manufacturing in six out of the 14 slave states. Only Ohio among the western states had a proportion over 10 per cent (13 per cent); the five other western states counted 5 per cent or less. Maryland and North Carolina reported higher proportions of women in their manufacturing establishments than Pennsylvania. (Pennsylvania counted many more workers—male and female—in manufacturing, of course, than any southern state.) [10]

One of the problems confronted by early manufacturers who sought to employ female labor was how to make such work acceptable to a predominantly rural society that was not used to having daughters leave home to work. The most famous—and most successful—answer were the mills around Lowell, Massachusetts, the locale of what foreign visitors and Americans alike referred to as "the Lowell girls." The idea was to provide dormitories on the grounds of the mills in which the daughters of farmers, who were recruited from a distance, would be housed near their new jobs. It was expected that the young women workers would thus have a community and acceptable housing, thereby relieving the anxiety of parents over their activities while absent from home. The dependence of the mills on women's labor is revealed by the high proportion of women who worked in them: 74 per cent in the largest company in 1836. About 96 per cent of the women workers were native, and more than 80 per cent were between 15 and 30 years of age. Significantly, almost three-quarters of the women at this mill lived in the company boarding house: only 25 per cent lived at other locations, and only one-ninth of the total actually lived at home. The boarding-house idea, in short, was essential, if sufficient women were to be attracted from the farms of New England. In their special environment, the working women of Lowell became the cynosure of every foreign visitor, who asked to view them as they read books to one another while tending the looms, and during their spare time composed poetry and published their own newspaper.[11]

This special, and as it turned out, short-lived, form of communal living had other consequences, as the recent researches of Thomas Dublin have shown. The Lowell girls developed sufficient sense of carmaraderie or occupational solidarity, if you will, that as early as 1834 and then again in 1836 they went on strike against wage cuts. The millowners, taken aback by the unanticipated consequences of their plan, denounced such a display of independence as not only unfeminine but ungrateful as well! The striking women, on the other hand, made quite clear that one reason they resented the wage cuts was that a loss of income reduced their sense of independence of family. For it must be remembered that these young women were living away from their parents and therefore probably did not contribute to total family income, as did other young women workers who lived at home. With reduced wages they would have to ask for help from family. The Lowell women strikers lost their strike in 1834, as well as the one in 1836, but the number who joined the second strike was more than double the number in the first. Moreover, the women stayed out longer the second time, and showed greater solidarity, suggesting that the work experience, particularly the proto-communal living, had developed a sense of unity among them.

The common housing arrangements at Lowell were only temporary, for the young native farm girls were replaced in the 1840s and 1850s by immigrant women. In 1836, for example, only 4 per cent of the women employed in one of the large Lowell firms were foreign-born; by 1860 about 60 per cent were, most of them Irish. By the end of the 1850s the millowners had given up on the boarding-house idea; it was no longer essential to provide such inducements in order to have farmers send their daughters out to work. In fact, with the increase in immigration at the end of the 1840s, much more cheap female labor was available. The majority of the mill-workers, however, were still female. Indeed, so well known was the propensity of millowners to hire women that Thomas Dublin found a high proportion of widows living in the town of Lowell. In 1860 half of the households were female-headed. This proportion held for the natives as well as the foreign-born, showing that the basis of the phenomenon was economic rather than ethnic.

Studies of other communities in which factory work was concentrated showed Irish women predominating in the work force after 1850. Only one-quarter of the women workers in the cotton textile mills in Cohoes, New York, near Albany, in 1860 had native fathers. Four out of five Irish girls between 15 and 19 in Cohoes worked in the mills that census year. Irish girls were also the group most likely to be working in the factories and shops in Poughkeepsie, New York, between 1860 and 1880. About 60 per cent of all Irish girls in the city between 15 and 20 years of age were working, a proportion noticeably higher than for German or native girls of the same ages. Generally speaking, the Irish were economically worse off than any other social group except blacks.[12] Black women, however, were usually not employed in factories or shops.

Despite the low wages and often poor conditions of work, to immigrant girls and their families a job in the mills was considered a step up, economically and socially. The newspaper in Cohoes, for example, complained that it was "next to impossible to get competent, reliable girls, who were willing to do housework at any price." For most young women, domestic service was the principal if not the only alternative to work in the mills. Such girls believed, the newspaper continued, "that as operatives in the mills they take a higher place in the social scale than is accorded them when they do housework. The fact is, they don't like the idea of being servants, or being treated as such, and unless compelled by lack of the employment of their choice they avoid it with scorn."[13]

Textiles were not the only manufacturing enterprises at midcentury in which women made up a majority or a substantial minority of the workers. In the so-called clothing industries, which included the manufacture of shoes, umbrellas, furs, and clothing proper, but not textiles, women in 1850 comprised almost 50 per cent of the 230,000 employed. By 1880 the proportion was down to 47 per cent, but the number of women workers was up to more than 200,000. Shoemaking had once been a male job because of the physical strength involved, but after the invention of the sewing machine and other machinery in the late 1840s, the number of women workers approached that of men. Between 1850 and 1900 the number of women working in manufacturing in general rose 500 per cent, yet, because that sector of the economy expanded so rapidly, women in 1900 still made up no more than 19 per cent of the total work force in manufacturing.

Important as women may have been in manufacturing, that was not the occupational category that engaged most women. Throughout the 19th century the single largest occupation of women was domestic service. In 1850 there were more women domestic servants than women in teaching and manufacturing combined. And this was so even though domestic service, as the Cohoes newspaper pointed out, was shunned like the plague by most women.

Again and again throughout the 19th century, writers on the subject of women's work tried to convince girls and young women that domestic service was not only a good way to earn money but also a way to stay within the home environment and prepare for eventual marriage. Helen Campbell, one of the best known of women economists of the late 19th century, told of the survey of 600 women workers who were asked why they did not become domestic servants. Almost invariably they listed "loss of freedom" as their reason. "This is as dear to women as to men," one woman told the interviewer, "although we don't get so much of it." Factory work might be hard, but unlike domestic service it lasted only a specified number of hours each day. Service, another woman worker said, offered "hurts to self-respect. One thing that makes housework unpleasant—chamberwork, for instance, and waiting on table—is that it is a kind of personal service, one human being waiting on another. The very thing you would do without a thought in your own home for your own family seems menial when it is demanded by a stranger." As the Cohoes newspaper writer had noted earlier, many girls disliked the menial character of service. "The very words 'service' and 'servant' are hateful," one girl told Helen Campbell. "It is all well enough to talk about service being divine, but that is not the way the world looks at it." Moreover, the young women workers complained that their lives were not their own as servants, that tasks were piled upon them without warning and that their friends were not welcome to visit at their places of service.[14] In short, domestic service was *too* much like home for young women; those intangibles they hoped to gain from working—independence and freedom—as well as income, were largely absent from domestic service.

When this widespread hostility among women to domestic service is combined with the knowledge that the wages for such work were invariably inferior to those for factory work, the large number of women who worked as domestic servants throughout the century takes on a special meaning. It suggests how severely limited the opportunities for women were. (And the women concerned were not only the foreign-born or blacks. In 1900 over a million women were counted in the census of that year as servants and waitresses, of whom 26 per cent were native whites of native white parents; another 19.2 per cent were native whites of foreign-born parents. About 27 per cent were blacks, and 28 per cent were foreign-born.) The large number of domestic servants also explains why the wages for women in all branches of the economy were lower than for men. There simply were more women seeking work than there were jobs for them outside domestic service. The reason for this will appear as we go along, for it had to do with more than simply the structure of the economy or the attitudes of employers.

Although the opening of new work opportunities for women may not have kept pace with the demand, the expansion of jobs for women during the 19th century was continuous. One source of these new opportunities was power-driven machinery, which reduced the need for heavy physical labor. Of equal importance as a source of jobs for women was the growth of cities. In fact, an important category of women's employment, like domestic service, was clearly the result of urban growth; cities were where the servants were wanted and employed. And after 1830 the number of urban dwellers shot up. Between 1830 and 1870, for instance, the urban population increased at the rate of 19 per cent each and every year on the average! Cities, especially larger ones, with their diversity of economic activities, generally provided a variety of jobs for women. In 1900, for example, almost 47 per cent of single women were in the labor force in cities of 50,000 or more, as compared with slightly over 25 per cent in the smaller cities of the country. Significantly, there were no such comparable differences between the two kinds of cities among the proportions of married, widowed, or divorced in the female working force.[15]

The number of women employed in manufacturing or domestic service, of course, only tells part of the story. A much more useful and meaningful statistical approach to the question of work in the lives of women is the proportion of all women who worked outside the home. In 1860 only about 10 per cent of white women ten years of age or older were engaged in paid labor. (At that date about 80 per cent of black women were working, principally as slaves in the southern states.) The figure for white women can be put another way, that is, that working women constituted about 10.2 per cent of the total American free labor force; once again, slave labor is not included. These figures, simply because they are general, conceal the wide variations in the proportion of working women among native and immigrant women and between women from middle- and lower-class families. As we have seen already, Irish girls were very highly represented in cotton textile factories and other kinds of work in towns like Cohoes and Poughkeepsie, New York. In Pittsburgh in 1880, one study has shown, 25 per cent of Irish girls between 15 and 19 years of age were working, as compared with fewer than 10 per cent of the native girls of the same age or 20 per cent of the German girls.

Native white girls often found that working was out of the question socially if economic necessity did not compel it. "I think a girl's life at my age [21] isn't the most pleasant by any means," wrote Amelia Lee Jackson, daughter in a well-to-do Boston family in the early 19th century; "she is in the most unsettled state: a young man can occupy himself with his business, and look forward to his life and prospects, but all we have to do is to pass our time agreeably to ourselves. I think everyone likes to feel the *necessity* of doing something, and I confess that I have sometimes wished I could be poor to have the pleasure of exerting myself." A young woman like Molly Dorsey, who was not wealthy but yet sufficiently above the necessity of working to avoid domestic service, complained, too, that the work she was able to do was boring, if only because it was done at home. At a time when she was sewing for a married woman in order to bring in some income to her family, she wrote in her diary, "I do often wish that I might be something more than a mere machine. There is something dull in sitting here day by day, planning this garment and making that, but it seems to be my destiny just now. There does not seem to be much that a girl can do" in a small town like Nebraska City in the 1850s, she concluded.[16]

The incidence of work outside the home varied not only with class and nativity; it also varied with marital state. Unlike men, women usually left the work force when they married. Thus there might be a substantial number of young women working prior to age twenty, but when the total number of women over age ten are counted, the proportion of working women is surprisingly low, being no more than 10 per cent in 1860. We shall return later to the question of the single versus the married working woman; here it is enough to notice that virtually none of the white women employed in manufacturing and domestic service or any other kind of work for that matter were married. Once this demographic fact is recognized, the paradox of the 1830s and 1840s to which Gerda Lerner has pointed dissolves. She has argued that "the slogan 'woman's place is in the home' " arose just at the time "when increasing numbers of poorer women *left* their homes to become factory workers," while the ladies stayed behind in the home.[17] It is true that during the 1830s, as we have seen in previous chapters, the cult of the family and the associated special role of women in the family were widely accepted. The modern family, as we have been referring to it in this book, certainly was flourishing during the years when women were moving into urban and factory work. But what Lerner and others who follow her interpretation ignore is that the women who were working, whether they were middle class or poor, were not married women—except for a very small number of free Negro women. The female workers who operated the machines, sold the goods, and performed the services in mid-19th-century America were overwhelmingly single women, waiting, and usually planning to be married. And generally when they did marry they, too, followed the cult of domesticity, that is, confined themselves to the task of child-rearing and housekeeping.

The economic basis of the cult of domesticity in the 19th century was that a married woman usually did not have to work for money, that she could live on her husband's wages if he was a city dweller, or on his income if he was a farmer. In neither case, however, did that mean that women did not work. Except for the very few rich, the great majority of married women worked hard at house maintenance and child-rearing. In characterizing the cult of the lady, Gerda Lerner has written that "idleness, once a disgrace in the eyes of society, had become a status symbol" in the new era of the 1840s. If it did, it did so for only a tiny fraction of women. It is true that the average middle-class wife and mother did not work as hard as the farm wife or the woman in the frontier family, but that was precisely why many women found the new companionate family of the city with its narrower array of home tasks for women an improvement. It is also why married women thought the ideal of a husband-companion, with themselves as the moral guardian of the family and the moral precep- tor of the children, desirable, even if, as the century wore on, increasing numbers of women did not find that situation totally satisfactory or per- sonally fulfilling. In fact, it was just because they did not that so many middle-class women formed or joined organizations and activities outside the home. As early as 1838, Sarah Grimké, abolitionist and feminist, called attention to how industry was helping to remove some of the labor a more primitive economy had imposed on women. "When all manufactures were domestic," she wrote in her *Letters on Equality,* "then the domestic func- tion might well consume all the time of a very able-headed woman. But nowadays . . . when so much of woman's work is done by the butcher and the baker, by the tailor, and the cook, and the gas-maker . . . you see how much of woman's time is left for other functions." [18] Although women's time free from domestic duties may have been increasing as the economy advanced, few married women joined the work force. And since married women of the working class did not seek employment either, it is clear that the steady increase in the number of women in the labor force throughout the 19th century depended almost entirely upon single women.

By the opening of the 20th century, the revolution in women's partici- pation in the economy that had begun in the 1820s had been completed in its broadest outlines. Historian William O'Neill has rightly called it "the most significant event in the modern history of women." [19] Women's eco- nomic opportunities were certainly not equal to those of men, neither in level of wages nor in access to positions of power or prestige. Yet by that date some women had moved into virtually all professions, if only tokenly, and into the great majority of occupations. In 1910, for example, women constituted almost a quarter of all workers in non-agricultural jobs, and in 1920 women were represented in all but thirty-five of the 572 occupa- tional classifications listed by the census. It is true that most women work- ers were concentrated in a fairly narrow range of occupations in manufac- turing, most of which had some relation to the kind of work they had done in the home, such as textiles or clothing manufacturing. But that is not the full story. Thousands of women worked in industries quite far re- moved from the traditional work of women. Among these were the more than 5000 in 1880 who worked in cigar factories, or the 21,000 women shoe and book-binding workers, or the 7000 employed in the making of boxes. On the other hand, it is worth noticing that several occupations that might have been thought to have been once in the home, like baking, cheese-making, and brewing, were, by the 1880s, almost entirely in the hands of male workers.

Still it is worth recognizing that most women who worked at the end of the 19th century were not employed in factories at all. In 1880, for example, four occupational categories—teachers; servants and laundresses; clerks and salespeople; and dressmakers, milliners, and seamstresses—accounted for four-fifths of all women engaged in non-farm employment. Of the categories the largest by far was servants and laundresses, as it would be well into the 20th century. In 1880 about 45 per cent of all gainfully employed women were engaged in what the census bureau termed domestic and personal service; in 1900 the proportion was no lower than 40 per cent. Manufacturing was the second largest category of working women; in 1880 and 1900 the proportion was slightly less than one-fourth of the total. If the picture of women's work in manufacturing is one in which there is a wide dispersion among the occupations, but a concentration of most women in a relatively few occupations, the statistical portrait of women in the professions is no different.[20]

Perhaps the most visible female profession in the 19th century was writing. Nothing has given that form of women's work more notoriety or public recognition than Nathaniel Hawthorne's famous outburst in 1855. "America is wholly given over to a damned mob of scribbling women," he wrote his publisher, "and, I should have no chance of success while the public taste is occupied with their trash."[21] The success of the women writers against whom Hawthorne railed was intimately connected to the development of the modern family. Women at home in the cities and with responsibilities confined largely to child-rearing and home maintenance had not only the necessary leisure but a new and imperious inducement to read, to learn more about rearing children, keeping a home, and catering to a husband. One measure of the interest women now took in learning about their domestic role was that between 1784 and 1860 at least one hundred magazines, most of which were devoted to women's interests, were founded. After 1830 the pace increased, thanks to improvements in printing that permitted cheaper and more frequent publication. Between 1830 and 1850, some 1150 novels by American authors alone were published in the United States. A large proportion of the authors and the readers were women; about one-third of all American novels published before 1820 were written by women. For it was the women of the middle-class family who bought and read the magazines and the novels by the "damned scribbling women." The magazine stories and novels, as a result, were primarily domestic in plot and character, that is, concerned with the home and women's part in it. These highly sentimental and didactic novels held great attraction for their readers.

Generally, the women who wrote and the women who read these admittedly third- or fourth-rate novels have not received much sympathy either from historians or literary critics. Their soft sentimentality has irritated the tastes of modern readers. Indeed, Ann Douglas in her recent *The Feminization of American Culture* has associated those women writers with the ministers of the first half of the 19th century and derided them both as the twin sources of modern American cultural anti-intellectualism. That these novels lacked intellectual rigor or depth no one can deny. But a closer scrutiny of the novels provides a somewhat different insight into the character and meaning of the women writers and their audience of urban, middle-class, white women.

Some years ago Helen Papashvily, and more recently, Sarah Lemmon, Mary Kelley, and Nina Baym have pointed out that the novels of E.D.E.N. Southworth, Caroline Hentz, Maria McIntosh, Amanda Douglas, Catharine Sedgwick, and Augusta Evans are not as devoid of insight into the minds of women as their Victorian sentimentality has led some to believe. It is true that the women in these novels are portrayed at the outset as submissive wives and that not infrequently the heroine is specifically said to be "not a disciple or pupil of Mary Wollstonecraft" or not a woman of spirit. She was, instead, an old-fashioned wife "who obeyed her husband." Yet, after immersing herself in these novels, Nina Baym refers to them as "woman's fiction," by which she means they were "written by women, addressed to women, and tell one particular story about women. They chronicle the 'trials and triumphs' . . . of a heroine, who, beset with hardships, finds within herself the qualities of intelligence, will, resourcefulness, and courage sufficient to overcome them." Indeed, Baym goes on to speak of these novels as displaying a quite overt, if 19th-century "feminism constrained by certain other types of belief that are less operative today." Men clearly play a less significant role than women in the lives of the heroines. "The traditional rescuing function of the lover is denied him," Baym notes. Elopement usually ends in a worse tyranny for the woman. In the fourteen novels of the 1850s which she studied, Baym "found only one thoroughly good man. . . . Most are of limited intelligence and overwhelming vanity. . . . The major repeated story is that of the struggle of the good woman against the oppression and cruelties, covert and blatant, of men."

In Amanda Douglas's *Out of the Wreck* the mistreated wife even sets forth to her mother-in-law why submission to a cruel husband is not to be endured and why abandoning him is justified. "It may be heresy, but I begin to think one law binding upon both. I cannot understand why I must live a miserable, distasteful life of privation to be shut out of all the society for which my early training fitted me, to be shunned like a moral leper when the crime is his. I think I have a right . . . to rescue myself and my children." And once on her own, she did prosper.[22] In short, it is quite possible that one of the sources of the popularity of these novels among women was not only their sentimentality but their offering, vicariously, a style of life that fitted the ideal of a strong woman in the family, one as competent in her personality as the man. In short, these novels not only spoke to the aspirations of many married women but reflected a reality of their lives. In the highly popular *Capitola* of E.D.E.N. Southworth one has a character who seemed to offer an aspiration as well. For Capitola was a young woman so dashing in manner and style as to be almost a young man. She dueled with men, outwitted, and outran them; she was, in short, a "hero." In 1859 *Capitola* rivaled *A Tale of Two Cities* in sales in the United States. There was, in short, more recognition of women's competence and influence in the home in these novels than has met the eye of Ann Douglas or Nathaniel Hawthorne.

That a relatively large number of women were writers reflected an important fact about professional careers for women, especially in mid-19th-century America. Not many professions were open to women. One woman writer referred to the "female professions" as "the instruction of youth; painting or art; literature; and the vocation of public entertainment— including actresses, singers, musicians and the like."[23] Writing lent itself to women because it permitted rather flexible hours, or at least the chance to be at home, important if the writer was a married woman, like Harriet Beecher Stowe, with several children. It was also a profession that a woman suddenly left a widow could enter upon without special training, providing, of course, she had some talent. Several of the women writers mentioned earlier were widows or the prime supporters of their families.

The profession that counted by far the most women in the 19th century was teaching. In 1870, for example, teachers made up 90 per cent of all professional women. At the time of the Civil War the typical teacher in American schools was already a woman, though that had not been true

twenty-five years before. In Massachusetts as early as 1834, women constituted 56 per cent of all teachers; by 1860 the proportion was 78 per
cent. By the end of the century fully three-quarters of all of the nation's
teachers were women.

The principal reason women were concentrated so heavily in teaching
was because it was so low paying. Women were able to replace men
because they would accept lower wages, even for the same work. As in
other kinds of work by women, the vast proprotion of women teachers
were single and young. In short, one of the first, if not the first, occupations
in which the practice of paying women less than men for the same work
got established was the profession of teaching. As we shall see in a subsequent chapter, differential pay for women derived, at least in part,
from the different kinds of jobs performed by the two sexes. But in teaching the jobs were the same yet the wages of women were invariably lower
than those of men.

Teaching attracted women because it was a socially acceptable job, even
in the beginning of the 19th century. It was, after all, an extension of
woman's traditional work as the rearer of children. As Catharine Beecher,
herself a dedicated teacher and writer of advice books, contended in 1853,
"it is ordained by infinite wisdom that, as in the family, so in the social
state, the interests of young children and of women are one and the same."
She recommended teaching as a way in which young women could prepare
themselves for "the great purpose of a woman's life—the happy superin-
tendence of a family." Although she was neither a feminist nor a suffragist,
Beecher did not hesitate to urge young women to take jobs as teachers.
Even in the conservative antebellum South, it was possible for a young
woman of good family to teach and to travel some distance to do it. When
a young woman of twenty-two planned to leave her home in Georgia to
teach at a plantation in Alabama in 1861, her grandmother was worried,
but there was no question that the young woman would go. "Sophie
seemed anxious to try and do something for herself," the grandmother
wrote to a relative, "and I consented to let her go, although it cost me
many bitter pangs and tears to have my poor child go so far from home to
teach." [24] After the Civil War teaching became a widely recognized occupation for southern women.

Recent research suggests that teaching was more important as an occupation in the lives of women than the number of women teachers at any
given time might suggest. A study of teachers in Massachusetts before
1860 asked how many white women between 15 and 60 years of age

worked as teachers at any specific time. The answer was only about 2 per cent of all working women. But when the study asked how many women worked at one time or another in the course of their lives as teachers, then the figure rose dramatically to 20 per cent. At this point there is no way of knowing whether Massachusetts was typical of other states or not. Nor should it be assumed that teachers came only from middle-class families. The Griffens in their study of Poughkeepsie, New York, for example, found that girls from working-class families were well represented among teachers. And a study made in 1911 showed that the father of the average woman teacher earned about $800 a year, a wage that placed him among skilled workers or a successful farmer rather than in the middle class.[25]

Women's entrance into the more prestigious—and better paying— professions of medicine and law was less easy and acceptable to men. Elizabeth Blackwell had to spend countless hours and many bottles of ink making inquiries and justifications for entrance into medical school in the 1840s. When Harvard Medical school admitted women in 1850, the male students compelled a reversal on the grounds that women would cause them to lose status, especially since blacks (another low-prestige group) had been admitted only shortly before. And as late as 1875 a well-known Harvard physician, Horatio Storer, objected to women medical students on the ground that "there is this inherent quality in their sex, month to month in each woman, that unfits her from taking those responsibilities which are to control questions often of life and death."[26]

Yet by the second half of the 19th century, as Dr. Mary Putnam Jacobi wrote in 1891, the question of women's admission to medical practice had been settled. At that date some 115 women had been admitted to medical societies, though women were not always able to practice in hospitals other than women's institutions. Even a small town like Poughkeepsie in 1870 counted three women physicians. In 1880 the U.S. census listed almost 2500 women physicians and surgeons, about 2.8 per cent of the nation's total. Not all of these, of course, any more than all of the men, were university trained. In fact, as late as the 1920s, a third of all medical schools still barred women.

The admission of women into law practice was considerably more delayed than into medicine, perhaps because medicine, like teaching, seemed to have some connection with woman's traditional role in the home, while the law had none. In any event, the first woman allowed to practice law in the United States was Arabella Mansfield of Iowa in 1869. She had been trained by her lawyer husband and was admitted to the bar by a liberal-minded judge who ignored the law which confined legal practice to "white male citizens." Ironically enough, that same year, Myra Bradwell, probably the best-known and most competent legal mind among women in the country—she was the editor of a prestigious legal journal—was denied admission to the bar in Illinois. However, three years later, in 1872, the Illinois legislature opened all professions to women. By 1881 there were 56 women lawyers in the country, thirty-one of whom had graduated from law school, not infrequently after a court fight to gain admission. In 1891 the number was up to 200, yet until well into the 20th century some law schools continued to exclude women. In short, women were hardly on an equal footing within the profession, not even in regard to admissions. But any barriers that had once absolutely kept all women from the professions had been breached beyond restoration.

The most galling discrimination against women, however, was not the limitations upon their entrance into, or practice of a profession, however severe these were, but the low pay women invariably received for their work. The average factory girl at the end of the 19th century earned above five or six dollars for a 60-hour week. These were the wages, incidentally, of an experienced, not a beginning, worker. At the same time an unskilled male manual laborer—the lowest level of male work—was earning on the average eight dollars a week. Domestic servants, four-fifths of whom were women and the largest single category of women workers, earned in 1900 between two and five dollars a week, and their work week could reach 72 hours, or 12 hours a day. Since women were concentrated in the unskilled or lesser skilled jobs, their wages were not only lower than men's on the average but were typically only half those of men. A study of some 150,000 employees made by the U.S. Bureau of Labor in the mid-1890s found only 800 cases where men and women were employed at roughly the same jobs. Yet in 600 of those 800 cases, where the work was pretty much the same, women's wages were still lower than men's, usually by a third.

The conditions under which women worked in the 19th and early 20th century were hardly ideal. Hours were long, wages were often inadequate for a comfortable life, ventilation, lighting, and safety precautions were usually poor, and, to make matters even less acceptable, most working women knew that they received lower wages than men. Withal there was less dissatisfaction from these objective facts than one would have expected. And the principal reason was also the most significant fact about working women throughout the 19th century and the first half of the 20th.

That is, that the overwhelming majority of white working women were young and single. Work outside the home was largely a temporary phenomenon in the lives of women. They abandoned it when they married.

The pattern runs all through the 19th century. Out of some thousand women employed at the Lawrence Corporation textile mills in Massachusetts in 1830, only thirty were married or widowed. In 1889, Carroll Wright, the head of the U.S. Bureau of Labor, made a thorough study of some 15,000 working women in 22 cities across the nation. He deliberately excluded from the survey textile workers and professional and semiprofessional women. Significantly, the interviewers were themselves women, thus enhancing the likelihood of accurate answers from the working women they questioned. Out of the 15,000 only 4.3 per cent were married and 5.6 per cent widowed, thus leaving 90 per cent single. Wright properly concluded that "the working women in our great cities are practically girls," for the study found that the modal age of the women was 18.[27] The average age at which these working girls began employment was 15 years and 4 months. About three-quarters of the women fell into the age group 14–25, suggesting that most of the women worked between seven and eight years before marrying. Although 81 per cent of the women were native-born, 91 per cent of those native women had fathers who had been born abroad. In short, young women workers were recruited at the end of the 19th century largely from immigrant families. The great proportion of them—86 per cent—still lived at home, and three-quarters of them either paid board or contributed their earnings to the domestic budget. These working women testified to the family character of work in the immigrant family, for one way in which the immigrant family, with a low-paid primary worker, was able to survive was by sending sons and daughters out to work. At the same time, many of the daughters must have seen marriage as a welcome release from the family and the obligation to help with its financial support.

On the other hand, simply because working women generally viewed their work as temporary, something that would be abandoned with marriage, they accepted wages and conditions few men could afford to. Being secondary workers in the family they were not impelled to seek more wages or better hours, as a father, or even a younger brother who would be working for the rest of his life, would be inclined to.[28]

A young woman's practice of leaving work when she married continued well into the 20th century. In 1890, for instance, amost 88 per cent of women working in nonagricultural jobs were single, widowed, or divorced; in 1920 the proportion had fallen only to 78 per cent. And in 1920, as earlier, most of the single women were living at home, presumably contributing to the family income. A study of eleven large cities in 1920 found that over 80 per cent of all working women, not counting live-in servants, lived at home.

Another way of looking at the relationship between marriage and work for women is to ask what proportion of married women were employed outside the home. Studies of individual 19th-century communities show that very few were. The Griffens found that in 1860 in Poughkeepsie, New York, 10 per cent of the native wives worked, while the figure for the Irish wives, despite the fact that a large proportion of their daughters were employed, was only 6 per cent. No more than 2 per cent of German wives worked. By 1880 the proportion was below 4 per cent for all groups, except for blacks. (This exception for black women will be discussed at greater length later in this chapter.) A study of Pittsburgh in 1880 found no more than 1 per cent of married native or immigrant wives working outside the home for pay. And at the turn of the century, only 2 per cent of Italian wives living in Buffalo, New York, went out to work. A sample of households drawn from the census in 1870 and 1880 for seven southern cities showed only a slightly different pattern. Only 4 per cent of married white women were working in 1870, and 7.3 per cent in 1880.

The picture is even more striking on the national level. In 1900, according to a census study, less than 4 per cent of married white women, regardless of nativity, worked outside the home. (For native white wives with native parents the proportion was 3 per cent; for native white wives with foreign-born parents the figure was 3.1 per cent; and for white foreign-born wives the ratio was 3.6 per cent.) Twenty years later the proportions had doubled, but for all three groups they were still low: 6.3 per cent of married native white women and 7.2 per cent of foreign-born wives were in the work force in 1920. (The proportion of black wives who were paid wages in that year was 32.5 per cent; they constituted more than a third of all working wives in the country.) The fact is that even as late as 1940 the proportion of white married women who worked outside the home was not greater than 12 per cent of the total.

Just because the typical woman worker in the 19th century was a young woman who would soon marry and leave the work force, Lucy Larcom, the most famous of the so-called Lowell girls, took a friend to task. "Don't you think it is getting a little tiresome, this *posing* as factory girls of the olden time?" she wrote toward the end of her life. "It is very much like politicians boasting of carrying their dinners in a tin pail in their youth. What if they did? . . . I am proud to be a working-woman, as I always have been; but that special occupation was temporary, and not the business of our lives, we all knew. . . ." It so happened that Lucy Larcom did not marry, but most of the factory girls with whom she had worked did. Lucy Larcom was really pointing to the fundamental fact of women's work-aspirations in the 19th century: If a woman wanted a career she had to forgo marriage. One measure of the fact was that in 1890 more than half of women doctors were single; an additional one-fifth were widowed or divorced, so that only about a quarter were living with husbands. A sample of 880 prominent women, mainly professional women, taken in 1913 showed that only a bare majority of them were married and less than half of those were mothers. Three-quarters of all women who earned Ph.D.s between 1877 and 1924 remained unmarried. And the census in 1920 revealed that only 12 per cent of all professional women were married.[29]

Because many professional women had more flexible schedules and sufficient income for domestic help and child care, the proportion of married women who worked as professionals was far above that for ordinary working women. As one working woman said about another woman her age, "she must be married, because she don't work."[30] Even in slum districts few married women were employed outside the home. A study made in 1893 in New York, Baltimore, Chicago, and Philadelphia showed that only 5 per cent of the New York wives were employed, and that was the highest proportion among the four cities.

The primary reason, of course, why married women, even those who were poor, did not hold an outside job was that women were the child-rearers. As Maria Van Vorst pointed out in 1903, in the course of her study on working women, "in those cases where the woman continues to work after marriage, she chooses invariably a kind of occupation which is inconsistent with child-bearing," that is, because the woman did not want children. Vorst made that point because she feared the effect women's working had upon the birth rate, but her generalization was sound, nonetheless. Even women who had a career often gave it up when they married because they thought it was not proper or possible for a woman to rear a child and pursue a job at the same time. Augusta Lewis, to take an extreme example, had been a leader among the women typesetters in the 1860s, becoming in time secretary of the International Union. But when she married in 1871 she dropped out of labor organizing entirely. (Ultimately, she bore six children and was active in works of charity.) Another union leader was Leonora Barry, a widow. She was an exceptionally successful organizer for the Knights of Labor in the 1880s, but when she married in 1890 for the second time, she resigned for good from the Knights. And when Alice Freeman, president of Wellesley College, married Professor George Palmer of Harvard in 1886, she resigned her position, too. Historian Eleanor Flexner, in explaining Leonora Barry's resignation, asserted that Barry had always thought that woman's place was in the home. And, in a sense, that was the heart of the matter. "Around the turn of the century," historian Robert Smuts observed, "when a married woman worked, it was usually a sign that something had gone wrong." Her husband was absent, crippled, or incompetent.

This attitude did not prevent married women from working under special circumstances or for brief periods early in their marriage. Charlena Anderson, whom we met in the first chapter, for example, gained the approval of her husband to work while he was away in Germany studying. "It would indeed be grand to get a place in a Normal School to teach German," he wrote in 1876, "even if you did not earn much the first year." His primary worry was that such work might impair her health. She, in turn, recognized that earning money to help him complete his studies was as temporary as it was useful. "You need not feel that you are a burden to all of us [by which she meant her parents, for she had no children at that point] . . . We had as soon loan our money to you as to anyone. I know I shall get mine again with good interest, won't I? You may say I have loaned you nothing, very true." Yet, when he returned to the United States and took a job, and they had children, Charlena gave up her work, just as most working women would upon marrying.[31]

Even for someone like Mary Hallock Foote, whose efforts as artist and writer were professionally and financially successful, the impetus to her working outside the home was necessity as much as internal drive. In 1888 she told her confidante Helena that she was now cooking along with her Chinese cook and enjoying it. "It is what I ought to have done long ago, intead of writing stories." A year later she returned to the subject, noting how much she had been enjoying reading Tolstoy and other writers. "I think I never should have written at all if I had not begun under money pressure and at a time I could not spend hours reading *great books.*" As a writer herself, with all the loneliness and self-doubt that the occupation entailed, she could well understand, she went on, why Tolstoy took pleasure in making shoes—"to do something that you know is needed and is as honestly and faithfully done must be very restful after beating the air in an effort to do something which no one really wants or would miss if it were never accomplished" Yet, once she was engaged upon her writing, "it is impossible not to find pleasure in doing one's best." In fact, in time she well recognized that there might be a real conflict within her and within Helena as well. "How do you *bear* it—Helena, my dear girl," she wrote in 1888, "—that constant thwarting and suppression of that side of your Nature, so strong and imperative really and so hidden, except in your rare work, when you have the time to work," for unlike Mary, Helena was not a published writer of note.

Five years later, when the need for income, because of her husband's incapacity increased, Mary Foote reopened the subject: "in the old days I used to regret my work as subsidiary to Arthur's—but alas, who knows when an engineer, who has spent ten years on his big stake in Idaho and lost it, may ever get in line again?" As a result, she was now intent on "making my work count as such as it can with the public. Hence my late recklessness about publicity. I am no longer the 'snob' I used to be about my work. I will never do less than my *best in the work itself,* but I am willing to caper and prance in the columns of personalities and show my middle aged visage like the rest of us, if it will bring in more dollars to my beloveds."

But the limits of what she would do to make money were quickly reached. When she was offered a fee of $100 for each of six talks "in select houses," she found the offer unacceptable, even though she admitted the offer was intended as a compliment. "There are all manner of ways for women to make money nowadays," she told Helena, "but surely this must be one of the hardest, and most trying. . . . Call me a snob if you will—to me it does not seem ladylike."[32] She was especially concerned about what her husband and children would say if she lectured. Certainly there were married women who did lecture and took on jobs that Mary Foote would have considered unladylike or embarrassing to husband and children. And there were married women physicians, lawyers, and educators who worked from choice rather than sheer necessity, but all of these women were the exceptions that proved the rule during the 19th century.

To married women, particularly those of working-class background and expectations, work outside the home was undesirable for at least two reasons. One was that such employment meant doing *two* difficult tasks; house maintenance and child-rearing on the one hand and filling the outside job on the other. The second objection was that most, if not all of the work available to women of the working class was monotonous, low paid, and without much future. Measured against that alternative, staying at home to care for children and husband, and keep a house, however arduous those tasks might be, had distinct advantages. Indeed, for most working-class young women, marriage must have been literally an excape from drudgery and monotony while offering at least the possibility that the life of wife and mother would bring love, companionship, and the joy of children. As Horace Greeley chauvinistically editorialized to members of the Typographical Union in 1854, when they attacked him for hiring women typesetters, "marry them, provide good homes, and earn means of living comfortably, and we'll warrant them never to annoy you thereafter by insisting on spending their days at the printing office setting type." [33] Marriage also meant escape from the control of parents. A husband might turn out to be as great a tyrant as a father, but at least he had been chosen, and a sensible young woman could exercise her intelligence on the choice. In any event, staying on the job usually meant that there would be little improvement in the character of work, and the possibility of winning a life-companion and having children would surely be foreclosed.

Simply because work for an educated woman intent upon a career was so different in content from that open to working-class women, there were conflicting differences in outlook between those women who sought to work with working-class women in organizations like the Women's Trade Union League or Consumers' League. As historian Nancy Shrom Dye has pointed out,[34] to the middle-class women work was often seen as liberating, but they did not recognize that for working-class women work was part of a family economic obligation and often did not bring freedom or independence. Moreover, it was often quite uninteresting, spiritually deadening, and perhaps rigorous and mechanical, especially when compared with the varied, if admittedly unending pre-industrial style of work of the home.

Perhaps the strongest evidence for the rule that the only married women who worked in the 19th century were those who were compelled to by economic necessity is the experience of black women. Throughout the late 19th and well into the 20th century, black married women participated in the work force at a rate several times that of white married women. During slavery, black women had been considered a part of the labor force, and perhaps as many as 90 to 95 per cent of black women slaves above the age of sixteen worked in the fields. Almost immediately after emancipation that proportion fell sharply as the legal coercive power of the masters was withdrawn. Economists Roger Ransom and Richard Sutch estimate that by the 1870s only a half to two-thirds of black women over 16 were working in agriculture, a drop of between 30 to 40 percentage points since slavery days.[35] Even after that drop, however, black women worked in greater proportions than white women. In 1880, for example, about 50 per cent of black women were in the labor force as compared with less than 15 per cent of white women. These figures are for women in general, not married women, but since most women of both races were married, the figures measure in broad terms the difference in the patterns. Studies of working women in particular cities have reported high proportions of black married women in the work force after emancipation. In New Orleans in the 1880s about 30 per cent of black wives worked; in Cambridge, Massachusetts, Nashville, Tennessee, and Atlanta, Georgia, in 1896, the proportions of black wives who worked ranged from 44 to 65 per cent, as against only 15 per cent of wives of Italian immigrants in Chicago.[36]

The high proportion of black wives in the work force even after emancipation is to be explained largely by the greater earnings of white families. Black women, whether married or single, had to work to supplement the lower earnings of husbands and fathers. What they worked at, however, happened also to be the lowest-paying occupations, principally washing clothes, domestic service, and agricultural labor. The Griffens in their study of Poughkeepsie, for instance, reported that 25 per cent of black women workers, regardless of marital status, in 1860 could be located in subsequent censuses as against only 12 and 14 per cent for other ethnic groups. This suggests that black women stayed longer in the work force or simply had so little mobility that they did not have as much opportunity to leave as white women. The Griffens also found that half of all black women held jobs in Poughkeepsie in 1880.

The propensity of black women to be in the work force to a greater degree than either immigrant or native women is evident in the census figures of 1900. That year slightly less than 15 per cent of white native women over 15 years of age were in the work force; 25 per cent of native white females with foreign-born parents and 19 per cent of foreign-born white women were working. These figures are to be compared with the 43 per cent of black women who were employed. In sum, black women were about twice as likely to work as white women, even if those white women were immigrants.

If the comparison is made by age groups, two additional measures of the greater participation of black women in work become evident, as perusal of the following table makes clear.

At the earliest age level more black girls went to work than in any of the other three groups; and at the oldest age level—that is, after menopause—over two-fifths of black women were still working though less than 13 per cent of white women were. These figures also remind us that a greater proportion of black wives worked than white wives. In 1900 over a quarter of black married women were in the labor force as compared with less than 4 per cent of all white wives, regardless of nativity. The three largest occupational categories for black wives in 1900 say much about the limited opportunities. The occupations were agricultural labor, domestic service, and laundry work; over 900,000 black women were employed in just these three categories.

Proportion of women employed, by ethnicity and race   1900 (in percentages)

Ages	Women of native parents	Women of foreign parents	Foreign-born women	Negro women
10–15	5.7	7.9	20.3	30.6
44–54	11.5	12.8	11.7	42.2

Source: *Census of 1900*, "Occupations," Special Reports, p. cxviii.

The usual explanation for the striking difference in the participation rates of white and black wives has been the lower income of black families. Recently, however, several studies of 19th- and 20th-century black women workers have offered additional explanations.[37] The principal reason for introducing other explanations is that, when family income is held constant for both races, the proportion of black women who work is still much higher than for white women. For example, a study of Italian and black women in 1896 revealed that, when the husbands of both groups of women earned $500 and more in a year, only 7 per cent of the Italian women worked, while around 30 per cent of the black women did. The explanation offered by the author of the study was that the difference might be accounted for by the fear among black women that because of racial discrimination their husbands would not be able to earn enough over a long period and thus the women thought it a form of insurance to be employed themselves, despite adequate incomes from the men. Another economic historian has made the additional suggestion that the propensity of black wives to work even when income from the husband was sufficient derives from their having learned how to combine work and family under the duress of slavery, and they continued to do so in freedom.

What role the slave experience played in bringing black married women into the work force is still not clear, but there is no question that well into the 20th century large numbers of black married women have worked as they did throughout the 19th century, under slavery and freedom alike. For example, in 1920, almost one-third of married black women, who lived with their husbands, were working, as compared with 6.5 per cent of married white women. As in the 19th century, these married black women worked at the lowliest jobs. Four-fifths of black married women were employed as domestic servants, farm laborers, or laundresses; in fact, they constituted more than one-quarter of *all* married women in the work force in 1920. Slightly more than 15 per cent of all married women who worked in 1920 were foreign-born.

Between 1920 and 1940 the trend for married black women moved in a direction opposite from that for married white women. By 1940 the proportion of white married women who worked outside the home was up to 11.9 per cent, a noticeable rise since 1920, but still encompassing only a very small proportion of all white married women in the United States. At that same date, the proportion of black married women who worked was *down* from 1920, suggesting that black women were still trying to get out of the work force and into the home, as they had been attempting to do ever since emancipation. Nonetheless, even in 1940, almost a quarter of black married women—or more than double the rate of married white women at that date—were still in the work force.

The principal conclusion to be drawn from these figures and comparisons is that right down to 1940 the great majority of women, insofar as they could, shaped their lives and their work around their families. It was, after all, the presence of children and husband that made working outside the home for married women difficult, if not impossible. That is why black married women so consistently sought to drop out of the labor force when they could afford to. It was possible for some professional women, or feminists like Elizabeth Cady Stanton, to urge women to assume careers or fill jobs outside the home, but only those women who had domestic servants, grown-up children, or no children could follow that advice, even if they overcame their husbands' and society's opposition. Of course, some women, like Stanton herself, were blessed with a sufficient supply of energy, organizing ability, and drive to take on both home and job.

It was the difficulty of combining the two full-time jobs of home and outside work that accounts for the opposition of even friends of working women to the employment of mothers outside the home. "If circumstances have given a woman a home and children," wrote Edith Lowry in a book published in 1911, which urged women to work, "they always must come first, but this does not mean the woman must do housework if conditions permit the employment of someone to do it," she added. And economist Helen Campbell, who devoted herself to defending the working girl and seeking to improve her lot, offered no argument against those who said the factory destroyed family life when the mother worked. "The employment of married women is fruitful of evil," she wrote in 1893, "and the proportion of these in Massachusetts is 23.8 per cent. Where ever this per cent is high," she warned, "infant mortality is very great." She fully approved an effort by the state of New Jersey to oppose "the employment of mothers of young children outside the home." Earl Barnes, another friend of working women, also cited the bad physical effects on children of working mothers. "Surely the ideal toward which we must work," he wrote in 1912, "is for the mother, during the period when she is bearing and rearing children, to be supported by the father of her children." Barnes, of course, completely supported the idea of young unmarried women working. Even as staunch a supporter of women's rights as John Stuart Mill thought that if married women worked they would be adding a further and unfair burden to their lives, not to mention what that work would subtract from their ability to care for children properly. "It is not," he wrote in the *Subjection of Women,* "a desirable custom that the wife should contribute her labour to the income of the family." It may have some advantages to her, but he thought when a woman married she "makes a choice of the management of a household, and the bringing up of a family, as the first call upon her exertions, during as many years of her life as may be required for the purpose, and that she renounces, not all other objects and occupations, but all which are not consistent with the requirements of this." And as late as 1964 the Women's Bureau officially announced that it was not the policy of the Bureau "to encourage married women and mothers of young children to seek employment outside the home. Home and children are considered married women's most important responsibilities."[38]

The implications of women's withdrawal from the labor force upon marriage were spelled out by Helen Marot, the executive secretary of the Trade Union League of New York, in 1913. "No one expects a woman to take her wage-earning seriously, or to consider it as a future occupation," she wrote quite accurately. "If she is a wage-earning wife or daughter, she is expected to change her work to suit home conditions and demands, which are seldom changed to suit her work. This attitude toward women wage earners is more serious in its effects on wages and her interest in the problems of her fellow workers than is the actual bearing of children," she concluded.[39]

A measure of the significance of the wife's withdrawal from the work force upon marriage is evident in the ways some wives sought to make up for their forgone income. One way was to take on so-called home work, either of the needle-trade variety, as many widows with small children, and poverty-stricken wives had to do, or some kind of service, such as washing, or running employment agencies. In 1902, for instance, two-thirds of the employment offices in big cities like New York, Boston, and Chicago were run by women in their homes. Another way married women undertook to contribute to family income without having to change family routine was to produce staples in their own homes. A U.S. Bureau of Labor study for 1889–92 of some 7000 working-class families reported that less than half of them bought bread, but almost all of them bought flour, an average of 1000 pounds of flour each year, from which presumably they baked the family supply of bread. Among the same 7000 working-class families, nearly 20 per cent took in boarders, a practice that was yet another way the working-class wife might help to support the family budget while staying at home.

All studies of communities in 19th-century America reported the prominence of boarding as a part of the life of families. The Griffens found that in Poughkeepsie at least 10 per cent of wives, regardless of ethnic background, took in boarders in 1880; Kleinberg reported that in Pittsburgh that same year the proportion was 13.4 per cent. Studies for other communities reported proportions reaching as high as 20 per cent. (In 1930, the figure was down to 11.4 per cent of families; today it is below 5 per cent.) The average figures seem to be between 15 and 20 per cent of families, although Ralph Mann in a study of two gold towns in California in 1860 and 1870 discovered that taking in boarders was very frequent, with perhaps a third or more of the families in the two towns doing so. The practice was sufficiently common in large cities for social workers often to warn against it, especially among immigrant families. The fear was that boarders threatened, by their strangeness, the proper cohesiveness of the family.[40]

Although the acceptance of boarders was related in part, at least, to the need to increase family income, that could not have been the sole reason.

Kleinberg, Mann, and the Griffens all have found that middle- and upper-class families also took in boarders, and sometimes in higher proportions than working-class families. Moreover, some of the merchants in the California gold towns who took in boarders also had servants. In fact, Mann notes that a woman who took in boarders was twice as likely to have servants as a woman who did not! Under such circumstances, a need for increased income could not have been the whole explanation. Mann guessed that in the mining communities in California one purpose besides increased income was to provide a place for a subordinate of the head of the household, such as a clerk or an apprentice. In short, there may have been an element of paternalism or social control operating. John Modell and Tamara Hareven in their study of boarding suggest a somewhat different, but related, explanation for the variations in the proportion of families who took in boarders. They noticed that the number of boarders varied with the life cycle of families. Families were more likely to take in boarders when they had empty rooms, after children had grown up or left, as well as when the family encountered greater expenses and thus would take in boarders for income. They also suggested that taking in boarders was a part of a migrating rather than an immigrating process. Boarders sought out families until they became settled in a city or new area. This would be consistent with the very high proportion of boarders Mann found in the two gold towns in the newly settled West.

On the whole, though, there is no doubt that increased family income was a significant part of the motivation among all those who took in boarders even if it was not the sole or even the primary motive. Modell and Hareven, for example, found that income from boarders was important in household budgets. Thus boarding was a way in which a married woman could stay at home and yet add to the family, though significantly not to her personal income.

In a sense, one might say that the taking in of boarders was a consequence of women's withdrawal from the labor force when they married. If so, it was certainly not the only consequence that flowed from that significant social practice. It also affected how women related to labor unions, how women perceived their lives as workers in cities and on farms, and how professional women accommodated marriage, family, and career. It is to these and other aspects of women's work that we turn in the next chapter.

XVI
Women at Work:
Unions, Farms, and Professions

Although women have been a part of the industrial system in the United States virtually from its inception, their relation to that system has always been different in certain fundamental ways from that of men. From the outset woman's employment was shaped around the family, while man's work, in a real sense, shaped the family. The family moved, lived, and functioned as man's work decreed; woman's employment, on the other hand, ceased when the family began, and from then on, as we have seen, it adjusted to the needs of the family, for the family was a woman's first responsibility.

This fundamental difference between the work of women and men also shaped other aspects of their relation to the expanding industrial world. It affected, as well as complicated, their attitudes and behavior toward trade unions, life on farms, and the professions and careers, to name three important ones. Let us look at each in turn.

The earliest trade unions, which began in the first two decades of the 19th century, were entirely male in membership. But as early as the 1830s women workers showed an interest in joining the male organizations or in forming their own. As a result the trade unions were confronted with the question of whether they should organize women along with men, or exclude them from the trade as well as from the unions. Often the answer depended on whether the women were already in the trade at the time organization was undertaken or whether they were entering an industry already organized. If the former, then women were usually accepted, if only because to exclude them would render the union's wage standard vulnera-

395

ble to competition from women workers. If the latter, then the women were likely to be shunned or excluded. This response, which was exhibited by certain unions even before the Civil War, was displayed also during World War I when male trade unionists welcomed women into the telephone and electrical workers' unions because women had been in those trades before unions had been established. But male welders, at the same time, insisted that women could not be permanent members of their union because in that occupation they would be taking men's jobs.[1]

When men wanted to exclude women from their unions or their trades, they often resorted to the stereotypes of the society, as happened with a leader of the Philadelphia Trades Association in 1835. In asking women to withdraw from the labor market he said that in doing so women would be "free from the performance of that kind of labor which was designed for man alone to perform." For if a woman confined herself to the home, she "will be able to attend to the cultivation of your mind, and impart virtuous instruction to your children. . . . And you who are unmarried can then enjoy those innocent amusements and recreations so essential to health and qualify yourselves for the more sober duties of wives, mothers, and matrons." The same appeal to the sanctity of the family was made at the other end of the century by an official of the Boston Central Labor Union in 1897. "The demand for female labor is an insidious assault upon the home; it is the knife of the assassin, aimed at the family circle," he warned. Even in a community like Cripple Creek, Colorado, where socialist unions dominated the town, the *Daily Press* offered as a measure of a decent wage for a male worker that it be "sufficient to keep his wife and children out of competition with himself."[2]

Despite the opposition of some male workers, women throughout the 19th century joined male unions or formed their own. Usually, however, the female organizations were local, formed principally to deal with specific grievances or causes, such as the wage cuts in 1834 and 1836 at the Lowell mills or the demand for better wages that caused hundreds of women workers to join the great shoemakers' strike at Lynn, Massachusetts, in 1860. The great majority of the national trade unions did not admit women. Between 1860 and 1880, for example, there were more than thirty national trade unions in the country, but only two of them admitted women—printers and cigarmakers. Women shoemakers formed a union of their own, the Daughters of St. Crispin. During its lifetime the organization established some 36 lodges across the country and held national conventions in four different years before it broke up (as did numerous men's labor organizations) in the devastating depression of 1873.

During the second half of the 19th century, as the number of working women continued to increase, organized labor had to take cognizance of them, if only because feminists like Susan B. Anthony were quite prepared to advocate strike-breaking if women were not admitted into unions. From the standpoint of organized labor, however, the mobilizing of women added just one more problem to the general difficulty of trying to establish unions. Throughout most of the history of organized labor in the United States the survival of unions has been precarious. Only a small handful of strong craft unions emerged alive after the depression of 1873, for example. And even a once-strong national labor organization like the Knights of Labor passed out of existence by the end of the century, in part, at least, because it undertook to organize women, blacks, and immigrants. The American Federation of Labor, created from a group of trade or craft unions in 1886, it is true, managed to hang on into the 20th century. But one reason it was able to survive was that it refused to go out of its way to include workers who might weaken its solidarity. For the fact of the matter was that the working class in America, unlike the working classes in more homogeneous European societies, had long been divided by race and ethnicity. In such a social order, to take on the organization of largely unskilled women, most of whom were not going to remain permanently in the work force anyway, bordered on the self-destructive in the eyes of many male union members and officials.

Officially, and according to the pronouncements of its leader Samuel Gompers, the American Federation of Labor favored organizing women, but in practice it was at best ambivalent and often dubious about the proposition. Certainly that was true of the membership. In 1898 and again in 1914, resolutions which advocated confining women to the home and discouraging them from working were seriously debated at conventions of the A. F. of L. Leonora Barry who was a general investigator for the 19th-century Knights of Labor, testified, too, that male workers were generally uncooperative toward women. In 1885 Terence V. Powderly, the leader of the Knights, had to remind the Order that organizing women was one of their founding principles. One early woman labor leader gave voice to the sense of frustration and injustice felt by many women in dealing with male coworkers. Although the women typesetters refused to act as strike-breakers, Augusta Lewis reported in 1871, "when there is no strike if we ask for women in union office we are told by union foremen 'that there are no conveniences for us.' " Yet when the women suffered the same hostility from employers for joining a union that the men did, the women were left without moral or other support from the male unionists. "It is the general opinion of female compositors," she concluded, "that they are more justly treated by what is termed 'rat' foremen, printers, and employers than they are by union men." [3]

During World War I, when women entered new occupations because the men left to join the army and navy, unions and individual rank-and-file members often objected. The locals of the Amalgamated Street and Electric Railway Employees in New York, Chicago, Cleveland, and Detroit in 1917 and 1918 fought the entry of the hundreds of women who became street-car conductors. Male machinists in Baltimore tried to drive off women welders with their torches and the sound of their riveting, usually with success.

To be fair to the male unionists, it needs to be recognized that women workers could be difficult to organize, even though, as has been mentioned, they sometimes organized themselves and did participate in strikes. A study of strikes at the opening of the 20th century reveals that unions made up primarily of women went out on strike much less frequently than male unions. A settlement worker at about the same time told a legislative committee one of the consequences which flowed from the fact that most working women were young women or girls who expected to leave work when they married: "You ask them if they belong to any kind of girls' club and they seem to be very much surprised if you mention any trades union or club for the raising of wages. I said to those two girls," the social worker continued, "Does it ever occur to you that your work ought, economically, to be worth more than ten dollars a week? But they said they didn't know, they were able to get so much; they didn't seem to have thought of the thing at all, in its large aspect." [4] Most of the women workers, of course, were not breadwinners but secondary earners for their families. And even when they were widows or women without husbands present, their very need to work as mothers precluded their having the time to get involved in the work of the union in their non-working hours. In short, women workers often did not have either the same stake in the job and the union the men did or else they did not have the time the men did for such activity. And just because women appeared to be such poor risks as workers, the male-dominated unions displayed little, or at least less, interest in organizing them, especially in an individualistic America, where organizing men was fraught with sufficient risk already. After all, that was why the A. F. of L. found it desirable, if not essential, to seek its members primarily among the skilled workers rather than the unskilled, among the white rather than the black, and among natives rather than immigrants.

The result was that trade unions did not take women seriously as workers. For years the A. F. of L. refused to spend money for organizing low-paid women workers. Not until 1918, for example, did Samuel Gompers agree to the demands of women trade unionists that the national organization hire a full-time woman organizer. And even a union as advanced in its outlook as the Amalgamated Clothing Workers accepted lower wages for women than for men, even though women comprised at least half of the total membership of the union. At Cripple Creek, Colorado, where the town was under the effective control of a powerful miners' union with socialist principles, the average wages of women were lower than men's even when they did the same job.

Nor did the unions take women seriously enough to admit them to leadership positions. No national union, not even those with substantial proportions of women members, included women among its leaders. The radical Industrial Workers of the World, which seemed to appreciate the part that women had played in the winning of the great Lawrence, Massachusetts, strike in 1912, gave women no part in the leadership of the local organizations. And despite the demands of women, the A. F. of L. refused to put two women on the national executive board during World War I. As late as 1940 only one female served on the 24-member executive board of the International Ladies' Garment Workers' Union, at a time when women constituted three-quarters of the membership. Helen Marot summed up the issue in 1914 when she said, "Labor union men are like other men: they are not eager to trust office-holding to women. Labor union women are like other women, they lack the courage and determination to overcome the prevailing attitude that women are unfit to assume executive responsibility." [5]

As the general hostility of male unions to the organization of women implies, most women workers remained unorganized. Although the Knights of Labor in the 19th century did seek to organize women, the total number was probably never more than 50,000 at any one time, and by 1888 it was probably no more than 12,000. By 1910 the total number of women workers organized by all unions was no more than 75,000, out of more than eight million women in the labor force.

That the fault for the poor showing lay more with the failure of union efforts than with the reluctance of women workers to join unions is suggested by the great upsurge in women members during the first two decades of the 20th century. The proportion of organized women workers doubled in those twenty years, going from 3.3 per cent to 6.6 per cent, a rate of increase twice that of men. Yet the number of women organized remained small compared with the total number of working women and the proportion of organized men. In 1920, for instance, out of 15 women industrial workers only one was in a union, while one out of five men was. At that date women constituted one-fifth of the non-agricultural labor force, but less than one-twelfth of organized workers.[6]

Women workers in general may have suffered because of the ambivalent attitudes and policies of the male-led unions, but those women who dedicated themselves to the organization of female workers suffered doubly. This was especially true of the working women associated with the Women's Trade Union League during the opening years of the 20th century. As working-class women themselves they believed in unions and in their class, but as feminists they were compelled to work against the sexism of male unionists on the one hand and the class snobbery of the middle-class feminists, who were also members of the WTUL, on the other. "Personally, I suffer torture dividing the women's movement into the Industrial Group and all the other Groups," wrote Leonora O'Reilly, a feminist and labor organizer. "Women, real women anywhere and everywhere are what we must nourish and cherish." Yet she resented the elitist attitudes she found at times among the middle-class "allies" in the Women's Trade Union League. Twice she resigned, only to rejoin. Pauline Newman, an organizer for the International Ladies' Garment Workers' Union and a committed feminist, found the middle-class feminists insensitive to the needs and interests of women workers. "My work is horrible," she complained to a friend in 1912. "The keeping sweet all the time and pleading for aid from the 'dear ladies' and the ministers is simply sickening." Fannia Cohn, another ILGWU organizer and feminist, complained from the other side of the divided allegiances experienced by these women. "The labor movement is guilty of not realizing the importance of placing the interest of women on the same basis as of men and until they will accept this," she predicted, "I am afraid the movement will be much hampered in its progress."[7]

Partly because the unions had much less interest in organizing and protecting the interests of women workers, many feminists and friends of women looked to other means. One such means was to enact laws specifically protecting women at work, such as limitations on hours of work, kinds of tasks, and hours and conditions of work for women. Although committed feminists like Susan B. Anthony as early as the 1860s opposed protective work laws for women because they seemed to set women apart from men, other women who were active in the labor movement usually supported such laws. The fundamental principle or justification was set forth in 1927 by the feminist and labor organizer Fannia Cohn when she wrote, "considering that very few women are as yet organized into trade unions, it would be folly to agitate against protective legislation."

One of the great triumphs of the association of women with the labor movement during the Progressive era had been the Supreme Court decision in the case of *Muller v. Oregon* in 1908. In his brief in that case, Louis Brandeis argued from specific and empirical evidence collected for him by women labor advocates that special protective legislation, in this particular case, limits on hours of work, were justified in order to protect women's health and safety. In distinguishing its position from that which it had taken against protective legislation in general, only three years before, the Court fell back upon the special dependence of women upon men. A woman "is properly placed in a class by herself," the court said, even though special legislation "could not be sustained" for men. "It is impossible to close one's eyes to the fact that she still looks to her brother and depends upon him."[8] The Court's decision opened the way for a host of protective laws in behalf of women on the state as well as the federal levels. In 1969, the Women's Bureau counted 46 states which had such laws on their statute books.

In the view of organizations dedicated to the interests of women workers, like the Consumers' League or the Women's Trade Union League, protective legislation could do for women what labor organizations ought to have done but had so far failed to do. Like a labor union, the state would now treat women as a group, securing gains for them collectively, rather than leaving them to bargain individually.

Many unions supported protective legislation for women because it could advance the special interests of men. As Otto Strasser of the Cigar Makers Union told a meeting of the International Union in 1879, "We cannot drive the females out of the trade but we can restrict this daily quota of labor through factory laws. No girl under eighteen should be employed more than eight hours per day; all over-work should be prohibited." At other times the unions supported protective laws for women for the same reason that Louis Brandeis and the Supreme Court had. Women were adults, wrote a columnist in the journal of the A. F. of L. in 1900, but it was useful to lump them under the law with children as protective legislation generally did, "because it is to the interest of all of us that female labor should be limited so as not to injure the motherhood and family life of a nation." [9]

The underlying justification for protective legislation for women was that women were different from men, and in such a way that the future of the country depended upon their ability to bear healthy children. That concern, moreover, was quite consistent with the character of the female work force, since the overwhelming majority of working women were unmarried and young, not yet mothers. Women's organizations generally accepted this social feminist outlook. The Consumers' League, for example, asserted that women had certainly the same rights as men, but that women were "not identical in economic or social function or in physical capacity" and thus ought not to be treated in the same way. Moreover, said Rose Schneiderman, one of the Women's Trade Union League leaders, if women were employed precisely as men were, those who worked "at the same hours of the day or night and receive the same pay might be putting their own brothers or sweethearts, or husbands out of a job." [10] This attitude may not have been consistent with a feminist philosophy, but few at the time took notice, so long as the suffrage still had to be won. Most women friends of protective legislation—like Rose Schneiderman herself—supported votes for women.

Once the suffrage had been achieved, however, the implicit contradiction between protective legislation and feminist ideology, which Susan B. Anthony had recognized from the outset, could not long be ignored. Indeed, the recognition was made within three years. For in 1923, Alice Paul, the militant suffragist who had organized the National Women's party following the ratification of the Nineteenth Amendment, announced a new feminist goal. She advocated the addition to the Constitution of an Equal Rights Amendment. The amendment would prohibit any kind of discrimination in law between men and women, even those, like the protective laws, which had been intended to help women. As Alice Paul ultimately was compelled to admit, the adoption of the Equal Rights Amendment would, in one stroke, wipe off the statute books of both the federal and state governments all the protective legislation that had been built up so painstakingly over the preceding fifty years. Those women who had spent the better part of their lives and countless hours of work obtaining those laws in behalf of working women were understandably outraged.

They could see no sense in what they considered a theoretical solution to a practical problem. "The cry Equality, Equality, where Nature has created inequality," thundered Florence Kelley of the Consumers' League, "is as stupid and as deadly as the cry Peace, Peace, where there is no Peace." To abandon special legislation in behalf of working women who had so little job protection as it was, Kelley said in 1923, would be to subject "wage-earning women to wage-earning men and to that subjection we are opposed in principle and practice. . . . On this subject we are immovable." [11] Florence Kelley was one of the two women who had gathered the economic and industrial data which had been the basis of Louis Brandeis's brief in *Muller v. Oregon*. Kelley spent the remaining ten years of her life fighting, in behalf of working women, the Equal Rights Amendment. She considered the proposed amendment a travesty of the hopes and the future of working women. The amendment, she predicted, would open up an immense amount of litigation, rendering the legal and constitutional consequences for women beyond prediction. Kelley was followed in her opposition to the ERA, as we have seen already in an earlier chapter, by the great majority of the suffragists.

As early as 1923 the issue between the old-line suffragists and Alice Paul's National Women's party in regard to protective legislation had reached such an impasse that the two groups appeared on opposite sides in cases before the Supreme Court. When the Court in *Adkins v. Children's Hospital* (1923) declared unconstitutional a minimum wage law for women, the National Women's party praised the decision as a victory for equal rights, while most women leaders throughout the country joined with labor and liberal groups in denouncing it as a retreat from *Muller v. Oregon*. The National Women's party had even filed a brief with the Court, prior to the decision, urging it to invalidate the minimum wage law. In 1936, in a New York state minimum wage case concerning women, it again filed a brief opposing the law, an action that evoked from the liberal *Nation* the observation that the party's position "is as always logically sound and theoretically progressive. Humanly, however, it is impractical and reactionary." And that was the view of most women and liberal-minded men on the question throughout the twenties and the thirties, indeed, right down to the 1970s. [12]

Only two groups took exception to the almost uniform belief in the validity and value of protective legislation for women. One was businessmen, who usually found such legislation costly or at least inconvenient. As early as 1923, for example, the National Association of Manufacturers came out for the Equal Rights Amendment, a fact the old social feminists and suffragists used gleefully against the amendment and Alice Paul's National Women's party.

The second major group of supporters of the ERA was business and professional women. They contended that laws and practices that purported to be helping women actually functioned in this case to keep women out of jobs they might like to enter. And there was evidence that when protective legislation went into effect women were in fact sometimes put out of jobs. In New York City, for example, some 700 women lost their jobs on the subway when laws against women's working during rush hours were enacted. And minimum-wage laws for women often resulted in women being replaced by men. White-collar and professional women especially objected to such laws because such blanket legislation often hit them individually. How could a woman aspire to becoming floor manager in a department store, for example, when the law limited the number of hours a woman might work in the name of protecting saleswomen and which precluded a woman's taking a managerial job in which the hours were longer? Or suppose a woman wanted to enter a trade like welding, which the law closed to her sex on the ground that most women could not perform such work? (As late as 1969, laws in at least 26 states categorically barred women from holding certain jobs on grounds of "protecting" them.) Florence Kelley, among others, recognized that the National Women's party was taking the side of business and of professional women against working women, thus exacerbating the class divisions among women. But that was neither the first nor the last time that women confronted the fact that their sex, like the other, was divided by class interests.

Although most women leaders in the nation stood behind protective legislation for another forty years or more, the conflict between them and the handful of committed feminists was a fundamental one. Women at the time the issue arose recognized it, too. The central point was highlighted by the resistance of the business and professional women. As they repeatedly emphasized, protective laws assumed a uniformity in women's capabilities and interests; it treated them collectively, rather than individually. What women opponents of protective legislation insisted upon was that their *individual* interests and talents be recognized and advanced as the opportunities arose rather than protect those attributes and abilities which they had in common with other women. Mary Beard recognized a part of the issue while obscuring another part when she wrote feminist Alma Lutz in 1937 that the Equal Rights Amendment "ran the risk of positively strengthening anachronistic competitive industrial processes; of supporting . . . ruthless laissez-faire; of forsaking humanism in the quest for feminism."[13] Mary Van Kleeck, a firm friend of working women, hit the nail on the head when she wrote as early as 1921 that the issue was really individualism, not laissez-faire, or middle class versus working class. "The feminist has an ideal for the home, the family, and children. She believes that all three would be improved by the greater freedom of the mother as an individual." Mary Van Kleeck opposed the feminist position, but she fully recognized why, by implication, the argument and the issue would surface again, a half-century later. "The freedom of the individual, and the release of powers suppressed by artificially imposed limitations, are [feminism's] goal," she pointed out.[14] This, of course, had been the driving impetus behind feminism all along, however it may have been obscured by social feminism or by those who wanted to expand women's range of activities without abandoning entirely the idea of separate spheres for the sexes.

The National Women's party lost its fight in the 1920s, but the conception of feminism for which it stood has become the operative philosophical position of the new feminist wave of the 1970s. The basic issues which that principle raises about the place of women in the family lie at the center, not only of the ratification of the Equal Rights Amendment but of the future of women and the family in America. Consequently, we shall have to return to the broader social implications of feminism in the last chapter.

By 1920 a majority of women lived in cities and towns, rather than on farms. Yet even at that date literally thousands of women who worked for wages were in farming. As late as 1880, for example, almost half a million women were employed on farms, a figure that included only those who were actually paid for their work, or worked as farmers or planters. It did not include the millions of women who were farm wives, whose work in the home might be onerous and almost unending and who in addition might work for days or even weeks in the fields, especially at particular times in the annual cycle of farm work. Because this labor in the home and in the field was unpaid it was not counted in the census figures on women's work. The great majority of women farm workers (that is, laborers) who were paid were black. In 1900, for example, there were 440,000 black women farm workers and 290,000 white. By 1930 the number of white women in agricultural labor (primarily as farmers) was still rising, reaching 345,000 that year, but at that date the number of black women had fallen to 420,000, a reflection of the migration of black families to northern cities like Detroit, New York, and Chicago, a trek which had begun during World War I.

Under slavery, black women had generally worked in the fields, and during the 19th century only in the South were white women used to working in the fields, mirroring, no doubt, the greater poverty of southern farmers, especially after the Civil War. A survey made in 1921 of some 900 farms in Nebraska, for example, showed that only 12.5 per cent of white women ever worked in the fields, while a comparable survey in South Carolina for the same year reported that 55 per cent of white farm women said that they worked on the crops for an average of 4.5 months of the year. That the cause was poverty is suggested by the additional information that the average number of wives of farm tenants who worked as farm laborers was twice that of wives of farm owners. The children of the two groups worked about in the same proportion, suggesting that when a farmer could afford to keep his wife out of the field work he did so.[15]

Even when a farm wife did not work in the fields her job was a heavy one, as it had been on the frontier or during an earlier and less developed stage of American agriculture. By the early years of the 20th century, whatever may have been the attitudes of farm wives earlier, to many women life on the farm seemed disadvantageous. The contrast of town or city life was now evident to all farm people, and the individual homestead farm did not shine in the comparison. In fact, there was sufficient discontent among farm women in the early 20th century for the Department of Agriculture in 1913 to conduct a survey of attitudes among 55,000 of its correspondents on farms. Many of the farmers' wives wrote directly, recording their attitudes and those of their neighbors. As one Iowa woman wrote, women want to feel "that they are partners in fact with their husbands and not looked upon as subordinates." In her opinion "the worst feature of farm work is too much work and too little pleasure. . . . The main cause for dissatisfaction of housewives is their isolation."[16]

Over and over again came the complaint of isolation and lack of diversion. Hardly a state was unrepresented by a reference to isolation. The absence of good roads, suggested one woman from Virginia, make women "almost 'shut ins' during the wintry season." A woman from Texas contended that "many farm women don't get off their own premises more than a dozen times a year. The fathers get so accustomed to the mothers' staying at home they seem to forget that they might enjoy a little rest and recreation," she asserted. "And the mother gets so accustomed to it she, too, seems to forget she is human." Farm life is undesirable, wrote a sixty-year-old woman from Georgia, because of the lack of human sympathy and cooperation. "The farmer's wife from the day she becomes a bride until the day of her death is the prop of the farm,"[17] she asserted. A woman who lived on an admittedly "splendid" 320-acre farm in Minnesota with "unlimited opportunities" still found her situation almost intolerable "on account of being so shut off from the outside world." Women have to stay home, she noted, while the man "is less subjected to the monotonous drudgery than is the woman." A similar comparison of the life of the farmer and that of the farm wife was made by a woman from New York: "The hardest phase of country life for the women in my neighborhood is the monotony, with no means or opportunity for any social life whatever. 'We are so isolated we can not even go to church on Sunday,' they all say to me. The country men do not care for the entertainments and amusements that the towns and cities offer. They meet among themselves at work more than the women do, and life is dreary indeed with never an afternoon or evening spent away from home." From an Ohio farm, too, came the complaint that "in all these years I have never had a vacation, never belonged to a club or any organization, and never went to church or to an entertainment; had not time to visit a neighbor—just worked early and late, with a snatch for reading between." A similar experience was echoed in Texas. "I have never been to a lecture, nor a play, nor show since marriage," she wrote, explaining it by a desire to save enough money to buy a home. "It has been a very monotonous road to travel. The women here in this county, where there is no help to be had, don't average a half dozen visits a year. Don't have time. I am making soap and catchup today."[18]

As these comments on the isolation of farm life suggested, an almost equally frequent objection was the heavy burden of work. The complaint was voiced especially by women living in the South, where many wives worked in the fields. From Florida, for example, came the observation that the "wife, if able to work, regardless of condition, makes a full hand at whatever the occasion demands—plowing, hoeing, chopping, putting down fertilizer, picking cotton, etc." Even where there was no field work, as a woman from Michigan made clear, work in the home could be backbreaking. "We do not feel so very much neglected by the department [of Agriculture] as by our men." Even on wealthy farms, with good and expensive equipment, "the women must still do the work much as their mothers before them did," she pointed out. "There are no modern conveniences for her, such as water in the house, bath, modern lights, vacuum cleaners, etc., and often not even such inexpensive things as oil stove, fireless cooker, washing machine, gasoline iron, bread mixer, and many such small items which help so much to lighten the women's work; while the men have all the modern machinery and farm implements their work requires." The woman writing the report did not blame the men for selfishness or even indifference; rather she ascribed the problem to men's lack of recognition of the large amount of work performed by farm women. A Colorado woman suggested that "the department should educate the farm men to the necessity of labor-saving devices for the household. Improvements in the farm home seem to fall behind improvements on the farm." [19] The farm woman's regimen was set forth succinctly by a woman from Pennsylvania. "I have in mind a small, delicate woman, with a family of small children who does all her own housework, milks four or five cows, cooks for extra help, carries from the spring all the water—no time to read a paper or book. Late to bed and early to rise, yet neither he nor she has any idea they could make her burden easier." Significantly, even those women who expressed satisfaction with their lives on the farm often said that the reason they felt that way was the decline in the amount of work they had to do at the time of the survey as compared with ten or twenty years earlier. The improvement was said to have come from the reduction in the number of hired hands they were expected to provide for, or because certain farm chores like making butter had been mechanized. [20]

Sometimes it has been contended by modern observers that on the farm the very importance of the woman in performing a myriad of tasks, not to mention her work in the field, gave her a function and therefore a status that was superior to that of the urban middle-class woman, many of whose economic functions had been taken over by industry. Though that interpretation might seem to be reasonable, neither these comments from farm women in the early 20th century nor the remarks of farm men in the 19th century seem to bear out the point. The work of the farm woman might be more varied and even more economically important than that of the urban middle-class housewife, but the division of labor by gender was about equally sharply drawn in both locales. The attitude of western men as spelled out by Thomas Dimsdale of Montana in the 1880s would have been quite acceptable to any eastern urbanite. "A woman is queen in her own home, but we neither want her as a blacksmith, a ploughwoman, a soldier, a lawyer, a doctor, nor any such professions or handicrafts." But, he went on, in their traditional roles as wives, mothers, and sisters, they were "the salt of the earth, the sheet anchor of society and the humanizing and purifying element in humanity. As such they cannot be too much respected, loved, and protected." [21]

Always, however, there was a gap between the ideal and the actual. Just as circumstances often threw women into jobs usually held by men in the colonial period, so the death of a husband or the loss of a family might well propel women into farm management or ownership. One such woman was Rachel O'Connor of Louisiana, who not only ran a large sugar plantation in the first decades of the 19th century but also managed to pay off the debts her husband and sons had left her. When a white overseer proved incompetent, she personally fired him and hired a black one. Her management of the plantation earned her money, with which she bought more land, and she successfully defended her property in court at least a dozen times. Bell Waller of Kentucky was not a plantation owner, but she did run her husband's farm while he pursued his profession as a lawyer. Her letters to her husband in the 1850s often refer to her running their farm. "You don't know how fast I am learning to farm," she wrote in 1852. "I believe I shall be a first rate farmer in a short time." Agnes Smedley, in her autobiographical novel, tells us of her grandmother in northern Missouri in the 1890s who ran her farm without a husband at all. "She milked the cows each morning and night with sweeping strength. . . . She carried pails of skimmed milk and slopped the hogs. . . . She awoke the men at dawn and she told them when to go upstairs to bed at night. She directed the picking of fruit . . . and she taught her girls how to can, preserve, and dry them for winter. In the autumn she directed the slaughtering of beef and pork, and then smoked the meat in the smokehouse." [22]

Not many women were as vigorous as Smedley's grandmother or as successful as Rachel O'Connor, but there were many women, in the North as well as in the South, after as well as before the Civil War, who undertook farming without the assistance of men. The Census of 1900 counted over 300,000 women as farmers, planters, or overseers, a figure that made farming the sixth largest occupation for women. Unlike farm labor, which employed almost a half million women, three-quarters of whom were black, a majority of women farmers in 1900 were white with native parents. In the deep South, for example, women farmers constituted over a quarter of all white native women gainfully employed in the region. In the Middle West that census year, about 8.3 per cent of all white native women workers were farmers.

Undoubtedly many women farmers and planters were widows working the land left by their husbands, but certainly many thousands of them were single women who had bought, or taken up land under the Homestead and other land acts. These laws did not permit married women to file a claim, but they did permit widows and single women to apply for land on the same basis as men. An examination of land-office records for counties in Colorado and Wyoming at the end of the 19th century and the opening of the 20th showed that about 12 per cent of the entries were made by women. In order to validate a claim a person had to establish a permanent dwelling and reside on the land for five years. Significantly, in this particular sample 42.5 per cent of the women claimants "proved up" their entries as compared with only 37 per cent of the men.[23]

A striking, if exceptional, illustration of one such woman homesteader was Sarah Show Wisdom, who as a recent widow with four children obtained a piece of land under the Homestead Act in western Nebraska in 1886. Once on the land she not only took her three school-age children to the rural school that was some miles away, with her baby strapped to her back, but she herself attended school until she was certified as a teacher. Meanwhile she "proved up" her entry by working it as a farmer and rancher. At that point she married again, only to have her second husband die in a blizzard while she was pregnant with her fifth child. Sarah Wisdom then undertook to "prove up" her husband's claim, added it to her own plot, continued her teaching, and later on entered claims for 320 more acres under the Kinkaid Act of 1904. She died at the age of 80.

Regardless of how arduous and demanding of time and effort the life of the farm woman may have been, it was always possible to combine work and family on a farm. Both occupations took place at the same site, as it were. When work for women moved outside the home, however, the only women who could follow it were those without family responsibilities or those who had no husband or no income. By the early years of the 20th century, although the great proportion of married women did not work outside the home, there was a sufficiently large number of married women who did, for whatever reason, that the combining of home and work was neither novel nor rare. In 1910, for example, over a million married women worked outside the home in non-agricultural jobs. One-fifth of them were employed as factory workers, clerks, or saleswomen, while another 30,000 were teachers, 13,000 were bookkeepers and accountants, almost 2000 managers of businesses, and about 300 college professors, to just name some of the different occupations. In short, literally hundreds of thousands of married women had entered upon industrial and professional careers before World War I.

Although many married women worked, the question of how to combine family and work was still a difficult one. "From the standpoint of the individual woman," wrote feminist thinker Jessie Taft in 1916, "the most hopeless problem, and the one which carried with it a long train of lesser difficulties, lies in the economic field. . . . Shall the young girl of today prepare for marriage or for wage-earning, for neither, or for both?" As a result of her training for a career, Taft continued, the college-educated young woman experienced a clash between her education and "the desire of the normal woman for a husband, children, and a home." Her education led her to work in the world while not preparing her for work in the home. Moreover, if she married she may regret it because "the wear and tear of domestic duties" will leave her at middle age "contented, settled down," with "all her possibilities for growth gone forever, even the desire to do, dead." Taft phrased the dilemma sharply: for the modern woman, alive to her potentialities and responsive to her education, yet "knowing in her heart that she could give a lifetime of happy association to the man she loved, and to society, healthy, normal children, the deadlock into which the present social order forces her is a cruel, blighting thing—a choice between a crippled life in the home or an unfulfilled one out of it." [24]

Not all feminists saw the conflict for the professional woman as pessimistically as Jessie Taft. Alice Henry, for example, in 1915 thought that for educated women combining motherhood and career was difficult, but "so many have solved the difficulties and have made the adjustment that it seems only a question of time when every professional woman may accept the happiness of wifehood and motherhood when it is offered to her without feeling that she has to choose once for all between a happy marriage and a successful professional career." Yet, she had to admit, if the problem was not impossible to solve for the professional woman, it was much more difficult for the working girl. No such accommodation between "domestic and industrial activities is in sight for her." For in the absence of adequate child care, only danger to the child would result from a young mother's working. "We know today how the health and the moral welfare of children fare when young mothers are prematurely forced back into the hard and exhausting occupations from which marriage has withdrawn them," Henry pointed out. And despite an optimism greater than Jessie Taft's, Alice Henry recognized that insofar as opportunities for work and careers for women are concerned, "single women are forging farther and farther ahead," while many a married woman "is finding herself between the upper and nether millstone." In fact, as domestic help became better paid the married woman often found her pursuit of career and family more and more costly and therefore more difficult to combine. Finally, Henry presciently observed, "the very function of sex, whose exercise enters into her relation with her husband, has complicated what could otherwise have been a simple partnership," that is to say, it results in children. "The helplessness of her children and their utter dependence upon her, which should have furnished her with an additional claim for consideration, have only tied her more closely and prevented her from obtaining that need of justice from society which a less valuable servant had long ago won." [25]

Obviously Alice Henry did not know how the question of combining family and career would be answered, but she seemed confident that it would be. Other forward-looking and thoughtful women seemed even more confident, just as the long battle for the suffrage was being finally won. "We cannot believe that it is fixed in the nature of things," wrote the *Smith College Weekly* in 1919, "that a woman must choose between a home and her work, when a man may have both. There must be a way out and it is the problem of our generation to find the way." [26]

During the 1920s, after the suffrage was achieved, the search for that way began in earnest. Part of the reason for the vigor of the effort was that many professional women were marrying. In 1910 only about 12 per cent of that class of working women had married; in 1930 the proportion was double that—almost a quarter of the whole. About 10 per cent of schoolteachers were married in 1920 and 18 per cent in 1930. "The question, therefore," asserted Virginia Collier in 1926 in her book *Marriage and Careers*, "is no longer, should women combine marriage with careers, but how do they manage it and how does it work?" Collier's book and other publications like it strikingly anticipated the message of Betty Friedan's *Feminine Mystique* of 1963. "I am burning up with energy and it is rather hard on the family to use it up in angry frustration," Collier quoted one woman who had gone out to work. Another woman cited by Collier candidly admitted, "I don't know what makes me do it," that is, work. "I only know I am happier when I am working." As another advice book observed, even the most devoted mothers did not want their children home all the time, as shown by their looking forward to the end of the summer vacation and the return of the children to school. "Mother love does not necessarily find it essential to express itself through changing diapers or washing out grass stains," wrote Alice Beals Parsons in *Woman's Dilemma* in 1926. "It is possible that the washing of diapers is no more essential to mother love than the grinding of corn into flour to make the bread the children are to eat" or the actual milking of the cow to get the baby's milk is necessary in order to demonstrate mother love, though at one time both tasks were part of a mother's work.[27]

The question of how to combine career or job and marriage was urgent in the 1920s also because so many women college graduates by then were marrying, as they had not at the end of the 19th century. Over 80 per cent of graduates from women's colleges were marrying in the 1920s as compared with 50 per cent thirty years before. A poll at Vassar College in 1923 revealed that 90 per cent of the woman students wanted to marry and only 10 per cent said they preferred careers without marriage. In 1925, in recognition of the new trend, Smith College set up an Institute To Coordinate Women's Interests, which was to experiment with ways of helping women to combine career and family. The Institute established or experimented with cooperative nurseries, communal laundries, shopping groups, and central kitchens. Smith's President William A. Neilson in 1927 made the concern official when he announced "that the outstanding problem confronting women is how to reconcile a normal life of marriage and motherhood with intellectual activity such as her college education had fitted her for." The board of trustees of Barnard College also took cognizance of the issue in 1932 in a practical way. It announced a policy of granting a six-month leave of absence with full pay to any woman faculty or staff member who was going to have a baby. In setting forth the policy, Dean Virginia Gildersleeve emphasized the underlying feminist principle. "Neither the men nor the women on our staff should be forced into celibacy, and cut off from that great source of experience, of joy, sorrow and wisdom, which marriage and parenthood offer."[28]

How effectively the new schemes would have worked and how deeply they would have reached socially were not to be learned. The Depression of the 1930s killed off not only these particular efforts but even the public discussion of how women might combine career and family on a reasonably egalitarian basis. On the contrary, as the Depression deepened, the most common experience of married women who worked was to be fired or denied jobs if they had working husbands. Several states and many municipalities simply barred married women from any job, on the plausible, though clearly illiberal, ground that during a period of widespread unemployment men needed work more than married women. The National Educational Association found that in 1930–31 some 77 per cent of 1500 school systems throughout the country refused to hire married women teachers and 63 per cent dismissed women teachers when they married. A New York Assemblyman as early as 1930 introduced a bill to tax heavily married women's personal income for the expressed purpose of driving them from the work force. "This will tend to eliminate unemployment," the Assemblyman explained, "by stopping married women from seeking employment." [29] Married women were asked to resign from the teaching staff of the University of Wyoming, and in Cincinnati and Columbus, Ohio, married women were systematically dismissed from teaching jobs. In 1932 the Federal government required a spouse to be let go if both worked for the government; almost invariably the law was applied against women only. Apparently these reactions were in conformity with popular attitudes, for in 1936 the Gallup poll reported that 82 per cent of Americans thought married women should not work if their husbands held a job.

The pessimistic shift in the ideological climate was already evident in 1934 in the comment of a Vassar alumna. "Twenty years ago we all believed in the economic independence of women. Domesticity was regarded with impatience. . . . We all expected to have careers and we all hoped to be distinguished. . . . It was part of the doctrine that we should marry and have children, but that these incidents should not stand in the way of our work. Marriage does not interfere with a man's work. A woman, too, should have both a rich personal life and a useful public career." [30] But by the thirties the search for the means to carry out the dream had been abandoned.

The implementation of the dream may have stopped, but the movement of women into the work force continued. In fact, between 1920 and 1940 women came to dominate the white-collar jobs that had begun to open up with the expansion of large-scale business enterprises during the 1920s. In 1910, for example, about 28 per cent of women were in non-manual occupations; by 1940 the proportion was up to 45 per cent. Stenography and typing went from fifth largest category of women's employment in 1910 to third in 1930. In 1910 women constituted 9.1 per cent of professional workers; just 20 years later, the proportion was over 14 per cent. Or put another way, in 1900 women made up less than 30 per cent of office workers; in 1940 they constituted 54 per cent. Between 1910 and 1940 women moved into the professions at a faster rate than men, and the number of women who were proprietors and managers (not including farmers) increased four times as fast as the number of men in those jobs, suggesting that women were making up for lost time.

On the whole, though, the increase in the number of professional women occurred largely in traditionally women's occupations like teaching and nursing. The number of women college teachers multiplied six times between 1910 and 1930, but in the same period the number of women entering medicine was 24 per cent *below* what it had been in 1910, and the number of dentists had increased no more than 2.6 per cent. (An exception was the increase in the number of lawyers and judges since 1910, a five-fold rise. But that profession had contained very few women at the beginning of the century.) The rise in the number of professional women during the 1920s was not at the expense of the more traditional categories of women's employment. In 1940, for example, women still constituted almost a quarter of the workers in manufacturing, and 93 per cent of those still in domestic service.[31]

The continued movement of women into the work force during the years between the two World Wars, however, did little to diversify women's occupations beyond what had been the case at the opening of the century. In 1940 women were presented in over 250 different occupational classifications, virtually all those enumerated by the census. In 1910 about 90 per cent of all working women fell into the 25 largest occupational classifications, that is, in only 10 per cent of the whole array of occupations. Thirty years later, in 1940, almost 88 per cent of all women workers still were to be found in the 25 largest classifications. At the top, as the biggest group in both 1910 and 1940, was domestic and personal service, as it had been all through the history of women's work outside the home. In 1920 and 1930 schoolteachers were in second place; by 1940, stenographers, typists, and secretaries had moved up to second place, reflecting the continued expansion of paperwork bureaucracy in business enterprises. In sum, on the eve of World War II most working women were still concentrated in the low-paying, semi-skilled, and unskilled jobs, the kinds they had filled ever since the industrial revolution had begun.

Contrary to what might have been anticipated, the Depression did not drive women out of the labor force, nor did it send them back to the home. The number of women working in 1940 was 25.1 per cent higher than it had been in 1930, while the increase for men was less than half of that—11.7 per cent. And in 1930, less than 12 per cent of married women were in the work force, but in 1940 the proportion was up almost to 15 per cent. Despite the continued rise in women's employment during the Depression, many who wanted to work could not find any. Perhaps as many as 20 per cent of all women normally employed were without work, or about 2 million. During the 1930s there was much concern that working women deprived men of jobs, but every government survey that looked into the matter concluded that segregation of work by gender was so pervasive that there was little actual replacement of men by women, despite the temptation offered employers by the lower wages customarily paid women.

On the other hand, the labor legislation enacted during the Depression years did help women, even though under the National Industrial Recovery Act of the New Deal at least a quarter of the codes drawn up for industry permitted women to receive lower minimum wages than men. And this often occurred in precisely those industries in which women were highly represented, such as the clothing and electrical industries. A state minimum-wage law, for example, raised wages of 84 per cent of female laundry workers in New York City in 1934, and New Deal legislation did the same for the textile workers, 40 per cent of whom were women. Despite the lower wages permitted for women in many industries under the NRA, wages for women in general rose more than for men, a measure once again of the great differential between the earnings of men and women. Hours, too, were reduced to a greater extent in those industries in which women predominated than in those in which males were in the majority. In boots and shoes, for example, the hours of work for women fell 16 per cent, while in the cement industry, which was principally male work, the drop in hours was only slightly more than 4 per cent. The principal explanation for the difference, of course, was that women were primarily employed in low-wage, long-hour industries. When legal minima or maxima were established, women profited more than men from the limitations. New Deal legislation made no consistent effort to even out the differences between the wages of men and women, but in some industries that was achieved. Yet not until after World War II, it is worth recognizing, was the principle of equal pay for equal work a public issue, much less a goal of policy. Even labor unions accepted wage differentials between the two sexes on the ground that such differences had always prevailed and that employers expected to calculate costs on that basis.

On the eve of World War II, in short, the chief patterns of women's work were remarkably similar to what they had been at the end of the 19th century, forty years before. Over four-fifths of working women were single and only temporarily in the work force prior to marriage; less than

15 per cent of all married women with husband present were employed, and at that a disproportionate share of the total were black women whose work was not only unskilled and low paid, but was chiefly compelled by low family income. Most working women were still engaged in a narrow range of occupations, most of which were traditional, such as unskilled factory, clerical, and sales work. Even the proportion that women constituted in the work force had not changed substantially since 1900. That year women comprised 18 per cent of the labor force; in 1940 the figure was 25 per cent. In other industrial countries women's proportion of the work force was frequently higher. In Britain in 1931, for example, almost 30 per cent of the labor force was female; in France in 1926, the proportion was slightly less than 37 per cent, and in Germany it was 36 per cent.

Within a decade, however, almost all of these characteristics changed dramatically. It would be the greatest alteration in the work patterns of American women since the late 19th century, when most jobs first became accessible to women. On the face of it, the sweeping changes during the decade of the 1940s seemed to be the culmination of the feminist revolution that had been under way for over a century. In fact, however, the meaning of the Second Tranformation in women's work was at once more complicated and less radical than that, as we shall see in the next chapter.

XVII

The Second Transformation
in Women's Work

The extent or character of the revolution in women's work after 1940 can be summarized best with a few figures. Within the space of ten years the pattern of women's work, with which we have become familiar in the last two chapters, reversed itself. Whereas as recently as 1940 married women had been barely a third of all working women, by 1950 married women made up 52 per cent of the group. Not quite as rapidly, but significant nonetheless, during the same span of years the proportion of married women who were in the work force increased. In 1940 only about 15 per cent of married women in the country were working; by 1960 the proportion had almost doubled; and by 1975 over 44 per cent of married women with husband present were in the labor force. Or, put in different terms, the number of married women entering the labor force between 1940 and 1975 rose more than two and a half times as fast as the number of married women in the country. This amazing increase in the number of married women who joined the work force during the 1950s and the 1960s also meant that for the first time in American history more women than men took jobs.

A second part of the transformation in the job patterns of women was that large numbers of mothers of young children now began to work outside the home. In 1940 less than 10 per cent of mothers with children under six held jobs; in 1950 the proportion was almost 12 per cent; by 1970 it was over 30 per cent and still rising. By 1975 the proportion was up to 36.6 per cent.

A third part of the great shift was that older women were now characteristic of the female work force, something that had not been true of white women workers before. (Black women often continued to work after marriage and on into rather advanced ages, even in the 19th century.) This development was a function, to be sure, of the entrance of large numbers of married women into the work force. Yet it is so striking that it deserves to be noted in its own right. In 1940, for example, 27.2 per cent of women between the ages of 35 and 44 were in the work force, but, by 1960, the figure was up to 42.6 per cent. Even more striking was the increase in the number of older women, those between 55 and 64, who went out to work in the years after World War II. In 1940 less than 17 per cent of such women held jobs, but, in 1960, 35 per cent did. How did this three-pronged revolution in the pattern of women's work come about, and what did it mean for women and the family?[1]

The immediate cause was undoubtedly the advent of World War II. Unlike World War I, which had no long-range effect upon the employment of women, World War II transformed the labor market. It is true that during World War I women entered a number of jobs that had been theretofore closed to them, such as street-car conductor, welder, or even non-combatant service in the army and navy. Doubtlessly many women, and many men, as a result, gained a new and broader perception of women's capacities as a result of women's new occupations during wartime. For under the demands of war men have often been willing to break the mold of social custom and allow gender roles to shift. But when one looks at the statistics of employment, either in numbers or in range of occupations, the situation in 1920 appears strikingly similar to that in 1910, suggesting that the war had little permanent or long-range effect upon women's work patterns, whatever effect it may have had on particular women or on women's participation in some occupational categories.

Probably the chief reason World War I had little effect upon women's employment in the long run was that it did not last long and did not demand much manpower. The great majority of men remained in their civilian jobs, and the draft never absorbed more than two million men. Moreover, the total period of U.S. participation, at the maximum, was no longer than 20 months. World War II, on the other hand, was a very different affair. Actual U.S. participation lasted almost four years, and the end came abruptly with the unexpected surrender of Japan. Thus the war economy lasted just about as long as the fighting; there was no tapering off. Even more important from the standpoint of women's work, and in contrast to the World War I experience, some 15 million men and women were taken into the armed forces from the civilian work force, leaving a wide range of opportunities for women not already in the work force or in the armed services.

Despite the recognition from hindsight of the war's great demands upon labor, at the outset of the conflict there was little anticipation that women's labor would be needed. Few women, for example, were mobilized in the early months. Between July 1941 and February 1942, for example, only 5 per cent of all workers who received preliminary defense-work training courses were women; and of some 700,000 workers given training in order to prepare others for defense work, only 1 per cent were women. No sooner did the need for more labor become evident than it also became clear that the traditional source of women's labor—single women—would be inadequate. Out of that realization came the decision to enlist the labor of married women. The Federal government mounted a propaganda campaign to convince married women, including those with small children, that it was now patriotic to work outside the home. "Our country was not built the soft way," one of the government brochures announced. "Women worked hard on the farms and in the households. They carried on in every war while their men were on the battlefield." But now they would be needed in the factories, as well. On still other occasions women were told bluntly that if they did not take a job in a war plant their men might well die from lack of ammunition on some "distant atolls . . . in the hot sun." [2] The propaganda was necessary since a preliminary government survey had discovered that, though 33 per cent of childless wives said they would be willing to take a job, only 19 per cent of wives with children were ready to. No more than 30 per cent of husbands thought it acceptable for their wives to work. Yet, despite these initial reservations and the no more than rather inadequate and poorly planned government assisted child-care facilities, women entered the work force in record numbers. (Most war-plant mothers apparently relied upon neighbors, relatives, or husbands for baby-sitters, rather than day-care centers or nurseries. That was the meaning, apparently, of the Gallup poll in 1943 that reported 56 per cent of mothers would not use government day-care centers even if they were provided free. They preferred more individual and personal care.) Between 1941 and 1944, some 6.5 million women took jobs; more than half of the new workers had previously been unpaid homemakers only. By May 1945, when the war in Europe was over, women workers constituted 57 per cent of all employed persons, an unprecedentedly high proportion. And for the first time, also, in American history, married white women had gone to work outside the home in large numbers. Almost half of all working women at that time were married, though, as recently as 1940, wives had constituted no more than 36 per cent of all working women.

Patriotism, it needs to be said, was not the only force bringing married women into the work place. For one thing, women were responding to the rise in wages, which the increased demand for labor spurred, especially since many families had experienced a fall in income after the male breadwinner had been taken into the armed forces. Many women also found that with their husbands gone there were fewer demands upon them at home for housekeeping services, and the fall in the birth rate consequent upon the husband's absence meant that child-care duties were reduced or, in the case of newly married women, not even begun. Finally, during the war recreational expenditures and vacations were played down, and opportunities for other kinds of activities for women were reduced, thus encouraging women to fill their time with paid work as they might not have done in more normal times.

Aside from bringing many new women workers, particularly the married, into the work force, the war's demand for labor resulted in an improvement in the status and the incomes of literally millions of women workers. Women moved into jobs that earlier had been out of their reach. At the close of the war, for example, a study by the Women's Bureau showed that two-thirds of women who had been employed in eating and drinking establishments at low wages and under poor conditions had transferred to better paying war-work. As early as 1942, over 600 laundries were forced to shut down because their women workers had left for better wages in war work and no replacements were available. Black women in particular benefitted from the opportunities that the new war industries and the withdrawal of large numbers of male workers opened up. Thousands of black domestic servants escaped into jobs with better pay and more regular and limited hours. The numbers of black women employed in agriculture, principally as farm laborers, declined 30 per cent between 1940 and 1945 as the women found new jobs in the expanding war industries. In 1940 there had been only 3000 black women employed in the metals, chemicals, and rubber industries; by 1945 the number had risen to 150,000, an increase of 5000 per cent! Black women employed by the government jumped from 60,000 to 200,000 during the four years of war.

Revolutionary as the increase in married women at work was, the change was primarily justified, in the minds of most Americans, by the goal of winning the war. And undoubtedly many married women themselves, as they went out to work, used that justification for their departure from traditional roles. After all, even during the 1920s and 1930s, friends of working women had generally counselled against any encouragement to mothers of young children, even those of the working class, to go out to work. A Gallup poll in 1936, just before the outbreak of World War II, had reported that three-quarters of women disapproved of a married woman's working. And during the war, when Congress was discussing the financing of child-care facilities for women with children who worked in war plants, the justification was the needs of the war. Senator Carl Hayden, a supporter of such child-care centers, remarked that "it is entirely proper that the Federal Government should appropriate child-care money because Congress declared war; child care is a war problem, support will cease with the end."[3] (And cease it did in February 1946.) As late as 1945 a *Fortune* poll reported that 63 per cent of Americans thought a woman should not work if her husband could support her. Moreover, the respondents made clear, rearing children was the primary job of women. And those conclusions were arrived at *after* four years' experience with a total work force made up largely of married women.

In the light of the emphasis, in previous American history, on the primary responsibility of married women to their families, it came as no surprise that in the first year after the end of the war 2.25 million women gave up their jobs voluntarily and another million were laid off in anticipation of returning male workers. Many observers, however, were not prepared for the 2.75 million women workers who joined the labor force at about the same time the others were leaving. As a consequence, the net decline in women workers was hardly more than half a million. In sum, the retreat of women from the work force that had been predicted just did not take place by 1946. Actually the predictions had ignored the contrary signs. Among those signs had been a Women's Bureau survey made during the war in which it was found that three-quarters of working women said that they wanted to retain their jobs when peace came. Some of them even said they saw no valid reason why they should give up their jobs to returning male veterans. Perhaps most revealing of all was the additional finding that the greatest enthusiasm for remaining at work was expressed by women over 45—the very group of women who in the 1950s and 1960s would comprise the largest number of new women workers. By 1960 the proportion of women between 45 and 54 who held jobs was greater than the percentage of women between 20 and 24 in the labor force; yet the latter age group in previous American experience had always contained the highest proportion of working women.

In the years after the war, occupational opportunities for women widened enormously. The number of women accountants and auditors tripled between 1940 and 1950 during a period when the number of males in the occupation increased barely 60 per cent. The number of women radio operators jumped ten times as fast as that of male operators during the same decade. The number of male welders doubled between 1940 and 1950, but the number of women in the occupation increased four and a half times. As one student of labor force statistics pointed out, the only categories of occupations in which women did not make striking advances between 1940 and 1950 were those in which they already were predominant or those in which neither women nor men wanted to work because the jobs were hazardous, strenuous, or disagreeable.

This movement of women into jobs heretofore closed to them for one reason or another accelerated during the 1960s. Unlike the fifties, the sixties was a period of great prosperity and increased popular and governmental concern about the civil rights and aspirations of minorities and women. Indeed, it was during this decade that the new feminist movement erupted. Between 1960 and 1970, as a result, the number of women carpenters went from 330 to 11,000, while the number of male carpenters grew by no more than 6000 in the same ten-year period. Women electricians jumped from 2500 to 8700; women machinists from 6700 to 11,800. By 1970 women machinists constituted 3 per cent of all machinists in the nation. A similar upsurge of women occurred in the professions. Women's share of the nation's lawyers rose from 2.4 per cent to 4.7 per cent; the number of engineers who were women increased from 7000 to almost 20,000 in ten years, a rate of increase 4.5 times that of men.

Despite these striking changes, many of which certainly were significant gains for women, the great majority of working women were still to be found at the lower levels of the economic pyramid. In 1973, for example, 34.1 per cent of all working women were in clerical jobs, slightly more than another one-fifth were in service occupations, of the one-sixth who were professionals a large proportion were teachers, and one-sixth were factory operatives. As a result, two authorities concluded in 1976 that "the working woman is a typist, maid, teacher, nurse, cashier, or saleswoman."[4] Despite the leaps forward during the 1960s and the high educational levels of women, remarkably few of them were in the skilled crafts or the professions. Yet the proportion of women graduating from college was higher than ever, and until 1970 the average 20th-century working woman had completed more years of schooling than the average working man. Even in 1973, barely half of white males in white-collar jobs had completed on the average four years of high school and more, while three-quarters of the women in that job category had. In service jobs twice as high a proportion of women had four years of high school education or more than men. But in all categories women were paid less than men. In short, even though women had flooded into the work force after 1945, the majority of working women were still to be found in occupations that were remarkably similar to those of 1940 or even of 1900, for that matter. The shifts in the participation rate of married and older women and the general upsurge in numbers, it is true, constituted real changes. But as far as occupations were concerned, the changes had been remarkably slight over the previous seventy years. The persistence of old occupational patterns was just one of four characteristics of women's work that continued after 1950 much as they had been in the late 19th century.

A second characteristic was the tendency of women to be concentrated in occupations in which few men were employed, or what economists speak of as job segregation by gender. As we have noticed in passing already, during the 19th century certain kinds of work were largely female, like domestic service, needle trades, and cotton textiles. By the same token, certain categories of work, like baking, steel manufacturing, and railroading, counted almost no women in them at all. During the 20th century the segregation of work by gender has been at least as pronounced and actually became more so. Sociologist Edward Gross has shown that, if an index of segregation is constructed for occupations, the degree of segregation by gender in 1960 was actually greater than in 1900! That is to say, more women would have had to change job categories with men in 1960 to equalize the proportion in each category than would have had to change jobs in 1900. Furthermore, the index of segregation by sex in 1960 is considerably higher, Gross shows, than job segregation by race.[5] It is true, as we have noticed earlier, that women have moved into occupations, especially since 1945, that were once filled largely by men, such as tobacco and shoe manufacture in the 19th century, and banking in the years after 1945. But the tendency in the 20th century, at least, has been for men to move out of the occupation, thus reconstituting the segregation.

Perhaps the most obvious cause, and consequence for women, of this long history of job segregation has been that women's wages have generally been lower than men's. This difference in wages is the third long-term characteristic of women's work in the American economy. The differential has prevailed in all categories of work and at all historical periods; it was true in the 19th century and it persists today. In 1960 the average wage for women in professional jobs was 64 per cent of men's; among sales personnel, women's wages were only 40.8 per cent of males'; among managers 57.6 per cent. The median wage or salary of white women in 1960 was 82.5 per cent that of black men, who, in turn, received incomes that were on the average only 60 per cent of white men's. Nor have the most recent alterations in women's access to a wider range of jobs or their higher participation rates reduced the differences. In 1945, for example, the median income of white women who worked full-time and all year round was 63 per cent of white men's; in 1973 the ratio was *down* to 57 per cent, and since that date it has declined still further. In short, despite the new opportunities for women and the new feminist consciousness among women, the wage differential between male and female workers is widening rather than narrowing.[6]

Part of the explanation for these different wages between the sexes, at least before 1940, is that women were generally not long-term participants in the work force. Since so many worked only until they married, they could be paid less, and many were, therefore, willing to accept less. Trade unions were, for the same reason, less interested in their cause. Another part of the explanation of why women's wages have remained lower on the average than men's is that they are concentrated in low-paying industries, again because they have often been short-term, rather than lifetime workers. The concentration in low-paying jobs also helps to explain why job segregation is so pronounced; men try to stay away from "women's work"; conversely, they try to keep women out of work that is traditionally theirs.

Further studies, however, suggest that these explanations are only part of the story. When all of these explanatory factors are held constant, the difference between male and female wages is reduced, but not eliminated. Simple discrimination, in short, is also a part of the explanation. At the time of the passage of the Equal Pay Act of 1963, numerous instances of women's being paid less money for performing exactly the same work as men were reported. In fact, until that act was passed, the idea that women by right ought to receive equal pay with men for the same work was not widespread at all. The American Federation of Labor had accepted the principle of equal pay in the 19th century, but the implementation was nil.

Many men argued that women did not need to be paid equal wages because so many of them were single women, not family breadwinners, even though that argument callously overlooked the hundreds of thousands of women who were in fact the sole support of their families, even in the 19th century. During World War II the National War Labor Board enunciated a policy of equal pay for equal work for women, but most employers paid no attention to it or set up classifications of jobs that would permit the old discrimination to persist under another rubric. General Electric, for example, simply redefined jobs as being "heavy" (male) or "light" (female) and then paid different wages, though in fact the work involved was identical for both sexes. Unions, too, during the war and after, although many thousands of their members were women, went along with the practice of paying different wages to women and men for the same work. During the 1940s and 1950s several states enacted laws mandating equal pay for equal work, but the Federal government did not do so until 1963 with the Equal Pay Act.

Differentials between men's and women's wages have prevailed in all of the industrial nations. But the gap has been noticeably greater in the United States than in any other industrial country. The reasons for the greater spread in the United States are not clear, but the international comparisons are striking. In 1968, for example, Great Britain, West Germany, Italy, and France all reported a gap between the average wages of men and women that was smaller than in the United States. In Britain women's wages were 60 per cent of men's; in France, 86 per cent; in Italy, 74 per cent; and in West Germany, 70 per cent. At that time women's wages in the United States were only 58 per cent of men's. Moreover, in all of the European industrial nations mentioned, the spread had narrowed since 1955, while in the United States it had widened. One possible explanation for the American anomaly is that a smaller proportion of working women in European industrial countries are in low-paying clerical jobs than in the United States.[7]

No class of working women has suffered more from the differential in wages than black women. In 1939 their median income was only 23 per cent of white men's and 37.9 per cent of white women's. After World War II, as occupational opportunities for black as well as white women improved, the gap narrowed. But even in 1960 the difference was still significant. By then the wages of black women on the average were up to 42 per cent of white men's and 70 per cent of white women's. A striking improvement occurred during the 1960s, thanks to improved geographical mobility, greater access to education for blacks in general and for black women in particular, and a general decline in racial discrimination. By 1973 the wages of what the census refers to as "minority race women"—but which is made up primarily of black women—came within striking distance of the wages of white women. That year their wages were 88.2 per cent of white women's. Furthermore, the improvement in black women's wages was accompanied by a substantial increase in their participation in the work force. As we have noted earlier, a greater proportion of black women has always worked principally because blacks are poorer and because a considerably higher proportion of black wives have worked outside the home. The changes over time are summarized in the following table:

Proportion of women in work force by race
(in percentages)

	White	*Non-White*
1900	17.2	41.2
1940	24.5	37.3
1950	28.4	37.1
1965	36.9	46.0

Source: Adapted from James A. Sweet, *Women in the Labor Force* (New York, 1973), p. 102.

Although it will be seen that the proportion of black women in the work force rose after the low point reached in 1950, the difference in the rates of white and black women is nonetheless narrowing because of the even faster increase in the work force participation rate of white women.[8]

Despite the undeniable improvement in the wages of black women, it is worth underscoring the point that the median earnings of black women are still below those of white women and of all men, black men included. In 1973 the median wage of minority men was 71.9 per cent of white men's, while white women's was 56.3 per cent and minority women's was 49.6 per cent. Moreover, the largest single occupational category for minority women in 1973 remained the service job, as it has been ever since emancipation in the 19th century. That year more than half of all minority women 35 years and older who worked were employed in service jobs. And two-fifths of those service employees were working in private households—that is, as domestic servants. In contrast, only 16 per cent of all white women who worked fell into the service job category.

The fourth persistent characteristic of women's work is that historically women have been discriminated against not only in the wages they received but also in the jobs they have had access to. We have already noticed this trend in the 19th and early 20th century when certain jobs were closed to them because the necessary training was denied them, as in the professions of law and medicine in the early 19th century and more recently in apprenticeships to skilled trades. Moreover, many labor unions have been hesitant about, or even hostile toward, accepting women members or cooperating with women in maintaining or improving their conditions of work. Until very recently, too, some jobs were effectively closed to women, even when the law was silent on the subject, on the ground that the work to be performed was unsuitable for women, such as in the military, mining, construction, police, and fire-fighting. Yet even in occupations in which women have long been represented in large numbers, such as in teaching or nursing, few women have been school principals, superintendents of education, or hospital administrators. Similarly, the strong and growing participation of women in the field of retail selling and in the lower echelons of business and banking has not resulted in more than a handful of women in managerial or executive positions or as bankers.

The great majority, if not all, of these time-worn denials of economic opportunity to women have been removed or substantially reduced by new equal opportunity laws and by consciousness-raising on the part of feminist groups during the 1960s and 1970s. The Civil Rights Act of 1964, several executive orders on the Federal level, and anti-discrimination legislation by the states, along with court decisions on both levels of government, have opened up virtually all jobs to women except the very few that are indisputably and legitimately sex-related such as locker-room attendant or male clothes' model. The new feminist consciousness and the courts' emphases upon legal equality of opportunity between the sexes have dismantled most of the special, protective legislation that had been enacted in behalf of women during the first forty years of the 20th century. The old battle between the militants of Alice Paul's National Women's party and the social feminists and suffragists of the 1920s has been resolved decisively in favor of the militants.

These, then, are the contours of the revolution in women's work since 1940. On one level it certainly seems like the achievement of the feminist goals. An increasing number of women are gaining economic independence as they flood into the work force, barriers to jobs have been beaten down by laws and feminist persistence, sexist attitudes have been successfully resisted and reversed. Much still remains to be done, to be sure. Wage differentials, for example, still persist. But on the whole it does seem that the economic basis for a feminist future has been laid. Or has it?

One reason for raising the question is the recognition that at the heart of the revolution in women's work lie several anomalies, which are worth examining. It has long been and still is a cliché of demography or social statistics that married women's participation in the work force is inversely related to income. The traditional and most respectable explanation, for example, why proportionately more black wives work outside the home than white wives is that their family incomes are lower. And virtually all studies of working wives, regardless of their race, show a close correlation between the proportion working and the level of family income. Yet during the 1940s and the 1960s wives entered the work force in great numbers, though those decades were characterized by generally rising family income. One interpretation that might be drawn from this overturning of the traditional relationship between working wives and income is that the reversal shows that women were now joining the work force for other than economic reasons, that they were responding to the argument that economic independence was desirable, and that therefore women's traditional involvement with the family was declining. Before we look any closer at that interpretation, however, let us examine a second anomaly in the post-1945 transformation.

Another accepted interpretation of the relationship between wives and work is that the presence of children, especially young children, has a strong inhibitory effect upon mothers' employment. Yet during the 1950s and early 1960s, the fertility of American women went steadily upward. In 1940 the fertility rate was 1.9, while in 1959 it was 2.3. In fact, the well-known "baby-boom" of the 1950s was occurring just as married women were leaving the home for outside employment in record numbers. At precisely the time Betty Friedan was writing her book and coining the phrase *The Feminine Mystique* to describe what she thought was an excessive involvement of women in the home, an ever-increasing number of married women were going out to work. Here, too, it is tempting to conclude that the demographic and economic facts seem to suggest that the mass of women, whatever the Friedans and other writers on the subject might contend, were in fact breaking out of the traditional bonds of home and motherhood, that they were finally repudiating the 19th-century doctrine of separate spheres.

From the beginning of the feminist movement in the early 19th century, the argument has been advanced that women, as human beings, not only deserved equality of economic opportunity but also that when married women gained economic independence, the relationships within the family would also become egalitarian. As Elizabeth Cady Stanton pointed out in 1870, it would work "a revolution." Charlotte Perkins Gilman, in her widely circulated book *Women and Economics* (1898), had developed that argument cogently and effectively. Now, half a century later, it was being acted upon by millions of married women. Wives, by the second half of the 20th century, outnumbered single women in the labor force, and in 1975 over a third of working women—36.6 per cent—had children under six years of age—that is, before the school years. (Actually, 32.7 per cent of women with children under three years of age were in the work force.)

Despite this apparent triumph of feminist economic ideology, however, there was very little change in the place or the position of women in the family. In fact, when the patterns of women's work in the present decade are looked at more closely, what emerges is the conclusion that, in spite of the transformation after World War II, women's relation to the family remained as primary and central as it had ever been. It was now combined with work, to be sure, but that outside job was secondary and supplementary to the family, which still remained the primary concern and sphere of most women.

The way in which women continued to mold their employment around their families comes through strikingly in a study of the 1960 census data. The conclusion of the economist authors was that women without children who worked outside averaged nearly two hours of work more per week than women who had children aged 14–17, while those women, in turn, averaged about two hours more work per week than women with children under 14. In short, the more dependent the children, the less likely the mother was to work. A more recent study based on the census of 1970 showed a continuing negative correlation between the presence of small children in the home and wives' participation in the labor force. The correlation was not as strong as in 1960, but it was still significant.[9] In sum, women continued to structure their work around what they perceived as their family responsibilities.

The same conclusion emerges from a comparison between the proportion of men and women who are in the labor force. Although today large numbers of women are employed, the proportion they constitute of all women is still far below that for men. In 1973 only 53.6 per cent of all women over 16 years of age were in the work force as against 83.7 per

cent of men. More revealing is the additional fact that women's participation in work is lower than men's at all age levels. The highest participation rate for women in 1973 was 74.3 per cent for the 20–24 age group;
for men in that same age group the participation rate was 92.1 per cent.
The obvious explanation for these differences between the sexes is that
marriage and involvement in their new families have caused the women to
withdraw from the work force or not to enter it in the first place.[10]

Even when marriage and family do not impel women to withdraw from
the job, they seem to cause them to reduce their availability for employment. In 1973, only 42 per cent of all working women were employed
full-time, all year round, as compared with 68 per cent of working men. It
is significant that almost half of the women who worked less than full-
time—47 per cent—told interviewers that their responsibilities at home
dictated their reduced hours of work. The reasons next in importance in
their responses were attendance at school (21 per cent) and unemployment
(16 per cent). In comparison, two-thirds of the men who did not work all
year round gave, as their primary reasons, education and unemployment.
It is true that the number of women who work full-time, all year round—
in the pattern analogous to men's—has risen dramatically since World
War II. The increase between 1950 and 1973 was 105 per cent. But that
rise, sharp as it is, seems to have reached its minimum. Since the middle
1960s the number of women working full time has risen at about the same
rate as the increase in the number of women workers.[11]

Once this continuing involvement of working women with the family is
recognized, women's increased participation in the work force after World
War II must assume a little different aspect than might seem to be the case
at first glance. Rather than signifying a repudiation of the traditional primacy of the family in the lives of married women, it betokens a continuing
involvement with the family, though that is now combined with work outside. The work, however, is clearly subordinated to the needs of the family; in fact, the work is often entered into for the purpose of supporting the
family, rather than increasing women's autonomy within the family.

One measure of the subordination of women's equality or autonomy
within the family is that even working women spent more time in housekeeping and family work than their husbands. A recent study of some
1400 families in upstate New York inquired as to the amount of housework performed by each family member. The women clearly did most,
running from a low of 3.5 hours a day when they were young, employed,
and without children, to a high of 12 hours a day when the wives were not

employed and with seven or more children, one of whom was a baby. The husbands' times averaged 1.5 hours a day.

Generally speaking, working wives see themselves as adding to the family income, not sustaining the family. (Here, of course, the subject is the majority of married women with husband present, not married women in general.) A study made in 1956, for example, showed that families with working wives tended to have more debt than those without working wives. Since the debts incurred were not for home mortgages, it seemed that wives were working to finance less durable goods, like cars, refrigerators, and TVs, items that did not require the wife to continue to work indefinitely. This secondary role that work played in the lives of most married women also helps to explain why most women did not work full-time, all year round. Again, their aim, apparently, was not to work for themselves, but for the family. The same conclusion emerges from a more recent analysis, made of families with and without working wives in the 1970s. This later study found that when total income was the same between families with and without working wives, spending was greater in families with working wives, principally because of the added costs incurred by the wife as an outside earner. But there was no increase in expenditures for durable goods. Wives were working, in short, not for a particular item for themselves, but for a general increase in income—that is, for the family as a whole.[12]

The continued orientation of women's lives to the family also explains why women over 45 constituted in the 1950s and 1960s the largest age group then entering the work force. They were women going to work after their children had been reared. It also accounts for the apparent paradox that the proportion of married women working was rising at the same time that the birth rate was going up. The women who were entering the work force were older women; it was the young women who were having the children. Finally, it is this centrality of the family in the lives of women, even among those who work, that helps to account for the many women who do not aspire to careers. Traditionally in American society, and short of a veritable revolution in current patterns of career lines, a professional career requires a separation from family responsibility, something most working women have not been prepared to make. A Harris poll in 1974 found that 60 per cent of all women, including young women, said they frequently felt that being a mother is as challenging as having a high occupational position. And only one-fifth said that they frequently hoped their daughters would have "more interesting careers outside the home" than they did.[13] As the patterns of women's work now stand, the increase in the number of married women in the work force has not caused them to abandon their traditional roles as the primary custodians of the home and the primary rearers of children. And so long as women do not abandon these roles, no matter how many of them work outside the home, men and the society at large will not find large numbers of working women objectionable. Undoubtedly some men have found their wives' hours and circumstances of work inconvenient, but that reaction is quite capable of being absorbed within the idea of the two spheres and the primacy of the home and family in women's lives. Moreover, the holding of a job by a woman, and especially by a wife, has often been essential for the physical comfort of the family and the achievement of its educational and consumer goals, thereby helping to counter-balance whatever inconvenience may result to the family from the absence of the wife and mother from the home. And certainly from the standpoint of the national economy women's work has been essential for its expansion and advancement. Yet in recognizing these contributions, we must not overlook the ways in which women have shaped and fitted their work around the family—a molding that is in stark contrast to men's shaping of the family around their work. And it is just this willingness of women to shape work to family that explains the undeniable social acceptance of women's paid work. In October 1973, for example, a public-opinion poll reported that 65 per cent of the population approved of a wife's working even if her husband's income was sufficient to support the family. Over 80 per cent of people under the age of 30 approved the idea.

The social acceptance of work for married women since 1945 is analogous to the earlier, if slow, acceptance of the suffrage for women. For a long time in the course of the 19th and early 20th century, it had been thought that women ought not to have the vote because it would surely disrupt the family. Once women began to vote, however, it soon became apparent that the ballot posed no serious threat to the family. In fact, it had little to do with intra-familial relations. Similarly it had long been believed that mothers of young children ought not to be in the work force, that it would weaken if it would not destroy the family. And when fertility was hard to control, for a mother to take a job outside the home did indeed make it difficult to attend to the proper rearing of children. As we have seen, only those 19th-century mothers worked whose husbands were incapacitated, absent, or incapable of earning a living. But when methods of fertility control improved and were widely disseminated, especially after

1950, and work for married women became available, more and more married women entered the labor market but without posing any threat to the family. For it soon became evident that, so long as married women were able or willing to assume the primary responsibility for the home along with a job outside the home, the traditional family was in no danger. The father remained the primary breadwinner, and the mother continued as housekeeper and principal child-rearer. Now, however, the family enjoyed the additional income from the working mother as a secondary earner.

None of these observations denies that many women—indeed a substantial minority of all women—have pursued careers out of interest and commitment to such aspirations and that many others have been compelled by poverty or economic necessity to support themselves and their families with full-time work. Nor do these observations deny that many women have suffered from discrimination when they sought to enter certain occupations or professions. No implication is intended, either, that women ought to refrain from careers or to cease to aspire to full-time work while rearing a family. And certainly there is no suggestion implied here that a woman ought to refrain from seeking to have her husband share equally the chores of the family if both of them pursue careers or jobs outside the home. The point is simply that compared with men the great majority of working women over the last century and a half have generally shaped their work around their family while, equally clearly, men have shaped their family life around their work. Why this pattern has persisted and what it means are among the questions that will have to be confronted in the next chapter. But the additional point that needs to be made is that a part of the argument of this book is that the difference between the work patterns of men and women noted here should be seen as a choice by women and not simply the result of male oppression or denial of equality of opportunity. That there were and are constraints on women's occupational choices goes without saying. But they are of the order that women were prepared to give up the pursuit of a career in order to have a family and marriage when it seemed too difficult or unrealistic to have both. In a sense, of course, that means that men's attitudes were not as egalitarian as they might theoretically be expected or hoped to be, but that is not the same as contending that women were prevented from pursuing a career by male fiat. Confronted with the social, psychological, or emotional costs of being unable to have children and family if she chose a career, the wife chose to opt for family and a secondary job, rather than a career. That was a constrained choice, to be sure, but a choice nonetheless.

Interestingly enough, students of working women in European history have also recognized the same centrality of the family in the lives of women as we have been noticing in the United States. "Working class women as a group," writes Patricia Branca, "never chose to make employment a primary means of identification in their lives. They rejected it when it conflicted with family-centered goals and welcomed it when it could supplement not only earnings but also the diversity of personal experience."[14] Although this statement is primarily intended to apply to working women in Europe before World War II, it applies quite neatly to the pattern we have described for women in the United States after 1945. For, though many more married women work today than in the past, the character of that work is but an extension of the pattern described by Branca for European working women of a much earlier period. The continuity is shown even more strikingly when it is recognized that in modern developing countries women's shaping of their work around their families is equally true. "Often the women themselves tend to prefer work in home industries or in service trades rather than in wage employment in large-scale industry," writes a modern student of women in developing countries. "The more flexible working hours in home industries are a great advantage for married women, and particularly for women with small children."[15]

Having looked at the patterns of women's work since 1945, we are now ready to examine more closely the implications these patterns hold for the future of women and for the future of the family in the United States. It is to the interrelations between women and the family that we turn in the next and final chapter. It is called woman's dilemma, for that is what confronts American women after two centuries of change in the family and in women's place.

XVIII

Woman's Dilemma

The increasingly important role that married women—especially mothers—now play in the labor force has caused many to wonder about where the American family is heading. For years it was almost an axiom of feminists and anti-feminists alike that when wives would enter the paid work force they would gain not only a sense of personal accomplishment but also a new sense of independence within the family that could not help altering traditional relationships. While the feminists looked forward to such gains, the anti-feminists deplored them. On the basis of what we have observed so far, however, neither the hopes of the one nor the fears of the other have been borne out. Women's work in the main is still shaped around the family, while the family is still shaped around the work of men—as has been the case ever since the First Transformation. To that extent the feminists have been disappointed. Yet the anti-feminists have not been proved completely right, either. For the rapid increase in married women's participation in the work force has been accompanied by other developments which are more to the liking of feminists. And though the connection between the changes in work patterns and the rise of a feminist movement in the 1960s is not easy to establish, that there is such a relationship seems reasonable. Let us look first at the revived feminist movement. What consequences has it had for women and for the future of the family in the United States?

A renewed feminist movement fairly burst upon the nation in the 1960s. Few women or men had predicted it, or even thought it likely. The surprise derived in substantial part from the over-selling of the suffrage in the first

436

decades of the 20th century. As we have seen already, the suffragists, in their desperate effort to gain the vote, had so enlarged the significance of the vote as a step in the achievement of women's equality that, once the Nineteenth Amendment was ratified, the tendency among most suffragists as well as the public at large was to think that the struggle for women's emancipation was over.

One sign of the overselling was the dismantling of the great suffrage organization itself. In its place was formed the League of Women Voters, an organization that was, to be sure, made up solely of women, but which explicitly eschewed taking stands solely on behalf of women. The League viewed women first as citizens and only secondarily as a sex in need of opportunities. In a sense, the League, like previous social feminist organizations such as the Women's Trade Union League and the Consumers' League, was not interested in equalizing opportunities for women. Its primary concern was to protect women. Hence during the 1920s and 1930s it worked with social workers and the government to shape social legislation helpful to women. The rationale behind such actions was that women were a special, disadvantaged group, more in need of protection than equality. And that was the reason that virtually all women's organizations during the 1920s and 1930s opposed the Equal Rights Amendment to the Constitution, which the National Women's party pressed upon Congress each year beginning in 1923.

The essential outlook of publicly active women in the decades after the achievement of the suffrage was neatly summed up in the activities and philosophy of Eleanor Roosevelt, certainly the most prominent woman in the nation during the 1930s and 1940s. No other President's wife in American history has been as socially aware and active as Eleanor Roosevelt, yet throughout her career she tailored her role to the traditional conception of women as helpmates to their husbands. Rather than simply let the home and family be the sole concern of a woman, Eleanor Roosevelt showed—as the social feminists of the 19th century had, too—that the world needed the moral power of women as much as the home did. In that way not only would the home be protected from outside forces harmful to it, but the world itself would be a better place for all. Like Jane Addams and other social feminists before her, Eleanor Roosevelt acknowledged differences between the sexes; indeed, it was just because women were different from men that they were needed in the world. Women brought to the world their own nurturing, warm, and supportive characters.

Even before Franklin Roosevelt became President, Eleanor Roosevelt was active in various social and political causes in New York City and New York state. During the 1920s, as later during the 1930s, she frequently took positions on social and political matters in advance of those of her more politically sensitive, and therefore more cautious, husband. His achievement of the presidency merely gave her a larger arena in which to assert her social feminism. Jim Farley, Roosevelt's Postmaster-General, for example, estimated that she personally brought some 4000 women into various jobs in the Post Office alone as part of her effort to include women in government. In order to encourage women reporters she did not allow male reporters to attend her press conferences during the White House years. After the death of her husband in 1945 she continued her active involvement with those interests of women that seemed to flow from their special characters as wives and mothers: peace, family relations, children, and health. She asserted no feminist ideology or outlook, though she offered to millions of women a model of what they could do in the world, though married and mothers. (Not all women appreciated the model, however, for to many she seemed to be neglecting her family and her husband just because she continued her social feminist works.)

Even without the undeniable influence of Eleanor Roosevelt, the Rooseveltian New Deal was an important force in expanding the influence of women in public life after suffrage. Thanks to the persistent efforts of an active woman politician like Molly Dewson, women gained an increasing number of positions within the councils of the Democratic party. In 1936 Dewson achieved her ambition of placing as many women as men on the important Platform Committee. Within the government, under the New Deal, a number of women filled important offices, beginning with Frances Perkins, a social worker from New York who became Roosevelt's Secretary of Labor and the first woman to be appointed to the Cabinet. It was revealing of attitudes toward feminism and women in those years that, although Perkins was opposed, and often ridiculed because of her sex, she did not consider herself a feminist and even refused to recommend public office to women. Instead, she made clear that she thought women ought to confine themselves to their traditional family roles. Among the other notable women who served conspicuously in the New Deal agencies were Hallie Flanagan, the head of the highly successful Federal Theater, Ruth Bryan Owen and Florence Harriman, who were ministers abroad, and Judge Florence Allen of the Federal Circuit Court. Moreover, simply because social workers were so frequently female, when New Deal agencies searched for staff, many women were appointed to middle- and lower-level executive jobs throughout the government. But again, the reason was unrelated to any drive toward equality. During those years it was generally assumed that the last barrier to women's emancipation had been leveled with the enactment of the suffrage. In fact, the very movement of a woman into the Cabinet or into the Federal judiciary seemed to prove that little, if anything, stood in the way of women's playing as large a role in public life as their talents and inclinations allowed.

A similar conclusion could have been drawn from the continued increase of women in the work force, even though, as we have seen, as late as 1940 less than 15 per cent of married women whose husbands were present then worked outside the home. And just because relatively few married women worked in the 1930s, the attempts on the part of some states to bar married women with husbands from public and other employment had little effect upon the total participation of women in the economy. In fact, during the 1930s more men were out of work in proportion to their role in the labor force than women. Women benefited from the new unionization drives of the 1930s, but not because of any feminist outlook on the part of either the A.F. of L. or the C.I.O. It just so happened that many women workers were concentrated in those industries which had not been organized before, but which, under pressure from the newly formed Committee on Industrial Organizations (C.I.O.), were now being brought into the labor movement. In sum, by the time of World War II the participation of women in the work force had neither revitalized nor sparked a feminist outlook among women. Indeed, aside from the National Women's party, which was minuscule in membership, there was no truly feminist organization in the whole country. Right down until the late 1960s, in fact, "feminist" was a dirty word, redolent of old maids, "blue-stockings," and man-haters.

Although the war drew literally millions of women into jobs and into the armed forces, no general feminist argument was made in justification. The massive movement of women, married as well as an unmarried, into the war effort was considered simply a response to an emergency, an activity that would be abandoned once the demands of the nation's war effort were met. It was in such an ideology-free atmosphere that large numbers of women in the postwar years took up jobs in the civilian economy. Ideology was absent, too, when married women began to move in great numbers into jobs outside the home in the 1950s. In fact, that was the decade of the baby boom and the new emphasis in the media upon home and traditional roles for women. The kickoff for the new attitude was a sensational—and popular—book *Modern Woman: The Lost Sex,* by Ferdinand Lundberg and Marynia Farnham, which appeared in 1947. Lundberg and Farnham made a frontal assault on all feminist assumptions, contending that women were unrealized and unfulfilled because feminist ideology—although almost none was to be seen—had tried to make them into men. During the 1950s the attack on women as workers outside the home mounted even as the number of married women in the work force rose. Historian Lynn White, Jr., then the president of Mills College, published his manifesto for a new education for women in 1950, *Educating Our Daughters.* He urged women's colleges, of which Mills was one, to "shake off their subservience to masculine values" and to produce a "distinctively feminine curriculum." By this he meant one geared to what most women did after college—that is, to care for home and children. He asked whether it was "impossible to present a beginning course in foods as exciting, and as difficult to work up after college, as a course in post-Kantian philosophy would be?" He thought it was not, providing the usual home economics emphasis upon bread-making and talk of proteins was dropped. "Why not study the theory and preparation of Basque paella, of a well-marinated shish-kebab. . . . A girl majoring in history or chemistry," he thought, "could well find time for one such course which, we may be sure, would do much to enliven her own life and that of her family and friends for years." Then he threw in what was to be the clincher: "It is rumored that the divorce rate of home economics majors is greatly below that of college women as a whole." Like Farnham and Lundberg, White believed that "the tragedy is not that our career-minded higher education has diverted some girls from marriage" but much worse than that, it has given them attitudes that have "prevented them from flinging themselves into the pattern of life which they had chosen. A symptom and a result is the small number of children they bear." In 1958 popular anthropologist Ashley Montagu, writing in the *Saturday Review,* announced that "being a good wife, a good mother, in short, a good homemaker is the most important of all occupations in the world. . . . I put it down as an axiom that no woman with a husband and small children can hold a full-time job and be a good homemaker at one and the same time."[1]

Signs that women were following some aspects of the new advice were evident in the upswing in the birth rate and in public-opinion surveys. Members of the class of '44, it was reported in the mid-fifties, produced more children in ten years than the members of the class of '21 had borne in a quarter of a century. In 1956 the *Ladies' Home Journal* published an article "The Plight of the Young Mother," in which a wife said that, in view of all her responsibilities in rearing three preschool children, her husband regretted his inability to afford a maid to help her. The apology brought forth from the wife the response, "Oh, fine, then what would I do all day?" [2]

Despite the celebration of home and children during the 1950s, however, the seeds of a feminist revival were germinating. The great outpouring of women—particularly wives and mothers—into jobs during the 1950s did not escape the attention of certain observers, however oblivious society at large may have been. For example, the Ford Foundation's study of women's work, published in 1957 under the title *Womanpower,* clearly recognized the significance of the changing patterns of work among women. And, though there was no hint of a feminist ideology or conclusion in the report, the study was obviously responding to the social changes that had been going on since 1945. The new John F. Kennedy administration in Washington in 1961, ambitious to leave its own mark upon the society, was also alert to the movement of married women into the work force. Not surprisingly, then, one of the first acts of the new President was to appoint a Presidential Commission on Women, with Eleanor Roosevelt as chairwoman. Roosevelt's appointment assured that the new Commission would not be feminist in either membership or intent.

The Commission's report in 1963 did nothing to change that expectation, even though by then Eleanor Roosevelt had died and been replaced by Esther Peterson, Director of the Women's Bureau. The Report certainly recognized the new and expanding role of married women in the economy, but it still asserted that a woman's primary role was as mother and wife. To strengthen the family, the report recommended special training of young women for marriage and motherhood. Significantly, it also took a stand against the Equal Rights Amendment, contending that the Fourteenth Amendment was sufficient protection for women's equality of opportunity. Only one member of the Commission, in fact, Marguerite Rawalt, later one of the founders of the National Organization for Women, actually supported the Equal Rights Amendment.

Despite the failure to take a feminist position, the President's Commission on Women nevertheless constituted a major turning point in the evolution of the modern women's movement. It was the first effort on the part of the Federal government to address the question of women in American society. That the time was ripe for such recognition was suggested by the rapid formation of similar commissions in the various states in the next few years. By 1967 all fifty states had set up commissions on the status of women.

The most immediate consequence of the Presidential Commission insofar as the Federal government was concerned was the enactment in June 1963 of the Equal Pay Act. It prescribed that women must receive pay equal to that of men when they performed the same work. It, too, was a landmark: the first piece of Federal legislation in American history prohibiting discrimination on the ground of sex. It still remains the only Federal law that deals with sex discrimination alone. Although today the principle of equal pay for equal work is the most widely accepted and least controversial aspect of the women' movement, the many years it took to get the principle written into law are worth remembering. As recently as World War II the principle was more honored in the breach than in the observance. Moreover, even after the passage of the Act resistance remained strong, as the hundreds of complaints filed by women in 1970 and 1971 against their employers testify. Despite its obviousness, in sum, the Equal Pay Act was a true milestone on the road to women's equality. (Great Britain passed such a law only in 1975.)

In 1963, the incipient woman's movement was overshadowed—and at the same time stimulated—by the escalating Civil Rights movement in behalf of blacks. Both the Kennedy and Johnson administrations were much more interested in pressing for black equality than for women's rights. But since arguments in support of equality of opportunity for one disadvantaged group were applicable to another, it was not long before women leaders began to draw an analogy and a remedy from the Negro Rights movement. Unexpected assistance for the cause of women's equality came from Congress in 1964, when women were included in the protections of the Civil Rights Act of that year. The explicit prohibition of discrimination on grounds of sex as of color, race, religion, and national origin was introduced by a conservative southern Congressman as a ploy to make passage of the Civil Rights bill more difficult. But when President Lyndon Johnson made it clear he wanted women's rights included, no further efforts were made to remove the provision. The Civil Rights Act of 1964 was surely the most significant single force behind the new feminist movement, for from then on women's equality of opportunity was endorsed by the Federal government.

There may have been legislative force behind the idea of women's equality, but was there the will to use the power provided in the law? After all, the constitutional and legal basis for Negro equality had long been present, but the civil rights agitation of the 1960s reminded Americans that without will legal authority was next to useless. The disappointing experience of blacks with Federal law, however, was not to be repeated with women, who, after all, were a much more numerous and vocal part of the population. Women themselves soon laid a social and intellectual basis for compelling the government to enforce the law. Among the several voices that helped to create an atmosphere favorable to women's rights, none was more influential and pointed than Betty Friedan's polemical book *The Feminine Mystique,* which appeared in 1963.

The book was an angry outburst from a highly intelligent woman who suddenly recognized that for too long she had accepted the idea that a middle-class woman's proper place was at home with her children even when that role was neither fully satisfying nor totally occupying. Cautiously steering away from an outright feminist argument, Friedan urged women to make a life for themselves outside of, and in addition to, their homes and families. (Nowhere in the book, significantly, did she call her cause "feminist.") She based her case not upon an appeal to abstract equality or feminism, but upon what she called "the problem that has no name,"—that is, the sense of frustration and lack of fulfillment many educated, middle-class women experienced as housewives.

Ironically enough, Friedan's book appeared just at that time in American history when more married women were leaving home for work than ever before. Yet, one might say, just because they were, *The Feminine Mystique* was social dynamite. Literally hundreds of thousands of women could make a connection between their lives as workers now, after years as wives and mothers, with what Friedan was saying. Many men, too, could see the connection between the claims of women and those of blacks, to whom they were being sensitized every day as the great Civil Rights movement of the 1960s lacerated the nation's conscience. *The Feminine Mystique* was only the first of several similar polemical works which honed to excruciating sharpness the case for women's equality. Among them were Alice Rossi's "Equality Between the Sexes: An Immodest Proposal," which appeared in 1964 in an issue, devoted to women in America, of the prestigious and influential magazine *Daedalus;* Kate Millett's *Sexual Politics* (1969); and Shulamith Firestone's *Dialectics of Sex* (1970).

Organizationally, too, the revived feminist movement owed its beginnings to Betty Friedan. Out of the royalties and prominence garnered from the financial success of the *Feminine Mystique,* Friedan organized the National Organization for Women in the fall of 1966 in Washington, D.C.

Present at the creation were thirty women and two men. Within a year, hundreds of women and men had joined the first truly feminist organization since the founding of the National Woman's party over half a century earlier. In a Bill of Rights for Women drawn up in 1967, NOW called upon the major political parties to support goals that would become the central principles of the women's movement in the 1970s. The two most striking—and most radical—were the advocacy of the Equal Rights Amendment and of "the right of women to control their reproductive lives." The second, of course, was ambiguous language denoting support of abortion as well as birth control. At that time an abortion was illegal in every state except when the mother's life was in danger.

By 1967, too, young educated women, who had not been especially attracted by Friedan's obviously middle-class organization, began to awaken to the issue of women's rights. The most dramatic example of that awakening occurred at the left-wing National Conference for a New Politics when militant blacks demanded 50 per cent of the seats as a recognition by whites of the justice of their cause. When women asked for a comparable representation in the light of their being 51 per cent of the population, they were summarily turned down. (The black Civil Rights leader Stokely Carmichael was reported to have said "the position of women in our movement should be prone.") The result of such relegating of women to subordinate places in the movement was that many young woman activists now saw the necessity for women to separate their cause from that of blacks or any political movement that was not devoted primarily to the interests of women. As one of the radical women said at the time of the Conference for a New Politics, "We intend to make our own analysis of the system, and put our interests first, whether or not it is convenient for the (male dominated) Left."[3] Although probably few of the young women who had moved into politics because of the Civil Rights movement of the 1960s knew it, this sudden recognition of the dangers of subordinating the cause of women to that of other minorities or policies was not a new experience for feminists. A century earlier Elizabeth Cady Stanton and Susan B. Anthony confronted it at the time of the ratification of the Fourteenth and Fifteenth amendments. They were then admonished to remember that "This is the Negro's Hour" and they must not confuse the issue by seeking the ballot, too.

By the opening years of the 1970s a number of organizations dedicated to pressing for equality for women had been formed in addition to NOW. Among them were the Women's Equity Action League, established in 1968 by academic and professional women, and the Women's Political Caucas, which, under the leadership of Friedan, Bella Abzug, Gloria Steinem, and Fannie Lou Hamer of Civil Rights fame, sought to open politics to feminist women. Groups of radical feminist women, like the Red Stockings and The Feminists, carried the argument to the extreme of having as little as possible to do with men, proclaiming them the enemy. Ti Grace Atkinson, one of the leaders of The Feminists, announced that, though she would be happy to debate or act with men for public purposes in behalf of women's rights, she would have nothing to do with men in her private life. The Feminists regarded heterosexual intercourse as oppressive and permitted only a third of their members to be married to or to live with men. As the ideology of The Feminists implied, one consequence of radical feminism was a forthright recognition of lesbianism. And so attractive was this ultimate appeal to sisterhood that for a time in the middle 1970s the issue threatened to divide irrevocably the women's movement. At the end of the decade, however, it was evident that, extreme as some ideologues of the movement might be, the great majority of women active in the cause were neither lesbians nor anti-male in outlook or intention. That this was so was evident at the highly successful national conference of several thousand women of all political and ideological persuasions held in Houston, Texas, in November 1977, to write a national agenda for women's rights. Significantly, the meeting was funded by the Federal government, an unprecedented sign of the success of the women's cause.

The remarkable rapidity with which the women's movement captured the allegiance of many women and men, as well as gaining the attention and support of the mass media, the academic community, government, and even business, was explained by several things. The increasing participation of married women in the work force was certainly a part of the explanation. And the general concern for equality which the Negro Rights Revolution sparked was certainly another. Then there was also a less easily recognized demographic fact, which was at once a consequence and a cause of the acceptance of women's rights. That was the unprecedentedly high proportion of women between the ages of 20 and 24 who were single. In 1974 the figure was 40 per cent, though in 1960 it had been only 28 per cent. Yet even the 1960 figure was the highest in the 20th century. Although the trend ran through all educational levels, it was especially noticeable among college-trained women. Later we will look again at this figure, since it also says something about women's attitudes toward marriage. But here its relevance is that it helps to account for women's interest in feminism, just as feminism may help to explain why young women were not marrying as young as they once had. So striking was the success of the women's movement that in 1978 veteran social-commentator David Riesman, in reviewing the great social upheavals of the late 1960s, told a British audience that the women's movement was "possibly the most lasting legacy of the . . . period of protests."[4]

That success, however, was not total. The most striking failure was the inability of the organized women's movement to add the Equal Rights Amendment to the Constitution. The amendment had been around for half a century before most women's organizations took an interest in it, as we have seen. So hostile were most women leaders and groups like organized labor to the ERA that it was plausibly alleged that one of the reasons President John F. Kennedy appointed his Commission on the Status of Women in 1961 was to head off the rising support for ERA in Congress. Both major parties had supported ERA in their platforms as early as 1944, and only the resistance of organized labor and most women leaders prevented it from being in the platforms of 1964 and 1968. To many women leaders, as Esther Peterson, the head of the President's Commission on Women, later remarked, the ERA was "a headache."[5] By endangering protective legislation for women it seemed only harmful to working women and of little use to professional women. It was for such reasons, too, that the Women's Bureau opposed the ERA throughout the 1960s. Then, under the leadership of Elizabeth B. Koontz, the first black woman to head the Bureau, a new turn was made. At Koontz's initiative, the Bureau in 1970 sponsored a conference on women which concluded with an endorsement of the ERA. That same year the Department of Labor itself reversed its long-standing opposition to the amendment. By 1972 the two houses of Congress had passed the amendment and sent it to the states. At that point ratification seemed relatively easy to accomplish, especially as the legislatures of several dozen states almost immediately voted for it. By the middle 1970s, however, one state legislature after another began to reject it, even though ratification lacked only a handful of states. By the summer of 1978 it became evident that the seven-year limit which had been placed upon the ratification period would expire before any of the remaining states would meet to act on the amendment. A quick campaign in behalf of extension of the time of ratification was successful, though not without acrimonious debate between proponents and opponents of the amendment. The opposition was measured in the limiting of the extension to only another three and one-half years.

The cause for the delay in ratification was complex and yet familiar. Part of the reason undoubtedly was that the amendment seemed to threaten some women as well as men. The remarks of Senator Sam Ervin, from North Carolina, who urged the Senate not to pass the amendment, probably reflected the view of many male opponents. "Keep the law responsible where the good Lord put it," he pleaded, "on the man to bear the burdens of support and the woman to bear the children."[6] It was significant that only Tennessee and Texas of all the states of the former Confederacy ratified the amendment; Tennessee state had been the single exception in the South's resistance to the Nineteenth Amendment sixty years before. The conservative South was still doubtful about the emancipation of women.

This time, too, women were active against the amendment, just as they had been in opposition to the suffrage. Phyllis Schlafly, a conservative Republican, had stumped the country for years telling women and legislators that the amendment would deprive them of their rights as wives and mothers and that it would, among other things, compel women to serve in the armed services in time of war. In some legislatures women members actually voted against ratification. A Gallup poll as late as July 1978 reported that a majority of the people in the country favored the ERA, including substantial proportions of men. But it was not without significance that more men than women supported the ERA. Forty-five per cent of women said that they either opposed the ratification or had no opinion. The women's movement, in short, was not able to overcome the fears of many women that the amendment would disturb or threaten their traditional place in the family, just as many women during the suffrage fight earlier in the century had feared its impact on the relation between husband and wife. Despite the contentions of Schlafly and other opponents, however, nothing in the ERA, any more than in the suffrage, would require individual women or men to alter their relations within marriage, though it would certainly facilitate changes in the direction of a wife's equality within marriage if that was what she wanted.

In a sense, the very success of the women's movement made it possible for opponents of the ERA to contend that the amendment was unnecessary. For, thanks to the Civil Rights Act of 1964, the various executive orders, and a series of judicial interpretations in favor of women's equality, all of the major barriers to equality of opportunity for women had already been removed without an ERA. The truth was that, despite the assertions from both sides, ratification of the amendment would not change much, so complete had been the legal and constitutional transformation brought about by the feminist revival. It was true, though, that passage of the ERA would imbed in the Constitution the legal basis for the feminist gains of the preceding decade and thus make their repeal difficult in the future. It would also hasten the removal of the few remaining legal obstacles to full equality of opportunity between the sexes.

Although the mass of women may not have been enthusiastic about the ERA, that fact ought not to leave the impression that the women's movement had not had a profound impact on large numbers of women. A poll by *Redbook* magazine in 1973 showed that 66 per cent of its readers favored the movement and 45 per cent admitted that it had raised their consciousness about women's opportunities. Less than 2 per cent of the women queried believed that women could realize their full potentialities by being a wife and mother only.[7] Here was as good a sign as any of the interaction between the movement of married women into the work force and the rise of the women's movement.

Readers of *Redbook,* however, were generally members of the middle class, and the prominence of that class in the new women's cause was one of its limitations. The women's movement was not able to transcend class or racial divisions among women. Throughout the history of feminism the problem of class divisions had always been present. During the earlier years of the 20th century there had been some efforts to link women of the working and middle classes. But not even those linkages now existed; in 1947, for example, the Women's Trade Union League had been disbanded at the suggestion of organized labor. The National Organization for Women, it is true, sought to attract ethnic and racial minority women into its ranks, but largely without success. And it probably was visionary to expect that women would be able to transcend class or race when men certainly had not succeeded in doing so. But, then, men did not have the common gender oppression that was believed to unite all women.

The heart of the matter was that feminism had always been a middle-class cause, so the new feminism, as represented by an organization like NOW was no exception. The interests of middle-class, college-educated women, who were at once the target of Betty Friedan's arguments and the source of her organization's membership, had concerns quite different from those of most working-class women. The sense of personal frustration that the *Feminine Mystique* spoke out against, and the appeal of careers that attracted many college-educated middle-class women to the women's movement, left working-class women largely untouched. A job to such women was considerably less attractive, however useful and even necessary it might be as a temporary or occasional source of family income. Sociologist Mirra Komarovsky reported in a study of working-class wives made at the end of the 1950s that "we find little evidence of status frustration among working-class wives. They accept housewifery," she concluded. She discovered no signs of that sense of frustration in the home that had been so prominent among middle-class wives she had studied earlier. A more recent, though impressionistic study of lower-middle-class women conducted by Louise Howe quoted a homemaker in the 1970s as asserting "that a lot of women are much better off married and at home than they would be at some low-paying job and they know this; they've usually worked before, after all. So when they hear some feminist writers or lawyers or something like that say that jobs are so terrific, they know that for the average woman that's a lot of baloney." Lillian Rubin in her recent study of working-class families in northern California pointed out that though the marriages which many young women of this class witnessed among their elders were hardly ideal, matrimony nevertheless often seemed better than the alternatives: "a job they hate, more years under the oppressive parental roof." Even when they continued to work after marriage—they considered it temporary. They simply did not see work outside the home as part of their role as they certainly considered it a part of men's lives.[8]

Demographer Judith Blake has pointed out that a very high proportion of women who work in the United States, regardless of their class, see work as temporary or hope to escape from it at some time. Her figures show that half or more of working women do not want to work, or desire part-time jobs. She cited a Harris poll of 1972 in which a national sample of women was asked how often they felt that "having a loving husband who is able to take care of me is much more important to me than making it on my own." Even among women under thirty, Blake reported, at least half said "frequently," while another 20 per cent said they felt that way occasionally. A fourth said "hardly ever." These data are also related to studies which show that a substantial proportion of husbands, even in the 1970s, tend to be less happy when their wives work. (Since a wife who does not work can usually be expected to devote more time to her husband's comfort, that reaction is not unexpected.) A 1973 survey of families in general found that when a wife worked full-time—that is, as a kind of career—38 per cent of husbands said they were "very happy in their marriage"; when the wives worked part-time the proportion rose to 45 per cent, and when the wives were at home the figure went up to 50 per cent. In short, for many non-professional women, whether from the working or middle classes, work outside the home might well seem to threaten their relation with their husbands. Moreover, the individualistic goals behind the women's movement did not have much appeal to them, since the jobs they would hold were rarely intrinsically interesting or fulfilling. And, as Helena Lopata has shown in her study of modern housewives, many middle-class women found deep satisfaction in their families and volunteer work. And despite the increased activity of women outside the home, the great majority of housewives she studied listed home and family activities ahead of any outside work, including church and community endeavors. Thus for many women, perhaps a majority, equality of opportunity in employment was not a real issue, especially if it seemed to compete with or threaten family relations.[9]

If a large proportion of women do not pursue their individuality as far as the modern women's movement counsels, that does not mean that the internal relationships within the family are not changing. Indeed, it is the thesis of this book that the modern family ever since its emergence at the beginning of the 19th century has been changing, often, as we have seen, under the influence of women's push for autonomy and individuality. In fact, over the last two centuries the changes within the family have frequently aroused alarm and comment. During the late 19th century the source of anxiety was the fall in the birth rate of the native, white middle class as compared with that of immigrants. And then at the opening of the 20th century the upsurge in divorce sparked a spirited national debate on the imminent demise of the family. In the 1920s and 1930s sociologists fretted over the fact that the family no longer seemed to have any economic function, such as it presumably had in pre-industrial days. "Even if the family doesn't produce thread and cloth and soap and medicine and food," sociologist William Ogburn rather defensively wrote in 1928, "it can still produce happiness." In our own time, despair over the future of the family has spawned such a mass of lugubrious studies that in 1977 the president of the Carnegie Corporation asked in the introduction to a new study on the family, "What happened and is happening to the American family? Is it still viable?"[10] During the early 1970s, radical psychologists like R. D. Laing and David Cooper proudly planned for *The Death of the Family,* as Cooper phrased it in a book with that title. They traced all that was wrong with children or society to the allegedly oppressive character of the nuclear, overly protective bourgeois family of industrial societies. At the same time, conservative psychologists like Urie Bronfenbrenner blamed the family for what was wrong with children and with society, but for just the opposite reasons: the family was too permissive, too uninvolved with child-rearing and mothering. "America's families and their children are in trouble," warned Bronfenbrenner in 1972. "Trouble so deep and pervasive as to threaten the future of our nation. The source of the trouble is nothing less than a national neglect of children and of those primarily engaged in their care: America's parents." In another article Bronfenbrenner ascribed the alienation of the young and the rise of juvenile crime to the increase in divorce, working mothers, and the single-parent household. A mother's continual presence in the household during a child's growing up, Bronfenbrenner insisted, was essential. He deplored the increasing tendency of women to be employed away from home even if they had small children.[11] And it will be recalled that in 1975 about a third of women with children under three years of age were in fact in the work force.

Radical social critics also found the American family defective. Historian Christopher Lasch reviewed the 20th-century literature on family sociology and psychology and found it, at the very least, conceptually confused. The argument of some sociologists that the family could divest itself of productive functions and still be a significant force in the lives of children Lasch thought wrong. "The so-called functions of the family form an integrated system," Lasch contended. Some functions cannot be abandoned without affecting all the others detrimentally. "The only function of the family that matters is socialization; and when protection, work, and instruction in work have all been removed from the home," he insisted, "the child no longer identifies with his parents and internalizes their authority in the same way as before, if indeed he internalizes their authority at all."[12]

There is no question that over the last two hundred years the family has been shedding, one by one, virtually all the functions it fulfilled in previous centuries. No longer is the family the principal place of learning for the child; it has long since ceased to provide either medical or psychological care, except of the most trivial kinds. Members of the family who need such help usually seek it elsewhere. It has been a century or more at least since religious life was centered at the family hearth or dinner table. Almost as many years have passed since the family ceased to be an economic unit in which members worked together to earn a collective living. The principal function of the modern family, at least over the last century and a half, has been to rear children and provide a haven, a place of rest, refreshment, and spiritual replenishment for its members. A sociologist put it well in the 1920s when he wrote that the function of the family was to "provide the best care for children, furnish a humanely satisfying affectional relationship and contribute to the personality development of parents and offspring."[13]

Modern critics of the family often deplore this loss of functions, but it is not at all clear that the loss has been severe or even important. It is quite possible that divestiture of functions has been a gain in that it has permitted a concentration upon the primary functions of the family without the distractions that must have occurred when the family was expected to be doctor, farmer, manufacturer, food preserver, tailor, baker, and carpenter as well as a source of affection, spiritual comfort, and teacher of values. To be everything may come close to being nothing. Once it is assumed that the primary function of the family is to provide love, support to children, and affection between spouses, it might be said that the modern family, unlike those of earlier ages, is for the first time free to perform its primary purposes without internal distraction. It is possible, in short, that not much of value has been lost at all.

In any event, at least one of the so-called lost functions seems to be returning. It is true that family members in industrial America have not worked in a common economic enterprise as most persons did when the typical family lived on a farm. Yet today, after the Second Transformation in women's work, it is hardly accurate to consider most wives as nonproducers. After all, almost half of American married women are now employed at some job outside the home. And in 1975 only about a third of families in which both spouses were present was the husband the sole breadwinner. (As recently as 1950, 56 per cent of such families counted the husband as the only earner.)[14] Moreover, as productive workers outside the home, married women are no less than in earlier times earners for the family. They work to contribute to the family, not to increase their individuality. In that way, at least, it is possible to view the new pattern of work for married women as a return to the pre-industrial one. In fact, English sociologists Michael Young and Peter Willmott have been so impressed with the similarity between the old, pre-industrial family and the new pattern of work for married women that they have coined a term to differentiate the two. Because they see the modern family as more egalitarian in the internal relationship between husband and wife they call it "the symmetrical family" to distinguish it from the male-dominated (patriarchal) family of previous centuries. They recognize what is true for the

American equivalent of the symmetrical family—namely, that, though husband and wife may still not be fully equal, they are more so than ever before, in part at least because the wife is employed. Most women, in short, are clearly productive members of the family today, even though they may not be independent. But then in the pre-industrial patriarchal family women were not independent, either. Finally, although the family of the 20th century may have changed in this respect from that of the 19th, its essential nature, which first became apparent in the early 19th century, has not altered. Women are still the primary child-rearers, even when they work, and the purpose of their work, in the main, is to support and advance the family, not to realize themselves as individuals.

There is another way in which the family today has changed while still retaining the essential features that emerged in the early 19th century. Affection between spouses and the love and care of children are still at the center of the modern family in America. But by the second half of the 20th century the center of gravity of the family has shifted from children to spouses. The cause for the change is at least twofold. One is that people of both sexes now live longer than ever before, and the other is that women now bear fewer children and have them closer together. A century ago, for instance, the average woman spent about twenty years in child-bearing and child-rearing—that is, until age 42, when her last child went off to school. Those years constituted about 51 per cent of her married life because the average husband died at age 56. By the middle of the 20th century, however, with fewer children and greater longevity for herself and her husband, a woman spent less than 20 per cent of her married life in such activities. Moreover, a century ago the average husband died two years before the average age of marriage of the family's youngest child. Thus, for most husbands and wives, there were at most only a few years together after family responsibilities had been met. During the second half of the 20th century, however, a husband's death, on the average, does not occur until he is almost 68, which, again on the average, is twenty years after the marriage of the couple's last child. Modern parents, in short, can expect a quarter of a century of life together without children at all—not to mention some forty years without small children. Surely this is quite a different intra-familial experience than Americans have known during most of the nation's history. (Women today can also expect some ten years of widowhood, on the average, as against a mere four years a century ago.) [15]

This long period during which couples live by themselves without children is so recent a social development that its meaning for the family has barely been studied at all. Some jaundiced observers have implied that an upsurge in marital disruptions will occur once the prop of children has fallen away. But figures as late as 1969 still show that the highest divorce rates are among ages 20 to 24, and there is no sign as yet of a rise among the so-called "empty nest" age groups. In fact, studies of marital happiness by age report that couples identify their period of greatest happiness as that after the children have left home for good. The years of child-rearing, on the other hand, are usually reported by parents as a time of tension and dissatisfaction, rather than of greatest happiness.

If one side of the modern family was that it provided an intense emotional ambience and support for its members, that gain carried a price: it could be lost. For if marriage was the ideal relationship and the home the ideal sanctuary, as so much of 19th-century advice literature insisted, then when marriage and family were disrupted the pain inflicted was that much greater. And for over a century now Americans have been aware of and worried about their rising divorce rate, which indeed has long been among the world's highest. Paradoxically, one reason divorces have become increasingly common is just that Americans have invested so heavily in marriage and family: when expectations are so high, it is inevitable that they will not be fully achieved. Even more important as a source of marital disruption is that modern marriage—that is, the kind which emerged at the end of the 18th century—has placed an increasingly heavy emphasis upon affection between spouses. When the family provided education, medical care, subsistence, and work, as well as love and companionship, divorce or separation was hardly the first thing one thought of when disagreements broke out between spouses. But when love is the purpose as well as the cement of marriage, a diminution of affection naturally leads to thoughts of dissolution. For what can be the justification of a modern marriage when love and companionship have fled? Moreover, as the opportunities for work for women increased, the practicality of escaping from an unsatisfactory marriage improved for women. And insofar as husbands objected to their wives' working, that, too, has increased the likelihood of divorce. At least one modern study has reported that as a wife's earnings increase so do the probabilities of marital break-up. The marriage least likely to disrupt is one in which a husband is clearly the sole breadwinner.

Today, the divorce rate in the United States is the highest in the world. Yet even that measure of the ease with which marriages are disrupted in this country does not tell the full story. In 1940, for example, there were twice as many married persons living apart from spouses as there were people listing themselves as divorced. And subsequent study found that the great proportion of those who were separated remained so. There is no reason to believe that the rate of separation has come down, though easier divorce laws may have reduced it somewhat. (The effect of changes in the law can be easily exaggerated, however. When California introduced a no-fault divorce law in the 1970s the rate of divorces spurted upward, but then fell back to the previous level.)

Divorce obviously has different meanings for the persons involved. For women seeking escape from an oppressive marriage, divorce offers a feminist solution, as we have noted already. For women without a means of support, divorce can be a traumatic experience. For women who are mothers, divorce usually imposes new and heavy burdens, and it affects most seriously a third party, the children. Divorce has its heartaches for men, too, but, since most men do not receive the children in a marital breakup and the great majority of men have jobs, the impact of divorce upon men generally is less severe than upon women or children.

The most obvious measure of the severity of the impact of divorce on women and children is that families headed by women are among the poorest in the country. In 1973, some 45 per cent of all families identified as living in poverty in the United States were headed by a woman. (More than half of all children living in poverty were in women-headed households.) Moreover, the number of mother-headed households is rising because more women with children are being divorced. In 1940 about 30 per cent of all white women who had been married and then had their union disrupted were childless. By 1970 the childless constituted only 18 per cent. Today, it would appear, women are more likely to take on the responsibility of children after divorce than they were earlier. In 1970, some 77 per cent of white women and 85 per cent of black women with children but without husbands maintained their own households. Yet as recently as 1940 only 45 per cent of white women and 40 per cent of black women did.[16]

Today more and more marriages that break up include children. For most of the history of divorce in the United States, the average number of children involved had been declining. In 1867, the earliest date for reliable national figures, the average number of children in a divorce in which children were involved was 2.1. But by 1900 the average was down to 1.87 children, and in 1932 it had decined further to 1.74. Considering the general fall in the birth rate that decline was to be expected. Less expected, however, has been the rise in the average since 1945. By 1955 the average number of children was 1.92, the highest since 1886. By 1967 the figure was 2.18 or slightly higher than that registered a century earlier.[17] When it is remembered that today couples have much more reliable methods of fertility control than couples in the 19th century, it would seem that modern Americans are not waiting to see how their marriage works out before having children.

The obvious effect is that, as far as children are concerned, more of them are being touched by divorce than ever before. Throughout the history of marriage, even before divorce became important, large numbers of children have had to suffer the loss of a parent through death. In fact, as we saw in Chapter VII, until very recently death was much more likely to remove a parent than divorce. As late as 1940, for example, over twice as many children lost a parent from death as from divorce. Not until 1965 did divorce surpass death as a cause for the loss of a parent. Thereafter, however, divorce has surged ahead. In 1970, for instance, some 60 per cent of children who lost a parent that year did so because of divorce. Consequently, that year only about 70 per cent of white children under 18 years of age were still living with their two natural parents who had been married only once. Among black children only 45 per cent were. It has been estimated that of children born in 1970, nearly 40 per cent of them will experience life in a one-parent household sometime before they reach 18 years of age.[18]

It is just this rising proportion of disrupted homes that gives substance to the fear that the modern American family is falling apart and failing to do its job. Yet, as sociologist Mary Jo Bane has pointed out, the effects of divorce on children are not clearly established. The adverse affects that past studies have turned up may well be consequences of poverty in conjunction with marital break-up rather than the result of divorce alone. Moreover, there is some evidence that children adjust fairly quickly to the discontinuities of divorce. From the standpoint of the children, an end to an unhappy marriage is probably preferable to living in a household characterized by tension and acrimony.

Despite the continued rise in divorce, however, there seems every reason to anticipate that both marriage and family will persist in the United States. For one thing, most marriages, despite the viewers with alarm, do not end in divorce—at least not yet. Moreover, marriage in the United States seems to be more popular than ever before. In 18th-century Andover, for example, about 10 per cent of women never married, even though at that time a woman had almost no alternatives to marriage. And, as we saw in an earlier chapter, between 10 and 11 per cent of women born in the last four decades of the 19th century failed to marry. Thereafter the proportion began to fall. Almost 95 per cent of women born between 1921 and 1925 had already married by age 50. Presumably a few more would marry after that. The proportion of Americans of both sexes who marry—between 90 and 95 per cent—may well be the highest proportion possible, given the difficulties of bringing compatible persons together.[19]

Even if the marriage rate is not the highest possible, it is certainly the highest in the world. In 1960 only one country came even close to the United States in the proportion of either sex of marriageable age who married. That country was Germany, where 81.1 per cent of males married, as compared with 88.2 per cent in the United States. But the high proportion for German males was a special case, being a function of the depleting effects of the war on the male population. This can be seen in that only 53.3 per cent of German women married as against 73.5 per cent of American women. In Spain that same year the marriage rate for men was 58.3 per cent and 45.9 per cent for women. Aside from the Germans, the closest any nation came to the marriage rate for males in the United States were the Japanese, with 75.1 per cent.[20]

Americans also lead the industrialized world in the youth of those who marry, a further sign of the popularity of marriage in this country. For most of American history prior to the 20th century, the age of marriage among men hovered around 25 and 26 years and around 22 for women. During the 20th century, however, the age has fallen, especially for men. In 1955, for example, the median age of marriage for men was 22, and 20 for women. In 1974 over 40 per cent of all 20-year-old women were already married. What is particularly striking about the low age of marriage among Americans is that the United States, of all the industrialized nations, also has the highest proportion of young people in higher education, a pattern that ought to raise, rather than lower the age of first marriage. Although there can be no doubt that these figures measure the popularity of marriage today among Americans, it ought also to be acknowledged that they probably also measure the unrealistic expectations of young Americans. As all statistics demonstrate, teenage marriages are especially prone to breakdown.

Finally, the popularity of marriage among modern Americans is most strikingly demonstrated by the high rate of remarriage among both sexes.

In 1970 only 3.6 per cent of divorced men aged 35–44 and only 5.5 per cent of divorce women of those ages had not remarried. Most divorced persons remarry within five years, and most keep themselves married: very few Americans have more than two marriages. Particularly striking during the 20th century is the rise in the rate of remarriage among women after widowhood or divorce. In 1910, for example, only 28.7 per cent of women between 50 and 54 who had lost their spouses remarried. In 1970 the rate of remarriage among the same age group was up to 45.2 per cent. What is notable about these particular figures is that the rise coincides rather closely with the movement of married women into the work force after 1950. As late as 1940 the proportion of the 50–54 age group who remarried was no more than 31.3 per cent, or an increase of less than three percentage points in the previous thirty years. But in the thirty years *after* 1940 the increase was almost 14 percentage points.[21] Since those were the years in which married women were entering the work force in large numbers, the coincidence suggests that the motive behind the upsurge in remarriage reflected the widened horizons of married women as a result of their working; they found husbands more easily, or at least were prepared to look for them! In any case, it does suggest that a husband's support was not the primary reason for the increase.

Because the remarriage rate is keeping pace with the divorce rate it follows that Americans are not rejecting marriage. When a particular marriage fails to meet their needs they end it, but continue to search for a better one. Moreover, as sociologist Kingsley Davis has pointed out, "they would rather risk a poor first marriage than to postpone marriage and they would rather get a divorce early than to continue a bad marriage."[22] Marriage as an institution may not be in the process of repudiation among Americans, but increasingly it is being shaped to individualistic purposes. For what the figures on divorce and remarriage tell us is that, among the increasing number of Americans whose marriages break up, the primary concern seems to be individual satisfactions; only secondarily are the interests of children or the endurance of an earlier decision about family formation taken into consideration. This change in priorities for children will be looked at again later in this chapter, for it suggests that an important alteration in the family since the 19th century may be in process.

Young women's attitudes toward marriage may also be changing, primarily because of the new opportunities that have recently been opened to women and the general influence of the women's movement. Sociological studies of age at first marriage show that when economic or job opportunities improve for women, age of marriage usually rises. And the increase in the median age of first marriage for women in 1970 over 1960 may well be explained by expanded economic opportunities for women. Another sign of a change in young women's attitudes toward marriage is that the number of single women among the 20–24 age group has been rising dramatically over the last fifteen years, as we noted in a different context some pages earlier. In 1974 a full 40 per cent of women in that age bracket were still single. Although the great majority of them will undoubtedly marry, it is unlikely that all will. If that should turn out to be the case, then one consequence of the new atmosphere for women in America over the last decade may well be a fall in the proportion of women who ever marry. That this shift, if it occurs, would be related to education and opportunity is suggested by the fact that about one-fifth of women between 35 and 44 years of age who also have some graduate education or an income of $20,000 or more in 1972 had not married. This figure is to be compared with the barely 5 per cent of women in that age bracket without college education who were still single.[23]

Whether this discrepancy is to be explained by the unwillingness of males to marry women of high education and earning power, as the demographer who reported the finding suggested, or by the lack of interest of women of that status in marriage at all, is not clear. But it is a fact that marriage as it is now constituted, other studies show, is generally more favorable to men than to women. Thus this postponement or outright rejection of marriage by educated women may be a sign of their pursuit of individuality, just as many college-educated women at the end of the 19th century also rejected marriage when it did not appear to accommodate their individual interest as women.

Although there have certainly been changes in marriage and the family over the last two hundred years, with more, perhaps, in prospect, that does not alter the essential argument of this chapter. The family in the second half of the 20th century still exhibits the main features that characterized the early 19th-century family. For, as historians of the family are finding out, the institution of the family is highly flexible and quite adjustable to social change. It is today, as it was two hundred years ago, the primary institution for the nurturing of children, and its essential interest for adults is that it provides affection, sexual expression, and companionship. This is the meaning to be drawn from the high proportion of persons who marry and then remarry almost immediately if divorce intervenes. As Kingsley Davis has observed, "with all the changes that urban-industrialism has brought, the basic principle of a family mode of population replacement has not been altered." [24] The persistence of earlier patterns is also mirrored in the fact that young people today stay at home longer than at any time in the past three hundred years. In 1974, for example, over 85 per cent of 18- to 19-year-old young men were living at home, and of those living away from home over half were already married. Among young women of that age bracket, if one leaves aside those who married—and women marry at younger ages than men—then only 9 per cent were living apart from their parents in 1974. In short, the trend toward keeping children at home longer, which began with the emergence of the modern family in the early 19th century, has continued. It will be recalled that the usual age for leaving home in colonial New England was perhaps as early as ten, while in the middle of the 19th century it was up to around fourteen or fifteen.

It is true that the late age of leaving does not tell us anything directly about the quality of the relationship between children and parents. But it is reasonable to assume that it is not a hostile one. This conclusion is warranted, too, because today's families are smaller than those in the past, a change that suggests more attention is being given to each child. Furthermore, studies show that, even when differences in income are taken into account, children in small families receive more education, obtain better jobs, and earn higher incomes than children from large families. Too much concentration of attention by parents upon children can have deleterious as well as positive effects, to be sure. But even that would not suggest any weakening of the emphasis upon the rearing of children with which the modern family began in the early 19th century.

It might be argued that the fall in the birth rate over the last quarter-century suggests that people are less, rather than more interested in children than in the past. Certainly with more reliable and more convenient contraception, fewer or no children at all is a real option for parents. By the 1920s and 1930s, the acceptance of contraception was widespread, and the methods, though not novel as compared with those of the 19th century, were better understood. Condoms were greatly improved by then and easily available in most drug stores, though always as an "under the counter" item. Thanks to the efforts of Margaret Sanger and birth-control organizations, the diaphragm became better known and was widely used by middle-class women. During the 1930s one of the great opponents of birth control, the Roman Catholic Church, endorsed the so-called rhythm method or what the 19th century called the "safe period." And by the 1930s use of that method had greater chance of success, since by then physicians could identify the correct infertile period of a woman's cycle, even if it was still difficult to locate its precise boundaries for any given woman. By the 1940s and 1950s virtually all of the state and Federal laws enacted during the 19th century to prohibit the dissemination of birth-control information were repealed or struck down by the courts. The most dramatic phase in the contraceptive revolution of the 20th century was the perfection of the anovulent pill, which had been for years the ambition of many friends of women, notably feminist philanthropist Katherine Dexter McCormick and scientist Gregory Pincus. By the 1960s, as a result, a married couple had at its disposal for controlling fertility a remarkable array of techniques, some of which delivered, when properly used, almost 99 per cent certainty. And one consequence was that the birth rate, which had fallen to its lowest point in the 1930s, began another sharp drop in the 1970s.

Significantly, however, despite the technical possibility of an increase in childlessness, that has not happened. The number of children per family has certainly declined over the last century, but the proportion of women giving birth to a single child or no child at all has hardly increased at all. Slightly more than 9 per cent of women born in 1846–55 had one child, while 11.7 per cent of mothers born in 1935–39 bore only a single child. What changed in the intervening years was that today only about a third of women bear more than three children, whereas a century ago a third of women bore seven or more children. (Of women born in 1935–39, only 7.3 per cent gave birth to seven or more children.) Furthermore, when women today are queried as to whether or not they want children, an overwhelming majority say "yes." In 1975, for instance, less than 5 per cent of women who were interviewed for that purpose said they wanted or expected to be childless. In the light of this evidence, sociologist Mary Jo Bane has concluded "that the vast majority of American women will continue to have at least one child."[25] And when one considers that the means today for having no children at all are so reliable, the present-day family's interest in children might well be considered to be higher than when the option of childlessness was much less practical.

A similar positive prognosis for the continuation of the family emerges from Lillian Rubin's examination of white working-class families in California in the early 1970s. She notes that even the young women in her study who became pregnant before marriage never considered abortion or not marrying; neither did the men. Marriage to these people, Rubin concluded, was a part of the achievement of womanhood and manhood.

However much the lives and even values of young men and women of this class may differ, she continued, "both are tied closely to marriage and parenthood." For most people, Rubin asserted more generally, "the issue is not *whether* the family has a future, but *what* that future will be like. For after all the questions are asked and the speculations are done, the unshakeable reality remains: most Americans of all classes still live in families and will continue to do so for the foreseeable future at least." Sociologist Kingsley Davis, writing in 1972, was no less convinced than Rubin that Americans, on the basis of their behavior, are firmly wedded to the family. The birth rate may be falling, he observed, but that does not mean the line will run off the bottom of the chart. Rather than comparing present-day urban birth rates with those in pre-industrial or rural days, as demographers and other worriers about the state of the family generally do, Davis advised that we should remember what the ordinary American well knows: behind all the abstract figures on the chart are real babies, and no society has ever done without them. It is unlikely that Americans will be the first.[26]

Psychologist Jerome Kagan predicts the continuance of the family for related reasons. He recently observed that, although modern young people may have drifted far from their families, they have found no other institution to replace the family. Without other groups to rely on, modern youth has greater freedom and "minimal constraints on autonomy of action," but the price is "loneliness and the unavailability of any person or group in which to invest strong emotion. It is for this reason that marriage and the creation of a new family are likely to experience a recrudescence in the West. We take as an axiom," Kagan continues, "that the self resists depersonalization. As modern environments make a sense of potency and individual effectiveness more difficult to attain, freedom from all affective involvements becomes more and more intolerable. Involvement with a family is the only viable mechanism available to satisfy that hunger."[27]

Looking at the modern family from the perspective of the last century, sociologist Peter Uhlenberg is no less sanguine about its future. After noting the rise in divorces and other signs of familial instability, he points out that in the 1970s a greater proportion of American women who reach 50 years of age achieve what today is thought to be the expected pattern of life than was true for women born as recently as 1870. (The expected pattern is that a woman and her husband are alive and married when the last child leaves the home to marry or pursue a career.) For men today that situation would also be true; moreover, the percentage of men who *never* marry today is less than half of that for men born in 1870. Uhlenberg's conclusion is that despite the changes in the family that everyone worries about, the "quantitative evidence does not support the notion of family disorganization and disintegration. An increasing proportion of the population lives out the life course almost wholly within a family context. In speculating on the future," he sums up, "one should not ignore the remarkable stability and adaptability of the American family during the past century of vast social change."[28]

If, then, the family is "here to stay," as Mary Jo Bane has also insisted in her recent book of that title, and as the facts of American social life seem to suggest, what effect does that have upon the realization of women's equality of opportunity? For, as has been evident throughout this book, an assumption of the modern family has always been that women are the primary child-rearers. As a result, there has been a fundamental tension, if not conflict, between the individualistic interests of women and those of the family. For the great majority of women that tension has not resulted in rupture, though at the same time it has certainly been the force which has gradually but significantly changed the relationship between husband and wife. Most married women now work outside the home. Yet at the same time their work is still largely shaped around the family. Insofar as it is, women's opportunities for self-realization on a par with men's are obviously limited. Certainly as things now stand, it is difficult if not impossible for most women to think about a career under such an intra-family arrangement—that is, to perceive work as enduring, personally important, and primary. Those women who have pursued careers along with family have had to make special arrangements, since by definition a career cannot be a part-time job or be interrupted for extended periods of child-rearing. The very fact that some professional women have had to exert extraordinary personal efforts and incur exceptional financial costs to combine career and family make it clear that such a solution is hardly practical for women in general. It provides no answer to the question of how to offer young women at the outset of their lives the same personal horizons that are routinely vouchsafed to young men.

One possible alternative is to recognize that the definition of career used here is one derived from the lives of men, not women. Ought we to assume that a career for a woman must be the same as for a man? Feminist sociologist Alice Rossi, along with other commentators on women's situation, does not think so. Beginning with the assumption that women's lives are inextricably bound up with not only the bearing but also the rearing of children, Rossi contended in a controversial article in the magazine *Daeda-lus* in 1977 that, if women are to have equality of opportunity, then the work patterns of the economy must be altered to fit her fundamental relationship to children and family. At the very least that solution would mean deliberately creating the kind of part-time work that would permit women to structure their work—and careers—around family responsibilities. It would also entail making it possible for a husband and wife to share a job, or so to restructure the work of a husband that he could assist with child-rearing. More than ten years earlier, Ellen and Kenneth Keniston had offered a similar solution. Like Rossi, the Kenistons were convinced that children needed individual care and saw women as best able to provide it. Hence they called for a third model of child-rearing, one "that epitomizes marriage *and* career instead of marriage or career." Unfortunately, the Kenistons did not make clear how the third model was to be realized. Rossi at least seized the nettle of utopianism and called for a radical restructuring of work. In 1977, when Kenneth Keniston headed a Carnegie Corporation study on children and the family, he came closer to Rossi's position. Work, he argued, not the family, ought to be reshaped to fit the needs of family. "It should no longer be assumed," he wrote, "that families are not the business of employers or public officials." [29] But here, too, no practical or specific ways to alter the order of things were laid out. Presumably he would support something along the lines of Rossi's part-time work for women and job-sharing. Yet if something so fundamental as restructuring the work patterns of a whole economy is necessary, then the proposal's practicality is called into question, at least for the immediate future. Moreover, if traditional work patterns must be abandoned to accommodate women's family responsibilities, then the work of most women will in fact be different from men's. Such a two-tiered career structure, it can be predicted, would leave women, once again, as inferiors and their work as second-best.

If a career is defined in the traditional or masculine way, the means for achieving equality of opportunity for women are no easier. One possibility is for women to fit in their careers with their husband's, as many career women have done in the past and do today. In that model a woman moves geographically when her husband's career demands it, and then at the new location picks up her own career as best she can. Since modern careers usually depend upon some geographical mobility for optimal achievement, under such an arrangement women's careers usually end up truncated, if not destroyed, since they have little or no opportunity for mobility. (It is possible, though much less common, for a woman to have the primary career, with the man following with his. But that option still leaves one person's career opportunity unequal.) Some modern career couples have modified this practice by taking turns in moving from job to job as opportunities arise. If the moves are made in strict rotation, both may lose out in the long run, at least as measured by achievement at high level posts. Yet as a way of combining career and family that model may well prove a serviceable solution for professional couples who cherish family as much as career success. In a variant of this model, couples live apart sometimes in different cities located in different states—for a portion of the week or year in order that each may be free to pursue job opportunities. Again, personal, not to mention financial, costs are high, though for high income couples with flexible and adjustable personalities, it is surely affordable.

Up to now nothing has been said about children, though obviously they are the heart of the problem of reconciling family and career. If both parents have careers—or full-time jobs, for that matter—who takes care of the children? If the answer is that both do—share and share alike—then both careers or jobs may suffer, and the result will be a compromise comparable with that worked out by the couples who alternated in their career moves. If both parents share in child-rearing, then both parents probably will sacrifice full success in the interest of family, too. And that, also, may become a recognized solution for many couples with children.

But long before that point is reached, the question of the husband's willingness to accept such a limitation on his own career or job will have to be faced. At this stage in the analysis, the problem is no longer peculiar to professional or career couples; it applies equally to any couple in which both parents want to work full-time. Michael Young and Peter Willmott, in their book *The Symmetrical Family*, refer to each parent in such a family as having two jobs rather than one. Under the old order in the 19th century, they note, the wife took care of the children and the household while the husband's job was outside the home. Then in the 20th century, as married women entered the paid work force, wives in effect took on a second job, while husbands continued to fill only one. But in a symmetrical family, as Young and Willmott see it, when husband and wife share house and child care as well as having jobs outside, each has two jobs.

When Young and Willmott wrote their book, they were optimistic bout the future of the symmetrical family, but so far, in the United States at least, that optimism has a thin basis in fact. As we saw in Chapter XVII, the general record of husbands' assuming household tasks, not to mention baby care, is pretty poor. There have been recent efforts, to be sure, to show that men have a kind of "paternal instinct," which encourages many men to want to share the care of children with their wives. James A. Levine, in his recent book *Who Will Raise the Children?*, provides some encouraging examples of male involvement in child-rearing. Yet even Levine has to admit that attempts to institutionalize and thereby encourage such behavior more broadly among fathers have been less than successful. For instance, he notes that though the Board of Education in New York City grants about two thousand maternity leaves each year, in the two years since September 1973, when men first became eligible for child-care leaves, only eight such leaves have been taken by fathers. In Seattle only one father has taken a child-rearing leave, and in Berkeley, California, where all municipal employees are eligible for such leaves, at the time Levine wrote not a single father had taken up the opportunity to stay home with his child.

Sociologist Mirra Komarovsky found that, though many American college men in the early 1970s said they believed in egalitarian marriages, they actually expected their wives to stay home to rear the children. They were willing to help, she reported, but certain tasks like diapering, washing, or cleaning they thought should not be expected of them. Jessie Bernard, another sociologist of the family, thought in 1972 that she saw signs of change in men's willingness to assume the care of children. In support of her contention she cited evidence from a popular TV show in 1970. But in subsequent years the evidence has been rather more negative than positive; there just have not been any signs that men are undertaking child care in substantial numbers or that they want to. As Lillian Rubin reported in her study of young white working-class families, men may help around the house, but they invariabley see such help as just that, not as responsibilities. "With all the talk about the changing structure of family roles," Rubin wrote, "a close look reveals that when it comes to the division of labor in the family, it's still quite traditional. Over and over, that's the story: He does man's work, she does woman's work."[30] In sum, if there is a strong desire on the part of men to share in child-rearing, it has not been very evident nor widely developed on any class level.

Sociologist William J. Goode has explained that the differences in attitudes and behavior regarding gender equality may be little more than apparent between working- and middle-class men. "Lower-class men concede fewer rights ideologically than their women in fact *obtain* and the more educated men are likely to concede *more* rights ideologically than they in fact grant. One partial resolution of the latter tension," Goode noticed, "is to be found in the frequent assertion from families of professional men that they should not make demands which would interfere with his *work:* He takes precedence as a professional, not as family head or as male; nevertheless, the precedence is his. By contrast, lower-class men demand deference as *men,* as heads of families." [31]

Nor have men in other industrial societies been more interested in personally bringing up children. One sociologist reported that, though it is Swedish government policy to enlist men in work at day-care centers, she did not find in visiting two dozen of such institutions in 1973 more than a single man at any of them. and even so most of the men were either conscientious objectors or older men.[32] Sweden, in short, also has had difficulty in tapping the "paternal instinct."

Another alternative to women as sole child-rearers, and the option most commonly advocated, is some form of institutional arrangement that would permit women to pursue work away from their children. Such institutional child care, usually under government auspices, has been the principal answer of feminists and other advocates of the expansion of career and work opportunities for women. The advocacy has been very recent, however. For as we have seen in earlier pages, prior to 1940 very few friends of women were prepared to defend the employment of mothers of small children, unless necessity compelled her to work. In some respects, Americans have come a long way toward recognizing the hard facts of life for many women—namely, that most married women now work and for reasons considerably more substantial than the need for "pin money." There was a time, and not so remote, either, when no income tax deductions were allowed to working mothers for child care on the ground that such a concession would encourage women to work outside the home! Yet at that time—in the 1950s—millions of mothers of small children were already working. But if that particular refusal to face the facts of women's work has now passed, the overall situation has not altered much. American governments are still reluctant to establish child-care centers, even though it is well recognized that over a third of children under school age are in families in which the mother is employed.

Part of the reason for that reluctance, it is necessary to recognize, is that most working mothers seem to be wary of institutional child care. It is felt, apparently, to be intrinsically inadequate. A study made in 1958, for example, found that only 2 per cent of children under 12 years of age of working mothers were in group-care units. The author of the study concluded, therefore, that such care was primarily an expenditure of upper-income families. A more detailed study made in 1965 of working mothers with at least one child under 14 reported that almost 46 per cent of the children were cared for at home—usually by fathers or by outsiders coming into the home. Another 16 per cent of the children were supervised in another home, and only 2.3 per cent of the mothers placed their children in a group-care center. Almost 88 per cent of the children under the age of six were cared for either in the home of the working mother or in the home of someone else. Less than 6 per cent were placed in a day-care center. Finally, a study in 1971 found only slight change in the pattern of parental behavior in this regard since 1965. At that date about 8 per cent of white working women placed their children in day-care centers; 15 per cent of black working women did. Well over half—56 per cent—of white working women used care at home by family members or others.[33]

A friend of the day-care-center solution might well argue that this limited recourse by mothers to such care stemmed from a dearth of facilities rather than from a lack of parental interest. But surveys of parental preferences and other signs suggest that cannot be the main reason. Regardless of quality, institutional care never is high on lists of parental preferences. Even more significant as a measure of how parents feel are the results of experiments with low-cost, high-quality institutional care. In all the instances studied, the parental response has been lower than expected. At Gary, Indiana, for example, the highest enrollment of children was 15 per cent of eligible preschoolers. In experiments where subsidies were offered, the results were much the same. And even group-care centers located at the work site of the mother, comparable with those widely established in some European countries, have not attracted the interest of working mothers.

Such a history has caused one authority on institutional child care to conclude in 1977 that "evidence accumulates to indicate much less interest on the part of parents in formal day-care centers than the public debate implies." Apparently the majority of mothers prefer to leave their children with relatives or known friends. Other professionals in the field are now becoming much less sanguine about child-care centers as quality institutions, for, to provide care of the level of quality that a mother as an individual routinely provides in her home, day-care centers would have to be much more lavishly funded than the society or the majority of parents is either able or willing to do. To pay for quality care, sociologist Mary Jo Bane has recently estimated, might well consume half the income of a working mother. From a perspective less friendly to women's aspirations, Selma Fraiberg has written that to provide the kind of care she thinks children deserve "we will need over 2,000,000 devoted and dedicated 'substitute mothers' with professional qualifications to serve the needs of 6,500,000 children under the age of six whose mothers are employed." At the moment such persons do not exist in such numbers.[34]

Furthermore, the experience of other industrial countries with institutional child care warns us against the easy assumption that the underdevelopment of institutional care is a peculiarly American deficiency. No country, including the Soviet Union and Sweden, the two societies which have made the heaviest commitment in this respect, has sufficient childcare facilities for all the children of working mothers. And though expense is undoubtedly an important reason in accounting for the disparity, the experience of a number of European countries suggests that it may also stem from the reluctance of women to place their children in such centers. A survey made in England in 1965, for example, showed that two-thirds of working women who were queried left their children with husbands or other relatives. About 2 per cent of children under two years of age, and about 12 per cent of children aged three and four, were in day nurseries there. These are figures somewhat higher than for the United States, but they are not substantially different. Alice Rossi in 1977 noted that "there is a drift in East European countries away from day-care centers for children less than three years old. Not only is such care extremely expensive—the younger the child is, the more costly its care—but there have been rumblings that all is not well in terms of the very young child's welfare in such group-care institutions." Some Czechoslovak researchers suggested that very young children's nervous systems are irritated by the noise and activity of others all day long. The Czechs, she points out, have begun to move "from group care to foster care in private homes and long-leave policies for employed mothers." Even among some Scandinavian countries interest in group care is low. Norway lags behind both Denmark and Sweden in number of facilities. And Finland, which in 1960 had the highest proportion of married women working and the highest proportion of women in universities of any industrial nation in the world, had virtually no child-care facilities at all. Only 2 per cent of Finnish working mothers placed their children in group care. How Finnish women are able to sustain such a high degree of work participation without group child care is an unanswered question. Gail Lapidus's recent scholarly book on women and work in the Soviet Union warns us that making institutional arrangements for women's family responsibilities can easily work against feminist goals. As she writes, "the conditions of female employment in the USSR are specifically designed to accommodate family responsibilities to a degree that is virtually unprecedented in industrial societies." But pregnancy leaves, arrangements for nursing infants during working hours, and exemption of pregnant women from heavy work or overtime or travel, she also notes, often result in women's continuing to shape their work around the family. Under such arrangements, Lapidus continues, "work satisfaction depends less on the content of the work itself than on its convenience in relation to family responsibilities." The higher rate of absenteeism among women than among men Lapidus attributes to women's responsibility for young children when they suddenly become ill. Men's work, on the other hand, is structured around the assumption that men have no responsibility for child or family care; they can even be expected to take work home with them. Not surprisingly, the bulk of the students in evening and correspondence courses in the Soviet Union are men. Nor is it unexpected, Lapidus pointedly observes, "that married women are seriously underrepresented in enterprise activities requiring additional commitments of time and energy, as well as in volunteer movements and in public affairs more generally." [35]

When this recent history of attempted solutions to the question of child care for families with working mothers is projected against the longer history of the family, one possible solution for the future of women and the family suggests itself. It is that we may well be at a point in the history of the family where the high level of child care, to which two centuries of the modern family has accustomed us, can no longer be sustained. For most of human history the care of children has been something performed by women in conjunction with many other tasks. Under the pre-industrial regime, in the main, there were few occasions for women to be physically separated from the child while these other tasks were being performed. Yet, given the variety and sheer physical demands of these other tasks, the mother was never able to concentrate the bulk of her time and attention upon her children. Only during the 19th and 20th centuries has child care been virtually a full-time occupation of mothers. Over the last quarter-century that pattern has been changing rapidly, as married women have sought other uses for their time and set other goals for their lives. Even during the 19th century there was tension between the family's interests and those of women as individuals. Although that tension most commonly manifested itself in relations between husband and wife, today it is most obviously, but certainly not exclusively apparent between women and children. One measure of it is the enduring debate over child-care centers and working mothers. In fact, the whole field of child psychology rests upon the assumption that the close supervision by a mother is indispensable for a child's successful passage into adulthood. Certainly that has been the burden of the widely influential work of John Bowlby during the 1960s, to mention only the best known. It has been recently and forcefully pressed upon us in Selma Fraiberg's book *Every Child's Birthright: In Defense of Mothering.* Her confidence in her position is almost unlimited. "In this century," she tells us, "we have come into knowledge about children and the constitution of personality that can be fairly placed among the greatest scientific discoveries in history."[36] The field of child study, in short, will provide little help in resolving the dilemma that confronts working mothers. On the contrary, it is likely to make more difficult the achieving of any further recognition of women's interest in activity outside the home.

The recognition and the realization of women's individuality in work will be difficult for an even more profound reason. The central values of the modern family stand in opposition to these that underlie women's emancipation. Where the women's movement has stood for equality, the family historically has denied or repudiated equality. For even in the companionate family of the 19th and 20th centuries, hierarchy has prevailed among father, mother, and children. Few families have treated them equally or assumed them to be equal, even today. Where the women's movement has called for a recognition of individualism, the family has insisted upon subordination of individual interests to those of the group. Even fathers have been expected to share their earnings with the other family members and to shape their lives to such an extent as to provide a living for the whole family. And, finally, where the women's movement has asked for a person to be judged on merit, the family has denied merit as a basis of membership, approval, or love. Indeed, the great appeal of the family has been that it accepts members simply because they are born into the group and not because of what they may achieve or contribute.

To point to these obvious contradictions is but another way of saying that the great values for which the family stands are at odds not only with those of the women's movement, but also with those of today's world. Democracy, individualism, and meritocracy, the values most closely identified with the last two centuries of Western history, are conspicuous by their absence from the family, even with its present modifications. Just because these modern values have been absent from the family, some commentators have called for the end of the family, or at least have predicted its dissolution on the ground that it is anachronistic.

But that conclusion is based upon only half the evidence, so to speak. For if the family, unlike the women's movement, does not reflect modern values, it does embody values that inhere in great social movements like nationalism, ethnicity, racial allegiance, and the great religions of the world. For those movements extol hierarchy and scorn equality and meritocracy. The family, in short, like the great traditional movements, is an anti-individualistic institution. In fact, its denial of individualism is the source of the family's strong attraction for many men and women today. For at least two centuries the best known alternative to the individualism, competitiveness, and egoism that infuse the modern, industrial and urban world has been the family. That has been its strongest appeal as individualism spread from country to country in the wake of commercial and industrial capitalism. As an ideal, at least, the family was truly a "haven in a heartless world," to use the title of Christopher Lasch's recent book. That is also why all the great utopian visions of the 19th and 20th centuries from Marxism, which is the most familiar, to the hippies of yesterday, have taken the family as their model of human order. In the face of an individualistic market economy, the family has seemed the epitome of true humanity and interrelatedness. The very slogan of Communism—"from each according to his abilities, to each according to his needs"—is not only the antithesis of a market economy's conception of human relations, but the central principle of family life. In short, aside from the evidence that Americans still consider the family a central institution in their lives, the very values for which it has stood over the years suggest that it will endure.

Simply because the family is deeply imbedded in American life and is unlikely to fade away, tension between it and the individual interests of women was inevitable. For some two centuries now, Americans have seen that tension rising. Most recently, with the movement into work of married women and particularly with the rise of the women's movement, the tension has reached a new height. Philosophically and practically the family and women's individuality are difficult to reconcile. Many women today find the realization of themselves as persons impossible to achieve within a family situation. Yet most women still consider a family relationship as more important to them than the realization of their own individuality. Obviously, how any individual woman perceives her future is up to her. The family, after all, is at bottom nothing more than a relation between a man and a woman and their offspring. What they work out for themselves as a mutually satisfying relation today depends in large part upon them. For some people that will mean a continuation of the established relation, with perhaps an opportunity for the woman to work outside the home, though for supportive rather than individualistic ends. For others it may mean abandoning family entirely in pursuit of complete individual fulfillment. The ideal goal, it would seem, would be one in which the values of family and the realization of women's individuality could be reconciled.

Will it be possible for women and men to work out some arrangements—call it family or something else—in which these two goals can be realized? Or must the historic drive for women's individuality stop short of full realization in the name of children, husband, and family? Never before has the tension been so evident or the room for maneuver so narrow. After two hundred years of development, both the future of the family and the fulfillment of women as persons are at odds as never before. Presumably a resolution will come in something less than another two centuries.

Notes

I The Emergence of the Modern American Family

1. William N. Stephens, *The Family in Cross-Cultural Perspective* (New York, 1963), pp. 15–19.
2. John Hajnal, "European Marriage Patterns in Perspective," in D. V. Glass and D. E. C. Eversley (eds.), *Population in History* (Chicago, 1965), pp. 101–4.
3. Philip J. Greven, Jr., *Four Generations: Population, Land, and Family in Colonial Andover, Massachusetts* (Ithaca, 1970), pp. 34, 117–20; Robert V. Wells, "Quaker Marriage Patterns in a Colonial Perspective," *William and Mary Quarterly*, 3rd Series, 24 (July 1972), 427, 430; John Demos, *A Little Commonwealth: Family Life in Plymouth Colony* (New York, 1970), p. 193, Table 4; Daniel Scott Smith, "The Demographic History of Colonial New England," *Journal of Economic History* 32 (March 1972), 177.
4. Natalie Zemon Davis, "Ghosts, Kin, and Progeny: Some Features of Family Life in Early Modern France," *Daedalus 106* (Spring 1977), 107; Lawrence Stone, "The Rise of the Nuclear Family in Early Modern England," in Charles E. Rosenberg (ed.), *The Family in History* (Philadelphia, 1975), pp. 45, 48–49.
5. Greven, *Four Generations*, pp. 222–23; Daniel Scott Smith, "Parental Control and Marriage Patterns: An Analysis of Historical Trends in Hingham, Massachusetts," *Journal of Marriage and the Family 35* (August 1973), 423–24; Robert A. Gross, *The Minutemen and Their World* (New York, 1976), pp. 211n, 235n.
6. Kathryn Kish Sklar, *Catharine Beecher: A Study in American Domesticity* (New Haven, 1973), p. 36; Ms. biography of Louis Alexander Janin, Box 20, Folder 22, Janin Family Collection, Huntington Library, San Marino, Ca.
7. Donald F. Danker (ed.), *Mollie: The Journal of Mollie Dorsey Sanford in Nebraska and Colorado Territories, 1857–1866* (Lincoln, 1959), p. 7; Robert Manson Myers (ed.), *The Children of Pride: A True Story of Georgia and the Civil War* (New Haven, 1972), p. 118.

8. Clarence Cook (ed.), *A Girl's Life Eighty Years Ago: Selections from the Letters of Eliza Southgate Bowne* (New York, 1887), p. 140; see also Janet Wilson James, "Changing Ideas about Women in the United States, 1776–1825," unpublished dissertation, Harvard University, 1954, p. 141; James R. McGovern, *Yankee Family* (New Orleans, 1975), p. 59.

9. Journal of Sarah Ripley Stearns, February 2, 17, May 26, October 24, 1810, February 1, November 10, 1812, Stearns Papers, Schlesinger Library, Radcliffe College; North Carolina planter's remark quoted in unpublished paper of Jane Turner Censer presented at meetings of Southern Historical Association, November 1977. I am indebted to Ms. Censer for permitting me to use the results of her research.

10. Hyland Rice to R. W. Waterman, September 25, 1871, Robert Waterman Papers, Bancroft Library, University of California, Berkeley; Censer's unpublished paper, Southern Historical Association, 1977.

11. Quoted in E. William Monter, "The Pedestal and the Stake: Courtly Love and Witchcraft," in Renate Bridenthal and Claudia Koonz (eds.), *Becoming Visible: Women in European History* (Boston, 1977), p. 123.

12. Robert C. Winthrop (ed.), *Life and Letters of John Winthrop* (2 vols., Boston, 1864), I, 247, 292; Stone, "Rise of the Nuclear Family," pp. 26–28, 30–31.

13. Lawrence Stone, *The Family, Sex, and Marriage in England, 1500–1800* (New York, 1977), pp. 318, 284.

14. *Ibid.,* p. 372.

15. Nancy F. Cott, "Eighteenth Century Family and Social Life Revealed in Massachusetts Divorce Records," *Journal of Social History* 10 (Fall 1976), 32; Nancy F. Cott, "Divorce and the Changing Status of Women in Eighteenth Century Massachusetts," *William and Mary Quarterly,* 3rd Series, *33* (October 1976), 586–614.

16. *Ibid.,* pp. 599–600, 613.

17. Herman R. Lantz *et al.,* "Pre-industrial Patterns in the Colonial Family in America: A Content Analysis of Colonial Magazines," *American Sociological Review 33* (June 1968), 413–26.

18. Quoted in Nancy F. Cott, *Bonds of Womanhood: "Women's Sphere" in New England, 1780–1835* (New Haven, 1977), p. 18. See also Michael Gordon and M. Charles Bernstein, "Mate Choice and Domestic Life in the Nineteenth Century Marriage Manual," *Journal of Marriage and the Family 32* (1970), 668–69.

19. Danker (ed.), *Mollie,* pp. 103, 113, 65.

20. Daniel Scott Smith and Michael S. Hindus, "Premarital Pregnancy in America, 1640–1971: An Overview and Interpretation," *Journal of Interdisciplinary History 4* (Spring 1975), 537–70; Herbert G. Gutman, *The Black Family in Slavery and Freedom, 1750–1925* (New York, 1976), pp. 64–65, 504, Table A-30.

21. Danker (ed.), *Mollie,* pp. 7, 20, 36, 47; Mary Cogswell to Weltha Brown, April 2, 1822, Brown Correspondence, Hooker Collection, Schlesinger Library, Radcliffe College; quotations from young man's diary in Ernest Earnest, *The American Eve in Fact and Fiction, 1775–1914* (Urbana, 1974); Diaries of

Anna Haskell, March 15, 1876, Haskell Family Collection, Bancroft Library, University of California, Berkeley.

22. Bernhard J. Stern (ed.), *Young Ward's Diary* (New York, 1935), pp. 10, 14–15, 18–19, 33, 35–37, 44, 80.

23. Hart-Clark Correspondence, especially Jerome Hart to Ann Clark, May 22, July 23, 1896, May 19, 1897, Ann Clark to Jerome Hart, May 22, 1896, April 1, 13, 1897, Bancroft Library, University of California, Berkeley.

24. Charlotte Perkins Stetson to Houghton Gilman, May 5, 3, 9, 13, 1898, Charlotte Perkins Gilman Papers, Schlesinger Library, Radcliffe College.

II Wives and Husbands

1. Herman R. Lantz, Jane Keyes, and Martin Schultz, "The American Family in the Pre-Industrial Period: From Base Line in History to Change," *American Sociological Review* 40 (February 1975), 29–30.

2. Alexis de Tocqueville, *Democracy in America*, ed. by Phillips Bradley (2 vols., New York, 1948), II, 213–14; Bremer quoted in Bernard Wishy, *The Child and the Republic: The Dawn of Modern American Child Nurture* (Philadelphia, 1968), p. 29; Hale quotation in Phillida Bunkle, "Sentimental Womanhood and Domestic Education, 1830–1870," *History of Education Quarterly* 14 (Spring 1974), 23.

3. William E. Bridges, "Warm Hearth, Cold World: Social Perspectives on the Household Poets," *American Quarterly* 21 (Winter 1969), 767. See also the cogent comments along similar lines in Nancy F. Cott, *The Bonds of Womanhood: "Woman's Sphere" in New England, 1780–1835* (New Haven, 1977), pp. 200–201.

4. Lantz *et al.*, "American Family in Pre-Industrial Period," pp. 26–27.

5. Quoted in Anne Firor Scott, *Southern Lady: From Pedestal to Politics, 1830–1930* (Chicago, 1970), p. 19; Donald F. Danker (ed.), *Mollie: The Journal of Mollie Dorsey Sanford in Nebraska and Colorado Territories, 1857–1866* (Lincoln, 1959), p. 126; William M. Hassler (ed.), *The General and His Lady: Civil War Letters of William Dorsey Pender to Fanny Pender* (Chapel Hill, 1962), p. 185.

6. Harriet Beecher Stowe to Calvin Stowe, May–June, July 19, 1844, Harriet Beecher Stowe Papers, Schlesinger Library, Radcliffe College.

7. Hassler (ed.), *General and His Lady*, pp. 39–40.

8. Clifford Merrill Drury (ed.), *First White Women over the Rockies* (3 vols., Glendale, Ca., 1963), II, 133.

9. Lucy Gray to Joshua Gray, June 2, 1823, Gray Correspondence, Hooker Collection, Schlesinger Library, Radcliffe College.

10. Quoted in Bernard Farber, *Guardians of Virtue: Salem Families in 1800* (New York, 1972), p. 183.

11. Lucy Gray to Joshua Gray, February 21, 1820, Gray Correspondence, Hooker Collection, Schlesinger Library, Radcliffe College.

12. Charlena Anderson to Melville Anderson, September 30, 1876, Anderson Papers, Stanford University Library.

13. Mary P. Poor to Henry V. Poor, July 19, 1846, June 7, 1847, June 6, 20, 1856, Poor Family Papers, Schlesinger Library, Radcliffe College.

14. Mary P. Poor to Henry V. Poor, July 9, August 18, 1863, January 20, 1870, Poor Family Papers, Schlesinger Library, Radcliffe College.

15. Mary Hallock Foote to Helena Gilder, March 20, 1896, Mary Hallock Foote Papers, Stanford University Library.

16. Sarah Bell Waller to Henry Waller, May 16, 1855, Waller Papers, Huntington Library, San Marino, Ca.; Charlena Anderson to Melville Anderson, December 2, 1876, Anderson Papers, Stanford University Library.

17. Danker (ed.), *Mollie,* p. 170.

18. Mary Hallock Foote to Helena Gilder, December 17, 1895, Mary Hallock Foote Papers, Stanford University Library.

19. Quoted in Richard L. Rapson, "The American Child as Seen by British Travelers, 1845–1935," *American Quarterly 17* (Fall 1965), 529–30.

20. Mary Beth Norton, *Liberty's Daughters: The Revolutionary Experience of American Women, 1750–1800* (Boston, 1980), chap. 2. I am indebted to Professor Norton for providing me with typescript pages of her book prior to its publication.

21. Henry V. Poor to Mary P. Poor, July 19, 1846, June 27, 1847, July 25, 1858, Poor Family Papers, Schlesinger Library, Radcliffe College.

22. Henry Waller to Sarah Bell Waller, August 6, June 13, 1840, June 24, 1853, Waller Papers, Huntington Library, San Marino, Ca.

23. Melville Anderson to Charlena Anderson, November 23, 1876, Anderson Papers, Stanford University Library.

24. Robert Manson Myers (ed.), *Children of Pride: A True Story of Georgia and the Civil War* (New Haven, 1972), pp. 941–42, 948, 956.

25. "Women Fit for Wives," by "A Country Parson," *Good Housekeeping,* November, 28, 1885, p. 51.

26. Andrew J. Rotter, " 'Matilda, for Gods Sake Write': Women and Families on the Argonaut Mind," *California Historical Quarterly 58* (Summer 1979), 139; Joseph Burt Holt to Emily Burt Holt, February 6, 1874, Holt-Messer Papers, Schlesinger Library, Radcliffe College.

27. Sam Leland to Minerva Leland, October 24, 1883, Minerva E. Leland Papers, Schlesinger Library, Radcliffe College; Juliet Janin to Louis Janin, September 4, 1847, Janin Family Collection, Huntington Library, San Marino, Ca.

28. *Good Housekeeping,* February 6, 1886, pp. 190–93.

29. Harriet Beecher Stowe to Calvin Stowe, August 1844, Harriet Beecher Stowe Papers, Schlesinger Library, Radcliffe College.

30. Mary Waterman Rice to Robert Waterman, February 29, 1876, Robert Waterman Papers, Bancroft Library, University of California, Berkeley.

31. Danker (ed.), *Mollie,* pp. 134, 158.

32. Sarah Bell Waller to Henry Waller, August 1, 7, 1852, Henry Waller to Sarah Bell Waller, December 8, 1856, Waller Papers, Huntington Library, San Marino, Ca.

33. Juliet Janin to Louis Janin, September 13, 1859, May 19, 1861, Janin Family Collection, Huntington Library, San Marino, Ca.

34. Juliet Janin to Louis Janin, June 3, 1863, Janin Family Collection, Huntington Library, San Marino, Ca.
35. Johnny Faragher and Christine Stansell, "Women and Their Families on the Overland Trail, 1842–1867," *Feminist Studies* 2 (February–March 1975), 153–54.
36. Danker (ed.), *Mollie*, pp. 33, 25, 124.
37. Quoted in Faragher and Stansell, "Women and Their Families," pp. 153, 158, 161–62.
38. *Ibid.*, p. 151.
39. Lillian Schlissel, "Women's Diaries on the Western Frontier," *American Studies 18* (Spring 1977), 88.
40. Raymond Lee Muncy, *Sex and Marriage in Utopian Communities in 19th-Century America* (Bloomington, Ind., 1973), p. 215.
41. Robert Griswold, "The Character of the Family in Rural California, 1850–1890," unpublished dissertation, Stanford University, 1979.
42. Quoted in Helena Znaniecki Lopata, *Occupation: Housewife* (New York, 1971), p. 108.
43. Ersel E. LeMasters, "The Passing of the Dominant Husband-Father," in Hans Peter Dreizel (ed.), *Family, Marriage, and the Struggle of the Sexes* (New York, 1972), pp. 107–8.

III Wife and Mother

1. Harriet Beecher Stowe to Calvin Stowe, May–June, May 23, 1844, Harriet Beecher Stowe Papers, Schlesinger Library, Radcliffe College.
2. Quoted in Anne Firor Scott, *Southern Lady: From Pedestal to Politics, 1830–1930* (Chicago, 1970), p. 32.
3. Harriet Beecher Stowe to Calvin Stowe, August 1844, Harriet Beecher Stowe Papers, Schlesinger Library, Radcliffe College.
4. Mary Hallock Foote to Helena Gilder, February 6, 1888, Mary Hallock Foote Papers, Stanford University Library.
5. Quoted in Johnny Faragher and Christine Stansell, "Women and Their Families on the Overland Trail, 1842–1867," *Feminist Studies* 2 (February–March 1975), 156.
6. Journals of Margaret Fowler Dunaway, Vol. I, Part 1, Part 2, April 26, 1929, Vol. II, Christmas time, 1931, Schlesinger Library, Radcliffe College.
7. Mary Hallock Foote to Helena Gilder, January 21, 1877, Mary Hallock Foote Papers, Stanford University Library.
8. Quoted in Catherine M. Scholten, "On the Importance of the Obstetrick Art: Changing Customs of Childbirth in America, 1760–1825," *William and Mary Quarterly*, 3rd Series, 34 (July 1977), 439.
9. Frances E. Kobrin, "The American Midwife Controversy: A Crisis of Professionalization," *Bulletin of the History of Medicine 40* (July–August 1966), 350–51. See also Judy Barrett Litoff, *American Midwives: 1860 to the Present* (Westport, Conn., 1978), chaps. 1 and 2.

10. Journal of Sarah Ripley Stearns, August 29, 1813, October 13, 1816, Stearns Papers, Schlesinger Library, Radcliffe College.

11. Elizabeth Dwight Cabot to Ellen Dwight, December 19, 1858, Hugh Cabot Collection, Section II, Elizabeth Dwight Cabot Papers, Schlesinger Library, Radcliffe College.

12. Paul H. Jacobson, "An Estimate of the Expectation of Life in the United States in 1850," *The Milbank Memorial Fund Quarterly 35* (April 1957), 198–99; Paul H. Jacobson, "Cohort Survival for Generations since 1840," *The Milbank Memorial Fund Quarterly 42* (July 1964), 38–39.

13. Elizabeth Dwight Cabot to Ellen Dwight, January 23, 1859, Hugh Cabot Collection, Section II, Elizabeth Dwight Cabot Papers, Schlesinger Library, Radcliffe College; Sarah Bell Waller to Henry Waller, July 22, 1855, Waller Papers, Huntington Library, San Marino, Ca.

14. Quoted in Anne Firor Scott, "Women's Perspective on the Patriarchy in the 1850s," *Journal of American History 61* (June 1974), 56–57; quoted in Scott, *Southern Lady,* pp. 38–39.

15. Mary Hallock Foote to Helena Gilder, July 10, 1880, Mary Hallock Foote Papers, Stanford University Library.

16. Clifford Merrill Drury (ed.), *First White Women over the Rockies* (3 vols., Glendale, Ca., 1963), II, 136, 227. I am indebted to Professor Lillian Schlissel of Brooklyn College for bringing this reference to my attention.

17. Sarah Bell Waller to Henry Waller, January 14, 1844, Waller Papers, Huntington Library, San Marino, Ca.

18. Elizabeth Dwight Cabot to Ellen Dwight, March 8, 1859, Hugh Cabot Collection, Section II, Elizabeth Dwight Cabot Papers, Schlesinger Library, Radcliffe College; Mary Hallock Foote to Helena Gilder, undated letter, *ca.* June 1877, March 6, 1887, Mary Hallock Foote Papers, Stanford University Library.

19. Harriet Beecher Stowe to Calvin Stowe, January 1, 1847, Harriet Beecher Stowe Papers, Schlesinger Library, Radcliffe College; Donald F. Danker (ed.), *Mollie: The Journal of Mollie Dorsey Sanford in Nebraska and Colorado Territories, 1857–1866* (Lincoln, 1959), p. 157.

20. Sarah Ripley Stearns Journal, Vol. 3, August 6, 1815, November 17, October 13, 1816, Stearns Papers, Schlesinger Library, Radcliffe College; Drury (ed.), *First White Women,* II, 296; Eliza Perkins to Weltha Brown, December 10, 1821, Brown Correspondence, Hooker Collection, Schlesinger Library, Radcliffe College.

21. Danker (ed.), *Mollie,* pp. 174–76, 179, 193.

22. Charlena Anderson to Melville Anderson, August 1, 1887, Anderson Papers, Stanford University Library.

IV Women and Children

1. Quoted in Arlene Skolnick, "The Limits of Childhood: Conception of Child Development and Social Context," *Law and Contemporary Problems 39* (Summer 1975), 44–45.

2. Peter Coveney, *Image of Childhood* (rev. ed., Baltimore, 1967), pp. 29, 80.

3. Barbara Garlitz, "The Immortality Ode: Its Cultural Progency," *Studies in English Literature, 1500–1900,* 6 (1966), 639–40, 647.

4. Peter Gregg Slater, *Children in the New England Mind: In Death and in Life* (Hamden, Conn., 1977), p. 163.

5. Quoted in Glenn Davis, *Childhood and History in America* (New York, 1976), p. 45.

6. Susan E. Hirsch, *Roots of the American Working Class: The Industrialization of Crafts in Newark, 1800–1860* (Philadelphia, 1978), pp. 41, 71; David Stern, Sandra Smith, and Fred Doolittle, "How Children Used To Work," *Law and Contemporary Problems* 39 (Summer 1975), 99–101.

7. Smith's unpublished study is summarized in James A. Henretta, "Families and Farms: *Mentalité* in Pre-Industrial America," *William and Mary Quarterly,* 3rd Series, 35 (January 1978), 29n; John F. Walzer, "A Period of Ambivalence: Eighteenth-Century American Childhood," in Lloyd de Mause (ed.), *The History of Childhood* (New York, 1975), pp. 357–58.

8. Nancy F. Cott, "Eighteenth Century Family and Social Life Revealed in Massachusetts Divorce Records," *Journal of Social History* 10 (Fall 1976), 29–30.

9. Lynne E. Withey, "Household Structure in Urban and Rural Areas: The Case of Rhode Island, 1774–1800," *Journal of Family History* 3 (Spring 1978), 46; Joseph F. Kett, *Rites of Passage: Adolescence in America. 1790 to the Present* (New York, 1977), pp. 123, 59.

10. Abigail J. Stewart, David G. Winter, and A. David Jones, "Coding Categories for the Study of Child-Rearing from Historical Sources," *Journal of Interdisciplinary History* 5 (Spring 1975), 701; Ruth H. Bloch, "American Feminine Ideals in Transition: The Rise of the Moral Mother, 1785–1815," *Feminist Studies* 4 (June 1978), 103–4, 109, 113; Ruth H. Bloch, "Untangling the Roots of Modern Sex Roles: A Survey of Four Centuries of Change," *Signs* 4 (Winter 1978), 251. Bloch takes a positive attitude toward the special role of mothers in the 19th century, for not only did it break tradition "by attributing to women strong moral authority" it also granted to them a field of specialty. "It entitled them to considerable autonomy within what came to be defined as the 'woman's sphere,' and it even helped to create both the legitimacy and the solidarity necessary for later, more successful, feminist agitation" ("American Feminine Ideals," p. 120).

11. Alexis de Tocqueville, *Democracy in America* ed. by Phillips Bradley (2 vols., New York, 1948), II, 192–95.

12. Statement from North Carolinian quoted in Jane Turner Censer, "Family Relationships and Power in Nineteenth Century North Carolina," paper presented at Southern Historical Association meeting, November 1977, pp. 2, 4; Robert Manson Myers (ed.), *The Children of Pride: A True Story of Georgia and the Civil War* (New Haven, 1972), pp. 568, 640, 783.

13. Julia E. Rollins Holt to Emily Burt Holt, November 11, 1873, March 28, 1875, P.S. from father; Joseph Burt Holt to Emily Burt Holt, March 21, 28, 1875, Holt-Messer Family Papers, Schlesinger Library, Radcliffe College.

14. Donald F. Danker (ed.), *Mollie: The Journal of Mollie Dorsey Sanford in Nebraska and Colorado Territories, 1857–1866* (Lincoln, 1959), pp. 63–64.

15. Henry Waller to Sarah Bell Waller, December 1856, Waller Papers, Huntington Library, San Marino, Ca.
16. Quoted in Bernard Farber, *Guardians of Virtue: Salem Families in 1800* (New York, 1972), p. 183.
17. William M. Hassler (ed.), *The General and His Lady: Civil War Letters of William Dorsey Pender to Fanny Pender* (Chapel Hill, 1962), p. 96.
18. Henry Waller tò Sarah Bell Waller, August 6, 1840, Waller Papers, Huntington Library, San Marino, Ca.; Hassler (ed.), *General and His Lady,* p. 91; Sam Leland to Minerva Leland, October 14, November 25, 1883, Minerva E. Leland Papers, Schlesinger Library, Radcliffe College.
19. William Buchan, *Advice to Mothers on the Subject of Their Own Health* (Boston, 1809), pp. 30, 67; Kathryn Kish Sklar, *Catharine Beecher: A Study in American Domesticity* (New Haven, 1973), p. 155.
20. Myers (ed.), *Children of Pride,* p. 1130; Clifford Merrill Drury (ed.), *First White Women over the Rockies* (3 vols., Glendale, Ca. 1963), II, 136–38, 138n, 144n. I am indebted to Professor Lillian Schlissel of Brooklyn College for bringing this reference to my attention.
21. Myers (ed.), *Children of Pride,* pp. 705, 758.
22. Sam Leland to Minerva Leland, October 24, 1883, Minerva E. Leland Papers, Schlesinger Library, Radcliffe College; Hassler (ed.), *General and His Lady,* pp. 103, 131.
23. Mary Waterman Rice to Robert Waterman, February 7, 1876, Robert Waterman Papers, Bancroft Library, University of California, Berkeley.
24. Quoted in Robert Sunley, "Early Nineteenth-Century American Literature on Child Rearing," in Margaret Mead and Martha Wolfenstein (eds.), *Childhood in Contemporary Cultures* (Chicago, 1955), p. 151; quotation from *Mother's Assistant* in Glenn Davis, *Childhood and History in America* (New York, 1976), pp. 50–51.
25. Bernard Wishy, *The Child and the Republic: The Dawn of Modern American Child Nurture* (Philadelphia, 1968), pp. 26–27.
26. Nancy Pottishman Weiss, "Mother, the Invention of Necessity: Dr. Benjamin Spock's *Baby and Child Care,*" *American Quarterly* 29 (Winter 1977), 522–24.
27. Sarah Ripley Stearns Journal, Vol. 3, February 19, 1815, October 13, 1816, Stearns Papers, Schlesinger Library, Radcliffe College.
28. Harriet Beecher Stowe to Calvin Stowe, May–June, 1844, Harriet Beecher Stowe Papers, Schlesinger Library, Radcliffe College.
29. Myers (ed.), *Children of Pride,* p. 641.
30. Drury (ed.), *First White Women,* II, 297–98; Sarah Bell Waller to Henry Waller, Waller Papers, Huntington Library, San Marino, Ca.
31. Journals of Margaret Fowler Dunaway, Vol. I, Part 1, October 26, no year, Part 2, March 8, 1929, Part 2, 1932, Journals of Margaret Fowler Dunaway, 1922–1943, Schlesinger Library, Radcliffe College.

V Inducting Children into the Social Order

1. Quoted in Lawrence Stone, "The Rise of the Nuclear Family in Early Modern England," in Charles E. Rosenberg (ed.), *The Family in History* (Philadelphia, 1975), pp. 36–37; Robinson quoted in John Demos, *A Little Commonwealth: Family Life in Plymouth Colony* (New York, 1970), pp. 134–35.

2. Quoted in David Hunt, *Parents and Children in History: The Psychology of Family Life in Early Modern France* (New York, 1972, orig. ed. 1970), p. 135; Byrd quotation in John F. Walzer, "A Period of Ambivalence: Eighteenth-Century American Childhood," in Lloyd de Mausse (ed.), *The History of Childhood* (New York, 1975), p. 369.

3. Quoted in Robert Sunley, "Early Nineteenth-Century American Literature on Child Rearing," in Margaret Mead and Martha Wolfenstein (eds.), *Childhood in Contemporary Cultures* (Chicago, 1955), pp. 159–60, 162.

4. Robert Manson Myers (ed.), *Children of Pride: A True Story of Georgia and the Civil War* (New Haven, 1972), p. 603.

5. *Ibid.,* p. 1077.

6. Mary Waterman Rice to Robert Waterman, December 5, 1875, Robert Waterman Papers, Bancroft Library, University of California, Berkeley; Juliet Janin to Louis Alexander Janin, September 4, 1847, Janin Family Collection, Huntington Library, San Marino, Ca.

7. Charlena Anderson to Melville Anderson, July 20, 1881, Anderson Papers, Stanford University Library. Emphasis added.

8. Quoted in Mary Patricia Ryan, "American Society and the Cult of Domesticity, 1830–1860," unpublished dissertation, University of California, Santa Barbara, 1971, p. 88; Larned quotation in Glenn Davis, *Childhood and History in America* (New York, 1976), p. 65.

9. Clifford Merrill Drury (ed.), *First White Women over the Rockies* (3 vols., Glendale, Ca., 1963), II, 197, 294–95.

10. Mary Waterman Rice to Robert Waterman, September 25, 1885, Robert Waterman Papers, Bancroft Library, University of California, Berkeley.

11. Harriet Beecher Stowe to Calvin Stowe, May 23, 1844, Harriet Beecher Stowe Papers, Schlesinger Library, Radcliffe College; The Wayland episode is reprinted in full in William G. McLoughlin, "Evangelical Childrearing in the Age of Jackson: Francis Wayland's Views on When and How To Subdue the Willfulness of Children," *Journal of Social History* 9 (Fall 1975), 35–39. On that version I have based my analysis.

12. Juliet Janin to Louis Alexander Janin, September 4, 1847, Janin Family Collection, Huntington Library, San Marino, Ca.

13. Charles Strickland, "A Transcendentalist Father: The Child-Rearing Practices of Bronson Alcott," *Perspectives in American History 3* (1969), 26.

14. Mary Gardiner Davis to Caroline Perkins Gardiner, October 1, 1860, Gardiner Family Papers, Schlesinger Library, Radcliffe College.

15. The whole episode is given in a long letter dated August 8, 1859.

16. Mary Gardiner Davis to Caroline Perkins Gardiner, October 1, 1860, Gardiner Family Papers, Schlesinger Library, Radcliffe College.

17. Catharine Sedgwick, *Home* (Boston, 1835), pp. 26–27; Bushnell quoted in Philip Greven, *The Protestant Temperament: Patterns of Childrearing, Religious Experience, and the Self in Early America* (New York, 1977), pp. 169–70.

18. Frank F. Furstenberg, Jr., "Industrialization and the American Family: A Look Backward," *American Sociological Review 31* (June 1966), 334–35; Sedgwick, *Home,* p. 27. Emphasis added.

19. Harriet Beecher Stowe to Calvin Stowe, May 23, 1844, Harriet Beecher Stowe Papers, Schlesinger Library, Radcliffe College; Juliet Janin to Louis Alexander Janin, July 26, 1845, Janin Family Collection, Huntington Library, San Marino, Ca.; Myers (ed.), *Children of Pride,* p. 1315.

20. Elizabeth Dwight to Ellen Twistleton, January 16, 1854, Hugh Cabot Collection, Section II, Elizabeth Dwight Cabot Papers, Schlesinger Library, Radcliffe College.

21. Quoted in Bernard Wishy, *The Child and the Republic: The Dawn of Modern American Child Nurture* (Philadelphia, 1968), pp. 126–27.

22. Mary Gardiner Davis to William H. Gardiner, August 13, 1859, Gardiner Family Papers, Schlesinger Library, Radcliffe College.

23. Myers (ed.), *Children of Pride,* pp. 942–43.

24. *Ibid.,* pp. 785, 1077, 1314–15.

25. Robert V. Wells, "Family History and Demographic Transition," *Journal of Social History 9* (Fall 1975), 12; Elizabeth Blackwell, *The Laws of Life: With Special Reference to the Physical Education of Girls* (London, 1859), pp. 20–24, 129–30.

26. *Ibid.,* pp. 138, 169–72.

27. Michael Ryan, *The Philosophy of Marriage and Its Social, Moral, and Physical Relations: With an Account of the Diseases of the Genito-Urinary Organs* . . . (3rd ed., London, 1839), pp. 65–66; John Harvey Kellogg, *Plain Facts for Old and Young* (Burlington, Iowa, 1881), pp. 182, 18–19.

28. *Ibid.,* pp. 19, 117–18.

29. Elizabeth Blackwell, *Essays in Medical Sociology* (2 vols., London, 1902), I, 242–43; Elizabeth Blackwell, *Human Element in Sex: Being a Medical Enquiry into the Relation of Sexual Physiology to Christian Morality* (2nd ed., London, 1884), p. 35.

30. Alan Macfarlane, *The Family Life of Ralph Josselin, a Seventeenth Century Clergyman: An Essay in Historical Anthropology* (Cambridge, Eng., 1970), p. 149.

31. Demos, *Little Commonwealth,* p. 124; Nancy F. Cott, "Eighteenth Century Family and Social Life Revealed in Massachusetts Divorce Records," *Journal of Social History 10* (Fall 1976), 25.

32. Myers (ed.), *Children of Pride,* p. 1118.

33. Donald F. Danker (ed.), *Mollie: The Journal of Mollie Dorsey Sanford in Nebraska and Colorado Territories, 1857–1866* (Lincoln, 1959), p. 3.

34. Tamara K. Hareven, "Family Time and Industrial Time: Family and Work in a Planned Corporation Town, 1900–1924," in Tamara K. Hareven (ed.),

Family and Kin in Urban Communities, 1700–1930 (New York, 1977), pp. 193–95.

35. Lydia Maria Child to "Louise," November 9, 1863, Loring Papers, Schlesinger Library, Radcliffe College. I am indebted for this reference to Professor Kirk Jeffrey, Jr., of Carleton College; Rebecca Root Buell to Weltha Brown, June 24, 1822, Hooker Collection, Schlesinger Library, Radcliffe College; Myers (ed.), *Children of Pride*, p. 1117; Danker (ed.), *Mollie*, pp. 131–32, 145.

36. Mary Waterman Rice to Robert Waterman, May 2, 1875, June 3, 1876, Robert Waterman Papers, Bancroft Library, University of California, Berkeley.

37. Mary Gardiner Davis to Caroline Davis, September 12, 1859, Mary Gardiner Davis to parents, October 3, 5, 1859, Gardiner Family Papers, Schlesinger Library, Radcliffe College; Myers (ed.), *Children of Pride*, p. 128.

38. Mary Gardiner Davis to William H. Gardiner, undated letter [1850s], Gardiner Family Papers, Schlesinger Library, Radcliffe College; Sam Leland to Minerva Leland, letters of 1883–84, especially June 17, November 25, December 9, 1883, Minerva E. Leland Papers, Schlesinger Library, Radcliffe College.

39. Myers (ed.), *Children of Pride*, pp. 910–15; Sarah Ripley Stearns, Journal, Vol. 3, October 31, 1813, Stearns Papers, Schlesinger Library, Radcliffe College; Danker (ed.), *Mollie*, pp. 84–86.

40. *Ibid.*, 174, 192–3; Mary Waterman Rice to Robert Waterman, March 5, 1886, Robert Waterman Papers, Bancroft Library, University of California, Berkeley.

VI   Under Stress: Families of Afro-Americans and Immigrants

1. Kenneth M. Stampp, *Peculiar Institution: Slavery in the Antebellum South* (New York, 1956), p. 342; see also C. Peter Ripley, "The Black Family in Transition: Louisiana, 1860–1865," *Journal of Southern History 41* (August 1975), 371.

2. Quoted in Eugene D. Genovese, *Roll, Jordan, Roll: The World the Slaves Made* (New York, 1974), pp. 477–78.

3. *Ibid.*, p. 481.

4. *Ibid.*, p. 478.

5. John W. Blassingame, *Black New Orleans, 1860–1880* (Chicago, 1973), p. 80.

6. Robert Manson Myers (ed.), *The Children of Pride: A True Story of Georgia and the Civil War* (New Haven, 1972), pp. 645–46.

7. Herbert G. Gutman, *The Black Family in Slavery and Freedom, 1750–1925* (New York, 1976), pp. 51, 145–49.

8. *Ibid.*, pp. 413–14, 426, 429.

9. Quoted in *ibid.*, p. 417.

10. *Ibid.*, pp. 114–17. Imaginative as Gutman's use of these plantation records undoubtedly is, as Stanley Engerman has pointed out, the accuracy of these records as sources for the paternity of the children is never discussed by Gut-

man. See Engerman, "Studying the Black Family," *Journal of Family History 3* (Spring 1978), 78–101. It is not clear, for example, how the master, who kept the records, ascertained the name of the father—by asking the mother, or by just assuming that the man she lived with was the father? The photographic reproductions of the lists that Gutman provides in his book offer no. clues on this matter. Failure to confront the issue is perhaps the weakest aspect of Gutman's effort to reconstruct the slave family.

11. Quoted in Genovese, *Roll, Jordan, Roll,* p. 467; Smalls is quoted in Gutman, *Black Family,* p. 63.

12. Gutman, *Black Family,* pp. 94, 115–17, 157, 180, 190, 420.

13. Paul A. David *et al., Reckoning with Slavery: A Critical Study in the Quantitative History of American Negro Slavery* (New York, 1976), pp. 143–45; Gutman, *Black Family,* p. 50.

14. *Ibid.,* p. 115; Maris A. Vinovskis, "The Demography of the Slave Population in Antebellum America," *Journal of Interdisciplinary History 3* (Winter 1975), 467.

15. William Robert Fogel and Stanley L. Engerman, *Time on the Cross: The Economics of American Negro Slavery* (2 vols., Boston, 1974), II, 116; David *et al., Reckoning with Slavery,* p. 111.

16. John W. Blassingame, *The Slave Community: Plantation Life in the Antebellum South* (New York, 1972), pp. 90–92.

17. Ripley, "Black Family in Transition," pp. 377–78.

18. Quoted in Genovese, *Roll, Jordan, Roll,* pp. 454–55.

19. Robert S. Starobin (ed.), *Blacks in Bondage: Letters of American Slaves* (New York, 1974), p. 58.

20. John W. Blassingame (ed.), *Slave Testimony: Two Centuries of Letters, Speeches, Interviews, and Autobiographies* (Baton Rouge, 1977), p. 19.

21. *Ibid.,* pp. 116–18.

22. Starobin (ed.), *Blacks in Bondage,* pp. 91–92.

23. *Ibid.,* pp. 89–90; Myers (ed.), *Children of Pride,* p. 1310.

24. Gutman, *Black Family,* pp. 344, 266–67; Ripley, "Black Family in Transition," p. 379.

25. Gutman, *Black Family,* pp. 123–39, 163.

26. Stampp, *Peculiar Institution,* p. 344.

27. Myers (ed.), *Children of Pride,* p. 643.

28. Quoted in Genovese, *Roll, Jordan, Roll,* p. 467.

29. Gutman, *Black Family,* pp. 186, 244.

30. *Ibid.,* pp. 64–65, 449; percentages calculated from figures provided in Table A-30, p. 504.

31. Paul J. Lammermeier, "The Urban Black Family of the Nineteenth Century: A Study of Black Family Structure in the Ohio Valley, 1850–1880," *Journal of Marriage and the Family 35* (August 1973), 44–56.

32. William Harris, "Work and Family in Black Atlanta, 1880," *Journal of Social History 9* (Spring 1976), 322; Gutman, *Black Family,* p. 496; Frank F. Furstenberg, Jr., Theodore Hershberg, and John Modell, "The Origins of the Female-Headed Black Family: The Impact of the Urban Experience," *Journal*

of *Interdisciplinary History* 6 (Autumn 1975), 219; Lammermeier, "Urban Black Family," p. 449n; Joseph A. Hill, *Women in Gainful Occupations 1870–1920,* (Census Monograph IX, Washington, D.C., 1929), p. 130; E. Franklin Frazier, *The Negro Family in the United States* (rev. and abr., Chicago, 1966), p. 103; Phillips Cutright, "Components of Change in the Number of Female Family Heads Aged 15–44: United States, 1940–1970," *Journal of Marriage and the Family* 36 (November 1974), 716.

33. Furstenberg *et al.,* "Origins of Female-Headed Black Family," pp. 223–33.
34. Harris, "Work and Family in Atlanta," p. 323; Elizabeth H. Pleck, "The Two-Parent Household: Black Family Structure in Late Nineteenth Century Boston," *Journal of Social History* 6 (Fall 1972), 3–31.
35. Crandall A. Shifflett, "The Household Composition of Rural Black Families: Louisa County, Virginia, 1880," *Journal of Interdisciplinary History* 6 (Autumn 1975), 235–60.
36. Frank L. Mott, "Portrait of an American Mill Town: Demographic Response in Mid-Nineteenth Century Warren, Rhode Island," *Population Studies* 26 (1972), 155; Daniel J. Walkowitz, "Working Class Women in the Gilded Age: Factory, Family, and Community Life Among Cohoes, New York, Cotton Workers," *Journal of Social History* 5 (Summer 1972), 489n, 478.
37. Daniel J. Walkowitz, "Statistics and the Writing of Working Class Culture: A Statistical Portrait of the Iron Workers in Troy, New York, 1860–1880," *Labor History* 15 (Summer 1974), 446–51; Susan E. Hirsch, *Roots of the American Working Class: The Industrialization of Crafts in Newark, 1800–1860* (Philadelphia, 1978), p. 57; Walkowitz, "Working Class Women," p. 477; Virginia Yans-McLaughlin, *Family and Community: Italian Immigrants in Buffalo, 1880–1930* (Ithaca, 1977), p. 209.
38. Tamara Hareven and Maris A. Vinovskis, "Marital Fertility, Ethnicity, and Occupation in Urban Families: An Analysis of South Boston and the South End in 1880," *Journal of Social History* 8 (Spring 1975), 84, 89; Laurence A. Glasco, "The Life Cycles and Household Structure of American Ethnic Groups: Irish, Germans, and Native-born Whites in Buffalo, New York, 1855," Tamara K. Hareven (ed.), *Family and Kin in Urban Communities, 1770–1930* (New York, 1977), p. 134.
39. Hirsch, *Roots of the American Working Class,* pp. 53–54, 61–62.
40. Susan J. Kleinberg, "Technology's Stepdaughters: The Impact of Industrialization upon Working Class Women, Pittsburgh, 1865–1890," unpublished dissertation, University of Pittsburgh, 1973, pp. 114–15; Margaret F. Byington, *Homestead: The Households of a Mill Town* (New York, 1910), pp. 60, 78, 108, 173.
41. Jane Addams, *The Long Road of Woman's Memory* (New York, 1916), p. 30.
42. William I. Thomas and Florian Znaniecki, *The Polish Peasant in Europe and America: Monograph of an Immigrant Group* (5 vols., Boston, 1920), V, 268.
43. Addams, *Long Road of Woman's Memory,* pp. 27–32.
44. Yans-McLaughlin, *Family and Community,* pp. 84–85.
45. Byington, *Homestead,* pp. 109, 114–15.
46. Thomas Kessner, *The Golden Door: Italian and Jewish Immigrant Mobility in*

New York City, 1880–1915 (New York, 1977), pp. 75–76; Barbara Klaz-cynska, "Why Women Work: A Comparison of Various Groups—Philadelphia, 1910–1930," *Labor History 17* (Winter 1976), 77–84; Yans-McLaughlin, *Family and Community,* pp. 205–6.

47. Stephan Thernstrom, *Poverty and Progress: Social Mobility in a Nineteenth Century City* (Cambridge, Mass., 1973), pp. 170–74, 205; John W. Briggs, *An Italian Passage: Immigrants to Three American Cities, 1890–1930* (New Haven, 1978), pp. 225–26; Elizabeth H. Pleck, "A Mother's Wages: Income Earning Among Married Italian and Black Women, 1896–1911," in Michael Gordon (ed.), *The American Family in Social-Historical Perspective* (2nd ed., New York, 1978), p. 449; Yans-McLaughlin, *Family and Community,* pp. 206, 251.

48. Quoted in *ibid.,* pp. 435–36.

49. Briggs, *An Italian Passage,* p. 229. Unlike Yans-McLaughlin, Briggs finds that Italian parents were as interested in their children's education as native parents. He concludes that they saw education as a means of social mobility for their children. *Ibid.,* p. 241.

VII Women Challenge the Family

1. Nancy F. Cott, *The Bonds of Womanhood: "Women's Sphere" in New England, 1780–1835* (New Haven, 1977), p. 182; Carroll Smith-Rosenberg, "The Female World of Love and Ritual: Relations Between Women in Nineteenth-Century America," *Signs 1* (Autumn 1975), 4–5.

2. Nancy Sahli, "Changing Patterns of Sexuality and Female Interaction in Late Nineteenth-Century America: Some Case Studies from the Feminist Movement," unpublished paper presented at Berkshire Conference on History of Women, Bryn Mawr, June 11, 1976, pp. 2–3. I am indebted to Ms. Sahli for permitting me to quote from her paper.

3. Private Journal of Sarah Watson Dana, November 13, 1833, Dana Family Papers, Schlesinger Library, Radcliffe College; Journal of Sarah Ripley Stearns, November 12, 1808, Stearns Papers, Schlesinger Library, Radcliffe College; Smith-Rosenberg, "The Female World of Love and Ritual," p. 26.

4. Diary of Emily M. Eliot, February 27, June 2, 1881, Morison Manuscripts, Schlesinger Library, Radcliffe College.

5. Elizabeth Dwight Cabot to Elizabeth Eliot, November 25, 1857, January 8, 1858, Hugh Cabot Collection, Schlesinger Library, Radcliffe College.

6. Smith-Rosenberg, "The Female World of Love and Ritual," p. 7.

7. Mary Hallock Foote to Helena Gilder, January 19, 1878, December 16, 1887, August 8, 1889, Mary Hallock Foote Papers, Stanford University Library.

8. Donald F. Danker (ed.), *Mollie: The Journal of Mollie Dorsey Sanford in Nebraska and Colorado Territories, 1857–1866* (Lincoln, 1959), pp. 44, 39.

9. Johnny Faragher and Christine Stansell, "Women and Their Families on the Overland Trail, 1842–1867," *Feminist Studies 2* (February–March 1975), 160, 159.

10. Mary Waterman Rice to Robert W. Waterman, March 1, 1874, Robert Waterman Papers, Bancroft Library, University of California, Berkeley.

11. Nancy F. Cott, "Eighteenth Century Family and Social Life Revealed in Massachusetts Divorce Records," *Journal of Social History 10* (Fall 1976), 26.

12. Diary of Clelia Mosher, undated but about 1919, Clelia Duel Mosher Papers, Stanford University Archives.

13. Quoted in William L. O'Neill, *Everyone Was Brave: The Rise and Fall of Feminism in America* (Chicago, 1969), p. 79; Anne Firor Scott, *Southern Lady: From Pedestal to Politics, 1830–1930* (Chicago, 1970, p. 153.

14. Daniel Scott Smith, "Parental Control and Marriage Patterns: An Analysis of Historical Trends in Hingham, Massachusetts," *Journal of Marriage and the Family 35* (August 1973), 425; Peter R. Uhlenberg, "A Study of Cohort Life Cycles: Cohorts of Native Born Massachusetts Women, 1830–1920," *Population Studies 23* (November 1969), 410–11; Daniel Scott Smith, "Family Limitation, Sexual Control, and Domestic Feminism in Victorian America," in Mary S. Hartman and Lois W. Banner (eds.), *Clio's Consciousness Raised* (New York, 1974), p. 121. See also Peter Uhlenberg, "Cohort Variations in Family Life Cycle Experience of United States Females," *Journal of Marriage and the Family 36* (May 1975), 284–92.

15. George H. Napheys, *The Physical Life of Woman: Advice to the Maiden, Wife, and Mother* (Philadelphia, 1871) p. 290.

16. Quoted in Jane Jerome Camhi, "Women Against Women: American Antisuffragism, 1880–1920," unpublished dissertation, Tufts University, 1973, p. 444.

17. Danker (ed.), *Mollie*, pp. 41, 62.

18. Scott, *Southern Lady*, p. 7; Mary Waterman Rice to Robert Waterman, September 4, 1874, Robert Waterman Papers, Bancroft Library, University of California, Berkeley.

19. Journal of Sarah Ripley Stearns, December 23, June 11, 1809, Stearns Papers, Schlesinger Library, Radcliffe College.

20. Diary of Elizabeth Dwight, February 24, 1853; Elizabeth Dwight to Ellen Twistleton, February 14, 1854, Hugh Cabot Collection, Schlesinger Library, Radcliffe College.

21. Quoted in Scott, *Southern Lady*, p. 89.

22. Computed from figures supplied in Stanley Lebergott, *Manpower in Economic Growth: The United States Record since 1800* (New York, 1964), Table A-10, p. 519.

23. Quoted in Smith-Rosenberg, "The Female World of Love and Ritual," p. 27.

24. *Ibid.,* p. 29.

25. Quoted in William G. Shade, "A Mental Passion: Female Sexuality in Victorian America," *International Journal of Women's Studies 1* (January–February 1978), 16.

26. Sahli, "Changing Patterns of Sexuality," pp. 3–4.

27. Edward Halsey Foster, *Catharine Maria Sedgwick* (New York, 1974), p. 107.

28. Catharine Sedgwick to Robert Sedgwick, August 15, 1813; to Charles Sedgwick, February 2, 1829; to Kate Sedgwick Minot, February 20, 1853; to

William Minot, October 5, 1851; to Kate Sedgwick Minot, August 4, 1856, Catharine M. Sedgwick Papers, Massachusetts Historical Society, Worcester. I am deeply indebted to Professor Mary Kelley of Dartmouth College for kindly lending me her notes from her own research on Sedgwick. See her fine article "A Woman Alone: Catharine Maria Sedgwick's Spinsterhood in Nineteenth-Century America," *New England Quarterly 51* (June 1978), 210–25.

29. Sarah Ripley Stearns Journal, March 3, 1809, Stearns Papers, Schlesinger Library, Radcliffe College.

30. Autobiographical Letter, January 2, 1887, Blackwell Family Papers, Schlesinger Library, Radcliffe College. I am indebted to Professor Kirk Jeffrey, Jr., of Carleton College for bringing this letter to my attention.

31. Quoted in Scott, *Southern Lady,* p. 23.

32. Cott, *Bonds of Womanhood,* p. 26n; Mary Waterman Rice to Robert Waterman, September 4, 1874, Robert Waterman Papers, Bancroft Library, University of California, Berkeley.

33. Quoted in Janet Wilson James, "Changing Ideas About Women in the United States, 1776–1825," unpublished dissertation, Harvard University, 1954, p. 132; quoted in Barbara J. Berg, *The Remembered Gate: Origins of American Feminism: The Woman and the City, 1800–1860* (New York, 1978), p. 247.

34. *Ibid.,* p. 247; Robert Manson Myers (ed.), *Children of Pride: A True Story of Georgia and the Civil War* (New Haven, 1972), pp. 442–44.

35. Dinah M. Mulock Craik, *A Woman's Thoughts About Women* (Leipzig, 1860), p. 7.

36. *Ibid.,* pp. 26–27.

37. *Ibid.,* pp. 14–15, 18–19.

38. *Good Housekeeping,* November 14, 1885, p. 22.

39. Quoted in Camhi, "Women Against Women," p. 266.

40. Vida Dutton Scudder, *On Journey* (New York, 1937), pp. 212–14.

41. Jessie Taft, "The Woman Movement from the Point of View of Social Consciousness," *Philosophical Studies of the University of Chicago* (Chicago, 1916), p. 10.

42. Herman R. Lantz, *Marital Incompatibility and Social Change in Early America* (Beverly Hills, Ca., 1976), pp. 15–27.

43. Hugh Carter and Paul C. Glick, *Marriage and Divorce: A Social and Economic Study* (Cambridge, Mass., 1970), p. 54. See also Nelson Manfred Blake, *The Road to Reno: A History of Divorce in the United States* (New York, 1962) and Carroll D. Wright, *A Report on Marriage and Divorce in the United States 1867 to 1886* (Washington, D.C., 1889).

44. Paul Harold Jacobson, *American Marriage and Divorce* (New York, 1959), pp. 120–21.

45. William L. O'Neill, *Divorce in the Progressive Era* (New Haven, 1967), pp. 6–7.

46. Department of Commerce and Labor, Bureau of Census, Special Reports, *Marriage and Divorce, 1867–1906,* Part I (Washington, D.C., 1909), p. 41.

47. Peter Uhlenberg, "Changing Configurations of the Life Course," in Tamara K. Hareven (ed.), *Transitions: The Family and the Life Course in Historical Per-*

spective (New York, 1978), pp. 73, 79; calculated from table in Jacobson, *American Marriage and Divorce,* p. 142.

48. Quoted in Blake, *The Road to Reno,* pp. 88–89.
49. Carter and Glick, *Marriage and Divorce,* p. 31.

VIII   Women in the Making of the Demographic Transition

1. Robert V. Wells, "Quaker Marriage Patterns in a Colonial Perspective," *William and Mary Quarterly,* 3rd Series, 29 (July 1972), 439–41; Philip J. Greven, *Four Generations: Population, Land, and Family in Colonial Andover, Massachusetts* (Ithaca, 1970), pp. 30–31, 111–12; Wilson H. Grabil, Clyde V. Kiser, and Pascal K. Whelpton, *The Fertility of American Women* (New York, 1958), p. 380.
2. Lynne E. Withey, "Household Structure in Urban and Rural Areas: The Case of Rhode Island, 1774–1800," *Journal of Family History 3* (Spring 1978), 38, 47–48; Robert Higgs and H. Louis Stettler, III, "Colonial New England Demography: A Sampling Approach," *William and Mary Quarterly,* 3rd Series, 27 (April 1970), 289–93. See also Stephanie Grauman Wolf, *Urban Village: Population, Community, and Family Structure in Germantown, Pennsylvania, 1683–1800* (Princeton, 1976), pp. 264, 269–70, for further signs of the fall in fertility at the end of the 18th century. Robert V. Wells, "Family Size and Fertility Control in Eighteenth Century America: A Study of Quaker Families," *Population Studies 25* (March 1971), 73–82.
3. Ansley J. Coale and Melvin Zelnick, *New Estimates of Fertility and Population in the United States* (Princeton, 1963), pp. 34–35.
4. See table in *ibid.,* p. 36. A recent demographic analysis of total fertility during the 19th century estimates that 68.5 per cent of the fall in fertility between 1800 and 1860 is attributable to deliberate effort by the couples and only 31.5 per cent to changes in the rate of marriages. See Warren C. Sanderson, "Quantitative Aspects of Marriage Fertility and Family Limitation in Nineteenth Century America: Another Application of the Coale Specifications," *Demography 16* (August 1979), 339–58.
5. Susan Bloomberg, Mary Frank Fox, Robert M. Warner, and Sam Bass Warner, Jr., "A Census Probe into Nineteenth Century Family History: Southern Michigan, 1850–1880," *Journal of Social History 5* (Fall 1971), 28; Wendell H. Bash," "Changing Birth Rates in Developing America: New York State, 1840–1875," *Milbank Memorial Fund Quarterly 41* (1963), 163, 180–81.
6. Richard A. Easterlin, "Factors in the Decline of Farm Family Fertility in the United States: Some Preliminary Research Results," *Journal of American History 63* (December 1976), 600–612.
7. Robert V. Wells, "Family History and Demographic Transition," *Journal of Social History 9* (Fall 1975), 1–19.
8. Philippe Ariès, "On the Origins of Contraception in France," in Orest and Patricia Ranum (eds.), *Popular Attitudes Toward Birth Control in Pre-Industrial France and England* (New York, 1972, orig. pub. 1953), pp. 13–20.
9. Natalie Zemon Davis, "Ghosts, Kin, and Progeny: Some Features of Family Life in Early Modern France," *Daedalus 106* (Spring 1977), 104.

10. Alice S. Rossi (ed.), _The Feminist Papers: From Adams to de Beauvoir_ (New York, 1973), pp. 10–11.
11. Richard J. Evans, _The Feminists: Women's Emancipation Movements in Europe, America, and Australasia 1840–1920_ (London and New York, 1977), p. 17. The question of when and why the new views emerge has been raised and canvassed recently in Randolph Trumbach, _The Rise of the Egalitarian Family_ (New York, 1978), pp. 3, 120–22, and in J. E. Crowley, _This Sheba, SELF: The Conceptualization of Economic Life in Eighteenth Century America_ (Baltimore, 1974), p. 152.
12. Roger Thompson, _Women in Stuart England and America: A Comparative Study_ (London, 1974), p. 263.
13. George H. Napheys, _The Physical Life of Woman: Advice to the Maiden, Wife, and Mother_ (Philadelphia, 1871), p. 91; Vincent J. Cirillo, "Edward Foote's _Medical Common Sense:_ An Early American Comment on Birth Control," _Journal of the History of Medicine and Allied Sciences 25_ (July 1970), 341; Norman E. Himes, _Medical History of Contraception_ (New York, 1970, orig. pub. 1936), pp. 265–66; J. Soule, _Science of Reproduction and Reproductive Control_ (New York, _ca._ 1856), pp. 12, 26–27; Charles Knowlton, _Fruits of Philosophy_ ed. by Charles Bradlaugh and Mrs. Annie Besant (3rd ed., London, 1878), p. 48.
14. Frank F. Furstenberg, Jr., "Industrialization and the American Family: A Look Backward," _American Sociological Review 31_ (June 1966), 337; E. Anthony Wrigley, "Reflections on the History of the Family," _Daedalus 106_ (Spring 1977), 76–77, 83.
15. L. F. E. Bergeret, _The Preventive Obstacle or Conjugal Onanism_ (New York, 1870), pp. 13–150; Augustus K. Gardner, _Conjugal Sins Against the Laws of Life and Health and Their Effects upon the Father, Mother and Child_ (New York, 1870), pp. 99–102; George M. Beard, _Sexual Neurasthenia: Its Hygiene, Causes, Symptoms and Treatment_ (New York, 1884), p. 127.
16. John Harvey Kellogg, _Plain Facts for Old and Young_ (Burlington, Iowa, 1881), p. 255; Linda Gordon, _Woman's Body, Woman's Rights: A Social History of Birth Control in America_ (New York, 1976), p. 149; P. Henry Chevasse, _Physical Life of Man and Woman; or, Advice to Both Sexes_ (Cincinnati, 1871), p. 425; Henry Gibbons, _On Feticide_ (n. p., n.d., _ca._ 1878), pp. 2–3; _New York Medical Journal 37_ (June 30, 1883), 715; James Foster Scott, _The Sexual Instinct: Its Use and Dangers as Affecting Heredity and Morals_ (New York, 1899), pp. 274–75; Cirillo, "Edward Foote's _Medical Common Sense,_" p. 345; Hall quoted in James Reed, _From Private Vice to Public Virtue: The Birth Control Movement and American Society Since 1830_ (New York, 1978), p. 178.
17. William Greenfield (trans.), _Marriage Physiologically Discussed_ (2nd ed., New York, 1839), pp. 79–83; Soule, _Science of Reproduction,_ pp. 16–17; A. M. Mauriceau, _The Married Woman's Private Medical Companion. . ._ (New York, 1847, reprinted by Arno Press, 1974), pp. 120–21.
18. Gardner, _Conjugal Sins,_ pp. 90–97.

19. Napheys, *The Physical Life of Woman,* pp. 93–94; Mauriceau, *Married Woman's Companion,* p. 116.
20. Paulina W. Davis, *A History of the National Woman's Rights Movement . . .* (New York, 1871), p. 82.
21. Frederick Hollick, *The Marriage Guide or Natural History of Generation* (New York, 1850), p. 334; Soule, *Science of Reproduction,* p. 37.
22. Napheys, *The Physical Life of Woman,* pp. 94–97.
23. Henry C. Wright, *Marriage and Parentage; or, The Protective Element in Man, as a Means to His Elevation and Happiness* (2nd ed., Boston, 1855), pp. 117–18; Mauriceau, *Married Woman's Companion,* p. 122.
24. Quoted in Gordon, *Woman's Body, Woman's Rights,* p. 104; Elizabeth Cady Stanton, *Eighty Years and More: Reminiscences, 1815–1897* (New York, 1971, orig. pub. 1898), p. 297; Theodore Stanton and Harriot Stanton Blatch (eds.), *Elizabeth Cady Stanton: As Revealed in Her Letters, Diary and Reminiscences* (2 vols., New York, 1922), I, 132–33.
25. E. B. Duffey, *The Relations of the Sexes* (New York, 1889), pp. 244–45.
26. *Ibid.,* pp. 284, 238.
27. *Ibid.,* pp. 242–43, 233–34.
28. Alice B. Stockham, *Tokology: A Book for Every Woman* (rev. ed., Chicago, 1887), pp. 323–26.
29. Elizabeth Edson Evans, *The Abuse of Maternity* (Philadelphia, 1875), p. 122; G. Stanley Hall, *Adolescence: Its Psychology and Its Relations to Physiology, Anthropology, Sociology, Sex, Crime, Religion, and Education* (2 vols., New York, 1904), II, 579.
30. Maris A. Vinovskis, "Socioeconomic Determinants of Fertility," *Journal of Interdisciplinary History* 6 (Winter 1976), 375–96; Tamara K. Hareven and Maris A. Vinovskis, "Patterns of Childbearing in Late Nineteenth-Century America: The Determinants of Marital Fertility in Five Massachusetts Towns in 1880," in Tamara K. Hareven and Maris A. Vinovskis (eds.), *Family and Population in Nineteenth Century America* (Princeton, 1978), pp. 85–125; Ray Erwin Baber and Edward Alsworth Ross, *Changes in the Size of American Families in One Generation* (Madison, 1924), especially pp. 64–67; on California families see S. J. Holmes, "The Size of College Families," *Journal of Heredity* 15 (1924), 407–15. See also Xarifa Sallume and Frank W. Notestein, "Trends in the Size of Families Completed Prior to 1910 in Various Social Classes," *American Journal of Sociology* 38 (November 1932), 398–408. Wells, "Family Size and Fertility Control," p. 76, shows that deliberate limitation of fertility must have been undertaken since mere change in age of marriage would not account for the change over time.
31. Quoted in Randolph Shipley Klein, *Portrait of an Early American Family: The Shippens of Pennsylvania Across Five Generations* (Philadelphia, 1975), p. 285, n.105; Cormany Diary, 1859–1865 in manuscript; held in private hands, p. 823. I am indebted to Professor James C. Mohr of the University of Maryland, Baltimore County, for this valuable reference from the Cormany diary.

IX Limiting Fertility

1. Pierre Goubert, "Historical Demography and the Reinterpretation of Early Modern French History: A Research Review," *Journal of Interdisciplinary History 1* (Autumn 1970), 44; E. A. Wrigley, *Population and History* (New York, 1969), p. 188.

2. Sarah B. Pomeroy, *Goddesses, Whores, Wives, and Slaves: Women in Classical Antiquity* (New York, 1975), p. 167; "pullbacks" are mentioned in Page Smith, *Daughters of the Promised Land: Women in American History* (Boston, 1970), p. 232; Calista Hall to Pliny Hall, 1849, Smelzer Family Papers, Cornell University Library.

3. Horatio R. Storer, "A Medico-Legal Study of Rape," *New York Medical Journal 2* (1865), 100; H. Arthur Allbutt, *The Wife's Handbook . . .* (3rd ed., London, 1886), p. 37; David M. Kennedy, *Birth Control in America: The Career of Margaret Sanger* (New Haven, 1970), p. 130.

4. James Ashton, *The Book of Nature; Containing Information for Young People Who Think of Getting Married, on the Philosophy of Procreation and Sexual Intercourse; Showing How To Prevent Conception and to Avoid Child-Bearing* (New York, 1865), pp. 38–39.

5. Frank De Witt Alexander, *Owners and Tenants of Small Farms in the Life of a Selected Community: A Cultural Analysis* (Nashville, 1938), p. 16. This reference was kindly brought to my attention by Professor David Danbom; James Reed, "Birth Control and the Americans, 1830–1970," unpublished dissertation, Harvard University, 1974, p. 18. I am indebted to Professor Reed for permitting me to see his dissertation before it appeared in book form: *From Private Vice to Public Virtue* (New York, 1978).

6. P. Henry Chevasse, *Physical Life of Man and Woman; or, Advice to Both Sexes* (Cincinnati, 1871), p. 23.

7. J. Marion Sims, *Clinical Notes on Uterine Surgery, with Special Reference to the Management of the Sterile Condition* (New York, 1871), p. 371.

8. Augustus K. Gardner, *Conjugal Sins Against the Laws of Life and Health and Their Effects upon the Father, Mother and Child* (New York, 1870), p. 182.

9. R. T. Trall, *Sexual Physiology: A Scientific and Popular Exposition of the Fundamental Problems in Sociology* (28th ed., New York, 1881), p. 206; Allbutt, *The Wife's Handbook*, p. 36; Linda Gordon, *Woman's Body, Woman's Rights: A Social History of Birth Control in America* (New York, 1976), pp. 219–20.

10. John W. Riley and Matilda White, "The Use of Various Methods of Contraceptives," *American Sociological Review 5* (1940), 896.

11. Paul A. David and Warren C. Sanderson, "The Effectiveness of Nineteenth-Century Contraceptive Practices: An Application of Microdemographic Modelling Approaches," International Economic History Association, *Seventh International Economic History Congress: Edinburgh, 1978* (Edinburgh, 1978), pp. 67–68.

12. James Reed, *From Private Vice to Public Virtue: The Birth Control Movement and American Society since 1830* (New York, 1978), p. 10.

13. William Greenfield (trans.), *Marriage Physiologically Discussed* (2nd ed., New York, 1839, from original of Jean Du Bois), pp. 87–92.

14. Frederick Hollick, *The Marriage Guide or Natural History of Generation* (New York, 1850), p. 340; An American Physician, *Reproductive Control, or a Rational Guide to Matrimonial Happiness . . . Reproductive Control the Only Antidote to the Early Decay of American Women, and the Increase of Poverty* (Cincinnati, 1855), p. 35.

15. Reed, *From Private Vice to Public Virtue*, p. 16.

16. William A. Alcott, *The Physiology of Marriage* (New York, 1972, 1865 ed.), pp. 180–81.

17. L. F. E. Bergeret, *The Preventive Obstacle or Conjugal Onanism* (New York, 1870), p. 12.

18. Tamara Hareven and Maris A. Vinovskis, "Marital Fertility, Ethnicity, and Occupation in Urban Families: An Analysis of South Boston and the South End in 1880," *Journal of Social History* 8 (Spring 1975), 86.

19. Virginia Yans-McLaughlin *Family and Community: Italian Immigrants in Buffalo, 1880–1930* (Ithaca, 1977), p. 105.

20. Hareven and Vinovskis, "Marital Fertility, Ethnicity," p. 89; Xarifa Sallume and Frank W. Notestein, "Trends in the Size of Families Completed Prior to 1910 in Various Social Classes," *American Journal of Sociology* 38 (November 1932), 404.

21. Mosher Survey, Clelia Duel Mosher Papers, Stanford University Archives.

22. William M. Hassler (ed.), *The General and His Lady: Civil War Letters of William Dorsey Pender to Fanny Pender* (Chapel Hill, 1962), pp. 114, 116, 118, 209.

23. Mary Hallock Foote to Helena Gilder, December 7, *ca.* 1876, *ca.* January 21, 1877, Folder 2, Mary Hallock Foote Papers, Stanford University Library.

24. Mary Hallock Foote to Helena Gilder, undated letter, numbered 15 in Folder 2-3, probably December 1877 or January 1878, Mary Hallock Foote Papers, Stanford University Library. I am indebted to Barbara Cragg of the University of Montana for bringing this valuable reference to my attention.

25. Quoted in Mary Armfield Hill Porter, "Charlotte Perkins Gilman: A Feminist Paradox," unpublished dissertation, McGill University, 1975, p. 223, n.48.

26. Sarah Bell Waller to Henry Waller, July 22, 1855; Henry to Sarah July 28, 1855, Waller Papers, Huntington Library, San Marino, Ca.

27. Hassler (ed.), *The General and His Lady*, p. 209; Mary P. Poor to Henry V. Poor, August 15, 18, 1863, Poor Family Papers, Schlesinger Library, Radcliffe College.

X Abortion: Women's Last Resort

1. Ely Van de Warker, *The Detection of Criminal Abortion and a Study of Foeticidal Drugs* (Boston, 1872), p. 7.

2. R. Sauer, "Attitudes to Abortion in America, 1800–1973," *Population Studies* 28 (March 1974), 54.

3. *Boston Medical and Surgical Journal* 51 (1854), 204–5; Horatio R. Storer and

Franklin Fiske Heard, *Criminal Abortion: Its Nature, Its Evidence and Its Law* (Boston, 1868), pp. 57–58; Frederick Hollick, *Marriage Guide or Natural History of Generation* (New York, 1850), p. 334.

4. Morse Steward, "Criminal Abortion," *Detroit Review of Medicine and Pharmacy* 2 (January 1867), 7–8.

5. G. Maxwell Christine, "The Medical Profession vs. Criminal Abortion," *Transactions of the Homeopathic Medical Society of the State of Pennsylvania, 1889* (Philadelphia, 1890), vol. 25, 70–72.

6. Van de Warker, *Detection of Criminal Abortion,* p. 8; James Foster Scott, *The Sexual Instinct: Its Use and Dangers as Affecting Heredity and Morals* (New York, 1899), pp. 293–94; James C. Mohr, *Abortion in America: The Origins and Evolution of National Policy 1800–1900* (New York, 1978), pp. 50, 254, 275 n.12; Linda Gordon, *Woman's Body, Woman's Rights: A Social History of Birth Control in America* (New York, 1976), p. 53.

7. Henry Gibbons, *On Feticide* (n.p., n.d., *ca.* 1878), pp. 15–16; John W. Trader, "Criminal Abortion," *St Louis Medical and Surgical Journal* 11 (November 1874), 587; *Boston Medical and Surgical Journal* 51 (1854), 204–5.

8. J. J. Mulheron, "Foeticide," *The Peninsular Journal of Medicine* 10 (September 1874), 386–87; Scott, *Sexual Instinct,* pp. 294–95; Mohr, *Abortion in America,* p. 101 and chap. 4 *passim.*

9. Sauer, "Attitudes to Abortion," pp. 55–56, 59.

10. " 'Why Not? A Book for Every Woman,' A Woman's View," *Boston Medical and Surgical Journal* 75 (1866), 275.

11. Joseph Taber Johnson, "Abortion and Its Effects," *American Journal of Obstetrics* 33 (1896), 91; S. K. Crawford, "Criminal Abortion," Illinois State Medical Society, *Transactions, 1872* (Chicago, 1872), 77–78; Elizabeth Edson Evans, *The Abuse of Maternity* (Philadelphia, 1875), p. 57.

12. Augustus K. Gardner, *Conjugal Sins Against the Laws of Life and Health and Their Effects upon the Father, Mother, and Child* (New York, 1870), p. 130; Storer and Heard, *Criminal Abortion,* p. 8.

13. John Harvey Kellogg, *Plain Facts for Old and Young* (Burlington, Iowa, 1881), p. 271; Gardner, *Conjugal Sins,* p. 125.

14. Van de Warker, *Detection of Criminal Abortion,* pp. 42–43.

15. Bernhard J. Stern (ed.), *Young Ward's Diary* (New York, 1935), pp. 140, 150–52, 174.

16. William M. Hassler (ed.), *The General and His Lady: Civil War Letters of William Dorsey Pender to Fanny Pender* (Chapel Hill, 1962), p. 203.

17. Robert Griswold, "The Character of the Family in Rural California 1850–1890," unpublished dissertation, Stanford University, 1979, pp. 210–11; Evans, *Abuse of Maternity,* p. 35.

18. David W. Louisell and John T. Noonan, Jr., "Constitutional Balance," in John T. Noonan, Jr. (ed.), *Morality of Abortion: Legal and Historical Perspectives* (Cambridge, Mass., 1970), p. 230.

19. *State v. Murphy* (1858), *New Jersey Reports,* 83, 630; Mohr, *Abortion in America,* p. 200 and chap. 5 in general.

20. Christine, "Medical Profession vs. Criminal Abortion," p. 71.

21. Quoted in Sauer, "Attitudes to Abortion," p. 59.
22. New York Medical-Legal Society, "Report on Criminal Abortion," *New York Medical Journal 15* (1872), 83–85; John P. Stoddard, "Foeticide—Suggestions Toward Its Suppression," *Detroit Review of Medicine and Pharmacy 10* (1875), 656.
23. "Report on Criminal Abortion," American Medical Association, *Transactions 22* (1871), 239–41.
24. Trader, "Criminal Abortion," p. 589; Scott, *Sexual Instinct*, p. 287; Gardner quoted in Carroll Smith-Rosenberg and Charles Rosenberg, "The Female Animal: Medical and Biological Views of Woman and Her Role in Nineteenth Century America," *Journal of American History 60* (September 1973), 350n.; Stewart, "Criminal Abortion," pp. 9–10.
25. *Satan in Society*, By a Physician (Cincinnati, 1873), pp. 124–25; Alice B. Stockham, *Tokology: A Book for Every Woman* (rev. ed., Chicago, 1887), p. 246.
26. E. H. Heywood, *Cupid's Yokes; or, The Binding Forces of Conjugal Life* (Princeton, 1887), p. 20; quotation from Foote in James Reed, *From Private Vice to Public Virtue: The Birth Control Movement and American Society since 1830* (New York, 1978), p. 16; Eliza B. Duffey, *The Relations of the Sexes* (New York, 1889, orig. pub., 1876), p. 274; Gordon, *Woman's Body, Woman's Rights*, p. 108.
27. A. M. Mauriceau, *The Married Woman's Private Medical Companion . . .* (New York, 1847), p. 169n.
28. Henry C. Wright, *The Unwelcome Child; or, The Crime of an Undesigned and Undesired Maternity* (Boston, 1858), pp. 35, 59.
29. *Ibid.*, pp. 75–85.
30. " 'Why Not? A Book for Every Woman,' " pp. 273–75.
31. Stockham, *Tokology*, pp. 250–51.
32. See Mohr, *Abortion in America*, pp. 241–43, where he argues that by the end of the 19th century single women and immigrant women were the majority of those resorting to abortion.
33. *New York Medical Journal 37* (June 30, 1883), 715.
34. Sauer, "Attitudes to Abortion," p. 61.

XI Women's Sexuality in 19th-Century America

1. Frederick Marryat, *A Diary in America, with Remarks on Its Institutions* (3 vols., London, 1839), II, 244–47.
2. William Acton, *The Functions and Disorders of the Reproductive Organs in Youth, in Adult Age, and in Advanced Life: Considered in Their Physiological, Social, and Psychological Relations* (Philadelphia, 1865), p. 133.
3. Richard T. Vann, "Toward a New Lifestyle: Women in Preindustrial Capitalism," in Renate Bridenthal and Claudia Koonz (eds.), *Becoming Visible: Women in European History* (Boston, 1977), p. 199; Book III, Chapter XXXII of *Gargantua and Pantagruel;* Keith Thomas, *Religion and the Decline of Magic* (London, 1971), pp. 568–69.

4. John S. Haller, Jr., and Robin M. Haller, *The Physician and Sexuality in Victorian America* (Urbana, Ill., 1974), pp. 92–94; Otho T. Beall, *"Aristotle's Master Piece* in America: A Landmark in the Folklore of Medicine, *William and Mary Quarterly,* 3rd Series, 20 (1963), 207–22.

5. Nancy F. Cott, "Eighteenth Century Family and Social Life Revealed in Massachusetts Divorce Records," *Journal of Social History* 10 (Fall 1976), 34–35.

6. Quoted in Haller, *Physician and Sexuality,* p. 96; William Greenfield (trans.), *Marriage Physiologically Discussed* (2nd ed., New York, 1839), pp. 23, 55; Charles Knowlton, *Fruits of Philosophy* (3rd ed., London, 1878), p. 55; A. M. Mauriceau, *The Married Woman's Private Medical Companion . . .* (New York, 1847), pp. 153–54.

7. Knowlton, *Fruits,* p. 25; Greenfield (trans.), *Marriage Physiologically Discussed,* pp. 21–22; Frederick Hollick, *The Matron's Manual of Midwifery, and the Diseases of Women During Pregnancy and in Child Bed* (New York, 1848), p. 16; Frederick Hollick, *Marriage Guide or Natural History of Generation* (New York, 1850), pp. 357–59.

8. Thomas Hersey, *The Midwife's Practical Directory or, Woman's Confidential Friend* (Baltimore, 1836), pp. 80, 83.

9. Acton, *Functions and Disorders* (1858), pp. 8–9; (1865), p. 134. Italics added.

10. John Harvey Kellogg, *Plain Facts for Old and Young* (Burlington, Iowa, 1881), pp. 178, 206, 209, 247, 221–26, 118.

11. Ely Van de Warker, "Impotency in Women," *American Journal of Obstetrics 11* (1878), 47; Charles Fayette Taylor, "Effect on Women of Imperfect Hygiene of the Sexual Function," *American Journal of Obstetrics 15* (1882), 161–63, 165, 167; William A. Hammond, *Sexual Impotence in the Male and Female* (Detroit, 1887), pp. 278–301.

12. Alice B. Stockham, *Tokology: A Book for Every Woman* (Chicago, 1887), p. 326; Nancy P. Cott, "Passionlessness: An Interpretation of Victorian Sexual Ideology, 1790–1850," *Signs 4* (Winter 1978), 219–36.

13. P. Henry Chevasse, *Physical Life of Man and Woman: or Advice to Both Sexes* (Cincinnati, 1871), pp. 73–74; Guernsey quotation may be found in Michael Gordon, "From an Unfortunate Necessity to a Cult of Mutual Orgasm: Sex in American Marital Education Literature, 1830–1940," in James M. Henslin (ed.), *Studies in the Sociology of Sex* (New York, 1971), pp. 58–59; James Foster Scott, *The Sexual Instinct: Its Use and Dangers as Affecting Heredity and Morals* (New York, 1899), p. 78.

14. James Ashton, *The Book of Nature; Containing Information for Young People Who Think of Getting Married, on the Philosophy of Procreation and Sexual Intercourse . . .* (New York, 1865), p. 34.

15. Elizabeth Edson Evans, *The Abuse of Maternity* (Philadelphia, 1875), pp. 118–19; Edward B. Foote, *Plain Home Talk* (New York, 1881), p. 631; E. H. Pratt, "Circumcision of Girls," *Journal of Orificial Surgery* 6 (March 1898), 391; Alvin Eyer, "Clitoridectomy for the Cure of Certain Cases of Masturbation in Young Girls," *International Medical Magazine* 3 (1894), 260; H. E. Beebe, "The Clitoris," *Journal of Orificial Surgery* 6 (July 1897), 10.

16. *Satan in Society,* By a Physician (Cincinnati, 1873), p. 149; H. Arthur Allbutt,

The Wife's Handbook . . . (3rd ed., London, 1886), p. 44; E. B. Duffey, *The Relations of the Sexes* (New York, 1889, orig. ed., 1876), p. 182.

17. Chevasse, *Physical Life of Man and Woman,* pp. 424–25; Kellogg, *Plain Facts,* p. 252.

18. James Marion Sims, *Clinical Notes on Uterine Surgery* (London, 1866), p. 369.

19. George H. Napheys, *Physical Life of Woman: Advice to the Maiden, Wife, and Mother* (Philadelphia, 1871), pp. 104–5.

20. Carl N. Degler, "What Ought To Be and What Was: Women's Sexuality in the Nineteenth Century," *American Historical Review* 79 (December 1974), 1479–90. The material in the text is based on this article.

21. Essay "Marriage" in Weld-Grimké Papers, Clements Library, University of Michigan, pp. 12–18. I am indebted to Professor Michael Johnson of the University of California, Irvine, for supplying me with the text of this valuable essay. Gerda Lerner assures me that the essay reflects the views of Sarah Grimké.

22. Hooker statement quoted in Linda Gordon, *Woman's Body, Woman's Rights: A Social History of Birth Control in America* (New York, 1976), p. 98; Theodore Stanton and Harriot Stanton Blatch (eds.), *Elizabeth Cady Stanton as Revealed in Her Letters, Diary and Reminiscences* (2 vols., New York, 1922), II, 210.

23. Bell Waller to Henry Waller, August 23, 1842, June 11, 1855, Waller Papers, Huntington Library, San Marino, Ca.

24. Charlotte Perkins Stetson to Houghton Gilman, May 11, 1898, Charlotte Perkins Gilman Papers, Schlesinger Library, Radcliffe College.

25. Duffey, *Relations of the Sexes,* pp. 204–6.

26. Elizabeth Blackwell *The Human Element in Sex: Being a Medical Enquiry into the Relation of Sexual Physiology to Christian Morality* (2nd ed., London, 1884), pp. 45–47.

27. Autobiographical Letter, January 2, 1887, Blackwell Family Papers, Schlesinger Library, Radcliffe College.

28. Ida C. Craddock, *Letter to a Prospective Bride* (Philadelphia, 1897), pp. 9–14.

29. William A. Alcott, *The Physiology of Marriage* (Boston, 1866), pp. 116–17.

30. John Cowan, *The Science of a New Life* (New York, 1870), pp. 116–17; R. T. Trall, *Sexual Physiology and Hygiene* (Glasgow and London, 1908), pp. 232–33.

31. Blackwell, *Human Element,* p. 31; Craddock, *Letter to a Bride,* pp. 7–9; Duffey, *Relations of the Sexes,* pp. 178, 96–97; Evans, *Abuse of Maternity,* p. 47.

32. Essay "Marriage" Weld-Grimké Papers, Clements Library, University of Michigan, p. 20; Dio Lewis, *Chastity; or Our Secret Sins* (Philadelphia, 1874), p. 80.

33. Essay "Marriage" Weld-Grimké Papers, Clements Library, University of Michigan, p. 3; Stanton quoted in Ronald G. Walters, *The Anti-Slavery Appeal: American Abolitionism After 1830* (Baltimore, 1976), p. 81; Elizabeth Blackwell, *Essays in Medical Sociology* (2 vols., London, 1902), I, 78, 253–54; Stockham, *Tokology,* pp. 47–48; Duffey, *Relations of the Sexes,* p. 97.

34. Quoted in James Reed, *From Private Vice to Public Virtue: The Birth Control Movement and American Society since 1830* (New York, 1978), p. 26.

35. Henry C. Wright, *The Unwelcome Child; or, The Crime of an Undesigned and Undesired Maternity* (Boston, 1858), p. 80; Kellogg, *Plain Facts,* p. 264; Lewis, *Chastity,* pp. 236–37.

36. Van de Warker, "Impotency in Women," pp. 38–39; Hammond, *Sexual Impotence,* p. 301; quoted in Nathan G. Hale, Jr., *Freud and the Americans: The Beginnings of Psychoanalysis in the United States, 1876–1917* (New York, 1971), p. 40; William M. McLaurey, "Remarks on the Relation of Menstruation to the Sexual Function," *American Journal of Obstetrics and Diseases of Women and Children* 20 (1887), 161.

37. Carry A. Nation, *The Use and Need of the Life of Carry A. Nation* (Topeka, 1908), pp. 62–64.

38. Blackwell, *Essays in Medical Sociology,* I, 54.

39. Denslow Lewis, *The Gynecologic Consideration of the Sexual Act* (Chicago, 1900), p. 7; Evans, *Abuse of Maternity,* p. 47; Wright, *Unwelcome Child,* pp. 5, 23, 87.

40. Stockham, *Tokology,* pp. 153–55.

41. Quoted in Emanie Sachs, *"The Terrible Siren," Victoria Woodhull (1838–1927)* (New York, 1928), p. 219.

42. Orson S. Fowler, *Sexual Science; Including Manhood, Womanhood, and Their Mutual Interrelations etc., as Taught by Phrenology* (Philadelphia, 1870), p. 682.

43. Duffey, *Relations of the Sexes,* pp. 208–9, 214; Craddock, *Letter to a Bride,* pp. 6–8, 12.

44. Trall, *Sexual Physiology,* p. 234.

45. Regina Markell Morantz, "Making Women Modern: Middle Class Women and Health Reform in 19th Century America," *Journal of Social History* 10 (June 1977), 497.

XII   Organizing To Control Sexuality

1. Elizabeth Edson Evans, *The Abuse of Maternity* (Philadelphia, 1875), p. 48; Ida C. Craddock, *Letter to a Prospective Bride* (Philadelphia, 1897), p. 9.

2. Carry A. Nation, *The Use and Need of the Life of Carry A. Nation* (Topeka, 1908), p. 188.

3. Quoted in Carroll Smith-Rosenberg, "Beauty, the Beast and the Militant Woman: A Case Study in Sex Roles and Social Stress in Jacksonian America," *American Quareterly* 23 (October 1971), 574–75.

4. *Ibid.,* p. 581.

5. *Ibid.,* p. 583.

6. Robert E. Riegel, "Changing American Ideas Toward Prostitution (1800–1920)," *Journal of the History of Ideas* 29 (July–September 1968), 448.

7. James Foster Scott, *The Sexual Instinct: Its Use and Dangers as Affecting Heredity and Morals* (New York, 1899), pp. 172–73; E. B. Duffey, *The Relations of the Sexes* (New York, 1889), p. 173; Caroline H. Dall, *The College, the*

Market, and the Court; or, Woman's Relation to Education, Labor, and Law (Boston, 1914, orig. pub., 1867), pp. 153–54.

8. Duffey, *Relations of the Sexes,* pp. 281–82.

9. *The Philanthropist Series,* No. 4, Barnes Collection, Stanford University Library.

10. David J. Pivar, *Purity Crusade, Sexual Morality and Social Control 1868–1900* (Westport, Conn., 1972), p. 102. I am indebted for much of the information on Social Purity to this innovative book.

11. Duffey, *Relations of the Sexes,* p. 224; Craddock, *Letter to a Bride,* pp. 12–16.

12. Pivar, *Purity Crusade,* pp. 150–55; George Elliott Howard, *A History of Matrimonial Institutions* (3 vols., Chicago, 1904), III, 198–200.

13. Evans, *Abuse of Maternity,* p. 128; Dall, *College, Market, and Court,* p. 81.

14. *Philanthropist Series,* No. 23, Barnes Collection, Stanford University Library; Dio Lewis, *Chastity; or, Our Secret Sins* (Philadelphia, 1874), pp. 44–47.

15. *Philanthropist Series,* No. 23.

16. The incident is described in Richard J. Evans, *The Feminists: Women's Emancipation Movements in Europe, America and Australasia, 1840–1920* (London and New York, 1977), pp. 77–78.

17. Evans, *Abuse of Maternity,* pp. 117–19.

18. John C. Burnham, "The Progressive Era Revolution in American Attitudes Toward Sex," *Journal of American History* 59 (March 1973), 901.

19. Peter T. Cominus, "Late Victorian Sexual Respectability and the Social System," *International Review of Social History* 8 (1963), 18–48, 217–50; and Steven Marcus, *The Other Victorians: A Study of Sexuality and Pornography in Mid-Nineteenth-Century England* (New York, 1966).

20. R. S. Neale, *Class and Ideology in the Nineteenth Century* (London, 1972), pp. 127–29, 132–36; Wells quotation in Daniel T. Rodgers, *The Work Ethic in Industrial America, 1850–1920* (Chicago, 1978), p. 118.

21. Lewis, *Chastity,* pp. 107–8; Elizabeth Blackwell, *Essays in Medical Sociology* (2 vols. London, 1902), I, 31.

22. Randall Collins, "A Conflict Theory of Sexual Stratification," *Social Problems* 19 (Summer 1971), 3–20, and Daniel Scott Smith, "Family Limitation, Sexual Control, and Domestic Feminism in Victorian America," in Mary S. Hartman and Lois W. Banner (eds.), *Clio's Consciousness Raised* (New York, 1974), pp. 119–36.

23. Robert Latou Dickinson and Lura Beam, *A Thousand Marriages: A Medical Study of Sex Adjustment* (Baltimore, 1940), p. 57.

24. Alfred C. Kinsey *et al., Sexual Behavior in the Human Female* (paper ed., New York, 1965), p. 359.

25. John S. Haller, Jr., and Robin M. Haller, *The Physician and Sexuality in Victorian America* (Urbana, Ill., 1974), p. 96.

XIII   The World Is Only a Large Home

1. Nancy F. Cott, *The Bonds of Womanhood: "Woman's Sphere" in New England, 1780–1835* (New Haven, 1977), p. 126; Keith Melder, "The Begin-

nings of the Women's Rights Movement in the United States, 1800–1840,"
unpublished dissertation, Yale University, 1964, pp. 69–71; Cedric B. Cowing,
"Sex and Preaching in the Great Awakening," *American Quarterly 30* (Fall
1968), 624–49; Nancy F. Cott, "Young Women in the Second Great Awakening in New England," *Feminist Studies 3* (Fall 1975), 16; Donald G. Mathews,
Religion in the Old South (Chicago, 1977), pp. 47, 110; William Forrest
Sprague, *Women and the West: A Short Social History* (Boston, 1940), pp.
59–61; Mary P. Poor to Henry V. Poor, April 16, 1870, Poor Family Papers,
Schlesinger Library, Radcliffe College.

2. Melder, "Beginnings of the Women's Rights Movement," p. 89; Mathews,
   Religion in the Old South, p. 102.

3. Janet Wilson James, "Changing Ideas About Women in the United States,
   1776–1825," unpublished dissertation, Harvard University, 1954, p. 165.

4. Edwin Wilbur Rice, *The Sunday-School Movement 1780–1917 and the American Sunday-School Union, 1817–1917* (Philadelphia, 1917; Arno Press ed.,
   1971), pp. 208–10; Journal of Sarah Stearns, Vol. 3, December 24, 1815,
   Stearns Papers, Schlesinger Library, Radcliffe College; Barbara J. Berg, *The
   Remembered Gate: Origins of American Feminism—the Woman and the City,
   1800–1860* (New York, 1978), p. 158.

5. Mathews, *Religion in the Old South,* pp. 104–5, 110; quoted in *ibid.,* pp. 193,
   256.

6. Ronald W. Hogeland, "Coeducation of the Sexes at Oberlin College: A Study
   of Social Ideas in Mid-Nineteenth Century America," *Journal of Social His-
   tory 6* (Winter 1972–73), 109–10; Carroll Smith-Rosenberg, "Beauty, the
   Beast and the Militant Woman: A Case Study in Sex Roles and Social Stress in
   Jacksonian America," *American Quarterly 23* (October 1971), 566; Berg,
   Remembered Gate, p. 229.

7. Quoted in Melder, "The Beginnings of the Women's Rights Movement," p.
   136.

8. *Ibid.,* p. 149.

9. *Ibid.,* pp. 182–83.

10. *Ibid.,* pp. 292–93, 230.

11. *Ibid.,* p. 185.

12. Cott, *Bonds of Womanhood,* p. 101; Joan Hoff Wilson, "The Illusion of
    Change: Women and the American Revolution," in Alfred F. Young (ed.), *The
    American Revolution: Explorations in the History of American Radicalism*
    (DeKalb, Ill., 1976), p. 409; Philip Alexander Bruce, *Institutional History of
    Virginia in the Seventeenth Century* (2 vols., New York, 1910), I, 457; Maris
    A. Vinovskis and Richard M. Bernard, "Beyond Catharine Beecher: Female
    Education in the Antebellum Period," *Signs: Journal of Women in Culture and
    Society 3* (Summer 1978), 863; Richard A. Easterlin, "Factors in the Decline
    of Farm Family Fertility in the United States: Some Preliminary Research
    Results," *Journal of American History 63* (December 1976), 602.

13. Carl F. Kaestle and Maris A. Vinovskis, "From Fireside to Factory: School
    Entry and School Leaving in Nineteenth Century Massachusetts," in Tamara
    K. Hareven (ed.), *Transitions: The Family and the Life Course in Historical
    Perspective* (New York, 1978), p. 160.

14. Hogeland, "Coeducation of the Sexes at Oberlin College," pp. 166, 175n, *passim.*
15. Quoted in Charlotte Williams Conable, *Women at Cornell: The Myth of Equal Education* (Ithaca, 1977), p. 67.
16. Quoted in William L. O'Neill, *Everyone Was Brave: The Rise and Fall of Feminism in America* (Chicago, 1969), p. 80.
17. Aileen S. Kraditor (ed.), *Up from the Pedestal: Selected Writings in the History of American Feminism* (Chicago, 1968), pp. 90–91.
18. Quoted in Thomas Woody, *A History of Women's Education in the United States* (2 vols., New York, 1929), II, 158; figures on increased enrollment taken from Debra Herman's unpublished dissertation, "College and After: The Vassar Experiment in Women's Education, 1861–1924," Stanford University, 1979, pp. 148–50.
19. Letters of Inquiry, from Sarah M. Perkins and Mrs. M. E. J. Gage in Vassar College Archives, Poughkeepsie, New York; Robert Manson Myers (ed.), *The Children of Pride: A True Story of Georgia and the Civil War* (New Haven, 1972), p. 950.
20. *New York Daily Tribune,* January 28, 1861, p. 4; quoted in Mabel Newcomer, *A Century of Higher Education for American Women* (New York, 1959), p. 32.
21. Quoted in William H. Chafe, *The American Woman: Her Changing Social, Economic, and Political Roles, 1920–1970* (New York, 1972), p. 104.
22. Melder, "Beginnings of the Women's Rights Movement," p. 123.
23. Joseph R. Gusfield, "Social Structure and Moral Reform: A Study of the Woman's Christian Temperance Union," *American Journal of Sociology 61* (November 1955), 231.
24. Mary Earhart, *Frances Willard: From Prayers to Politics* (Chicago, 1944), pp. 141–43.
25. Quoted in Anne Firor Scott, *Southern Lady: From Pedestal to Politics, 1830–1930* (Chicago, 1970), p. 149; Earhart, *Frances Willard,* pp. 142, 177.
26. *Ibid.,* p. 154.
27. Andrew Sinclair, *Prohibition: The Era of Excess* (London, 1962), pp. 112–23; quoted in Aileen S. Kraditor, *The Ideas of the Woman Suffrage Movement, 1890–1920* (New York, 1965), p. 59.
28. O'Neill, *Everyone Was Brave,* p. 149.
29. Mary Ritter Beard, *Women's Work in Municipalities* (New York, 1915), pp. 221–22.
30. O'Neill, *Everyone Was Brave,* pp. 142–43.
31. *Ibid.,* pp. 143–44.

XIV   The Suffrage Fight: The Last Step Was Really the First

1. Quoted in James M. McPherson, "Abolitionists, Woman Suffrage, and the Negro, 1865–1869," *Mid-America 47* (January 1965), 44; Susan B. Anthony and Ida Husted Harper (eds.), *The History of Woman Suffrage* (4 vols., Rochester, N.Y., 1902), IV, 148; 1893 quotation from Aileen Kraditor, *Ideas of the Woman Suffrage Movement, 1890–1920* (New York, 1965), p. 131.

2. Eleanor Flexner, *Century of Struggle: The Woman's Rights Movement in the United States* (Cambridge, Mass., 1959), p. 294.

3. Anthony and Harper, (eds.), *History of Woman Suffrage,* IV, 455, 458.

4. David Morgan, *Suffragists and Democrats: The Politics of Woman Suffrage in America* (East Lansing, Mich., 1972), p. 41.

5. William O'Neill, *Everyone Was Brave: The Rise and Fall of Feminism in America* (Chicago, 1969), p. 143.

6. Kraditor, *Ideas of the Woman Suffrage Movement,* p. 263.

7. Quoted in Robin Miller Jacoby, "The Women's Trade Union League and American Feminism," *Feminist Studies 3* (Fall 1975), 129.

8. Linda Kerber, "The Republican Mother: Women and the Englightenment—an American Perspective," *American Quarterly 28* (Summer 1976), 187–205.

9. Harriet H. Robinson, *Loom and Spindle or Life Among the Early Mill Girls . . . ,* (New York, 1898), pp. 86–87; quotation taken from Keith Melder, "The Beginnings of the Women's Rights Movement in the United States, 1800–1840," unpublished dissertation, Yale University, 1964, p. 390; Marvin E. Gettleman, *Dorr Rebellion: A Study in American Radicalism: 1833–1849* (New York, 1973), p. 168n.

10. Henry Waller to Sarah Bell Waller, August [no day] 1840, Waller Papers, Huntington Library, San Marino, Ca.

11. Julie Roy Jeffrey, "Women in the Southern Farmers' Alliance: A Reconsideration of the Role and Status of Women in the Late Nineteenth-Century South," *Feminist Studies 3* (Fall 1975), 77–81; Robert C. McMath, Jr., *Populist Vanguard: A History of the Southern Farmers' Alliance* (New York, 1977), p. 67.

12. Annie L. Diggs, "The Women in the Alliance Movement," *Arena 6* (July 1892), 161–79; Morton Keller, *Affairs of State: Public Life in Late Nineteenth Century America* (Cambridge, Mass., 1977), p. 573.

13. Quotation from Hoover in Richard Jensen, "Family Career, and Reform: Women Leaders of the Progressive Era," in Michael Gordon (ed.), *The American Family in Social-Historical Perspective* (New York, 1973), p. 93; World statement quoted in Peter H. Odegard, *Pressure Politics: The Story of the Anti-Saloon League* (New York, 1928), p. 95.

14. Carrie Chapman Catt and Nettie Rogers Shuler, *Woman Suffrage and Politics: The Inner Story of the Suffrage Movement* (New York, 1926), p. 134; Morgan, *Suffragists and Democrats,* p. 162.

15. *Ibid.,* p. 161; Frederick C. Luebke, *Immigrants and Politics: The Germans in Nebraska, 1880–1900* (Lincoln, 1969), p. 129.

16. Quoted in Jeffrey, "Women in the Southern Farmers' Alliance," p. 79.

17. Elizabeth Oakes Smith, *Woman and Her Needs* (New York, 1851), pp. 24, 27, 63–64; Caroline H. Dall, *College, the Market, and the Court; or, Woman's Relation to Education, Labor, and Law* (Boston, 1914, orig. ed., 1867), p. 360.

18. Anthony and Harper, (eds.), *History of Woman Suffrage,* IV, 189–90; Jacobi quotation in Ellen Du Bois, "The Radicalism of the Woman Suffrage Movement: Notes Toward the Reconstruction of Nineteenth-Century Feminism," *Feminist Studies 3* (Fall 1975), 66.

19. Dall, *College, Market, and Court,* p. 378; Paulina W. Davis, *History of the National Woman's Rights Movement . . .* (New York, 1971), pp. 60–63.

20. Dall, *College, Market, and Court,* pp. 128–29.

21. Katharine Du Pre Lumpkin, *Emancipation of Angelina Grimké* (Chapel Hill, 1974), p. 168; Josephine Goldmark, *Impatient Crusader: Florence Kelley's Life Story* (Urbana, Ill., 1953), p. 18.

22. Du Bois, "Radicalism of the Woman Suffrage Movement," p. 68; private quotation from suffragist in T. A. Larson, "Woman Suffrage in Western America," *Utah Historical Quarterly 38* (Winter 1970), 8; Anthony and Harper, (eds.), *History of Woman Suffrage,* IV, 45.

23. Alice Henry, *Trade Union Woman* (New York, 1973, orig. ed., 1915), p. 260.

24. Ross Evans Paulson, *Women's Suffrage and Prohibition: A Comparative Study of Equality and Social Control* (Glenview, Ill., 1973), p. 139.

25. Janet Zollinger Giele, "Social Change in the Feminine Role: A Comparison of Woman's Suffrage and Woman's Temperance, 1870–1920," unpublished dissertation, Radcliffe College, 1961, pp. 120–25, 142–49.

26. *Ibid.,* p. 161; Henry, *Trade Union Woman,* p. 262.

27. Jane Jerome Camhi, "Women Against Women: American Antisuffragism, 1880–1920," unpublished dissertation, Tufts University, 1973, p. 352.

28. Constance Rover, *Women's Suffrage and Party Politics in Britain, 1866–1914* (London, 1967), pp. 170–71; quotation from *Indianapolis Journal* in Camhi, "Women Against Women," p. 91.

29. *To the Honorable Members of the Legislature of the State of Illinois* (1897) in *Why Women Do Not Want the Ballot.*

30. Ann Watkins, "For the Twenty-two Million: Why Most Women Do Not Want To Vote," *The Outlook,* May 4, 1912, 26–30.

31. Blackwell quotation in Giele, "Social Change in the Feminine Role," p. 115; other quotations in Kraditor, *Ideas of the Woman Suffrage Movement,* p. 63; Carl N. Degler, "Charlotte Perkins Gilman on the Theory and Practice of Feminism," *American Quarterly 8* (Spring 1956), 21–39.

32. G. E. Jones, "Impediments to Woman Suffrage," *North American Review 109* (August 1909), 158; Grace Duffield Goodwin, "The Non-Militant Defenders of the Home," *Good Housekeeping 55* (July 1912), 77; Margaret C. Robinson, "The Feminist Program," *The Unpopular Review 5* (1916), 319–20.

33. Mrs. H. A. Foster, *Taxation and Representation,* Pamphlet No. 43 in *Why Women Do Not Want the Ballot;* Letter from Mrs. Clara T. Leonard to Massachusetts Legislative Committee, 1884, in *Why Women Do Not Want the Ballot,* Pamphlet No. 9; Alice N. George, "Women Suffrage Must Fail," *Independent 84* (October 11, 1895), 59; untitled address to 1894 New York State Constitutional Convention, Brooklyn Auxiliary, New York State Association Opposed to the Extension of the Suffrage to Women, Pamphlet No. 2 in *Why Women Do Not Want the Ballot;* Foxcroft quotation in Camhi, "Women Against Women," p. 60.

34. George, "Women Suffrage Must Fail," p. 59; Frances J. Dyer, *A Remonstrance,* An Address before Committee on Election Laws at State House, Boston, January 27, 1903, Pamphlet No. 51 in *Why Women Do Not Want the Ballot;* Helen Kendrick Johnson, *Woman and the Republic: A Survey of the*

Woman-Suffrage Movement in the United States and a Discussion of the Claims and Arguments of Its Foremost Advocates (New York, 1897), pp. 315–16.

35. Caroline F. Corbin, "Suffrage and Industrial Independence," Leaflet No. 10 in *Why Women Do Not Want the Ballot,* II.
36. Quoted in Camhi, "Women Against Women," pp. 296–97.
37. Priscilla Leonard, *Woman as a Municipal Factor,* Pamphlet No. 44 in *Why Women Do Not Want the Ballot;* quotation from *Anti-Suffragist* in Camhi, "Women Against Women," pp. 113–14.
38. John D. Buenker, "The Urban Political Machine and Woman Suffrage: A Study in Political Adaptability," *The Historian 33* (February 1971), 273.
39. Quoted in Kraditor, *Ideas of the Woman Suffrage Movement,* pp. 70, 64.
40. Catt and Shuler, *Woman Suffrage and Politics,* p. 107.

XV Women's Work: The First Transformation

1. Quoted in Julia Cherry Spruill, *Women's Life and Work in the Southern Colonies* (paper ed., New York, 1977), p. 82.
2. *Ibid.,* p. 81.
3. Edith Abbott, *Women in Industry: A Study in American Economic History* (New York, 1910), p. 11.
4. Eugenie Andress Leonard, *The Dear-Bought Heritage* (Philadelphia, 1965), pp. 421, 449, 458, 471; Joan Hoff Wilson, "The Illusion of Change: Women and the American Revolution," in Alfred F. Young (ed.), *The American Revolution: Explorations in the History of American Radicalism* (DeKalb, Ill., 1976), pp. 395–96.
5. Leonard, *Dear-Bought Heritage,* pp. 440–41.
6. Mary Beth Norton, "Eighteenth Century American Women in Peace and War: The Case of the Loyalists," *William and Mary Quarterly,* 3rd Series, *33* (July 1976), 386–409.
7. Nancy F. Cott, *The Bonds of Womanhood: "Woman's Sphere" in New England, 1780–1835* (New Haven, 1977), p. 43.
8. Rolla Milton Tryon, *Household Manufactures in the United States, 1640–1860: A Study in Industrial History* (Chicago, 1917), pp. 131, 161, 167; Helen L. Sumner, *History of Women in Industry in the United States,* Vol. IX in *Report on Condition of Woman and Child Wage-Earners in the United States* (19 vols., Washington, D.C., 1910), p. 37.
9. Quoted in *ibid.,* p. 14.
10. Stanley Lebergott, *Manpower in Economic Growth: The American Record since 1800* (New York, 1964), pp. 125, 129–30; for statistics see J. D. B. De Bow, *Statistical View of the United States . . .* (Washington, D.C., 1854), and U.S. Census, 1860, *Manufactures.*
11. I am especially indebted in this section to two articles by Thomas Dublin, "Women, Work, and the Family: Female Operatives in the Lowell Mills, 1830–1860," *Feminist Studies 3* (Fall 1975), 30–39, and "Women, Work and

Protest in the Early Lowell Mills: 'The Oppressing Hand of Avarice Would Enslave Us'," *Labor History 16* (Winter 1975), 99–116.

12. Daniel J. Walkowitz, "Working-Class Women in the Gilded Age: Factory, Family and Community Life Among Cohoes, New York, Cotton Workers, *Journal of Social History 5* (Summer 1972), 469; Clyde and Sally Griffen, *Natives and Newcomers* (Cambridge, Mass., 1978), pp. 231–32.

13. Walkowitz, "Working Class Women in the Gilded Age," p. 476.

14. Helen Campbell, *Women Wage-Earners: Their Past, Their Present, and Their Future* (Boston, 1893), pp. 238–42.

15. Stanley Lebergott in Lance Davis *et al.*, *American Economic Growth: An Economist's History of the United States* (New York, 1972), p. 196.

16. Cott, *Bonds of Womanhood*, pp. 52–53; Donald F. Danker (ed.), *Mollie: The Journal of Mollie Dorsey Sanford in Nebraska and Colorado Territories, 1857–1866* (Lincoln, 1959), p. 98.

17. Gerda Lerner, "The Lady and the Mill Girl: Changes in the Status of Women in the Age of Jackson," *Midcontinent American Studies Journal 10* (Spring 1969), 12 and *passim*.

18. Quoted in Ronald G. Walters, *The Anti-Slavery Appeal: American Abolitionism after 1830* (Baltimore, 1976), p. 100.

19. William L. O'Neill, *Everyone Was Brave: The Rise and Fall of Feminism in America* (Chicago, 1969), p. 147.

20. The foregoing figures on women's employment are garnered from a variety of published sources, principally the printed census reports for 1880 and 1900. A convenient entry to the masses of statistics in the census of 1880 is *Compendium of the Tenth Census* (Washington, D.C., 1883); the best analysis is Joseph A. Hill, *Women in Gainful Occupations, 1870–1920* (Census Monograph IX, Washington, D.C., 1929). See also Stanley Lebergott, "Labor Force and Employment, 1800–1960," in National Bureau of Economic Research, *Output, Employment and Productivity in the United States after 1800* (New York, 1966).

21. Quoted in Herbert Ross Brown, *The Sentimental Novel in America, 1789–1860* (Durham, N.C., 1940), p. 104.

22. *Ibid.*, p. 105; Nina Baym, *Woman's Fiction: A Guide to Novels by and about Women in America, 1820–1870* (Ithaca, 1978), pp. 22, 18, 39, 115; Helen Papashvily, *All the Happy Endings* (New York, 1956), pp. 185–86. Even Ann Douglas and Nathaniel Hawthorne admired the popular woman novelist who went under the name of Fannie Fern. Hawthorne wrote his publisher in 1855 that he thought her novel *Ruth Hall* had bite and fire and showed what women could do when they "throw off the restraints of decency and come before the public stark naked." Quoted in Ann D. Wood, "The Scribbling Women and Fannie Fern: Why Women Wrote," *American Quarterly 23* (Spring 1971), 3.

23. Dinah M. Mulock Craik, *A Woman's Thoughts about Women* (Leipzig, 1860), p. 33.

24. Quoted in Kathryn Kish Sklar, *Catharine Beecher: A Study in American Domesticity* (New Haven, 1973), p. 182; Robert Manson Myers (ed.), *The Chil-*

dren of Pride: A True Story of Georgia and the Civil War (New Haven, 1972), p. 647.

25. Richard M. Bernard and Maris A. Vinovskis, "The Female School Teacher in Antebellum Massachusetts," *Journal of Social History 10* (March 1977), 332–45; C. and S. Griffen, *Natives and Newcomers*, p. 241; Robert W. Smuts, *Women and Work in America* (New York, 1959), p. 49.

26. Quoted in Annie Nathan Meyer, *Woman's Work in America* (New York, 1891), p. 182.

27. Carroll D. Wright, *Working Women in Large Cities* (Washington, D.C., 1889), p. 62.

28. Michael B. Katz, in his *People of Hamilton, Canada West: Family and Class in a Mid-Nineteenth-Century City* (Cambridge, Mass., 1975), p. 273, notices that young women in Hamilton in the 19th century also left work when they married. Katz contrasts the pattern he has found with that reported by Michael Anderson for Preston in Lancashire, England, where some 28 per cent of women with husbands present were in the work force in the 19th century. Katz calculated that no more than 2 per cent of Hamilton wives worked. Katz's puzzlement as to the differences between Preston, England, and Hamilton would probably have dissipated had he made his comparison with other North American cities.

29. Harriet H. Robinson, *Loom and Spindle or Life Among the Early Mill Girls* (New York, 1898), pp. 177–78; Smuts, *Women and Work*, p. 51; Richard Jensen, "Family, Career, and Reform: Women Leaders of the Progressive Era," in Michael Gordon (ed.), *The American Family in Social-Historical Perspective* (New York, 1973), pp. 275–76; William H. Chafe, *The American Woman* (New York, 1972), p. 100.

30. Mrs. John Van Vorst and Marie Van Vorst, *The Woman Who Toils Being the Experiences of Two Gentlewomen as Factory Girls* (New York, 1903), p. 82.

31. Melville B. Anderson to Charlena, September 14, 1876; Charlena Anderson to Melville, October 29, 1876. Anderson Papers, Stanford University Library.

32. Mary Hallock Foote to Helena Gilder, May 23, 1888, June 6, 1887, February 14, 1888, undated letter about August 1894, March 27, 1893. Mary Hallock Foote Papers, Stanford University Library.

33. *New York Tribune*, July 17, 1854.

34. Nancy Schrom Dye, "Creating a Feminist Alliance: Sisterhood and Class Conflict in the New York Women's Trade Union League," *Feminist Studies 2* (Number 2/3, 1975), 31.

35. Roger L. Ransom and Richard Sutch, *One Kind of Freedom: The Economic Consequences of Emancipation* (Cambridge, Eng., 1977), p. 233. Herbert Gutman, *The Black Family in Slavery and Freedom 1750–1925* (New York, 1976), pp. 167–68, makes the same point from literary evidence.

36. John W. Blassingame, *Black New Orleans, 1860–1880* (Chicago, 1973), p. 93; Elizabeth H. Pleck, "A Mother's Wages: Income Earning Among Married Italian and Black Women, 1896–1911," in Michael Gordon (ed.), *The American Family in Social-Historical Perspective* (2nd ed., New York, 1978), p. 493.

37. *Ibid.*, pp. 498–50; Claudia Goldin, "Female Labor Force Participation: The

Origin of Black and White Differences, 1870 and 1880," *Journal of Economic History 37* (March 1977), 90–91, 101.

38. E. B. Lowry, *Herself: Talks with Women Concerning Themselves* (Chicago, 1911), chap. 23; Campbell, *Women Wage-Earners*, pp. 90–91; Earl Barnes, *Women in Modern Society* (New York, 1912), p. 147; John Stuart Mill, *Subjection of Women* (London, 1906), pp. 107–9; Judith Hole and Ellen Levine, *Rebirth of Feminism* (New York, 1971), p. 57.

39. Helen Marot, *American Labor Unions, by a Member* (New York, 1914), p. 72.

40. C. and S. Griffen, *Natives and Newcomers*, pp. 235–36; Susan J. Kleinberg, "Technology's Stepdaughter, the Impact of Industrialization upon Working Class Women, Pittsburgh, 1865–1890," unpublished dissertation, University of Pittsburgh, 1973, p. 251; John Modell and Tamara Hareven, "Urbanization and the Malleable Household: An Examination of Boarding and Lodging in American Families," *Journal of Marriage and the Family 35* (August 1973), 467–79; the data on the two California gold towns of Grass Valley and Nevada City are drawn from the as yet unpublished researches of Professor Ralph Mann of the University of Colorado at Boulder. I am indebted to Professor Mann for letting me use his material prior to its publication.

XVI   Women at Work: Unions, Farms, and Professions

1. John P. Andrews and W. D. P. Bliss, *History of Women in Trade Unions*, Vol. X in *Report on Condition of Women and Child Wage-Earners in the United States* (19 vols., Washington, D.C., 1911), p. 45; Maurine Weiner Greenwald, "Women Workers and World War I: The American Railroad Industry, a Case Study," *Journal of Social History 9* (Winter 1975), 154–73.

2. Andrews and Bliss, *History of Women in Trade Unions*, p. 48; Alice Kessler-Harris, "Where Are the Organized Women Workers?" *Feminist Studies 3* (Fall 1975), 97; Elizabeth Jameson, "Imperfect Unions: Class and Gender in Cripple Creek, 1894–1904," in Milton Cantor and Bruce Laurie (eds.), *Class, Sex, and the Woman Worker* (Westport, Conn., 1977), p. 175.

3. Quoted in Eleanor Flexner, *Century of Struggle: The Woman's Rights Movement in the United States* (Cambridge, Mass., 1959), p. 136.

4. *Report of the Special Committee of the Assembly . . . To Investigate the Condition of Female Labor in the City of New York, January 16, 1896* (Albany, 1896), p. 85.

5. Helen Marot, *American Labor Unions, by a Member* (New York, 1914), p. 68.

6. Kessler-Harris, "Where Are the Organized Women Workers?", p. 92; James J. Kenneally, "Women and Trade Unions, 1870–1920: The Quandary of the Reformer," *Labor History 14* (Winter 1973), 55.

7. Nancy Schrom Dye, "Creating a Feminist Alliance: Sisterhood and Class Conflict in the New York Women's Trade Union League," *Feminist Studies 2* (Number 2/3, 1975), 35; Alice Kessler-Harris, "Organizing the Unorganizable:

Three Jewish Women and Their Union," *Labor History* 17 (Winter 1976), 14–15, 19.

8. 208 *U.S. Reports*, p. 412.

9. Gladys Boone, *The Women's Trade Union Leagues in Great Britain and the United States* (New York, 1942), p. 49; Kessler-Harris, "Where Are the Organized Women Workers?", p. 101.

10. William H. Chafe, *The American Woman* (New York, 1972), pp. 128–29.

11. J. Stanley Lemons, *The Woman Citizen: Social Feminism in the 1920s* (Urbana, Ill., 1973), p. 185; Josephine Goldmark, *Impatient Crusader: Florence Kelley's Life Story* (Urbana, Ill., 1953), p. 185.

12. Lemons, *The Woman Citizen*, pp. 189–90; Chafe, *The American Woman*, p. 127.

13. *Ibid.*

14. Mary Van Kleeck, "Women and Machines," *Atlantic Monthly* 77 (February 1921), 255, 258.

15. Stanley Lebergott, *Manpower in Economic Growth: The American Record since 1800* (New York, 1964), p. 71; Mary Meek Atkeson, "Women in Farm Life and Rural Economy," *Annals* of the American Academy of Political and Social Science, 142 (May 1929), 189.

16. U.S. Department of Agriculture, Report Number 103, *Social and Labor Needs of Farm Women* (Washington, D.C., 1915), pp. 5–6, 13. I am indebted to Professor David Danbom of North Dakota State University at Fargo for bringing this source to my attention.

17. *Ibid.*, pp. 68–70, 16, 14.

18. *Ibid.*, pp. 13, 11–12, 16.

19. *Ibid.*, pp. 48, 25, 27–29.

20. *Ibid.*, pp. 44, 16–22.

21. Quoted in T. A. Larson, "Women's Role in the American West," *Montana, the Magazine of Western History* 24 (July 1974), 11.

22. The story of Rachel O'Connor is told with affection in Avery O. Craven, *Rachel of Old Louisiana* (Baton Rouge, 1975); Sarah Bell Waller to Henry Waller, August 11, 1852, Waller Papers, Huntington Library, San Marino, Ca.; Agnes Smedley, *Daughter of Earth* (Old Westbury, N.Y., 1973), p. 19.

23. Robert W. Smuts, *Women and Work in America* (New York, 1959), p. 10; Sheryl Patterson-Black, "Women Homesteaders on the Great Plains Frontier," *Frontiers* 1 (Spring 1976), 67–68, 71.

24. Jessie Taft, "The Woman's Movement from the Point of View of Social Consciousness," *Philosophical Studies of the University of Chicago* (Chicago, 1916), pp. 1–3.

25. Alice Henry, *The Trade Union Woman* (New York, 1973; orig. pub. 1915), pp. 188–89, 225, 242–43.

26. Quoted in Peter Gabriel Filene, *Him Her Self: Sex Roles in Modern America* (New York, 1975), p. 141.

27. Virginia MacMakin Collier, *Marriage and Careers: A Study of One Hundred Women Who Are Wives, Mothers, Homemakers, and Professional Workers . . .* (New York, 1926), pp. 9–10, 17–19; Alice Beal Parsons, *Woman's Dilemma* (New York, 1926), p. 267.

28. The quotation from Neilsen is in *Review of Reviews*, 1927, p. 665; the one from Gildersleeve is reported in Sophinisba P. Breckinridge, *Women in the Twentieth Century* (New York, 1933), pp. 122–23. See also Frank Stricker, "Cookbooks and Lawbooks: The Hidden History of Career Women in Twentieth Century America," *Journal of Social History 10* (Fall 1976), 1–19, and Chafe, *The American Woman*, pp. 100–102.

29. Quoted in Lemons, *The Woman Citizen*, p. 230.

30. Quoted in Richard Jensen, "Family, Career, and Reform: Women Leaders of the Progressive Era," in Michael Gordon (ed.), *The American Family in Social-Historical Perspective* (New York, 1973), p. 269.

31. The principal sources for these pages on the character of the work force are Mary Elizabeth Pidgeon, *Women in the Economy of the United States of America* (Washington, D.C., 1937) and Janet Hooks, "Women's Occupations Through Seven Decades," *Women's Bureau Bulletin* No. 218 (Washington, D.C., 1951).

XVII The Second Transformation in Women's Work

1. Convenient sources for statistics on women's work patterns, which I have drawn upon here and elsewhere are: *Handbook on Women Workers, 1975,* Women's Bureau Bulletin #297 (Washington, D.C., n.d.), especially pp. 15–16, 18; *A Statistical Portrait of Women in the United States.* Current Population Reports, Special Studies, Series P-23, #58, U.S. Department of Commerce, Bureau of the Census (Washington, D.C., 1976), p. 31; Valerie Kincade Oppenheimer, *The Female Labor Force in the United States: Demographic and Economic Factors Governing Its Growth and Changing Composition* (Berkeley, 1970), p. 8.

2. Quoted in Chester W. Gregory, *Women in Defense Work During World War II* (New York, 1974), p. 32.

3. Quoted in Virginia Kerr, "One Step Forward—Two Steps Back: Child Care's Long American History," in Pamela Roby (ed.), *Child Care—Who Cares?* (New York, 1973), p. 165.

4. Juanita Kreps and R. John Leaper, "Home Work, Market Work, and the Allocation of Time," Juanita M. Kreps (ed.), *Women and the American Economy: A Look at the 1980s* (Englewood Cliffs, N.J., 1976), p. 70.

5. Edward Gross, "Plus ça change . . . ? The Sexual Structure of Occupations Over Time," *Social Problems 16* (Fall 1968), 198–208.

6. See especially the revealing table in *Handbook on Women Workers*, p. 136.

7. Juanita Kreps, *Sex in the Marketplace: American Women at Work* (Baltimore, 1971), p. 91n.

8. James A. Sweet, *Women in the Labor Force* (New York, 1973), p. 102.

9. William G. Bowen and T. Aldrick Finegan, *The Economics of Labor Force Participation* (Princeton, 1969), pp. 100–101; Judith M. Fields, "A comparison of Intercity Differences in the Labor Force Participation Rates of Married Women in 1970 with 1940, 1950, and 1960," *The Journal of Human Resources 11* (Fall 1976), 574.

10. *Handbook on Women Workers*, p. 51.

11. *Ibid.*, pp. 51–53.
12. *Ibid.*, pp. 173–74; Stanley Lebergott, *Manpower in Economic Growth: The American Record since 1800* (New York, 1964), pp. 66–68; Myra H. Strober, "Wives' Labor Force Behavior and Family Consumption Patterns," *American Economic Review 67* (February 1977), 410–17; Myra H. Strober and Charles B. Weinberg, "Working Wives and Major Family Expenditures," *Journal of Consumer Research 3* (December 1977) 141–47.
13. Judith Blake, "The Changing Status of Women in Developed Countries," *Scientific American 231* (September 1974), 144.
14. Patricia Branca, "A New Perspective on Women's Work: A Comparative Typology," *Journal of Social History 9* (Winter 1975), 147.
15. Ester Boserup, *Woman's Role in Economic Development* (New York, 1970), p. 114.

XVIII   Woman's Dilemma

1. Lynn White, Jr., *Educating Our Daughters. A Challenge to the Colleges* (New York, 1950), pp. 77–78, 101; Ashley Montagu quoted in William H. Chafe, *American Woman: Her Changing Social, Economic, and Political Roles, 1920–1970* (New York, 1972), pp. 206–7.
2. Quoted in Peter Gabriel Filene, *Him Her Self: Sex Roles in Modern America* (New York, 1975), pp. 190, 193.
3. Carmichael quoted in Chafe, *American Woman*, p. 233; radical woman quoted in Filene, *Him Her Self*, pp. 224–25.
4. (London) *Times Higher Education Supplement*, May 5, 1978.
5. Judith Hole and Ellen Levine, *Rebirth of Feminism* (New York, 1971), p. 19.
6. Quoted in *ibid.*, p. 76.
7. Lois W. Banner, *Women in Modern America: A Brief History* (New York, 1974), p. 246.
8. Mirra Komarovsky, *Blue-Collar Marriage* (New York, 1967), p. 49; Louise Kapp Howe, *Pink Collar Workers: Inside the World of Women's Work* (New York, 1977), pp. 200, 229–30; Lillian Breslow Rubin, *Worlds of Pain: Life in the Working-Class Family* (New York, 1976), pp. 41, 45.
9. Judith Blake, "The Changing Status of Women in Developed Countries," *Scientific American 231* (September 1974), 144; Mary Jo Bane, *Here To Stay: American Families in the Twentieth Century* (New York, 1976), p. 28; Helena Znaniecki Lopata, *Occupation: Housewife* (New York, 1971), pp. 47–48, 374.
10. Quoted in Paula S. Fass, *The Damned and the Beautiful: American Youth in the 1920s* (New York, 1977), p. 97; Kenneth Keniston, and the Carnegie Council on Children, *All Our Children: The American Family Under Pressure* (New York, 1977), p. ix.
11. Urie Bronfenbrenner, "Who Cares for America's Children?" in Louise Kapp Howe (ed.), *The Future of the Family* (New York, 1972), p. 139; Urie Bronfenbrenner, "The Origins of Alienation," *Scientific American 231* (August 1974), 53–61.

12. Christopher Lasch, *Haven in a Heartless World: The Family Besieged* (New York, 1977), pp. 131–32.
13. Quoted in Fass, *Damned and the Beautiful*, p. 97.
14. Howard Hayghe, "Families and the Rise of the Working Wives—An Overview," *Monthly Labor Review* (May 1976), p. 16.
15. Robert V. Wells, "Demographic Change and the Life Cycle of American Families," in Theodore K. Rabb and Robert I. Rotberg (eds.), *The Family in History: Interdisciplinary Essays*, (New York, 1973), pp. 89–90; Bane, *Here To Stay*, p. 25.
16. *Handbook on Women Workers, 1975*, Women's Bureau Bulletin #297 (Washington, D.C., n.d.), p. 141; Phillips Cutright, "Components of Change in the Number of Female Family Heads Aged 15–44; United States, 1940–1970," *Journal of Marriage and the Family* 36 (November 1974), 717; Bane, *Here To Stay*, p. 13.
17. Alexander Plateris, "100 Years of Marriage and Divorce Statistics, United States, 1867–1967," Department of Vital and Health Statistics, Series 21, No. 24, National Center of Health Statistics (U.S. Department of Health, Education and Welfare, December 1973), p. 45.
18. Kingsley Davis, "The American Family in Relation to Demographic Change," Charles R. Westoff and Robert Parke, Jr. (eds.), *Demographic and Social Aspects of Population Growth* (Washington, D.C., 1972), I, 255; Paul Glick, "Some Recent Changes in American Families," *Current Population Reports*, Special Studies, Series P-23, #52 (U.S. Department of Commerce, Bureau of the Census, Washington, D.C., 1976), p. 10; Bane, *Here To Stay*, p. 13.
19. *Ibid.*, p. 22.
20. Hugh Carter and Paul C. Glick, *Marriage and Divorce: A Social and Economic Study* (Cambridge, Mass., 1970), p. 18.
21. Glick, "Some Recent Changes," p. 6; Donald J. Bogue, *The Population of the United States* (Glencoe, Ill., 1959), p. 242; Bane, *Here To Stay*, p. 34.
22. Davis, "The American Family," p. 262.
23. Glick, "Some Recent Changes," pp. 3–5.
24. Davis, "The American Family," p. 263.
25. Bane, *Here To Stay*, pp. 8–10.
26. Rubin, *Worlds of Pain*, pp. 5, 67–68; Davis, "The American Family," p. 262.
27. Jerome Kagan, "The Child in the Family," *Daedalus* 106 (Spring 1977), 54.
28. Peter Uhlenberg, "Changing Configurations of the Life Course," in Tamara K. Hareven (ed.), *Transitions: The Family and the Life Course in Historical Perspective* (New York, 1978), pp. 94–95.
29. Ellen and Kenneth Keniston, "An American Anachronism: The Image of Women and Work," *American Scholar* 33 (Summer 1964), 374–75; Keniston, *All Our Children*, p. 122.
30. Sarane Spence Boocock, "The Role of the Parent: Problems and Prospects," in Victor C. Vaughan and T. Berry Brazelton (eds.), *The Family—Can It Be Saved?* (Chicago, 1976), p. 261; Jessie Bernard, "Changing Family Life Styles: One Role, Two Roles, Shared Roles," in Louise Kapp Howe (ed.), *The Future of the Family* (New York, 1972), pp. 245–46; Rubin, *Worlds of Pain*, p. 102.

31. William J. Goode, *World Revolution and Family Patterns* (New York, 1970), pp. 21–22.
32. Boocock, "Role of the Parent," p. 261.
33. Glen G. Cain, *Married Women in the Labor Force: An Economic Analysis* (Chicago, 1966), p. 18; *Handbook on Women Workers,* 1975, p. 34; Suzanne H. Woolsey, "Pied Piper Politics and the Child-Care Debate," *Daedalus 106* (Spring 1977), 130.
34. *Ibid.,* pp. 135–36; Bane, *Here To Stay,* p. 83; Selma Fraiberg, *Every Child's Birthright: In Defense of Mothering* (New York, 1977), pp. 87–88.
35. Alice S. Rossi, "A Biosocial Perspective on Parenting," *Daedalus 106* (Spring 1977), 31, n.36; Marjorie Galenson, *Women and Work: An International Comparison* (Ithaca, 1973), pp. 43–44, 50, 67, 105; Gail Warshofsky, *Women in Soviet Society: Equality, Development, and Social Change* (Berkeley, 1978), p. 279.
36. Fraiberg, *Every Child's Birthright,* p. 112.

Index